INTERPARLIAMENTARY COOPERATION IN THE COMPOSITE EUROPEAN CONSTITUTION

This collection analyses the place and the functioning of interparliamentary cooperation in the EU composite constitutional order, taking into account both the European and the national dimensions. The chapters join the recent scholarship on the role of parliaments in the EU after the Treaty of Lisbon. The aim of this volume is to highlight the constitutional significance of interparliamentary cooperation as a permanent feature of EU democracy and as a new parliamentary function as well as to investigate the practical side of this relatively new phenomenon. To this end the contributors are academics and parliamentary officials from all over Europe.

The volume discusses the developments in interparliamentary cooperation and its implications for the organisation and procedures of national parliaments and the European Parliament, for the fragmented executive of the EU, and for the democratic legitimacy of the overall EU composite Constitution. These issues are examined by looking at the EU legislative process, the European Semester and the Treaty revisions. Moreover, the contributions take into account the effects of interparliamentary cooperation on the internal structure of parliaments and analyse the different models of interparliamentary cooperation, ie from COSAC to the new Interparliamentary Conference on Stability, Economic Coordination and Governance in the European Union provided by the Fiscal Compact.

Volume 1 in the series Parliamentary Democracy in Europe

Parliamentary Democracy in Europe

Parliamentary democracy is at the core of all modern European constitutions. In representing the people, national parliaments are traditionally viewed as the primary centres for democratic deliberation and decision-making. Yet with the rise of international and supranational organisations, this national democratic frame is increasingly challenged.

What, then, is the role and task of national parliaments today? And how has European integration affected them? The European Union itself is founded on the idea of 'representative democracy'. Citizens are directly represented in the European Parliament, but Union democracy is equally based on indirect forms of representation; and because of this, Union democracy indirectly relies on the good functioning of national democratic institutions. What, then, is the role and relationship between the European and the national parliaments in the democratic functioning of the Union? Do they exercise distinct or complementary functions?

This new Hart Series on 'Parliamentary Democracy in Europe' aims to address these questions. Encompassing monographs and edited collections, it offers new insights into rules and conventions shaping parliaments and parliamentary democracy in Europe.

Series Editors

Nicola Lupo
Robert Schütze

Interparliamentary Cooperation in the Composite European Constitution

Edited by
Nicola Lupo
and
Cristina Fasone

•HART•
OXFORD • LONDON • NEW YORK • NEW DELHI • SYDNEY

HART PUBLISHING

Bloomsbury Publishing Plc

Kemp House, Chawley Park, Cumnor Hill, Oxford, OX2 9PH, UK

HART PUBLISHING, the Hart/Stag logo, BLOOMSBURY and the Diana logo are trademarks of Bloomsbury Publishing Plc

First published in Great Britain 2016

Paperback edition 2018

A catalogue record for this book is available from the British Library.

Library of Congress Cataloging-in-Publication data

Names: Lupo, Nicola, editor. | Fasone, Cristina, editor.

Title: Interparliamentary cooperation in the composite European constitution / edited by Nicola Lupo and Cristina Fasone.

Description: Oxford ; Portland, Oregon : Hart Pub. Ltd, 2016. | Series: Parliamentary Democracy in Europe ; volume 1 | Includes bibliographical references and index.

Identifiers: LCCN 2016000212 (print) | LCCN 2016009772 (ebook) | ISBN 9781782256977 (hardback : alk. paper) | ISBN 9781782256984 (Epub)

Subjects: LCSH: European Union countries—Politics and government. | Legislative bodies—European Union countries. | European Union. Conference of Community and European Affairs Committees of Parliaments

Classification: LCC JN30 .I595 2016 (print) | LCC JN30 (ebook) | DDC 342.24/057—dc23

LC record available at http://lccn.loc.gov/2016000212

ISBN: PB: 978-1-50992-442-4
HB: 978-1-78225-697-7

Typeset by Compuscript Ltd, Shannon

To find out more about our authors and books visit www.hartpublishing.co.uk. Here you will find extracts, author information, details of forthcoming events and the option to sign up for our newsletters.

Acknowledgements

This book is a result of a series of initiatives organised by the LUISS Center for Parliamentary Studies (CESP) in Rome: namely, a Summer school on parliamentary democracy in Europe organised together with the LUISS School of Government and funded by the European Commission as a Jean Monnet Module 2013–2015 (no 2012-2881), and a series of workshops promoted in Rome to coincide with the semester of the Italian presidency of the European Union. All the initiatives were characterised by the active involvement of officials of national and European parliaments, together with scholars, mainly lawyers (specialised in EU law, constitutional law and comparative law) and political scientists. This volume, the first in the new series on *Parliamentary Democracy in Europe*, reflects this approach, as the sixth part is entirely composed of contributions written by practitioners.

The editors are grateful to Robert Schütze for his constant encouragement, to Hart Publishing, especially Sinead Moloney for having put her trust in this project, since the beginning, and to Luca Bartolucci for the editorial help.

A warm thanks goes to all the authors who agreed to send their chapters and contributions, all written between January and July 2015, and to be involved in a continuous dialogue with the two co-editors.

Finally, the editors are grateful to Andrea Manzella and Melina Decaro, President and Director respectively of the LUISS CESP.

Contents

Part IV: Euro-national Parliamentary Procedures

Part V: Old and New Interparliamentary Conferences

Part VI: Debating the Role of COSAC

List of Contributors

Antonia Baraggia is Postdoctoral Fellow in Constitutional Law at the Department of National and Supranational Public Law, University of Milan. She has also been Visiting Fellow at Fordham University School of Law. She holds a PhD in Public Law from the University of Turin. She serves as one of the members of the Affiliates Advisory Group of the Younger Comparativists Committee (YCC), American Society of Comparative Law. Her research interests include citizenship, bicameralism, the role of courts in protecting human rights and within the euro-zone crisis, and the right to education considered in a comparative perspective. She has authored several articles on these topics, including most recently 'Conditionality Measures within the Euro Area Crisis: A Challenge to the democratic principle?' (2015) 4(2) *Cambridge Journal of International and Comparative Law*, and 'Paths of Dialogue Between the ECJ and Constitutional Courts on Fundamental Rights Protection: A Still-Puzzling Scenario' (2015) 24(1) *Tulane Journal of International and Comparative Law.*

Leonard FM Besselink is Full Professor of Constitutional Law at the University of Amsterdam. He studied at the University of Leiden (Netherlands) and the Johns Hopkins School of Advanced International Studies (Bologna Centre). He holds a doctorate in social and political sciences from the European University Institute, Florence (Italy), and is a member of the Royal Dutch Society of Sciences and Humanities. He is co-editor in chief of the *European Constitutional Law Review* and he has published extensively in matters of comparative law and EU law. Recent publications include *The Eclipse of the Legality Principle in the European Union* (ed) (Kluwer Law International, 2010). He is one of the authors of the Report on *National Constitutional Avenues for Further EU Integration* prepared for the European Parliament's Committees on Legal Affairs and on Constitutional Affairs, 2014.

Nathalie Brack is Professor, Department of Political Science and CEVIPOL, Université libre de Bruxelles. She is also Visiting Professor at the College of Europe. She holds a PhD in political sciences from the Université libre de Bruxelles where she teaches European politics and legislative studies. Her research interests include Euroscepticism, the European Parliament, legislative studies and the linkage between citizens and representatives in Europe. She recently published *L'euroscepticisme au Parlement européen. Stratégies d'une opposition anti-système au coeur des institutions* (Larcier, 2014), and co-authored *How the EU works* (Ashgate, 2014) (with O Costa).

Davide Alberto Capuano is Counsellor of the Italian Senato della Repubblica and Head of the Secretariat of the Committee on EU Policies (2014). He also worked for the International Affairs Department of the Senate (2003–2013) and headed the Interparliamentary Relations Office (2009–2013). Other experiences saw him as an official of the Italian Authority of the Stock Exchange (2000–2003) and as a practicing lawyer (1997–1999). His published writing includes 'The role of national parliaments in the legislative process of the EU. A view from the Italian Parliament' in M Cartabia, N Lupo and A Simoncini (eds), *Democracy and Subsidiarity in the EU* (Il Mulino, 2013), and 'La nuova governance economica europea. I risvolti sulle procedure parlamentari italiane' (with E Griglio) in N Lupo and A Manzella (eds), *Il sistema parlamentare euro-nazionale* (Giappichelli, 2014).

Ian Cooper is a Jean Monnet Fellow in the Robert Schuman Centre for Advanced Studies at the European University Institute in Florence, Italy. Previously, he was Senior Researcher at ARENA, Centre for European Studies at the University of Oslo and Research Associate at the Department of Politics and International Studies (POLIS), University of Cambridge. A Canadian, he holds a PhD in Political Science from Yale University. His current research is focused on the collective role of national parliaments in the European Union. His recent work has appeared in the *Journal of Common Market Studies*, *West European Politics* and the *Journal of European Public Policy*. He is currently writing a monograph putting forth the argument that national parliaments together constitute a 'virtual third chamber' within the political system of the European Union.

Adam Cygan is Full Professor of EU Law, University of Leicester and Director of the LLM in EU Law by distance learning at the School of Law. Professor Cygan's work focusses on the relationship between national parliaments and EU institutions, with a particular emphasis upon the process of decision making. It explores the challenges that national parliaments face with securing effective accountability within the legislative process and the limits of subsidiarity monitoring as mechanism through which to improve legislative legitimacy. He has recently published a monograph titled *Accountability, Parliamentarism and Transparency in the EU: The Role of National Parliaments* (Edward Elgar, 2013) and is the author of several articles on the topic.

Bruno Dias Pinheiro is Head of Unit in charge of the Parliamentary TV Channel and Official Journal at the Portuguese Parliament (Assembleia da República) and previously was Permanent Representative of the Portuguese Parliament to the EU and its Representative at the Presidential Troika of the COSAC Secretariat. He holds a master degree in International Relations (European Affairs) from the Institute for Social and Political Sciences of the Technical University of Lisbon. He was Adviser in the Cabinet of the State Secretary for European Affairs, Ministry of Foreign Affairs, Principal Adviser for the President of the Diplomatic Institute of the Ministry of Foreign Affairs and associate researcher at the Portuguese Institute for International Relations and Security (IPRIS), Lisbon. He is finalising an essay (with I Cooper) on 'The representatives of national Parliaments to the EU'.

Thibaud Deruelle is a PhD student in European Politics at the University of Exeter. He is currently working on a dissertation on the role of policy learning in the regulation of health crises in the EU. After obtaining an MA in European Studies from the Institut d'Etudes Européennes in Strasbourg and from the College of Europe in 2009 and 2010 respectively, Thibaud held a temporary position as an administrator at the Directorate for relations with national parliaments in the European Parliament in Brussels (2011–2012), and then became Academic Assistant at the Department of European and Political Administrative Studies of the College of Europe, Bruges (2012–2015).

Antonio Esposito is a Counselor of the Italian Chamber of Deputies. After working for more than a decade at the EU Affairs Department, he is currently Head of the Secretariat of the Speaker. He has published articles and essays on EU affairs, especially on the role of national parliaments in the European constitutional framework and on comitology. His most recent publications include 'La legge 24 dicembre 2012, n. 234, sulla partecipazione dell'Italia alla formazione e all'attuazione della normativa e delle politiche dell'UE. Parte I, Prime riflessioni sul ruolo delle Camere', *Federalismit.it*, 2013, and 'La cooperazione interparlamentare: principi, strumenti e prospettive' in A Manzella and N Lupo (eds), *Il sistema parlamentare euro-nazionale. Lezioni* (Giappichelli, 2014).

Cristina Fasone is Assistant Professor of Comparative Public Law, Department of Political Science, LUISS Guido Carli University, Rome. She holds a PhD in Comparative Public Law from the University of Siena and was previously Max Weber Postdoctoral Fellow (2013–2015), Max Weber Programme and Law Department, European University Institute, Florence, where she is also a Visiting Fellow and one of the coordinators of the project on 'Constitutional Change through Euro-Crisis Law'. She has been Visiting Researcher at the Georgetown University Law Center, Washington DC (USA) and Erasmus Mundus Visiting Scholar at the Victoria University of Wellington (New Zealand). Her research focuses on parliaments and constitutional courts in the EU and in the Eurozone crisis, parliamentary committee systems and forms of government (*Sistemi di commissioni parlamentari e forme di governo* is the title of her monograph (Cedam, 2012)), and regional parliaments. She has authored several essays on these topics, including 'European Economic Governance and Parliamentary Representation. What Place for the European Parliament?' (2014) 20(2) *European Law Journal* 164–85.

Diane Fromage is Assistant Professor of EU Law, Faculty of Law, University of Utrecht and was previously Max Weber Postdoctoral Fellow (2014–2015), Max Weber Programme and Law Department, European University Institute, Florence. She holds a PhD in Law and in Institutions, Administrations and Regional Policies from the University of Pavia and the Pompeu Fabra University of Barcelona (joint degree). Previously, she was an Associate Lecturer at the Catholic University of Lille and at Pompeu Fabra University (where she also coordinated an EU ALFA project for the promotion of human rights in Latin America), and a Research Fellow at the Max Planck Institute for Comparative Public Law and International Law, Heidelberg. Her research focuses on national and regional parliaments in the European Union which she has addressed from both a national and a European perspective. On this topic she has recently authored 'The Second Yellow Card on the EPPO Proposal: An Encouraging Development for Member State Parliaments?' in the *Yearbook of European Law* (2015) and a monograph entitled *Les Parlements dans l'Union Européenne après le Traité de Lisbonne. La participation des parlements allemands, britanniques, espagnols, français et italiens* (L'Harmattan, 2015).

Christiana Fryda has been a permanent member of the COSAC Secretariat since 1 January 2014. She was previously a permanent representative of the House of Representatives of the Republic of Cyprus to the European Parliament in Brussels. She had previously served as an officer in the European Affairs Service of the House of Representatives of the Republic of Cyprus. She is a lawyer by training with an LLB from the University of Bristol (UK) and an LLM in European and International Law from the University of Sheffield (UK). Her publications include, amongst others, a chapter titled 'The House of Representatives and the challenge of Cyprus' accession to the EU' in Achilles Aimilianides (ed), *Policy Proposals—Cyprus After Accession to the EU* (Power Publishing, 2005). She has also, for some time, been writing literary reviews for Cyprus' culture magazine *Anev*.

Marco Goldoni is Lecturer in Legal Theory at the University of Glasgow and Part-time Researcher at the Institute for State and Law of the Academy of Sciences of the Czech Republic. He holds a PhD in Legal Philosophy from the University of Pisa and a PhD in European Law from the University of Antwerp. His publications concern mostly the intersection between law and politics, treated through the perspectives of constitutional law and theory, EU public law and political philosophy. He is the author of *La Dottrina costituzionale di Sieyès* (Firenze University Press, 2009) and co-editor of *Hannah Arendt and the Law* (Hart Publishing, 2012). His current research focuses on European constitutional law and in particular on the relationship between European institutions and national parliaments.

Francisco Gómez Martos is Visiting Professor at the Adam Mickiewicz University in Poznan, Faculty of Political Sciences and Journalism. He was previously an Official of the European Parliament, Head of the Institutional Cooperation Unit at the European Parliament's Directorate General for Presidency, Directorate for relations with national parliaments. For ten years he has been a Professor of Public Finance at the Universidad Autónoma de Madrid and is currently a collaborator with the Institute of European Studies of the FUSL (Faculté Universitaire Saint-Louis) in Brussels and a lecturer at public agencies, universities and business schools in Spain, France and Italy. He has published numerous articles on economic policy and the European Union in *El País* and other newspapers and magazines.

Katarzyna Granat is a Junior Research Fellow and a Marie Curie Fellow at Durham University Law School. During the 2014–2015 academic year, she was Emile Noël Fellow at New York University (NYU), Jean Monnet Centre. She completed her PhD on 'The Role of National Parliaments in the Policing of the Subsidiarity Principle' at the European University Institute, Florence. She holds an LLM from this institution as well as a Masters of Law from the University of Warsaw. She was previously a visiting researcher at the London School of Economics and at the Max Planck Institute for Comparative Public Law and International Law, Heidelberg. She has interned at the Court of Justice of the European Union in Luxembourg (chambers of Judge M Safjan), at the European Court of Human Rights in Strasbourg, as well as in public institutions and private practises in Warsaw and Berlin. Her research interests concern EU law, European parliamentarism, comparative constitutional law and federalism (she is an affiliated member of the 'Neo-federalism' project at Durham Law School). On these topics she has authored 'Yellow card, but no foul: The role of the national parliaments under the Subsidiarity Protocol and the Commission proposal for an EU regulation on the right to strike' (2013) 50 *Common Market Law Review* 115–44 (with F Fabbrini) and 'Institutional Design of Member States for Ex Post Subsidiarity Scrutiny' in M Cartabia, N Lupo and A Simoncini (eds), *Democracy and Subsidiarity in the EU* (Il Mulino, 2013).

Anna-Lena Högenauer is a research associate in the Institute of Political Science at the University of Luxembourg. She holds a PhD in Politics from the University of Edinburgh. She works on multi-level governance, interest representation and the Europeanisation of parliaments. She has been a member of the OPAL (Observatory of Parliaments after the Lisbon Treaty) project and is currently an active member of the Erasmus Network on Parliamentary Democracy in the EU (PADEMIA). She was co-editor of the OPAL Online Paper Series from 2013–2014 and book review editor for Regional and Federal Studies from 2012–2015.

She is currently the co-editor of PADEMIA's Online Papers on Parliamentary Democracy. Her recent publications include various articles on regional executives and national parliaments in *Comparative European Politics*, the *European Political Science Review*, *Regional and Federal Studies* and *West European Politics*.

Davor Jančić is a Senior Researcher in EU Law at the TMC Asser Institute The Hague, Faculty of Law, University of Amsterdam. Prior to this, he was a British Academy Newton Fellow at the Department of Law, London School of Economics and Political Science (LSE), and Assistant Professor in Constitutional and European Law at Utrecht University Law School. He holds a PhD on the role of national parliaments in the EU from Utrecht University. Dr Jančić has been a Visiting Scholar at SciencesPo Paris, LSE, University of Lisbon and Max Planck Institute for Comparative Public Law and International Law in Heidelberg. In 2011, he won the Europe Award from the Montesquieu Institute, The Hague, for an article published in the *European Constitutional Law Review*, and in 2010 received an honourable mention from the Ius Commune Research Network for an article published in the *Columbia Journal of European Law*. His most recent publications include 'The Game of Cards: National Parliaments in the EU and the Future of the Early Warning Mechanism and the Political Dialogue' (2015) 52(4) *Common Market Law Review* 939–76, 'Transatlantic Regulatory Interdependence, Law and Governance: The Evolving Roles of the EU and US Legislatures' (2015) 17 *Cambridge Yearbook of European Legal Studies* 334–59, and 'Globalizing Representative Democracy: The Emergence of Multilayered International Parliamentarism', (2015) 38(2) *Hastings International and Comparative Law Review* 197–242.

Nicola Lupo is Full Professor of Public Law and deputy director of the Centre for Parliamentary Studies at LUISS Guido Carli University in Rome. At LUISS School of Government he is Director of the master program 'Parliament and Public Policies', of the Summer School on 'Parliamentary Democracy in Europe' and of the Erasmus+ Master in Parliamentary Procedures and Legislative Drafting (EUPADRA). He was counsellor at the Italian Chamber of Deputies (1997–2005), member of the Prime Minister's Simplification Unit (2006–2008) and of the Drafting Committee of the Commission for Constitutional Reform (2013). He has been a visiting scholar at George Washington University Law School (US), the Institute of Advanced Legal Studies in London, the Institut d'Etudes Europeénnes at the Université Libre de Bruxelles, the Australian National University in Canberra and at the Department of Politics of the University of Sheffield. His publications concern sources of law, parliamentary rules of procedures, legal drafting, budgetary procedures, regional councils and parliaments in the EU. He has co-authored a textbook on Italian parliamentary law (with L Gianniti), *Corso di diritto parlamentare* (2nd edn, Il Mulino, 2013), and he has recently co-edited both *Democracy and Subsidiarity in the EU* (Il Mulino, 2013) (with M Cartabia and A Simoncini) and *Comparative Law in Legislative Drafting* (Eleven International Publishing, 2014) (with L Scaffardi).

Giuseppe Martinico is Associate Professor of Comparative Public Law at the Scuola Superiore Sant'Anna, Pisa. Prior to joining the Scuola Sant'Anna, he was García Pelayo Fellow at the Centro de Estudios Politicos y Constitucionales (CEPC), Madrid, and Max Weber Fellow at the European University Institute, Florence. He holds a PhD in Law from the Scuola Superiore Sant'Anna (Sant'Anna School of Advanced Studies), Pisa, Italy, where he also conducted two years of postdoctoral research. In Pisa he also serves as the editor of *STALS*.

He has also held the position of visiting researcher at the University of Barcelona, Université de Montréal, University of Geneva, King's College, London, and the Tilburg Institute of Comparative and Transnational Law (TICOM). He is Researcher at the Centre for Studies on Federalism, Turin, and member of the editorial board of *Perspectives on Federalism*. He is the author of several books and essays in English, Italian and Spanish, including *The Tangled Complexity of the EU Constitutional Process: The Frustrating Knot of Europe* (Routledge, 2012) and *Historias del País de las Hadas. La jurisprudencia constitucionalizadora del Tribunal de Justicia, Civitas* (Thomson-Reuters, 2015) (with L Gordillo).

Andreja Pegan is Associate Researcher at the Chair of Legislative Studies, Chamber of Deputies/University of Luxembourg. She holds a PhD in Political Science from the University of Luxembourg, where in March 2015 she defended her thesis entitled 'An Analysis of Legislative Assistance in the European Parliament'. Her main research interests concern the legislative staff in the European Parliament, parliament and foreign affairs and interparliamentary cooperation. Her publications include 'Traités internationaux et le parlement luxembourgeois' (with A Spreitzer and A Husain) in P Poirier (ed), *Autonomie et rôle du parlement luxembourgeois* (Larcier, 2014).

Cesare Pinelli is Full Professor of Public Law in the Faculty of Law of the University of Rome 'Sapienza'. He is a former member of the Executive Committee of the International Association of Constitutional Law (2004–2010) and an expert of the 'Commission for Democracy through Law' (Venice Commission), Council of Europe. He has authored several publications in Italian and in English, French, Spanish, Portuguese and German, including 'The Populist Challenge to Constitutional Democracy' (2011) 7(1) *European Constitutional Law Review*, 'Parliamentarism' (with AW Bradley) in M Rosenfeld and A Sajo (eds), *The Oxford Handbook of Comparative Constitutional Law* (Oxford University Press, 2012), and 'Constitutions' (with Y Hasebe) in M Tushnet, T Fleiner and C Saunders (eds), *Routledge Handbook of Constitutional Law* (Routledge, 2013).

Kolja Raube is Senior Researcher at the Leuven Centre for Global Governance Studies, as well as programme coordinator and lecturer in the 'Master of European Studies: Transnational and Global Perspectives' at the Centre for European Studies (KU Leuven). He holds a PhD in Political Science from the University of Hamburg. His research interests focus on EU Foreign Policy, especially with a view to coherence and legitimacy. He has been Visiting Professor at Kobe University (Japan) and is the author of several publications on EU external policies and its parliamentary dimension, including articles in the *Journal of European Integration, European Foreign Affairs Review, The Hague Journal for Diplomacy* and the *Cambridge Review of International Relations.*

Mendeltje van Keulen is parliamentary clerk of the European Affairs Committee and head of the EU advisory staff of the House of Representatives of the States-General of the Netherlands (Tweede Kamer). Previously she worked as senior researcher at the Netherlands Institute for International Relations 'Clingendael', the Netherlands Scientific Council for Government Policy (WRR) and in the European Parliament. She regularly publishes and lectures on EU policy making by governments and national parliaments, is Visiting Lecturer at Leiden University, and co-authored the academic textbook *Analyzing EU policy* (Palgrave Macmillan, 2011) (with Esther Versluis and Paul Stephenson). Her PhD, *Going*

Europe or Going Dutch (Amsterdam University Press, 2005) discussed strengths and weaknesses of national interest representation in the EU.

Jan Wouters is Full Professor of International Law and International Organizations, Jean Monnet Chair *Ad Personam* on EU and Global Governance and founding Director of the Institute for International Law and of the Leuven Centre for Global Governance Studies, an interdisciplinary centre of excellence, at the University of Leuven (KU Leuven). He is a Member of the Royal Academy of Belgium for Sciences and Arts, is President of the United Nations Association Flanders Belgium, and practises law as *Of Counsel* at Linklaters, Brussels. He is Editor of the *International Encyclopedia of Intergovernmental Organizations*, Deputy Director of the *Revue Belge de Droit International* and an editorial board member of ten international journals. He has published widely on international, EU, corporate and financial law. His recent books include *The EU's Role in Global Governance* (Oxford University Press, 2013) (with B Van Vooren and S Blockmans), and *National Human Rights Institutions in Europe* (Intersentia, 2013) (with K Meuwissen). He is co-ordinator of a large-scale FP7 Programme FRAME, 'Fostering Human Rights Among European (External and Internal) Policies' and of the InBev-Baillet Latour EU China Chair at KU Leuven.

Introduction

Parliaments in the Composite European Constitution

CRISTINA FASONE AND NICOLA LUPO

I. THE HARD TASK OF BEING A PARLIAMENT IN THE EUROPEAN UNION TODAY …

THE FACT THAT since the end of the Second World War in Europe and elsewhere legislatures have undergone a series of deep transformations as far as concerns their way of functioning and the exercise of their powers, is something repeatedly asserted by scholars.[1] The rise of the rule-making powers of the executives, the increasing globalisation and internationalisation of politics and policies, the Information and Communications Technology revolution and the launching of new forms of citizen participation in political decisions are only a few factors underlying a trend that challenges the main assumption of what a legislature is and how it is deemed to perform its tasks.

The European Union (EU) constitutes an interesting laboratory in which to see how a significant number of parliaments—according to the theories proposing a distinction between parliaments and congresses, depending on whether they are placed within parliamentary or presidential systems[2]—deal with their evolving role in contemporary times.[3]

[1] P Norton, 'Parliaments in the 21st century: The representative challenge', *Lectio magistralis at the Italian Chamber of Deputies* (2012), available at: www.amministrazioneincammino.it, and J Pollak, 'Compounded representation in the EU. No country for old parliaments?' in Sandra Kröger (ed), *Political Representation in the European Union. Still democratic in times of crisis?* (Abingdon, Routledge, 2014) 19.

[2] On this point, see A Kreppel, 'Typologies and Classifications' in Shane Martin, Thomas Saalfeld, and Kaare W Strøm (eds), *The Oxford Handbook of Legislative Studies* (Oxford, Oxford University Press, 2014).

[3] T Raunio, 'National Parliaments and European Integration: What We Know and Agenda for Future Research' (2009) 15 *Journal of Legislative Studies* 317.

On the one hand, the impressive transfer of legislative and budgetary powers to the European institutions has pushed parliaments of the EU Member States[4]—called 'national parliaments' (NPs) by the European Treaties—to adapt their functions and organisation in a rather unique way compared to what happens in the rest of the world. Initially represented also in the European Parliament (although originally called European Parliamentary Assembly) through their members, since 1979, when this institution was directly elected for the first time, they have not enjoyed any direct representation at European level.

On the other hand, the European Parliament, one of the very few cases of a supranational parliament directly elected by the people,[5] has seen its own powers dramatically increased in the last 30 years, acquiring at first budgetary functions and later on legislative functions (now on an almost symmetric basis with the Council),[6] together with a progressively greater influence on the appointment of the European Commission (even 'electing' its president, according to article 17 TEU).[7]

The Treaty of Lisbon, sometimes enthusiastically defined as the 'Treaty of parliaments',[8] has aimed at strengthening the role of parliaments, both in terms of the law-making powers of the European Parliament and the participation and information rights for national parliaments. Parliaments were seen in their traditional representative function, as essential—although not exclusive—channels of communication between national public opinions and the European institutions, in order not to leave it uniquely to Member States' executives, decisively reinforced thanks to the European integration process.

The referendums of 2005 in France and the Netherlands on the constitutional treaty has undoubtedly showed—among other things—the negative effects that can derive from a detachment of EU policies from public opinions, although limited to some of its Member States. One of the reactions therefore was to insist, in the aftermath of the failure of the constitutional treaty, on the mainly representative nature of the European Union democracy, founded both on the European Parliament and the national parliaments. The need for the good functioning of both representative channels has been clearly highlighted by the Treaties (Articles 10 and 12 TEU) and recognised through the formation of constitutional

[4] It is remarkable that the term 'national' re-appears, in the European treaties, precisely in the very discipline addressed to those who, with more neutral terms, could have been called the 'Parliaments of the Member States': see N Lupo, 'National and Regional Parliaments in the EU decision-making process, after the Treaty of Lisbon and the Euro-crisis' (2013) 5 *Perspectives on Federalism* E-1–28, E-9.

[5] The Mercosur Parliament and the Parliament of the Andean Community are equally elected, although by no means they have a set of functions and powers comparable to those of the EP. cf O Costa, C Dri and S Stavridis (eds), *Parliamentary Dimensions of Regionalization and Globalization. The Role of Inter-parliamentary Institutions* (New York, Palgrave MacMillan, 2013).

[6] For the first steps along this path see O Costa, *Le Parlement européen, assemblée délibérante* (Bruxelles, Éditions de l'Université de Bruxelles, 2001); P Settembri and C Neuhold, 'Achieving Consensus Through Committees: Does the European Parliament Manage?' (2009) 47 *Journal of Common Market Studies* 127.

[7] On the debate regarding the correctness of the referral to an 'election', given the absence of more than one alternative choice, see S Fabbrini, *Which European Union? Europe after the Euro-crisis* (Cambridge, Cambridge University Press, 2015) 155–56, and A Manzella, 'Il parlamentarismo europeo al tempo della globalizzazione' (2015) 4 *Federalismi.it*: www.federalismi.it p 3 ff.

[8] Dutch *Tweede Kamer*, 'Ahead in Europe. On the role of the Dutch House of Representatives and national parliaments in the European Union' *Final Report on Democratic Legitimacy*, 9 May 2014, p 8.

conventions, like the so-called 'political dialogue' between national parliaments and the European Commission, introduced in 2006.[9]

Notwithstanding the generous provisions of the Treaty of Lisbon regarding parliaments, new threats loomed up on the horizon of the parliaments of Europe. Assessed as a whole, the developments that have taken place in the EU since 2009 have challenged their role. In particular, the impairment of the democratic credentials of the European Parliament and the Eurozone crisis have contributed to making their lives particularly complicated in their respective domestic contexts.[10]

Indeed, when the ratification of the Treaty of Lisbon was still ongoing, the European Parliament was subject to a harsh attack on the part of the German Constitutional Court against its very nature as a democratic parliamentary body. The empowerment of the European Parliament, coupled with the application of the principle of degressive proportionality (Article 14 TEU) to its composition, which in the view of the German Court would alter the principle of 'one man, one vote' in particular to the detriment of German citizens, the most under-represented in this legislature, makes the 'Assembly for Europe' not fully democratic.[11] This is why the German Bundestag, which in contrast to the European Parliament could truly represent the German people, and Bundesrat, in their domains, must retain control over any explicit or implicit competence conferral to the European Union in the cases listed by the Court and even regardless of formal treaty revisions.

Likewise, the Eurozone crisis has hit both the European Parliament and national parliaments' democratic legitimacy. The former, because of the limited competence it has in the field of economic governance, has certainly not been a prominent player during the crisis and, even less so, in some crucial activities, like the creation of rescue funds and the negotiation of bailout programmes (whereas in the definition of the Euro-national budgetary procedures through the European Semester and the Banking Union it has been actively involved).[12] The lack of responses provided to the citizens of Europe by this institution, in particular against the grip of austerity, in addition to the weaknesses of a truly transnational electoral campaign, despite the experiment of the Spitzenkandidaten, and the rise of populist and Eurosceptic movements in 2014, led to the lowest electoral turnout ever in the history of the European elections (42.61 per cent).[13]

[9] See D Chalmers, G Davies and G Monti, *European Union Law*, 3rd edn (Cambridge, Cambridge University Press, 2014) 129, and, more specifically, D Jančić, 'The Barroso Initiative: Window Dressing or Democracy Boost?' (2012) 8 *Utrecht Law Review* 78. Although unilaterally granted by means of a letter from the then Commission President Barroso, the procedure was agreed with COSAC. And maybe following the same procedure, the political dialogue is going to be updated and extended by the Juncker Commission. See the chapter by M Goldoni, 'The Instrumental Value of Horizontal Parliamentary Cooperation: Subsidiarity Review and the Political Dialogue', Chapter 9 in this volume.

[10] For the European Parliament the domestic context can be identified with the institutional system of the European Union as well as with the relationship with the European voters.

[11] See the decision on the Treaty of Lisbon by the German Constitutional Court, Second Senate, *2 BvE 2/08*, 30 June 2009.

[12] C Fasone, 'European Economic Governance and Parliamentary Representation. What Place for the European Parliament?' (2014) 20 *European Law Journal* 164.

[13] Although the percentage has dropped by less than 0.3% from 2009 to 2014. Source: statistics available on the website of the European Parliament, at: www.europarl.europa.eu/elections2014-results/en/turnout.html. On the Spitzenkandidaten experience, see N Peñalver García and J Priestley, *The Making of a European President* (Palgrave, Abingdon, 2015).

Moreover with few exceptions and although potentially enabled to oversee their executive,[14] national parliaments have found themselves unable to deal properly, in terms of parliamentary debate, with careful scrutiny and well-informed deliberation on the intergovernmental agreements negotiated during the crisis: the European Financial Stability Facility, the Treaty on the European Stability Mechanism (ESM), the Fiscal Compact and the agreement on the Bank Resolution Fund.[15] The pressure put on them by the governments, individually and collectively through the Eurogroup, the European Council and the Euro Summit, and on some occasions also by the European Central Bank and the International Monetary Fund, has not left much choice to national legislatures that often have jointly discussed these measures or passively voted for them. The parliaments of the Member States that have benefited from financial assistance and support within (Cyprus, Greece, Ireland, Italy, Portugal and Spain) or outside the Eurozone (Hungary, Latvia[16] and Romania) were even more constrained in the autonomy of their budgetary decisions and in the adoption of structural reforms. The only counter-weight to this (forced) parliamentary passivity has been represented either by Constitutional and Supreme Courts, for example in Germany, Portugal and Estonia,[17] or by Eurosceptic parties, which tended to move the debate outside and sometimes even against parliamentary assemblies.

Perhaps the most acute challenge to representative democracy entrenched in parliamentary institutions has been launched in the case of the 2015 Greek—last minute—referendum. The bypassing of the Greek Parliament was determined by many factors: first, its inability to elect a President of the Republic, which led to new parliamentary elections in January 2015; second, the electoral success of the Eurosceptic party SYRIZA, which made the adoption of the required austerity measures extremely difficult; third, the illusion, created by the government in office, of letting the Greek people directly decide on their own future through a referendum, called in 10 days, and held on 5 July 2015.[18] When a third bailout programme was finally agreed upon by the Euro Summit on 12 July 2015—the choice being between bankruptcy and potential exit from the Eurozone, on the one hand, and staying within the Eurozone, re-opening banks and receiving financial assistance, on the other—the Parliament was again requested to vote on, to our knowledge, the most comprehensive package of reforms negotiated with the Troika in the shortest period of time: just … one week.[19] While the Greek Parliament 'approved' these reforms, which were

[14] E Griglio and N Lupo, 'Parliamentary Democracy and the Eurozone Crisis' (2012) 1 *Law and Economics Yearly Review* 314.

[15] See A Maatsch, 'Limited and asymmetrical: approval of anti-crisis measures (EFSF, ESM, and TSCG) by national parliaments in the Eurozone' in C Fasone, D Fromage and Z Lefkofridi (eds), *Parliaments, public opinion, and parliamentary elections in Europe*, (2015) 18 *EUI Max Weber Working Paper Series*, and C Fasone, 'Eurozone, non-Eurozone and "troubled asymmetries" among national parliaments in the EU. Why and to what extent this is of concern' (2014) 6 *Perspectives on Federalism*, in R Castaldi and G Martinico (eds), Special Issue on 'The Never-Ending Reform of the EU: Another Chain in the Semi Permanent Treaty Revision Process?', p 1.

[16] Latvia joined the Eurozone afterwards, only on 1 January 2014.

[17] C Fasone, 'Taking budgetary powers away from national parliaments? On parliamentary prerogatives in the Eurozone crisis' (2015) 37 *EUI Law Working Paper Series*, cadmus.eui.eu/handle/1814/36658.

[18] See X Contiades and A Fotiadou, 'The Greek Referendum: Unconstitutional and Undemocratic', *Constitutional Change Thorugh Euro Crisis Law*, European University Institute, Law Department, 7 July 2015: eurocrisislaw.eui.eu/news/the-greek-referendum-unconstitutional-and-undemocratic-by-xenophon-contiades-and-alkmene-fotiadou/.

[19] See the detailed lists in the Euro Summit Statement of 12 July 2015: eurocrisislaw.eui.eu/wp-content/uploads/2015/07/20150712-eurosummit-statement-greece.pdf. They include, for instance, the reform of the pension and fiscal systems and the adoption of the Code of Civil Procedure.

a pre-condition for the rescue programme to be in operation, other parliaments of some of the creditor countries, such as the Austrian, Estonian, Finnish and German Parliaments, were voting to authorise their governments to start the negotiations on granting financial assistance to Greece, according to their national constitutional requirements.[20]

II. ... AND A WAY FORWARD: THE DEVELOPMENT OF INTERPARLIAMENTARY COOPERATION

What do all these developments tell us in terms of the role of the European and national parliaments in the European Union? Interestingly enough and precisely when the role of the European Council and the Council has grown substantially in deciding the strategies as well as the concrete measures to face the financial crisis in Europe[21] and when the margins of manoeuvre of many parliaments were restrained in their own domestic context, there has been a blossoming of interparliamentary meetings, forums and conferences on different topics and purposes and with a variable-asymmetric participation.

While in the domestic arenas, although to a different degree depending on the Member State, national parliaments have tried to strengthen their scrutiny of the executives in the field of EU affairs and to set up new committees or administrative structures that could support a gradual shift from (sole) law-making to a greater oversight function especially on European policies, they have devoted their attention to the external dimension of their activities, in an incremental way.

In spite of the traditional competition between the European Parliament and national legislatures and the different degrees of commitment they show towards their cooperation, at least every week the parliaments of Europe meet all together or in smaller formations (by policy interest or by region) in Brussels, in other European capitals as well as virtually on the Internet.[22] They exchange information, necessary to better oversee the many executives existing in the European Union, and try to coordinate their positions on the most salient issues wherever possible.

[20] A first comparative picture is offered by V Kreilinger, 'Asymmetric parliamentary powers: the case of the third rescue package for Greece', 19 August 2015, available at: www.delorsinstitut.de/en/allgemein-en/asymmetric-parliamentary-powers-the-case-of-the-third-rescue-package-for-greece/. On the French case, where the government just involved the Assemblée Nationale to approve a general political declaration, ie even a negative vote would not have hampered the government from continuing the negotiations with Greece, see D Fromage, 'The ESM and National Parliaments: France', *Constitutional Change Through Euro-Crisis Law*, 28 July 2015: eurocrisislaw.eui.eu/news/the-esm-and-national-parliaments-france-by-diane-fromage/.

[21] See U Puetter, *The European Council and the Council. New intergovernmentalism and institutional change* (Oxford, Oxford University Press, 2014); J White, 'Politicizing Europe: The Challenge of Executive Discretion' in SB Hobolt and O Cramme (eds), *Democratic Politics in a European Union under Stress* (Oxford, Oxford University Press, 2014) 87 ff; S Fabbrini, above n 7, 45ff; D Howarth and L Quaglia, 'The New Intergovernmentalism in Financial Regulation and the European Banking Union' in CJ Bickerton, D Hodson and U Puetter (eds), *The new intergovernmentalism. States and Supranational Actors in the Post-Maastricht Era* (Oxford, Oxford University Press, 2015) 146–62.

[22] See D Fromage, 'A mapping of recent trends in interparliamentary cooperation within the EU' in C Fasone, D Fromage and Z Lefkofridi (eds), *Parliaments, public opinion and parliamentary elections in Europe*, (2015) 18 *EUI Max Weber Working Paper Series*, http://cadmus.eui.eu/handle/1814/37462.

While the multiplication of interparliamentary meetings raises concerns as to their effectiveness and the cost for their organisation, it also shows that parliaments are re-inventing their role through interparliamentary cooperation—that now also has legal bases in the European Treaties (article 12 TEU, articles 9–10 Protocol No 1, Protocol No 2 and the Fiscal Compact)—in between the domestic and the supranational arenas. Given the variety of the formats that interparliamentary cooperation can take on, ie, permanent or ad hoc-temporary, asymmetric or 'all inclusive', generalist or policy-oriented, etc, and its direct link with the issue of democratic legitimation of the European Union, the phenomenon of interparliamentary cooperation deserves a more careful academic analysis, which this book aims to provide.

To this end, the following research questions are dealt with in the chapters that follow in the volume, each of them addressing one or more of these questions according to their focus: 1) What are the instruments and aims of interparliamentary cooperation and are they achieved? 2) To what extent do parliaments contribute to the development of the composite European Constitution through interparliamentary cooperation? 3) Is interparliamentary cooperation helping in reconciling European and national democratic systems? 4) Is interparliamentary cooperation increasing the executives' accountability and political responsibility in a Euro-national parliamentary system?[23]

III. THE CONCEPTUAL FRAMEWORK

A. The Ongoing Debate on the Role of Parliaments in the Composite European Constitution

The book aims to cover a topical debate in EU constitutional law,[24] which originates from the present difficulty in finding new patterns of parliamentary interaction at European level now that national parliaments have been provided with powers of direct intervention in the EU, in particular through the scrutiny of the principle of subsidiarity, ie, the early warning system (EWS).

Such difficulty has also been highlighted by the political, institutional and technical discussions concerning interparliamentary cooperation, which was deemed to have a marginal institutional impact in the past, but today, as said, is expressly acknowledged as a permanent feature of EU democracy by EU Treaties and the Fiscal Compact.

The volume does not focus on interparliamentary cooperation in itself. It aims first and foremost at analysing the effects of interparliamentary cooperation on the institutional actors directly and indirectly involved, at national as well as at European level—namely, on national parliaments and the European Parliament, in terms of organisation and procedures, but also on the fragmented executive of the EU, composed of national

[23] For a more detailed definition of the Euro-national parliamentary system, see Section II.B below and the Conclusion in this volume.

[24] A Von Bogdandy and J Bast, *Principles of European Constitutional Law*, 2nd edn (Oxford and München, Hart Publishing and Verlag CH Beck, 2011); R Schütze, *European Constitutional Law* (Cambridge, Cambridge University Press, 2012); R Bin, P Caretti and G Pitruzzella, *Profili costituzionali dell'Unione europea* (Bologna, Il mulino, 2015); K Tuori, *European Constitutionalism* (Cambridge, Cambridge University Press, 2015).

governments, with their different ministries by policy area, the European Commission, the Council, the European Council and, to some extent, also the independent agencies and authorities.[25]

Indeed, the fragmented executive is a very important institutional feature of the EU, which interparliamentary cooperation is requested to deal with. The fragmented nature of the executive of the EU often induces national and European governments to share, but also to escape from and dissolve their political responsibility, in relation to their own parliament as well as to citizens.[26] It weakens the traditional instruments of parliamentary scrutiny and oversight, as the responsibility for the policies carried out is not clearly traceable to a single executive body.

In particular, intergovernmental institutions and bodies, like the European Council and the Euro Summit, cannot be effectively controlled either by the European Parliament or by national parliaments: the first is substantially devoid of powers to directly oversee these bodies, while at best the latter are able to check whether national government members actually pursue their national interests in those forums.

In this context, interparliamentary cooperation is one of the ways whereby a form of political responsibility and/or democratic accountability can be revived: building connections among different parliaments has often helped in reconstructing how decisions have been taken far away from the national scene and has unveiled some documents/positions that a single national executive did not want to disclose to its parliament and citizens.

This complex set of relationships is investigated by looking at the EU as a composite Constitution,[27] grounded at the same time on the Constitutions of the Member States and on the European Treaties (by which we refer to TEU, TFEU, Charter of fundamental rights, and EU-related treaties like the Fiscal Compact and the Treaty on the European Stability Mechanism), as the framework of analysis. National Constitutions and European Treaties recognise each other—in the European clauses of national Constitutions and in several Treaties' references to national constitutional law, respectively—therefore self-restraining their original sovereign power and giving rise to a composite Constitution.

Given this interpretation of the EU as a composite constitutional order, the roles of parliamentary institutions placed at different levels of government also become strongly intertwined. Thus, in order to fully grasp the reality of a Euro-national parliamentary dimension, we must look dynamically at the horizontal relationship between national parliaments, at each of them embedded in a specific form of government (and consequently with their executive branch), as well as at their relationship with the European Parliament and the EU institutions exercising the executive power.

So far scholarly articles and books dealing with parliaments in the EU have looked at them from the viewpoint of the problem of the democratic deficit,[28] the theory of

[25] D Curtin, 'Challenging Executive Dominance in European Democracy' (2014) 77 *Modern Law Review* 1.

[26] B Crum and D Curtin, 'The Challenge of Making European Union Executive Power Accountable' in S Piattoni (ed), *The European Union. Democratic Principles and Institutional Architectures in Times of Crisis* (Oxford, Oxford University Press, 2015) 63.

[27] LFM Besselink, *A Composite European Constitution* (Groningen, Europa Law Publishing, 2007).

[28] A Føllesdal and S Hix, 'Why There is a Democratic Deficit in the EU: A Response to Majone and Moravcsik' (2006) 44 *Journal of Common Market Studies* 533.

delegation,[29] the theory of representation,[30] and the theory of legal and political constitutionalism,[31] especially when an attempt was made to look at parliaments from the perspective of political theory or philosophy.

In the case of national parliaments, by far the most studied procedure since the entry into force of the Treaty of Lisbon has been the EWS, although different conclusions have been reached about its suitability and effectiveness and the scope of the scrutiny of the principle of subsidiarity.[32] There are also books on how national parliaments have been affected by the process of European integration, in terms of procedures and organisation and in terms of the relationship with the executive, in a comparative perspective.[33] Finally, there are contributions on interparliamentary cooperation in international politics, which look at the phenomenon from the point of view of international relations, in Europe and beyond.[34]

However, there is not much scholarship aiming to see whether interparliamentary cooperation is able to reconcile the European and the national dimensions of parliamentary democracy in the EU and to analyse it in relation to the role that the executives play in the composite European Constitution. By contrast, the starting point of this volume is that a reconciliation between the national and the European dimensions of parliamentary democracy is required in order to preserve the democratic legitimacy and accountability of the current decision-making processes in the EU. These processes take place partly within the Member States and partly within EU institutions (also composed of members pertaining to domestic institutions, in the cases of the Council and the European Council). Thus, individually taken, each national parliament and the European Parliament hold only a portion of the relevant information and powers that enable them to oversee the fragmented executive of the EU.

Given the wording of the Treaties and the developing institutional practice, interparliamentary cooperation can even be detected as a new parliamentary function, jointly exercised by national parliaments and the European Parliament. However, it does not constitute an autonomous channel of parliamentary legitimation and representation of the EU, but

[29] G Majone, 'Europe's "Democratic Deficit": A Question of Standards' (1998) 4 *European Law Journal* 5; B Rittberger, *Building Europe's Parliament: Democratic Representation Beyond the Nation State* (Oxford, Oxford University Press, 2005).

[30] D Friedrich and S Kröger (eds), *The Challenge of Democratic Representation in the European Union* (New York, Palgrave MacMillan, 2012).

[31] M Goldoni, 'The Early Warning System and the Monti II Regulation: The Case for a Political Interpretation' (2014) 10 *European Constitutional Law Review* 90, based on the account of political and legal constitutionalism provided by R Bellamy, *Political Constitutionalism: A Republican Defence of the Constitutionality of Democracy* (Cambridge, Cambridge University Press, 2007).

[32] I Cooper, 'A "Virtual Third Chamber" for the European Union? National Parliaments after the Treaty of Lisbon' (2012) 35 *West European Politics* 441; P De Wilde, 'Why the Early Warning Mechanism does not Alleviate the Democratic Deficit' (2012) 6 *OPAL Online Paper*; P Kiiver, *The Early Warning System for the Principle of Subsidiarity: Constitutional Theory and Empirical Reality* (London, Routledge, 2012); F Fabbrini and K Granat, '"Yellow card, but no foul": The role of the national parliaments under the Subsidiarity Protocol and the Commission proposal for an EU regulation on the right to strike' (2013) 50 *Common Market Law Review* 115.

[33] A Maurer and W Wessels (eds), *National Parliaments on their Ways to Europe. Losers or Latecomers?* (Baden Baden, Nomos Verlag, 2001); K Auel and A Benz, 'The politics of adaptation: The Europeanisation of national parliamentary systems' (2005) 11 *The Journal of Legislative Studies* 372; S Brouard, O Costa and T König (eds), *The Europeanization of Domestic Legislatures: The Empirical Implications of the Delors' Myth in Nine Countries* (New York, Springer, 2012).

[34] B Crum and JE Fossum (eds), *Practices of Inter-parliamentary Coordination in International Politics: The European Union and Beyond* (Colchester, ECPR Press, 2013).

rather an instrument which could help the two ordinary channels for parliamentary representation to find better ways to exercise their functions and to design more coordinated strategies of parliamentary oversight.[35]

B. A Euro-national Parliamentary System

The often inconsistent evaluations of the EWS and the harsh debates characterising, in particular, the setting up of the new interparliamentary conferences on foreign, security and defence policy and economic and financial governance, derive—it is argued in this book—from the co-existence of very different ideas and theoretical frameworks concerning the role of parliaments in the EU. Which are and which should be the respective roles of national parliaments and the European Parliament are still matters of concern in the EU institutional debate, both at academic and political levels.

As for the political debate, recipes for the strengthening of European democracy differ very much. Some require a further increase of the powers of the European Parliament. Others ask for the introduction of a veto power (often called 'red card') upon a certain number of national parliaments (or even a single one).[36] Further opinions argue in favour of a revival of an old proposal: that is, the setting up of a new parliamentary assembly, composed of representatives of national parliaments, limited to the Eurozone Member States.[37]

As for academic debate, as is well known, the federalist approach is very much in favour of strengthening the authority and powers of the European Parliament as the supranational democratic institution par excellence, but usually overlooks the democratic contribution of the national parliamentary dimension to the EU integration process.[38] For the rest, at the national level, each government is accountable to its respective parliament, also on EU matters and, according to the federalists, no direct role should be exercised by national parliaments at European level.

According to other scholars, by contrast, the main channel for the democratic legitimacy of the EU still relies on national parliaments, as the nation state and its bodies are to be deemed the main locus of constitutional and democratic accountability of the EU regulatory powers.[39] This approach moves to proposals aimed at increasing the national parliaments' role in EU decision-making, either through Treaty amendments, or else through the introduction of new constitutional conventions (called 'green card' or 'enhanced political

[35] E Griglio and N Lupo, *Strengths, Weaknesses, Opportunities and Threats of Interparliamentary Cooperation in the EU*, paper presented at the 13ème Congrès national—Association française de Science politique, 22–24 June 2015, Aix-en-Provence.

[36] Cf D Cameron, UK Prime Minister, *A New Settlement for the United Kingdom in a reformed European Union*, Letter to Donald Tusk, President of the European Council, 10 November 2015, https://www.gov.uk/government/uploads/system/uploads/attachment_data/file/475679/Donald_Tusk_letter.pdf.

[37] E Griglio and N Lupo, 'Towards an asymmetric European Union, without an asymmetric European Parliament' (2014) 20 *LUISS SOG Working Papers*; D Curtin and C Fasone, 'Differentiated Representation: Is a Flexible European Parliament Desirable?' in B de Witte, E Vos and A Ott (eds), *Between Flexibility and Disintegration: The State of EU law today* (Cheltenham, Edward Elgar Publishing, 2016), forthcoming.

[38] D Marquand, *Parliament for Europe* (London, Jonathan Cape, 1979).

[39] PL Lindseth, *Power and Legitimacy: Reconciling Europe and the Nation-State* (Oxford, Oxford University Press, 2010); D Chalmers, 'Democratic Self-Government in Europe. Domesticating Solutions to the EU Legitimacy Crisis', *Policy Network Paper*, 15 May 2013, 5 ff; R Bellamy and S Kröger, 'Domestic the Democratic Deficit? The Role of National Parliaments and Parties in the EU's System of Governance' (2014) 67 *Parliamentary Affairs* 437.

dialogue') encouraging, in the wake of the experience of the 'political dialogue', a more proactive role for them.[40]

Recently Ben Crum and Erik Fossum have proposed a new paradigm for understanding parliamentary democracy in the EU, its strengths and weaknesses, according to the idea of a 'multilevel parliamentary field'.[41] They argue that parliamentarism in the EU has to be put in context: since the EU develops as a multilevel system of government, it is exactly within this framework that the contributions of national parliaments and the European Parliament to EU democracy have to be assessed. Both dimensions of parliamentarism are important, and even more so their mutual relationship. Although the idea of a 'multilevel parliamentary field' appraises the significance of interparliamentary cooperation, it does not include in this dynamic the interplay with the EU fragmented executive, which nevertheless in our view is a crucial feature for understanding the role of parliaments in the composite European Constitution.[42]

Indeed, the legitimacy of the European constitutional order, particularly after the Treaty of Lisbon and the new economic governance, depends on the nature and functioning of a more complex set of parliamentary and interinstitutional relationships that can be divided up for explanatory purposes as follows: the relationship between each national parliament and its government; the relationship between national parliaments that parallels the relationship between national executives; the relationship between the European Parliament and the EU executive; the relationship between the European Parliament and the national parliaments.

This arrangement is what this book defines as the 'Euro-national parliamentary system', where each set of relationships listed above has to take into account all the others as inherent to the composite nature of the EU constitutional order. This very idea of a 'Euro-national parliamentary system', of which interparliamentary cooperation is a crucial component and which considers the role of the executive as the first point of reference for parliamentary action, is the approach followed by the editors and is the starting point of this volume.[43]

In other words, the concept of the 'Euro-national parliamentary system' moves from the model of the 'multilevel parliamentary field' coined by Crum and Fossum, but goes further. It is composed of both European and national procedures and based upon the idea that the functions of representation, policy-setting and oversight—traditionally attributed to every legislature—are now necessarily networked and shared among the different parliaments in the EU.[44]

Differently from the previous model, which relied on the concept of the 'field', in which every parliament is called upon to play rather freely its own game,[45] the model proposed

[40] C Fasone and D Fromage, 'National parliaments and the EU Commission's agenda: limits and recent developments of a difficult partnership' in C Fasone, D Fromage and Z Lefkofridi (eds), *Parliaments, public opinion and parliamentary elections in Europe*, (2015) EUI Max Weber Working Paper Series; N Lupo, 'Iniziativa legislativa e ruolo dei parlamenti nazionali nel sistema istituzionale dell'Unione europea' in R Mastroianni and A Maffeo (ed), *L'iniziativa dei cittadini europei* (Napoli, Editoriale scientifica, 2015) 13ff.

[41] B Crum and JE Fossum, 'The Multilevel Parliamentary Field: a framework for theorizing representative democracy in the EU' (2009) 1 *European Political Science Review* 249.

[42] See section II.A above.

[43] Cf A Manzella and N Lupo (eds), *Il sistema parlamentare euro-nazionale. Lezioni* (Torino, Giappichelli, 2014).

[44] A Manzella, 'La cooperazione interparlamentare nel "Trattato internazionale" europeo' *Astrid-online.it*, 22 February 2012.

[45] And even to fight one against one another within what has been named 'the multi-level parliamentary battlefield': see A Herranz Surálles, 'The EU's Multilevel Parliamentary (Battle)Field: Explaining Inter-parliamentary Cooperation and Conflict in the Area of Foreign and Security Policy' (2014) 37 *West European Politics* 957.

here uses the concept of the 'system'—intended, according to the general system theory, as a set of elements standing in interrelation to one another and with the environment[46]—and refers to more structured inter-institutional relationships, not exclusively concerning parliaments. The fulfillment of this idea calls for the development of parliamentary and inter-institutional procedures, both bilateral and multilateral, which are not only able to structure the relationships among parliaments into a real and effective 'system', but also between each parliament and its own executive at national level (whose relevance for EU democracy is acknowledged by article 10 TEU).

One of the factual elements on which this model is founded is, in fact, that in the Constitutions of all the EU Member States, with the only exception of Cyprus, the government is held responsible before the parliament (or at least a chamber thereof).[47] This means that most of the EU chambers are called upon to exercise a function of scrutiny and direction of their own government, including on EU affairs.[48] Far from being external to the EU institutional system, these relationships are an essential part of the composite European Constitution. Furthermore, alongside interparliamentary cooperation and the relationships that the European Parliament entertains with the EU as well as national institutions, they build the structure on which the Euro-national parliamentary system is founded.

C. The Increasing Legalisation of Interparliamentary Cooperation and its Effects on the Composite European Constitution

Interparliamentary cooperation is therefore not just a marginal element of the activity of every national parliament of the EU, but a vital dimension of the Euro-national parliamentary system. The constitutional role of each legislature in the EU is defined not only by its national Constitution, but also by the 'European powers' attributed to it by the Treaties or other sources of EU law and international law.[49]

[46] See L von Bertalanffy, *General System Theory* (New York, George Braziller Inc, 2003 [1968]).

[47] M Olivetti, 'Parlamenti nazionali nell'Unione europea' in *Digesto discipline pubblicistiche*, Aggiornamento V (Torino, Utet, 2012) 498. More specifically, cf A Emilianides, O Chrostou and C Ioannou, 'The Cypriot Parliament and EU Affairs' in C Hefftler et al (eds), *The Palgrave Handbook of National Parliaments and the European Union* (Basingstoke, Palgrave MacMillan, 2015) 479–93.

[48] For an accurate comparative analysis, from which a very diversified picture emerges, see Hefftler et al (eds) ibid n 47 and especially K Auel, O Rozenberg and A Tacea, 'Fighting Back? And, If So, How? Measuring Parliamentary Strength and Activity in EU Affairs', ibid, 60–93.

[49] N Lupo, 'I poteri europei dei Parlamenti nazionali: questioni terminologiche, classificazioni e primi effetti' in A Manzella and N Lupo (eds), *Il sistema parlamentare euro-nazionale. Lezioni* (n 43 above) 108–13. M Olivetti, above n 47, 523 ff, speaks, instead, of 'functions of national parliaments in the European Union' (own translation from Italian), following the Treaty of Lisbon. Most likely, behind this nominal distinction lies a different understanding of the way national legislatures are deemed to exercise these functions or powers. Indeed, according to Nicola Lupo, each national parliament, individually, is able to determine its level of commitment and the degree of involvement in the EWS, the political dialogue, the Treaty revisions and even in interparliamentary cooperation. In other words, national parliaments can have different views on what concerns the objectives and the *finalité* of the European powers outlined in the Treaties and protocols, and this is considered perfectly plausible and legitimate. By contrast, Marco Olivetti tends to see the 'European functions' of national parliaments and their active exercise as being both instrumental to the 'good functioning of the EU' (article 12 TEU). Hence, the use of these functions and procedures cannot be left entirely to the discretion of national parliaments when and how to exercise them. Their *finalité* is embedded in the Treaty and its fulfillment requests the active pro-EU involvement of all parliaments.

Yet, the role of interparliamentary cooperation in theory and in practice is often overlooked. This is not a new phenomenon, but only recently is it gaining more attention from scholarship. Indeed, the rise of interparliamentary cooperation happened rather gradually but its legalisation has intensified only recently.

The EU Speakers' Conference started meeting on a regular basis every two years in 1975 and then, from 1999, in the aftermath of the entry into force of the Treaty of Amsterdam, every year. By the same token, the Conference of parliamentary committees dealing with European affairs (COSAC) was established in 1989 at a crucial juncture for the evolution of the process of European integration, in between the fall of the Berlin Wall and the gradual reunification of Germany and the 'revolution' put forward by the Treaty of Maastricht.[50]

Since then, after the unique experience of the Assises in 1990—praised by the European Parliament while having been rejected by national parliaments[51]—and the two Conventions (1999–2000 and 2001–03), national parliaments have taken on a new lease of life in Europe, at least if we look at legal documents. They have been empowered by the Treaty of Lisbon to be informed and to directly participate in the European policy-making and 'higher law making'[52] (ie, through treaty revisions), up to the point of delaying, vetoing, or even proposing legislation, as the recent 'green card' initiative by the House of Lords, joined by other 17 parliamentary chambers, shows.[53]

In other words, there has been an increasing legalisation of this phenomenon by means of EU primary law, EU legislation, national law and parliamentary rules of procedure that signals the importance of its development. Yet it is not easy to analyse interparliamentary cooperation or even to classify its different legal manifestations.

First, most interparliamentary forums and conferences lack transparency and receive almost no media coverage. Thus, there is not enough awareness by the public or scholars that every week bilateral or multilateral meetings among parliaments take place in the EU, both at national and European level.

Secondly, it remains unclear what legal effects interparliamentary cooperation is entitled to produce. In principle, this cooperation is not able to lead to the adoption of resolutions that are binding, especially for non-parliamentary actors. To some extent, depending on the parliament, parliamentary delegations lack the power to bind their own assembly or to make commitments on their behalf.

[50] See JHH Weiler, first, in 'The Transformation of Europe', (1991) 100 *Yale Law Journal* 2403, 2474–83, and, then, Weiler, 'Europe After Maastricht—Do the New Clothes have an Emperor?' (1995) *NYU Jean Monnet Center for International and Regional Economic Law and Justice.*

[51] E Barón Crespo, 'Parliamentary democracy and the Treaty of Lisbon' (2012) 1 *OPAL Online Paper* 7–10.

[52] B Ackerman, *We the People, Volume 1: Foundations* (Cambridge MA, Harvard University Press, 1991).

[53] See UK House of Lords, European Union Committee, and co-signatories, 'Letter to the European Commission', *Food waste: a proposal by national parliaments to the European Commission*, 22 July 2015, available at: www.parliament.uk/documents/lords-committees/eu-select/green-card/green-card-on-food-waste.pdf. The co-signatories of the 'green card' are: the Bulgarian National Assembly, the Croatian Parliament, the Cypriot House of Representatives, the Czech Chamber of Deputies and Senate, the Danish Parliament, the French National Assembly and Senate, the Hungarian National Assembly, the Italian Senate, the Latvian Saeima, Lithuanian Seimas, Luxembourgish Chamber of Deputies, the Maltese House of Representatives, the Dutch Tweede Kamer, the Portuguese Assembleia da República, the Slovakian National Council, and the UK House of Lords. The Czech Senate and the Danish Parliament confirmed their support to the 'green card' only afterwards, on 27 August and on 10 September respectively. See also, UK House of Lords, European Union Committee, 'The referendum on UK membership of the EU: assessing the reform process', *3rd Report of Session 2015–16*, 28 July 2015, available at: www.publications.parliament.uk/pa/ld201516/ldselect/ldeucom/30/30.pdf, 21–23, regarding the support the House of Lords asks to the Government for the 'green card' initiative.

However, the debates taking place in the framework of interparliamentary cooperation, the constant exchange of views and best practices among parliaments, the informal coordination that is achieved by means of the EWS have deeply affected the organisation and the procedures of the parliaments concerned, the positions and the ideas of some MPs, as well as, in a few cases, policy outcomes.

The limitations of interparliamentary cooperation in general, in the EU and beyond, have been pointed out at length by the few publications on the topic.[54] These limits are the proliferation of interparliamentary forums without a clear design, and the lack of both an ordered development and a process of institutionalisation, whereby the objectives to be achieved and the tasks assigned are anything but clear.

A second type of limit consists in the lack of political willingness on the part of MPs, coming from very different political backgrounds and parties, to be actively involved in interparliamentary cooperation, as there is no incentive here for the success of their political career and re-election.[55] Hence, very often, not only the management of but also political inputs to interparliamentary cooperation are provided by parliamentary officials, thus leading to a sort of bureaucratisation of the instrument.[56] By the same token, interparliamentary cooperation is often accused of encompassing high costs against a substantial lack of effectiveness.

Nevertheless, both criticisms need to be specifically assessed in the light of the actual practice, which is examined in this volume. At present, as far as concerns the unbalanced cost-benefit relationship affecting interparliamentary cooperation, one can just highlight that parliaments are ineffective and inefficient only to a certain extent, since the fulfillment of their representative function nonetheless requires time and resources to be used for the sake of organising and engaging with debates and exchanges of opinions regarding issues of public interest. Regarding the second limit referred to, ie, the lack of political willingness and administrative activism, it can be observed that the 'European powers' are attributed not to MPs themselves, but to national parliaments as institutions, therefore including their parliamentary administrations, which indeed play an important intermediation function, between politics and technical expertise. The extent to which MPs ask for the assistance of and delegate tasks to parliamentary officials on documents and draft legislation almost always with a high level of complexity is nonetheless very variable, and depends also on the degree of Europeanisation of these officials and on the qualitative and quantitative features of parliamentary administrations.

[54] C Decaro and N Lupo (eds), *Il 'dialogo' tra parlamenti: obiettivi e risultati* (Rome, LUISS University Press, 2009); C Fasone, 'Interparliamentary Cooperation and Democratic Representation in the European Union' in S Kröger and D Friedrich (eds), above n 30; O Costa, C Dri and S Stavridis (eds), above n 5; C Lord, 'The European Union: Parliamentary Wasteland or Parliamentary Field?' in B Crum and JE Fossum (eds), above n 34, 235–49.

[55] See K Auel and T Christiansen, 'After Lisbon: National Parliaments in the European Union' (2015) 38 *West European Politics* 261 and the emphasis they put on political motivation besides institutional capacities to explain the use by national parliaments of their new powers under the Treaty of Lisbon.

[56] N Lupo, 'Il ruolo delle burocrazie parlamentari alla luce dei mutamenti dell'assetto istituzionale nazionale e sovranazionale' (2012) 54 *Rassegna parlamentare* 51, 88–89; T Christiansen, A-L Högenauer and C Neuhold, 'National Parliaments in the Post-Lisbon European Union: Bureaucratization rather than Democratization?' (2014) 12 *Comparative European Politics* 121; A-L Högenauer and C Neuhold, 'National Parliaments after Lisbon: Administrations on the Rise?' (2015) 38 *West European Politics* 335.

However, as has been highlighted, parliaments of the twenty-first century are very different institutions from their predecessors in the nineteenth and early-twentieth century. Most importantly, parliaments are placed in a different institutional landscape, which is not only and sometimes not primarily national. Now set within multiple and variable relationships, with their governments, subnational actors, other parliaments, supranational and international organisations, parliaments—it has been argued—have been called upon to develop an international networking function, in addition to the classic parliamentary functions.[57]

This picture is even clearer within the composite European Constitution, where parliaments, at every level of government, are asked to contribute to the good functioning of the EU.[58] As national and European policies become more and more intertwined, only a coordinated and cooperative control of the Euro-national decision-making, between national parliaments and the European Parliament, can ensure effective democratic oversight of the fragmented EU executive. Thus, the national and European parliamentary dimensions are today incomplete if standing alone—each focused either on the purely national or European side of the story—unless they are reconciled, mainly through interparliamentary cooperation.

The book intends to highlight the potential that interparliamentary cooperation has for the development of a composite European Constitution, where—it is supported—the legitimacy of institutional arrangements and procedures depends primarily on the quality of the relationship developed among institutional actors placed at different levels of government. Moreover, the approach taken into account in the volume, that of the Euro-national parliamentary system, challenges the usual understanding of interparliamentary cooperation as something that is for parliaments only; rather it is also very much affected by the executive–legislative relationship and thus by the forms of government, at both EU and national level.

IV. STRUCTURE AND RATIONALE OF THE VOLUME

This collective volume analyses the place and functioning of interparliamentary cooperation in the composite European Constitution. It discusses the developments in interparliamentary cooperation, before and after the Treaty of Lisbon, and its implications for the organisation and procedures of national parliaments and the European Parliament, for the fragmented executive of the EU, and the democratic legitimacy of the overall EU institutional system.

The volume aims to provide a bridge between scholars (of different origins and backgrounds) and practitioners focused on parliamentary studies in the European context. It relies largely on a series of seminars and lectures organised in the framework of the LUISS Guido Carli University School of Government's Summer School on Parliamentary Democracy in Europe, in Rome, a Jean Monnet Module generously funded by the European Commission (2013–15), and in the context of the LUISS Center for Parliamentary Studies.

[57] T Raunio, 'The Gatekeepers of European Integration? The Functions of National Parliaments in the EU Political System' (2011) 33 *Journal of European Integration* 303, who adds the networking function to those original five parliamentary functions described by Walter Bagehot [1867], *The English constitution* (Oxford, Oxford University Press, 2009).

[58] This is clearly spelled out for national parliaments in Art 12 TEU, after the Treaty of Lisbon.

The choice of the authors of the chapters responds to the aim to ensure a threefold overall balance: first, between academics and practitioners, with the latter focusing in particular on the most institutionalised forum of interparliamentary cooperation in the EU, the Conference of parliamentary committees dealing with EU affairs (COSAC); secondly, between young scholars and senior academics; and thirdly, between the different methodological approaches of constitutional law, EU law, international law, legal theory, political science and international relations, which are complementary to each other when studying legislatures. The predominant approach followed, nevertheless, is legal, ie, based on the analysis of written and unwritten rules and on a normative assessment of their application.

The chapters included in this volume cover a variety of different and crucial developments occurring after the Treaty of Lisbon, although most of them make use of a diachronic comparison with the pre-Lisbon arrangements in order to describe, explain and elaborate on the changes.

These issues are examined in the context of the European decision-making processes, namely the legislative process and the European Semester, on the one hand, and the Treaty revisions, on the other, by looking at the effects of interparliamentary cooperation on the internal structure of parliaments and at the models of interparliamentary cooperation that can be detected, on the basis of the EU Treaty provisions and protocols.

The book consists of six parts. The first part investigates the role of parliaments, ie, the European and national Parliaments, in the EU understood as a composite European constitutional order and in comparison with an inherent feature of the EU legal architecture, namely interjudicial cooperation, which has received much more attention from scholars. Leonard Besselink highlights that national parliaments do not always behave according to the ideal place assigned to them in a composite Constitution and investigates some of the causes for such a mismatch. He focuses in particular on a traditional institutional account of democratic legitimation, which is deemed unsatisfactory and not able to explain the current developments of parliamentary democracy in Europe. Rather, we should move beyond the usual (national) 'democratic legitimation chain' and emphasise the significance in terms of transparency and accountability of parliamentary scrutiny and mandating systems by national parliaments as well as their involvement in implementing EU law, besides the interplay with democratically legitimated EU institutions. In his chapter Giuseppe Martinico provides an overview of the different paths of interaction among institutional actors at national and supranational level by looking first at the relationship between conflicts and cooperation among judges and then exploring the category of 'dialogue'. He then applies the metaphor of the 'dialogue' to parliaments in the EU and develops a comparison between the informal and more formalised relationships established among judges with the rise of interparliamentary cooperation in the EU. Not only can similarities be found in the relatively stable, interdependent and non-hierarchical relationships and in the organisational arrangements, but also in the functions performed through this cooperation and in the detection of a sort of political control of constitutionality of EU legislative proposals by national parliaments through the EWS. Although clear differences between the two phenomena can equally be noticed—starting from the background of the actors, their nature and discretion—according to Martinico, interparliamentary cooperation and inter-judicial dialogue 'work in tandem' to protect national and transnational goods.

The second part of the book deals with interparliamentary cooperation in the EU Treaty revisions, considering here the role of parliaments in the past 'constitutional' Conventions of 1999–2000 and 2002–03 and in those which might be convened in future according to Article 48 TEU: within the ordinary revision procedure, when Treaty amendments are agreed just within an intergovernmental conference; and in the framework of the new simplified revision procedures. Cesare Pinelli's chapter analyses the two cases of European Conventions held up to now—the Convention that drafted the Charter of fundamental rights of the EU and the Convention on the future of Europe—as examples of interparliamentary cooperation. Although the Conventions were also composed of representatives of national governments, the Commission and other European institutions and bodies—which were crucial to shaping the results of the collective work—the greatest part of their members were national MPs or MEPs. In the light of the achievements of the Convention on the Future of Europe concerning the role of national parliaments and the European Parliament in the EU, Pinelli considers whether and to what extent the format of the Convention, now briefly depicted in the EU Treaties, can become a model for interparliamentary conferences. In her chapter Katarzyna Granat deals with the role of national parliaments in the simplified Treaty revision procedures of Article 48.6 and 48.7 TEU, in particular on whether interparliamentary cooperation has been developed or can be developed in this framework. Indeed, according to the simplified revision procedures each national parliament is entitled to exercise a veto power on such Treaty revisions for up to six months from when the amendment was proposed. After an overview of the national rules implementing the Treaty provisions of the simplified revision procedures, the chapter focuses on the amendment to article 136 TFEU as a case study to test the implications for interparliamentary cooperation and for the overall contribution of national parliaments to the good functioning of the EU.

The third part of the volume analyses interparliamentary cooperation in the ordinary life of the EU, eg within the EU legislative process, from the standpoint of the impact this cooperation has on the organisation of parliaments. Antonia Baraggia's chapter deals with different challenges deriving from the European powers conferred by EU Treaty provisions on bicameral legislatures, which represent almost half of the national parliaments in the EU. It considers a series of questions posed by the participation of bicameral legislatures in interparliamentary cooperation—for instance the composition and the size of national parliamentary delegations and the weight the second chambers should have in the delegation—because of their structure and powers, primarily in relation to the national executive. Likewise, in the EWS in bicameral legislatures each chamber is assigned one vote by Protocol No 2 annexed to the Treaty of Lisbon, although their internal balance and democratic credentials can vary a lot from one Member State to another. These issues are analysed by Baraggia, taking into account the increasing activism second chambers show in EU affairs compared to lower chambers. Diane Fromage then considers how interparliamentary cooperation, in particular after the Treaty of Lisbon, has influenced a particular aspect of the internal organisation of national parliaments, ie, their standing committees. It is argued that, after the setting up of the European Affairs Committees (EACs) in 1989, when COSAC was established, with different structures, sizes and powers depending on the national legislature, the current phase has been characterised by a change in the balance between these committees and the sectoral committees competent by policy so far as concerns their involvement on EU issues. The increasing number of specialised interparliamentary meetings alongside the creation of sectoral interparliamentary conferences without any hierarchy or order of precedence nevertheless pose questions as to whether a (re)concentration of interparliamentary activities in the hands of EACs is needed. Then, in the chapter by Nathalie Brack and Thibaud Deruelle the attention is devoted to other crucial bodies for parliamentary organisation and activities, political groups, and the role they play in interparliamentary cooperation. The chapter focuses in particular on the European Parliament's groups, analysing their degree of involvement and the constraints faced when they (informally) coordinate their action at European level and between the national and the supranational levels. The case study of political groups in the European Parliamentary Week is examined and, on this basis, it is concluded that, at least in this forum, interparliamentary cooperation has been increasingly politicised and turned towards more technical issues. By the same token, interests, resources and political opportunity appear to be the main factors explaining the asymmetric involvement of political groups in the interparliamentary cooperation. In the final chapter of this section, Andreja Pegan and Anna-Lena Högenauer analyse administrative interparliamentary cooperation, understood as the support that parliamentary administrators provide to members of parliament in interparliamentary cooperation but also including the contacts between parliamentary bureaucracies. Since the Treaty of Lisbon, this cooperation has acquired a permanent or semi-permanent organisation, as in the case of national parliamentary representatives, the COSAC's Secretariat and the European Parliament's Directorate for Relations with National Parliaments, while at the same time exchanges have occurred also on an ad hoc basis, for example in the framework of the EWS, and have been no less significant in terms of support provided to MPs and MEPs and coordination of parliaments' positions.

The fourth part of this volume, which is closely linked to the third one, examines the procedural dimension of interparliamentary cooperation, in particular in the context of the EWS for the control of compliance with the principle of subsidiarity and in the procedures stemming from the new economic governance. Marco Goldoni's chapter deals with the EWS and the political dialogue as potential tools for interparliamentary cooperation. Indeed, while the EWS assigns a power to each national parliament individually, only when a certain number of parliaments issue reasoned opinions is the Commission forced to re-examine the proposal. This tension between the individual and collective exercise of the power is coupled by the tension between the cooperative or veto use of the subsidiarity review that, by contrast, is lacking in the political dialogue. After having examined the two yellow cards issued by national parliaments and the different readings of them put forward by scholars regarding interparliamentary cooperation, the chapter looks at ongoing developments in the use of political dialogue up to the proposal for a 'green card', and in the conclusion makes an argument against the unlimited and unconstrained rise of asymmetric interparliamentary cooperation in the EU. Davor Jančić's chapter, instead, analyses the involvement of national parliaments in the procedures surrounding the Economy and Monetary Union (EMU). It first considers the position of national parliaments in the aftermath of the adoption of the Six-pack, the Fiscal Compact and the Two-pack and then elaborates on the actual use of the parliamentary channels of participation in the EMU and the European Semester. According to Jančić, from an overall evaluation of the composite EU fiscal law-making process it can be concluded that national parliaments have been able to counter the restriction of their autonomy during the Euro crisis by exploiting a variety of different constitutional tools, and one of them is interparliamentary cooperation itself.

The fifth part focuses on (old and new) interparliamentary conferences, which are the predominant structural format of interparliamentary cooperation. The first chapter in this part, by Adam Cygan, is devoted to COSAC; by far the most institutionalised forum of interparliamentary cooperation in the EU, although its positions and functions have changed over time. For example, while the ratification process for the Constitutional Treaty was still ongoing, COSAC fostered a collective exercise among parliaments of the EWS on an experimental basis, but later on the Treaty of Lisbon excluded any competence regarding the principle of subsidiarity from the COSAC's mandate. This chapter assesses what the results of COSAC's activities have been so far, its current 'existential crisis', also due to the setting up of other interparliamentary conferences, and its prospective developments (also taking into account the analyses and proposals advanced in the last part of the volume). Chronologically the second EU interparliamentary conference to be set up, in 2012, was the Interparliamentary Conference for the Common Foreign and Security Policy and the Common Security and Defence Policy. The chapter by Jan Wouters and Kolja Raube deals with the cooperation between national parliaments and the European Parliament in the context of European security governance. In spite of its peculiar status and given the decidedly intergovernmental domain covered, the Interparliamentary Conference has been seen as a test case for further interparliamentary settings in EU governance. Based on the first two years of its existence, the chapter puts forward the thesis that the work of this Conference, as it stands, is mainly about mutual information exchange and network building. Cooperation in respect of the latter is undermined by unresolved status questions and the lack of a common understanding on what accountability of the EU executives exactly entails. Nevertheless, information exchanges with executives in an interparliamentary context, for example with the High Representative of the European Union for Foreign Affairs and Security Policy, are seen by the authors as added value to the overall parliamentary dimension of the EU's foreign and security policy. Ian Cooper sheds light on the newest interparliamentary conference, established in 2013, the Interparliamentary Conference on Stability, Economic Coordination and Governance in the European Union (also called the 'Article 13 Conference'), which so far has been at the centre of controversy regarding its composition, size, objectives and powers. The chapter runs through the short but intense history of this Conference until November 2015, when its Rules of procedure were eventually adopted. It examines the role of the EU Speakers' Conference in this process and compares the opinions of different national parliaments and the European Parliament on the shape this body should take. It concludes that, while many crucial issues regarding the Conference have been gradually addressed, the exact 'mandate' of the Conference, ie, whether it is supposed to be just a discussion forum or is expected to perform an oversight function, is yet to be defined. At the end of this series of chapters on interparliamentary conferences, is the one on the EU Speakers' Conference. Indeed, although it is the oldest, as this Conference was created shortly before the European Parliament became a directly elected assembly, it was only a few years ago, while the ratification process for the Treaty of Lisbon was ongoing, that the EU Speakers' Conference started to play a new and only partially unexpected role, ruling the (dis-)order of interparliamentary cooperation. After a brief description of the historical evolution of this Conference, the chapter by Cristina Fasone considers the developments concerning the Conference from two points of view. The first looks at the Conference as a representative body. The second deals with its role of 'leader' of interparliamentary cooperation in the EU, to provide guidelines for interparliamentary cooperation and to coordinate the multiplicity of interparliamentary activities. The third perspective regards the role of the EU Speakers' Conference in providing an input to set up new interparliamentary conferences, and even in determining some of their rules of procedure. The chapter discusses whether the present developments are deemed to endure and if this is desirable.

Finally, the sixth part of the book collects the contributions of parliamentary officials of the European and national parliaments on the evolution of the role of COSAC, especially in the development of interparliamentary cooperation and in the Europeanisation of national parliaments. This part is seen as a necessary complement to the academic studies presented in the other five parts of the volume, given the rather peculiar place of this Conference in interparliamentary cooperation. COSAC, which has been in operation for 25 years and has witnessed the most lively period of the European integration process, definitely looks very different from the small conference it was in 1989. It is now the only interparliamentary conference to be provided for by the European Treaties, has 'Europeanised' and 'trained' national parliaments to practise the EWS and the political dialogue with the European Commission, as pointed out by Davide Alberto Capuano, and has adapted to a new reality in which the number of parliaments involved, due to the eastward enlargement, and their powers at the different levels of government have changed dramatically, as observed by Francisco Gómez Martos regarding the European Parliament. This evolution has required structural transformations, like the creation of a permanent COSAC Secretariat, as highlighted by Christiana Fryda, but has also led to the setting up of new and more specialised interparliamentary conferences—analysed in the fifth part of the volume—which have inevitably constrained the role of COSAC. It is not by chance that in their contributions both Bruno Dias Pinheiro and Antonio Esposito refer to a COSAC identity crisis, and Mendeltje Van Keulen supports the idea to reshape this conference as a more dynamic venue. Looking at the case of COSAC through the lens of actors, like parliamentary officials, who have been involved in its developments and put forward important proposals for its reform, is thus a way to review the overall evolution of interparliamentary cooperation in the last quarter of a century after its setting up.

As anticipated, the choice of a combination of theoretical analysis and studies based on the development of parliamentary institutional practice, on which only parliamentary officials can shed some light, is one of the methodological keys of this book. Indeed, the phenomenon under investigation, interparliamentary cooperation, in its procedures and decision-making, is not very well known by the public and usually parliamentary officials remain the main keepers of the memory of interparliamentary activities and meetings. The insights presented by the officials enrich the academic discussions and can be highly valued by the scholarly community.

Given the intensification and multiplication of interparliamentary activities, there is also a need to conceptualise this phenomenon, so as to detect its implications and effects on EU and national constitutional law. Interparliamentary cooperation is usually labelled either as a form of parliamentary 'tourism' or as an exercise in diplomatic attitudes with more or less no policy-making effects or legally binding outcomes, and thus, according to some scholars and politicians, it does not deserve much consideration. However, as this volume sets out to demonstrate, there is strong evidence from the legal point of view and from the current practice that this is no longer the case, in particular after the experience of the two Conventions, the Treaty of Lisbon and the reform of European economic governance. As we seek to argue in the concluding chapter, using the model of the Euro-national parliamentary system, if taken seriously and developed consistently with the principles of the composite European Constitution, the procedures and the structures linking the many parliaments of the EU can play a decisive role in European democracy.

Part I

The Role of Parliaments and Interparliamentary Cooperation in the European Union

1

The Place of National Parliaments within the European Constitutional Order

LEONARD FM BESSELINK

I. INTRODUCTION

This chapter is about the place of national parliaments in the composite European constitutional order.[1]

First, the chapter explains that the kind of European constitutional order in which national parliaments have a role to play is 'composite' in nature, in contrast with conceptualisations of the relations between the national orders and the order of the European Union in terms of hierarchically structured 'levels', whether it is a two-level or multi-level order. Then, it elaborates on the specific place of national parliaments within that European constitutional order, which – it is argued – can be traced both in law and in institutional practice. Subsequently, the fact that national parliaments do not always act at in accordance with the role they would ideally have in a 'composite constitution' is highlighted and assessed. This requires an enquiry into the causes of the divergence between an understanding of parliaments' role within a 'composite constitution' and the practical behaviour of some parliaments. One such cause that is discussed in this chapter is the traditional institutional account of democratic legitimation. For that reason, the 'challenge of democracy' is

[1] This essay was presented as opening lecture at the Summer School on Parliamentary Democracy in Europe, Third edition on 'The Europeanisation of national parliaments', Rome, 14–25 July 2014. It draws significantly on and elaborates earlier work, in particular 'National Parliaments in the EU's Composite Constitution: a Plea for a Shift in Paradigm' in P Kiiver (ed), *National and Regional Parliaments in the European Constitutional Order* (Groningen, Europa Law Publishing, 2006) 117–31.

discussed, before drawing some brief conclusions on the problem of parliamentary legitimation in the European Union.

II. WHAT KIND OF 'EUROPEAN CONSTITUTIONAL ORDER'?

The year 2014 saw the fiftieth anniversary of the *Costa v ENEL* judgment of the Court of Justice of the European Union (CJEU),[2] which was not celebrated and hardly paid any attention by scholars. The previous year the fiftieth anniversary of the equally famous, but constitutionally less decisive, judgment of the Court of Justice in the case of *Van Gend en Loos* was celebrated with much pomp and circumstance, particularly at the Court itself.[3]

These two judgments are considered to be of a constitutional nature: they established rights of individuals under European law against public authorities, rights that could be invoked by individuals in national courts (*Van Gend en Loos*) and that can be upheld in court against contrary national legislation (*Costa v ENEL*).

Since they were issued, these two judgments have provoked much scholarly speculation as to the way in which the relationships between the national and the European legal orders must be viewed. This is also what is attempted here, when the European constitutional order is said to be 'composite' in nature. A distinction is made between this 'composite' character of the relations between the European and national legal orders, and the view that looks at these orders in terms of 'levels'.

Let us take the two famous judgments just mentioned as a starting-point to illustrate this distinction. The two judgments point in different directions. The Court has held that the European legal order is autonomous. Because national legal orders claim constitutional autonomy as well, one might think of the two types of orders as standing side by side, juxtaposed, in a kind of dualist or, in more fashionable terms, 'pluralist' manner.

In the view of most EU lawyers, however, this 'pluralist' image of the relations between European and national law is outweighed by an image that is more hierarchical, and is associated with issues of primacy and supremacy, the topic of *Costa v ENEL*. The gist of *Costa v ENEL* was, after all, that European law trumps contrary national law; European law out-ranks national law; European law is of a 'higher' rank, 'superior', or—to use the language of the 1960s—European law is 'supranational' law, that is to say 'above' national law. From these metaphors an overall picture emerges of the existence of various 'levels' that relate to each other as 'higher' and 'lower' levels.

Fifty years later the term 'supranational' law has gone almost totally out of fashion. The mood of the day is neither that of monism or dualism, but rather that of 'pluralism': a 'feel good' term that is not always clear as to what it is supposed to mean.[4]

[2] See Case 6/64, *Flaminio Costa v ENEL*, 15 July 1964, ECLI:EU:C:1964:66.

[3] See Case 26/62, *NV Algemene Transport- en Expeditie Onderneming van Gend en Loos v Nederlandse Administratie der Belastingen*, 5 February 1963, ECLI:EU:C:1963:1. See the proceedings of the conference organised at Court of Justice, on *Fiftieth Anniversary of the Judgment in* Van Gend en Loos *1963–2013*, organised by Antonio Tizzano, Juliane Kokott, Sacha Prechal, 13 May 2013, and available at: curia.europa.eu/jcms/upload/docs/application/pdf/2013-12/qd30136442ac_002.pdf. On this decision see also the contributions, by P Pescatore, B De Witte, F C Mayer and B Halbertstam, in M Pojares Maduro and L Azoulai (eds), *The Past and Future of EU Law: The Classics of EU Law Revisited on the 50th Anniversary of the Rome Treaty* (Oxford, Hart Publishing, 2010) 1–36.

[4] On the various readings of the 'pluralist paradigm', see M Avbelj and J Komárek (eds), *Constitutional Pluralism in the European Union and Beyond* (Oxford, Hart Publishing, 2012).

It is preferable to use the expression of a 'composite constitutional order', a term derived from the French language writings of Ingolf Pernice[5] and which has been used in Italy also by Giacinto Della Cananea,[6] although in what follows, the expression is not necessarily used in the way these two scholars have applied it.

When using the alternative term of a 'composite' constitutional order, one must be aware of the limitations of this metaphor. In adopting the expression of a 'composite' constitutional order, there is no ambition to try to describe reality in full. Not everything in the relations between the Union and the Member States can be understood in terms of the composite nature of those relations. But yet the idea of a 'composite' order creates another way of looking at reality that changes our understanding and the meaning that is attached to that reality. Things cannot be understood without a coherent way of looking at them; and such ways of viewing reality determine the understanding of the reality.

The idea of the European order as a 'composite' order needs further explanation. Primarily it expresses the hypothesis of a constitutional order that is comprised of a plurality of legal orders. These are primarily the EU legal order and the constitutional orders of the Member States, at any rate for the purpose of this chapter. However, these are not the *only* relevant legal orders in the EU-Member State context where, among the notable other (partial) legal orders, at least the ECHR must be mentioned. Each of these orders in various manners partakes of other legal orders. They presuppose each other's existence and together form a compound,[7] that is to say each is a component within a larger order that comprises the various legal orders.

The relation between these orders is not a relation of simple hierarchy. They are characterised by a more dynamic equilibrium that goes beyond the simple static dominance of one legal order over the other. The dynamics are visible in the practice of legislatures and are authoritatively determined by courts within their respective jurisdictions.

Let us apply this conceptual scheme to *Costa v ENEL* judgment and its progeny.

Saying that relations are not hierarchical and also that the idea of a composite constitutional order is an alternative to the 'levels' paradigm, is not at all a denial of the legal situation, both normatively and factually, that EU law can trump contrary national law. The point is rather that saying, as the Court has done since *Costa v ENEL*, that European law has 'primacy' over national law is somehow not representing the full picture. It leaves out the plain fact that national constitutional orders do not unconditionally share this point of view. All Member States in fact do accept primacy of EU law as regards ordinary statute law, but the vast majority do not accept the Court of Justice's view of unconditional primacy of EU law over national constitutional law. This is true at least as regards the primacy of EU law over core principles and provisions of national constitutional law, which have been challenged in some judgments of the Court of Justice (*Internationale Handelsgesellschaft*, *Simmental II*, and, more recently, *Winner Wetten* and *Melloni*).[8]

[5] I Pernice and F Mayer, 'De la constitution composeè de l'Europe' (2000) 36 *Revue trimestrielle de droit européen* 623–47.

[6] G Della Cananea, *L'Unione europea. Un ordinamento composito* (Roma/Bari, Laterza, 2003) 107.

[7] S Fabbrini, *Compound Democracies: Why the United States and Europe Are Becoming Similar* (Oxford, Oxford University Press, 2010), indeed, refers to the word 'compound' to identify the *ensemble* of the EU and the Member States' system; likewise the US federation and its federated entities.

[8] See Case 11/70, *Internationale Handelsgesellschaft mbH*, 17 December 1970, ECLI:EU:C:1970:114; Case 106/77, *Amministrazione delle Finanze dello Stato v Simmenthal (No 2)* [1978] ECR 629, 9 March 1978;

There are other elements confirming the composite nature of the European legal order, some of which are 'built in' to the Treaties from the very beginning in such a manner that this compositeness can be said to be 'constitutional'. Obvious examples are the preliminary reference procedure to the CJEU and the legislative instrument of the European Directives.

First, in the preliminary reference procedure national and European courts cooperate to resolve a case, each deciding a certain part, and in the end it is up to the national court to come to an integral judgment, applying the interpretation of EU law as determined by the CJEU. There is a division of labour, but this division of labour can only be fully understood within the context of the process as a whole, to which various actors contribute across the boundaries of the EU and national legal orders. National judges fulfil the role of judges of EU law and, reciprocally, the Court of Justice needs to be activated by national judges while deciding national cases, in which EU law has to be applied.[9]

The instrument of the Directive presupposes the mutual existence and constructive role of Member State constitutional organs within the EU order, in a legislative process across boundaries of Union and national legal orders. Not only the executive, but also the national parliament, is in essence then both a national organ and acts as the national legislature, whose procedures are governed by national constitutional rules, and at the very same time they act as the European legislature. Again, the division of labour can only be fully understood within the context of the process as a whole. Notwithstanding this structural element, the European dimension of the national legislatures' role and function took some time to be acknowledged. This was facilitated—as will be highlighted in the next sections—through the recent conferral of some 'European functions' on national parliaments and the express recognition of their contribution to the good functioning of the EU (Article 12 TEU).[10]

All this could be elaborated much further and more examples could be given, but it is now time to turn, more specifically, to the place of national parliaments within the 'composite constitutional order of Europe'.

III. PARLIAMENTS IN THE 'COMPOSITE CONSTITUTIONAL ORDER OF EUROPE'

First a few points of clarification need to be made on how looking at parliaments from the perspective of Europe as a composite constitutional order differs from looking at it from

Case 409/06 *Winner Wetten GmbH v Bürgermeisterin der Stadt Bergheim* [2010] ECR I-8015, 8 September 2010; Case 399/11, *Stefano Melloni v Ministerio Fiscal*, ECLI:EU:C:2013:107, 26 February 2013, on which, see LFM Besselink, 'The Parameters of Constitutional Conflict after Melloni' (2014) 39 *European Law Review* 531–52.

[9] See T de la Mare and C Donnelly, 'Preliminary rulings and EU legal integration: evolution and stasis' in P Craig and G De Búrca (eds), *The evolution of EU law*, 2nd edn (Oxford, Oxford University Press, 2011) 363–406; G Martinico, *The Tangled Complexity of the EU Constitutional Process: The Frustrating Knot of Europe* (Abingdon, Routledge, 2013) 107–61; and M Dicosola, C Fasone and I Spigno, *The preliminary reference to the Court of Justice of the European Union by Constitutional Courts* (2015) special issue in 16(6) *German Law Journal*.

[10] See, among others, P Kiiver, *The National Parliaments in the European Union. A Critical View on EU Constitution-Building* (The Hague, Kluwer, 2006) 47 and N Lupo, 'National parliaments in the European integration process: re-aligning politics and policies' in M Cartabia, N Lupo and A Simoncini (eds), *Democracy and Subsidiarity the EU. National Parliaments, Regions and Civil Society in the Decision-Making Process* (Bologna, Il Mulino, 2013) 107–32.

the perspective of the EU as made up of different 'levels'. It is better to start with the latter: the view that there are separate constitutional levels that essentially exclude each other.

A. The Multi-level Perspective

In the 'levels' view, it is typical to think in terms of an EU level, where we have a European Parliament which fulfils the role of representative of the European citizens (article 14 TEU), while the national parliaments fulfil their role at the national level. The European Parliament is there to control and legitimise the European Commission; the national parliament is supposed to control the national representatives in the Council and European Council. This can be read into Article 10 TEU, particularly its second paragraph, although—as is shown below—it can also be read differently:

> Article 10
> 1. The functioning of the Union shall be founded on representative democracy.
> 2. Citizens are directly represented at Union level in the European Parliament.
> Member States are represented in the European Council by their Heads of State or Government and in the Council by their governments, themselves democratically accountable either to their national Parliaments, or to their citizens.

According to the 'multi-level' view, the framework of analysis for the role of parliaments is essentially dualist: there are two sorts of power centre, one at European level and the other at the level of the national parliaments. This is a 'multi-level' approach, in that two constitutional levels co-exist which do not influence each other (or if they do, they do so only indirectly).

In line with this view, the prevailing pre-Lisbon analysis of the democratic deficit was that the deficit is the result of a transfer of powers from one level to another, whereby the democratic control which existed at one level, the national level, after the transfer no longer exists at that national level, while it does not in an equivalent way come to exist at the other level, the European level: hence the occurrence of a 'democratic deficit'.[11]

Inherent in speaking of 'transfer', instead of, for instance, 'attribution' or, more neutrally, 'conferral' of powers, is the idea that once a previously national power has moved to the European level, it has somehow 'disappeared' at the national level. The disappearance of a relevant amount of decisional power of national parliaments, importantly their legislative power, was not compensated for by that power shifting to a European Parliament. At the European level, at that time, legislative power was mainly exercised by the Council. This had as a consequence that national governments, represented in the Council, became pivotal actors to the detriment of national parliaments. Not the parliaments in the national capitals, but Brussels decided.[12]

[11] See *Report drawn up on behalf of the committee on Institutional Affairs on the democratic deficit in the European Community*, PE Doc No A 2-276/87 (1 February 1988) [the *Toussaint Report*] and G Majone, 'Europe's "Democratic Deficit": The Question of Standards' (1998) 4 *European Law Journal* 5–28.

[12] A Moravcsik, 'In Defence of the "Democratic Deficit": Reassessing Legitimacy in the European Union' (2002) 40 *Journal of Common Market Studies* 603–24 and D Curtin, *Executive Power of the European Union: Law, Practices, and the Living Constitution: Law, Practice, and Constitutionalism* (Oxford, Oxford University Press, 2009) 28–46.

This type of analysis implies that democracy is thought of as being either in one place, the national level, or in the other, the EU level, and that these levels are mutually exclusive, autonomous and separate. A seeming paradox is that the two levels are in a sense separate from each other, but at the same time it essentially leads to a situation in which one level must outweigh or even supersede the other. This is so, because the 'centre of gravity' within the system can only exist at one level at a time: the levels cannot be co-extensive.

This is in part reinforced by the approach taken by most, but not all, national parliaments before 2006 (and some of them still now take this approach). Parliamentary scrutiny and parliamentary mandating of EU decision-making took as their starting point the information that the government provided, not the information that was provided by the EU institutions. The scrutiny was focused on the national level only and was governed by national notions of ministerial responsibility for acts of the national representatives, and also for their acts within the EU institutions.[13] In line with this, the aim of the parliaments was that which is typical of the parliamentary system, ie that ultimately the parliamentary system is geared to the power of voting out a minister or government, or in practice for the parliamentary majority: to keep the government (and its ministers) in power.[14] So also when it concerns the scrutiny and mandating of ministers as regards EU decision-making, it was neatly within the boundaries of domestic parliamentary control, so within the confines of the national parliamentary system. Again, separateness is dominant.

While parliaments operated within the prevailing multi-level paradigm, mostly thinking and acting within a level which is separate from the EU level, the executives had already long overcome this approach, and thus in many cases successfully avoided effective parliamentary oversight. The 'democratic deficit' is not so much—or not only—a legitimacy deficit in terms of legislative power, but more a deficit in parliamentary political oversight and control. While parliaments stayed put within their own neatly nationally fenced-off compartments, the executive developed into a strongly interwoven, complex administrative network. Key roles are played by individual ministers, and of course by national civil servants making trips to Brussels, in which they can freely and directly discuss matters with their European counterparts, sometimes with a clear mandate from their bureaucratic superiors, but often with a vague mandate or none at all.[15]

And the European institutions themselves remained quite far beyond the horizon of most national parliaments. From the viewpoint of national parliaments, the European institutions were mainly seen as technical bodies detached from national politics and problems, not least because it was often in the interest of the national executives to deny any political responsibility, blaming the EU and Brussels for decisions they, or their predecessors, have contributed to taking.

[13] An early example is the Danish cabinet crisis early in 1973, which was caused by the EC Council decisions on the prices of bacon, which triggered the famous Danish parliamentary mandating system. On the Danish case, see M Buskjœr Christensen, 'The Danish Folketing and EU Affairs: Is the Danish Model of Parliamentary Scrutiny Still the Best Practice?' in C Hefftler et al (eds), *The Palgrave Handbook of National Parliaments and the European Union* (New York, Palgrave Macmillan, 2015) 275–78.

[14] Also here, Denmark, with its minority governments, is the classic example.

[15] See GJ Brandsma, *Backstage Europe: Comitology, Accountability and Democracy in the European Union. Dissertation* (Utrecht, Universiteit Utrecht, 2010).

B. The 'Composite Order' Perspective

The same legal developments can also be looked at in other terms than those of separate 'levels'. For this, one must take the Union not as merely 'Brussels' (Commission, European Council and Council), or as 'Brussels and Strasbourg' (to include the European Parliament metaphorically). If the EU constitutional order is a more truly composite legal order than is apparent in the 'levels' approach, the situation turns from a focus on single and separate sites of democracy to a more polycentric, or, so to say, a composite one.

National parliaments are not isolated at the national level within the national system, then, but must be considered part of the larger EU constitutional order. This should imply that they also play a role within the broader EU framework. This role is not constrained to the national arena, but is a role in the broader European arena. This broader vision opens up new perspectives for national parliaments. For one thing, they can actively approach EU institutions and rely on information provided by others than the national governments only. This was formalised in Protocol No 1 annexed to the Treaty of Lisbon[16] and has become even more important in the context of the 'early warning system' of the parliamentary subsidiarity review of EU draft legislative acts under Article 12 TEU and Protocol No 2. Before the entry into force of the Treaty of Lisbon, in fact, at least in some Member States information on EU documents and legislative proposals was not transmitted in a timely manner to the national parliament. This occurred, on the one hand, because the time limits are tight and not all governments prepare their information, reports and assessments in time to be able to share these with parliament; and on the other hand, because it was not in governments' interest to disclose and share all the information with their parliament (and thus expose it to national public opinion).

If national parliaments are viewed as independent actors within the broader European order, this also creates possibilities of accountability of the EU institutions to those actors. Thus, national parliaments can invite representatives of the institutions and hold them in one way or another to account for the work of the institutions.[17] A good example of this is shown by Commission President Barroso and his Commissioner Ms Wallström, who made a point of touring the capitals not only to visit the governments, but also the parliaments. A lively example of such holding to account can be found in the debate between Barroso and the French *Assemblée Nationale* around the time of the plans for a Services Directive (the 'Bolkenstein Directive' as it was known at the time).[18]

In a broader, more encompassing constitutional order, *national* members of the executive can also be held to account beyond what they themselves have done and failed to do as a *national* actor. Notably they can be held to account for the acts of the Council in all its

[16] D Jančić, 'The Barroso Initiative: Window Dressing or Democracy Boost?' (2012) 8 *Utrecht Law Review* 78–91 and PG Casalena, C Fasone and N Lupo, 'Comment on Protocol No 1, on the role of national parliaments in the European Union annexed to the Treaty of Lisbon' in HJ Blanke and S Mangiameli (eds), *The Treaty on European Union (TEU). A Commentary* (Vienna-New York, Springer, 2013) 1529–634.

[17] B Crum and D Curtin, 'The Challenge of Making EU Executive Power Accountable' in S Piattoni (ed), *The European Union: Democratic Principles and Institutional Architectures in Times of Crisis* (Oxford, Oxford University Press, 2015).

[18] To get an impression of the very lively debate in January 2006, which was an important news item on French television, see the clip at: lci.tf1.fr/france/2006-01/barroso-tance-france-malade-imaginaire-4856716.html. For the full debate, see www.assemblee-nationale.fr/international/barroso.asp.See also A Crespy, *Qui a peur de Bolkestein? Conflit, resistances et démocratie dans l'Union européenne* (Paris, Economica, 2012).

formations. A minister is not only a national functionary, representing the Member State in the Council: as a member of the Council he is also a representative of the Council of the EU when he appears in the national parliament. Logically, he will need not only to explain what he did as an individual member, but also to explain the sense or non-sense of a Council decision, thus rendering the Council and its decisions accountable in the national arena, where such decisions usually have the most decisive effect. When both national parliaments and members of national executives are viewed as integral parts of the European system, the latter can no longer hide behind having voted against a measure. Instead, it becomes a matter of taking responsibility for the outcome of the vote.

IV. COMPOSITENESS IN LAW AND PRACTICE

Both the TEU since Lisbon and practice provide further clues for such a broadening of the context in which national parliaments can act. A few of them, as entrenched in Treaty provisions, are pointed out in this section.

A very general clue is the provision on the values on which the EU is based.[19] These are—to use the concise words of the older provision (Article 6(2) TEU) preceding the present Article 2 TEU—the principles of liberty, democracy, respect for human rights and fundamental freedoms, and the rule of law, *principles which are common to the Member States*. Notice the composite nature of the foundation of the EU: the EU is founded on the values 'common to the Member States', a striking example of the complementariness of Union and Member States, that includes democracy as a founding value both of the Union and of the Members States. Given the largely prevalent parliamentary nature of democracy in the Member States (except in Cyprus, the Member States all have either a parliamentary, or a 'rationalised parliamentary' *cum* semi-presidential system), this points to the importance of the institution of parliaments to the European democratic legal order.

Another relevant provision is that on the duty of the Union to respect the Member States' 'national identities', which was already mentioned in passing. This provision has been part of the EU Treaty since the Treaty of Maastricht, and has now been formulated in a more articulated manner as the duty to respect the Member States' 'national identities inherent in their fundamental structures, political and constitutional' (Article 4(2) TEU).[20] It has become justiciable at the CJEU since the entry into force of the Lisbon Treaty.[21] It suffices

[19] More precisely, according to Art 2 TEU, 'The Union is founded on the values of respect for human dignity, freedom, democracy, equality, the rule of law and respect for human rights, including the rights of persons belonging to minorities. These values are common to the Member States in a society in which pluralism, non-discrimination, tolerance, justice, solidarity and equality between women and men prevail'.

[20] See M Claes, S Imamovic, LMF Besselink and J Herman Reestman, 'National Constitutional Avenues for Further EU Integration, Study', European Parliament, Directorate General for Internal Policies, Policy Department C: Citizens' Rights And Constitutional Affairs, Legal Affairs Committee, Constitutional Affairs Committee, PE 493.046 EN, Brussels, March 2014, 277 *passim*, electronically available at: www.europarl.europa.eu/RegData/etudes/etudes/join/2014/493046/IPOL-JURI_ET%282014%29493046_EN.pdf 8-18.

[21] Prior to the Lisbon Treaty, Art 46 TEU (Nice Treaty version; Art K from Maastricht to Amsterdam) limited the judicial power of the CJEU to the TEU provisions it enumerated. The identity clause of Art 6(3) TEU (Nice version; Art F3 from Maastricht to Amsterdam) was not among them. On this matter, see LFM Besselink, 'Respecting Constitutional Identity in the EU. A Case Note to ECJ (Second Chamber), Case C 208/09, 22 December 2010, *Ilonka Sayn-Wittgenstein v Landeshauptmann von Wien*' (2012) 49 *Common Market Law Review* 671, 678–79.

to say that the Treaty reference to national identities may be understood in two ways, each of which corresponds to one of the two paradigms outlined, the 'multi-level' and the 'composite order' paradigms.

First, the provision can be read in accordance with the distinct 'levels' approach as meaning that the national system is guarded from the European level, the latter not being allowed to interfere with the national constitutional order. Thus, the national level is fenced off from the European level. Parliaments, which are undoubtedly fundamental to the political and constitutional structure of the Member States, are then restricted to their own national level, even when they deliberate on EU matters and EU decision-making.

An alternative way of interpreting this provision is to understand it as a recognition of the importance and relevance of the values inherent in the constitutional structures of the Member States to the EU constitutional order. Parliaments are a crucial element in the constitutional structure of the political and constitutional order of the Member States of the European Union and for the Union itself. Parliaments' role in legitimating democratically the exercise of power by public authorities in this view must also concern the exercise of power in the framework of, and on the basis of, EU decisions. National parliaments are not necessarily constrained only to whatever national authorities do or do not do within the remit of their responsibility, or to the extent of their accountability towards the national parliament in a strictly national one-to-one relationship. National parliaments also have a role to play in the structure of the EU itself.

This reading is reinforced by other provisions of the Treaty. Since Lisbon an explicit clue is found in Article 10(2), second sentence, TEU, which was cited above, but which for convenience is reproduced again here:

> Member States are represented in the European Council by their Heads of State or Government and in the Council by their governments, themselves democratically accountable either to their national Parliaments, or to their citizens.

This confirms what has been clarified above concerning the role of national parliaments and their role in holding members of the Council and European Council to account for acts in and of these councils.

Furthermore, Article 12 TEU is at the very centre of the present analysis on national parliaments and the compositeness of the European constitutional order:

> Article 12
>
> *National Parliaments* contribute actively to the good functioning of the *Union*:
>
> (a) through being informed by the institutions of the Union and having draft legislative acts of the Union forwarded to them in accordance with the Protocol on the role of national Parliaments in the European Union;
> (b) by seeing to it that the principle of subsidiarity is respected in accordance with the procedures provided for in the Protocol on the application of the principles of subsidiarity and proportionality;
> (c) by taking part, within the framework of the area of freedom, security and justice, in the evaluation mechanisms for the implementation of the Union policies in that area, in accordance with Article 70 of the Treaty on the Functioning of the European Union, and through being involved in the political monitoring of Europol and the evaluation of Eurojust's activities in accordance with Articles 88 and 85 of that Treaty;

(d) by taking part in the revision procedures of the Treaties, in accordance with Article 48 of this Treaty;
(e) by being notified of applications for accession to the Union, in accordance with Article 49 of this Treaty;
(f) by taking part in the inter-parliamentary cooperation between national Parliaments and with the European Parliament, in accordance with the Protocol on the role of national Parliaments in the European Union. (emphasis added)

First it has to be noted that the provision opens by saying that 'national parliaments contribute actively to the good functioning *of the Union*'; they do so by using all the powers and functions summed up under (a) to (f). So being informed by the EU institutions sub-paragraph (a) contributes not merely to the good functioning of the Member State institutions but to the good functioning of *the Union*. Scrutiny is, in other words, not a matter of fulfilling a *national* constitutional mandate only; it is also fulfilling an *EU* mandate.

The wording of Article 12 sub-paragraph (b) TEU brings out neatly that the provisions on subsidiarity can be read in the light of the idea of the European constitutional order as a composite order. Indeed, subsidiarity is a principle which applies to the *EU* institutions and its agencies and other bodies (see Article 5(3) TEU),[22] but, alongside supranational institutions, it is the *national* parliaments that scrutinise, determine and supervise whether the EU institutions apply it correctly.[23]

The significant element, and it is confirmed by Article 6(1) of the Protocol on the application of the principles of subsidiarity and proportionality, is that national parliaments (or chambers thereof) are placed in a direct and unmediated relation to the European institutions. According to this protocol, national legislatures do not address their views on a draft EU measure (so-called 'reasoned opinions') to their own national government, nor are their views to be transmitted by their governments, but rather they immediately communicate with the EU institutions.[24] National parliaments are thus made actors with an independent role of their own within the EU constitutional system.

The EU institutions must take reasoned opinions of the national parliaments into account (Article 7(1) Protocol No 2) on the application of the principles of subsidiarity and proportionality). If a certain threshold is met (as a rule, a third of the votes of the number of parliaments and chambers), they can force the Commission to reconsider the proposed legislative act (Article 7(2) Protocol No 2), and in the event that a higher threshold

[22] According to Article 5(3) TEU, '[u]nder the principle of subsidiarity, in areas which do not fall within its exclusive competence, the Union shall act only if and in so far as the objectives of the proposed action cannot be sufficiently achieved by the Member States, either at central level or at regional and local level, but can rather, by reason of the scale or effects of the proposed action, be better achieved at Union level.

The institutions of the Union shall apply the principle of subsidiarity as laid down in the Protocol on the application of the principles of subsidiarity and proportionality. National Parliaments ensure compliance with the principle of subsidiarity in accordance with the procedure set out in that Protocol'.

[23] As is mentioned below, there is also a role for the Court of Justice under Protocol No 2. This notwithstanding, it should be noted that the Commission, in its handling of national parliaments' reasoned opinions, has on occasion acted as arbiter of the subsidiarity test in determining whether subsidiarity objections of national parliaments are admissible or not, eg by qualifying an alleged 'subsidiarity' objection as a presumable 'proportionality' objection outside the scope of Protocol No 2. This is not in accordance with Article 12 TEU.

[24] This remains the case in the legal systems that require a transmission *also* to the Government of the reasoned opinions expressed.

(half of the votes) is met, the measure—if the Commission upholds the proposal—can only be adopted under a specific procedure (Article 7(3) Protocol No 2).

That this system of subsidiarity review makes national parliaments an integral part of a truly composite constitutional order is further borne out by another feature of the subsidiarity protocol: the power to bring actions for annulment on grounds of subsidiarity to the CJEU has been given to national parliaments as independent actors (Article 8 Protocol No 2). It provides that the CJEU shall have jurisdiction in cases 'notified by [the Member States] in accordance with their legal order on behalf of their national Parliament or a chamber of it', when the parliament involved brings the claim that an Union measure infringes the principle of subsidiarity.

These are the most important provisions on the role of national parliaments. There are other explicit and implicit provisions that guarantee the input of national parliaments, for instance whenever the Treaty refers to the requirement of adopting a decision in accordance with national constitutional procedures.[25] These national constitutional procedures usually guarantee, to a larger or more limited extent, requirements of information or approval of the national parliament before a representative of the Member State in question can cooperate in the adoption of the relevant EU measure. This chapter will not go into any of these, just as the provisions in national constitutions, legislation and parliamentary practices that are not mentioned in primary EU law but have a similar effect are not examined here.[26]

At this point it is important to add, that also *outside* the framework of the European Treaties practices have developed to enhance the participation of the parliaments in EU decision-making. The most important of these is the so-called Barroso initiative that was started in 2006: the non-legally binding political dialogue with the national parliaments. Under this practice EU legislative proposals or documents are sent by the Commission directly to the parliaments and, in turn, these are invited to present their views to the Commission directly. These views, usually, take the form of an opinion or a 'reasoned opinion', as is the case in the subsidiarity review. In a sense it extends the scope of the 'Early Warning System' of subsidiarity review, in as much as parliaments are invited also to provide political assessments on other aspects than subsidiarity in the narrower technical sense. It presupposes direct interaction of parliaments with the Commission.[27] And this in

[25] In the TEU: Arts 42(2), 48(4), 48(6), 49, second paragraph, 54(1) and 55(2); in the TFEU: Arts 25(2), 218(8), 223(2), 262, 311, third paragraph, 357, first paragraph; Statute of the ECB, Art 40.2. The duty to notify national parliaments (outside Protocols Nos 1 and 2) is also provided for in TEU: Arts 48(2), 48(7), 49; in TFEU: Arts 70, 71, 81(3), 352(2).

[26] Famous examples are the Italian *Legge 24 dicembre 2012, no 234, Norme generali sulla partecipazione dell'Italia alla formazione e all'attuazione della normativa e delle politiche dell'Unione europea*, which we may consider the Italian European Union Act; the UK's European Union Act 2011; and Art 23(1a) to (7), of the German Constitution (*Grundgesetz*), as well as the *Integrationsverantwortungsgesetz* and the *Gesetzüber die Zusammenarbeit von Bundesregierung und Deutschem Bundestag in Angelegenheiten der Europäischen Union*, as well as the *ESM-Finanzierungsgesetz*. For further references about these and other Member States, see Leonard Besselink, Monica Claes, ŠejlaImamović, Jan Herman Reestman, National Constitutional Avenues for Further EU Integration (n 20 above) at 263–73.

[27] I Cooper, 'The Watchdogs of Subsidiarity: National Parliaments and the Logic of Arguing in the EU' (2006) 44 *Journal of Common Market Studies* 281–304; D Jančić, 'Representative Democracy across Levels: National Parliaments and EU Constitutionalism' (2012) 8 *Croatian Yearbook of European Law and Policy* 227; M Goldoni, 'The Early Warning System and the Monti II Regulation: The Case for a Political Interpretation' (2014) 10 *European Constitutional Law Review* 90 and Goldoni 'The Instrumental Value of Horizontal Parliamentary Cooperation: Subsidiarity Review and the Political Dialogue' Chapter 9 in this volume. According to others, the two procedures should be clearly separated: see P Kiiver, *The Early Warning System for the Principle of Subsidiarity: Constitutional*

turn presupposes the existence in national parliaments of a procedure for parliamentary scrutiny of EU decision-making.

For the subsidiarity review and the political dialogue to be successful, they require parliaments to view themselves as actors within the broader encompassing European order. But for this to take place, national institutions should see themselves as part of a greater constitutional whole, of which they each constitute a part and in which they have a role to play. This whole does not consist of two more or less separate, mutually exclusive levels, but something much more inclusive and coordinated; as regards the sources of democratic legitimacy, something that is not a matter of one body pushing out another, but is rather based on the cooperation between national parliaments and the European Parliament. So the image is not one of two mutually exclusive political centres, but something more polycentric.

However, this legal framework is not fully reflected in common practice yet. The practice under the Early Warning System and of the Barroso Initiative shows that not all parliaments and certainly not all chambers of parliaments actively engage in the political dialogue and in an intense scrutiny of EU decision-making comparable to that in national decision-making.[28] Why do remnants of the 'levels approach' persist in the national parliaments? In order to address this question the next section deals with what can be called the challenge of democracy within a composite constitutional order.

V. THE CHALLENGE OF DEMOCRACY WITHIN A COMPOSITE CONSTITUTIONAL ORDER

Democracy is one of the greatest challenges—if not the greatest—of European integration, and indeed of internationalisation and globalisation; a challenge of which not all the implications are fully understood, let alone any satisfactory solutions available. Everything argued here is therefore necessarily tentative.

As academics we can lament that parliaments do not behave in ways which we would normatively expect them to behave. The new setting that has arisen since the end of the twentieth century has led to cognitive dissonance, so the excuse might be. The possible causes of this dissonance, however, require further examination. Of course, there are practical explanations why not all national parliaments and their chambers fully engage in the European political discourse outside the confines of their own national constitutional framework. Insufficient resources in terms of expertise, parliamentary time for debate, and too little support of parliamentary committees to cope with a new and huge information overload are real problems.

Theory and Empirical Reality (Abingdon, Routledge, 2012) 103 and F Fabbrini and K Granat, '"Yellow Card, but no Foul": The Role of the National Parliaments under the Subsidiarity Protocol and the Commission Proposal for an EU Regulation on the Right to Strike' (2013) 1 *Common Market Law Review* 115.

[28] Hefftler et al (eds), *The Palgrave Handbook of National Parliaments and the European Union* (n 13 above) at 153–666. See also European Commission, *Annual Report 2013 on Relations Between the European Commission and National Parliaments*, COM(2014) 507 final, Brussels, 5 August 2014, pp 4–7 and European Commission, *Annual Report 2013 on Subsidiarity and Proportionality*, COM(2014) 506 final, Brussels, 5 August 2014, p 4.

All this may not explain more fundamentally the reluctance or even resistance of national parliaments to engage as European actors or to do so more fully. The hypothesis presented here involves the nature and legitimation of the exercise of public authority by parliaments.

This legitimation is generally considered to exist in the fact that they have been elected by the citizens as an electorate, and this provides action and inaction by the elected to be democratically legitimated. On the European continent there is the further consideration, based in constitutional theory, of the 'sovereignty of the people': all power emanates from the people, and all institutions exercising public authority over citizens should therefore be based on a popular mandate. The *Bundesverfassungsgericht* uses the expression *Legitimationskette*, 'chain of legitimation'. This is in principle a two- or three-stage chain: from the people to parliament, and from parliament to the executive. In reality, governments create—usually based on parliamentary legislation—further steps in the chain: for instance by setting up independent agencies. This removes such agencies further away from the people; they are at least three steps removed from the people. Moreover, the whole point of agencies is that they are shielded from, and hence at a distance from, the ordinary political process, as is the case, for example, with competition authorities and central banks. Here the problem is not that their origin cannot be traced back ultimately to the electorate. Rather, what can be detected is the absence of normal accountability feedback from the institution (agency) backwards to its intermediate principal (executive), to the latter's principal (parliament), and finally to the people (or at any rate the electorate), because the agency does not owe responsibility to its principal and cannot be held to account by its principal. Even in cases in which there is some form of accountability, we should notice the decreasingly democratic character that is attributed to institutions that are three steps or more removed from the people.

As regards the establishment of an international organisation, the situation seems somewhat similar. And the same must be said about the EU, based as it is on treaties principally negotiated and exclusively concluded by executives, albeit under approval of parliament and occasionally covered by popular referendum. It is true that since the Treaty of Lisbon the 'ordinary revision procedure' takes a 'convention' as the main source of procedure,[29] but even then the subsequent intergovernmental conference has the true power to determine which amendments shall be put to the Member States, each of whom are to approve or reject them in accordance with their national constitutional procedures.[30]

A number of things can be said about reasoning in terms of this chain of legitimation. First, the chain becomes too long if it goes beyond the steps from the 'people' (or electorate) to parliament, to the government. Secondly, the chain must not be a one-way but a two-way system for democracy to be able to work properly.

At the time of the Constitution for Europe, one tried to solve part of the legitimation problem of the EU, by creating a direct mandate from the people, through a constitutional act, and ideas of a Europe-wide referendum were floated. But the Constitution for Europe was in the end not based on such a Europe-wide popular referendum. To the contrary, if failed because it was voted down decisively in the French referendum.[31] So the idea of the

[29] See the chapter by C Pinelli, 'The Convention Method', Ch 3 in this volume.

[30] See Art 48(2) to (4) TEU.

[31] It was also defeated in the Netherlands, but this was not decisive, as experience teaches that negative referenda outcomes in smaller Member States are usually overridden in a subsequent referendum.

Union being based on a popular constitutive act is for all intents and purpose one that does not adequately reflect reality. Or, worse, it is incorrect: the Union is not based on a popular constitutive act either of the people or peoples of Europe; it remains mainly a product of the co-operating Member State executives.

Indeed, throughout the history of European integration there have been referenda in various Member States, often with a positive outcome, particularly surrounding the accession by a new Member State, or about a State's remaining in the Union, as was the case even in the UK, when it had only shortly beforehand become a member of the European Communities.[32] By now in 19 out of the 28 Member States there have been referenda on the EU or directly related thereto; mostly they have concerned membership of the EU, membership on the basis of the treaties as we now know them, or on alternatives for them. But as long as a third of the Member State populations have not at any time had the chance to participate directly, this is insufficient to conclude that it can be a popular constitutive act of the Union.

In the absence of a popular constitutive act, we would have to look for a *parliamentary* basis, thus creating a derivative democratic basis, in order to remain within the traditional 'chain of legitimation' as here represented. Potentially this could be the Union Parliament (ie the European Parliament) or the national parliaments.

Although under the present Treaty the European Parliament can propose amendments to the Treaty and must be heard on proposed amendments by the European Council (article 48(2) and (3) TEU), it neither has the monopoly to initiate treaty amendments, nor does it have decisive powers. Only under the procedure to switch from unanimity to qualified majority and from the special legislative procedure to the ordinary legislative procedure, do the relevant decisions require the 'consent' of the European Parliament (article 48(7) TEU). So the European Parliament provides no democratic legitimacy to a *constitutive* act under the EU Treaty, albeit that it does indeed provide a direct parliamentary basis for the day-to-day functioning of the Commission and for the adoption of legislation for which co-decision (now ordinary legislative procedure) is required.

What about the national parliaments? Unlike the European Parliament, they do provide some democratic legitimacy to the Union, based as it is on the national parliaments' approval of the founding Treaties and the treaties amending them. This legitimacy is *derivative* in nature as regards the constitutive, founding act of the EU. As to its daily functioning the situation is the opposite from that of the European Parliament: national parliaments do not provide direct legitimacy to the same extent as the European Parliament, since there is no *decisive*, legally binding and sanctioned accountability relation between the Union institutions and the national parliaments. National parliaments cannot send home any of the Union's institutions or their officials (except the national ministerial representative in the Council).

So, in terms of the mechanism of the democratic legitimation chain, there is no single and ultimate site of legitimacy. We must conclude that a more direct and solid democratic mandate along the lines of the legitimation chain is therefore lacking for the EU at the moment.

[32] The referendum in the UK on the continued membership of the then European Economic Community was held on 5 June 1975. For a full list of referenda on European integration, see the following webpage at the website of the Danish Parliament: english.eu.dk/en/faq/faq/referendums.

VI. CONCLUSIONS

Where does this leave us? It is possible to affirm that under the current circumstances the democratic legitimacy of the Union is *composite* in nature.

The European Parliament provides legitimation primarily on a day-to-day basis as far as the Commission and secondly as far as most of the legislation is concerned, but not in terms of foundational legitimacy when we think of this in terms of the 'chain of legitimation'. By the same token, national parliaments primarily provide the Union with derivative foundational legitimacy. It is only secondarily that national parliaments provide legitimacy to the extent that they actively scrutinise the Union's work. Even then, they do so under conditions of a weak accountability relation in as much as it is sanction-less. In other words, if national parliaments are dissatisfied with the feedback provided by EU institutions represented by their officials, they do not have any sanctions at their disposal to enforce their views. There is a division of labour, but only by understanding the complementary nature of these elements can we understand the legitimacy of the order as a whole.

What are then the prospects for a democratic European order, and in particular for the national parliaments in such an order?

Perhaps we may have to think in other terms than those of the 'democratic legitimation chain'. And moreover, we should perhaps not think of 'foundational legitimacy'—provided by a constituent power, *pouvoir constituent originaire*—and ordinary day-to-day political legitimation—provided by the constituted powers, *pouvoirs constitués*—as concepts that are functionally very different. From a functional perspective we may even have to give up on that distinction as fundamental to constitutional thought.

The ultimate 'rule of recognition'[33] lies not necessarily in sovereignty of the people as the only redeeming source of legitimacy. This could just as well lie in the preparedness to accept the exercise of public authority, also if that authority is based in EU law. There are various historical examples of this. One of them is the United Kingdom, of which it is impossible to say when there ever was an original constituent power.[34] But also the history of the *Grundgesetz* makes clear that even in the Federal Republic its authority derives from its subsequent acceptance, not from the historical circumstances under which it was adopted.

Acceptability of the exercise of authority can and must also be fostered by the extent to which representatives of the citizens have been involved in the EU decision-making that is the basis of the exercise of a particular act of public authority, be it at more constitutive moments in which primary law is adopted or amended, or in the course of 'ordinary' day-to-day decision-making. So here, the importance of parliamentary scrutiny and mandating systems by national parliaments should be emphasised, as mechanisms to enhance transparency and enabling accountability, ultimately creating legitimacy: legitimacy that may even be created in the absence of original legitimacy. As pointed out in the first part of this chapter, feedback from the EU to national parliaments would be a considerable improvement in the line of upward accountability in the scheme from the people to

[33] The reference is obviously to HLA Hart, [1961] *The Concept of Law*, 3rd edn (Oxford, Oxford University Press, 2012). For an application to the US Constitution see M Adler and KE Himma (eds), *The Rule of Recognition and the U.S. Constitution* (New York, Oxford University Press, 2009).

[34] See B Ackerman, 'Three Paths to Constitutionalism—and the Crisis of the European Union' (2015) 45 *British Journal of Political Science* 705.

parliaments to executives to the Union. As recounted earlier in this chapter, this is precisely what the EU Treaty provides for since Lisbon.

National parliaments are important also—and this is often forgotten in treatises on the role of national parliaments in the Union—because of the fact that most of the EU legislation and decision-making results in the exercise of power by *national* public authorities: the application, implementation, execution and enforcement of EU law takes place mostly in the Member States.

A national authority that applies, implements or enforces Union law is both a *national and* a *European* authority, as is appropriate in a composite constitutional order. And if that exercise of authority can be said to be based both on a democratic legitimation by EU institutions *and* by national parliaments, this is most fitting in a democratic composite constitutional order.

2

Interjudicial Dialogue and Interparliamentary Dialogue in the Constitution of the Union

GIUSEPPE MARTINICO[*]

I. DIALOGUE AS A FRAMEWORK OF ANALYSIS

THIS CHAPTER LOOKS at the features of interparliamentary cooperation, recognised by European Treaties provisions since the 1990s, in comparison with the so-called 'interjudicial dialogue' in the EU. Both phenomena have been growing and intensifying in the last two decades, although they show rather different legal objectives and effects.

The idea of interjudicial dialogue has immediately been the target of criticism. In the Canadian context, for instance, it was argued that 'Dialogue theory offers a means of rationalising this world of judicial interpretative supremacy'.[1]

This criticism is also due to the frequent ambiguity with which it has been employed and by the polysemy of its formula. Such a polysemy can be explained in light of the massive and very interdisciplinary literature interested in the phenomenon: theorists of communication and argumentation, legal theorists, constitutional law scholars, public international law and EU law scholars and comparative law scholars represent just some of the contributors in the history of this concept.

[*] I would like to thank my friends and colleagues Diane Fromage and Katarzyna Granat for their help. The usual disclaimers apply.

[1] G Huscroft, 'Rationalizing Judicial Power: The Mischief of Dialogue Theory' (2008), available at: papers.ssrn.com/sol3/papers.cfm?abstract_id=1083685.

A reference mark in the literature is represented by a famous article by Slaughter,[2] in which the author examined the 'form, function, and reciprocity of the [judicial] communication', introducing some of the classifications still used in the debate. As for the function of judicial communication she distinguished between a strategic and normative function of dialogue, stressing that it is aimed at 'enhancing the effectiveness of supranational tribunals'; 'enhancing the persuasiveness, legitimacy or authority of individual judicial decisions'; ensuring the 'collective deliberation'; 'cross-fertilisation'; 'assuring and promoting acceptance of reciprocal international obligations'.[3]

Slaughter also insisted on the degree of reciprocity between interlocutors, which is key in fully-fledged dialogue. When dialogue meets Parliaments, then the degree of uncertainty increases and indeed dialogue between legislatures is an ambiguous phenomenon, known by different formulae ('parliamentary diplomacy', 'interparliamentary cooperation'), which however presents a certain interest if analysed as a perspective through which it is possible to investigate the relations among legal orders (following what has been done in respect of interjudicial dialogue).[4] To a certain extent this applies to the EU as well, although in this context, especially thanks to the Lisbon Treaty, there has been a partial codification of the phenomenon.

This chapter is structured as follows. First, I shall present the structure of the EU constitutional architecture which will help us understand the incentives that actors operating in a multilevel structure might have for dialogue. Secondly, I shall move from the structure to the behaviour of the actors operating in such a multilevel context, trying to identify at least three types of interactions: cooperative, competitive and conflictual. I shall focus on the cooperative interactions and, within them, I shall pay particular attention to dialogue. This scheme has been applied to judicial actors mainly, while in this chapter I shall try to adapt some of these considerations to parliamentary actors. In this sense this chapter may be read as a sort of research agenda rather than a mature account of these phenomena.

II. THE STRUCTURE OF THE EUROPEAN COMPLEX LEGAL ORDER

Why should actors cooperate? The rationale for cooperation can be primarily sought in the incentives that a given scenario might offer. In order to explore this point (the 'why' level) it is necessary to say a few words about the structure of the European context. This account will help us understand why isolation is not an option for actors (judges, parliaments) working in the EU context.

There is no doubt that the current EU constitutional architecture is provided with a multilevel governance system. This has been extensively explored by scholars who paid less attention to its complex structure. Indeed, EU constitutional law responds to its complex nature. By 'complex' I do not mean simply 'complicated'; complexity is much more,[5] since

[2] AM Slaughter, 'A Typology of Transjudicial Communication' (1994) 29 *University of Richmond Law Review* 99.

[3] Slaughter (n 2 above), 99.

[4] S Cassese, 'La funzione costituzionale dei giudici non statali. Dallo Spazio giuridico globale all'ordine giuridico globale' (2007) *Rivista trimestrale di diritto pubblico* 609.

[5] The *mot-problème* (E Morin, *Introduzione al pensiero complesso* (Milano, Sperling & Kupfer, 1993), and E Morin, *Conoscenza della conoscenza* (Milano, Feltrinelli, 1989)) 'complexity' is used in several ways. Millard, for

it refers to a general category that has caused a fundamental shift in the history of social and experimental sciences. By applying the idea of complexity developed by Morin to the supranational context, it might be argued that the European Union is a complex legal order for certain reasons. The first one, which is also the most superficial, is an etymological reason. In fact, complexity comes from the Latin *complexus* which means 'interlaced' and the European legal order is based on a constitutive 'knot'[6] which ties the law of the EU Treaties to that of the Member States' Constitutions. A confirmation of this is given by the wording of those European Treaties which refer to the national legal orders (for instance Articles 6 TEU and 4(2) TEU) and by the existence of many European clauses included in the national constitutions.[7] These provisions are the channels through which a continuous exchange of legal materials between the national and supranational levels occurs.[8]

In this sense, constitutional complexity is of course indebted to some scholarly views on the European Union, namely multilevel constitutionalism and constitutional pluralism.[9] From the former it borrows the idea of the Constitution understood as the outcome of the dialectic between the national and the supranational legal systems, as a process whose shape depends on the mutual exchange between EU and national legal materials.[10] At the same time, constitutional complexity highlights how the interconnection between legal orders fosters interpretative competition, emphasising the importance of constitutional conflicts. These aspects, and particularly the hot issue of constitutional conflicts, seem to be neglected by the theory of multilevel constitutionalism,[11] at least in the first works by Pernice.[12]

instance, recalls at least four different meanings of the word complex (E Millard, 'Eléments pour une approche analytique de la complexité' in M Doat, J Le Goff and P Pédrot (eds), *Droit et complexité. Pour une nouvelle intelligence du droit vivant* (Rennes, Presses Universitaires de Rennes, 2007) 141). Among other things, complexity is also meant as interdependency of the objects with regard to their relative autonomy: in this paper I focus on the relative autonomy of the legal orders (national, supranational and international) in the multilevel system.

[6] G Martinico, *The Tangled Complexity of the EU Constitutional Process: The Frustrating Knot of Europe* (Abingdon, Routledge, 2012).

[7] See M Claes, 'Constitutionalizing Europe at its Source: The "European Clauses" in the National Constitutions: Evolution and Typology' (2005) 24 *Yearbook of European Law* 81.

[8] In order to define this phenomenon I elsewhere (Martinico, n 6 above) used the concept of constitutional *synallagma*. Although this concept has been widely employed in contract theory, in the economy of this work I am going to limit myself to the etymologic level without endorsing a contractual theory for the reading of EU constitutional dynamics.

[9] On constitutional pluralism, see: N MacCormick, 'Beyond the sovereign state' (1993) 56 *Modern Law Review* 1; M Poiares Maduro, *The European Court of Justice and the European Economic Constitution* (Oxford, Hart Publishing, 1998) 31. See also: N Walker, 'The Idea of Constitutional Pluralism' (2002) 65 *Modern Law Review* 317; M Poiares Maduro, 'Contrapunctual Europe's constitutional pluralism in action' in N Walker (ed), *Sovereignty in Transition* (Oxford, Hart Publishing, 2003), 501; M Poiares Maduro, 'Interpreting European Law: Judicial adjudication in a context of constitutional pluralism' (2007) 1 *European Journal of Legal Studies*. For a comparison between the different visions of constitutional pluralism, see M Avbelj and J Komarek (eds), 'Four visions of constitutional pluralism' *EUI Working Paper* 2008/21 (2008), available at: cadmus.iue.it/dspace/bitstream/1814/9372/1/LAW_2008_21.pdf.

[10] This Constitution is the result of a steady coordination of two legal orders; national and supranational. From a dynamic point of view this interplay (as Pernice said, the national and supranational legal systems are 'closely interwoven and interdependent', I Pernice, 'Multilevel Constitutionalism in the European Union' (2002) 27 *European Law Review* 511, 514) is well represented by Article 6 TEU, which refers to the national constitutional traditions as a part of the European legal order.

[11] L Besselink, *A Composite European Constitution/Een Samengestelde Europese Constitutie* (Groningen, Europa Law Publishing, 2007) 6.

[12] Partly different is the discourse in Franz Mayer's works, see, for instance, F Mayer, 'The European Constitution and the Courts. Adjudicating European constitutional law in a multilevel system' *Jean Monnet Working Paper* 9/03 (2003), available at: centers.law.nyu.edu/jeanmonnet/archive/papers/03/030901-03.pdf.

That is why scholars have accused this reconstruction of giving an optimistic and misleading representation of the reality.[13]

On another level, one may conceive the EU as complex because its legal system shares some features with complex systems in natural sciences, namely non-reversibility, non-reducibility, unpredictability, non-determinability (*rectius*, non-determinism).[14] Elsewhere I tried to show how these categories can be applied to the EU legal system.[15]

To this end, I understood by the term 'complex', a system composed of several interconnected or interwoven (as the etymology of the word 'complex' suggests) constitutional levels/poles. Against this background, the European Constitution is understood as a *composite entity*,[16] made of constitutional principles developed at the European level and complemented by (common) national constitutional principles. In this sense, one could argue that in such a context national laws as well as European law partake in defining the European constitutional law. This type of constitution presents a hybrid nature: some of its component principles have been codified over the years in the wording of the Treaties (one could view the Charter of Fundamental Rights of the EU as a codification of those principles recognised by the Court of Justice of the EU (CJEU) in its dialectic with the national Constitutional Courts), whilst others remain unwritten (the principle of direct effect, for example). As for the genesis of these principles, they can be seen as the outcome of the dialectic between levels, namely between the interpreters of these levels, the CJEU and the national Constitutional Courts. The European Constitution thus results from a combination of national and supranational constitutional materials.

Their interactions between levels/poles create a kind of additional information which is not visible to an external observer (in this sense one could say that in complex systems there is no Laplace's demon).[17] New properties that cannot be explained from the properties of individual elements emerge as a result of the interactions among levels/poles. Such features are usually called emergent properties and correspond to those constitutional principles that cannot be entirely reduced to the national or supranational levels. In this sense a complex system should not be understood as a mere sum of its components, but as something characterised by an added value which is the product of all the interactions among them. The idea of emergent properties refers to those entities that '"arise" out of more fundamental entities and yet are "novel" or "irreducible" with respect to them'.[18] The emergence of these properties is frequently associated with evolutionary dynamics which shape and

[13] M Luciani, 'Costituzionalismo irenico e costituzionalismo polemico' (2006), available at: www.rivistaaic.it/old_site_aic/materiali/anticipazioni/costituzionalismo_irenico/index.html.

[14] For a complex system, non-reversibility is the impossibility of returning to the status quo spontaneously and precisely. Unlike reversible processes, in fact, where from the final condition it is possible to return to the starting condition, complex systems are non-reversible due to the non-linearity of the evolution. Non-reducibility implies that the result of the relationship among diversities does not present itself as a mere sum of the latter but is rather something different. Unlike what happens in a deterministic system, in a complex adaptive system it is difficult to foretell or foresee the evolution of the system by looking at the starting position. Complex systems do not follow necessary and univocal laws according to a linear concept of the evolution based on the dialectic of cause/effect.

[15] G Martinico, 'The Tangled Complexity of the EU Constitutional Process: On Complexity as a Constitutional Theory of the EU' (2012) 31 *Yearbook of European Law* 198.

[16] Besselink (n 11 above).

[17] I Prigogine and I Stengers, *Order Out of Chaos: Man's New Dialogue with Nature* (New York, Bantam, 1984).

[18] T O'Connor and HY Wong, 'Emergent Properties' in EN Zalta (ed), *The Stanford Encyclopaedia of Philosophy* (Spring, 2012, edn), available at: plato.stanford.edu/entries/properties-emergent/#EmeSub.

reshape the natural order stemming from the different types of interactions possible among actors operating at the different levels/poles.

Without going into detail, here, I can limit myself to the idea of reducibility, according to which the European legal order is not reducible to the sum of legal provisions at various levels. I mean that, for example, it is impossible to 'find' the legal basis for the principles of primacy and direct effect in the wording of the Treaty or in the letter of the national constitutions; in this respect these principles may be defined as the emergent properties of the EU legal system. In *Van Gend en Loos*,[19] and *Costa*[20] in fact, the CJEU found the roots of such principles in the 'spirit' of the Treaties and, also, in the indirect will of the states signing the Treaties.[21] A consequence of the impossibility of tracing these principles back to the wording of a univocal primacy clause,[22] for instance, has underscored the role of courts. My assumption is that this context exalts the case-by-case judicial approach to solving legal conflicts between rules; this responds to the idea of non-determinability of the European Union legal order; and this also explains the importance their decisions have had for the evolution of such an order, thanks to their incremental and flexible nature.

Another building block of complex systems comes from studies on chaos theory[23] (both complexity studies and chaos theory share a non-deterministic approach), which conceives the relationship between order and disorder as fundamental to the evolution of the complex system. In other words, as Le Goff put it when writing about the relation between complexity and labour law: 'Comme si s'on optait pour la technique homéopathique de lutte contre le mal par le mal lui-même, le désordre devenant paradoxalement vecteur d'ordre'.[24]

I dealt[25] with this issue when exploring the role played by constitutional conflicts in the life of the Union. Unlike constitutional pluralism, complexity does not present a normative proposal for adjusting or neutralising constitutional conflicts[26] between constitutional supremacy and EU law primacy, conceiving them as elements of disorder.[27]

[19] Case C-26/62 *NV Algemene Transport- en Expeditie Onderneming van Gend en Loos v Nederlandse Administratie der Belastingen*, [1963] ECR 3.

[20] Case C-6/64 *Flaminio Costa v ENEL* [1964] ECR 1141.

[21] Case C-26/62 *Van Gend en Loos.*

[22] Scholars have identified at least four different meanings of primacy/supremacy in CJEU case law. Moreover, the notion of primacy enshrined in Art I-6 of the Constitutional Treaty seems to be different from that used by the CJEU. See for example M Claes, *The National Courts' Mandate in the European Constitution* (Oxford, Hart Publishing, 2006) 100–111. In order to find a solution to this ambiguity, some scholars have devised a 'law of laws'; see WT Eijsbouts and LFM Besselink, 'Editorial: "The Law of Laws"—Overcoming Pluralism' (2008) 4 *European Constitutional Law Review* 395.

[23] For instance see: I Prigogine, *Le leggi del caos* (Roma/Bari, Laterza, 2008). SH Kellert, *In the Wake of Chaos: Unpredictable Order in Dynamical Systems* (Chicago IL, University of Chicago Press, 1993). On chaos theory and the EU see: AM Russo, 'La territorial cross-border cooperation "attraverso lo specchio" del diritto transnazionale: Alice diventa regina e il sogno svanisce' (2013) 14 *Diritto Pubblico Comparato ed Europeo* 515, 518.

[24] J Le Goff, 'Le droit du travail, terre d'élection de la complexité' in M Doat, J Le Goff and P Pédro (eds) (n 5 above), 106.

[25] Martinico (n 6 above), 110 et seq.

[26] Especially when referring to the works of Maduro and Kumm, constitutional pluralism is also characterised by a strong normative position aimed at neutralising possible constitutional conflicts. Going beyond its descriptive value, Maduro's view presents a strong normative character. It does not limit itself to describing what constitutional pluralism is, but attempts to provide some solutions for better coordination among judges (M Poiares Maduro, n 9 above). A similar observation may be made with regard to Mattias Kumm's works, especially his principle of 'best fit' (M Kumm, 'The jurisprudence of constitutional conflict: Constitutional supremacy in Europe before and after the Constitutional Treaty' (2005) 11 *European Law Journal* 262).

[27] Attempting to reduce complexity would mean killing it, especially taking into account the risk of holism present in these theories. On this see P Eleftheriadis, 'Pluralism and Integrity' (2010) 23 *Ratio Juris* 365, 387.

In this sense constitutional complexity can provide 'an analogical foundation for that new paradigm of legal theory',[28] and in this particular field it can describe how the authority of EU law impacts on the domestic constitutional systems and how the constitutional systems react by challenging a complete unification. Since unpredictability is one of the basic features of a complex system, it is impossible within the logic of constitutional complexity to foresee the evolution of the EU system.

Another important difference between constitutional complexity and constitutional pluralism is the different functions played by constitutional conflicts in the two paradigms. Disagreement and conflicts represent what disorder is for complex systems in natural sciences.[29] Consistently with the tradition of complexity studies (and even with a certain branch of political science scholars),[30] conflicts (as a form of disorder) are conceived as factors of—constitutional in our case—transformation.

Whilst authors like Maduro and Kumm, as we noted, attempted to provide a set of principles aimed at neutralising constitutional conflicts, seeing them like a hindrance in the path towards the coherence of the system, constitutional complexity conceives of possible collisions between different levels as the driving force behind new constitutional development, since it takes into account the potentially positive aspects at least of certain forms of constitutional conflict.

Against this, order and disorder thus interact, favouring the emergence of social changes and the renovation of the organisation. Finally, like some complex systems in natural sciences, the European Union legal order is adaptive, it reflects 'an ability to adapt through the emergent characteristic of self-organization, which comes from the interdependency of their individuals or agents, a.k.a. sub-systems'.[31] In other words, the European Union legal order develops through non-constructivist dynamics.

III. FROM THE STRUCTURE TO THE ACTORS: THE IDEA OF DIALOGUE

After having explored the meaning and the potential of constitutional complexity when applied to EU law it is time to move from the structure of this complex legal order to the consequences that such a structure has on the actors operating at the different levels/poles of this legal order.

The general idea is that in an order which is characterised by shared legal norms (ie common constitutional traditions, some of the general principles of EU law), that are the product of the constitutional synallagma, interpreters cannot work in an isolated manner (what Delmas Marty calls '*l'isolement impossible*').[32] On the contrary, they have to interact with the other actors operating at different levels.

[28] J Ruhl, 'Complexity theory as a paradigm for the dynamical law-and-society system' (1995–96) 45 *Duke Law Journal* 851.

[29] See A Montuori, 'Foreword: Edgar Morin's path of complexity' (2008), available at: www.academia.edu/213724/Edgar_Morins_Path_of_Complexity, XXXIV.

[30] J Knight, *Institutions and social conflict* (Cambridge, Cambridge University Press, 1992).

[31] M Schneider and M Somers, 'Organizations as complex adaptive systems: Implications of Complexity Theory for leadership research' (2006) 17 *The Leadership Quarterly* 351, 355.

[32] M Delmas Marty, *Le pluralisme ordonné. Les forces imaginantes du droit* (Paris, Seuil, 2006) 39.

Constitutional pluralism has emphasised this aspect but the cooperative spirit inspiring the principles of contrapuntal law,[33] for instance, captures just a part of the phenomenon.

'Interactions' may cover a broader range of actions (cooperative, competitive, conflictual), with cooperation being just one of these.

In this chapter I will try to present some of these kinds of interactions produced by the EU constitutionalisation process, paying particular attention to cooperative dynamics. In order to do that, first I shall focus on judges (but of course other actors could be taken into account), employing as viewpoint the perspective of national actors that play a fundamental role in the multilevel legal system as we will see. In order to present this idea, I will introduce my idea of judicial dialogue.

When one thinks about 'dialogue' in EU law, the preliminary ruling mechanism comes to mind but despite its importance in the economy of the evolution of EU law, the preliminary ruling mechanism does not exhaust all the forms of dialogue that can be used by courts in the multilevel legal system.

A terminological caveat should be made at this point. The metaphor of dialogue has been widely used by the literature and this concept is variously understood in different meanings; a vehicle for legal transplants, an informal means of communication between judicial and political bodies, or a new paradigm of judicial relations between actors not belonging to the same legal order.[34] Recently some authors[35] have attempted to define the essence of the idea of 'dialogue' better by identifying some key elements that should be present when talking about a proper dialogue. However, this notion is still considered by many authors to be misleading and foggy.[36] For all these reasons in this chapter I am going to adopt more neutral language, writing of 'judicial interactions', ie episodes of contact (intentional or

[33] Maduro (n 9 above), 501–37.

[34] See the different contributions collected in the volume: F Fontanelli, G Martinico and P Carrozza (eds), *Shaping Rule of Law through Dialogue: International and Supranational Experiences* (Groningen, Europa Law Publishing, 2009). On dialogue as a vehicle for legal transplants, see: D Barak-Erez, 'An International Community of Legislatures?' in RW Bauman and T Kahana (eds), *The Least Examined Branch: The Role of Legislatures in the Constitutional State* (Cambridge, Cambridge University Press, 2006) 532. The literature on judicial dialogue is very large: Cassese (n 4 above); Y Shany, *The Competing Jurisdictions of International Courts and Tribunals* (Oxford, Oxford University Press, 2003); Y Shany, *Regulating Jurisdictional Relations between National and International Courts*, (Oxford, Oxford University Press, 2007); C L 'Heureux-Dube, 'The International Judicial Dialogue: When Domestic Constitutional Courts Join the Conversation' (2001) 114 *Harvard Law Review* 2049; AM Slaughter, 'A Global Community of Courts' (2003) 44 *Harvard International Law Journal* 191; S Choudry, 'Globalization in Search of Justification: Towards a Theory of Comparative Constitutional Interpretation' (1999) 74 *Indiana Law Journal* 819, 821; A McCrudden, 'A Common Law of Human Rights? Transnational Judicial Conversations on Constitutional Rights' (2000) 20 *Oxford Journal of Legal Studies* 499; A Stone Sweet, *On Law, Politics and Judicialization* (Oxford, Oxford University Press, 2002); A Stone Sweet, *Governing with Judges: Constitutional Politics in Europe* (Oxford, Oxford University Press, 1992); A-M Slaughter, 'Judicial Globalization' (2000) 40 *Virginia Journal of International Law* 1104; R Hirschl, *Towards Juristocracy, the Limits and the Consequence of the New Constitutionalism* (Cambridge MA, Harvard University Press, 2004); GN Tate and T Vallinder (eds), *The Global Expansion of the Judicial Power* (New York/London, New York University Press, 1995); MR Ferrarese, 'When National Actors Become Transnational: Transjudicial Dialogue between Democracy and Constitutionalism' (2009) 9 *Global Jurist Frontiers* 1; M Claes, M de Visser, P Popelier, and C Van de Heyning, *Constitutional Conversations in Europe. Actors, Topics and Procedures* (Cambridge, Intersentia, 2012).

[35] A Torres Pérez, *Conflicts of Rights in the European Union: A Theory of Supranational Adjudication* (Oxford, Oxford University Press, 2009) 118.

[36] For instance, see: G de Vergottini, *Oltre il dialogo fra le Corti* (Bologna, Il Mulino, 2010); E D'Alterio, *La funzione di regolazione delle corti nello spazio amministrativo globale* (Milano, Giuffrè, 2010) 194.

casual) between courts, which may differ in their degree of intensity, results and typology. Within the notion of 'dialogue' Luc Tremblay proposed an interesting distinction between dialogue as a conversation and dialogue as deliberation. The former implies a conversation that does not have a specific purpose in mind; this is the case of a casual meeting between friends talking about trivialities, while the latter is aimed at a specific purpose and attempts to achieve a common agreement, solving problems collectively.[37] In this context, even 'conflicts' (and constitutional conflicts[38] in particular) can be traced back to the idea of judicial interactions.[39] Within this macro-group it is possible to distinguish between cooperative and competitive judicial interactions, by specifying the particular features of the second typology.

Against this background, 'dialogue' can be conceived as a *species* of the *genus* 'judicial interaction', characterised by the presence of some specific features, namely the existence of differing viewpoints, symmetry between the interlocutors (ie one's lack of complete authority over the other), mutual recognition and respect, equal opportunity to participate, and continuity over time.[40]

This view has many merits, first of all it is a selective notion which excludes other forms of interactions and which helps scholars understand the very essence of dialogue. At the same time, if taken too rigidly, it risks setting aside forms of influence that could be relevant according to other definitions. This point has been stressed by Tzanakopoulos, according to whom dialogue

> could thus be defined as 'influence' (exercised by the decision of one court on the reasoning and decision of another), or as 'reaction', or even better, criticism and rejection (by one court of the reasoning or decision of another). All this, in the process of 'engagement' with another court's decision.[41]

I think that these two views can be reconciled: indeed sometimes interpretative conflicts can serve to trigger a real dialogue.[42] More in general, two interlocutors can have an exchange of views even if the result of this is not full agreement: if you take the argument of your

[37] L B Tremblay, 'The Legitimacy of Judicial Review: The Limits of Dialogue between Courts and Legislatures' (2005) 3 *International Journal of Constitutional Law* 617.

[38] On constitutional conflicts, Kumm (n 26 above).

[39] On the importance of conflicts in pluralistic systems, see: D Halberstam, 'Constitutional Heterarchy: The Centrality of Conflict in the European Union and the United States' in J Dunoff and J Trachtman (eds), *In Ruling the World? Constitutionalism, International Law and Global Governance* (Cambridge, Cambridge University Press, 2009) 326.

[40] For this conception of judicial dialogue, see Torres Pérez (n 35 above). According to another definition, 'Dialogue can be defined as an exchange of views between two interlocutors on a given subject. One interlocutor puts forward a position or makes a claim. The other interlocutor engages with that position or claim, either agreeing or disagreeing, in whole or in part, and puts forward another, addressing the first interlocutor. The latter then, or another interlocutor, engages with the last position or claim, and so forth. Judicial dialogue is such an exchange of views between courts, in the first instance, and might even extend to an exchange of views between judges serving in the same court': A Tzanakopoulos, 'Judicial Dialogue as a Means of Interpretation', *Oxford Legal Studies Research Paper* No 71/2014 (2014), available at: papers.ssrn.com/sol3/papers.cfm?abstract_id=2497519. However in that paper the author goes beyond this definition.

[41] Tzanakopoulos (n 40 above).

[42] See the Solange saga for instance. It started with the famous *Solange I*: Case 2 BvG 52/71 Bundesverfassungsgericht: Federal Constitutional Court [1974] 2 CMLR 540.

interlocutor into account and give reasons explaining your disagreement, it is possible to define this exchange as dialogue.[43]

IV. PARLIAMENTARY DIALOGUE

It is not the first time that the idea of dialogue has been applied to Parliaments. Among others, this idea has been developed by Barak-Erez who explores the dialogue among legislatures as a vehicle for legal transplants.[44]

Even the EU Institutions are familiar with the formula of 'political dialogue' introduced by the Barroso Commission, a phenomenon which goes beyond the mere interparliamentary dialogue since it involves the Commission as well.[45] Are judicial and interparliamentary dialogue comparable?

In order to address this question it is necessary to look at the incentives these actors have. From this point of view, what has been written above concerning judges can be argued with regard to Parliaments as well (to a certain extent, at least). Parliaments have similar incentives to interact in a complex system and this has been explained by Manzella and Lupo, among others, by employing the formula 'euro-national parliamentary system'[46] to refer to the progressive construction of a compound parliamentary arena ('that is to say, it being constituted both by the EU Treaties and by the Constitutions of the Member States').[47] The EU Treaties, especially after the coming into force of the Lisbon Treaty, are rich in provisions referring to the role of national Parliaments and because of that scholars have written about some European powers conferred on them.[48]

As Van Rompuy said: '[m]aybe not formally speaking, but at least politically speaking, all national parliaments have become, in a way, European institutions',[49] and Article 12 of the TEU is very clear on this when saying that they 'contribute actively to the good functioning of the Union'.[50] The Early Warning System (EWS) is perhaps the most important

[43] See the examples coming from the UK Supreme Court with regard to the case law of the European Court of Human Rights: *R v Horncastle and Others* [2009] UKSC 14, para 11 and *Manchester City Council v Pinnock* [2010] UKSC 45, para 48. On these cases see: C Murphy, 'Human Rights Law and the Challenges of Explicit Judicial Dialogue', *Jean Monnet Working Paper* (2012), available at: www.jeanmonnetprogram.org/papers/12/1210.html.

[44] Barak-Erez (n 34 above). See also: D Barak-Erez, 'Legislation as Transplantation' in N Lupo and L Scaffardi (eds), *Comparative Law in Legislative Drafting. The increasing importance of dialogue amongst parliaments* (The Hague, Eleven, 2014) 17 and MR Ferrarese, 'Il dialogo tra Parlamenti e il dialogo tra corti: nuove tendenze del costituzionalismo' in C Decaro and N Lupo (eds), *Il 'dialogo' tra Parlamenti: obiettivi e risultati* (Roma, Luiss University Press, 2009) 317.

[45] europa.eu/rapid/press-release_IP-09-1368_en.htm.

[46] A Manzella and N Lupo (eds), *Il sistema parlamentare euro-nazionale. Lezioni* (Torino, Giappichelli, 2014).

[47] Manzella and Lupo (eds) (n 46 above), 270–71.

[48] N Lupo, 'I poteri europei dei Parlamenti nazionali: questioni terminologiche e primi effetti' in Manzella and Lupo (eds) (n 46 above), 101.

[49] Speech by President Herman Van Rompuy to the Interparliamentary Committee meeting on the European Semester for Economic Policy Coordination, Brussels, 27 February 2012, EUCO 31/12 PRESSE 68 PR PCE 26.

[50] Article 12 TEU: 'National Parliaments contribute actively to the good functioning of the Union: (a) through being informed by the institutions of the Union and having draft legislative acts of the Union forwarded to them in accordance with the Protocol on the role of national Parliaments in the European Union; (b) by seeing to it that the principle of subsidiarity is respected in accordance with the procedures provided for in the Protocol on the application of the principles of subsidiarity and proportionality; (c) by taking part, within the framework of the area of freedom, security and justice, in the evaluation mechanisms for the implementation of the Union policies in that area, in accordance with Article 70 of the Treaty on the Functioning of the European Union, and through

confirmation of this role and, not by coincidence, in light of it scholars have described national Parliaments as 'a "virtual third Chamber" for the European Union'.[51] Prior to the Lisbon Treaty, instead:

> For a long time, especially after 1979, the word 'Parliament' in the European integration process has been used rather exclusively to refer to the European Parliament ... Both national and subnational Parliaments, indeed, were not deemed relevant neither in the institutional architecture, nor in the EU decision-making processes. National parliaments were completely covered by their respective Governments, at least in the day-to-day decisions, centered on the Council (of ministers). And, internally, European affairs were almost always considered as a part of foreign affairs, therefore mainly inside the powers of the Government (except for the ratification of the Treaties).[52]

Indeed, contrary to what many argue, over recent years national Parliaments have benefited from important 'window opportunities' offered by EU Treaties and this was the point made even by the German Constitutional Court in its famous Lisbon decision,[53] which has been considered as a Euro-sceptical judgment. However the German Court did not understand the Lisbon Treaty as being inconsistent with its basic norm: on the contrary, it considered the national legislation's[54] strengthening of the rights of the German chambers to be unconstitutional.[55] The judgment is based on a strong criticism addressed to the German Parliament—the real custodian, together with the other national Parliaments, of democracy in the EU context—since it easily gave up competences, not exploiting the possibility offered by the Lisbon Treaty and not being aware of the chambers' fundamental task,[56] as, for instance, in paragraph 411 of the judgment the German Constitutional Court observes: 'Bundestag and Bundesrat must take into account that they must exercise their responsibility for integration in numerous cases of dynamic development of the Treaties'.[57] This is an

being involved in the political monitoring of Europol and the evaluation of Eurojust's activities in accordance with Articles 88 and 85 of that Treaty; (d) by taking part in the revision procedures of the Treaties, in accordance with Article 48 of this Treaty; (e) by being notified of applications for accession to the Union, in accordance with Article 49 of this Treaty; (f) by taking part in the interparliamentary cooperation between national Parliaments and with the European Parliament, in accordance with the Protocol on the role of national Parliaments in the European Union'.

[51] I Cooper, 'The Watchdogs of Subsidiarity: National Parliaments and the Logic of Arguing in the EU' (2006) 44 *Journal of Common Market Studies* 281–304; I Cooper, 'A "Virtual Third Chamber" for the European Union? National Parliaments after the Treaty of Lisbon' (2012) 35 *West European Politics* 441. I Cooper, 'Bicameral or Tricameral? National Parliaments and Representative Democracy in the European Union' (2013) 35 *Journal of European Integration* 531.

[52] N Lupo, 'National and Regional Parliaments in the EU decision-making process, after the Treaty of Lisbon and the Euro-crisis' (2013) 5 *Perspectives on Federalism* E-1, E-5.

[53] Lisbon Case, BVerfG, 2 BvE 2/08 from 30 June 2009, available at: www.bundesverfassungsgericht.de/entscheidungen/es20090630_2bve000208.html.

[54] The subject-matter of the case was represented by three distinct statutes: first of all, the Act Approving the Treaty of Lisbon, secondly, the Act Amending the Basic Law (Articles 23, 45 and 93) and finally, the Act Extending and Strengthening the Rights of the German Federal Parliament (Bundestag) and the German Federal Council of States (Bundesrat) in European Union Matters.

[55] Para 406 of the Lisbon judgment: 'The Act Extending and Strengthening the Rights of the Bundestag and the Bundesrat in European Union Matters (Extending Act) infringes Article 38.1 in conjunction with Article 23.1 of the Basic Law insofar as rights of participation of the German Bundestag and the Bundesrat have not been elaborated to the extent required'.

[56] In a similar way R Caponi, 'Democrazia, integrazione europea, circuito delle corti costituzionali (dopo il Lissabon-Urteil)' (2010), available at: www.astrid-online.it/rassegna/12-04-2010/Caponi_LissabonUrteil_Riv-Dir-Pubbl-Com.pdf.

[57] *Lisbon Case*, BVerfG, 2 BvE 2/08 of 30 June 2009, available at: www.bundesverfassungsgericht.de/entscheidungen/es20090630_2bve000208.html.

important case since it shows the existing risks behind the choice of relying on national Parliaments as the watchdog of the multilevel system. Nevertheless, even before the Treaty of Lisbon scholars stressed the important function performed by national Parliaments in the EU[58] and, more generally, since the beginning of the Union it has been clear that the European Parliament was not created to operate in a vacuum. This has also created a sort of rivalry or competition with national Parliaments, as Kiiver pointed out:

> The relation between the national parliaments and the European Parliament is a tricky one. It is tempting to state that they are allies, in that they have the joint task of parliamentarizing the European Union. On the other hand, we may note that there is an undeniable potential for structural rivalry between the two tiers of parliamentarism. This not only concerns conflicting claims for exclusive popular representation in the European Union, it also concerns diverging long-term interests.[59]

This phenomenon is consistent with the picture described above, as we have seen interactions in a complex system can be cooperative, competitive or even conflictual and the interactions between Parliaments do not depart from this trend. Looking at cooperative interactions, scholars have noticed the importance of Protocol 1,[60] especially Articles 9 and 10.[61] More in general, today interparliamentary cooperation in the EU develops through different channels (Conference of Community and European Affairs committees of Parliaments of the European Union—COSAC; Joint Parliamentary Meetings, Joint Committee Meetings, Meetings of Sectoral Committees etc) but it is sufficient to refer to recent works here without going into detail.[62]

More recently, new arenas of 'second generation'[63] have been created: the Interparliamentary Conference for the Common Foreign and Security Policy and the Common Security and Defence Policy (CFSP/CSDP),[64] which gathers delegations of the national Parliaments

[58] L Besselink, 'National Parliaments in the EU's Composite Constitution: A Plea for a Shift in Paradigm' in P Kiiver (ed), *National and Regional Parliaments in the European Constitutional Order* (Groningen, Europa Law Publishing, 2006) 119. D Jančić, 'Representative democracy across levels? National Parliaments and EU Constitutionalism' (2012) 8 *Croatian Yearbook of European Law and Policy* 227; N Lupo, 'Parlamento europeo e parlamenti nazionali nella costituzione "composita" dell'UE: le diverse letture possibili' (2014) *Rivista AIC*, available at: www.rivistaaic.it.

[59] P Kiiver, 'The composite case for National parliaments in the European Union: who profits from enhanced involvement' (2006) 2 *European Constitutional Law Review* 227.

[60] Protocol on the Role of National Parliaments in the European Union, [2004] OJ C310/204.

[61] Art 9: 'The European Parliament and national Parliaments shall together determine the organisation and promotion of effective and regular interparliamentary cooperation within the Union'.

Art 10: 'A conference of Parliamentary Committees for Union Affairs may submit any contribution it deems appropriate for the attention of the European Parliament, the Council and the Commission. That conference shall in addition promote the exchange of information and best practice between national Parliaments and the European Parliament, including their special committees. It may also organise interparliamentary conferences on specific topics, in particular to debate matters of common foreign and security policy, including common security and defence policy. Contributions from the conference shall not bind national Parliaments and shall not prejudge their positions'.

[62] C Fasone, 'Interparliamentary Cooperation and Democratic Representation in the European Union' in S Kröger and D Friedrich (eds), *The Challenge of Democratic Representation in the European Union* (Basingstoke, Palgrave Macmillan, 2012) 41.

[63] D Fromage, 'Parlamento Europeo y Parlamentos nacionales después del Tratado de Lisboa y en un contexto de crisis: ¿Un acercamiento de grado diverso según el ámbito?' in P Andrés and JI Ugartemendia (eds), *El Parlamento europeo: ¿esta vez es diferente?* (IVAP, 2015) 223.

[64] Decisions of the EU Speakers's Conference at its meetings in Brussels, on 4–5 April 2011 and in Warsaw, on 20-21 April 2012, establishing an Inter Parliamentary Conference for the Common Foreign and Security Policy (CFSP) and the Common Security and Defence Policy (CSDP): www.europarl.europa.eu/webnp/cms/pid/1932.

of the EU Member States and the European Parliament[65] and the Interparliamentary Conference on Economic Governance of the European Union, established by Article 13 of the Treaty on Stability, Coordination and Governance (TSCG).[66] This mushrooming of phenomena has suggested the existence of a 'Multilevel Parliamentary Field',[67] an arena which seems to represent dynamics similar to those observed with regard to judicial actors.

V. A POSSIBLE RESEARCH AGENDA: COMPARING INTERPARLIAMENTARY AND INTERJUDICIAL DIALOGUE

The goal of this chapter was to look at the common features of interjudicial dialogue and so-called interparliamentary cooperation, recognised by European Treaties provisions since the 1990s.

As recalled these two phenomena have been growing and intensifying in the last two decades, and in order to carry out this research I structured this piece into three parts. First of all, I outlined the structure of the EU constitutional architecture in order to understand the incentives that actors in a multilevel structure might have for dialogue. Secondly, I moved from the structure to the behaviour of the actors operating in such a multilevel context and I focused on cooperative interactions. In this section I shall look at interparliamentary cooperation by sketching a first attempt of comparison between the latter and interjudicial dialogue.

Does interparliamentary cooperation look like interjudicial dialogue? The answer depends (of course) on the definition of dialogue adopted.

For instance, many of the activities that scholars label 'parliamentary diplomacy'[68] resemble the activity performed through the so-called judicial networks but on this scholars are split: according to Claes and de Visser, for example, these meetings are relevant and sometimes work as important channels to enable a proper dialogue between judges and judiciaries,[69] since 'extrajudicial exchanges, both in writing and via personal contacts, score much higher as they allow for a free exchange of ideas and arguments on a more equal footing and even give room for deliberation on common issues'.[70]

On the contrary, these formal or informal meetings of judges have not been included in his notion of dialogue by Tzanakopoulos: indeed, while, on the one hand these meetings 'may be important for the formation of the judges' understanding and opinions on the interpretation of rules of (international) law',[71] on the other hand

[65] J Wouters and K Raube, 'Europe's common security and defence policy: the case for interparliamentary scrutiny', *Leuven Centre for Global Governance Studies Working Paper* (2012) 1.

[66] Art 13 TSCG: 'As provided for in Title II of Protocol (No 1) on the role of national Parliaments in the European Union annexed to the European Union Treaties, the European Parliament and the national Parliaments of the Contracting Parties will together determine the organisation and promotion of a conference of representatives of the relevant committees of the European Parliament and representatives of the relevant committees of national Parliaments in order to discuss budgetary policies and other issues covered by this Treaty'.

[67] B Crum and JE Fossum, 'The Multilevel Parliamentary Field: a framework for theorizing representative democracy in the EU' (2009) 1 *European Political Science Review* 249.

[68] C Decaro, 'Esiste la diplomazia parlamentare?' in C Decaro and N Lupo (eds), *Il 'dialogo' tra Parlamenti: obiettivi e risultati* (Roma, Luiss University Press, 2009) 315–19.

[69] M Claes and M de Visser, 'Are You Networked Yet? On Dialogues in European Judicial Networks', 3 *Utrecht Law Review* (2012) 100.

[70] Claes and de Visser, n 70, 106.

[71] Tzanakopoulos n 40.

> [dialogue] is neither accessible to the legal researcher nor can its impact be easily demonstrated on publicly available evidence. It is thus easier to ascertain the presence and effects of interjudicial dialogue when these are evident through referencing, discussion and cross-citation of foreign court decisions in domestic court judgments.[72]

However, when coming back to the features of a proper dialogue noted above one can notice that these networks sometimes present that element of 'continuity over time' and 'lack of complete authority over the other' that Torres Pérez[73] stressed in her monograph. In fact, for Claes and de Visser these phenomena respond to the concept of network defined by Börzel as:

> a set of relatively *stable* relationships which are of *non-hierarchical* and *interdependent* nature linking a variety of actors, who share common interests with regard to a policy and who exchange resources to pursue these shared interests acknowledging that cooperation is the best way to achieve common goals (emphasis added).[74]

However, even those who do not consider these judicial networks or other forms of meetings (either between members of Parliaments or of Judiciaries) as expressions of dialogue can find other analogies between interparliamentary and judicial cooperation, especially if we consider scholarship that looks at the EWS as 'an invitation to national parliaments and to their EACs in particular, to investigate, judge, influence and censure the legislative proposals of the Commission'.[75] This way, the EWS looks like a sort of political control of constitutionality whose dynamics resemble those characterising the preliminary ruling mechanism, ie the centre of attention for scholars interested in interjudicial dialogue in EU law.[76]

Going beyond EU law, well-known studies have shown important differences between interparliamentary and interjudicial dialogue, differences that are connected to the features of the actors involved in these interactions:

> First, as noted, individual legislators are motivated to look for inspiration in foreign legislation mainly when the legislation touches on value issues, such as the recognition of same-sex marriages. In matters requiring expertise, the parties to the international dialogue are the professionals who draft the laws. Second, the so-called dialogue often assumes the form of a monologue, namely, countries adopting foreign models of legislation usually do not serve as legislation models for other

[72] Tzanakopoulos (n 40 above).

[73] Torres Pérez (n 35 above), 118 et seq.

[74] T Börzel, 'What's So Special About Policy Networks? An Exploration of the Concept and Its Usefulness in Studying European Governance', *European Integration online Papers* No 16 (1997) available at: eiop.or.at/eiop/pdf/1997-016.pdf.

[75] M Goldoni, 'The Early Warning System and the Monti II Regulation: The Case for a Political Interpretation' (2014) 10 *European Constitutional Law Review* 90, 106. For a different understanding of the EWS see: K Granat, *National Parliaments and the Policing of the Subsidiarity Principle*, Phd thesis defended at the European University Institute (on file with author), especially at 120 et seq. See also: F Fabbrini and K Granat, '"Yellow card, but not foul": The role of the National parliaments under the subsidiarity Protocol and the Commission proposal for an EU Regulation on the right to strike' (2013) 50 *Common Market Law Review* 115. On the EWS see also: G Barrett, 'Monti II: The subsidiarity review process comes of age … or then again maybe it doesn't' (2012) 19 *Maastricht Journal of European and Comparative Law* 595, C Fasone, 'Parlamenti nazionali e controllo di sussidiarietà: il secondo cartellino giallo sull'istituzione della Procura europea' (2014) *Quaderni Costituzionali* 165.

[76] Elsewhere I tried to cast light on forms of judicial dialogue other than the mechanism governed by Art 267 TFEU. See G Martinico, 'Judging in the Multilevel Legal Order: Exploring The Techniques Of "Hidden Dialogue"' (2010) 21 *King's Law Journal* 257.

countries. Eastern Europe adopted Western models of legislation but has never been viewed as a relevant source of legal inspiration by American lawyers or legislators. The judicial community, by contrast, is more egalitarian. Because this is a professional community, worthy precedents from small countries can be a source of inspiration also to judges active in countries that are politically and economically more powerful. Third, even when legislatures use the information regarding laws in other countries, they do not limit the scope of their learning to the legislative arena. A legal principle originally introduced in the exporting country by way of judicial interpretation will sometimes be adopted in the importing country by way of legislation. In other words, legislators refer to any relevant source of inspiration, without granting priority to the principles created by their legislative counterparts.[77]

In light of these considerations, which emphasise the absence of a common background for the international Community of Legislatures and[78] the lack of a sufficient degree of 'variety' in the exchanges between Parliaments (this would be too unilateral, which is why she uses the formula 'monologue'), Barak-Erez argues 'the dynamics of legislation influencing foreign legislative initiatives should rather be described as based on inspiration without a community'.[79]

Another important difference is given by the nature of the actors: while Parliaments are often conceived as provided with legislative discretion, on the contrary

courts are in general reactive institutions: they are called upon to adjudicate on the initiative of the parties that come before them. They thus react on the initiative of the parties, rather than on their own initiative, to the positions taken by other courts ... They may not be allowed to consider *proprio motu* points not raised by the parties.[80]

Finally, there is another possible difference connected to the 'reactive' nature of courts: interjudicial dialogue is supposed to start from concrete cases, while interparliamentary dialogue often deals with a broader object, even with entire policies sometimes. Interjudicial dialogue (at least for those who believe that courts should decide 'one case at a time')[81] is supposed to be thus evolutionary and incremental, without a constructivist design behind it,[82] while Parliaments are frequently depicted as the bearers of a general and abstract will. Very often this distinction does not correspond to reality but offers a good basis for a deeper analysis.

77 Barak-Erez (n 34 above).

78 'Judges and rights activists share a common background—either professional (in the case of judges) or ideological (in the case of human rights activists)—as well as similar value systems. By contrast, members of legislatures in different countries do not share a common background. At most, and only to a limited extent, members of parties with similar ideologies have a shared background (conservatives, socialists, "green" parties, and so forth). Moreover, members of legislative bodies feel accountable mostly to their constituents. This is their most significant link and the only one that can guarantee their professional future. Members of legislative bodies are also less exposed to their colleagues in other countries. Leading party members may take part in delegations visiting other legislatures, but most legislators stay at home. International institutions encouraging cooperation between legislatures for the purpose of mutual learning and experience sharing do not seem to be relevant to the daily work of ordinary legislators ...', Barak-Erez (n 34 above).

79 Barak-Erez (n 34 above) 545.

80 Tzanakopoulos (n 40 above).

81 To borrow the title of a famous book: C Sunstein, *One Case at a Time: Judicial Minimalism on the Supreme Court* (Cambridge MA, Harvard University Press, 2001).

82 'A conception which assumes that all social institutions are, and ought to be, the product of deliberate design': FA Hayek, *Law, Legislation and Liberty*, vol 1, *Rules and Order* (London, Routledge, 1973) 5 et seq. The dualistic structure of Hayek's thought links the idea of constructivism to that of order, which can be conceived in two different ways: order as κόσμος (spontaneous order) and order as ταξις (constructed order).

However these differences should not be overstated: interparliamentary and interjudicial dialogue may work in tandem to improve the protection of transnational constitutional goods or to face those challenges that present a cross border nature (among others, new technologies, counter-terrorism).

Consequently these kinds of phenomena should not be conceived as antithetical and mutually exclusive: on the contrary, in Canada the idea of dialogue originated from a desired exchange between courts and legislatures with regard to Article 33 of the Canadian Charter of Rights and Freedoms.[83]

More in general, as it was pointed out by Ferrarese,[84] nowadays Parliaments are at a crossroads between the necessity to preserve the specificity of their domestic democratic systems and the need to open themselves to other 'voices' coming from other democracies. In this field, interparliamentary dialogue can give an added value either by codifying or by challenging what transnational judicial dialogue produces. If once most American Congressmen[85] did not have a passport, isolation is not an option in today's globalised world.

[83] PW Hogg and A Bushell, 'Dialogue Between Courts and Legislatures (Or Perhaps the Charter of Rights Isn't Such a Bad Thing After All)' (1997) 35 *Osgoode Hall Law Journal* 75.

[84] Ferrarese (n 44 above) 331.

[85] Ferrarese (n 44 above) 329–30.

Part II

Treaty Revisions

3

The Convention Method

CESARE PINELLI

I. INTRODUCTORY REMARKS: THE CONVENTION METHOD AND BEYOND

IN THE AFTERMATH of the 2004 EU Constitutional Treaty's approval, it was affirmed that 'No matter how one evaluates the product of its work, the Convention on the Future of Europe has marked a turning point in the history of European integration'.[1]

Such assumption referred to the *procedure* adopted for the Constitutional Treaty's approval. While the previous EU treaties had been exclusively held by national governments through the exertion of the treaty-making power within the Conference of the Representatives of the Governments of the Member States (IGC), the Constitutional Treaty had been approved in the same manner, thus complying with the then Article 48 TEU, but on the basis of a draft adopted by a body called 'the Convention', composed of members of national

[1] R Dehousse and F Deloche-Gaudez, 'The Making of a Transnational Constitution: An Institutionalist Perspective on the European Convention' (2005) 2 *Les Cahiers européens de Sciences Po.*

parliaments, the European Parliament (EP), representatives of national governments and the Commission, where MPs and MEPs together made up the body's huge majority.

Such change must be related to the deep influence that the treaty revision procedure exerted on the whole debate on the EU's structure and scope. With such a procedure in use, those conceiving the EU as an international organisation felt at home in defining the EU Member States as 'Master of the treaties', whereas those noticing the EU's supranational features could only rely on the functions that the EU had progressively acquired. Resorting to the Convention for the adoption of a treaty draft was thus likely to appear as an historical 'turning point' of the aforementioned debate, challenging the 'Master of the treaties' thesis also on the grounds of the treaty revision procedures that represented its ultimate bulwark.

Ten years later, it is possible to evaluate the implications of that event, given the insertion of the Convention method into the final version of Article 48 TEU. So far, the issue arises of how, and to what extent, such method affects the TEU and the TFEU revision procedure on legal grounds. Further reflection is needed on the scope of the joint participation of the European and national Parliaments in the decision-making process that lies at the core of resorting to a Convention. Finally, that participation will be compared with inter-parliamentary cooperation, as provided for in Title II of Protocol No 1 and Article 13 of the Treaty on Stability, Coordination and Governance (TSCG), or emerging from practice. A brief account will be given of the latter's potential and difficulties, with a view to inquiring into whether the Convention method has anticipated further developments in the EU institutional system.

II. WHY MEMBER STATES WERE FORCED TO ABANDON THE PURELY INTERGOVERNMENTAL APPROACH TO THE TREATY REVISION PROCEDURES

The suggestion of adopting the Convention method with respect to the EU treaty revision procedure goes back to the EP Resolution of 10 February 1994 containing an EU Constitution draft that was preceded inter alia by the following statement:

> [The EP]
>
> D. …
>
> 2. Proposes that a European convention bringing together the Members of the European Parliament and the parliaments of the Member States of the Union should be held prior to the Intergovernmental Conference scheduled for 1996 in order to adopt, on the basis of a draft Constitution to be submitted by the European Parliament, guidelines for the Constitution of the European Union, and to assign to the European Parliament the task of preparing the final draft.

Such solution clearly reflected the EP's preference both for an EU constitutionalisation and for its own direct involvement in the related procedure, that was far from being shared by the Member States as represented in the Council. However, the suggestion to convene a European convention with a view to adopting a draft Constitution anticipated to a certain extent the decisions taken by those States in the following decade. Why, then, did the latter change their mind within a relatively short time?

It is worth recalling that, while the 1957 Treaty of Rome establishing the European Community was subject only to limited amendments over a period of more than 30 years, the 1993 Maastricht Treaty launched a series of major changes, namely the 1997 Amsterdam Treaty and the 2000 Nice Treaty, each of which had barely come into force when a new IGC was prepared. Such a pattern was not only strikingly in contrast with the incremental changes affecting the *méthod communautaire*, but intrinsically revealed the failure of the Conferences to meet the challenges engendered by the Union's establishment. In particular, the IGC leading to the Nice Treaty has its origins in the shortcomings of the 1997 Amsterdam IGC, which was unable to reach an agreement on the institutional issues on its agenda.[2] Given the EU enlargement and the new functions that it had acquired from the Maastricht Treaty onwards, the most troublesome issues were the simplification of the treaties and the reform of the institutional framework, both of which were left unresolved by the successive IGCs.

On the other hand, the debate on the European democratic deficit demonstrated that the crisis of the traditional communitarian assessments affected the procedures adopted for the revision of the treaties no less than the institutional framework.

A fresh start was therefore required both for functional and democratic reasons, although Member States were forced to do it rather than being convinced of the inadequacy of the treaty revision procedures.

III. THE CONVENTION ON THE CHARTER OF FUNDAMENTAL RIGHTS OF THE EUROPEAN UNION

A first step towards the Convention method was taken at the Cologne European Council of June 1999.[3] A Convention, composed of representatives of the Heads of State and Government and the President of the Commission, as well as members of the European Parliament and national parliaments, was entrusted with the task of elaborating a draft of a Charter of Fundamental Rights of the European Union's citizens, containing the rights guaranteed by the ECHR and derived from the constitutional traditions common to the Member States, together with the rights of the Union's citizens, taking into account the economic and social rights contained in the European Social Charter and the Community Charter of the Fundamental Social Rights of Workers. The Tampere European Council of October 1999 specified that the Convention would be composed of 15 representatives of national governments, one representative of the President of the Commission, 16 Members of the EP designated by itself and 30 members of national parliaments designated by the national parliaments themselves.

According to one of its members, the Convention 'in fact worked like a melting-pot in which the whole process of drawing up the Charter was characterised by full representation and equal treatment for all and each of its members', and opted for 'complete and immediate transparency of the discussion and documents', thus drawing a clear 'distinction between a constitutional and a diplomatic procedure'.[4] First and foremost the Convention

[2] G Milton and J Keller-Noellet, 'The Immediate Origins of the European Constitution' in G Amato, H Bribosia and B de Witte (eds), *Genesis and destiny of the European Constitution* (Bruxelles, Bruylant, 2007) 28.

[3] It might be recalled that during the XX COSAC, that met in Berlin on 30 May–1 June 1999, German MEP Elmar Brok suggested that a special Convention, involving national parliaments and the European Parliament, should be convened to draft a European Charter of Fundamental Rights.

[4] A Manzella, 'The Convention: a new model for constitution making' *Europeos—Institutional reforms in the European Union. Memorandum for the Convention*, Rome 2002, 167–68.

broadly interpreted its mandate of elaborating the Charter draft. While affirming that the purpose of the Charter consists in 'making those rights more visible', not in creating them anew (nor in extending the existing ones), the Preamble did comply with the original Cologne European Council's mandate. Nevertheless not all the rights contained in the Charter's text were already recognised as fundamental principles of the EU. As has been noted, 'The Charter did not invent any new rights, but certainly smuggled into the Union some that had not been previously contemplated as Union rights per se',[5] with the effect that no jurist 'would refuse to recognise the innovatory capacity inherent in that Convention's "recognition" of the rights, its exclusions and inclusions, the exchanges set in motion by virtue of contiguity'.[6] This discrepancy with the status quo ante was never questioned by the European Council. It is true that the Charter was only 'proclaimed' at the Nice IGC, and that the issues raised by some Member States about the Charter's status under EU law were surmounted only with the Lisbon Treaty. But these did not affect the Convention's legitimacy in broadly interpreting its original mandate. On the contrary, from the beginning that experience was viewed as a positive precedent, thus paving the way to the 'Convention on the Future of Europe' (Convention II).

IV. THE LAEKEN DECLARATION AND THE WORKINGS OF THE CONVENTION ON THE FUTURE OF THE UNION

The choice to adopt the Convention method on more demanding grounds, namely with a view to concurring to the treaties' reform, had already been taken at an informal meeting of Foreign Ministers in September 2001, under the Belgian Presidency,[7] establishing the premises for the 'Laeken Declaration on the future of the European Union' adopted by the European Council on December 2001. It was based on two main points. First it raised the questions arising from the reform of the treaties, namely those of their simplification and of a possible distinction 'between a basic treaty and the other treaty provisions', of whether the Charter should be included in the basic treaty and the EC should accede to the ECHR, and finally that of the EU's constitutionalisation, in the following terms:

> The question ultimately arises as to whether this simplification and reorganisation might not lead *in the long run* to the adoption of a constitutional text in the Union. What might the basic features of such a constitution be? The values which the Union cherishes, the fundamental rights and obligations of its citizens, the relationship between Member States in the Union? (emphasis added).

The emphasis here added to the words 'in the long run' is meant to point out that the drafting of a constitutional text was not among the immediate objectives of the envisaged reform. This caution was due to the fact that in the EU political environment the term 'constitution' had been hitherto 'rigorously banned, as evoking developments that were highly controversial and firmly opposed'.[8]

[5] F Fontanelli, 'The European Union's Charter of Fundamental Rights two years later' (2011) 3 *Perspectives on Federalism* 25.

[6] Manzella (n 4 above) at 176.

[7] See Milton and Keller-Noellet (n 2 above) at 41.

[8] GL Tosato, 'Simplification of the Treaties as a constitutional process', *Institutional reforms in the European Union. Memorandum for the Convention* (2002) 183.

Moreover, '[i]n order to pave the way for the next Intergovernmental Conference as broadly and openly as possible', the Laeken Declaration convened a Convention 'to consider the key issues arising from the Union's future development and try to identify the various possible responses'. The Convention, it was further specified,

> will draw up a final document which may comprise either different options, indicating the degree of support which they received, or recommendations if consensus is achieved. Together with the outcome of national debates on the future of the Union, the final document will provide a starting point for discussions in the Intergovernmental Conference, which will take the ultimate decisions.

Two elements deserve attention here. The explicit reference to the alternative between 'consensus' reached on 'recommendations' and the indication of 'different options', that was the method of deliberation already used by Convention I, but not recommended to it by the Cologne and Tampere European Councils.[9] Such reference made it clear that Convention II should not decide through votes, so as to avoid the emergence of a certain majority or veto powers. The Laeken Declaration was also clear in establishing that 'the final document' would amount to the 'starting point' of the IGC's discussion culminating in 'the ultimate decisions'. This was, of course, the most relevant difference from the outcome of Convention I.

Finally, as far as concerns the composition of Convention II, the Declaration reports that the European Council appointed the Chairman and two Vice-Chairmen, adding that

> the Convention will be composed of 15 representatives of the Heads of State or Government of the Member States (one from each Member State), 30 members of national parliaments (two from each Member State), 16 members of the European Parliament and two Commission representatives.

The proportion among the parliamentary and governmental components was thus identical to that of Convention I.

Since the first Convention II meeting, it was unanimously presumed by its members that the 'Final document' would consist of a Constitutional Treaty draft: the issue was not that of evaluating whether the simplification and reorganisation of the treaties might lead 'in the long run' to the adoption of a constitutional text, but that of drafting such a text. Once again, as in case of Convention I, the caution with which the IGC had circumscribed the Convention's mandate was surmounted.

However, the mission of Convention II acquired a more pronounced political dimension than that of Convention I, as demonstrated inter alia by the composition of the former, many members of which had held leading political roles in their own country, starting from its chairman, the former President of the French Republic, and its vice-chairmen, former Prime Ministers of Italy and Belgium. On the other hand, unlike Convention I, Convention II would provide only a draft text that would be submitted to the IGC.

Both these features appear to be of paramount importance for an understanding of how the Convention method would later be stabilised within the EU treaty-making procedure. While the Convention's function consisted in the political appreciation and deliberation of crucial EU issues, namely those affecting the revision of the treaties, the outcome of its workings was conceived as a premise to those of the IGC. A balance was thus sought

[9] F Deloche-Gaudez, 'La Convention européenne sur l'avenir de l'Europe: ruptures et continuités' in *Genesis and destiny of the European Constitution* (n 2 above) at 61.

between the democratic implications of the Convention's establishment and the tradition of international law that was entrenched in the EU treaty-making procedure.

Attention should also be paid to the influence of the different institutional components in the decision-making processes of Convention II. It depends on a series of criteria that go beyond that of the number of each component, among which feature internal homogeneity and the capacity to interact with the other components. For the purposes of this inquiry, it is worth recalling that, in spite of the size of their group, amounting to 53 per cent of the Convention's members, the members of national parliaments were unable to reach a common position on the main issues, including that of strengthening the role of national parliaments within the EU, while the EP's delegates, comprising only 15 per cent of the Convention's members, were far more homogeneous and active in a series of issues, apart from that of defending the EP's prerogatives within the Union. Moreover, the fact that MPs and MEPs represented together 86 per cent of the Convention members appeared almost irrelevant, since these components managed to put forward joint proposals only toward the end of the Convention's work, with the aim of countering the demands of the national governments.[10]

These elements reflect not only the different institutional role of the EP and the national parliaments within the EU system, but also their respective internal homogeneity and they should not be neglected in our analysis, to the extent that the outcome of the Convention method depends on practice, rather than on 'the law in the books'.

V. HOW THE CONVENTION METHOD WAS INSERTED INTO EU PRIMARY LAW

How was the Convention method inserted into EU primary law? It is worth recalling the 2007 Lisbon Treaty's version of Article 48 TEU, which entered into force in December 2009:

> 1. The Treaties may be amended in accordance with an ordinary revision procedure. They may also be amended in accordance with simplified revision procedures.
>
> *Ordinary revision procedure*
>
> 2. The Government of any Member State, the European Parliament or the Commission may submit to the Council proposals for the amendment of the Treaties. These proposals may, inter alia, serve either to increase or to reduce the competences conferred on the Union in the Treaties. These proposals shall be submitted to the European Council by the Council and the national Parliaments shall be notified.
>
> 3. If the European Council, after consulting the European Parliament and the Commission, adopts by a simple majority a decision in favour of examining the proposed amendments, the President of the European Council shall convene a Convention composed of representatives of the national Parliaments, of the Heads of State or Government of the Member States, of the European Parliament and of the Commission. The European Central Bank shall also be consulted in the case of institutional changes in the monetary area. The Convention shall examine the proposals for amendments and shall adopt by consensus a recommendation to a conference of representatives of the governments of the Member States as provided for in paragraph 4.

[10] On this see Dehousse and Deloche-Gaudez, n 1 above.

The European Council may decide by a simple majority, after obtaining the consent of the European Parliament, not to convene a Convention should this not be justified by the extent of the proposed amendments. In the latter case, the European Council shall define the terms of reference for a conference of representatives of the governments of the Member States.

4. A conference of representatives of the governments of the Member States shall be convened by the President of the Council for the purpose of determining by common accord the amendments to be made to the Treaties.

The amendments shall enter into force after being ratified by all the Member States in accordance with their respective constitutional requirements.

5. If, two years after the signature of a treaty amending the Treaties, four fifths of the Member States have ratified it and one or more Member States have encountered difficulties in proceeding with ratification, the matter shall be referred to the European Council.

Simplified revision procedures

6. The Government of any Member State, the European Parliament or the Commission may submit to the European Council proposals for revising all or part of the provisions of Part Three of the Treaty on the Functioning of the European Union relating to the internal policies and action of the Union.

The European Council may adopt a decision amending all or part of the provisions of Part Three of the Treaty on the Functioning of the European Union. The European Council shall act by unanimity after consulting the European Parliament and the Commission, and the European Central Bank in the case of institutional changes in the monetary area. That decision shall not enter into force until it is approved by the Member States in accordance with their respective constitutional requirements.

The decision referred to in the second subparagraph shall not increase the competences conferred on the Union in the Treaties.

7. Where the Treaty on the Functioning of the European Union or Title V of this Treaty provides for the Council to act by unanimity in a given area or case, the European Council may adopt a decision authorising the Council to act by a qualified majority in that area or in that case. This subparagraph shall not apply to decisions with military implications or those in the area of defence.

Where the Treaty on the Functioning of the European Union provides for legislative acts to be adopted by the Council in accordance with a special legislative procedure, the European Council may adopt a decision allowing for the adoption of such acts in accordance with the ordinary legislative procedure.

Any initiative taken by the European Council on the basis of the first or the second subparagraph shall be notified to the national Parliaments. If a national Parliament makes known its opposition within six months of the date of such notification, the decision referred to in the first or the second subparagraph shall not be adopted. In the absence of opposition, the European Council may adopt the decision.

For the adoption of the decisions referred to in the first and second subparagraphs, the European Council shall act by unanimity after obtaining the consent of the European Parliament, which shall be given by a majority of its component members'.

Such text results from a series of subsequent additions to the version contained in the Constitutional Treaty draft proposed by the Convention. That draft contained only the 'ordinary revision procedure' as reported above, with the exception of the sentence 'These proposals [for the amendment of the Treaties] may, inter alia, serve either to increase or to reduce the competences conferred on the Union in the Treaties', and the explicit provision that the Council of Ministers transmit the proposals for amendment to the European Council.

The IGC convened to discuss the draft Constitution added in the 'Treaty establishing a Constitution for Europe' (see, respectively, Article IV-444 and Article IV-445), the two forms of 'simplified revision procedure' now provided for in Article 48, paragraph 7 and Article 48, paragraph 6, TEU. Both have the function of 'bridging provisions', or so called '*passerelles*', for they do not need any formal initiation of the Treaty amendment procedure by a Convention or an IGC.

According to a number of scholars, such addition demonstrated that national governments were concerned about the risk that 'the lengthy procedures and elaborate democratic safeguards contained in the ordinary revision procedure would make Treaty amendment even of a limited character almost impossible to achieve'.[11] However, the Constitutional Treaty draft accompanied the ordinary revision procedure that required the convening of a Convention with a further one, giving the European Council the opportunity to 'decide by a simple majority, after obtaining the consent of the European Parliament, not to convene a Convention *should this not be justified by the extent of the proposed amendments*' (emphasis added). Such procedure has led to the conclusion that, 'if the nature of the revision does not justify the setting-up of a cumbersome Convention', the European Council is in the condition to decide

> such a change of track by a simple majority but subject to the consent of the European Parliament, which is of course an effective means of ensuring that the European Council will not abuse this possibility of acting 'quickly', without calling a Convention.[12]

The addition of the simplified revision procedures by the IGC that approved the Constitutional Treaty reflects rather the need to overcome even an IGC in the respectively reported fields (Part Three TFEU, and TFEU and Title V TEU in the reported cases).

Finally, the Lisbon Treaty added the clause to the provisions concerning the ordinary revision procedure that the proposed amendments 'may, inter alia, serve either to increase or to reduce' the EU's competences, with the aim of reassuring those Member States fearing that integration was leading ultimately to a 'United States of Europe'.[13]

VI. ANALOGIES AND DIFFERENCES BETWEEN THE TREATY REVISION PROCEDURES AS PROVIDED FOR IN ARTICLE 48 TEU

Article 48 TEU poses many questions, some of which appear directly connected with the aim of exploring the relevance of the Convention method, as provided for in the first amending ordinary procedure, vis-à-vis the other amending procedures.

[11] E Denza, 'Article 48 [Treaty Revision Procedures]' in HJ Blanke and S Mangiameli (eds), *The Treaty on European Union (TEU). A Commentary* (Berlin-Heidelberg, Springer-Verlag, 2013) 1339.

[12] B de Witte, 'The European Treaty Amendment for the Creation of a Financial Stability Mechanism' (2011) 6 *European Policy Analysis* 3.

[13] Denza (n 11 above) at 1347.

Two main theses have been put forward in this respect. According to the first,

> The word 'ordinary' does not signify that this procedure will be the one that is most commonly used, but rather that it is the default procedure which must be used when the conditions for using the simplified procedures are not met.[14]

Other scholars, on the contrary, have asserted that, while the Convention will probably be the body responsible for examining future revision projects, the simplified provisions are made conditional on whether the Convention method is 'not … justified by the extent of the proposed amendments', and also on the approval of the European Parliament.[15]

It should appear sufficiently clear that resorting to the Convention method presupposes that the proposed amendments concern those parts of the treaties (TEU and TFEU) that involve the most significant choices in the EU. This assumption is first justified by a textual analysis. Article 48 not only subordinates the European Council's subsidiary decision not to convene a Convention to whether it 'is not justified by the *extent of the proposed amendments*' (emphasis added), but also circumscribes the resorting to the simplified revision procedures to the case of amendments concerning, respectively, 'all or part of the provisions of Part Three of the Treaty on the Functioning of the European Union relating to the internal policies and action of the Union' (paragraph 6), and 'Where the Treaty on the Functioning of the European Union or Title V of this Treaty provides for the Council to act by unanimity in a given area or case', or 'Where the Treaty on the Functioning of the European Union provides for legislative acts to be adopted by the Council in accordance with a special legislative procedure' (paragraph 7).

The preference for the Convention method vis-à-vis further forms of procedure does not depend only on the extent of the proposed amendments. Article 48 makes it in fact clear that proposals for amendments serving 'either to increase or to reduce the competences conferred on the Union in the Treaties' should be examined only through the ordinary procedure (paragraph 2), since the decisions adopted through the special procedure aimed at amending Part Three TEU 'shall not increase the competences conferred on the Union' (paragraph 6), and those adopted under paragraph 7 concern rendering the procedural requirements affecting certain cases or sectors smoother (from unanimity to qualified majority, or from special legislative procedure to ordinary legislative procedure), that are as such unable to alter the competences conferred on the Union. Hence it follows that the discretionary powers given to the decision-makers are greater in the case of the ordinary revision procedure, that usually presupposes the resorting to the Convention method.

Such resorting is thus rendered compulsory in the event of treaty changes that involve the most important issues and/or presuppose the power of increasing the EU competences. That choice presupposes that the Convention method is provided for with a unique democratic legitimacy, namely the connection between democratic legitimacy and the exertion of political power lying at the core of contemporary constitutionalism. Once referred to the EU system, such connection of course needs to be adjusted with the concurrent legitimacy of the Member States, expressed through the rules of the unanimous approval of the EU treaties by the IGC's members and the related unanimous ratification by the Member States. Therefore, as has been affirmed,

[14] De Witte (n 12 above) at 3.

[15] M Urrea Corres, 'The New Treaty Revision Procedure and the Entry into Force of the Constitutional Treaty' (2002) available at: www.law.nyu.edu/sites/default/files/upload_documents/urreacorres 12.

> Combining the Convention method (for preparing the reform) with the diplomatic method (for its approval) not only improves the efficacy of the revision procedure, but also indirectly strengthens the legitimacy of the reforms made, since the use of both the Convention and the Intergovernmental Conference reproduces the two legitimacies on which the Union is based: that flowing from its citizens and that of the Member States.[16]

The question might also be posed of the relationship between the two stages of such procedure. On legal grounds, the IGC is not bound to implement the amendments adopted by the Convention, not only because these amount to '*a recommendation*' (Article 48, paragraph 3), but also because the IGC is convened 'for the purpose of *determining* by common accord the amendments to be made to the Treaties'(emphasis added) (Article 48, paragraph 4). However, on factual grounds, the experience of the two Conventions has led to the conclusion that 'the task of the Intergovernmental Conference may be reduced to one of mere technical and political fine tuning of those reforms proposed by the Convention'.[17]

However, the ordinary revision procedure comprehending resorting to a Convention appears the most cumbersome among the four revision procedures provided for in Article 48 TEU. Against such background, the ordinary revision procedure initiated by the European Council whenever the convening of a Convention 'should not be justified by the extent of the proposed amendments', no less than the two simplified procedures, reflects the common need to simplify treaty change, although Article 48 TEU makes it clear that such need overcomes that of convening a Convention only in the already mentioned circumscribed premise.

On the other hand, whenever it prioritises the need for simplification, Article 48 TEU does not leave the revision procedures at the disposal of national governments, be it the IGC or the European Council. On the contrary, both the EP and the national parliaments do maintain certain prerogatives. In particular, according to Article 48, paragraph 3, the European Council should obtain the consent of the former before deciding 'not to convene a Convention', and the latter are called to ratify the treaty amendments that were approved by the IGC. Article 48, paragraph 6 entrusts the EP with the task of proposing amendments to the provisions of Part Three TFEU relating to the internal policies and action of the Union, and with that of being consulted by the European Council before the latter adopts the related decision, while national parliaments are once again called upon to ratify that decision. Finally, as for the European Council's decisions taken under Article 48, paragraph 7, which do not need ratification, the corresponding initiatives are notified to national parliaments, each of which may exert a veto power within six months of the day of such notification, and the European Council's decisions are conditioned by the EP's consent.[18]

So far, even in the revision procedures different from that requiring the Convention method, Member States are not likely to maintain their role of 'Master of the treaties'. Nevertheless, the participation of the EP and the national parliaments differs strikingly from that affecting the Convention method. While in the latter case MEPs and MPs a) are gathered together, b) belong to an ad hoc body, and c) are called upon to exert a positive role in the decision-making process, in the former case the EP and national parliaments a1) are

[16] Urrea Corres (n 15 above) at 15.

[17] ibid.

[18] On this see K Granat, 'Interparliamentary Cooperation and the Simplified Revision Procedures' Ch 4 in this volume.

insulated one from the other, b1) are called upon to exert a role as institutions, rather than being represented in a different body by some of their members, and c1) are provided only with veto or negative powers (with the sole exception of the EP's initiative provided for in Article 48, paragraph 6).

VII. INTERPARLIAMENTARY COOPERATION UNDER PROTOCOL NO 1 TO THE TREATY OF LISBON AND THE TREATY ON STABILITY, COORDINATION AND GOVERNANCE

It is now worth adding that, under EU primary law, interparliamentary cooperation is not exhausted by the participation of MEPs and MPs at the Convention, although only the latter are included in a formal decision-making procedure.

The text of Title II of Protocol No 1 TFEU, is in fact devoted to 'Interparliamentary cooperation', providing that 'The European Parliament and national Parliaments shall together determine the organisation and promotion of effective and regular interparliamentary cooperation within the Union' (Article 9), and that

> A Conference of Parliamentary Committees for Union Affairs may submit any contribution it deems appropriate for the attention of the European Parliament, the Council and the Commission. That conference shall in addition promote the exchange of information and best practice between national Parliaments and the European Parliament, including their special committees. It may also organize interparliamentary conferences on specific topics, in particular to debate matters of common foreign and security policy, including common security and defence policy. Contributions from the conference shall not bind national Parliaments and shall not prejudge their position' [Article 10].

While clearly enhancing their mutual cooperation, Protocol No 1 leaves to the European and the national representative assemblies the modes of organising such cooperation, departing from that between the EP and the already well-established COSAC (Conférence des organes spécialisés dans les affaires communautaires). Unlike the joint participation of the MEPs and MPs at the Convention as provided for in Article 48 TEU, these modes are therefore meant to remain on informal grounds. They are not somehow connected with the formal EU procedures, as confirmed by the provision that the conference's outputs are not binding for national parliaments. However, since the formal recognition and regulation of previously informal agreements, procedures and devices have frequently characterised the course towards European integration, a similar development should not be excluded prima facie in this case either.

To this end, a brief account will be given of the recent evolution of interparliamentary cooperation, with a view to highlighting its problems as well as its potential perspectives in the EU's institutional framework.

A premise is however needed. The years following the Lisbon Treaty's entry into force have been marked by the Eurozone's crisis management, and the measures taken with regard to this by the EMU, the EMU Member States and the EU. The European Council here played a role resembling that of the monarch in continental Europe's regimes of the nineteenth century,[19] with the difference, however, that the former consists of the Heads

[19] C Franzius, *Europaeisches Verfassungsrechtsdenken* (Tuebingen, Mohr & Siebeck, 2010) 58.

of State or Government of the EU Member States. The traditional balance between the supranational and intergovernmental features of the EU institutional system has thus clearly shifted towards the prevalence of the latter.[20]

Furthermore, the legal instruments provided in the EU system were not always adequate for the issues emerging from the Eurozone's crisis. While at the European Council meeting of 24–25 March 2011, article 136 TFEU was amended according to the simplified revision procedure as laid down in Article 48, paragraph 6, TEU, with a view to establishing the European Stability Mechanism (ESM), the ESM itself was established by a treaty among the Eurozone Member States as an intergovernmental organisation under public international law with its seat in Luxembourg. International law was then used as a tool to avoid the normal constraints of the EU legal order, including judicial review, subsidiarity control and decision-making procedures.[21] Moreover, first and foremost, the fact that an international treaty, the 'Treaty on Stability, Coordination and Governance' (TSCG), or the so-called 'Fiscal Compact', was signed on 2 March 2012 by the EU Member States (with the exception of the United Kingdom and the Czech Republic) revealed that these States were forced to abandon the original plan to amend the EU treaties according to the procedures laid down in Article 48 TEU that required unanimity.

While dictating rules concerning the debt of the EMU Member States, already anticipated by the Six-pack, the Fiscal Compact entrusts the Commission with the task of monitoring their compliance through 'proposals and recommendations' (see Article 7 TSCG) during the procedures of the respective budget approvals, with the effect of putting strong constraints on the traditional budgetary prerogative of national parliaments, if not of causing its 'substantial alienation'.[22] Once again, however, there appears a reference to interparliamentary cooperation: Article 13 TSCG establishes that

> As provided for in Title II of Protocol (No. 1) on the role of national Parliaments in the European Union annexed to the European Union Treaties, the European Parliament and the national Parliaments of the Contracting Parties will together determine the organisation and promotion of a conference of representatives of the relevant committees of the European Parliament and representatives of the relevant committees of national Parliaments in order to discuss budgetary policies and other issues covered by this Treaty.[23]

Just a few months later, in a thorough re-organisation plan by the EU economic governance, the 'Report of the Four Presidents' further emphasised that the 'Close involvement of the European parliament and national parliaments will be central, in the respect of the community method. Protocol No. 1 on the role of national parliaments in the EU offers an appropriate framework for interparliamentary cooperation'.[24]

Against such background it was argued that interparliamentary cooperation

[20] O Cramme, 'The worrying inevitability of EU intergovernmentalism' (2012) *Policy Network*.

[21] De Witte (n 12 above) at 8.

[22] A Manzella, 'Is the EP legitimate as a parliamentary body in EU multi-tier governance?', European Parliament, Directorate-General for Internal Policies, *Challenges of multi-tier governance in the EU*, Workshop, 4 October 2012, at 37.

[23] On this see I Cooper, 'The Interparliamentary Conference on Stability, Economic Coordination and Governance in the European Union (the "Article 13 Conference")', Chapter 13 in this volume.

[24] The Report of the Presidents of the European Council, of the Commission, of the Eurogroup, and of the European Central Bank, 'Towards a Genuine Economic and Monetary Union' was delivered in Brussels on 26 June 2012.

> stretches and strengthens the wire of the parliamentarisation of the EU, involving not only the European Parliament, but also strongly implicating national parliaments as co-promoters of the policies, as subjects which are co-bound by common limits (like the balanced budget) and as subjects being part of conferences and conventions',

and that the increasing use, in the new texts, of a 'parliamentarism by committees' might lead to a 'new representative institutional dimension' capable of balancing inter alia the 'verticalisation that occurred in the economic governance of the Union'.[25]

A different picture is given by those scholars that, while considering interparliamentary cooperation to be an important instrument for guaranteeing 'early coordination and alignment of parliamentary budgetary work beyond the borders of the individual Member State', doubt 'the effectiveness of framing such interparliamentary cooperation within the only moderately successful model of the COSAC', as implicitly suggested in Article 13 TSCG.[26] In the same vein, other authors emphasise the need to balance the verticalisation which took place in the EU's economic governance through the democratic devices of such cooperation, but admit that the envisaged solution is still far from being exploited to its full potential.[27]

As we shall see, recent developments are likely to confirm these assumptions.

VIII. THE DIFFICULT BEGINNING OF THE INTERPARLIAMENTARY CONFERENCE ON ECONOMIC AND FINANCIAL GOVERNANCE

It is worth premising that interparliamentary cooperation is not exhausted by the COSAC and the Conference established by Article 13 TSCG. It includes various bodies, among which are the Conference of Speakers which gathers together the speakers of the national parliaments and the EP's President, and the interparliamentary committees organised both by the EP and the national parliament of the country holding the rotating Presidency, including the Inter-Parliamentary Conference for the CFSP and the CSDP. These bodies, whose meetings usually take place every six months, might indeed establish the premises for creating irreplaceable opportunities for networking, exchange of information and best practices among the committees of the European and the national assemblies, although the size of the conferences might deter their members from speaking up, or even from attending the meeting.[28]

At least, any evaluation whatsoever of the performances of such committees depends on the objectives that these are believed to pursue, within a range that goes from the exchange of information among their members to that of balancing through democratic devices and procedures the technocratic and 'vertical' dimension of EU economic governance.

[25] Manzella (n 22 above) at 38.

[26] I Pernice, M Wendel, LS Otto, K Bettge, M Mlynarsky and M Schwarz, *A Democratic Solution to the Crisis. Reform Steps towards a Democratically Based Economic and Financial Constitution for Europe* (Baden-Baden, Nomos Verlag, 2012) 118.

[27] S Piedrafita, 'EU Democratic Legitimacy and National Parliaments', *CEPS* Essay No 7, 25 November 2013, p 6, and Y Bertoncini and A Vitorino, 'Réformer la "gouvernance" européenne. Pour une fédération des Etats Nations plus légitime et plus efficace' (2014) *Etudes et Rapports*—Notre Europe 69, further proposing the establishment of an 'Eurozone subcommission' in the EP.

[28] S Piedrafita (n 27 above) at 8.

The latter might be included, in particular, among the objectives of the Conference provided for in Article 13 TSCG.

Its first steps, however, appear far from encouraging great expectations.

The Nicosia Speakers' Conference of 21–23 April 2013 prepared a draft of the Rules of Procedure of the Interparliamentary Conference on Economic and Financial Governance, whose first meeting was provided for in October 2013, under the Lithuanian Presidency of the Council. While establishing that 'the composition and size of each delegation rests upon each Parliament', the draft clearly showed a number of difficulties in finding a good compromise on such issues. As for its competences, the Conference was defined as a 'framework for debate and exchange of information and best practices on matters of economic and financial governance of the EU and shall maintain a special focus on the budgetary issues and procedures covered by the TSCG', adopting 'non-binding conclusions'. The Conference was thus conceived as a simple forum for discussion, rather than as a unique opportunity for Europeanising from a democratic perspective the parliamentary control exercised on the budget at the national level.

The impression appears thus justified that the draft of the Rules of Procedure was 'a missed opportunity because of its design flaws', with the implication that 'national parliaments have, once again, failed to be collective actors at the EU level'.[29] Nor have these Rules been approved in the following meetings,[30] with the effect of confirming that Conference's weakness.[31]

IX. THE DIVIDES AMONG NATIONAL PARLIAMENTS AND BETWEEN THEM AND THE EUROPEAN PARLIAMENT

These difficulties are due to structural rather than contingent reasons. As has been observed, interparliamentary cooperation does not amount to a zero-sum game, where more competences for national parliaments mean fewer competences for the EP and vice versa, but it can help to fill a control gap, provided, however, that 'their constituting parliaments overcome their old reflexes'.[32] Accordingly, the circumstance that MEPs and MPs rarely put forward joint proposals during the Convention's work (see section IV above) appears the symptom of rival visions of the EU institutional system. Nor has the Eurozone's crisis management composed such rivalries. On the contrary, the already mentioned rise of intergovernmentalism has challenged the EP's as well as the Commission's role, while the contextual adoption of the TSCG, with the herein provided EU surveillance procedure on national budgets, has introduced a direct connection between the Commission, albeit for the moment, on behalf of the European Council, and national parliaments. These shiftings have to a certain extent affected the respective roles of the EP and national parliaments within the EU institutional assessment, tending to invert the Lisbon Treaty's approach, where an enlargement

[29] V Kreilinger, 'The New Inter-parliamentary Conference for Economic and Financial Governance', (2013) 100 *Policy Paper—Notre Europe* 17.

[30] As it results from the Presidency Summary of the Rome Conference of 29–30 September 2014: 'In the last session the Conference discussed the draft rules of procedure presented by the Italian Parliament. Taking into account the positions expressed by the delegations, the Presidency will submit the delegations new draft rules' (Point 7).

[31] On this see Cooper, n 23 above.

[32] Kreilinger (n 29 above) at 17.

of the EP's functions was accompanied by a more nuanced reference to the contribution of national parliaments to European integration.

Hence might derive the dilemma that follows:

> More Europeanization heading towards a federal European state ... will mean less power for national parliaments. And *vice versa*: the emergence of stronger interests of Member States within European integration will increase the importance of national parliaments as European actors.[33]

Irrespective of the predictions that it might authorise with regard to the EU institutional developments, that dilemma provides an analytical tool to describe the range of tensions among the EP and national parliaments, that interparliamentary cooperation ambitiously attempts to overcome.

But conflicts and differences do emerge also between national parliaments. While some derive from their structural heterogeneity,[34] further processes of differentiation emerged from the Eurozone's crisis management.

The divide between Euro and non-Euro Member States as set down in the EU treaties since the establishment of the EMU appears insufficient to comply with the challenges ensuing from that crisis. Apart from the frequent suggestion to introduce separate bodies or sessions for the Eurozone's Member States within the EP, new political divergences have arisen between national parliaments according to the respective State's adherence to the common currency.

A further differentiation appears even more dangerous, depending on whether the Euro Member States receive or provide financial assistance through the different rescue mechanisms. While the former seem to be 'more responsive to the demands of unelected institutions and the financial markets than to those of their public',[35] donor countries, on the contrary, urge for a parliamentary approval of the financial guarantees issued by governments. Here emerges, in particular, 'the German exception'. Since the 2010–13 the *Bundesverfassungsgericht*'s decisions requiring that whichever financial measure concerning the different rescue mechanisms must be explicitly approved by the *Bundestag*, a clear asymmetry has affected the Eurozone countries with respect to the exertion of parliamentary powers related to the budgetary authority. Its fundamental implications for the democratic legitimacy of the EU and EMU policy-making appear beyond any doubt.[36] It should only be added that, unlike the well-known EU democratic deficit, such asymmetry threatens the EU and EMU democratic legitimacy to the extent that it jeopardises the principle of equal treatment of Member States, namely a foundational principle of the EU irrespective of whatever opinion one may have about its nature, be it that of an international organisation, a confederation, or a federation of nation states.[37]

[33] M Zalewska and OJ Gstrein, 'National Parliaments and their Role on European Integration: The EU's Democratic Deficit in Times of Economic Hardship and Political Insecurity' (2013) 28 *Bruges Political Research Papers* 20.

[34] See N Lupo, 'National Parliaments in the European integration process: re-aligning politics and policies' in M Cartabia, N Lupo and A Simoncini (eds), *Democracy and subsidiarity in the EU. National parliaments, regions and civil society in the decision-making process* (Bologna, Il Mulino, 2013) 107.

[35] R Fox, 'Europe, Democracy and the Economic Crisis: Is It Time to Reconstitute the "Assises"?' (2012) 65 *Parliamentary Affairs* 464.

[36] O Höing, 'Differentiation of parliamentary powers. The German Constitutional Court and the German Bundestag within the financial crisis', *Democracy and subsidiarity in the EU* (n 34 above) at 261.

[37] C Pinelli, 'La giurisprudenza costituzionale tedesca e le nuove asimmetrie fra i parlamenti nazionali dell'eurozona' (2014), *Costituzionalismo.it*.

X. HAS THE CONVENTION METHOD ANTICIPATED INTERPARLIAMENTARY COOPERATION'S DEVELOPMENTS?

These elements suffice to demonstrate why the outcomes of interparliamentary cooperation, particularly of the Conference provided for in Article 13 TSCG, are unlikely to go beyond free discussion, exchange of information and spread of best practices among the assemblies concerned. These are of course good developments from the perspective of European integration, but do not necessarily lead to an institutionalisation of the EP-national parliaments' relationship. We might even ask ourselves how the Convention method could have anticipated an evolution of that sort. The fact that MEPs and MPs did not reach a common position during the Convention's workings should be taken into account even more so while considering that the interparliamentary conferences are expected to take place only twice a year. Furthermore, it is difficult to imagine how any interparliamentary cooperation could be institutionalised against the background of the current tensions affecting the whole EU fabric, including the differentiation processes arising between national parliaments.

4

Interparliamentary Cooperation and the Simplified Revision Procedures

KATARZYNA GRANAT

I. INTRODUCTION

IN CONTRAST WITH the past, the Lisbon Treaty sought to address the issue of amendments of the Treaties by linking the aspiration that all institutions should be included as the EU changes with the difficulties that this can pose in the enlarged EU of 28 Member States.[1] Moreover the 'democratic deficit' concerns at the time led to the inclusion of the Convention and national parliaments in the revision procedure, helping to 'democratise' future reform projects.[2] Article 48 TEU reflects these ideas by providing for two processes: ordinary and simplified revision procedures. The latter one, which is the subject of this contribution, is a novel procedure and simplified in the sense that it does not demand calling a Convention or an intergovernmental conference and aims at accelerating Treaty revisions,[3] and at the same time brings 'democratisation' by involving national parliaments.

In fact, national parliaments were involved in the amendment procedure since the Treaty on the European Union, signed in Maastricht in 1992, demanded ratification by the Member States 'in accordance with their respective constitutional requirements'.[4] In addition,

[1] P Craig, *The Lisbon Treaty, Revised Edition: Law, Politics, and Treaty Reform* (Oxford, Oxford University Press, 2013) 438.

[2] M Urrea Corres, 'The New Treaty Revision Procedure and the Entry into Force of the Constitutional Treaty' (2007) Global Fellows Forum, New York University 12 available at: www.law.nyu.edu/sites/default/files/upload_documents/urreacorrespaper.pdf.

[3] Craig, *The Lisbon Treaty* (n 1 above) 451.

[4] Art N TEU, now Art 48 TEU.

the representatives of national parliaments participated in the works of the European Convention that was entrusted with the preparation of a draft Treaty establishing a Constitution for Europe.[5] However, the novelty of the Lisbon Treaty in this respect can be seen not only in the new types of revision procedures, but also in the direct highlighting of the involvement of national parliaments in the amendment of the Treaties. Specifically, Article 12(d) TEU states that 'national Parliaments contribute actively to the good functioning of the Union by taking part in the revision procedures of the Treaties, in accordance with Article 48 of this Treaty'.

Under Article 48(6) TEU national parliaments participate in simplified revision procedures when their approval is demanded in accordance with the constitutional requirements of the Member States for the entry into force of European Council decisions. Under Article 48(7) TEU national parliaments may oppose a European Council initiative that would allow an act to be adopted according to procedures other than those laid down in the Treaties, specifically allowing the Council to act by qualified majority instead of unanimity or to switch from special to ordinary legislative procedure.

While the participation of national parliaments in the Early Warning System (EWS) established in Protocol No 2 to the Lisbon Treaty seems to be the main new source of involvement of national parliaments at the EU level and the one on which the most academic research is focused,[6] this chapter will inquire into the functions of national legislators within the treaty revision procedures. The design of these procedures in the Lisbon Treaty allows a single national parliament to veto the amendment when the amendment has to be approved according to national procedures that involve an agreement of the parliament or to oppose the so-called general passerelle. These options show the individual character of the involvement of national parliaments. In this respect, this chapter will give an overview of simplified revision procedures in selected Member States: the UK, Germany, Poland, Italy and France. This sample reflects different patterns of parliamentary control of European Council meetings.[7] Although this chapter does not directly deal with the control of the European Council decisions, they are central to the simplified treaty revision and the strength of parliamentary control of those acts might be reflected in the design of national procedures of parliamentary involvement in the simplified revision procedures. This chapter will also inquire whether the involvement of national parliaments shows any potential for cooperation between national parliaments. In consequence, this chapter will reflect whether the participation of national parliaments in the simplified treaty revisions and interparliamentary cooperation on the very same field create a synergy contributing to the good functioning of the EU as proclaimed by Article 12 TEU.

[5] See at: european-convention.europa.eu/EN/organisation/organisation2352.html?lang=EN.

[6] See M Cartabia, N Lupo and A Simoncini (eds), *Democracy and Subsidiarity in the EU. National Parliaments, Regions and Civil Society in the Decision-Making Process* (Bologna, Il Mulino, 2013), Parts II and IV; M Goldoni, 'The Early Warning System and the Monti II Regulation: The Case for a Political Interpretation' (2014) 10 *European Constitutional Law Review* 90; F Fabbrini and K Granat, '"Yellow card, but no foul": The role of the national parliaments under the Subsidiarity Protocol and the Commission proposal for an EU regulation on the right to strike' (2013) 50 *Common Market Law Review* 115.

[7] W Wessels et al, 'Democratic Control in the Member States of the European Council and the Euro zone summits' available at: www.europarl.europa.eu/RegData/etudes/etudes/join/2013/474392/IPOL-AFCO_ET(2013)474392_EN.pdf.

The chapter first describes the relevant provisions in the Treaties highlighting the involvement of national parliaments. It then describes in detail the national procedures for implementing the simplified revision procedures in selected Member States. The chapter then moves on to focus on the effects of Article 48(6) and 48(7) TEU for interparliamentary cooperation, illustrating this particular aspect using the amendment of Article 136 TFEU as a case study. Finally, the chapter investigates the potential implications of interparliamentary cooperation in simplified treaty revisions for the overall good functioning of the EU (Article 12 TEU).

II. SIMPLIFIED REVISION PROCEDURES IN THE LISBON TREATY

The new, simplified type of treaty revision procedures are anchored in Article 48 TEU. They were first proposed in the same form in the Constitutional Treaty.[8] The following sections give a brief overview of the procedures.

First, Article 48(6) TEU provides that a Member State government, the European Parliament (EP) or the Commission may put forward a proposal in the European Council to revise all or part of the provisions of Part Three of the TFEU, which is a major section relating to the internal policies and action of the Union. This type of amendment is hence excluded, for example with regard to provisions concerning EU principles; provisions on non-discrimination and citizenship; or those concerning association of the EU with the overseas countries and the Union's external action. The relevant decision to amend the Treaties is adopted unanimously by the European Council after consulting the EP and the Commission and, if the amendment at stake concerns the monetary area, the European Central Bank (ECB). Importantly, the decision of the European Council 'shall not increase the competences conferred on the Union in the Treaties'. The European Council decision does not enter into force 'until it is approved by the Member States in accordance with their respective constitutional requirements'.[9]

According to De Witte, 'the European founding treaties distinguish themselves from the usual multilateral treaties by the *express mention* (in Art. 48 [TEU]) that ratification of a treaty amendment must happen "in accordance with constitutional requirements" of the parties'.[10] The rationale for this provision is to guarantee 'the protection of the national constitutional division of powers which the governments cannot set aside'.[11] Without the Article 48 TEU procedure, as De Witte argues, the national governments could have amended the Treaties informally by an '"ordinary" parallel agreement' and hence could have omitted European constitutional guarantees expressed in Article 48 TEU (the participation of the national parliament).[12] In addition, if the national governments would

[8] The counterpart of Art 48(6) TEU is Art IV-445 of the Constitutional Treaty and Art 48(7) TEU is Art IV-444 of the Constitutional Treaty. During the IGC in November 2003, already after the European Convention had concluded its work, the Italian presidency proposed that instead of individual opposition a threshold or a number of parliaments could block the revision. See Naples Ministerial Conclave: Presidency proposal, CIG 42/03 25.11.2003 at 38.

[9] Art 48(6)(2).

[10] B De Witte, 'Treaty revision in the European Union: constitutional change through international law' (2004) 35 *Netherlands Yearbook of International Law* 51, 74.

[11] ibid, 56.

[12] ibid.

not follow Article 48 TEU they would act in the violation of national constitutional law requiring the approval of the national legislature.[13]

Member States' ratification procedures tend to share the same elements, such as referendum or parliamentary authorisation to ratify which allows the parliament to control the authority capable to sign the treaty (the executive).[14] The vote in parliament is in fact, as Closa puts it, 'an inalienable component of ratification procedures', and although the parliaments cannot make reservations on EU treaties, the possibility that a national parliament will refuse to grant authorisation hangs over the negotiations process.[15] Nonetheless, the data on the EU Treaty ratification process shows that neither such variables as different positions on EU integration within the coalition government, qualified majorities necessary to authorise the ratification, or the participation of a second chamber, nor a change of parliamentary majority through an intervening election have been a hurdle in the ratification process in the past.[16] Hence while parliaments are a participant in the ratification process, they are not the obvious veto-player suspects.

Secondly, Article 48(7) TEU establishes the so-called general passerelle,[17] which was first proposed in the Constitutional Treaty.[18] De Witte labels the procedure of general passerelle a 'genuine measure of flexibility in treaty amendment', since it allows for a 'further deepening of integration ... without the need for setting up an IGC and, above all, without the need for constitutional ratification of these changes by all the Member States separately'.[19] Specifically, the European Council, acting by unanimity and with the consent of the absolute majority of the EP,[20] may decide to authorise the Council to change its decision-making procedure from unanimity to a vote by qualified majority. This change may concern the areas provided in the TFEU and Title V of TEU regarding the EU's external action and Common Foreign and Security Policy.[21] This type of revision has hence a broader scope than the Article 48(6) TEU procedure. Similarly, the European Council may decide that a legislative act is adopted under the ordinary legislative procedure instead of the special legislative procedure (applicable to the TFEU provisions).[22]

The general passerelle explicitly embraces a role for national parliaments. First, both Article 48(7)(3) TEU and Article 6 of Protocol No 1 grant national parliaments information rights on the planned use of the general passerelle. Specifically, the European Council

[13] ibid.

[14] C Closa, *The Politics of Ratification of EU Treaties* (Abingdon, Routledge, 2013) 46 ff. See that Closa uses the notion of ratification and approval alternately with regard to the simplified revision procedures (at 31–32).

[15] ibid, 47.

[16] ibid, 49–62.

[17] There is also a number of specific passerelle clauses (or bridging clauses) which provide for the possibility to change the voting/legislative procedure directly in the treaty text (eg Art 31(3) TEU, Art 81(3) TFEU, Art 153(2) TFEU, Art 192(2) TFEU, Art 312(2) TFEU, Art 333(1)–(2) TFEU). They provide for some procedural particularities with respect to the general passerelle clause. For example, they do not grant a veto to national parliaments (except for Art 81(3) TFEU), as well as some of them provide for a unanimous decision by the Council instead of the European Council.

[18] See Art IV-444(3) Constitutional Treaty. Also previous treaties contained some passerelles but they were rarely used. See J-C Piris, *The Lisbon Treaty. A Legal and Political Analysis* (Cambridge, Cambridge University Press, 2010) 107.

[19] De Witte, 'Treaty revision in the European Union' (n 10 above) 80.

[20] Art 48(7)4 TEU.

[21] Excludes decisions with military implications or concerning defence.

[22] Art 48(7)(2) TEU.

is obliged to notify national parliaments of its intention to adopt an act according to a changed procedure a minimum of six months before the European Council adopts its decision. Within six months of the notification date, a national parliament may oppose the initiative of the European Council and in this case the decision at stake will not be adopted. To be clear, Article 48(7)(3) TEU describes the opposition by a national parliament to the European Council initiative—not to the decision. The decision is adopted only after the six-month period has elapsed and if national parliaments did not oppose the initiative. Hence between the notification to parliaments and the end of the six-month period for parliaments' opposition the document at stake is a *draft* European Council decision, since the European Council may adopt the decision only in the absence of opposition.

So far, Article 48 TEU has been applied three times for amendments of the Treaties. The ordinary revision procedure was used both for the amendment of Protocol No 36 with regard to additional seats in the EP for the period of the 2009–14 parliamentary term[23] and in order to add the Protocol on the concerns of the Irish people on the Treaty of Lisbon ('Irish Protocol') to the TEU and TFEU.[24] The only simplified treaty revision so far took place for the amendment of Article 136 TFEU and will be studied in more detail below.

The design of Article 48(6) and 48(7) TEU grants a role to national parliaments at the final stage of the revision procedure. In contrast, the ordinary revision procedure allows for direct involvement of the representatives of the national parliaments in the examining of the amendments proposed to the Treaties in cases when the Convention is convened.[25] This characteristic of the Convention method of treaty revision is arguably increasing the input legitimacy of the EU by decreasing the lines of accountability between the citizen and the agents conducting the negotiations and enhancing the number of represented interests.[26]

Some differences between Article 48(6) TEU and the general passerelle should be also noted. For example Kiiver points out that the Article 48(7) TEU procedure 'is not strictly speaking a ratification of a Treaty amendment but a veto right *against* a Treaty amendment' in contrast to the ratification (ordinary revision procedure) or approval (simplified revision procedure) carried out by the Member States 'in accordance with their respective constitutional requirements'.[27] It is hence argued by some authors that since Article 48(7) TEU does not demand a 'positive approval' of the European Council decision it is further from a classic conclusion of international treaties, although ultimately the revision still depends on the willingness of each Member State.[28]

[23] European Council Decision 2010/350/EU of 17 June 2010 on the examination by a conference of representatives of the governments of the Member States of the amendments to the Treaties proposed by the Spanish Government concerning the composition of the European Parliament and not to convene a Convention, [2010] OJ L160, p 5–9.

[24] European Council Decision 2013/106/EU of 11 May 2012 on the examination by a conference of representatives of the governments of the Member States of the amendment to the Treaties proposed by the Irish Government in the form of a Protocol on the concerns of the Irish people on the Treaty of Lisbon, to be annexed to the Treaty on European Union and to the Treaty on the Functioning of the European Union, and not to convene a Convention, [2003] OJ L60, pp 129–30.

[25] Art 48(3) TEU.

[26] T Risse, M Kleine, 'Assessing the Legitimacy of the EU's Treaty Revision Methods' (2007) 45 *Journal of Common Market Studies* 69, 75.

[27] P Kiiver, *The Early Warning System for the Principle of Subsidiarity. Constitutional theory and empirical reality* (London, Routledge, 2012) 10.

[28] H-J Cremer, 'Art 48 EUV' in C Calliess and M Ruffert (eds), *EUV/AEUV Kommentar*, 4th edn (München, CH Beck, 2011) Rn 14.

III. OVERVIEW OF NATIONAL PROVISIONS ON THE ROLE OF PARLIAMENTS IN THE TREATY REVISION

The aim of this section is to show in greater detail how the simplified revision procedures are structured in selected Member States: the UK, Germany, Poland, Italy and France. The inquiry into these five Member States is justified by the different patterns of parliamentary control of European Council meetings put forward in a study led by Wolfgang Wessels.[29] Although this chapter does not directly concern the control of the European Council decisions, those decisions are at the centre of the simplified treaty revision and the strength of parliamentary control of those acts might be reflected in the design of national procedures of parliamentary involvement in the simplified revision procedures. Accordingly, Poland represents the 'Europe as usual' model, which follows on the system of scrutiny established for ordinary legislation. The UK exemplifies the 'government accountability' model, centered on plenary sessions after the summits to question the government policy. France is located between an 'expert' model of scrutiny based on an ex-ante and ex-post control by European Affairs Committees and the 'policy-maker' represented by Germany, which emphasises the ex-ante control. Finally, Italy with the new scrutiny powers of the parliament over the European Council meeting represents the strongest model of scrutiny.[30] The next sections give an overview of the national procedures for the Treaty amendment in the chosen Member States and whether they correspond with the strength of those parliaments in the scrutiny of European Council decisions.

A. United Kingdom

In the UK, the European Union Act 2011 regulates in great detail the national procedure for the simplified treaty revision in Article 48(6) and (7) TEU. With regard to Article 48(6) TEU, section 3(1) of the European Union Act provides that the decision of the European Council has to be approved by Act of Parliament (statute) and in a referendum.[31] With regard to the revision procedure under Article 48(7) TEU, section 6(1) of the European Union Act demands that before the Minister of the Crown votes in favour of the European Council decision, the draft decision must be approved by Act of Parliament (statute) and in a referendum.[32] The requirements are hence identical for both procedures of simplified treaty revision. The relevant distinction is that in Article 48(6) TEU procedure the parliament is involved only *after* the European Council decision is taken and needs to be approved by the Member States in accordance with their respective constitutional requirements, while under the Article 48(7) TEU procedure the parliament has to approve the draft decision

[29] Study directed by Wessels and Rozenberg distilled altogether seven different models of parliamentary control of European Council meetings on the basis of three criteria such as timing, locus, and significance of parliamentary control. See Wessels, 'Democratic Control in the Member States' (n 7 above).

[30] The study originally included Italy in the 'Europe as usual' group. However since December 2012 Law n° 234/2012 introduced ex ante and ex post control of the European Council meetings, which often includes the prime minister and may also take place in a plenary session.

[31] For a detailed analysis of cases in which a referendum will be necessary see S Peers, 'The UK's European Union Bill' (2010) 12 *Statewatch Analyses* 8, available at: www.statewatch.org/analyses/no-111-uk-eu%20bill.pdf.

[32] ibid, 10.

before the prime minister votes in favour of it in the European Council. This is connected to the fact that, as Paul Craig explains, the 'strategy' of the framers of the European Union Act was to introduce the approval by Act of Parliament or referendum as a 'pre-condition' for the general passerelle.[33] In this situation however, the right to oppose the European Council initiative granted by Article 48(7)(3) TEU 'is unlikely to be needed', and hence no national provisions have been introduced for this procedure.[34] Indeed, it seems rather improbable that the parliament would use the veto after approving a draft decision in an Act of Parliament, unless the political majorities at stake would change, which is improbable taking into account the short six-month period foreseen for the parliaments.

B. Germany

In Germany, the Bundestag and the Bundesrat have to be informed about the revisions of the Treaties. Specifically, §9(1) of the Act on Cooperation between the Federal Government and the German Bundestag in matters concerning the European Union (EUZBBG)[35] states that the Bundestag has a right to deliver an opinion on proposals and initiatives for decisions on the opening of negotiations to make amendments to EU Treaties. Moreover, before the final decision on the treaty amendment is taken, the federal government should 'reach an agreement with the Bundestag'. Knowing the opinion of the Bundestag, the federal government may however take a divergent decision justified by good reasons of foreign or integration policy.[36] Similarly, the Annex to §9(1) of the Act on Cooperation between the Federal Government and the German Länder in Matters concerning the European Union (EUZBLG) indicates with regard to Article 48 TEU in general that the federal government informs the Bundesrat about its position and about the further negations as far as the interests of the Länder are at stake.[37]

The procedure for approval of the simplified treaty revision is further specified in the German Integrationsverantwortungsgesetz of 2009 (Responsibility for Integration Law).[38] With regard to the Article 48(6) TEU procedure §2 IntVG provides that a statute (Gesetz) in accordance with Article 23(1) of German Basic Law is necessary for the approval of European Council decisions. In short, approval by the Bundestag together with the consent of the Bundesrat is necessary.

[33] See further P Craig, 'The European Union Act 2011: Locks limits and legality' (2011) 48 *Common Market Law Review* 1915, 1930. In addition, Craig questions the legality of the pre-conditions making the approval conditional upon national constitutional requirements in cases where the Treaty does not foresee it directly, 'there is no warrant for acceptence of such a power [of national parliament and the national electorate] in any of the deliberations on Treaty reform, nor is there any warrant for accepting that Member States can unilaterally arrogate such a power to themselves'.

[34] Annex to the Thirteenth Bi-annual Report on Developments in European Union Procedures and Practices Relevant to Parliamentary Scrutiny: Replies of National Parliaments and the European Parliament (May 2010) 511.

[35] Gesetz über die Zusammenarbeit von Bundesregierung und Deutschem Bundestag in Angelegenheiten der Europäischen Union, Bundesgesetzblatt Jahrgang 2013 Teil I Nr 36.

[36] §9(2) EUZBBG.

[37] Gesetz über die Zusammenarbeit von Bund und Ländern in Angelegenheiten der Europäischen Union, vom 12. März 1993 (Bundesgesetzblatt Teil I Seite 313); zuletzt geändert durch das Gesetz vom 22. September 2009 (Bundesgesetzblatt Teil I Seite 3031).

[38] Gesetz über die Wahrnehmung der Integrationsverantwortung des Bundestages und des Bundesrates in Angelegenheiten der Europäischen Union (Integrationsverantwortungsgesetz) vom 22. September 2009 (IntVG).

For the Article 48(7) TEU procedure, according to §4(1) IntVG an approval of the parliament in form of statute is necessary before the German representative approves or rejects the European Council initiative. Without such statute, the German representative in the European Council is obliged to reject the European Council initiative. This regulation is hence similar to the British one. This solution is due to the Lisbon judgment of the German Federal Constitutional Court which indicated that the right of national parliaments to oppose a passerelle under Article 48(7)(3) TEU

> is not a sufficient equivalent of the requirement of ratification; therefore the approval by the representative of the German government always requires a law within the meaning of Article 23.1 second sentence, and if necessary third sentence, of the Basic Law. It is only in this way that the German legislative bodies exercise their responsibility for integration in a given case and also decide whether the level of democratic legitimation is still high enough to accept the majority decision.[39]

German law distinguishes however between the statute necessary for the consent or rejection by the German representative to the European Council decision[40] and the self-standing right of the German parliamentary chambers to oppose the European Council's initiative.[41] Specifically, §10(1) IntVG states that (only) the Bundestag may oppose the general passerelle when the initiative touches upon exclusive competences of the Bund.[42] In all other cases, meaning those not concerning the exclusive competences of the federation, German law allows both the Bundestag and the Bundesrat to oppose the amendment at stake, without requiring any common position. Subsequently, the President of the Bundestag or of the Bundesrat accordingly informs the President of the European Council about the opposition and notifies the German government about this.[43]

C. Poland

In Poland, any decision of the European Council according to Article 48(6) TEU demands ratification.[44] The Polish Constitution provides for three types of ratification procedure; among those, two demanding the prior agreement of the parliament expressed in a statute and one which does not require such approval. These two procedures are relevant here since they relate to international treaties concerning Poland's membership of an international organisation or conferrals of competences of organs of state authority in some matters to an international organisation.[45]

[39] Bundesverfassungsgericht, Order of 30 June 2009—2 BvE 2/08, Lisbon Treaty, para 319.

[40] §4(1) IntVG.

[41] §10(1) IntVG.

[42] The specification about the 'exclusive competences of the Bund' seems to limit the scope of objection and the rights of the Bundesrat under Art 48(7) TEU.

[43] §10(2) IntVG.

[44] Art 12(2a), Ustawa z dnia 14 kwietnia 2000, o umowach międzynarodowych.

[45] Art 89(1) and Art 90(1) of Polish Constitution. The choice of an appropriate procedure for the simplified treaty revision with regard to Article 136 TFEU was at the heart of the Polish Constitutional Court's Decision. See Trybunał Konstytucyjny, K 33/12, judgment of 26 June 2013; K Granat, 'Approval of Article 136 TFEU Amendment in Poland: The Perspective of the Constitutional Court on Eurozone Crisis law' (2015) 21 *European Public Law* 33.

With regard to the general passerelle, both chambers of the parliament have to agree to it in a statute.[46] Accordingly, a motion of the government based on the parliament's statute is passed to the President of Poland who takes the decision on Poland's position in the case at stake. This motion obliges the government's representative in the European Council to vote in favour of the European Council initiative or to abstain from the vote. If the President does not take any decision on the position of Poland, the Polish representative in the European Council should reject the European Council initiative. Hence, there is no possibility that the Polish representative in the European Council will vote in a way that the Polish parliament did not approve of. If the President did not take any decision, it would have the same effect as parliament's opposition. The only problematic case is when the parliament is in favour of the amendment but the President takes no action and hence the representative would have to vote against. Yet, some indication on how such cases could be solved gives the Constitutional Tribunal which decided that although the Polish Constitution designates the President as 'the supreme representative of the Republic of Poland and the guarantor of the continuity of State authority' the President and the national government should cooperate with regard to the position of Poland during the meetings of the European Council to ensure uniformity in relations with the EU and its institutions.[47]

The right to oppose a European Council decision is regulated separately in the Rules of Procedures of both chambers of the Polish Parliament. In the Sejm, the initiative to raise the veto remains with the European Affairs Committee but the final decision is taken by the plenary.[48] In the Senat, the relevant parliamentary committee prepares an opinion which is then also discussed and voted on in the plenary.[49]

In consequence, similar to the German one, the Polish system offers both the necessity that the parliament agrees to the passerelle in a statute before the vote in the European Council as well as a direct repetition of the treaty provisions granting parliaments an opportunity to raise their opposition.

D. Italy

In Italy the new Law 234/2012 on Italy's participation in EU affairs mandates that the government informs both chambers of parliament about initiatives concerning the simplified revision procedure according to Article 48(6) and (7) TEU.[50] If the European Council decision demands the prior approval of the Member States according to their constitutional rules, the Italian government transmits such a decision to then be approved by the

[46] Art 14(1), Ustawa z dnia 8 października 2010, o współpracy Rady Ministrów z Sejmem i Senatem w sprawach związanych z członkostwem Rzeczypospolitej Polskiej w Unii Europejskiej.

[47] Case Kpt 2/08, judgment of 20 May 2009, OTK ZU 2009/5A/78. See also A Łazowski, 'Half full and half empty glass: The application of EU law in Poland (2004–2010)' (2011) 48 *Common Market Law Review* 503, 517. The case focused more specifically on who (the President or the Prime Minister) should attend the European Council meetings as the representative of Poland. If it was decided that the President attends the European Council meeting, she should cooperate with the government. One could hence conclude that the 'cooperation sprit' could go beyond the issue of attendance of a meeting and concern also with regard to European Council decisions.

[48] Art 34(4)(c), Art 148b(1)11b, Art 148b(4); Art 148ca, Rules of Procedure of the Sejm.

[49] Art 75f and Art 75g, Rules of Procedure of the Senate, demanding an absolute majority of senators in order to pass the veto for a general passerelle in contrast to the default simple majority.

[50] Art 11(1) Law 234/2012.

chambers.[51] Specifically, with regard to the Article 48(6) TEU procedure the government submits within 30 days of the European Council decision to the chambers a draft statute approving the decision of the European Council.[52] According to Article 80 of the Italian Constitution, the parliamentary chambers authorise in form of a statute the ratification of international treaties and no referendum is admissible for laws authorising the ratification of international treaties as per Article 75 of the Constitution.

With regard to the general passerelle, the Italian provisions repeat the text of Article 48(7) TEU by stating that the parliamentary chambers should take the decision within six months from the moment of the transmission of the act at stake.[53] In case of a negative decision of both chambers, the chambers should inform the European Council and the government of their decision. Hence, different to Germany, the UK and Poland, the Italian parliament has only its Treaty right to oppose the passerelle, but prior agreement of the parliament in form of a statute is not necessary for the approval of the decision in the European Council by the Italian representative.

E. France

In France, Article 88(7) of the French Constitution grants the National Assembly and the Senate the right to oppose 'any modification of the rules governing the passing of acts of the European Union in cases provided for under the simplified revision procedure for treaties'. This provision was added as a consequence of the Lisbon decision of the French Constitutional Council,[54] which followed the reasons of its prior decision on the Constitutional Treaty. Specifically, with regard to Article IV-445 of the Constitutional Treaty (Article 48(6) TEU) the Council identified the parliamentary authorisation according to Article 53 of the French Constitution as the approval demanded 'in accordance with the respective constitutional requirements of the member states'.[55] Article 53 of the French Constitution provides for an approval of EU Treaties by an act of parliament.

With regard to Article 48(7) TEU (Article IV-444 of the Constitutional Treaty) the decision of the French Constitutional Council mandates that constitutional amendment is necessary 'in the absence of any national ratification procedure making it possible to review the constitutionality of said laws';[56] and in 'order to allow [the parliament] to exercise its prerogative'.[57] The particularities of the right to oppose are indicated in the Rules of Procedure of the National Assembly and of the Senate. In the Assembly, the motion opposing the passerelle must be signed by at least one tenth of the members of the chamber within six months of the transmission of the initiative,[58] while in the Senate any senator may table a motion to oppose a European Council initiative within four months of its transmission

[51] Art 11(3) Law 234/2012.
[52] Art 11(4) Law 234/2012.
[53] Art 11(5) Law 234/2012.
[54] Conseil constitutionnel, Decision n 2007-560 DC du 20 decembre 2007, paras 26–29.
[55] Conseil constitutionnel, Decision n 2004-505 DC du 19 novembre 2004, para 36.
[56] ibid, para 35.
[57] ibid, para 41.
[58] Art 151-12(3), Rules of Procedure of Assemblée nationale.

to the chamber.[59] To pass, the motion to oppose has to be adopted by each of the chambers and in case of rejection, no motion against the same initiative can be drafted again in the Assembly or Senate.[60] Hence, the right of the French parliament to oppose demands an agreement of both chambers of the parliament, which is also clearly stated in the French Constitution.

In sum, France, similar to Italy, does not demand a prior approval by statute before the representative votes in the European Council. Moreover, in the same vein as Italian law, the French provisions demand a joint decision of the chambers to veto the general passerelle.

The examples studied here show some significant differences in the regulation of the simplified treaty revision procedure at the national level. While with regard to Article 48(6) TEU the revision of the Treaties demands the consent of parliament in all cases (or referendum as in the UK), the main differences concern the general passerelle procedure. These include the necessary consent of the parliament needed for the initiative to be approved by the national representative in the European Council (the UK, Germany, Poland) or whether an opposition to that European Council initiative is regulated at the national level. The latter aspect is present in Italy and France, but also in Germany and in Poland which hence exhibit both types of safeguards in a form of a parliamentary statute and as an opposition. Moreover, national regulations differ on whether a joint decision of the chambers is necessary for the opposition.

The national regulations explored in this chapter prove that there is some link between the practice of scrutiny of European Council summits and the necessity of an act of parliament allowing the executive to vote in favour of the passerelle in the European Council. For example, the 'policy-maker' model of the German parliament explains the additional safeguard in a form of a statute granted to this parliament, similarly as in the UK which is based on the governmental accountability to the parliament. In Poland which exhibits the weak 'Europe as usual' model, a prior statute is necessary, which means that for a passerelle an additional hurdle was put in place. In Italy, on the contrary, the strong ex ante and ex post scrutiny of European Council decisions may seem to be a sufficient safeguard and hence there is no requirement of a prior statute in Italy. This reasoning might be similar for the lack of prior statute in France, which places itself not far from Italy in Wessels' model. In sum, because the stronger models of oversight of European Council decisions (Germany and Italy), as well as the weaker ones (Poland, the UK and France) have taken different approaches to the prior statute requirement, there does not seem to be much of an overlap with the categories of Wessels' study. Hence, the passerelle might present a very special case of parliamentary scrutiny of EU affairs.

The broader explanation of the additional safeguards might be however connected with the view of the German Constitutional Court in the Lisbon judgment that '[i]t would be incompatible with the constitutional requirement of a parliamentary decision if the requirement of a time-limit could construe in concrete terms the possible silence on the part of the legislative bodies as their approval'.[61] In other words, the principle of parliamentary involvement requires active, explicit approval by the legislatures in order to allow the government to support the revision of the treaty. This argument of the German Court could also be behind the procedures introduced in the UK and in Poland.

[59] Art 73i(1), Rules of Procedure of Sénat.

[60] Art 151-12(9), Rules of Procedure of Assemblée nationale; Art 73i(1)(8) Rules of Procedure of Sénat.

[61] Bundesverfassungsgericht (n 39 above) para 320.

Under Article 48(7) TEU, the paradox of providing for both the statute necessary for the approval or rejection of the decision in the European Council (stemming from national law) and the right to opposition (stemming from EU law but specified in national law) is that the former 'consumes' the latter. If a statute is necessary for the approval of a European Council decision by the member of the executive, then there is no need for the parliament to have a separate right to oppose European Council initiatives. In other words the parliament may express its opposition simply by not giving its consent in the form of the statute necessary for the German representative to vote in favour. There is basically no chance that the parliament will grant a consent for a national representative to vote in favour of adoption of the European Council decision when it would also plan to use its right to oppose expressed in Article 48(7)(3). The main difference here is arguably 'psychological': where a statute is needed for the vote of the representative in the European Council, it will be still the Head of State or government that vetoed the passerelle. This is also typical of many decisions taken under unanimity in the legislative process. In contrast the right to oppose comes from the parliament directly, which adds drama, as is the institution democratically linked directly with its citizens.

The final remark concerns the notion of 'national parliament' applied in Article 48(7) TEU. In contrast to the possibility of issuing reasoned opinions under the EWS, which explicitly grants such a right to a national parliament and to a chamber thereof, the general passerelle indicates that a national parliament may oppose a European Council initiative. In consequence it seems that in the case of bicameral parliaments (see the example of France and Italy above) a joint opinion of both chambers is necessary.[62] On the contrary, in some of Member States there is explicitly no plan to adopt a joint position at all (the Netherlands),[63] or national provisions are not provided for and hence in line with the Treaty a joint position of the chambers will be necessary (Poland). Yet, because most of the studied national systems introduced a distinct parliamentary veto on the government's decision in the Council, the need for a joint position of both chambers under Article 48(7)(3) might be rather rare.[64]

IV. INSTITUTIONAL POSSIBILITIES OF INTERPARLIAMENTARY COOPERATION

Both types of the treaty revision procedure focus on an individual parliament. First, the simplified revision procedure on the basis of Article 48(6) TEU refers to the approval by the Member States in accordance with their respective constitutional requirements, which includes an approval by a national parliament. Secondly, the general passerelle is directly oriented towards an individual parliament by granting it a right to opposition. In fact, both of the simplified treaty revision types allow a single parliament to stop revisions of

62 See especially in Spain, where Art 8(2) of Ley 24/2009 directly states that both chambers of the Spanish parliament have to ratify the proposed opposition. Hence, if one chamber disagrees with the ratification, there will be no opposition to the European Council initiative from the Spanish parliament. See also Annex to the Thirteenth Bi-annual Report on Developments (n 34 above) 464.

63 For example in the Netherlands. See Annex to the Thirteenth Bi-annual Report on Developments (n 34 above) 349.

64 This issue was signaled by House of Lords, Select Committee on European Union, Tenth Report, Session 2004–05, para 3.16.

the Treaties: an approval by all Member States is necessary for the entry into force of an approved European Council decision in the first case and the European Council may adopt a decision only '[i]n the absence of opposition' of national parliaments in the second case. These cases are also different from the EWS. Although the EWS allows a national parliament to draft a reasoned opinion on subsidiarity violation grounds, it does not grant opposition rights to individual parliaments unless certain thresholds of numbers of reasoned opinions are met. An element of similarity between the EWS and the simplified treaty revision procedure is however that both grant national parliaments a 'negative' blocking role in the EU decision-making process, in contrast to proposing their own initiatives.[65] How can we hence reconcile the single-parliament-centered and negative role of national legislatures with the possibility of interparliamentary cooperation?

Interparliamentary cooperation seems to play an important role post-Lisbon. Crum and Fossum note a growing trend of cooperation within the 'multilevel parliamentary field' encompassing national and supranational parliamentary institutions participating in the EU decision-making process.[66] Their assessment of this cooperation is positive: as 'parliaments are increasingly oriented to one another; each is becoming an intrinsic part of the others' operating environment'.[67] The interparliamentary networks are distributed according to bilateral–multilateral and formal–informal lines.[68] This chapter will focus on multilateral networks, including formal and informal networks which can offer relevant forums of interparliamentary cooperation by simplified revision procedures.

First, the EU Speakers' Conference aims at 'safeguarding and promoting the role of parliaments and carrying out common work in support of the interparliamentary activities'.[69] It meets at least once a year and involves the speakers of parliaments of EU Member States and the EP's President.[70] The Interparliamentary EU information exchange, IPEX, was created in 2006 following the recommendations of this conference.[71] Since June 2011, when the new version of the IPEX platform was launched, it includes inter alia a possibility for national parliaments to make known its opposition in accordance with Article 48(7) TEU and 81(3) TFEU. The second relevant forum for parliamentary cooperation from the perspective of this chapter is the Conference of the EU affairs committees of the national parliaments and the representatives of the EP (COSAC). The COSAC, as indicated in Article 10 of Protocol No 1, 'promote[s] the exchange of information and best practice between national Parliaments and the European Parliament'. Thirdly, the informal network of the permanent representatives of the national parliaments in the EP (NPRs) 'facilitate[s]

[65] One of the proposals for a positive contribution of national parliaments in the EU is the 'green card' proposed by the House of Lords that a number of national parliaments working together makes constructive policy or legislative suggestions. See House of Lords, European Union Committee, 9th Report of Session 2013–14, para 58.

[66] B Crum and JE Fossum, 'Introduction' in B Crum and J Erik Fossum (eds), *Practices of interparliamentary coordination in international politics* (Colchester, ECPR, 2013) 5ff.

[67] B Crum and JE Fossum, 'Conclusion' in B Crum and JE Fossum (n 66 above) 252.

[68] A Buzogány, 'Learning from the best? Interparliamentary networks and the parliamentary scrutiny of EU decision-making' in B Crum and JE Fossum (eds), *Practices of interparliamentary coordination in international politics* (Colchester, ECPR, 2013).

[69] Art 2 of the Stockholm Guidelines for the EU Speakers' Conference, available at: www.ipex.eu/IPEXL-WEB/euspeakers/getspeakers.do.

[70] See C Fasone, 'Ruling the (Dis-)order of Interparliamentary Cooperation? The EU Speakers' Conference', Chapter 14 in this volume.

[71] See the History of EU Speakers's Conference at: www.ipex.eu/IPEXL-WEB/euspeakers/getspeakers.do.

informal, day-to-day cooperation',[72] and provides information to national members of the parliament on EU issues.[73] Specifically, NPRs report on EU developments and political issues on a weekly basis or ad hoc on urgent matters or such matters that are interesting only for a limited number of MPs.[74] Högenauer and Neuhold indicate that national representatives play a representational function, by building relationships between members of parliaments and EU institutions, such as organising visits of national MPs to the EP, liaising with the national MEPs or participating in interparliamentary conferences.[75] Finally, NPRs enable a 'bridge-building function across national parliaments' by directly exchanging information across national parliaments about the stance of their national parliament on a specific issue.[76] This was already visible in the case of cooperation for gaining enough votes to trigger a 'yellow card' against the Monti II proposal under the EWS where the NPRs played a leading and effective role.[77]

The following section explores the possible fora and ways of interparliamentary cooperation by national parliaments within the simplified revision procedure. The sections below will elaborate on these issues taking the amendment of Article 136 TFEU as a case study.

V. CASE STUDY OF ARTICLE 136 TFEU AMENDMENT

In October 2010, at the time of the deep Eurozone crisis, EU Heads of State or Government agreed that Member States should establish 'a permanent crisis mechanism to safeguard the financial stability of the euro area as a whole' 'in order to ensure balanced and sustainable growth' in the EU.[78] To this effect, 'a limited treaty change' was required, yet without modifying Article 125 TFEU (the so-called 'no bail-out' clause).[79] In December 2010, the Belgian government put forward a proposal for revising Article 136 TFEU concerning the adoption of measures for Euro-zone Member States by the Council ensuring the functioning of economic and monetary union. In March 2011, within the simplified revision procedure under Article 48(6) TEU the European Council adopted Decision 2011/199 to amend Article 136 TFEU accordingly.[80] The newly inserted paragraph 3 states that

[72] V Knutelská, 'Cooperation among national parliaments: an effective contribution to EU legitimation?' in B Crum B and JE Fossum (n 66 above) 38.

[73] A-L Högenauer and C Neuhold, 'National Parliaments after Lisbon: Administrations on the Rise' OPAL Online Paper Series 12/201316, available at: www.opal-europe.org/index.php?option=com_content&view=article&id=76&Itemid=108. See also Anna-Lena Högenauer and Andreja Pegan, 'The role of parliamentary administrations in interparliamentary cooperation', Chapter 8 in this volume.

[74] Eleventh Bi-annual Report on Developments in European Union Procedures and Practices Relevant to Parliamentary Scrutiny (May 2009) 28.

[75] Högenauer and Neuhold, 'National Parliaments after Lisbon' (n 73 above) 16.

[76] ibid.

[77] See I Cooper, 'A yellow card for the striker: national parliaments and the defeat of EU legislation on the right to strike' (2015) 22 *Journal of European Public Policy* 1406, 1412.

[78] European Council, Conclusions, 28–29 October 2010, EUCO 25/1/10, point I 2.

[79] ibid.

[80] European Council Decision 2011/199/EU of 25 March 2011 amending Article 136 of the Treaty on the Functioning of the European Union with regard to a stability mechanism for Member States whose currency is the euro, [2011] OJ L91, p 1–2.

> Member States whose currency is the euro may establish a stability mechanism to be activated if indispensable to safeguard the stability of the euro area as a whole. The granting of any required financial assistance under the mechanism will be made subject to strict conditionality.

The question whether the requirements of Article 48(6) TEU for a valid treaty amendment were met was subject to the judicial review by the European Court of Justice (CJEU) within the procedure of preliminary reference from the Supreme Court of Ireland.[81] Specifically, the CJEU had to review whether the amendment concerned provision of Title III of TFEU and whether it did not increase the competences conferred on the Union in the Treaties. With regard to the first matter, the CJEU stated that while the Decision 2011/199 amends a provision of Part Three of the TFEU (Article 136 TFEU) it 'formally satisfies' the condition imposed by Article 48(6) TEU that the simplified revision procedure may concern solely provisions of that treaty part,[82] and in addition, does not affect any other provision of the Treaty, especially in Part One in the area of monetary policy.[83] Regarding the increase of competence condition, the Court found that Decision 2011/119 in itself does not confer any new competence on the EU and does not create a legal basis which would enable the EU to undertake an action which was not possible before the amendment.[84] In sum, the CJEU declared Decision 2011/199 valid.

In the meantime, following Article 48(6) TEU, the Decision 2011/199 required approval by Member States 'in accordance with their respective constitutional requirements' in order to enter into force.[85] The need for parliamentary cooperation with regard to the Article 136 TFEU amendment arose at the point of the approval procedures due to the complexity of the Eurozone related reforms at the time. The issue at stake was that in addition to the revision of the Lisbon Treaty, two new intergovernmental treaties were also agreed to and put for ratification. The first of them, the Treaty Establishing the European Stability Mechanism launches a new financial institution, the European Stability Mechanism (ESM)

> to mobilise funding and provide stability support under strict conditionality, appropriate to the financial assistance instrument chosen, to the benefit of ESM Members which are experiencing, or are threatened by, severe financing problems, if indispensable to safeguard the financial stability of the euro area as a whole and of its Member States.[86]

Although the ESM Treaty was 'closely intertwined' with the amendment of Article 136 TFEU,[87] the CJEU underlined in its *Pringle* judgment that Member States may conclude and ratify the ESM Treaty before the entry into force of Decision 2011/199.[88] Secondly, the Treaty on Stability, Coordination and Governance (TSCG) signed enshrining the

[81] Case 370/12 *Pringle v Government of Ireland and Others* ECLI:EU:C:2012:756. See also B De Witte and T Beukers, 'The Court of Justice approves the creation of the European Stability Mechanism outside the EU legal order: Pringle' (2013) 50 *Common Market Law Review* 805.

[82] ibid, para 46.

[83] ibid, para 47–69.

[84] ibid, para 73.

[85] In fact all the national parliaments approved the Decision 2011/199 before the Pringle judgment. None of the Member States held a referendum. See: www.europarl.europa.eu/RegData/etudes/note/join/2013/462455/IPOL-AFCO_NT(2013)462455_EN.pdf.

[86] Art 3 ESM Treaty.

[87] K Tuori and K Tuori, *The Eurozone Crisis. A Constitutional Analysis* (Cambridge, Cambridge University Press, 2014) 145.

[88] Pringle (n 81 above) para 185.

so-called fiscal compact with a requirement for national budgets that the annual structural government deficit does not exceed 0.5 per cent of GDP at market prices was under ratification at the same time as the amendment of Article 136 TFEU.[89]

The highly relevant issues of the financial crisis that the Lisbon Treaty amendment and the two new treaties dealt with and the complexity of the approval and ratification processes of three different legal instruments made it difficult for national parliaments to understand the scope of change. In order not to stay in the dark about the relevant issues surrounding the new legal mechanisms directed against the Eurozone crisis, some interparliamentary cooperation was initiated in order to gather information and monitor the ratification process. The idea to launch interparliamentary cooperation was a 'consensual decision' addressing many requests that the national parliamentary representatives received from national parliaments (especially the French parliament, the German Bundestag and the Portuguese parliament), institutions and academia.[90] On the side of the NPRs in Brussels the idea of creating a special database containing all the relevant information on the state of play within the ratification of Article 136 TFEU amendment, but also the ESM and the TSCG Treaty was especially pursued by the representatives of the Austrian, Portuguese and Spanish parliaments in Brussels.[91] This database was being updated 'in real time' by the respective national parliamentary representatives in Brussels, reflecting the status of ratification of the Article 136 TFEU, ESM Treaty and the TSCG. In this respect, the database was useful for the parliaments in order to know 'whether the ratification of the European Council decision or of the new treaties was high on the agenda in a specific national parliament'.[92] At the same time, the EP AFCO committee kept, in cooperation with, among others NPRs in Brussels, its own database which was following the ratification processes at national level.[93] In sum, the exchange of information was 'intensive' and presented a 'good rehearsal of interparliamentary cooperation in real time'.[94]

In contrast to this, COSAC did not seem to function as a relevant forum for interparliamentary cooperation during the amendment of Article 136 TFEU. The revision of the Treaties was not an item on the COSAC agenda and remained only on the sidelines of the proceedings. For example, the XLV COSAC's ordinary meeting in May 2011 in Hungary and the XLVII COSAC Chairpersons' meeting in January 2012 in Copenhagen discussed Eurozone crisis related issues.[95] However, none of the COSAC Bi-annual reports addressed the question of Article 136 TFEU amendment.[96]

[89] Art 3 TSCG.

[90] Interview with BA Dias Pinheiro, former NPR for the Assembleia da República (Portugal), January 2015.

[91] ibid.

[92] ibid.

[93] See document 'Article 136 TFEU, ESM, Fiscal Stability Treaty. Ratification requirements and present situation in the Member States' requested by the European Parliament's Committee on Constitutional Affairs at the Directorate General for Internal Policies at 10 available at: www.europarl.europa.eu/RegData/etudes/note/join/2013/462455/IPOL-AFCO_NT(2013)462455_EN.pdf.

[94] Interview with BA Dias Pinheiro (n 90 above).

[95] 'The way to recovery: Economic governance, Europe 2020 Strategy and European Semester; point of debate, Programme of the XLV COSAC meeting; 'The sovereign debt crisis, European Economic Governance and democratic accountability' at COSAC XLVII Chairpersons, 29–30 January 2012, Copenhagen, Denmark: www.cosac.eu/denmark2012/meeting-of-the-chairpersons-of-cosac-29-30-january-2012/.

[96] Compare Eighteenth COSAC Bi-annual Report on EU Practices and Procedures which addressed the question of the TSCG ratification and possible role of Art 13 TSCG conference.

In the same vein, the EU Speakers' Conference did not address the Article 136 TFEU amendment. In contrast, the ratification of the TSCG Treaty was an important point on the agenda of the conference: the participants 'shared information on the ratification of the Treaty and the implementation of its provisions in Member States'.[97]

In sum, as the current practice of interparliamentary cooperation shows with regard to the EWS, the network of the permanent representatives of the national parliaments in Brussels remains the crucial forum.

VI. CONTRIBUTION TO THE GOOD FUNCTIONING OF THE EU

Article 12 TEU states that '[n]ational parliaments contribute actively to the good functioning of the Union' and lists specific functions of national parliaments from the Lisbon Treaty, including both themes of this contribution: participation in the revision procedures of the Treaties, in accordance with Article 48 TEU, and participation in interparliamentary cooperation between national parliaments and with the EP, in accordance with Protocol No 1. As argued by Kiiver, although oddly drafted, Article 12 TEU presents 'an attempt to upgrade the visibility of national parliaments in a prominent part of the EU Treaty'.[98]

Yet, what is much more at stake here than the visibility of parliaments is that their participation is *meaningful* for the EU decision-making process, with an important, useful quality or purpose. In a sense this is much more visible in the EWS where the reasoned opinions may lead to changes in the draft legislative acts proposed by the Commission, at different stages of the process. Similarly, interparliamentary cooperation in the EWS turned out to be very useful for reaching the 'yellow card' thresholds. In contrast the involvement of national parliaments in both types of the simplified revision procedures has a much more ex-post character, since the parliaments participate in the approval of an amendment or can oppose to an already drafted initiative of the European Council. Nonetheless, the position of national parliaments in these procedures is much more powerful and individualistic than under the EWS, as even a single parliament can block the entire amendment procedure. In this sense the participation of parliaments has very serious consequences.

The simplified revision procedure can be meaningfully enhanced by the interparliamentary cooperation, which was depicted in the case of the Article 136 TFEU amendment, where the cooperation focused on the exchange of information 'in real time' on highly complex issues of the Eurozone crisis. Although it might be hard to measure the impact of interparliamentary cooperation in the case at stake, in fact, the approval of the European Council decision was successful. Interparliamentary cooperation in this field may hence offer a counterbalance to the negative role of parliaments in the revision of the Treaties by sharing information on the stage of the amendment process and enhancing the understanding of the complex revision procedures, such as in the area of the Eurozone crisis.

[97] Presidency Conclusions of the EU Speakers' Conference, Warsaw, 20–21 April 2012 at p 5 available at: www.ipex.eu/IPEXL-WEB/euspeakers/getspeakers.do?id=082dbcc530b1bef60130b6491e6c001d.

[98] Kiiver, *The Early Warning System* (n 27 above) 6. Barnard and Peers add that this provision is 'descriptive rather than prescriptive'. See C Barnard and S Peers, *European Union Law* (Oxford, Oxford University Press, 2014) 138.

VII. CONCLUSION

This chapter has studied the role of national parliaments within the simplified revision procedures of Article 48(6) and 48(7) TEU. These new provisions introduced by the Lisbon Treaty grant individual parliaments a prominent role in the revision of the Treaties. Specifically, under Article 48(6) TEU, an amendment enters into force only if approved according to national constitutional requirements, which in the current EU involves a national legislature in all the Member States. Similarly, within the general passerelle of Article 48(7) TEU, a successful revision demands that none of the national parliaments opposes the procedural change in the decision-making process.

The overview of different national designs of the simplified revision procedures shows some divergence mostly in the approval of the 'general passerelle' at national level. Specifically, the studied jurisdictions Germany, Poland, Italy and France (except for the UK) provided for the general passerelle by adopting national provisions to this effect. However, in addition to that the UK, Germany and Poland introduced a requirement of a parliamentary statute necessary for the relevant national representative to vote in favour of the passerelle in the European Council.

This chapter has also studied the possibility for national parliaments to cooperate within the simplified revision procedures. As the example of the Article 136 TFEU amendment shows, national parliaments did pursue an increased exchange of information with regard to the approval of the new provision. The exchange helped national parliaments to follow 'in real time' the complex issues around different Eurozone related changes, namely the ESM Treaty and the TSCG, which were under ratification in addition to the Article 136 TFEU amendment. Finally, such interparliamentary cooperation seems to contribute to the good functioning of the EU as expressed in Article 12 TEU, by offering a meaningful way for parliaments to participate in the revision process as informed actors, as well as providing a counterbalance to the rather negative blocking role of national parliaments in the revision process.

Part III

Parliamentary Organisation in the Ordinary Constitutional Life of the European Union

5

Bicameralism and Interparliamentary Cooperation

ANTONIA BARAGGIA

I. INTRODUCTION

AS IS WELL known, the Treaty of Lisbon has opened a new chapter in the history of national parliaments within the EU legal system. The 'losers of integration'[1] regained a pivotal role as drivers of integration, considered both as individual institutions and as a collective subject of the so-called EU multilevel parliamentary field.[2]

A pivotal role in these ongoing developments is represented by interparliamentary cooperation, which is, however, one of the most controversial and lesser known aspects of the EU integration process.[3] This statement is even truer regarding the role of the 'second chambers' in the interparliamentary dialogue.

In fact, the Treaty of Lisbon, when addressing the theme of the participation of national parliaments in EU affairs, seems to be blind to the unicameral or bicameral structure of national parliaments. Except for the number of votes assigned to each parliament in the early warning system (EWS), according to Article 7 of Protocol No 2 annexed to the Treaty of Lisbon, there is no formal distinction between the role and the weighting in EU affairs

[1] See especially A Maurer and W Wessels (eds), *National Parliaments on their Ways to Europe: Losers or Latecomers?* (Baden-Baden, Nomos, 2001), KH Goetz and JH Meyer-Sahling, 'The Europeanisation of national political systems: Parliaments and executives' (2008) 3 (2) *Living Reviews in European Governance.*

[2] B Crum and JE Fossum, 'The multilevel parliamentary field: a framework for theorizing representative democracy in the EU' (2009) *European Political Science Review* 249–71. J Pollak and P Slominski, 'EU parliaments after the Treaty of Lisbon: towards a parliamentary field?' in B Crum and J E Fossum (eds), *Practices of interparliamentary coordination in international politics* (Colchester, ECPR Press, 2013).

[3] See A Esposito, 'La cooperazione interparlamentare: principi, strumenti e prospettive' in A Manzella and N Lupo (eds), *Il sistema parlamentare euronazionale* (Torino, Giappichelli, 2014).

of national first and second chambers. The Treaty speaks generally of 'national parliaments', without any reference to the unicameral and bicameral systems adopted by Member States.

Moreover, even legal scholars do not seem to pay any specific attention to the role of second chambers within the EU parliamentary system. The literature on interparliamentary cooperation, with a few exceptions,[4] is focused on the general category of national parliaments and is indifferent to their internal structure.

It is even questioned whether second chambers have a different, more specialised role in EU matters from that of first chambers. Certainly, if they do not have one yet formally, it is an interesting lens through which to look at the role of second chambers and especially at the recent reforms implemented in several Member States on this issue.

This chapter intends to shed light on the penumbra in which European second chambers seem to be confined, arguing that there could be a specific role for these chambers and for cooperation among them, in particular when they represent different interests from those of the first chamber, as happens, for example, in the case of federal/regional second chambers.

To this extent, the chapter will describe the European landscape of second chambers, which is characterised by deep diversification rather than homogeneity (as in the case, more or less, of the first chambers). In this variety of bicameralism lies one of the most prominent problems in addressing the theme of the role of second chambers in Europe, since it is not possible to compare radically different institutions, such as the German Bundesrat, the UK House of Lords, the Italian Senate, the French Senate, and the Polish Senate.

Beyond this complexity, however, one has to consider other elements that suggest that an investigation of the role of second chambers in interparliamentary cooperation may not be in vain. In particular it has to be evaluated whether, at the EU level, the second chamber is often much more active than its national sister house, the first chamber. I will examine the data on the participation of national parliaments in political dialogue and in the EWS, which clearly provides for a primary role for second chambers within the EU landscape. I argue that second chambers may play a fundamental role within the development of cooperation among parliaments in Europe, first because they are chambers of expertise—as I will show—by looking inside the organisation of the parliamentary structure of some of them. Given this feature of second chambers, it can be deduced that even if at a national level they seem to be weaker than first chambers, they can strengthen their role within the EU landscape, both towards their respective governments and the EU institutions. This is the case, for example, with the UK House of Lords.

However, looking at the interparliamentary cooperation fora, the COSAC above all, but also the more recent Conference on Economic and Financial Governance of the European Union,[5] second chambers are not recognised as distinct institutions: the composition of national delegations is left to the determination of each Member State, the rules of procedure of the interparliamentary institutions remaining silent on the weight that has to be given to each chamber in bicameral systems.

[4] P Kiiver, *The early warning system for the principle of subsidiarity* (Abingdon/New York, Routledge, 2012).

[5] Established by art 13 of the Treaty on Stability, Coordination and Governance in the Economic and Monetary Union. (COSAC—Conférence des organs spécialisés dans les affaires communautaires (Conference of Community and European Affairs Committees)).

After an in-depth analysis of the lights and shadows of the participation of second chambers in interparliamentary cooperation, the chapter will make suggestions on developing real cooperation between second chambers, particularly those sharing the same representative criteria (federal/regional second chambers), considering such cooperation as an effective resource to address the EU democratic disconnect.[6]

II. BICAMERALISM IN THE EU. A RUGGED LANDSCAPE

Before entering into the middle of the theme of interparliamentary cooperation, a terminological premise is necessary.

As already mentioned, the Treaty of Lisbon and the Annexed Protocols use the expression 'national parliaments' to refer to the participation of the representative assemblies of each Member State in EU decision-making.

The definition of national parliament for this purpose is not as uniform as it would appear at first sight. As Kiiver pointed out, the EU meaning of national parliaments includes several grey-area cases, such as the Belgian one,[7] for example, where, according to Declaration 51 of the Lisbon Treaty, even regional parliaments are considered, 'in terms of the competences exercised by the Union as components of the national parliamentary system or chambers of the national Parliament'.

In the light of the Belgian exception, one might wonder if the definition of national parliament is left to the autonomy of each single constitutional order or if it has to be an autonomous Union concept.[8] In this regard, it seems reasonable to observe, as Olivetti does, that 'the notion of "national Parliament" is not completely defined by European law, but is derived from national constitutional law, that fills the gap left by the European notion'.[9]

With regard to the different features that the notion of national parliaments can assume in each Member State, it seems clear that the main difference is that between unicameral and bicameral systems. However, even within the two main categories, the notion of parliament may vary significantly.[10] This is even more true of bicameral parliaments, where the origins, functions, raison d'être, and powers of the second chamber can be very different. There are also a very few cases where constitutions 'stipulate that the legislature is unicameral but create institutions that have the characteristics of a second chamber'.[11] Examples

[6] P Lindseth, *Power and Legitimacy: Reconciling Europe and the Nation-State* (Oxford, Oxford University Press, 2010) 31. According to the Author, the democratic disconnect is a 'disconnect between the exercise of the supranational regulatory power and its ultimate sources of legitimacy at national level'.

[7] See M Romaniello, 'Beyond the constitutional "bicameral blueprint": Europeanisation and national identities in Belgium' in M Cartabia, N Lupo and A Simoncini (eds), *Democracy and Subsidiarity in the EU* (Bologna, Il Mulino, 2013) 285.

[8] Kiiver, *The early warning system* (n 4 above) 55.

[9] M Olivetti, 'The Role of National Parliaments' in H-J Blanke and S Mangiameli (eds), *The Treaty on European Union* (Heidelberg, Springer, 2013) 473; N Lupo, 'National parliaments in the European integration process; re-aligning politics and policies' in Cartabia (n 7 above) 107–32.

[10] The nature and functions of a Parliament are determined not only by its constitutional position, but also by other systemic elements, as, for example, the characters of the political system, the role of political parties, the political culture (majoritarian or consensual). See M Olivetti, 'The Role of National Parliaments' (n 9 above) 475.

[11] P Norton, 'Adding Value? The Role of Second Chambers' (2007) 15 *Asia Pacific Law Review* 3, 12.

falling in this category include, besides some non-EU countries, the EU itself.[12] According to a view shared by several scholars,[13] in the institutional design of the EU, there is one parliament but the legislative power given to the Council of Ministers makes the latter a sort of second chamber. It can be recalled, without getting into an-depth analysis of this point, that within this approach, the national parliament has been considered by legal scholars as a sort of 'virtual third chamber'[14] of the EU.

However, for the purpose of this contribution, within the broader concept of bicameralism, I will adopt a classical definition of national parliament and thereof of the second chamber, analysing systems in Europe in which the parliament is composed, effectively, of two different branches.

The European Union's 28 national parliaments and 41 chambers can be included in this definition. In fact, 13 national parliaments are bicameral while 15 are unicameral (some of them have changed from bicameral to unicameral).[15]

The 13 with bicameral systems are Austria, Belgium, the Czech Republic, France, Germany, Ireland, Italy, the Netherlands, Poland, the United Kingdom, Romania, Spain, and Slovenia.

Trying to capture a common feature of these second chambers is a difficult task. Since the elements that determine the differences between these institutions encompass political cultures, second chambers' structures are based on the composition of these cultures and the powers allocated to the chambers.

Is it possible, however, to categorise these second chambers based on their composition, tracing an ideal spectrum from authentic federal second chambers (as in the German and Austrian[16] Bundesräte), in which the representation is based only on the federal principle, to 'national' second chambers, in which the representation does not differ significantly from that of the lower chamber (as in Poland, in the Czech Republic and Italy). Even if the representation is different, it may not be an expression of federal interests but of local interests (French and Dutch Senates), or corporative/sectoral interests (Irish Senate).[17] There are also non-elective second chambers (UK House of Lords). Within the spectrum defined by these archetypes, other institutional solutions can be identified regarding the composition of second chambers, which can be defined as 'mixed' because they are based on a combination of the different criteria, as in Belgium[18] Spain[19] and Slovenia.[20]

[12] Other countries falling in this category are Botswana and Iran.

[13] See S Fabbrini, 'Intergovernmentalism and Its Limits: Assessing the European Union's Answer to the Euro Crisis' (2013) 46 *Comparative Political Studies* 1003 and R Schütze, *European Union Law* (Cambridge, Cambridge University Press, 2015), 60.

[14] I Cooper, 'A "Virtual Third Chamber" for the European Union? National Parliaments after the Treaty of Lisbon' (2012) 35 *West European Politics* 441.

[15] This is the case of Greece (1935), Denmark (1953), Sweden (1971) and Portugal (1976).

[16] Even if we will not analyse this model, it cannot be ignored among the federal second chambers. In the Austrian model of bicameralism members of the Bundesrat are designated indirectly by the Länder's legislative assembly (Landtage). The nine Länder of Austria are represented proportionally in the Bundesrat, so that the more densely populated Länder have more seats in the Bundesrat.

[17] The members of the Irish Senate are 60, 11 of which appointed by the Prime Minister. The other members are elected: 43 by specific vocational panels and 6 by the graduates of two universities.

[18] The Belgian Senate is composed of 50 Senators designated by the Parliaments of the federated entities and 10 coopted Senators.

[19] The Spanish Senate is composed, mainly of members directly elected by the population and by a residual quota of members appointed within the Legislative Assemblies of the Autonomous Communities.

[20] The National Council has 40 members who are elected by indirect suffrage by interests organisations (representatives of employer, of employees, of farmers, crafts, etc) and by local communities.

This great variety of models represents an element that one needs to consider carefully while addressing the theme of interparliamentary cooperation among second chambers. In fact, this heterogeneity could make the development of cooperation among such chambers more difficult, mainly because no common ground of interests (for example, regional or social ones) shared by these chambers can be found and therefore there are no real grounds for dialogue between them. Therefore, if we were looking for an alliance of second chambers capable of influencing EU policies, we would not find much evidence.

This does not mean, however, that second chambers cannot have a specific weight within the European parliamentary system, as, for example, can be seen in the fact that among the most active chambers in political dialogue with the Commission and in issuing reasoned opinions within the EWS, there are several second chambers.[21] The latter seem to play a fundamental role in tackling both the democratic deficit and the legitimacy deficit of the EU, despite, paradoxically, their being often accused of being non-democratic institutions.

Since second chambers are commonly considered debating institutions, before dealing with their specific role in EU interparliamentary cooperation, their 'controversial' nature has to be highlighted.

A. Second Chambers as Controversial Institutions

The existence of second chambers is a highly debated issue in political and legal theory.[22] The controversial nature of second chambers is even confirmed by the several attempts made at reform of bicameralism recently by different countries within and outside of Europe.[23]

Highlighting the problematic issue of second chambers, some scholars argued that 'many countries choose not to have one, others have them but then do away with them, and still others keep them but are engaged in an apparently incessant dialogue about how they should be reformed'.[24]

Two of the main contested issues are their role and their legitimation.

Regarding the first, whether second chambers are useful institutions or if they are in fact redundant and useless compared to first chambers is a question often asked. This issue encompasses the theme of the functions of second chambers, which is one of the most debated issues in the field.

One of the classical justifications of bicameralism concerns, as is well known, their role as chambers of 'second thought', where bills can be also considered by a wiser legislative assembly.

[21] See Report from the Commission. Annual Report 2013 on Relations between the European Commission and National Parliaments.

[22] J Uhr, 'Bicameralism' in RAW Rhodes, SA Binder and BA Rockman (eds), *The Oxford Handbook of Political Institutions* (Oxford, Oxford University Press, 2008).

[23] For a recent overview of the ongoing reforms of bicameralism, see J Bethge, 'Bicameralism and its Discontents' at: www.verfassungsblog.de, 12 October 2014. Among the countries in which the existence of a second chamber is questioned there are: Canada, Ireland, the UK, Italy and Belgium.

[24] SC Patterson and A Mughan, *Senates, Bicameralism in the contemporary world* (Columbus OH, Ohio State University, 1999) 338.

The second function to be considered is that of the representation of different groups that may be underrepresented or even absent within the first chamber. Second chambers are common in federal systems, where the states/regional interests need to be represented (even if, as it is well known, this relation is not necessary, there being federal states that adopt a unicameral parliament). Second chambers may also represent different social classes, linguistic minorities, or even religious ones.

In other words, what makes second chambers useful is the fact that they can extend the range of actors involved in political decision-making. As it is argued in this chapter, this feature establishes an important role for the second chambers within EU decision-making and within the interparliamentary dialogue, namely the representation of local/regional interests in the EU space.

If the role of second chambers can be considered as a positive added value to cope with the EU democratic disconnect the issue of their legitimacy, on the contrary, presents some obstacles in terms of making second chambers protagonists in the European parliamentary field.

In fact, while first chambers are democratically elected by direct elections, second chambers are often appointed or elected indirectly, and often they over-represent certain sections of society, becoming, paradoxically, a kind of unrepresentative and non-democratic institution.[25]

Given this picture, one can ask: can such debated and controversial assemblies have the same weight as first chambers within the EU democracy? Or should they be assessed in a different way, so that they would be a kind of secondary chamber subordinate to the first one?

B. 'The Dark Side of the Moon'. Second Chambers as a Resource Against the EU Democratic Disconnect

The debate over the EU democratic deficit or its democratic disconnect has been traditionally focused on the two main channels of representation at EU level: the role of the EU parliament and the role of national parliaments in legitimising their respective governments.[26] Therefore, the focus has traditionally been on the study of national parliaments with respect to the national form of government, and on their capacity to control and influence their executives acting at EU level in the Council of Ministers and the European Council.[27] Moreover, because of the prominence of the role of governments in EU decision-making, legal and political scholars have depicted national parliaments as the losers of integration and the victims of a general phenomenon of de-parliamentarisation in the EU space.[28]

[25] M Russell, *The Contemporary House of Lords* (Oxford, Oxford University Press, 2013) 62.

[26] About the possible different interpretations of the relationship between the European Parliament and national parliaments, see N Lupo, 'Parlamento europeo e parlamenti nazionali nella Costituzione "composita" nell'UE: le diverse letture possibili' (2014): www.rivistaaic.it, also in A Ciancio (ed), *Nuove strategie per lo sviluppo democratico e l'integrazione politica in Europa* (Rome, Aracne, 2014) 365–96.

[27] Already in the Treaty of Nice the solution of the democratic deficit has been found in strengthening the powers of national parliaments to direct and control the European policy of their governments, see M Olivetti, 'The Role of National Parliaments' (n 9 above) 476.

[28] For the analysis of the deparliamentarisation thesis, see J O'Brennan and T Raunio, 'Introduction: Deparliamentarization and European integration' in J O'Brennan and T Raunio (eds), *National Parliaments within the Enlarged European Union: From' victims' of integration to competitive actors*? (Abingdon, Routledge, 2007) 1–26.

It is not surprising, therefore, that in this landscape, no particular attention has been paid to the role of second chambers, which are often not even politically linked to their respective governments and are weaker than lower chambers.

However, the perspective changed with the provision of the Treaty of Lisbon and Protocol No 1, which provide for the direct and non-mediated participation of national parliaments in the EU decision-making process.

The mark of such an evolution is the parliamentary control of the EU institutions' compliance with the principle of subsidiarity through the EWS.

It is exactly in this revival of the powers of participation of national parliaments that second chambers, despite their controversial nature, can play a fundamental role in the multilevel parliamentary field, giving voice to particular groups of interests that otherwise would be underrepresented or not represented at all at the EU level.

This is true particularly when second chambers represent local/regional bodies. In this way, in fact, regional governments/legislatures may have a powerful and effective role in influencing the EU decision-making process, tackling the issue of the so-called blindness[29] of EU institutions towards the 'Europe of the regions'. In fact, even if the role of regional governments has been empowered over time, it nevertheless still takes second place to the role of Member States. The strengthening of the role of second chambers could represent the opportunity by which regional/sub-national entities can participate actively in EU affairs, bringing the EU even closer to its citizens.

The German Bundesrat, even if it is a very peculiarly defined second chamber—because of its composition, it is more of a second government[30] than a second legislative chamber—is, however, a good example of a second chamber through which regional governments can participate effectively in the EU political process.

It is not by chance that even in Italy, where, as is well known, the Senate has exactly the same function as the first chamber and is not representative of the regions, the reform proposals are aimed at transforming it into a regional body, with specific tasks regarding the participation of Italy's regions in EU affairs.[31]

Strengthening the role of territorial second chambers would, in other words, contribute to reducing at least part of the democratic disconnect that still affects the EU. As Benz argues,

> as long as we cannot assume that European citizens develop a strong sense of community, horizontal trust and a certain degree of solidarity among their fellow citizens all across Europe, intermediary institutions and processes linking the national demoi are of particular relevance to make democracy work.[32]

[29] S Weatherill, 'The Challenge of the Regional Dimension in the European Union' in S Weatherill and U Bernitz, *The Role of Regions and Sub-National Actors in Europe* (Oxford/Portland OR, Hart Publishing, 2005) 1–31.

[30] See L Violini, *Bundesrat e Camera delle Regioni. Due modelli alternativi a confronto* (Milano, Giuffrè, 1989).

[31] According to the constitutional bill aiming to reform the Italian Senate (AS n° 1429), the second chamber is defined as an institution of connection between the EU and the national state and its sub-national bodies. Moreover it contributes to the decision-making and to the implementation of EU Acts and policies, and evaluates their impact. On this reinforcement of the Senate in EU affairs, see F Clementi, 'Non un Senato "federale" ma un Senato "federatore". Prime note sul disegno di legge di riforma costituzionale del Governo Renzi' (2014): www.federalismi.it. For a more skeptical evaluation of the effectiveness of such provision, see E Catelani, 'Riforme costituzionali: un compromesso in una logica unitaria' (2014): www.osservatoriosullefonti.it.

[32] A Benz, 'Linking Multiple Demoi. Interparliamentary relations in the EU' (2011) *IEV-Online* 11.

It may look like a paradox: institutions whose legitimacy and existence are debated at national level, as mentioned above, can become instruments of democratic legitimation in the EU space. But it is not a contradiction. The role of national parliaments, both unicameral and bicameral, is a fundamental pillar of the future of the EU's democratic legitimacy. As Weiler argued,[33] the reaffirmation of 'the importance, even primacy of the national communities as the deepest source of "legitimacy" of the integration project' will be a decisive moment in the evolution of the EU construct.

III. ON THE TRAIL OF THE ROLE OF SECOND CHAMBERS IN INTERPARLIAMENTARY COOPERATION

Even the studies about interparliamentary dialogue within the EU after the Lisbon Treaty are mainly focused on the concept of 'national parliament', without paying specific attention to the role played by each single chamber in bicameral systems.

In effect, with the exception of the Association of European Senates,[34] which is, however, an informal forum for interaction between EU second chambers, there has not yet been developed an institutionalised interparliamentary dialogue between the second chambers within the EU.

Even looking at the main instrument of formalised interparliamentary dialogue, the Conference of Parliamentary Committees for Union Affairs of Parliaments of the European Union (COSAC), it seems that the bicameral structure of national parliaments is just a nuance of the concept of national parliament, without having a particular emphasis in interparliamentary cooperation. This is clear when examining the rules of procedure of COSAC, which set out that for the composition of the committees, each national parliament will be represented by a maximum of six members of its Committee(s) for Union Affairs and that each parliament will determine the composition of its own delegation.

The possible bicameral structure of a parliament is not even mentioned and the power of determining the composition of national delegations is given to the national parliaments themselves, leaving open the possibility that a second chamber will not be represented within COSAC.

Even the recent Interparliamentary Conference on the Economic and Financial Governance of the European Union, a sort of 'Parliament for the Eurozone',[35] seems to ignore the internal composition of the national parliaments. More precisely, it is composed of delegations from the relevant committees of the national parliaments of the EU Member

[33] JHH Weiler, 'Europe in crisis—on "political messianism", "legitimacy" and the "rule of law"' [2012] *Singapore Journal of Legal Studies* 268.

[34] The Association of European Senates brings together second chambers from European states. It supports the development of relations between its members and promotes the bicameral system in parliamentary democracy. Its goals also include strengthening European identity and fostering an awareness of European ideals. Members of the Association of European Senates are: the Belgian Senate, the House of Peoples of the Parliamentary Assembly of Bosnia-Herzegovina, the Federal Council of Germany (Bundesrat), the Senate of the French Republic, the Italian Senate, the First Chamber of the States General of the Netherlands, the Federal Council of Austria (Bundesrat), the Polish Senate, the Romanian Senate, the Federation Council of the Federal Assembly of the Russian Federation, the Swiss Council of States, the National Council of Slovenia, the Spanish Senate, the Senate of the Czech Republic, and the House of Lords of the United Kingdom.

[35] A Manzella, 'Parlamento europeo e parlamenti nazionali come sistema' (2015), in: www.rivistaaic.it, 12.

States and the European Parliament. Moreover, lacking rules of procedure, there is no clear provision given for the membership: the composition and size of delegations shall be determined by each parliament.[36]

In other words, the participation of bicameral legislatures in interparliamentary cooperation poses still unanswered questions on the composition and size of national parliamentary delegations and on the weight second chambers should have in such delegations because of their structures and powers.

However, despite the lack of a specific role within the formal conference on interparliamentary dialogue and despite their internal weakness compared to the lower chambers, at the EU level, and in particular in the EWS and in the political dialogue with the European Commission, second chambers seem to have gained strength and authority, being among the most active assemblies for the number of opinions and reasoned opinions sent to the EU's institutions.

A. Second Chambers and the Early Warning System. Critical Issues

The commitment of national parliaments to EU affairs is formally prescribed by Protocol No 1 on the role of national parliaments and by Protocol No 2 on the application of the principles of subsidiarity and proportionality.

I will focus, in particular, on the provisions regarding the participation of national parliaments in the EWS, provided, respectively, by Article 3 of Protocol No 1 and Articles 6 and 7 of Protocol No 2.

As is well known, any national parliament or any chamber of a national parliament may, within eight weeks from the date of transmission of a legislative act, send to the presidents of the EU Parliament, the Council, and the Commission a reasoned opinion stating why it considers that the draft in question does not comply with the principle of subsidiarity. For our purposes, it is interesting to underline the distinction that the protocols make between unicameral and bicameral systems. Article 7.1 of Protocol No 2, assigns each national parliament two votes, but in the case of a bicameral parliamentary system, each of the two chambers has one vote.

As argued, this provision led to sub-national bodies participating through second chamber representatives in the control of compliance with the principle of subsidiarity: 'in those systems, therefore, it may be stated that one of the two votes is attributed to protect regional-local interests, even though formally attributed to one of the chambers that in any case are to be considered bodies of the federation'.[37]

This provision, which seems to ensure the democratic control by sub-national entities of EU affairs, nevertheless possesses some problematic issues, concerning those systems, such as in Italy, where the second chamber is not representative of regional bodies. In those cases

[36] See I Cooper, 'Parliamentary oversight of the EU after the crisis: on the creation of the "article 13" interparliamentary conference', 21/2014, *Working Papers Series, Luiss Guido Carli School of Government*. N Lupo, 'La Conferenza interparlamentare sulla governance economica e finanziaria: la deludente attuazione dell'art. 13 del Fiscal Compact' (2014) 1 *Quaderni costituzionali* 113–15.

[37] S Mangiameli and P Colasante, 'Protocol No. 2' in H-J Blanke and S Mangiameli (eds), *The Treaty on European Union* (Heidelberg, Springer, 2013) 1714.

the participation of the latter in the early warning system and the related procedures are left to the determination of the particular Member State, the influence of regional entities being weaker than that provided by the second chamber.

Moreover, the equality of the lower and upper chamber may be problematic. Under the EWS, they are considered as equals, although usually the lower chamber plays a dominant role, being, for example, involved with its government through the the potential vote of no confidence. Even in the legislative process, second chambers usually have a secondary role: with the exception of the Italian Senate, embedded in a symmetric bicameral system and having, therefore, the same powers of the first chamber,

> the Netherlands is the only country that grants its upper chamber an absolute veto in the legislative process in all cases, and even then the upper chamber votes only after the lower chamber has adopted a bill and does not enjoy the power to initiate or amend a bill.[38]

The internal balance and the democratic credentials of second chambers, in other words, can vary a lot from one Member State to another.

Moreover, since there is no provision seeking coordination between the chambers of a bicameral parliament in case of discord between them, the vote of the first chamber weighs less than the chamber of a unicameral parliament. In this way, the first chamber is 'penalized for being trapped inside a bicameral system'.[39]

Probably the fairest solution would be to allow the first chamber 'to cast both votes, irrespective of what the senate does, while reserving one vote for the senate in case it wants to act alone'.[40]

Otherwise, in order to maintain one vote for each chamber, a form of intra-parliamentary cooperation within the two chambers could be prescribed, which should lead to a common position, expressed by the vote assigned to both chambers.

What is certain is that, besides the most problematic issues, second chambers 'enjoy a voice that is completely out of proportion with the voice that they have when legislative competences actually are domestic'.[41] The EWS grants second chambers co-equality with the first chambers in terms of voting weight so that they do not have to fight for it themselves. In this regard there is an emblematic case of a second chamber whose role in the EWS, despite the Treaty provisions, has been reduced by a national decision. The Slovenian National Council (the second chamber of the Slovenian parliament) has very limited functions in EU affairs, mainly consultative.[42] Therefore the Slovenian Constitution, in regulating the participation in EU affairs, does not even mention the National Council, but it only addresses the relations between the government and the first chamber. Moreover, even the Law on Relations between the National Assembly and the Government (LRNAG), amended

[38] Kiiver, *The early warning system* (n 4 above) 65.

[39] ibid.

[40] ibid. A very peculiar (and complex) system has been adopted in Belgium, where the two votes are assigned depending on the legislative competence, respectively of the Federation or of the subnational entities. See T Delreux and F Randour, 'Belgium: Institutional and Administrative Adaptation but Limited Political Interest' in C Hefftler, C Neuhold, O Rozenberg and J Smith (eds), *The Palgrave Handbook of National Parliaments and the European Union* (Basingstoke, Palgrave Macmillan, 2015) 153–69.

[41] Kiiver, *The early warning system* (n 4 above) 65.

[42] See M Romaniello, *Upper Chambers in EU Parliamentary Democracies*, PhD dissertation, courtesy of the Author (2014) 97.

after the entry into force of the Lisbon Treaty, does not consider the role of the National Council in EU affairs. On the basis of this asymmetry in the domestic and European provisions on the National Council's participation in the EU decision-making process, the latter appealed to the Constitutional Court claiming the unconstitutionality of the LRNAG and arguing that the provisions of the Treaty of Lisbon and the annexed Protocols 'gave rise to changes in the domestic organization of parliamentary scrutiny of EU affairs in such a way as to put both houses of parliament on an equal footing'.[43] Moreover the National Council claimed that it already participated to interparliamentary cooperation through the COSAC together with the National Assembly, while its role in the domestic system of parliamentary scrutiny on EU affairs was confined to a marginal and merely consultative one.[44] The Constitutional Court, however, by its decision U-I-17/11, on 18 October 2012, did not strike down the domestic legislation, ruling that the Treaty provisions do not interfere with the domestic organisation in providing for the participation of each chamber inEU affairs, which is a national prerogative.[45]

Even though the Slovenian case shows that the equal consideration of first and second chambers under the Treaty of Lisbon and the annexed Protocols is quite problematic in the light of the domestic legislation, this may however be 'a rather smart design for reasons of both principle and practical effect'.[46]

This seems to be confirmed even by the Commission's statistics on the participation of national parliaments in the EU, which will be addressed in the following section.

B. Second Chambers and the Early Warning System. Facts and Figures

The discrepancy between the role given by the Treaty of Lisbon to second chambers and their weight in the domestic sphere clearly emerges when looking at the statistics on the second chambers' participation in the EWS and in the political dialogues held with the EU Commission.

If one considers the EU Commission's annual reports on the relations with national parliaments from 2010 to 2013[47] it is quite evident that second chambers are particularly active in EU participation, in several cases much more than their respective first chambers. Looking at the number of opinions[48] and reasoned opinions[49] issued each year by second

[43] S Kajnč Lange, 'Slovenian Parliament and EU Affairs: Strong Formal Powers Awaiting Interests and Capacity to Be Used' in Hefftler, Neuhold, Rozenberg and Smith (n 40 above) 654.

[44] ibid.

[45] M Romaniello, *Upper Chambers in EU Parliamentary Democracies* (n 42 above) 97.

[46] Kiiver, *The early warning system* (n 4 above) 65.

[47] Report from the Commission, Annual Report on Relations between the European Commission and National Parliaments, Brussels, COM(2011) 345 final, COM(2012) 375 final, COM(2013) 565 final and COM(2014) 507 final.

[48] Considering the period 2010–13, among the most active chambers in issuing opinions to the Commission there are: the Italian Senate (respectively 71 opinions in 2010, 76 in 2011, 96 in 2012, 36 in 2013), the Czech Senát (respectively 29, 43, 46, 64 opinions), the German Bundesrat (23, 33, 59, 40), the Austrian Bundesrat (13, 7, 12, 9) and the UK House of Lords (12, 16, 16, 18).

[49] The trend of reasoned opinions is significantly different from that of opinions, and is more difficult to evaluate, first of all because the former are much fewer than opinions in general. However even in this case second chambers are often more active than the first chambers. In particular we can mention the German Bundesrat (3 reasoned opinions in 2010, 1 in 2011, 5 in 2012 and 3 in 2013), the Austrian Bundesrat (respectively 2, 1, 3, 6) and the French Senate (3, 1, 7, 4).

chambers, in fact, there is no doubt that they play a prominent role both in the political dialogue and in the EWS.

However, it has been argued that beyond the absolute numbers, the picture is much more complex. Despite being univocal, in fact, the participation of second chambers in EU affairs varies considerably from one bicameral system to another. Scholars[50] have distinguished at least four different situations: second chambers active both in the political dialogue and in the EWS (Germany, Austria, France); second chambers more active in the political dialogue than in the EWS (Italy, Czech Republic, UK); second chambers acting on equal footing with the first chamber (Spain, Ireland, Netherlands, Poland); and second chambers only marginally involved in EU affairs (Slovenia, Belgium). The EU Commission's annual reports on the relations with national parliaments in 2013,[51] seems to confirm the prominent role played by the first and the second group of chambers. With regard to political dialogue, the Senate of the Czech Republic, the German Bundesrat, the Italian Senate, and the UK House of Lords are among the most active chambers, with 64, 40, 36, and 18 opinions issued to the Commission, respectively. These numbers are even more impressive when compared to those related to the first chambers: the Czech Republic Poslanecká sněmovna issued 8 opinions; the German Bundestag, 0; the Italian Chamber of Deputies, 6; and the House of Commons, only 5.

The same trend, even if on a smaller scale, can be observed regarding the subsidiarity control mechanism. Also in this case, in fact, second chambers are particularly reactive: the Austrian Bundesrat issued 6 reasoned opinions (the Nationalrat issued 2); the French Senate, 4 (the Assemblée nationale, 1); the German Bundesrat, 3 (the Bundestag, 0); and the Italian Senate, 2 (the Chamber of Deputies, 0).

Even the data about reasoned opinions issued in 2014 seem to give back a similar picture.[52] Except for the House of Lords and the Dutch Eerste Kamer, which did not submit any reasoned opinion (while the House of Commons submitted 3 and the Twede Kamer, 2), all the other second chambers which issued reasoned opinions have exceeded the related first chambers. The Austrian Bundesrat sent 4 reasoned opinions (the Nationalrat, 1), the French Senate, 3, while the Assemblée nationale, only 1, the German Bundesrat, 1 and the Italian Senate, 2, while the Bundestag and the Chamber of Deputies none; last but not least the Polish and Czech Senate issued 1 reasoned opinion each, while their first chambers did not send any opinions. In few cases (Belgium, Ireland, Romania and Slovenia) neither the first nor the second chamber sent reasoned opinions.

Although the role of second chambers appears to be prominent also in the EWS, the differences between second and first chambers in absolute terms are less evident for reasoned opinions than for opinions in general. It is not so surprising if one looks at the fact that the former are just a small minority compared to the latter, and many chambers do not adopt reasoned opinions at all. Regarding specifically bicameral systems, the reason for the relatively less intense activity of second chambers in issuing reasoned opinions (compared

[50] Romaniello, *Upper Chambers in EU Parliamentary Democracies* (n 42 above) 86.

[51] Report from the Commission. Annual Report 2013 on Relations between the European Commission and National Parliaments, Brussels, 5.8.2014, COM(2014) 507 final.

[52] The synthetic data of 2014 have been inferred from the *State of Play on reasoned opinions and contributions submitted by national Parliaments under Protocol no 2 of the Lisbon Treaty*, Brussels, respectively: 8 January 2014, 29 January 2014, 5 March 2014, 9 April 2014, 9 September 2014, 15 October 2014, 18 November 2014 and 9 December 2014.

to the political dialogue) might be related to problems of coordination. Second chambers 'in federal systems often have to coordinate with regional parliaments, which may lead to problems in terms of the eight-week deadline for reasoned opinions'.[53]

However, what is important to underline here is that in several cases, there is a sort of asymmetry in the commitment of the two branches of legislative power in bicameral systems, second chambers being more reactive even if in the domestic domain they play a marginal role. Despite the fact that the variegated landscape of second chambers prevents the making of any generalisation, as Kiiver argued, 'a "rise of the Senates" is one of the possible phenomena that we may well witness as the EWS becomes more established'.[54]

Considering such a trend, it is interesting to look at the reasons that may lie behind it. These will be addressed in the next section.

C. Second Chambers. A Special 'Vocation' for EU Affairs?

There are different orders of reasons—both common to different parliamentary systems and specific to particular national systems—that may explain the role the second chamber has carved out in EU matters.

The first one deals with the peculiar nature of second chambers, which are generally not involved in a confidence relationship with their respective governments, being for this reason less politically committed, and being chambers of expertise.

Such characteristics can be found in the House of Lords, the German Bundesrat, the French Senate, and the Irish Seanad.

In all these systems, second chambers are formally placed outside the circuit of general political direction, and for this reason, they can act more independently than the lower ones within the EU.

A reason related to the relationship between parliaments and cabinets might be also that

> lower chambers profit from closer contacts to the government both in terms of information as well as in terms of influencing EU policy making in the Council through holding their government to account. For second chambers, the political dialogue seems to be one of the few instruments to make their voice heard at the EU level, especially if no breach of subsidiarity is apparent.[55]

Moreover, second chambers often are chambers of expertise, whose membership is determined by different criteria (for example, expertise and representation of interests) than mere political belonging and loyalty. The peculiar membership of second chambers is a functional element that has transformed them into privileged interlocutors within the EU. This is, for example, the direction the recent Italian Senate's reform has taken. The Bill proposal portrayed a Senate as the chamber that is primarily put in charge of participation in EU law-making and of the creation of links between the supranational level and the regional one.

A second reason is the asymmetry in the functions of second chambers (not always or not all involved in the legislative process, as noted above), which may give them more space

[53] E Mastenbroek et al, 'Evaluating national parliamentary control of EU decision making after the Lisbon Treaty' (2014): www.houseofrepresentatives.nl, p 31.

[54] Kiiver, *The early warning system* (n 4 above) 66.

[55] E Mastenbroek, 'Evaluating national parliamentary control' (n 53 above) 31.

and time to scrutinise EU legislative acts. It seems that while at the national level, the second chamber carries less weight than the first one does, it can gain a fundamental and primary role at the supranational level.

The third order of reasons that may explain the activism of second chambers in the EU is that they have developed a sort of specialisation in such matters, being qualified as chambers of particular expertise. Moreover, even their internal organisation, through the systems of specialised committees, may influence their efficiency.

D. The Role of Parliamentary Committees. Case Studies of the House of Lords and the Italian Senate

A key role in evaluating the activity of national parliaments in the scrutiny of EU legislation is played by the procedural and institutional organisation of each chamber. In particular, it is fundamental to assessing by which parliamentary committees[56] scrutiny processes are undertaken and the depth of their involvement and powers.

In all of the Member States' parliaments, European Union Committees[57] charged with the parliamentary control on EU affairs have been established by constitution or by law, or even by the rules of procedure of the chamber in question. However, as Kiiver[58] pointed out, 'the role, the status, competence and composition of these European Affairs Committees differs greatly from one national parliament to another'. Moreover, even when established, the role of an EU committee may be not exclusive: there are cases of overlapping matters between EU committees and other existing specialised ones. In those cases, the role of the EU committee may differ, depending on the internal rules of procedures of each parliament or chamber.

For Member States with a bicameral system, in most cases there is a European Affairs Committee (EAC) in each chamber, although in a few cases (Ireland and Spain), a joint committee composed of members from both chambers has been established.

Two opposing models of scrutiny of EU acts have been identified regarding the role of the committee:[59] a centralised scrutiny, where all EU-related matters are examined by the EU committee, and a decentralised model, where EU scrutiny activity is shared by the EU committee and the sectoral ones, that can provide specific expertise in the different issues dealt with by the EU.

A second distinction is made by the so-called 'mandate-based system', where parliaments are more interested in influencing the position of their respective governments, and the 'document-based system', where the parliament and its committee are more interested in the detailed examination of EU acts.[60]

[56] For an in-depth analysis of the role of Committees in a comparative perspective, see C Fasone, *Sistemi di Commissioni Parlamentari e Forme di Governo* (Padova, Cedam, 2012).

[57] A well-studied case is that of the EU Committe in Denmark: F Laursen, 'The Role of National Parliamentary Committees in European Scrutiny: Reflections based on the Danish Case' in K Auel and A Benz, *The Europeanisation of Parliamentary Democracy* (London/New York, Routledge, 2013) 110.

[58] P Kiiver, *The National Parliaments in the European Union—A Critical View on EU Constitution Building* (The Hague, Kluwer Law International, 2006) 47.

[59] ibid.

[60] On the different kind of scrutiny see COSAC, *Seventh bi-annual report: Developments in European Union Procedures and Practices* (2007), www.cosac.eu.

Having sketched the main issues of the role of committees in EU scrutiny, I will now focus on the case studies of the House of Lords and the Italian Senate in order to show that committees plays a central function in making these second chambers one of the most active in EU participation.

(i) The EU Committee of the House of Lords

The European Union (EU) Committee was the first committee established in the House of Lords, in 1974.[61] It is a meaningful example of how the role of a committee may be determined by a national chamber's influence on and power over EU affairs. This EU committee is, in fact, considered one of the most influential committees, both nationally and at a European level. At a national level, in particular, the government always considers the EU committee's proposals and recommendations very carefully because of the experience and expertise of committee members. This is due mainly to its internal organisation and to some rules, like the scrutiny reserve, by which UK ministers may not agree to any proposal in the Council of Ministers until the committee has finished its scrutiny.

Also the officials of the European Commission and of other national parliamentary institutions read regularly the Committee's reports.

One of the peculiarities of this EU committee is that it operates through a set of six sub-committees, each focused on one policy field (Economic and Financial Affairs, Agriculture, Fisheries, Environment and Energy, Home Affairs, Health and Education, etc). This system involves about 70 peers supported by 24 specialist staff.[62] After an EU document has been sent by the government to the EU committee, the scrutiny is carried out intensively by the sub-committee with responsibility for the relevant policy area. It is for the sub-committee then to decide how to scrutinise the document. The sub-committees meet on a weekly basis when the house is in session and consider proposals in detail. A substantially similar procedure is carried out for the subsidiarity scrutiny function within the EWS.

The main difference between the EU Committee of the House of Lords and of the House of Commons is that the latter 'puts its energy into filtering all EU policy proposals for their importance, in order to draw these to the attention of the House as necessary'.[63] The Lords Committee, on the other hand, selects a small number of topics for more in-depth scrutiny. As Cygan noticed, 'only a very few proposals of the approximate 1200 deposited in Parliament each year are subject to detailed examination. On average each subcommittee will conduct three inquiries each year/parliamentary session'.[64]

Given also the short term of eight weeks prescribed by the Treaty for the EWS, this efficient organisational structure explains how the House of Lords' expertise on EU affairs and their scrutiny in the EWS is more effective than that of the House of Commons. It is true to the extent that the EU committee represents the most elaborate system of national parliamentary scrutiny of EU legislation in the EU.[65]

[61] See Russel, *The Contemporary House of Lords* (n 25 above) 212.

[62] ibid.

[63] ibid.

[64] A Cygan, 'Scrutiny of EU legislation in the UK Parliament: the first thirty years ... and beyond?' in J O'Brennan and T Raunio (n 28 above).

[65] M Russell, *The Contemporary House of Lords* (n 25 above) 212.

(ii) *The Committee on European Union Policies of the Italian Senate*

The Italian Senate is quite a unique model in the comparative landscape, since it is an example of perfect bicameralism: in other words, the Senate carries out the same functions as the first chamber with no differentiation at all.

Further, the representation of the two chambers, except for the senators for life, is exactly the same: they are elected by the entire population of the nation (even if using different electoral systems and the active and passive electorate is different, being 18–25 years and 25–40 years old, respectively).

Moreover, the Senate is involved in the political circuit by being linked to the executive branch, as in the case of the lower chamber, through the instrument of the vote of confidence. The government has to resign if either the Senate or the Chamber of Deputies refuses to grant it a vote of confidence. This provision also seems quite strange in the comparative landscape. However, despite this uniqueness of the Italian Senate, as has been already mentioned, it is one of the most active chambers in EU scrutiny, much more than the Chamber of Deputies.

For various reasons, I argue that also in this case, the institutional arrangement is fundamental to explaining the success and the activity of this chamber in the EU landscape. Also in the Italian Senate an EU affairs Committee (the 14th Committee) has been established. According to article 23 of the Rules of procedures of the Senate, the committee has a general competence on the scrutiny of the activity and of the acts of the EU. Moreover it maintains the relationship with the European Parliament and with COSAC. However, it is not the only player in EU affairs. At the heart of the control of respect of the principle of subsidiarity, in fact, are the sectoral committees, while the Committee on EU policies can only express an opinion on an analysis carried out by the merit committee. Only in the event that the merit committee is silent, may the committee on EU policies, in default, directly express an opinion to both the government and the EU institutions.[66]

The crucial difference between the procedure adopted by the Senate and the Chamber of Deputies is that the latter reserves subsidiarity scrutiny for the EU affairs committee only, while assigning the sectoral committees the scrutiny of EU documents on all other grounds. This solution, even if it intends to create a coherent design, may be too complex and Byzantine to function effectively.[67]

Moreover even the composition of the 14th Committee of the Senate may favour its particular commitment in EU affairs. All members of the Committee belong to one of the other sectoral Committees of the Senate. This kind of a double membership gives the Committee, at the same time, both a clear sensibility towards EU issues and a qualified expertise in each of the different sectoral fields represented in the other Committees.

As is clear, the Italian Senate model is quite different to that of the House of Lords (and it cannot but be, given the different systems of bicameralism), but they share a common feature: their participation in the EU affairs needs both a high level of EU expertise and of technical expertise. This is the main reason that allows second chambers, often addressed

[66] See N Lupo, 'I Parlamenti nazionali nell'Unione europea e il principio di sussidiarietà: qualche suggestione per la Camera dei deputati' (2014): www.amministrazioneincammino.luiss.it, p 10.

[67] ibid.

as chambers of greater expertise than the lower ones, to represent valid interlocutors of the EU institutions and competitive actors in the EU.[68]

IV. THE MISSING PIECE. INTRA-PARLIAMENTARY COOPERATION IN BICAMERAL SYSTEMS

As seen in the previous sections, even if second chambers are particularly active in participating in EU affairs, interparliamentary cooperation between them needs to be strengthened and developed.

In achieving such a goal, I argue that a preliminary step is necessary: the development of intra-parliamentary cooperation between first and second chambers at a national level. What is meant by intra-parliamentary cooperation is the institutionalised exchange of a range of information, cooperation, and coordination, and even agreement on positions to take on specific EU matters.

In looking for this kind of cooperation in bicameral systems in Europe, it has to be concluded that national parliaments have not yet developed any best practices in this regard,[69] except for those parliaments that have a bicameral committee for EU affairs. Typically, 'it is seen that lower and upper houses have different procedures and role conceptions vis-à-vis the EWS. Also, the understanding of subsidiarity may be different'.[70] Moreover, in such cases as the German one, the cooperation with the second chamber is lower than with the other parliaments in Europe.[71]

Usually each chamber has different procedures, independent powers, and even different conceptions about the role of the chamber in EU decision-making.

There are, nevertheless, few exceptions. In the Netherlands there is soft cooperation between the EACs' staff and at the administrative level for coalition building on EU matters, particularly in cases of lack of agreement regarding the EWS. This kind of technical coordination, however, seems to be quite ineffective.

The most successful example in the field of intra-parliamentary cooperation is Austria. Here the Bundesrat and the Nationalrat share their administrative staff for EU matters, easing the communication between both chambers. But it is, as already mentioned, an extraordinary case in the comparative landscape of bicameral systems.

This general lack of intra-parliamentary cooperation is not a secondary element, because it makes more difficult even the development of interparliamentary cooperation and the emergence of national parliaments as collective subjects of EU integration, despite the Treaty of Lisbon appearing to encourage such developments by the promotion of interparliamentary cooperation.

Definitively, as Lupo sharply observes, the difficulties in inter and intra-parliamentary cooperation testify to the fact that parliaments are by definition complex and articulate institutions, and therefore it is not easy to make them engage in dialogue, particularly if

[68] O'Brennan, Raunio, 'Introduction: Deparliamentarization and European integration'.

[69] Mastenbroek, 'Evaluating national parliamentary control' (n 53 above) 54.

[70] ibid, 31.

[71] ibid, 54.

there are no formal procedures that require a kind of confrontation between the national state interest and the European one.[72]

V. TOWARDS NEW ROUTES FOR THE ROLE OF SECOND CHAMBERS WITHIN THE EU?

If interparliamentary cooperation is a fleeting concept, it is even more elusive if looking exclusively at the role of second chambers.

Second chambers are still debated institutions, whose existence is at stake in many bicameral systems. However, today more than ever, 'processes of collective decision-making need to allow for the political expression of societal differentiation and diversity and bicameralism is a crucial mechanism in this regard'.[73]

This is even truer in the euro-national parliamentary system, where second chambers seem to have emerged as the dynamic interlocutors of EU institutions, showing a commitment to acting outside their national boundaries as 'supplementary watchdogs of national and subnational prerogatives'.[74]

Even if at a national level, they are considered as weaker chambers compared to the lower ones, their role seems to be amplified and strengthened within the EU space. Although the protagonists of interparliamentary cooperation are apparently national parliaments, with no particular attention being paid to second chambers, their role is not to be underestimated. While Europe still suffers from the so-called democratic disconnect, one cannot but look to second chambers as extraordinary resources which allow for the expressing of certain aspects of political pluralism and disagreement and which are able to reflect the complexity of societies that are internally heterogeneous and organised in politically self-governing sub-entities.[75]

It is not by chance that second chambers seem to have developed a particular expertise in EU matters, and, following some recent trends of reforms, are considered as favoured leaders for participation in EU affairs.

Further, the data I have provided regarding the degree of interaction with EU institutions through the political dialogue and the EWS clearly testify to this euro-vocation of second chambers.

Of course there is a great variation among second chambers in the degree of specialisation in EU affairs, in the organisational provisions to manage the scrutiny of EU acts, and in the capacity of influencing their respective governments.

For this reason, I would suggest here the strengthening of EU commitment of second chambers through the development of interparliamentary cooperation between those of them that share the same kind of representation (for example federal/regional/local ones). In order to move in this direction, one can look at the creation of clusters of interest

[72] N Lupo, 'Parlamento europeo e parlamenti nazionali nella costituzione "composita" nell'UE: le diverse letture possibili' (2014): www.rivistaaic.it, p 13.

[73] J von Achenbach, 'Bicameralism and Political Legitimacy' (2014): www.verfassungsblog.de.

[74] Olivetti, 'The Role of National Parliaments' (n 9 above) 517.

[75] See von Achenbach, 'Bicameralism and Political Legitimacy' (n 73 above).

conferences where second chambers with similar interests may hold informal meetings to discuss specific policy issues.[76]

Moreover second chambers have to further develop their expertise in EU affairs, distinguishing their role from that of most politically characterised lower chambers. The key of bicameralism should remain that of differentiation even in the EU legal space, because, both at national and EU level, 'if a second chamber offers nothing different from the first, then it is redundant and every cost incurred in its establishment and maintenance is wasted'.[77]

For all these reasons, second chambers need to find and follow new routes in interparliamentary cooperation in order to make their role as the representatives of plural interests at EU level more visible and strong and in this way to really make Europe an 'ever-closer union'.[78]

[76] More in general on the creation of 'regional clusters cooperation' due to the great variations shown by national parliaments, see Benz, 'Linking Multiple Demoi' (n 32 above) 12. See also Esposito, 'La cooperazione interparlamentare: principi, strumenti e prospettive' (n 3 above) 174; House of Lords, European Union Committee, 'The Role of National Parliaments in the European Union', 9th Report of Session 2013–14: www.parliament.uk, p 39.

[77] J Waldron, 'Bicameralism' (2012), *NYU School of Law, Public Law Research Paper no 12-19*, quoting J Bentham, 'Letter to his fellow citizens of France, on House of Peers and Senate', 1830: www.oll.libertyfund.org.

[78] R Bellamy, '"An Ever Closer Union Among the Peoples of Europe": Republican Intergovernmentalism and *Demoi*cratic Representation within the EU' (2013) 35 *Journal of European Integration* 499.

6

Standing Committees in Interparliamentary Cooperation in the Post-Lisbon Era: Towards the End of the European Affairs Committees' Predominance?

DIANE FROMAGE*

I. STANDING COMMITTEES AT THE CORE OF INTERPARLIAMENTARY COOPERATION

THIS CHAPTER AIMS to analyse the role played by the standing committees of national parliaments in interparliamentary cooperation since the entry into force of the Lisbon Treaty.

Indeed, even if standing committees are now at the centre of the efforts of interparliamentary cooperation, originally they were absent from it; the first forum with such a purpose was the Speakers' Conference created in 1963.[1] However, this original focus on the houses' speakers and not on committees can be explained by the fact that, at the time, only the German Bundesrat had a specific European Community (EC) Affairs Committee.[2] Such an absence of institutional adaptation from the then six EC Member States can largely be explained by three factors.

* I am thankful to the members of the thematic group on Governance, Constitutionalism and Democracy of the Max Weber Programme at the European University Institute for their insightful comments on previous versions of this chapter. I also thank Werner Vandenbruwaene for the useful information he provided on Belgium.

[1] See C Fasone, 'Ruling the (Dis-)Order of Interparliamentary Cooperation? The EU Speakers' Conference', Ch 14 in this volume.

[2] All information regarding the date of creation of European Union Affairs Committees is extracted from the COSAC's website [last updated February 2013]: www.cosac.eu/commissions-des-affaires-europ/.

First, the European integration process was only at its beginning and hence much less advanced and intrusive for the Member States than it is today.

Secondly, provided that the EC was originally conceived as based on a traditional international agreement, the main competence for its management lay with the executives of the Member States, without, in general, any parliamentary agreement or involvement being necessary.[3] As a consequence of the latter, national parliaments had not yet been granted extended rights of control or even information in this field. Hence, not only did European Affairs Committees (EACs) not exist, but neither the other sectoral committees nor the plenary could exercise any control of EU matters either. For instance, at the beginning of the European integration process, the Dutch parliament was mostly informed about the progress of European integration during the debates on annual budgets and the general reports by the ministry of foreign affairs.[4] In contrast, the Luxembourg Chamber of deputies, at the beginning of the 2000s, still did not have any provision, in its rules of procedures, for its involvement in the European Union's and the European Communities' affairs. Its involvement was hence possible through informal procedures.[5] The German Chambers, though, were formally guaranteed some rights to information when the Treaties of Rome were approved in 1957.[6] However, in practice, this information long remained incomplete.

Thirdly, until 1979 the European Parliament was composed of delegations of national parliaments so that the need for the establishment of an EC affairs committee may have appeared less salient.[7] For all these reasons, committees became important in the field of interparliamentary cooperation (only) in the 1980s: when this cooperation was strongly reinforced, it was indeed EC Affairs Committees, and not the speakers, that were granted the most preeminent role.

Nowadays, committees' importance is such that the European Parliament (EP) declared shortly after the entry into force of the Lisbon Treaty that 'The establishment of a systematic political dialogue at committee level on important subjects of common concern is a sine qua non of interparliamentary cooperation'.[8] Nonetheless, as will be underlined in this chapter, the EP may have had a specific type of cooperation in mind, one that would provide its standing committees with inputs from national parliaments rather than one that might allow for an exchange of information and best practices among legislatures placed on an equal footing, as is the case in certain arenas for interparliamentary cooperation today.

Additionally, the question of the role played by parliamentary standing committees in interparliamentary cooperation is further justified by the importance that has formally

[3] On Germany for instance: M Obrecht, *Niedergang der Parlamente? Transnationale Politik im Deutschen Bundestag und der Assemblée nationale* (HAL, 2009) 147.

[4] BJS Hoetjes, 'The Parliament of the Netherlands and the European Union: Early Starter, Slow Mover' in A Maurer and W Wessels (eds), *National Parliaments on their ways to Europe: Losers or Latecomers*? (Baden-Baden, Nomos, 2001) 347.

[5] D Bossaert, 'The Luxembourg Chamber of Deputies: From a Toothless Tiger to a Critical Watchdog?' in A Maurer and W Wessels (eds), *National Parliaments on their ways to Europe: Losers or Latecomers*? (Baden-Baden, Nomos, 2001) 303f.

[6] Art 2, Law for the ratification of these Treaties.

[7] Indeed, it is the introduction of the direct elections to the European Parliament that invited the French chambers to create *Délégations* for EC affairs in 1979. These delegations, however, had very limited powers and remained dependent, up until their mutation into *Commissions* in 2009, on the permanent sectoral committees which, by adopting the *Délégations*' resolution or conclusions proposals, could grant them effect.

[8] European Parliament, *Report on 'Interparliamentary Relations between the European Parliament and National Parliaments under the Treaty of Lisbon' 2010–2011* (2011) 17.

been granted to them in the European integration process: interestingly, whereas the Speakers' Conference is the oldest forum in this field, it is COSAC, established in 1989, that was institutionalised in the Treaty of Amsterdam and can, hence, be considered to be, or to have been at least, the most important forum for interparliamentary cooperation.[9]

Even if in recent years we have seen the emergence of two additional interparliamentary conferences—the Common Foreign and Security Policy (CFSP) Conference in 2012 and the Article 13 Conference[10] in 2013—clearly the most well-known institutionalised forum for interparliamentary cooperation in the European Union (EU) is still COSAC. In fact, although it is not specifically mentioned in the EU Treaties, as it used to be until the Treaty of Lisbon, it is the only forum for interparliamentary cooperation addressed directly in the Treaties.[11] In contrast, the other article devoted to interparliamentary cooperation makes a general reference to the fact that 'The European Parliament and national Parliaments shall together determine the organisation and promotion of effective and regular interparliamentary cooperation within the Union',[12] without any specific mention of committees; this article actually provides a legal basis for the general competence of organisation and coordination of national parliaments, which the European Parliament had already previously attributed to the EU Speakers' Conference.[13] By the same token, article 12 TEU devoted to the role of national parliaments in the EU also refers to interparliamentary cooperation but there is no specific mention of the parliamentary bodies that are deemed to take part in this cooperation either. Arguably, it would not have been possible or desirable for the Treaties to define the forms of interparliamentary cooperation in more detail. First, because this task falls within the institutional autonomy of Member States, and their parliaments, which neither necessarily have the same sectoral division among standing committees nor have even the same number of committees. Secondly, anchoring all details and the personality of the committees or the participating bodies in the Treaties could have immobilised the situation as it was at the time of the negotiations of the Lisbon Treaty by not allowing for later modifications. Finally, the oldest forums for interparliamentary cooperation, that is the Speakers' Conference and COSAC, have functioned with no Treaty basis over several decades, which implies that introducing a reference to committees in the Treaties was not a necessity.

As will be developed further below, the choice to create the two latest interparliamentary conferences on the basis of article 9 and not on that of article 10 has resulted in these new arenas for interparliamentary cooperation enjoying autonomy and in the EACs having lost the exclusive leadership they had enjoyed since 1989, in the framework of interparliamentary conferences at least. There exist too other forums of (formalised) interparliamentary relationships: since 1991, the European Parliament has expressed its will to cooperate with national parliaments' committees and this possibility was institutionalised in the EP

[9] See the contribution by BA Dias Pinheiro, 'The Role of COSAC in the Changing Environment of National Parliaments in the EU: An Identity Crisis?' Ch16 in this volume.

[10] This conference was, eventually, officially named the 'Interparliamentary Conference on Stability, Economic Coordination and Governance in the European Union' by the Speakers' Conference held in Rome in April 2015. The name has been confirmed by the rules of procedure of this conference, eventually adopted in November 2015. However, in this chapter it shall be referred to as the Article 13 Conference, which is its unofficial denomination as the adoption of the rules of procedure of the conference took place after this chapter was finalised.

[11] Art 10, Protocol No 1. Article 10 of Protocol No 1 now simply refers to 'A conference of Parliamentary Committees for Union Affairs' but this is undoubtedly a reference to COSAC. In any event, this change does not have any consequence in practical terms.

[12] Art 9, Protocol No 1.

[13] A Esposito, 'La Cooperazione Interparlamentare. Principi, Strumenti e Prospettive' in A Manzella and N Lupo (eds), *Il sistema parlamentare euro-nazionale* (Torino, Giappichelli, 2014) 142.

rules of procedure in 2010.[14] Some Joint Parliamentary Meetings (JPMs), convened by the European Parliament and the parliament of the country holding the EU Council's presidency were organised in the past as well, although no such meeting has taken place since 2011[15] and Joint Committee Meetings (JCMs), gathering EP committee(s) and the equivalent committees from the national parliaments, are regularly set up (once or twice a year) by the EP and the parliament of the Member State holding the EU Council's presidency. In addition to these possibilities, any committee of the European Parliament may decide to invite the corresponding national parliaments' committees to participate in its workshops, hearings and ordinary meetings. In fact, as will be seen below, this type of interparliamentary cooperation has intensified in recent years. The parliament of the Member State holding the EU Council presidency may additionally decide to organise, alone, interparliamentary meetings in its premises.

Furthermore, the EP's interest in the development of relationships with national parliaments in the post-Lisbon era is also visible in the creation of the steering group on relations with national parliaments in 2009.[16] Some of the recommendations it issued in 2011 in fact concerned the future developments of meetings with national parliaments at committee level.[17] The Lisbon Treaty, in introducing the Early Warning System (EWS) within whose framework national parliaments have to coordinate with each other and send their opinions to the EP, has also established a new avenue for interparliamentary cooperation and, in doing so, has changed the relationship existing between EACs and sectoral committees.

Given the limited role of leader assumed by the Speakers' Conference—that created the new CFSP Interparliamentary Conference and the Article 13 Conference, among others, but eventually did not approve the rules of procedure of the latter despite numerous hesitations in this regard—the major part of the relationships between parliaments can indeed be said to take place at committee level. This notwithstanding, not all types of relationship take place with the same purpose: whereas within interparliamentary conferences and in the framework of the meetings organised by the presidency parliament, national parliaments and the European Parliament are on an equal footing in their debates and exchange of best practices, in the case of the interparliamentary meetings at the initiative of the European Parliament, the purpose is a different one. In that case, the European Parliament seeks input from national parliaments and is consequently not bound in any way. It can use the information provided as it sees fit.

In this context, this chapter argues that the new period which started with the entry into force of the Lisbon Treaty has in fact been characterised by a new balance in the involvement of EACs and sectoral committees in interparliamentary cooperation, in accordance

[14] The EP suggested that the chairmen of Member States' parliaments' sectoral committees should be permanently invited to the corresponding committee meetings in the EP and vice versa. M Larhant, 'La Coopération Interparlementaire dans l'UE. L'heure d'un Nouveau Départ?' (2005) *Notre Europe policy paper* p 8.

[15] Besides, the registration rates of the JPMs declined in the last years in which they were organised. K Gattermann, 'Opportunities, Strategies and Ideologies: The Incentives of European Parliament Political Groups for Inter-Parliamentary Cooperation' (2014) *OPAL Online papers 16/2014*, p 13.

[16] European Parliament, Directorate for relations with national parliaments: www.europarl.europa.eu/webnp/cms/pid/1905.

[17] For instance, the steering group recommended the creation of a comprehensive calendar of activities and noted that 'Overlapping or inappropriate accumulation of interparliamentary meetings should be avoided in the interest of an efficient and mutually successful cooperation with national parliaments'. Steering Group on national parliaments, *Recommendations to the Conference of Presidents* pp 2–3.

with the 'specialisation' currently operating in interparliamentary cooperation in general. This specialisation is visible, for instance, in the 'trend for interparliamentary cooperation to move away from all-embracing conferences debating wide-ranging topics such as "The Future of Europe" towards more specialist meetings at the committee level or even between rapporteurs and spokespersons'.[18] In fact, this mirrors a tendency currently operating within national parliaments. While EACs generally play the central role in carrying out the scrutiny of EU policies[19] and 'serve as the interface between government and parliament',[20] scrutiny of EU affairs in national parliaments might actually be currently 'moving away from a concentration on a few select EU affairs specialists and EACs … to MPs who are experts in certain policy fields and members of sectoral committees'.[21] Changes towards the specification of the forums of interparliamentary cooperation in whose framework EACs are at the edge of being replaced by sectoral committees are in motion, although they are, so far, only beginning. This is because the EACs are only involved within COSAC, which has long been considered an only partially successful experience within the Early Warning System (for some of them at least, as will be underlined in section II.B below), and during their visits to the EP (section II). In contrast, the forums for interparliamentary cooperation involving sectoral committees are blossoming and include the creation of two new sectoral interparliamentary conferences, numerous meetings with the EP, among others (section III). In this context, as will be highlighted in the concluding remarks (section IV), the role played by standing committees in interparliamentary cooperation, and the balance among them, appear to be at a juncture, while the emergence of numerous forums for interparliamentary cooperation at committee level do raise the question of a need for (re)concentration and definition of their goals.

II. EUROPEAN AFFAIRS COMMITTEES' LIMITED ROLE IN INTERPARLIAMENTARY COOPERATION

As I highlighted in the introduction, EACs played a major role in interparliamentary cooperation during the two decades following the creation of COSAC in 1989. Nonetheless, this predominance has been eroded by the creation of two new interparliamentary conferences analysed in section III. The marginalisation of these general committees is further a consequence of the numerous and recurrent criticisms of COSAC (II.A); the introduction of the EWS for the control of the respect of subsidiarity, in whose framework EACs play a major role, has not sufficed to balance this situation as this System is, in fact, of limited effectiveness (II.B). Therefore, EACs appear to be losing ground in this framework (II.C).

[18] C Hefftler and K Gattermann, 'Interparliamentary Cooperation in the European Union: Patterns, Problems and Potential' in C Hefftler et al (eds), *Palgrave Handbook of National Parliaments and the European Union* (Basingstoke, Palgrave Macmillan, 2015) 95.

[19] A Buzogány, 'Learning from the Best? Interparliamentary Networks and the Parliamentary Scrutiny of EU Decision-Making' in B Crum and JE Fossum (eds), *Practices of Inter-Parliamentary Coordination in International Politics: The European Union and beyond* (Colchester, ECPR Press, 2013) 17.

[20] J Pollak, 'Compounded Representation in the EU. No Country for Old Parliaments?' in S Kröger (ed), *Political representation in the European Union. Still democratic in times of crisis?* (Abingdon/New York, Routledge, 2014) 25.

[21] Hefftler and Gattermann (n 18 above) at 98.

A. COSAC as a Flawed Forum for Interparliamentary Cooperation

Since the creation of COSAC in 1989, EACs have had the main and most visible role in interparliamentary cooperation. This may, in fact, have had two-fold effects: on the one hand, it provided a response to the ever closer integration process but, on the other, it might also have provoked changes in the balance among parliamentary committees within parliaments by providing an incentive for the creation of EACs where they did not exist.[22]

Since its foundation, COSAC has, nonetheless, been subject to varied and numerous criticisms and it appears that, more than 25 years after its creation, it still has difficulties in defining—and, in reality, finding—its own role.[23] Indeed, the question of its future and its role has been the subject of regular reflections.[24] The EP itself underlined recently that 'some existing forums of interparliamentary relations are in need of some reflection as to their future [and that] COSAC is the body which can be cited as a notable example in this respect'.[25] This is not the place for a reminder of the reasons usually put forward for these shortcomings—such as, for instance, COSAC's mixed composition of MPs and MEPs who have different institutional positions and agendas—that are inherent to the functioning of COSAC.[26] Rather, this analysis focuses on the different nature of the EACs, which are brought together within COSAC with no consideration of the differences deriving from their composition and their institutional position in their national parliaments, since this may have contributed to the difficulties COSAC is facing.

With regard to their composition, and without aiming here at mirroring the reality of the 28 Member States,[27] some examples will be given that illustrate the existing diversity. The Belgian delegation attending COSAC meetings stems from the Federal Advisory Committee on European Affairs, composed of members of the two Belgian federal assemblies and of MEPs.[28] In contrast, in France, each of the two chambers has and, in fact, must have, its own EAC since the constitutional reform that took place on 4 February 2008.[29] However, these two EACs have a special status that derives from the fact that they are not permanent committees which, in turn, allows their members to be simultaneously members of another (permanent) committee, whereas this 'double hat' is prohibited for the members of the permanent committees.[30] The Romanian EAC is peculiar in that it is common to

[22] See A Cygan, 'COSAC: Birth, Evolution, Failures and Perspectives', Chapter 11 in this volume, on the lack of EACs in some parliaments at the beginning of COSAC.

[23] See on COSAC the chapter by A Cygan, 'COSAC: Birth, Evolution, Failures and Perspectives' (Chapter 11), and the Sixth Part in this volume.

[24] Among others during the VII meeting organised in Copenhagen, 3–4 May 1993, the XV meeting held 15–16 October 1996 in Dublin or in the 21st bi-annual report adopted in June 2014. This is also highlighted by O Costa and M Latek, 'Paradoxes and Limits of Interparliamentary Cooperation in the European Union' (2001) 23 *Journal of European Integration* 139.

[25] European Parliament, *Report on 'Interparliamentary Relations between the European Parliament and National Parliaments under the Treaty of Lisbon' 2009–2014. Annual Report 2013/2014* (April 2014) 20.

[26] These questions are addressed in-depth in the contributions on COSAC contained in this volume.

[27] Such a thorough study is contained in Hefftler and Gattermann (n 18 above) and T Freixes Sanjuán et al (eds), *Constitucionalismo Multinivel y Relaciones entre Parlamentos* (Madrid, Centro de Estudios Políticos y Constitucionales, 2013).

[28] www.senate.be/english/fedadv_en.html.

[29] Constitutional law no 2008-103.

[30] See on the fact that the EACs are not, in fact, committees in the sense of permanent committees: O Dord, 'Vers un Rééquilibrage des Pouvoirs Publics en faveur du Parlement' (2009) *Revue française de Droit constitutionnel* 1 108.

both chambers and its members, contrary to the French case, cannot be simultaneously members of any other parliamentary committee.[31] In the UK House of Commons, the Scrutiny Committee, which participates in COSAC and whose members are permanent, will typically sift the EU documents for political or legal importance whereas the three European Committees, whose members are nominated on an ad hoc basis depending on the subject-matter, will examine the content of the proposals.[32]

A similar diversity exists in terms of the role EACs assume within their parliaments. For instance, the Belgian Federal Advisory Committee on European Affairs normally witnesses the 'debates on high politics issues … whereas debates on the day-to-day issues are conducted in the sectoral committees', where the issues of high politics are of the kind dealt with at European Council level whereas those of low politics are of the kind discussed at EU Council level.[33] On the other hand, although the status of the French EACs has been enhanced following the entry into force of the Lisbon Treaty, it is still secondary. In the National assembly, the EAC is in a better position than in the Senate[34] since its resolutions can now be approved tacitly if the sectoral committee does not examine it within a limited time period of one month.[35] By contrast, in the Senate, the EAC is only competent to examine a legislative proposal if the sectoral committee competent in the policy area affected does not decide to do so, thus being in a rather weak position.[36] The same applies to the EAC of the German Bundestag which, in fact, examines EU legislative proposals in very rare cases.[37] In Spain, the exact opposite is the rule, given the almost complete predominance of the Joint Committee on EU affairs in this area.[38] In Estonia too the EAC 'plays a pivotal role in the coordination of parliamentary work on EU affairs'.[39] The same goes for Denmark, where the sectoral committees have to go through the EAC to be able to mandate the government, as the EAC centralises all initiatives in this sense and where, hence, there is a 'centralization of EU affairs within the EAC, with a less significant role than other parliamentary bodies such as the plenary and sectoral committees',[40] although now sectoral committees have to deliver an opinion on a legislative proposal, a Green Paper or a White Paper if so required by the EAC and, in practice, their involvement in EU affairs varies.[41]

[31] J Freixes Montes, 'Rumanía' in Freixes Sanjuán et al (n 27 above) 770.

[32] House of Commons, *The European Scrutiny System in the House of Commons* (2015) 6, 11.

[33] T Delreux and F Randour, 'Belgium: Institutional and Administrative Adaptation but Limited Political Interest' in C Hefftler et al (eds), *The Palgrave Handbook on National Parliaments and the European Union* (Basingstoke, Palgrave Macmillan, 2015) 155.

[34] In the general scrutiny of EU affairs. This is different in the framework of the participation of the Senate in the EWS.

[35] Art 151-6 rules of procedure of the National Assembly.

[36] Art 73 fifth rules of procedure of the Senate.

[37] O Höing, 'With a Little Help of the Constitutional Court: The Bundestag on Its Way to an Active Policy Shaper' in Hefftler et al (n 18 above) 195.

[38] Law 24/2009.

[39] P Ehin, 'The Estonian Parliament and EU Affairs: A Watchdog That Does Not Bark?' in Hefftler et al (n 18 above) 517.

[40] M Buskjoer Christensen, 'The Danish Folketing and EU Affairs: Is the Danish Model of Parliamentary Scrutiny Still Best Practice?' in Hefftler et al (eds), *The Palgrave Handbook on National Parliaments and the European Union* (Basingstoke, Palgrave Macmillan, 2015) 277.

[41] ibid, 278.

Though this analysis does not represent the reality in all Member States, it is certainly the case from the examples given that COSAC, in spite of treating all EACs strictly identically, in fact brings together parliamentary committees which are very dissimilar. This may actually account, at least partially, for the many difficulties COSAC has been facing since its creation.

B. European Affairs Committees as the Main Actors of an Only Partially Effective Means of Cooperation, the Early Warning Mechanism

Since the entry into force of the Lisbon Treaty in December 2009, the EWS has represented a new avenue for interparliamentary cooperation. Indeed,

> National Parliaments [are called to] contribute actively to the good functioning of the Union … by seeing to it that the principle of subsidiarity is respected in accordance with the procedures provided for in the Protocol on the application of the principles of subsidiarity and proportionality.

Protocol 2 on the application of the principles of subsidiarity and proportionality defines how this control should be carried out and establishes, accordingly, the features of the EWS. While this chapter does not aim at analysing the role played by national parliaments as 'guardians of subsidiarity', which has attracted scholars' attention widely,[42] it remains that the thresholds needed for the activation of this System—at least one third of the total number of votes allocated to national parliaments—require national parliaments to cooperate, or at least to inform each other of their intentions. In a vertical dimension, given the fact that article 6 Protocol no 2 foresees that

> Any national Parliament or any chamber of a national Parliament may, within eight weeks from the date of transmission of a draft legislative act, in the official languages of the Union, send to the Presidents of *the European Parliament*, the Council and the Commission a reasoned opinion stating why it considers that the draft in question does not comply with the principle of subsidiarity (emphasis added),

there is room for the development of interparliamentary cooperation in a vertical dynamic too.

In this context, Member States' parliaments have made diverging choices as to which of their committees—with the involvement of other committees and of the plenary or not—shall adopt reasoned opinions and as to how they exchange information with other (national) parliaments. An analysis of the 41 chambers existing to date in the 28 Member States[43] reveals that the plenary is involved in a minority of cases and such an involvement is possible in an even smaller number of them.[44] This is the case in the European Parliament too where the procedure designed to treat the reasoned opinions received does not foresee

[42] See Ch 9 by M Goldoni in this volume and, among many others, P Kiiver, *The Early Warning System for the Principle of Subsidiarity: Constitutional Theory and Empirical Reality* (Abingdon, Routledge, 2012); T Raunio, 'Destined for Irrelevance? Subsidiarity Control by National Parliaments' (2010) *Real Instituto Elcano Working Paper 36/2010.*

[43] This analysis is based on the relevant information contained on the website of the European Parliament directorate for relations with national parliaments: (www.europarl.europa.eu/webnp/webdav/site/myjahiasite/shared/Publications/subsidiarity%20procedures/Table%20internal%20procedures%20for%20subsidiarity%20check%2008.04.13.pdf), on the COSAC website (www.cosac.eu/country-specific-subsidiarity/) and on the platform for EU interparliamentary exchange (IPEX) website (www.ipex.eu/IPEXL-WEB/parliaments/neparliaments.do).

[44] The plenary is always involved in 16 of the 41 chambers whereas this is a possibility in 12 of the 41 chambers.

any involvement of the plenary and where a certain centralisation in the Committee on legal affairs, which can also submit recommendations on this matter to the sectoral committees during the legislative procedure, is visible.[45] When national parliaments transmit reasoned opinions to the EP, these are first examined by the Committee on Legal Affairs and then forwarded to the committees responsible for the affected policy area.[46] Hence, the interparliamentary cooperation established in the framework of the EWS is rather taking place among committees.

In this framework as well, EACs play a major role since they are involved in all but three chambers,[47] and in a large majority of them[48] bear (or can bear) the main responsibility for the preparation of the reasoned opinions. In contrast, in eight cases they are simply involved and do not have the main responsibility. This classification provides an overview of the main tendencies. However, some systems have specificities that make the definition of the role of each type of committee—EACs and sectoral committees—uneasy. For instance, in the French chambers, the EACs draft the reasoned opinions that are forwarded to the responsible sectoral committee for discussion and potential adoption. However, if this sectoral committee does not examine the proposal within a defined timeframe, the opinion previously adopted by the EAC automatically becomes the opinion of the House (unless a vote in plenary is requested). Hence, the EAC formally has only a secondary responsibility but, in practice, can be the main organ responsible for the adoption of a reasoned opinion. In the Italian Senate too the role played by the EAC is peculiar. The EAC will examine the respect of the principle of subsidiarity, transmit its assessment to the competent standing committee(s) and if it (or they) do not adopt any resolution within 15 days, the EAC may request that its resolution be transmitted to the EU institutions.

As regards the sectoral committees on the other hand, their participation is much more limited: they hold the main responsibility in subsidiarity matters in 11 cases and are involved in nine further chambers.

It can therefore be said that the introduction of the EWS has reinforced the EACs' role in interparliamentary cooperation and that sectoral committees only play a marginal role by participating in the procedure in only half of the Chambers. Such an outcome is, however, not surprising given the composition of most EACs. As has been highlighted in the French case, but this is also true of Estonia for instance,[49] EACs may in fact be the only committees bringing together MPs from different sectoral committees. Besides, the characteristics of the EWS require national parliaments to be able to act seamlessly and on proposals affecting all policy areas. By bringing together members of different sectoral committees, EACs secure expertise in many different domains and familiarity with EU affairs; both elements are particularly needed in order to succeed in approving a reasoned opinion in the short period of eight weeks provided for this purpose by the European Treaties.

This positive note should, however, be qualified in the perspective of the role played by EACs in interparliamentary cooperation in the EU. The EWS has only been activated twice

[45] Art 42-2 rules of procedure.

[46] Art 42-3 rules of procedure.

[47] The EAC is not involved in the Dutch House of Representatives, in the Dutch Senate and in the Luxembourg Chamber of Deputies.

[48] 30.

[49] Ehin (n 39 above) at 517.

since the entry into force of the Lisbon Treaty[50] and critiques of its efficiency and proposals for reforms have been numerous and recurrent.[51] Thus, even if EACs do play a major role in this framework, their potential influence in the field of EU affairs through this means is rather limited.

C. European Affairs Committees Losing Ground in Interparliamentary Cooperation

The preceding analysis has examined the frameworks for interparliamentary cooperation in which the EACs play a major role and it has shown that, in fact, on the one hand, EACs cooperate in forums devoid of a demonstrated efficiency—this is particularly true of the EWS and less so of COSAC—and that, on the other hand, this deficiency may actually be due to the numerous differences existing among EACs. EACs are treated as identical parliamentary bodies, whereas their composition and their institutional position are varied. If for instance the various understandings parliaments have with regard to the aim or the desired form interparliamentary cooperation should take are also taken into account, it results that COSAC especially is unlikely to ever become an effective forum for any form of cooperation going beyond the exchange of information and best practices.

Additionally, this situation is challenged by the blossoming of other, more specialised, forums of interparliamentary cooperation.

III. THE BLOSSOMING OF THE FORUMS OF INTERPARLIAMENTARY COOPERATION AMONG SECTORAL COMMITTEES AS AN ADDITIONAL THREAT TO EUROPEAN AFFAIRS COMMITTEES

The multiplication of the forums for interparliamentary cooperation taking place at committee level results first of all from the creation of two new sectoral conferences (A). Additionally, the presidency parliament also organises interparliamentary meetings among sectoral committees (B), while meetings between the EP and NPs have intensified at committee level (C), so that the erosion of the EACs' predominance in interparliamentary cooperation is visible (D).

A. European Affairs Committees' Importance Eroded by Other Interparliamentary Conferences

The creation of the two new interparliamentary conferences—CFSP and Article 13 Conferences[52]—in 2012 and 2013 has challenged the privileged position EACs had enjoyed

[50] The first yellow card concerned the 'Monti II' proposal (COM(2012) 130) while the second was issued regarding the proposal for the establishment of the European Public Prosecutor's Office (COM(2013) 534 final).

[51] The latest attempt in this sense being the establishment of a working group on improving the 'yellow card' procedure led by Polish Sejm whose aim it is to reflect on this question. For more information: oide.sejm.gov.pl/oide/en/index.php?option=com_content&view=article&id=14900&Itemid=946.

[52] See on these Conferences respectively the contributions by J Wouters and K Raube, 'The Interparliamentary Conference on Common Foreign and Security Policy: A Quest for Democratic Accountability in EU Security Governance', and by I Cooper, 'The Interparliamentary Conference on Stability, Economic Coordination and Governance in the European Union (the 'Article 13 Conference')', Chapters 12 and 13, respectively, in this volume.

so far in the efforts of interparliamentary cooperation. COSAC is no longer the only forum with such a purpose, its general focus is now challenged by more specialised arenas, and this can lead it to an 'identity crisis'. Although the two new conferences are still in a consolidation phase and are far from being exempt from any flaw, they have the potential to further marginalise EACs in daily interparliamentary cooperation in the future. This is all the more true as other forums for interparliamentary cooperation in the framework of EUROPOL and EUROJUST could be put into place soon,[53] and other similar arrangements could follow in other policy areas.

On the other hand, so far, this potential of marginalisation of EACs is only virtual because the revised rules of procedure of the CFSP Conference were, for instance, only adopted in April 2015 and, most importantly, because the Article 13 Conference only adopted its rules in November 2015: even the size of the participating delegations could not be agreed on by the EP and national parliaments. Further to these questions related to the functioning of the conferences, the issue of their lack of permanent secretariat should be highlighted. The Member State holding the Council presidency is in charge of the organization of the meeting taking place during this half of the year, and of the good functioning of the secretariat of the conference in cooperation with the Member State assuming the preceding and the next presidencies, as used to be the case for COSAC until it was awarded a permanent administrative structure.

The Article 13 Conference also suffers from the competition existing between the EP and national parliaments, visible in the EP's will to host systematically one of the two annual Conferences for example.

Additionally, the very legal basis chosen for the introduction of these conferences has led to a (cognizant?) marginalization of COSAC and, thereby, of EACs. This derives from the fact that Protocol No. 1 annexed to the Treaties entails two dispositions which could have served as a basis for the creation of the two new interparliamentary conferences: articles 9 and 10. The choice to create the new interparliamentary conferences on the basis of article 10 Protocol No. 1,[54] that is below the umbrella of COSAC, could have led to the indirect reinforcement of the role assumed by the EACs of each Chamber since even if EACs had been excluded from the actual conferences, they would still have been supervising the activities of the two other interparliamentary conferences. In contrast, the main consequence of the preference finally given to article 9 has been that that the EP may be granted a more important role than national parliaments within these two sector-specific conferences and, even more important for the present analysis, that EACs have been fully excluded from this framework.

However, in spite of these flaws, both sectoral interparliamentary conferences are particularly needed. Recent developments at the borders of the EU and the abolition of the Western European Union parliamentary assembly make the reinforcement of the CFSP

[53] Cooperation already takes places on an irregular basis and the French National assembly and Senate insisted on the need to put in place arrangements for the democratic accountability of EUROPOL and EUROJUST. European Parliament, see n 25 above, at 19 and COSAC, *20th Bi-Annual Report* (October 2013) 21.

[54] As Article 10 provides that 'A conference of Parliamentary Committees for Union Affairs may submit any contribution it deems appropriate for the attention of the European Parliament, the Council and the Commission ... It may also organise interparliamentary conferences on specific topics, in particular to debate matters of common foreign and security policy, including common security and defence policy'.

Conference particularly pressing. Besides, since the adoption of the Eurocrisis law—in whose framework the responsible standing committees have become more and more involved in the scrutiny of EU affairs –, it is desirable that the Article 13 Conference replaces COSAC in whose framework attempts to exchange information and best practices in this policy area originally took place.[55]

All in all, given the state of the current efforts to set up the CFSP Conference and the Article 13 Conference—which bring sectoral committees together –, they do not (yet) seem to be a serious threat to the predominance of EACs that has existed since 1989 in this field, but they are likely to become one in the future when they manage to function effectively. However, the mere existence of these two conferences, and the fact that the EU Speakers' Conference was not confirmed in its role of leader, as it eventually did not approve the Article 13 conference's rules of procedure, indicates that sectoral committees are likely to become key actors in the efforts for more interparliamentary cooperation. The mandate of the two sectoral conferences is much better defined than that of COSAC and they affect areas—foreign and security policy and economic policy—closely bound to national sovereignty whereas COSAC treats of EU affairs in general.

B. Committees in the Meetings Organised on Member States' Initiative

It is usual for the parliament holding the EU Council rotating presidency to organise alone, i.e. without the European Parliament, interparliamentary meetings at committee level in its capital. Although the EP does not co-organise, MEPs do participate in these forums. In fact, some presidencies, such as for example Ireland in 2013 and Italy in 2014, even created websites dedicated to the parliamentary dimension, showing its importance.

With the creation of the CFSP Conference, the usual meeting of the chairpersons of the foreign affairs and defence committees has now been abandoned, but other meetings still continue to take place with the involvement of different sectoral committees. A recent tendency towards the reduction of this kind of interparliamentary cooperation seems to be emerging though: while previous presidencies had organised five to six such meetings at committee level (for example Spain in 2010, Poland in 2011, Ireland and Lithuania in 2013), in 2014 and in 2015 the Greek, the Italian and the Latvian presidencies have limited their number to three.[56] The creation of the two new interparliamentary conferences, together with the introduction of the European Parliamentary Week by the EP in 2013, may explain these developments which, therefore, must not necessarily be seen negatively. In fact, the reduction of the number of meetings organised by the presidency parliament could also be interpreted as a consequence of the growing number of ICMs convened by the EP, shown in the following paragraph.

The identity of the organising standing committees varies depending on the priorities of the presidency in question. For instance, the Latvian parliament brought together the standing committees on employment and economic and digital affairs whereas the Italian

[55] For instance, its 18th bi-annual report addressed the issue of 'the Treaty on Stability, Coordination and Governance in the Economic and Monetary Union and the role of Parliaments' whereas its 19th bi-annual report gathered information on the European Semester 2013.

[56] Information extracted from the presidencies' websites.

one favoured fundamental rights, agriculture and small and medium-sized enterprises, and employment, research and innovation. This variety in the topics addressed certainly makes EU affairs more salient and interesting for individual MPs, especially for those of the presidency parliament, hence participating in the reduction of the European democratic deficit and bringing the EU closer to its citizens. In daily parliamentary business, EU affairs have little attraction for MPs and many still prefer to focus on their primary parliamentary functions at the national level. On the other hand, at the same time this political choice is made at the expense of the potential participation of all national parliaments: on certain topics, some national parliaments may simply decide not to attend the meetings because they do not feel concerned or because it is not an issue for their Member States (and their constituencies). Thereby the potential remedy to the European democratic deficit may be more limited.

Moreover, note that, obviously, the parliament of the Member State holding the EU Council presidency does not have the monopoly of the organisation of interparliamentary meetings at committee level: the other 27 Member States may also take the initiative as, for instance, the Dutch Tweede Kamer did in January 2015.[57] In this framework, the variety of the meetings organised but, and most importantly, the lack of transparency existing around this informal interparliamentary cooperation make it impossible to identify definite patterns regarding the identity of the participating standing committees. However, observe that some of these meetings are organised with regularity in preparation for COSAC, and hence bring EACs together, whereas others, taking place on an ad hoc basis, may bring together members of the EACs and/or of the standing committees affected by the discussed topic, as it was the case during the interparliamentary meeting organised by the French National Assembly on 17 September 2014.[58]

Furthermore, there exist other formalised forms of cooperation among a more reduced number of Member States, such as for example the Visegrád group, so that, in the end, parliaments and their committees are highly solicited. As a consequence, and given the always more pressing necessity to use resources effectively, a reduction of the meetings organised by the parliament of the Member State holding the EU Council presidency may, in fact, appear to be a positive development. This is so also because standing committees are, and should be, first and foremost national parliamentary organs. Given the importance the European integration process has now gained for the daily parliamentary tasks of control of the executive and approval of national legislation, and bearing in mind the lack of interest MPs had long shown for EU affairs, their growing participation in the existing forums for interparliamentary cooperation is in fact welcome indeed. But their primary task remains in their capital, for now at least, since the European Union is still an association of sovereign states.

[57] This interparliamentary meeting was organised in order to debate 'Selecting dossiers from the annual work programme' and 'Improving the yellow card procedure' (*Background paper* by R Leegte, Tweede Kamer der Staten-Generaal) and the EAC Chair of the British House of Lords requested that the 'green card' should be included on the agenda too. *Discussion paper* prepared by Lord Boswell of Aynho, Chairperson of the House of Lords EU Select Committee, 19 January 2015.

[58] Transcription of the meeting organised at the initiative of an MP member of the EAC and of the standing committee concerned by the legislative proposal discussed, that of the European Public Prosecutor's Office: www.assemblee-nationale.fr/14/europe/c-rendus/c0154.asp#P16_377. See, further on this question of the informal interparliamentary cooperation: D Fromage, 'Increasing Interparliamentary cooperation in the EU: Current Trends and Challenges' (forthcoming) *European Public Law*.

C. Committees in the Bilateral Relationships with the European Parliament

As mentioned in the introduction, interparliamentary cooperation takes place in a vertical dynamic with the EP too. In this framework, committees develop bilateral relationships with the European legislature, either collectively when they are jointly invited to Brussels, or individually when they either attend EP committee sessions or visit the EP. As remarked by K Neunreither, these forums offer far more possibilities than COSAC meetings organised only twice a year with the participation of six MPs per Member State.[59]

The EP regularly hosts, at the initiative of one or more of its committees, Interparliamentary Committee Meetings (ICMs). In contrast, the number of parliamentary and committee meetings organised jointly by the EP and the parliament of the Member State holding the EU Council's presidency (Joint Parliamentary Meetings (JPMs) and Joint Committee Meetings (JCMs) respectively) has been decreasing. No JPM has been held since 2012, but this might be explained by the fact that, according to the EP, 'they have limited direct impact on the on-going parliamentary activity and are suited for more general discussions'; in fact, they were introduced after the Constitutional Treaty was rejected to 'invigorate the debate on European integration'.[60]

On the contrary, the number of ICMs—which are the responsibility of the EP alone—has been growing steadily, which could account for a demand by MPs and MEPs for more frequent exchanges among specialists.[61] This form of interparliamentary cooperation does, in fact, grant a major, and growing, role to sectoral committees; in 2012, 10 meetings were organised[62] whereas there were 17 in 2013.[63] An analysis of the identity of the organising committees reveals that two committees, the Foreign Affairs Committee and the Civil Liberties, Justice and Home Affairs Committee, currently tend to organise more ICMs than the other EP committees but, in general, most committees occasionally take such an initiative. A few of them, such as for instance the Internal Market and Consumer Protection Committee or the Fisheries Committee, do not usually hold ICMs though.[64] These meetings are now planned further in advance and, hence, advertised with more anticipation: 'The whole process of prior consideration and validation of planned ICMs aims at better coordination of interparliamentary activities and the avoidance of overlaps. To this end, this calendar includes as well the interparliamentary activities of the presidency Parliament'.[65] Still, there appears to be some need for reflection as to their format and purpose,[66] and it will be necessary to observe how this tendency evolves, particularly after the latest EP elections held in 2014.

In any case, the ongoing trend speaks in favour of the reinforcement of sectoral committees—although this affects only some of them, both at national and at European

[59] K Neunreither, 'The European Parliament and National Parliaments: Conflict or Cooperation?' (2005) 11 *Journal of Legislative Studies* 471.

[60] European Parliament (n 25 above) at 19–20.

[61] Hefftler and Gattermann (n 18 above) at 98.

[62] European Parliament, *Report on 'Interparliamentary Relations between the European Parliament and National Parliaments under the Treaty of Lisbon' 2012* (2012) 9.

[63] European Parliament (n 25 above) at 13.

[64] Information extracted from the agendas and reports available on the EP directorate for the relations with national parliaments' website.

[65] European Parliament (n 25 above) at 21.

[66] ibid, 21.

level—and not of EACs. It also corresponds to a thirst for more effective and specialised exchanges which will allow the committees of the EP to collect the opinions represented by their national counterparts. As mentioned in the introduction, while this development can be considered positive in the sense that it eventually leads to an end of the rivalry that had long existed between EP and national parliaments, and allows MEPs to adopt legislation that corresponds to the true needs of EU citizens, still national parliaments are in weak position. The participating national committees have no guarantee of seeing their opinion taken on board and they have to bear the cost of these visits, without even being sure that numerous MEPs will participate. It has been the case in the past that MPs travelled to Brussels to participate in a committee meeting with only very few MEPs! The question of the interest of individual MEPs is a real issue here, in their willingness both to participate in ICMs and to organise them. In fact, in 2014, 32 of the 37 chambers that responded considered that there was a need for improvement with respect to the meetings organised in the EP's premises.[67] The main issues identified by national parliaments related to the duration of their intervention, the content, the duration of the meetings and the choice of keynote speakers.

National parliaments and the EP also cooperate in another forum: national parliaments' delegations regularly visit the EP. Unfortunately the corresponding data are only available in a minority of cases.[68] However, this form of interparliamentary cooperation seems to be highly appreciated by parliamentarians, as their reduced format and limited requirements in terms of organisation allow for both a deeper dialogue and more flexibility.[69] In 2012, 42 visits were organised among which 13 originated from EACs while the others involved other committees, speakers, officials as well as other kinds of participants.[70] In 2013, similar proportions remained.[71] Given the fact that only just over half of the organised visits are in fact visits by parliamentary committees, there seems to be a fair share of them between the EACs and the sectoral committees. It should however be noted that this format of interparliamentary cooperation presents the limitation of including only a few parliamentary chambers—19 in 2013.[72] The EP notes in this sense that

> This is all the more surprising since in this type of meeting national Parliamentarians have the opportunity to set their own agenda and conduct discussions with key players in the European Parliament over matters which are of interest to them.

The absence of participation of the other Chambers could be explained by budgetary constraints or perhaps even more so by a lack of parliamentary interest, given the fact that the possibility to hold video-conferences exists and that it would therefore be possible to organise bilateral meetings at least at reduced costs.[73] In sum, this may also be the consequence of the EP's attitude towards national parliaments in general as is particularly illustrated in

[67] COSAC, *21st Bi-annual Report* (June 2014) 24.

[68] The European Parliament started producing reports on its relationship with national parliaments in 2010 and only the two latest reports contain detailed information on this topic.

[69] European Parliament (n 8 above) at 12–13.

[70] European Parliament (n 62 above) at 18–19.

[71] European Parliament (n 25 above) at 28–29.

[72] ibid, 14.

[73] So far, only the EP and the German Bundestag have the technical equipment to support meetings with numerous channels.

the context of the interparliamentary conferences where it generally seeks to dominate and wants to be reserved a special preponderant position.

These issues notwithstanding, interparliamentary cooperation at committee level with the EP seems to be a popular tool with actually a growing number of ICMs, and hence growing exchanges with sectoral committees and a move towards a more democratic Union, during the last legislature (2009–14).

D. Towards the End of the European Affairs Committees' Predominance

The preceding analysis of the current state of play in these three fields of interparliamentary cooperation hence seems to indicate that none of them is yet fully threatening the predominance of the EACs, although there is a clear tendency to move in this direction. As will be developed in the concluding remarks, these tendencies may actually be the expression of different needs and purposes of interparliamentary cooperation.

IV. CONCLUDING REMARKS

This chapter has clearly highlighted the predominance of parliamentary committees in attempts for more interparliamentary cooperation.

The preceding analysis has shown that EACs, though having been at the centre of the efforts for interparliamentary cooperation over several decades, are in fact, currently, losing ground in this field, and this holds notwithstanding the fact that they assume the main role in the implementation of the newly introduced EWS. As mentioned in section II of this chapter, the different nature and role assumed by EACs in general makes it unlikely that COSAC will ever become an effective forum for interparliamentary cooperation. Arguably, EACs do play a central role in the framework of the EWS but the potential of this system is in itself rather limited. In addition to these issues, sector-specific committees are gaining ground in this field through the creation of two new interparliamentary conferences from whose framework EACs are strictly excluded. Sector-specific committees additionally meet within the framework of the numerous meetings organised by the presidency parliament and, most importantly, by the EP. Although the EACs' predominance in this field is not yet fully ended, it is seriously threatened by these recent trends.

The framework for the exchanges at committee level is therefore an ever evolving one, influenced, for instance (but not solely), by the priorities of each parliament when its Member State holds the rotating presidency; other factors may also play a role.

First, the need for the organisation of large parliamentary debates which had motivated the creation of JPMs after the Constitutional Treaty failed to be adopted may explain why, as this need disappeared, these meetings stopped being organised too.

Secondly, the tendency towards the organisation of more formalised meetings in the framework of interparliamentary conferences may account for the reduction of the number of meetings organised by the presidency of the Member State holding the EU Council presidency. Their co-existence with other interparliamentary meetings organised at committee level by other Member States on an ad hoc and informal basis may also explain this decrease.

Thirdly, while the profile of the organised meetings is still varying, there are fewer joint initiatives between the EP and the national parliament of the Member State holding the EU Council presidency. Initiatives for ICMs and for bilateral parliamentary visits to the EP are flourishing, and very much liked, whereas JCMs and JPMs are decreasing or even disappearing for the latter. Obviously this tendency can be explained by organisational factors: given the fact that these joint meetings are co-chaired by the EP and the parliament of the country holding the EU Council presidency, they necessarily require demanding coordination and logistic efforts for the two organising bodies, whereas both of them do not really have the need to go through this procedure given the possibility they have to organise meetings on their own. These practical aspects notwithstanding, this thirst for independence shown by the national and the European legislatures may also be an expression of their conflict of interests in this field. Even if, arguably, dissension exists among Member States too, the European Parliament seems to be reluctant to cooperate in the areas in which its own institutional position is not secured by the Treaties as is, for instance, the case in the economic and the CFSP areas.[74]

As regards the distribution of competence among the different committees (EACs vs sectoral committees), the developing tendency towards a tighter implication of sectoral committees and the emergence of two new interparliamentary conferences is leading to the EACs becoming less important in this field. This tendency does not, nevertheless, necessarily imply that EACs will cease to exist. Rather, as is logical, both EACs and sectoral committees may actively—and, to a certain extent, equally—become involved in interparliamentary cooperation, only in different arenas and with different purposes. Whereas the creation of two specialised interparliamentary conferences, when and if they become fully functional, may in fact deepen COSAC's 'identity crisis', the division of responsibilities between EACs and sectoral committees in other fields makes some sense. EACs would then continue to deal with the issues of subsidiarity, which have an impact on many policy areas, and with other general European questions, while sectoral committees would engage with the EP and try to exercise political influence in specific policy areas within the framework of the ICMs and sectoral interparliamentary conferences, and of the meetings organised by the presidency parliament. Such a move would contribute to a reduction in the democratic gap between the EU and its citizens. In fact, such an evolution is desirable, as it could lead to national parliaments collectively holding to account, or, at least, hearing the corresponding European executive organs. A possibility in this sense would be for national parliaments to become inspired by the evolution and the consequent specialisation experienced by the EU Council and, in fact, in the future the forums for interparliamentary cooperation—eventually in the form of sectoral conferences headed by COSAC and the EU Speakers' Conference—could mirror the different Council configurations. National parliaments could then, collectively, debate the decisions taken by the Council instead of solely holding their national representative to account at national level as is currently the case.

This possibility actually poses the question of the aim of cooperation among national and European parliamentary committees. If committees seek to develop their influence at EU level in this way, they may be successful but some obstacles exist. They can be successful

[74] D Fromage, 'Parlamento Europeo y Parlamentos Nacionales después del Tratado de Lisboa y en un Contexto de Crisis: ¿Un Acercamiento de Grado Diverso según el Ámbito?' in P Andrés Sáenz de Santa María and JI Ugartemendia (eds), *El Parlamento Europeo: ¿Esta Vez es Diferente?* (Oñati, IVAP, 2015).

mostly in three ways: first, by, acting as a temporary and variable second chamber. Secondly by, in their exchanges with the EP, explicating their position(s) and convincing the European legislature. Their option would then be to manage to agree on a common position, consequently sent to the EU Commission: this position having been granted the approval of several Chambers—and, ideally, powerful ones too—the chances that the Commission will take due account of the observations transmitted are indeed higher than if each of the national parliaments had written to the EU institution on their own. However, these positive effects may be hampered by the lack of consensus among national parliaments on a specific topic or by the fact that MPs participating in interparliamentary forums participate in their own name only without having the possibility to act as representatives of their respective chambers.

If, in contrast, interparliamentary meetings are meant to be places for the exchange of information or forums of reflection—that is, if their goal is slightly less ambitious—then the need for their institutionalisation is far less pressing. More transparency and better coordination are, still, highly desirable so that parliaments, through their committees, comply with their 'communication function' towards their citizenries and so that the highest attendance rate possible is guaranteed through the avoidance of overlap. Such an evolution is indeed particularly needed in the view of the current situation.

It seems that, as long as there are contrasts in the understandings that national parliaments and/or the European Parliament have as to the actual function of interparliamentary cooperation, it will be difficult for it to be an effective instrument for parliamentary influence, although the openness of the addressee institution surely plays a role too. If it managed to be an efficient means for the exchange of information and for common reflections among specialists issued from the sectoral committees, whose outcomes were easily accessible, this would already be a positive achievement capable of potentially enhancing the democratic legitimacy of the EU.

7

Towards a More Politicised Interparliamentary Cooperation? The European Parliament's Political Groups and the European Parliamentary Week

NATHALIE BRACK AND THIBAUD DERUELLE

I. INTRODUCTION

THE SEARCH FOR parliamentary legitimacy is an intrinsic tropism of the European integration. Although the 'Monnet Method'[1] was built on a functionalist perspective of the integration process, a common parliamentary assembly was adjoined and national parliaments were the original pool from which the members of the common assembly were selected. In a sense, the very beginning of parliamentary legitimacy in the EU was based on interparliamentary cooperation, with an assembly comparable to the one to be found in the Council of Europe, the OSCE (Organization for Security and Co-operation in Europe), or the OECD (Organization for Economic Cooperation and Development). Interparliamentary cooperation became, however, more complex in the EU than in other polities or international organisations. This is mainly due to the role of the European Parliament (EP) in this cooperation. If the setting remains horizontal, with a strong prevalence

[1] Based on the functionalist theory of spillover, the 'Monnet Method' broadly refers to a gradual process of European integration, relying on functional needs and a 'small steps' approach towards communitarisation of policy fields.

of Members of national parliaments, it looks like a classic form of cooperation in an international organisation. But if the EP is introduced into the equation, things become more complicated depending on its role. Indeed, the key question is to know whether the EP is a chamber among others or takes the lead (or patronage), transforming interparliamentary cooperation into a form close to a federal experience.

With the first direct election of the EP, a double trend was triggered: national parliaments became losers of European integration while the EP has been progressively empowered. Indeed, European integration led to a strengthening of the national executives and national parliaments were progressively sidelined in this new 'post sovereign, polycentric and incongruent' political system.[2] At the same time, the EP has been gradually empowered: with each treaty reform, national governments have granted new legislative or budgetary powers to the EP as a way to compensate for the democratic deficit of the EU.[3] While one of the tropes of the European integration process was the parliamentarisation of the decision-making process, this evolution was in favour of the EP rather than national parliaments. Indeed, the EP and national parliaments were competitors for the provisions of democratic legitimacy and rivals for voters' attention.[4] And for a long time, the different promoters of EU integration were betting on a parliamentary strategy supporting a strong European Parliament rather than an increased involvement of national parliaments.

The situation has evolved recently. The Lisbon treaty ended a long process of constitutionalisation and strengthened the powers of parliaments in the European political system, establishing a multilevel parliamentary field.[5] The EP has been once again granted new powers but due to a discursive shift, national parliaments are now seen as key players to reduce the EU's democratic deficit. Their direct involvement in EU affairs has therefore been institutionalised.[6] At the same time, the Eurozone crisis and its management raised new concerns about the parliamentary and democratic legitimacy of the EU.[7] Indeed, the technocratic and intergovernmental character of the crisis management led to a further empowerment of the executives.[8] Parliaments have been side-lined whereas the core instruments of the new EU economic governance have major effects on the budgetary powers of national parliaments.[9] As noted by Berthold Rittberger,

> many of the measures to reform the EU's fiscal and economic governance architecture have been criticized for undermining the prerogatives of national parliaments as well as for sidestepping

[2] P Schmitter, 'Imagining the Future of the Euro-Polity with the Help of New Concepts' in G Marks, F Scharpf, P Schmitter and W Streeck (eds), *Governance in the European Union* (London, Sage, 1996) 136.

[3] O Costa and P Magnette, 'Idéologies et changement institutionnel dans l'Union européenne. Pourquoi les gouvernements ont-ils constamment renforcé le Parlement européen?' (2003) 9 *Politique européenne* 49.

[4] K Auel and T Christiansen, 'After Lisbon: National Parliaments in the European Union' (2015) 38 *West European Politics* 261.

[5] B Crum and E Fossum, 'The Multilevel Parliamentary Field: a framework for Theorising representative democracy in the EU' (2009) 1 *European Political Science Review* 249.

[6] Auel and Christiansen, n 3 above.

[7] R Fox, 'Europe, Democracy and the Economic Crisis: Is it Time to Reconstitute the Assises?' (2012) 65 *Parliamentary Affairs* 463; S Puntscher Rickmann and D Wydra, 'Representation in the European State of Emergency: Parliaments against Governments?' (2013) 35 *Journal of European Integration* 565.

[8] G Majone, 'From Regulatory State to a Democratic Default' (2014) 52 *Journal of Common Market Studies* 1216.

[9] K Auel and O Höing, 'National Parliaments and the Eurozone Crisis: Taking ownership in difficult times' (2015) 38 *West European Politics* 375.

the EP. Still the reforms of the EU's economic and fiscal governance architecture do not constitute a parliament-free space.[10]

Indeed, the risk of de-parliamentarisation gave incentives to parliaments to use interparliamentary cooperation to counterbalance the dominance of executives, and diverse forums of parliamentary cooperation emerged or were renewed.[11] One of these initiatives is the Interparliamentary meeting on the European Semester as part of the European Parliamentary week.[12] Organised on an annual basis, this meeting brings together national parliamentarians from across the EU to discuss first and foremost the annual growth survey and the European Semester. The EP is the leading actor of this process: it organises the meetings in Brussels, which are chaired by the President of the European Parliament (when it meets in its plenary form) or by the Chairpersons of the EP committees. As such, this type of interparliamentary cooperation is not new, but its organisation on a regular basis, and the precision of its goals, compared to other existing settings, made it an institutionalised instrument of interparliamentary cooperation.

A burgeoning literature has emerged in the last few years to understand the new provisions of the Lisbon treaty and the new impulse for interparliamentary cooperation, the involvement of national parliaments in EU affairs as well as the role of the EP in economic governance and its relations with national parliaments.[13] But this literature tends to consider parliaments as unitary actors and to focus on inter-institutional relations (among national parliaments and between them and the EP).[14] So far, only limited attention has been paid to the informal aspects of interparliamentary cooperation and more particularly, to the role of political parties and groups, whereas intra-party links seem to be the most frequent contacts between the EP and national parliaments.[15]

Building on this research, this chapter aims at exploring the role of EP political groups in fostering interparliamentary cooperation. While their importance is uneven across the political spectrum, large groups can be expected to be involved in an informal but significant coordination between the national and EU levels in order to increase their influence through political parties. Based on interviews with EP civil servants and staff members of several EP groups as well as the observation of the third European Parliamentary Week, the chapter underlines a developing trend: interparliamentary cooperation has evolved towards increased technicality and a politicisation of the issues discussed during meetings.

[10] B Rittberger, 'Integration without Representation? The European Parliament and the Reform of Economic Governance in the EU' (2014) 52 *Journal of Common Market Studies* 1174.

[11] D Fromage, 'A mapping of recent trends in interparliamentary cooperation within the EU' in C Fasone, D Fromage and Z Lefkofridi (eds), *Parliaments, Public Opinion, and Parliamentary Elections in Europe* (2015) EUI Max Weber Working Paper 2015/18.

[12] See also the chapter by D Jančić, 'Parliamentary Involvement in the Economic and Monetary Union after the Euro Crisis' Ch 10 in this volume.

[13] C Fasone, 'European Economic Governance and Parliamentary Representation. What Place for the European Parliament?' (2014) 20 *European Law Journal* 164; C Hefftler, C Neuhold, O Rozenberg, J Smith and W Wessels (eds), *The Palgrave Handbook of National Parliaments and the European Union* (Basingstoke, Palgrave MacMillan, 2014); B Rittberger, n 9 above; See also (2014) 20(1) *Journal of Legislative Studies* Special Issue: 'Connecting with the Electorate? Parliamentary Communication in EU Affairs'.

[14] K Neunreither, 'The European Parliament and National Parliaments: Conflict or Cooperation?' in K Auel and A Benz (eds), *The Europeanization of Parliamentary Democracy* (London, Routledge, 2006).

[15] E Miklin and B Crum, 'Interparliamentary contacts of Members of the European Parliament. Report of a Survey' (2011) 08 Recon Online Working Paper; O Costa and M Latek, 'Paradoxes and limits of interparliamentary cooperation in the European Union' (2001) 23 *Journal of European Integration* 139.

This chapter is structured around three main sections. The first one provides an overview of the literature on interparliamentary cooperation as well as a review of the various forms of interparliamentary cooperation. It shows that the literature has followed the ebbs and flows of interparliamentary cooperation but also that it tends to overlook the role played by EP groups and more generally, political parties. The second part shows a shift in interparliamentary cooperation due to the Eurozone crisis. With the creation of the European Semester and the European Parliamentary Week, interparliamentary cooperation has become more pragmatic, specialised and focused on expertise. The last section examines the diverging involvement of EP groups and the constraints they face. It shows that there are three key elements to understanding their varied engagement in interparliamentary cooperation: their interests, resources and political opportunity.

II. DEVELOPMENT OF INTERPARLIAMENTARY COOPERATION IN THE EU AND AS A FIELD OF STUDY OF EUROPEAN INTEGRATION

The involvement of national parliaments in EU affairs has been at the centre of major recent studies,[16] from their lack of involvement in EU affairs to the institutionalisation of their role with the Lisbon treaty. It is interesting to see the development of interparliamentary cooperation as parts of different narratives, or strategies to foster EU integration. The solutions presented have relied almost solely upon interparliamentary cooperation.

In 1989, the Conference of Parliamentary Committees for Union Affairs (COSAC) was created as an initiative of national parliaments: the cooperation was made at parliamentary committee level. The practice of committees on EU affairs was generalised in the EU9, and their representatives would meet during interparliamentary meetings held every six months. For almost 20 years, COSAC would be the alpha and omega of parliamentary cooperation in the EU, establishing in a lasting way the practice of meetings at community level. There is an extensive literature on this issue.[17]

However, since the 1990s, the literature has also pointed out the lack of transnational coordination beyond COSAC and the limits of interparliamentary cooperation, mainly due to the absence of interest of national parliamentarians in forging meaningful links with the EP or in associating MEPs to their work.[18] Scholars have been tackling the topic in the light of the Europeanisation of national parliaments, be it in terms of agenda-setting or in terms

[16] Auel and Christiansen, n 3 above; Auel and Höing, n 8 above; J Neyer, 'Justified Multi-level Parliamentarism: Situating national parliaments in the European Polity' (2014) 20 *Journal of Legislative Studies* 125; T Raunio, 'The gatekeepers of European integration? The Functions of National Parliaments in the EU political system' (2011) 33 *Journal of European Integration* 303; I Cooper, 'A Virtual Third Chamber for the European Union? National Parliaments after the Treaty of Lisbon' (2012) 35 *West European Politics* 441.

[17] A Cygan, *Accountability, Parliamentarism and Transparency in the EU* (Cheltenham, Edward Elgar, 2013); M Latek, 'Le poids des traditions parlementaires nationales dans le développement de la coopération interparlementaire. La participation française et britannique à la COSAC' (2003) 9 *Politique européenne* 143; K Neunreither, 'The Democratic Deficit of the European Union: Towards Closer Cooperation between the European Parliament and the National Parliaments' (1994) 29 *Government and Opposition* 299; L Tordoff, 'The conference of European affairs committees: A collective voice for national parliaments in the European Union' (2000) 6 *Journal of Legislative Studies* 1. See also the contributions in the Sixth Part of this volume.

[18] M Larhant, 'La coopération interparlementaire dans l'UE' (2005) 16 *Notre Europe Policy Paper*.

of practices, and have made case studies to assess the involvement of each chamber in EU affairs.[19] De facto this approach underlined the differences among national parliaments but also the competition between the EP and national parliaments. These studies tend to consider national parliaments as one compact unit of analysis rather than tackling the topic of their interactions at the horizontal level.[20]

The convention for the European Constitution brought new solutions for national parliaments. Some advocated strongly for an EU senate of national parliaments and both advocates of further integration and parts of the Euro-sceptics found common ground on the empowerment of national parliaments in EU affairs, although for different reasons. Indeed, most of the advocates of further EU integration favoured new solutions to alleviate the democratic deficit and legitimise the EU while some Euro-sceptics saw an opportunity to repatriate powers to the national level. National parliaments have been gradually considered as a whole rather than the sum of their different parts.[21] Their role was thus increasingly studied under the light of comparative politics and their democratic input compared to the EP's one until the entry into force of the Lisbon treaty.[22] As outlined earlier, national parliaments have been a tool for conceptualising and assessing the democratic deficit as well as a way for fixing it.

The Lisbon treaty and the creation of the early warning system mechanism on the principle of subsidiarity[23] have provided new opportunities for the national parliaments. According to Andreas Maurer and Wolfgang Wessels, the concept of de-parliamentarisation has called for a phenomenon of 're-parliamentarisation'. Thus, from 'losers' of the integration, national parliaments have become 'latecomers'.[24] And the literature has mirrored those changes closely. While interparliamentary cooperation had been criticised for its lack of results, the principle of individual votes for each chamber led researchers to increasingly focus their attention on the way national parliaments deal with their new prerogative and less on their interactions.[25]

The recent developments related to the Eurozone crisis and the establishment of the European Semester have brought new subjects to study the relations between national

[19] K Auel and A Benz, 'The Politics of Adaptation: The Europeanisation of National Parliamentary Systems' (2005) 11 *Journal of Legislative Studies* 372; O Costa and M Latek, n 14 above; J Karlas, 'National Parliamentary Control of EU Affairs: Institutional Design after Enlargement' (2012) 35 *West European Politics* 1095.

[20] P Schmitter, 'Imagining the Future of the Euro-Polity with the Help of New Concepts' in G Marks et al (eds), *Governance in the European Union* (London, Sage, 1996).

[21] A Fraga, 'After the Convention: The future role of National Parliaments in the European Union (and the day after … nothing will happen)' (2005) 11 *Journal of Legislative Studies* 490.

[22] T Jans and S Piedrafita, 'The Role of National Parliaments in European Decision-Making' (2009) 1 *Eipascope*; J-V Louis, 'The Lisbon Treaty: The Irish "No". National Parliamentsand the Principle of Subsidiarity—Legal Options and Practical Limits' (2008) 4 *European Constitutional Law Review* 429; P Kiiver, 'Legal Accountability to a Political Forum? The European Commission, the Dutch Parliament and the Early Warning System for the Principle of Subsidiarity', *Maastricht Faculty of Law Working Paper* 2009–8.

[23] I Cooper, 'The Watchdogs of Subsidiarity: National Parliamentsand the Logic of Arguing in the EU' (2006) 44 *Journal of Common Market Studies* 289.

[24] A Maurer and W Wessels (eds), *National Parliaments on their ways to Europe: Losers or latecomers*? (Baden Baden, Nomos, 2001).

[25] R Matarazzo and J Leone, 'Sleeping beauty Awakens: The Italian Parliament and the EU after the Lisbon Treaty' (2011) 46 *The International Spectator* 129; C Neuhold, 'Late wake-up call or early warning? Parliamentary participation and cooperation in light of the Lisbon treaty' (2011) UACES Conference, London; T Raunio, 'National Parliaments and European Integration: What we know and Agenda for Future research' (2009) 15 *Journal of Legislative Studies* 317.

parliaments and the EP. Scholars have underlined how interparliamentary cooperation has increased due to the crisis and its management, and has been fostered under the patronage of the EP.[26]

In a nutshell, the study of interparliamentary cooperation in the EU has long been divided into the two approaches: on the one hand, studies have analysed the horizontal cooperation between national parliaments through studies of the only existing forum: COSAC (and to some extent IPEX (the InterParliamentary EU information eXchange) and network of parliamentary representatives). On the other hand, following the Lisbon Treaty, scholars have focused on the interactions between parliaments and the EU institutions, mainly the EP and the Commission. But as mentioned, the literature tends to consider parliaments as unitary actors. And while EP political groups are key organs for interparliamentary cooperation,[27] apart from a few exceptions, there have been very few studies on the partisan variable of interparliamentary cooperation. Focusing on the Joint Parliamentary Meetings (JPMs) between 2005 and 2011, Katjana Gattermann examined the role of the EP in fostering a greater involvement of its political groups in interparliamentary cooperation.[28] She shows that political parties have varying interests in maintaining a dialogue with national parliamentarians. Eric Miklin focuses on the Austrian case to show that there is a varying engagement of political parties in transnational cooperation that can be explained by the parliamentary status and ideology of the party.[29]

Building on this literature, this chapter seeks to unveil the role of political groups in interparliamentary cooperation and identify what explains the differentiated involvement of EP groups and their behaviour in terms of intra-party coordination. To do so, it will focus on a new type of parliamentary cooperation—the Interparliamentary Meetings on the European Semester—which aims not only to foster interparliamentary cooperation but also to present a joint opinion to the Council of the EU. It is assumed that the Interparliamentary Meeting can be considered as a momentum for interparliamentary cooperation and a window of opportunity for political groups to adopt more proactive behaviour. Hence, the main hypothesis is that EP groups' differentiated approach cannot be reduced to a matter of preferences but reflects their different access to resources and how their involvement may be maximised.

In addition to that, the chapter will test several additional expectations. First, we expect that the third European Parliamentary Week underlines a developing trend towards an increase in technicality and a politicisation of the debate. This trend results in a shift of the EP's groups' political priorities in terms of interparliamentary cooperation. Secondly, we assume that political groups represent an alternative model to the engine of interparliamentary cooperation. Therefore, we expect groups' behaviour to be influenced by their size.

[26] Auel and Christiansen, n 3 above; K Auel and T Raunio, 'Introduction: Connecting with the Electorate? Parliamentary Communication in EU affairs' (2014) 20 *Journal of Legislative Studies* 1; I Cooper, 'Parliamentary oversight of the EU after the Crisis: On the Creation of the "Article 13" Interparliamentary Conference', *LUISS Working Paper Series SOG*-WP21; C Sprungk, 'A New type of Representative Democracy? Reconsidering the role of national parliaments in the EU' (2013) 35 *Journal of European Integration* 547.

[27] Costa and Latek, n 14 above.

[28] K Gattermann, 'Opportunities, Strategies and Ideologies: The Incentives of European Parliament Political Groups for Inter-parliamentary cooperation' (2014) 16 *OPAL Online Paper Series*.

[29] E Miklin, 'Interparliamentary Cooperation in EU affairs and the Austrian Parliament: Empowering the Opposition?' (2013) 19 *Journal of Legislative Studies* 22.

In other words, we anticipate that large groups will be more involved in interparliamentary cooperation. Lastly, without bypassing the institutional aspect of the EP patronage, political groups pursue a strategy of maximisation: they seek to increase their influence on national parties as well as in the EP.

III. INTERPARLIAMENTARY COOPERATION AND THE ECONOMIC AND BUDGETARY CRISIS: TOWARDS PRAGMATISM, INCREASED TECHNICALITY ... AND POLITICISATION?

In his interim report 'Towards a genuine Economic and Monetary Union',[30] the then-President of the European Council Herman Van Rompuy outlined that the democratic oversight of the Eurozone governance, in its core aspects, lies within the responsibility of national legislatures. In doing so, he was referring to the European Semester and most particularly the Commission's Annual Growth Survey, which identifies objectives to fulfil the priorities for the EU as set by the Commission. The Annual Growth Survey is always discussed in the Council and the European Parliament before being endorsed by the Spring European Council, giving strategic guidance on the priorities to be pursued. The focus here lies on another step: the Interparliamentary Meeting on the European Semester, which prepares recommendations for the European Council.

The Interparliamentary Meeting was created as a democratic oversight of the budgetary surveillance as crafted in the so-called 'Six-pack'.[31] The technical aspect of the cooperation became salient before the EP focused its effort on indicating clearly the issues that should be on the agenda of the future interparliamentary meetings, underlining a growing trend of pragmatism in interparliamentary cooperation.[32] The texts provide the following design:[33]

> in line with the legal and political arrangements of each Member State, national parliaments should be duly involved in the European Semester and in the preparation of stability programmes, convergence programmes and national reform programmes in order to increase the transparency and ownership of, and accountability for the decisions taken.[34]

[30] H Van Rompuy, 'Towards a genuine Economic and Monetary Union', 5 December 2012.

[31] The 'six-pack' refers to a set of six EU laws (listed below), the first four on fiscal policy and the last two on macroeconomic imbalances:

Regulation (EU) No 1175/2011 of the European Parliament and of the Council of 16 November 2011 amending Council Regulation (EC) No 1466/97 on the strengthening of the surveillance of budgetary positions and the surveillance and coordination of economic policies. [2011] OJ L306/12.

Council Regulation (EU) No 1177/2011 of 8 November 2011 amending Regulation (EC) No 1467/97 on speeding up and clarifying the implementation of the excessive deficit procedure. [2011] OJ L306/33.

Regulation (EU) No 1173/2011 of the European Parliament and of the Council of 16 November 2011 on the effective enforcement of budgetary surveillance in the euro area. [2011] OJ L306/1.

Council Directive 2011/85/EU of 8 November 2011 on requirements for budgetary frameworks of the Member States. [2011] OJ L306/41.

Regulation (EU) No 1176/2011 of the European Parliament and of the Council of 16 November 2011 on the prevention and correction of macroeconomic imbalances. [2011] OJ L306/25.

Regulation (EU) No 1174/2011 of the European Parliament and of the Council of 16 November 2011 on enforcement measures to correct excessive macroeconomic imbalances in the euro area. [2011] OJ L306/8.

[32] S&D group staff member, interviewed in Brussels on 19 February 2015.

[33] Regulation (EU) No 1173/2011 of the European Parliament and of the Council of 16 November 2011 on the effective enforcement of budgetary surveillance in the euro area. [2011] OJ L306/1.

[34] Council Regulation (EU) No 1177/2011 of 8 November 2011 amending Regulation (EC) No 1467/97 on speeding up and clarifying the implementation of the excessive deficit procedure. [2011] L306/33.

The Interparliamentary Meeting on the European Semester may be seen as a series of Interparliamentary Committee Meetings (ICMs) held at the same time, and packed with 'plenaries' organised as introduction and conclusion sessions. It is thus the sophistication of existing practices, ie the organisation of JPMs and ICMs.[35] The main difference between those two settings is the chair; while JPMs are co-chaired by corresponding chairpersons from the EP and the chamber(s) of the country exercising the rotating presidency of the Council, ICMs are organised only on the initiative of the parliamentary committees of the EP.

The Meeting is actually a concomitant ICM for the EP's Economic and Financial Committee (BUDG), Economic Policy Committee (ECON) and Employment Committee & the Social Protection Committee (EMPL). Moreover, the President of the EP, the President of the Commission and the President of the European Council participate in the event. The choice of this model, which gives the upper hand to the EP in the organisation of these meetings, should be seen not only as a sign of its empowerment but also as an insurance for the ECON committee that the interparliamentary cooperation will provide an input on the national budgets' oversight that will go beyond a symbolic democratic input.

This search for increased technicality and political input may also be underlined in the difference between the Interparliamentary Meeting on the European Semester and the 'Article 13 Conference'. It is important to briefly explain the negotiations that led to article 13 of the TSCG. This article refers to Title II of Protocol no 1 of the Lisbon Treaty. But the title is composed of two different articles, each of them calling for a different design of interparliamentary cooperation. The first one (article 9) model refers to an 'ICM-type' meeting (with a clear patronage of the EP) while the second model (article 10) refers to the COSAC-type meeting. No choice was made between those two articles in article 13 of the TSCG—which was negotiated in the same period when the 'Six-pack' was adopted. This shows that during the negotiation of the TSCG, the concerns of democratic accountability were addressed, but the issue of increasing technicality was not decisive in drafting article 13. The difference also lays in the scope[36] and output of these meetings:[37] while the Article 13 Conference discusses budgetary policies and other issues covered by the TSCG,[38] the role of the Interparliamentary Meeting on the European Semester is to provide an input to the Council of the EU following the annual growth survey.[39]

The EP has thus been an important actor in crafting the Meeting, pushing for an increased technicality and assuming the patronage of interparliamentary cooperation. But the ECON,[40] EMPL[41] and BUDG[42] committees also played a role in shaping the Interparliamentary Meeting on the European Semester or in its organisation. These committees (and the EP as a whole) could benefit from the technical input of this joint ICM. However the political aspect of the questions dealt with by the Interparliamentary Meeting

[35] EP civil servant, DG for Presidency, interviewed in Brussels on 17 February 2015.

[36] EP civil servant, DG for Presidency, interviewed in Brussels on 17 February 2015.

[37] Article 13 Treaty on Stability Convergence and Governance in the Economic and Monetary Union.

[38] Although in the light of the current practice, this still remains not entirely clear: see I Cooper, 'The Interparliamentary Conference on Stability, Economic Coordination and Governance in the European Union ("The Article 13 Conference")', Ch 13 in this volume.

[39] EP civil servant, DG for Presidency, interviewed in Brussels on 17 February 2015.

[40] Economic and Monetary Affairs Committee of the European Parliament.

[41] Committee on Employment and Social Affairs of the European Parliament.

[42] Budgets' Committee of the European Parliament.

on the European Semester should not be underestimated. National budgets' oversight is an increasingly salient issue in Europe and which is very delicate in some Member States where public opinion is very sensitive about the consequences of the European Semester. Beyond the empowerment of the EP and the struggle for increased technicality, politicisation is an important element to understand the European Parliament's political groups in the Interparliamentary Meeting on the European Semester.

IV. POLITICAL GROUPS' BEHAVIOUR TOWARD THE INTERPARLIAMENTARY MEETING ON THE EUROPEAN SEMESTER: DIFFERENTIATED APPROACHES, CONSTRAINTS AND OPPORTUNITIES

So far, research has tended to concentrate on interparliamentary cooperation by focusing on the formal and institutional relations. But parties are important actors within parliaments and intra-party links are the main channel for the contacts between national parliaments and the EP.[43] In principle, political groups do not have a specific mandate to become patrons or federate national parliamentarians invited to the meeting. In practice, interparliamentary meetings such as COSAC, JPMs or the Interparliamentary Conference for the Common Foreign and Security Policy and the Common Security and Defence Policy show that divisions among parliamentarians are most likely to occur along national than political lines. This section will therefore concentrate on the differentiated involvement of EP groups in interparliamentary cooperation and the constraints they face.

A. Intra-Party Cooperation. Differentiated Approaches and Their Success

The literature on political parties shows that the linkage between national parties and MEPs has gradually become stronger and that national parties now pay more attention to their MEPs.[44] Interparliamentary contacts can be seen as a resource for MEPs, their national party and their political group in order to increase their influence on the decision-making process. And as most national delegations are too small to have an impact on the EP's deliberation, parties rely on the cooperation and resources of EP groups to maximise their impact.[45] We can thus expect that EP political groups are engaged in cooperation with national members of parliaments, especially from their political family but also that there will be considerable variation between party families.

The survey by Eric Miklin and Ben Crum confirms that indeed most interparliamentary engagement proceeds through political parties on the initiative of MEPs (rather than MPs) and that there is a significant difference between the two main EP groups. They found

[43] E Miklin and B Crum, 'Interparliamentary contacts of Members of the European Parliament. Report of a Survey' (2011) 8 *RECON Online Working Paper*.

[44] T Raunio, 'Losing Independence of Finally Gaining Recognition? Contacts between MEPs and National Parties' (2000) 6 *Party Politics* 211; T Raunio, 'National Parliaments and European Integration: What we know and Agenda for future research' (2009) 15 *Journal of Legislative Studies* 317; T Raunio, 'Open List, Open Mandate? Links between MEPs and Parties in Finland' (2007) 8 *Perspectives on European Politics and Society* 131.

[45] C Lord, 'The aggregating function of political parties in EU decision-making' (2010) 5/3 *Living Reviews in European Governance* 5.

that MEPs from the Socialist and Democrat Group (S&D) are more regularly involved in coordination with their national parties as well as with EP parties from their party family. In comparison to the European People's Party group (EPP), they are more interested in developing a common position on EU issues but are also more prone to criticise the lack of attention paid by the national party to EU affairs.[46]

The data from the EPRG Survey of 2010 confirms that there is indeed considerable variation among the different EP groups in terms of contact with the national parties and parliaments. Table 1 displays several elements. First, there are frequent intra-party contacts in the 'multilevel parliamentary field': 51 per cent of the MEPs have weekly contact with their national party, almost 30 per cent with national parliamentarians as well as with their national party leadership. 40 per cent have monthly contact with MPs and almost 50 per cent have monthly contact with the national party executive. Secondly, there is considerable variation across the different groups. It is not surprising that small and marginal groups (such as the Europe and Freedom and Democracy (EFD) and the European United Left/ Nordic Green Left (EUL/NGL)) as well as non-attached members have the most frequent contact with their national parties due to their attitudes towards European cooperation and the fact that it is usually party leaders and key figures who take the seats in the EP. Thirdly, if we focus on the two main groups, these data contradict the findings of Miklin and Crum: the EPP seems more involved in interparliamentary coordination than the S&D. EPP members have more frequent contact with national parliamentarians, national party executives and member of their national party than S&D members. This finding is corroborated by interviews with representatives from the two largest groups: the EPP tends to prioritise interparliamentary cooperation and can rely on its past experiences in intra-party coordination while S&D involvement is in its infancy. Finally, the data displayed in table 1 confirm that intraparty coordination is by far the most frequent link between national and the European parliaments.

The EPRG survey data show a strong linkage between national parties and MEPs. More importantly, they show that intra-party cooperation is a phenomenon that is spread across all groups. The fact that small and marginal groups seem to be most frequently in touch with national parliamentarians and party representatives confirms—so far—part of the hypothesis. However, intra-party linkage is only one of the different facets of interparliamentary cooperation: the data presented above focus on personal and individual linkage rather than on groups' organisation. They give a general picture of the 'day-to-day' linkage and indicate that these links are first and foremost about national parties' affiliations. However, taking the lead and assuming a 'patronage' of interparliamentary cooperation require more than a strong linkage with national parties. The following part of this chapter will investigate how the Interparliamentary Meeting, as a *momentum*, creates opportunities and constraints for political groups.

[46] Miklin and Crum, n 42 above.

Table 1: Intraparty coordination and relations to national parliaments

	At least once a week (%)	At least once a month (%)	At least every 3 months (%)	At least once a year (%)	Less often (%)	No contact (%)
Contacts frequency with MPs from my national parliament						
EPP	28.6	41.3	19	3.2	4.8	3.2
S&D	20	41.8	32.7	5.5	0	0
ALDE	30	43.3	16.7	0	10	0
Greens/EFA	40	26.7	26.7	6.7	0	0
ECR	12.5	62.5	25	0	0	0
EUL/NGL	16.7	66.7	16.7	0	0	0
EFD	60	20	10	0	10	0
NA	60	0	0	20	0	20
Total (N = 192)	28.6	40.1	22.4	3.6	3.6	1.6
Contact frequency with national party executives						
EPP	25	51.6	15.6	1.6	3.1	3.1
S&D	23.6	52.7	14.5	5.5	1.8	1.8
ALDE	30	53.3	6.7	6.7	3.3	0
Greens/EFA	26.7	26.7	40	6.7	0	0
ECR	0	50	25	25	0	0
EUL/NGL	50	33.3	0	0	0	0
EFD	50	50	0	0	0	0
NA	80	20	0	0	0	0
Total (N = 193)	28	48.7	15	4.7	2.1	1.6
Contact frequency with members of the national party						
EPP	54.7	35.9	3.1	1.6	3.1	1.6
S&D	44.4	50	5.6	0	0	0
ALDE	51.7	37.9	10.3	0	0	0
Greens/EFA	46.7	33.3	6.7	6.7	6.7	0
ECR	25	62.5	12.5	0	0	0
EUL/NGL	60	20	20	0	0	0
EFD	70	30	0	0	0	0
NA	80	20	0	0	0	0
Total (N = 190)	51.1	40	5.8	1.1	1.6	0.5

Source: David Farrell, Simon Hix and Roger Scully (2011) 'EPRG MEP Survey Dataset: 2011 Release'

B. Constraints and Opportunities: Ideological Approach, Political Strategy, Administrative Resources

The political salience of the Interparliamentary Meeting on the European Semester is nevertheless an opportunity for political groups to seize. Partisan division among national parliamentarians, especially along the majority/opposition axis, are more easily drawn, which offers a window of opportunity for political groups to assume a role of patron.

However, this window of opportunity may vary from one group to another. Three variables are relevant in this respect:

1. The size of the group in the EP as well in the national parliament: the larger the group, the more administrative resources it can claim and the larger the pool of national parliamentarians it could cooperate with.[47]
2. The political group's interest in interparliamentary cooperation and its path dependency: the longer is the practice, the more developed it should be.
3. The political opportunity to adopt a proactive strategy towards interparliamentary cooperation.

Building on these variables, the most proactive group in interparliamentary cooperation would be a group which tackles this issue with an approach close to that of a club[48] with a strong record of inclusivity and which behaviour is motivated by both ideological and political incentives.

(i) Size and Logistics

As underlined by the interviewee from the EPP, size matters.[49] The most important challenge of interparliamentary cooperation is to maintain a stable network. There is a constant turnover of national parliamentarians in Europe and this perpetual movement requires strong logistical efforts. Moreover, the number of national parliamentarians they are able to access varies a lot from one group to another. In this respect, the EPP is the group with the strongest potential to assume a proactive role in interparliamentary cooperation. It is the largest group in the EP and is able to reach out to the most important pool of national parliamentarians in the Union because of the current political majorities in the Member States. The S&D comes right behind it, being the second largest group in the European Parliament, but also the second group in terms of possible parliamentarians to reach out to. Both groups have a structured administration dedicated to relations with national parliaments. While the S&D has a Special Adviser for Relations with National Parliaments, the EPP has a more political approach, with a vice-Chair for Relations with National Parliaments in the EPP Bureau (currently Esther de Lange (NL)) as well as members of the staff entirely dedicated to this task.

However, smaller groups may encounter difficulties. A staff member of the EFDD[50] group explains the lack of means at their disposal, but also the narrow number of parliamentarians

47 EP civil servant, DG for Presidency, interviewed in Brussels on 17 February 2015.
48 ibid.
49 EPP group staff member, interviewed in Brussels on 26 February 2015.
50 Europe of Freedom and Direct Democracy.

they are able to establish a contact with. This finding is true for other smaller groups such as EUL/NGL, the Greens and ECR.[51] In all those cases, national parliamentarians are unevenly represented in Member States and the cost of their efforts represents a bad pay-off in terms of benefits. Small and marginal groups, despite a strong intra-party linkage, cannot cope with the advantages that larger groups have access to, due to their size and resources. During the interviews conducted in the EP, it was made clear that marginal groups see a genuine interest in fostering interparliamentary cooperation; however their lack of administrative means leads them to focus on intra-party linkage rather than attempting to assume a patronage.[52] The case of ALDE[53] is interesting as it has long been the third largest group in the European Parliament, with a relatively significant staff. However, even with this staff resource, the scope of their opportunity for interparliamentary cooperation remains narrow, as the pool of national parliamentarians at their disposal remains small.

The first variable shows that the opportunity is only significant enough for the two biggest political groups: the EPP and the S&D. By their size and the opportunities they can reach out to national parliamentarians and they are more likely to be involved in interparliamentary cooperation and eventually take initiatives. The interviews and the observation data of the third European Parliamentary Week confirm this finding. If all groups are officially involved by the EP's Directorate for Relations with National Parliaments in the preparation of the parliamentary week, only the two largest ones have the resources to have permanent staff following and preparing interparliamentary meetings. Hence, the next two subsections will focus only on these two groups.

(ii) Interest in Interparliamentary Cooperation and Path Dependency

The EPP has a strong record in terms of efforts to promote interparliamentary cooperation, with the organisation of the meetings of group coordinators. The EPP secretariat has been investing time and resources in promoting and preparing for interparliamentary cooperation for quite some time. Considering interparliamentary cooperation as a political priority, in 2007 the group created an organ to deal with the issue, and since 2009 one of the vice-presidents of the EPP has been in charge of relations with the national parliaments and travels often to meet national parliamentarians. Before each official interparliamentary meeting, the EPP seeks to determine a common line among its members from national and the European parliaments. And the group also organises various events such as the summits of the presidents of the parliamentary groups belonging to the EPP, twice a year, or that of the EPP's network on EU affairs.

The same involvement can be noticed in the European Parliamentary Week. There were preparatory meetings among parties from the EPP to decide on a common position and to maximise the EPP's input during the parliamentary week. And during the event as such, there were informal gatherings such as lunch, organised by the group to foster intra-party coordination. There is thus a strong path dependency in the EPP group and a structured network.

[51] European Conservatives and Reformists.
[52] EFDD group staff member, interviewed in Brussels on 17 February 2015.
[53] Group of the Alliance of Liberals and Democrats for Europe.

The PSE has a less strong record, and parliamentary cooperation is a more recent priority in the group. For a long time, interparliamentary cooperation has not been a priority for the S&D group; this was attributed to a lack of political tradition by our interviewees.[54] While the EPP was developing a strategy to bring together its political family and to structure its network of MPs, the S&D group was focusing its efforts on gaining influence within the EP rather than extending its influence outside the institution. Whilst the interviewees attest to a shift in the groups' preferences, the interest for interparliamentary cooperation has still room to develop. For instance S&D did not invest in upstream preparations of the parliamentary week and there did not seem to be any special event or meetings organised by the group for the occasion.

While the two groups have different approaches, especially during the last mandate, they share a similar proactive attitude towards interparliamentary cooperation. This may find an explanation in the fact that both groups are in the coalition supporting the Juncker Commission.[55] As such, they are both concerned with assuming a leading and proactive role in the functioning of the institution—in this respect, the S&D group has been through a rapid evolution. There are also exchanges of good practices between the two groups,[56] in terms of structure and logistics.

(iii) Political Opportunity

The evolution of interparliamentary cooperation towards more pragmatism and increased technicality had a decisive importance in encouraging the S&D group to focus more on interparliamentary cooperation[57] and in maintaining their efforts in the case of the EPP. Both groups welcome the evolution of the cooperation on more technical and precise issues, citing the Interparliamentary Meeting on the European Semester as an example. The COSAC model is seen as too general and unfruitful when it comes to putting forward measures and the subsidiarity check is seen as unpractical and limited in motivating national parliaments' input.

Assuming the 'patronage' of interparliamentary cooperation is a strategic tool, with more precise topics debated with national parliaments and recommendations passed on to the European Council, national parliamentarians can be used as a relay and/or a support to the group's position. The EPP has the most sophisticated approach with preliminary meetings to establish a common political line with national parliamentarians. Interparliamentary cooperation can be thus seen as a means of empowerment. It was underlined by a member of the administrative staff of the EP[58] and corroborated by a staff member of the S&D[59] group that there is a current rise of the political groups in the institution: they dominate the agenda and MEPs hire more and more specialised people, while the secretariat has seen its influence decrease.[60] The proactive behaviour of political groups is thus a process of

[54] S&D group staff member, interviewed in Brussels on 19 February 2015.
[55] ibid.
[56] EPP group staff member, interviewed in Brussels on 26 February 2015.
[57] S&D group staff member, interviewed in Brussels on 19 February 2015.
[58] EP civil servant, DG for Presidency, interviewed in Brussels on 17 February 2015.
[59] S&D group staff member, interviewed in Brussels on 19 February 2015.
[60] A Pegan, *An Analysis of Legislative Assistance in the European Parliament*, PhD Thesis, University of Luxembourg, March 2015.

appropriation of a part of the inter-institutional relations of the institution. Moreover it corroborates the idea of path dependency for the S&D: the definitive goal of the group is still to gain in importance within the EP, however the patronage of interparliamentary cooperation is seen as an appropriate means by which to reach this goal. Political opportunity and groups' traditional strategy are easily wed in the framework of the Interparliamentary Meeting.

To sum up, groups are subject to constraints vis-à-vis interparliamentary cooperation, especially in terms of logistics, means and number of MEPs and MPs. The evolution of the S&D group also underlines an important point: being part of the coalition may be seen as an incentive to assume a form of patronage in interparliamentary cooperation. Eventually, the increased technicality of meetings such as the Interparliamentary Meeting on the European Semester is a political opportunity that groups are interested in seizing.

Table 2: Constraints and behaviour explanation for political groups

Variables	Groups	
	EPP	S&D
Administrative resources	Very strong	In development
Interest and path dependency	Welcoming and proactive—Constant since the Lisbon Treaty	More welcoming since the Juncker Commission
Political opportunity	The increased technicality and pragmatism is seen as a strong opportunity to use interparliamentary cooperation in order to gain/maintain influence within the EP.	

V. CONCLUSION

Interparliamentary cooperation has attracted much attention lately. The Lisbon treaty, also known as the 'treaty of parliaments',[61] evidenced a shift in the involvement of national parliaments in EU affairs. The status of national parliaments changed, from losers to latecomers, as they started to be seen as a potential tool to remedy the EU's democratic deficit. In addition to that, the EP has started to use interparliamentary cooperation to strengthen its position and its legitimacy, especially since the start of the Eurozone crisis. The risk of a de-parliamentarisation due to the side-lining of parliaments in the management of the crisis has triggered a new appetite for interparliamentary cooperation and new forums emerged.

It remains to be seen how this shift is interpreted by the EP. With the Lisbon treaty, it seems that there are competing approaches within the EP as to the best strategy to include national parliaments in the EU's decision-making, and as a result, the patronage of the EP has become more complex. While the COSAC setting is increasingly challenged, the new forms of interparliamentary cooperation focus on more technical but also more political

[61] See for instance: European Parliament, 'Report on Interparliamentary Relations between the European Parliament and national parliaments under the Treaty of Lisbon, 2009–2014', Annual Report 2013–14; A Herranz-Surrallés, 'The EU's Multilevel Parliamentary (Battle)Field: Inter-parliamentary Cooperation and Conflict in Foreign and Security Policy' (2014) 37 *West European Politics* 957.

issues, be it cooperation in foreign and security policy or in budgetary and economic issues. This increased technicality and politicisation of the interparliamentary meetings have opened a window of opportunity for an enhanced involvement of EP political groups. Although often neglected by the literature, intra-party links are one of the most frequent forms of interparliamentary cooperation. As we have shown in this chapter, MEPs are regularly in contact with members of national parliaments as well as members of their national political parties. And the main EP groups seek to enhance their influence by promoting multilevel cooperation within their respective political families. As such, group politics has developed as an informal means of interparliamentary cooperation without bypassing the institutional aspects of the EP's patronage, and represents an alternative model to the engine of interparliamentary cooperation.

The main hypothesis is confirmed, what can be considered as momentum in interparliamentary cooperation is an opportunity for political groups to adopt more proactive behaviour. Their differentiated approach may not be summed-up as a matter of mere preferences but lays in their different access to resources and how their involvement may be maximised. However, EP political groups have differentiated approaches and strategies towards interparliamentary cooperation. As it has been shown here, three main variables help in explaining this difference. First, EP groups face constraints in terms of size and resources. Larger groups have more resources to engage in interparliamentary cooperation and are therefore more involved. Secondly, the interest and experience of an EP group in such cooperation is crucial: involvement in interparliamentary cooperation requires the political will to do so, which explains the diverging strategy of the S&D in comparison to the EPP. Finally, the context also plays a role. As mentioned, the evolution of interparliamentary cooperation towards more pragmatism and increased technicality was decisive in encouraging the S&D to increase intra-party links.

One last aspect can be underlined with the S&D case: interparliamentary cooperation is more and more attractive for the EP's political groups because the practice is much more important in the EP itself. The importance of political groups in this type of cooperation depends on their ability to tag onto the general functioning of the institution. Despite the fact that interparliamentary cooperation is still considered to be a matter of interinstitutional relations, this chapter has shown that large groups increasingly claim ownership of this process. In doing so, it suggests that studies should continue opening the Pandora's box that is the European Parliament and its relations with national parliaments. And a promising avenue for future research is to adopt a partisan approach to investigating interparliamentary cooperation.

8

The Role of Parliamentary Administrations in Interparliamentary Cooperation

ANDREJA PEGAN AND ANNA-LENA HÖGENAUER

I. INTRODUCTION

COMPARED TO INTERPARLIAMENTARY cooperation between members of parliament (MPs), there is limited knowledge on interparliamentary cooperation at the administrative level, ie, cooperation between administrators or the un-elected officials working in parliament.[1] Parliamentary administrators have played a role in interparliamentary cooperation already in the 1950s, when the European Parliament (EP) was known as the Common Assembly of the European Coal and Steel Community (ECSC). Even before the ECSC Common Assembly was set up, the parliamentary Secretaries General of the EU founding member states supported the ECSC in devising an independent parliamentary administration.[2] For the first two decades of European integration, national parliaments (NPs) seconded a number of their officials to the ECSC to technically run the plenary session of the Common Assembly (eg, stenographic assistance).[3] National parliaments had even offices at the premises of the EP.[4] This can be considered an early example of administrative cooperation between national parliaments and the EP—a long time before interparliamentary contacts between members of national parliaments and the EP were regularised in the 1990s (eg, through the Conference of the European Affairs Committees, COSAC) and institutionalised with the Maastricht, Amsterdam and Lisbon Treaties.

[1] For exceptions see A-L Högenauer and C Neuhold, 'National Parliaments after Lisbon: Administrations on the Rise' (2015) 38 *West European Politics* 335, 354 and A-L Högenauer and T Christiansen, 'Parliamentary Administration in the Scrutiny of EU Decision-Making' in C Heffler, C Neuhold, O Rozenberg and J Smith (eds), *The Palgrave Handbook of National Parliaments and the European Union* (Basingstoke, Palgrave Macmillan, 2015).

[2] A Pegan, 'An Analysis of Legislative Assistance in the European Parliament (DPhil thesis, University of Luxembourg, 2015).

[3] S Guerrieri, 'L'amministrazione parlamentare dell'Assemblea comune della Ceca all'Assemblea delle tre Communità' (2000) 8 *Storia amministrazione costituzione—Annale ISAP* 134, 156.

[4] Interview with Guy Vanhaeverbeke, Honorary Director of the EP, 14/10/2012 and 11/11/2012.

Therefore, it is not surprising that scholars and practitioners agree that administrative contacts are one of the most successful forms of interparliamentary cooperation.[5] Away from the political spotlight, administrative contacts occur in confidence. Administrators are able to communicate the perspective of their parliament and pass on informal messages, which can ease the political dialogue between parliamentary chambers. Hence, this chapter seeks to address the question to what extent interparliamentary cooperation takes place on the administrative level.

For this purpose, the chapter provides an overview of administrative interparliamentary cooperation in the EU between parliaments of the EU's 28 Member States and the EP. In this chapter, 'administrative parliamentary cooperation' is understood as the support parliamentary administrators provide to members of parliament in interparliamentary cooperation (eg, COSAC, interparliamentary meetings, etc), but also contacts between administrators per se. The chapter is structured in the following way. The first section is about administrative actors and structures in parliament that are involved in interparliamentary cooperation or that have resulted from this cooperation. These consist mainly of the network of parliamentary officials, also known as national parliamentary representatives or NPRs, the staff of the Conference of the European Affairs Committees (COSAC) and the EP's Directorate for Relations with National Parliaments. The second section is about the activities of administrative actors in interparliamentary cooperation. Here the focus is on the support that administrators provide for interparliamentary cooperation on the political level. The chapter also deals with interparliamentary relations aimed at administrative cooperation (eg, EU Interparliamentary Exchange). Finally, it describes the added value of interparliamentary cooperation in the Early Warning System (EWS) and the scrutiny of EU legislation. The chapter shows that intensive parliamentary administrative activity has developed around the EU. Some of the activities are based on established practices that exist also outside the European context, such as support for delegations of parliamentarians. Others are exclusive to EU Integration, such as the COSAC Secretariat and the liaison officers of national parliaments in Brussels.

II. THE ORGANISATION OF COOPERATION BETWEEN PARLIAMENTARY ADMINISTRATIONS

The activities of members of parliament in interparliamentary cooperation are mainly organised by the EP and the national parliament holding the Presidency ('Presidency Parliament') with support from the other two parliaments, which take part in the 18-months Presidency of the EU Council ('Parliamentary Troika' or 'Presidency Troika'). The scope of respective responsibilities of the Troika and the European Parliament is in general well defined, but overlaps for specific events, such as the organisation of the Conference on the

[5] Bodies within National Parliaments Specialising in European Affairs, available at: bookshop.europa.eu/is-bin/INTERSHOP.enfinity/WFS/EU-Bookshop-Site/en_GB/-/EUR/ViewParametricSearch-Dispatch; C Fasone, 'Interparliamentary Cooperation and Democratic Representation in Europe' in S Kröger and D Friedrich (eds), *The Challenge of Democratic Representation in the European Union* (Basingstoke, Palgrave Macmillan, 2012); K Neunreither, 'The European Parliament and National Parliaments: Conflict or Cooperation' (2015) 11 *Journal of Legislative Studies* 466, 489; Interview with an EP Official in Brussels, 30/03/2015.

Common Foreign and Security Policy and the Conference on Economic Governance.[6] The administrative services of the EP, but in particular the ones of national parliaments are wary of each other's interference in the competences of one another.[7] This is in particular true for national parliaments, who are disadvantaged compared to the EP in terms of the experience with the organisation of events in a multilingual setting and the logistical services that come with it. It seems that a certain degree of 'mistrust' exists between national and European parliamentary administrations, which mirrors the situation at the level of members of parliament.[8] This 'mistrust' is rooted not only in the different level of management experience, but also in the more general discussion on which legislative goals should be achieved on the European level and which ones are better left to national institutions.

Parliamentary administrators are loyal to their respective parliaments and work according to this logic.[9] Having said that, it has to be acknowledged that parliamentary administrators tend to agree that on a personal level the administrative relations between parliaments are open and successful.[10] The next sections review the following administrative actors and structures: the Network of Liaison Officers, COSAC Secretariat and the Directorate for Relations with NPs.

A. The Network of Liaison Officers of National Parliaments in Brussels

The Network of Liaison Officers consists of representatives at the administrative level, which the national parliaments of the EU send to Brussels. In 1991, the Danish parliament was the first parliament to post an official in Brussels as liaison officer for EU affairs.[11] At the time, his office was in the Belgian parliament. Over time, more and more parliaments sent liaison officers, especially since the 2000s. Today, 26 out of 28 national parliaments (ie, the equivalent of 35 out of 39 parliamentary chambers) have one or more liaison officers in Brussels (Figure 1). With the exception of the German liaison officers, they are hosted by the European Parliament in the direct proximity of the Directorate for Relations with NPs.[12] Most of them have worked for their parliament for several years before being sent to Brussels, and thus have a thorough understanding of the working and priorities of their parliament.[13]

[6] See, respectively, J Wouters and K Raube, 'The Interparliamentary Conference on Common Foreign and Security Policy: A Quest for Democratic Accountability in EU Security Governance' (Ch 12), and I Cooper, 'The Interparliamentary Conference on Stability, Economic Coordination and Governance in the European Union (The "Article 13 Conference")' (Ch 13), both in this volume.

[7] Interview with a COSAC official in Brussels, 13/10/2011; Interview with an Honorary Director of the EP in Luxembourg 23/10/2012; EP Official in Brussels 30/3/2015, n 5 above.

[8] Neunreither, 'The European Parliament and National Parliaments: Conflict or Cooperation', n 5 above; Fasone, 'Interparliamentary Cooperation and Democratic Representation in Europe', n 5 above.

[9] Högenauer and Christiansen 'Parliamentary Administrations in the Scrutiny of EU Decision-Making', (n 1 above) at 119.

[10] EP Official 30/3/2015, n 5 above.

[11] Interview with a Parliamentary Liaison Officer in Brussels, 09/10/2010.

[12] The German parliament sends not only a civil servant, but also representatives for the political parties. As the European Parliament only provides a limited number of offices per parliament, they could not be hosted in the EP. C Neuhold and A-L Högenauer, 'Administrators networking EU affairs? The role of parliamentary officials in interparliamentary coordination and control' presented at the EUSA Biennial Conference in Baltimore on 9–11 May 2013; EP Official in Brussels 30/3/2015, n 5 above; Interview with a Parliamentary Liaison Officer in Brussels, 12/01/2012.

[13] Interview with a Parliamentary Liaison Officer in Brussels, 31/05/2012; Interview with a Dutch EAC clerk, 9/01/2012.

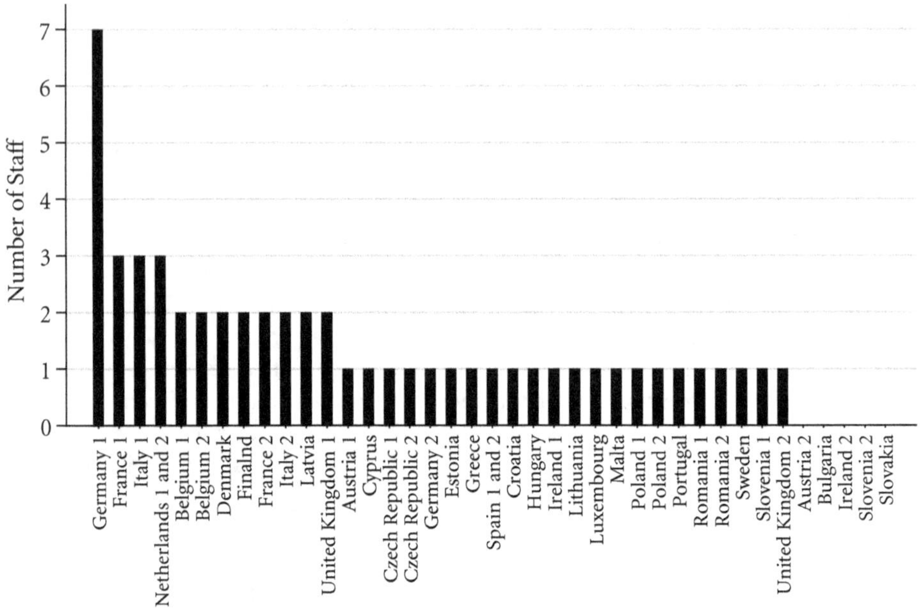

Figure 1: Number of Staff in the Liaison Offices of NPs in Brussels

Source: National Parliament contacts in April 2015 (see footnote 25).
Note: The number of staff includes liaison officers, deputies, assistants and trainees. The number after each country stands for lower (1) or upper (2) chambers of parliament.

The tasks of the liaison officers in Brussels revolve strongly around a central information function.[14] First, they gather information on new and ongoing EU policy initiatives, especially on the basis of the priorities defined by the sectoral and/or European Affairs Committees of their parliaments.[15] This involves both informal communication via phone or email, and—in many cases—regular newsletters.[16] Secondly, the liaison officers establish and maintain a network of contacts with the European Parliament and the European Commission as part of the political dialogue and their information-gathering activities.[17] Thirdly, the liaison officers allow national parliaments to exchange information and coordinate their activities on a frequent basis. For this purpose, they meet every Monday in so-called 'Monday Morning Meetings', but the fact that their offices are located on the same corridor also facilitates informal discussions.[18] The COSAC Secretariat, which is discussed

[14] C Neuhold and A-L Högenauer, 'Administrators networking EU affairs? The role of parliamentary officials in interparliamentary coordination and control', n 12 above; Interview with a Parliamentary Liaison Officer in Brussels, 13/10/2011; COSAC Official, 13/10/2011, n 7 above.

[15] BA Dias Pinheiro, 'The Treaty of Lisbon and the adaptation of national Parliaments to the challenges of European integration: the case of the permanent representatives of Parliaments to the EU institutions' (2012) available at: www.repository.utl.pt/handle/10400.5/5124.

[16] Parliamentary Liaison Officer, 12/01/2012, n 12 above; Parliamentary Liaison Officer, 31/05/2012, n 12 above.

[17] cf MW Bauer, 'Impact of Administrative Reform of the European Commission: Results from a Survey of Heads of Unit in Policy-making Directorates' (2009) 75 *International Review of Administrative Sciences* 459.

[18] Parliamentary Liaison Officer, 12/01/2012, n 12 above.

in the next section, is part of these Monday Morning Meetings and has its offices also on the same corridor. Finally, the liaison officers fulfil a limited representative function when they organise meetings between their MPs and European officials and politicians. But they do not 'lobby' the institutions themselves and emphasise that the multi-party nature of their parliaments requires them to observe strict neutrality.[19]

B. Presidency Troika and COSAC Staff

One important element in interparliamentary cooperation is COSAC, the Conference of the European Affairs Committees of the national parliaments of the EU Member States and the European Parliament. First established in May 1989, COSAC now has a legal basis in the European Treaties (Protocol No 1 to the Treaty of Lisbon). Its aim is to strengthen the role of national parliaments in EU affairs through the exchange of best practices and by fostering interparliamentary debate on important political topics. Today, COSAC meets biannually. Each parliament is represented by six members, and the national parliaments of candidate countries can each send three observers.[20] The core activities of COSAC are political in nature and consist of conferences of national MPs and members of the EP (MEPs) on topics of current interest. These conferences are supported by the COSAC Secretariat and the European Affairs Committee secretariat of the Presidency Parliament).[21] The COSAC Secretariat is composed of officials of the parliaments of the three Member States that assure the Council Presidency and a permanent staff member.[22] The officials coming from the Parliamentary Troika are thus temporarily delegated to COSAC and return to their parliaments after 18 months.[23] The exact number of these temporary members varies over time, as it is up to each parliament to decide how many resources it is willing to commit to COSAC.[24] In the period between July 2014 and December 2015 (Presidency Troika of Italy, Latvia and Luxembourg), the COSAC Secretariat consisted of five temporary delegates from Italy, Latvia and Luxembourg.[25]

In addition, the COSAC Secretariat has one permanent member of staff, who has to be a parliamentary official and who is appointed for a renewable two-year term. The permanent member of staff usually also has a background as liaison officer of a national parliament in Brussels, and has thus experience in networking with different parliaments.[26] The procedure for the appointment of the permanent member is laid down in the COSAC Rules

[19] Interview with a Parliamentary Liaison Officer in Brussels, 24/01/2013; COSAC Official, 13/10/2011, n 7 above; Parliamentary Liaison Officer, 12/01/2012, n 12 above.

[20] Art 3, European Parliament, Rules of Procedure of the Conference of Parliamentary Committees for Union Affairs of Parliaments of the European Union, [2011] OJ C299/1–9. L Tordoff, 'The conference of European affairs committees: A collective voice for national parliaments in the European Union' (2000) 6 *The Journal of Legislative Studies* 1, 8.

[21] Art 8.7, Rules of Procedure of COSAC, n 20 above; see also C Fryda, 'The role of the COSAC Secretariat Within the Evolving Landscape of Interparliamentary Cooperation: Challenges for the Future', Chapter 17 in this volume.

[22] Art 9.1, Rules of Procedure of COSAC, n 20 above.

[23] Art 9.2, Rules of Procedure of COSAC, n 20 above.

[24] COSAC Official, 13/10/2011, n 7 above.

[25] National Parliament contacts in April 2015, available at: www.europarl.europa.eu/relnatparl/en/about/contacts.html.

[26] COSAC Official, 13/10/2011, n 7 above.

of Procedure. The candidate is proposed by the Presidency Troika, and confirmed by the Chairpersons of the European Affairs Committees.[27] The selection of the permanent member is not free from political inferences, where parliaments have an interest in promoting the appointment of their candidate.[28] Finally, the European Parliament sends one representative to the COSAC Secretariat, who usually also changes every 18 months in respect to the rotation of national parliamentary administrations and to avoid giving the EP representative any advantage compared to national parliament representatives.[29]

While COSAC has had regular meetings since the 1990s, the Secretariat itself was only established in 2003, when it became clear that the staff of the European Affairs Committees of the parliaments in the Troika could not provide sufficient support.[30] By setting up a secretariat, interparliamentary relations achieved a formal structure. This is not redundant, given the debate among politicians whether and how interparliamentary cooperation should be formally institutionalised.[31] While the COSAC Secretariat is only an administrative structure, it is a step towards formal institutionalisation.

As in the case of the liaison officers of the national parliaments, the European Parliament provides the offices for the COSAC Secretariat. The temporary members of the COSAC Secretariat are paid by their home countries, as it is their responsibility to support COSAC during their Troika Presidency.[32] The permanent member is co-financed by the national parliaments through voluntary contributions.[33]

The COSAC Secretariat receives its political guidance from the COSAC Presidency (ie, the three parliaments of the Presidency Troika), or follows the decisions of the COSAC meetings. It works mainly in English and French (and the COSAC website reflects this). In practice, in the daily organisation of COSAC, English is particularly important as a working language.[34] The key points of contact for the COSAC Secretariat are the liaison officers of national parliaments in Brussels, as these are the easiest to reach.[35] Direct contact with the parliamentary administrations in the national capitals is relatively rare. An exception is the preparation of the biannual COSAC meetings, which require pre-preparatory meetings with the parliamentary administration in those capitals.[36]

C. The European Parliament's Administration

Compared to national parliaments, the EP relatively quickly dedicated permanent administrative resources to the development of interparliamentary relations. The European Union

[27] Art 9.3, Rules of Procedure of COSAC, n 20 above.

[28] COSAC Official, 13/10/2011, n 7 above.

[29] Interview with an EP Official, 26/01/2012.

[30] C Neuhold, 'Trans-national bureaucratic networks in the EU: The role of parliamentary officials in interparliamentary coordination and control' presented at the EUSA Conference in Boston on 5–7 March 2015.

[31] C Bengtson, 'Interparliamentary cooperation within Europe' in J O'Brennan and T Raunio (eds), *National Parliaments within the Enlarged European Union. From 'victims' of integration to competitive actors* (London and New York, Routledge, 2007) 53.

[32] COSAC Official, 13/10/2011, n 7 above.

[33] Art 9.5, Rules of Procedure of COSAC.

[34] COSAC Official, 13/10/2011, n 7 above.

[35] See, in particular, the Part Six of this volume presenting a debate on the role of the COSAC.

[36] ibid.

d funding to the EP for relations with national parliaments for the first time in 1990. The budget, which became operational in 1991, can be used for facilitating the exchange of information (including EPCRD and IPEX),[37] analysing information, training schemes for officials and study visits to the EP.[38] Figure 2 shows the yearly appropriations and real outturns. On average, the EP has spent 200,000 euro per year between 1991 and 2013. The most was spent in 2007 (almost 800,000 euro), while the least financial resources were used in 1991 (50,000 euro). Given the fact that the EP houses the COSAC Secretariat and national parliamentary liaison officers, it can be said that the EP carries the major financial burden of interparliamentary cooperation.

D. Directorate for Relations with National Parliaments

In the same year as the first financial resources were appropriated for interparliamentary cooperation, the EP's political bodies decided to set up an administrative service for relations with national parliaments.[39] This service was at first organised at a unit level and operated in the Directorate-General (DG) for Committees and Delegations in recognition of the key role to be played by committees in interparliamentary contacts.[40] In 2003, the unit was upgraded into a directorate, which still functioned under a DG dedicated to committees (DG IPOL). Since 2009, the unit is known as the Directorate for Relations with National Parliaments, and operates within DG Presidency.

Organisationally, the Directorate is split into two units. One of the units specialises in institutional cooperation, which includes relations with NPRs in Brussels and interparliamentary assemblies (eg, the Parliamentary Assembly of the Council of Europe), the organisation of Joint Parliamentary and Joint Committee Meetings, issues relating to COSAC, the EU Speakers' Conference, ECPRD and IPEX. The second unit specialises in legislative dialogue, which mainly involves the oversight of interparliamentary activities of EP committees (including the maintenance of a Directory of Corresponding Committees in national parliaments), but also parliamentary scrutiny (eg, subsidiarity checks).[41] In 2014, the Directorate comprised 12 staff at the administrator level (AD level/officials) and 10 staff at the secretarial/assistant level (AST rank).[42] Apart from an interest in inter-institutional relations, no particular expertise is required such as, for example, is required in some committee secretariats (eg, Economic Affairs or Legal Affairs Committees).[43] Since its establishment in the 1990s, the number of administrators in the Directorate for relations with NPs

[37] On these two networks see in detail section II.D below.

[38] The EP has at its disposal two other items for interparliamentary cooperation in Chapters 3 and 10 of the Annual Budget. For example, Item 3043 is dedicated to joint parliamentary committees. However, these two chapters are not limited to cooperation with national parliaments, but also with parliaments of third countries. Therefore, a distinction between interparliamentary cooperation between EU parliaments and the EU with third parliaments is not possible.

[39] European Parliament's 1991 Directory, published by the Directorate-General for Committees and Delegations in Luxembourg.

[40] Neunreither, 'The European Parliament and National Parliaments: Conflict or Cooperation', n 5 above.

[41] EP Official in Brussels 30/3/2015, n 5 above.

[42] Organisational Chart of the Directorate for Relations with National Parliaments, available at www.europarl.europa.eu/relnatparl/en/about/contacts.html.

[43] EP Official in Brussels 30/3/2015, n 5 above.

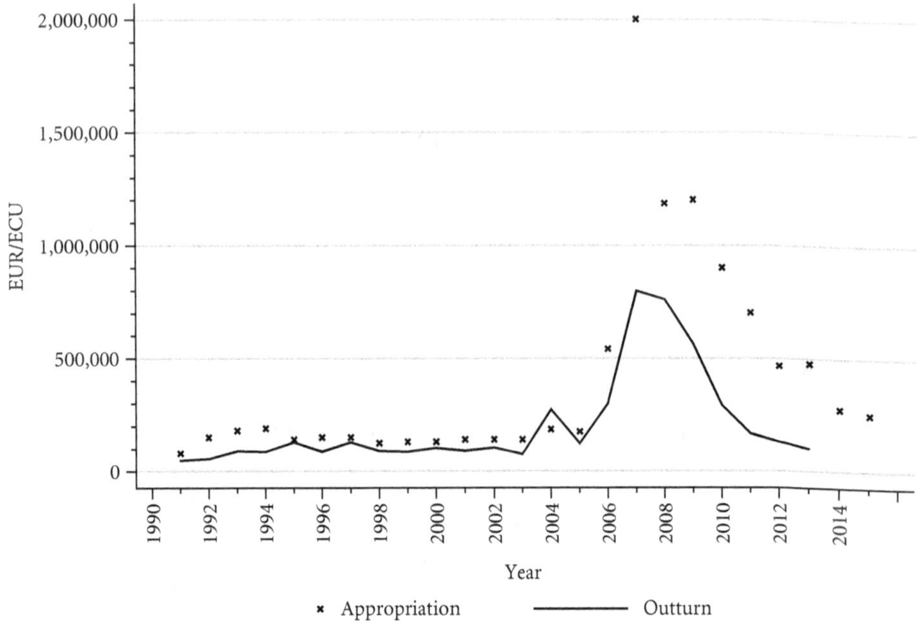

Figure 2: EU Budget Appropriations and Outturns for Relations with National Parliaments
Source: EU Annual Budgets 1991–2015, Item 3249 (Item 2993 before 2003)

has tripled, which signifies the extent to which the EP has invested in fostering contacts with national parliaments. The number of staff in NPs is quite different compared to the EP, as only a handful of chambers (ie, both chambers in Germany, UK and Italy, and the upper houses of Romania and France) dedicate more than 10 staff working on EU Affairs.[44]

The general mission of the Directorate is to act as a coordinating body and a platform of information between the EP and national parliaments. In this sense it occupies a unique role in interparliamentary relations. Not only does it support the work of MEPs, but it also makes sure that the voice of NPs is heard inside the EP.[45] The main task of the Directorate is to facilitate contacts between the committees of the EP and national parliaments, such as working visits by standing committees and interparliamentary meetings.[46] In addition, the Directorate cooperates with parliaments from Member States holding the EU Presidency, organises bilateral (study) visits and advises the EP's political bodies (eg, Conference of Presidents, Conference of Committee Chairs, etc), MEPs and other departments within the EP's General Secretariat in their relations with national parliaments. The extent of the Directorate's involvement depends on the solicitation from the EP's committees and MEPs. As the Directorate is based in Brussels, it is likely to be informed and involved in

[44] Högenauer and Christiansen 'Parliamentary Administrations in the Scrutiny of EU Decision-Making', (n 1 above) at 125.
[45] EP Official in Brussels 30/3/2015, n 5 above.
[46] ibid.

interparliamentary activities in the EP's headquarters. It is, by contrast, less involved when MEPs visit national parliaments outside the premises of the EP.[47]

III. INTERPARLIAMENTARY ACTIVITIES

A. COSAC Activities

The activities of COSAC develop around its biannual meetings and the exchange of best practices. The main tasks of the COSAC Secretariat include the preparation and the coordination of the agendas of COSAC meetings. Most of the agenda items are usually proposed by the Presidency Troika, and a few items are related to current events.

The second and related important task is the preparation of the biannual reports of COSAC, which are a key tool for the exchange of best practice on parliamentary procedures. For example, the priorities of the Polish Presidency in 2011 were the multiannual financial framework and the review of parliamentary procedures two years after the changes introduced by the Lisbon Treaty. How well had parliaments adapted to the new opportunities? What were successful ways of adaptation and could other parliaments learn from those? For the biannual report, the COSAC Secretariat thus had to draw up questions that reflected those priorities. The Presidency Troika provides guidelines for this, such as the size of the report, the topics to be included; sometimes it even suggests some precise questions that it wants to see included.[48] But the COSAC Secretariat then has to propose the precise questionnaire and has to make sure that comparable data can be collected. In addition, the COSAC Secretariat can play the role of initiator by proposing potentially interesting items. Thirdly, the COSAC Secretariat analyses the responses of national parliaments and draws up the actual reports. Finally, the COSAC Secretariat acts as the institutional memory, by maintaining the COSAC's website, by drawing up minutes of meetings and by archiving this information.[49]

B. Interparliamentary Meetings and Conferences

Interparliamentary meetings and conferences are frequent forms of contact between members of NPs and the EP. In this type of relations parliamentary administrators are responsible for the organisation and the support to respective delegations of parliamentarians (eg, preparation of briefings). The responsibility for the organisation will vary depending on the type of meeting. While the EP is exclusively responsible for the organisation of Interparliamentary Committee Meetings (ICMs), the Parliamentary Troika (ie, the Presidency Parliament in particular) organises Joint Parliamentary Meetings (JPMs), Joint Committee Meetings (JCMs) and Interparliamentary Conferences in collaboration with the EP.

[47] EP Official, 26/01/2012, n 29 above.
[48] COSAC Official, 13/10/2011, n 7 above.
[49] ibid.

(i) Interparliamentary Committee Meetings

ICMs bring together members of parliament from specialised committees in the EP and national parliaments. They take place at the premises of the EP and on a topic selected by MEPs. Their organisation is carried out by the EP's Directorate for Relations with National Parliaments and the secretariat of the EP committee which initiated the ICM. Since the main duty of committee secretariats is the management of legislative and own-initiative reports, rather than interparliamentary matters, the Directorate for Relations with NPs is an important partner for committees in the organisation of ICMs.[50] In order to effectively organise interparliamentary activities, the Directorate for Relations with NPs and the relevant committee services of the EP (ie, DG IPOL and DG EXPO) have set up a modus operandi, which delineates each other's responsibilities.[51] The main logistical organisation falls under the Directorate for Relations with NPs (eg, distribution of invitations, preparation of a list of participants, catering, etc), while committee secretariats assist MEPs in the substantive preparation of the meetings (eg, set up of the agenda). The Directorate for Relations with NPs contributes to the ICM's agenda insofar as it discusses the relevance of the subjects for NPs.[52]

(ii) Joint Parliamentary Meetings and Joint Committee Meetings

Compared to ICMs, Joint Parliamentary Meetings (JPMs) and Joint Committee Meetings (JCMs) take place less frequently. Both are organised by the Presidency Parliament in partnership with the EP, which also hosts the events at its premises. As for the case of ICMs, the EP's Directorate for Relations with NPs plays an important organisational role, while the agenda is coordinated together with the administrators of Presidency Parliaments.[53] Since JPMs bring together delegations of parliamentarians of the EU's parliaments to discuss broad aspects of political issues, they are specifically suitable for fostering relations between parliamentarians of the same political families. Accordingly, one can expect a large presence of officials from parties and parliamentary party groups. Compared to contacts between civil servants in parliament, there is less information on the relations between party and parliamentary party group officials. When such contacts occur, they are organised by the secretariats of parties and parliamentary party groups and not necessarily by the central administrations of parliaments.[54] In addition, the administrative capacity of parliamentary groups varies. Among the parliamentary groups in the EP, only the European People's Party has an administrative unit taking care of relations with NPs. This could be one of the reasons why the Group of European People's Party has the best-developed relations with parties from NPs.

[50] EP Official in Brussels 30/3/2015, n 5 above.
[51] ibid.
[52] ibid.
[53] ibid.
[54] ibid.

(iii) Interparliamentary Conferences

Interparliamentary Conferences are a relative novelty in interparliamentary activities. The organisation of the two that have thus far been established (ie, the Interparliamentary Conference on Common Foreign and Security Policy and the Common Security and Defence Policy and the Interparliamentary Conference on Economic Governance, set up in 2012 and 2013, respectively) does not differ substantially from other interparliamentary meetings (eg, Rules of Procedure of the Conference on CFSP). Both conferences are held biannually. Compared to ICMs, only one of the JPMs and JCMs meetings is held in the EP (Brussels), while a second one is held in the country of the Presidency Parliament. Hence, the logistical burden to organise these meetings falls either on the EP (Directorate for Relations with NPs) or the Presidency Parliament.

Administrators thus have some influence on organisational arrangements, discussions on the agenda and the drafting of the rules of procedure. However, beyond that, parliamentary administrations do not play a role in the substantive policy-related discussions during interparliamentary meetings.[55] This is expected given that most of these events are dedicated to interparliamentary cooperation between politicians and not parliamentary administrators. However, administrative contact does occur in the activities we describe next.[56]

C. Bilateral Visits to the European Parliament

One of the most frequent forms of interparliamentary cooperation is bilateral visits from national parliaments to the EP. Compared to interparliamentary meetings, delegations from national parliaments consist either of members of parliament or administrators (Figure 3). Bilateral visits give therefore the floor to formal administrative interparliamentary cooperation, which targets specific issues of collaboration between administrations. The visits are not limited to the EU's national parliaments only, but are also organised for countries preparing to join the EU.[57] In 2008, there were, for example, five such visits, which brought to the EP more than 40 officials from the Former Yugoslav Republic of Macedonia, Serbia, Montenegro, Turkey and Kosovo.[58] These numbers are, however, relatively low compared to visits from the EU's national parliaments. In 2008, the EP has for instance hosted more than 220 officials in a total of 36 bilateral visits. In 2013, the EP received more than 160 administrators and 120 members of parliament.[59] As Figure 3 shows, bilateral visits

[55] The administrators of NPs are involved insofar as they brief their members and accompany them to Brussels. In several instances this support is often provided by NPRs.

[56] C Neuhold, 'Trans-national bureaucratic networks in the EU: The role of parliamentary officials in interparliamentary coordination and control', n 30 above.

[57] National Parliaments European Parliament Yearbook 2008, available at: www.europarl.europa.eu/webnp/webdav/site/myjahiasite/shared/Publications/Yearbook/Yearbook%202008.pdf; National Parliaments European Parliament Yearbook 2009, available at: www.europarl.europa.eu/webnp/webdav/site/myjahiasite/shared/Publications/Yearbook/Yearbook%202009.pdf.

[58] These five visits are not included in Figure 3, which includes only visits from the EU's national parliaments.

[59] Annual Report 2013/2014 on Interparliamentary relations between the European Parliament and national Parliaments under the Treaty of Lisbon, available at: www.europarl.europa.eu/webnp/webdav/site/myjahiasite/shared/Publications/Annual%20report/Relations%20with%20National%20Parliaments%20-%20Annual%20Report%202013.pdf.

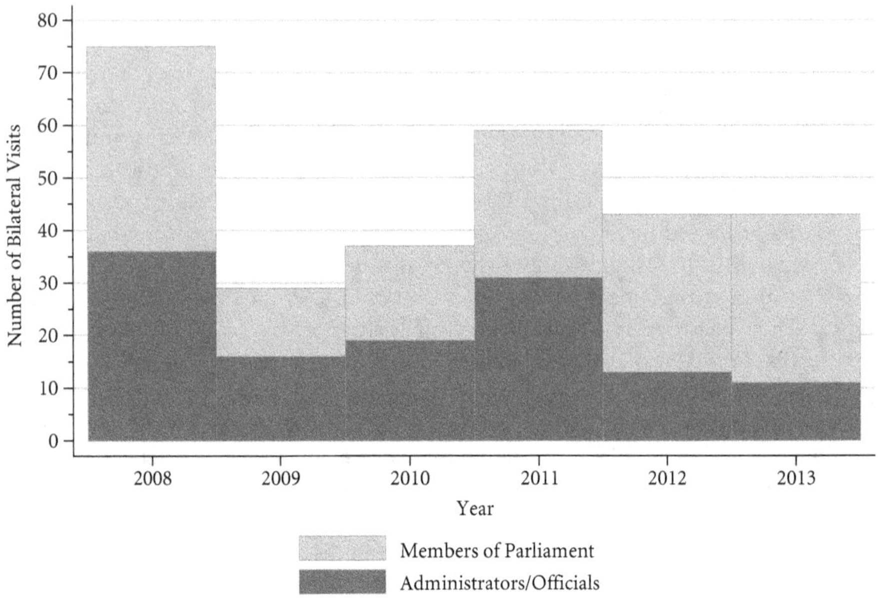

Figure 3: Bilateral Visits to the EP

Source: Yearbook 2008 (n 55), Yearbook 2009 (n 55), Yearbook 2010 (n 58) and Annual Report 2013/14 (n 57)

of administrators from national parliaments are numerically as important as visits from members of parliament.

Bilateral visits (either from administrators of politicians) are always organised by the EP at the request of individual chambers. This means that NPs shape the agenda. Visits take the form of working meetings, study visits, guided tours or trainings. Some of them are dedicated to the preparation for the EU rotating Presidency. In 2010, there were 19 such visits from the Polish parliament in order to prepare for its Presidency.[60] In general, bilateral visits consist of officials from committees on EU-related issues, and a mixed group of administrators and officials working for parliamentary groups.[61] The latter are however limited in number compared to the former.

National parliaments are not equally represented in bilateral visits to the EP and some chambers are more active than others. In 2013, six national parliaments sent their officials to the EP.[62] Three visits were from the British House of Commons,[63] two from the Swedish Riksdagen, the Danish Folketingetm, and Dutch Tweede Kamer, one from the Estonian Riigkogu and the Austrian Nationalrat.

Since 2008, the EP has also organised thematic administrative visits. Unlike bilateral visits, these visits do not target specific requests from national parliaments. The purpose

[60] National Parliaments European Parliament Yearbook 2010, available at: www.europarl.europa.eu/webnp/webdav/site/myjahiasite/shared/Publications/Yearbook/Yearbook%202010.pdf.

[61] Yearbook 2009, n 55 above.

[62] Annual Report 2013–14, n 57 above.

[63] One of the three visits was organised together with the House of Lords.

is rather to gather together officials from different national parliaments on issues of cross-parliamentary interest, such as protocol, library services, plenary activities, communication with citizens, etc. In the period between 2008 and 2010, there have been 20 such visits for a total of more than 500 administrators. Such visits offer the opportunity for contact between officials from different NPs and the EP at the same time.

D. Information and Documentation Networks

The exchange of information and documentation is at the core of the European Centre for Parliamentary Research and Documentation (ECPRD) and the InterParliamentary EU Information eXchange (IPEX). Both of these networks are connected with European integration. The ECPRD was established on the initiative of the Conference of Speakers of European Parliamentary Assemblies in 1977. Members of the ECPRD are the EP, the Parliamentary Assembly of the Council of Europe (PACE) and parliaments of the EU and Council of Europe Member States.[64] The ECPRD Directors are appointed by the Secretaries General of the EP and PACE.

IPEX is, on the other hand, a network exclusive to the parliaments of the EU.[65] It is mainly dedicated for the use of national parliaments as a point of contact for the scrutiny of EU draft legislative proposals. The Secretaries General of national parliaments each appoint up to two IPEX correspondents, who are responsible for uploading documents relating to the subsidiarity check of EU draft legislative proposals.[66] IPEX is co-financed by the EP and national parliaments. The EP appropriates from its own budget funds for securing the IPEX's website domain; while national parliaments co-finance the salary of an officer, who centrally oversees IPEX's operations.[67] The objectives of the platform are decided by the EU Speakers' Conference, while the Secretaries General approve the working guidelines. The IPEX Chairmanship and Board prepare IPEX's background work.[68] Besides an important instrument for the exchange of documents, IPEX functions also as a venue for networking between administrators. Meetings for IPEX correspondents are organised annually and include activities such as training, workshops and a plenary session. Unlike the website of the ECPRD, the documents on the IPEX website are freely available to the public.[69] As a result, IPEX has become a source of information for EU citizens as well.

[64] The parliaments of Israel, Canada and Mexico have an observer status in the ECPRD. Statutes of the European Centre for Parliamentary Research and Documentation, available at: ecprd.secure.europarl.europa.eu/ecprd/navigation.do?section=3.

[65] Note that candidate countries can also participate.

[66] Art 8, IPEX Guidelines as approved by the meeting of the Secretaries General of the EU Parliament at the Meeting of Secretaries General on 14 March 2015 in Rome, available at: www.ipex.eu/IPEXL-WEB/widgets/download.do?widgetId=082dbcc5312cf97d013147b139360ad7&fileId=082dbcc5312cf97d013147b2166d0ad9. Based on information on the IPEX website, only seven chambers have appointed two administrators as IPEX correspondents, while most of them have only one correspondent. The Dutch upper chamber is the only chamber which did not appoint an IPEX correspondent (situation in March 2015).

[67] Art 9, Art 10 IPEX Guidelines, n 66 above.

[68] Art 4, Art 5 IPEX Guidelines, n 66 above.

[69] See the Conclusion of the EU Speakers' Conference held on 7–8 April 2014 in Vilnius, Lithuanian, available at www.ipex.eu/IPEXL-WEB/euspeakers/getspeakers.do.

E. Meetings of the Secretaries General of the EU Parliaments

Like the Speakers' Conference, which dates back to the 1960s and 1970s, the meetings of Secretaries General were one of the first formal administrative relations that were established in the scope of EU interparliamentary cooperation. The Secretaries General of EU parliaments meet in order to prepare the annual EU Speakers' Conference. Meetings occur annually and a few weeks before the Conference of Speakers. They are organised by the Presidency Troika and take place in the country which presided over the EU Council in the second half of the year. The preparation is therefore in the hands of national parliaments and the EP does not play a particular role.

The annual meeting lasts two days. The programme includes presentations, debates and social events. Compared to the administrative networks, such as the ECPRD or IPEX, the meetings of Secretaries General are not limited to technical cooperation. They serve as a platform for discussing the agenda of the upcoming EU Speakers' Conference on politically relevant topics, such as the economic crisis, human rights, foreign affairs, etc. In addition, they provide a venue for exchanging best practices, when Secretaries General present individual reports on different issues (eg, the development of political dialogue, coordination of EU affairs, the scrutiny of draft proposals on EU law, etc). The Secretaries General are responsible for overseeing the lower levels of administrative cooperation. For this purpose they have the power to appoint the IPEX Chair and Board, adopt guidelines for the operations of IPEX, etc. Therefore, administrative interparliamentary cooperation follows a strict logic of hierarchy, where the leeway of action and mandate to discuss political matters varies according to the level of seniority in the administration. This administrative hierarchy reflects the hierarchy that exists between corresponding types of political coordination.

F. Scrutiny of EU Draft Legislation: The Early Warning System

As it has been seen for the case of COSAC contributions, most of the results of interparliamentary activities are not formally binding. With the entry into force of the Lisbon Treaty in 2009, national parliaments were given a formal right under the Early Warning System (EWS).[70] Through the EWS national parliaments are mandated to scrutinise the compliance of draft EU legislation with regard to the principle of subsidiarity. This right is exercised through so-called reasoned opinions and contributions, which are issued by individual NPs and their chambers. As is well known, when one third of all the chambers issue a reasoned opinion detecting a violation of the principle of subsidiarity by a legislative proposal, a so-called 'yellow card' is reached and the European Commission is obliged by law to review the proposal.[71] It can maintain, amend or withdraw the proposal.[72]

[70] See Protocols No 1 and 2 annexed to the Treaty of Lisbon.

[71] Art 7, Protocol No 2.

[72] Since the access of Croatia one third of votes amounts to 19 out of 56 chamber votes.

(i) *National Parliamentary Administrations in the Early Warning System*

Reasoned opinions and other contributions are prepared by national parliaments, where parliamentary administrators can play a considerable role in the scrutiny of EU proposals.[73] In particular, parliamentary administrators are responsible for an extensive range of tasks. They often pre-select potentially problematic EU legislative proposals for scrutiny, gather and summarise information, provide procedural and legal advice and sometimes even draft reasoned opinions.[74] While the role of parliamentary administrators in the EWS can vary between chambers, almost all NPs' parliamentary administrators play a role that goes beyond technical support, which indicates a certain level of convergence.[75] A very common activity of administrators is the pre-selection of documents for scrutiny.[76]

The important role that parliamentary administrators carry out as non-elected officials has led to the assumption that the scrutiny of EU politics escapes the political control from elected officials or members of parliament.[77] Although parliamentary administrators play an extensive role, evidence collected thus far shows that parliamentarians delegate tasks to staff selectively. Especially those parliaments that have well-staffed party groups and generous allowances for MPs' assistants use these 'politicised' administrators to maintain a grip on the scrutiny of EU legislation.[78]

(ii) *Interparliamentary Aspects*

While the preparation of reasoned opinions is not an interparliamentary activity per se, interparliamentary activities are important for their effective use.[79] Thus far, national parliaments have found it difficult to reach the threshold necessary for the yellow card due to different priorities and some NPs' inactive use of the EWS. For example, some parliaments did not call reasoned opinions 'reasoned opinions' or did not clearly argue in terms of subsidiarity, which would lead their reasoned opinions to be discarded. Here, COSAC made great efforts to help national parliaments to adapt their approaches to avoid those problems.[80] For instance, it organised so-called 'subsidiarity tests' between 2006 and 2009 that allowed national parliaments to prepare for subsidiarity review. It is still an important platform for discussions on the ideal format and content of reasoned opinions.

In addition, reaching a yellow card requires cooperation between NPs. In order to mount a successful challenge to an EU proposal, national parliaments have to coordinate their

[73] Högenauer and Neuhold, 'National Parliaments after Lisbon: Administrations on the Rise', n 1 above; Högenauer and Christiansen 'Parliamentary Administrations in the Scrutiny of EU Decision-Making', n 1 above.

[74] Högenauer and Neuhold, 'National Parliaments after Lisbon: Administrations on the Rise', n 1 above at 341–42.

[75] ibid, 344, 348.

[76] ibid, 344.

[77] T Christiansen, A-L Högenauer and C Neuhold, 'National Parliaments in the post-Lisbon European Union: Bureaucratization rather than Democratization?' (2014) 12 *Comparative European Politics* 121, 140.

[78] T Winzen, 'Bureaucracy and Democracy: Intra-Parliamentary Delegation in European Union Affairs' (2014) 36 *Journal of European Integration* 777, 695; A Strelkov, 'Who Controls National EU Scrutiny? Parliamentary Party Groups, Committees and Administrations' (2015) 38 *West European Politics* 355, 374.

[79] I Cooper, 'The Interparliamentary Conference on Stability, Economic Coordination and Governance in the European Union (The "Article 13 Conference")', Ch 13 in this Volume.

[80] COSAC Official, 13/10/2011, n 7 above.

activities and motivate each other to join in the effort of reaching a yellow card. In this respect the liaison officers of NPs in Brussels play an important role.[81] In the two instances where national parliaments were successful in reaching the threshold for a yellow card (the Monti II and EPPO Regulations), liaison officers in Brussels played the part of coordinators and motivators.

(iii) Monti II Regulation

The first example of a yellow card is the so-called Monti II Regulation, which proposed to limit the right to organise collective action, including the right to strike. Before the eight-week EWS deadline expired, 12 reasoned opinions amounting to 19 votes were adopted. The Danish parliament had identified Monti II early on as a priority and drafted a reasoned opinion. The Danish liaison officer quickly distributed an English version of the reasoned opinion to other parliaments so that they would have a blueprint in case they too wanted to adopt one.[82] In addition, the Danish parliament could use a conveniently timed COSAC meeting to push the issue on the agenda, as they held the COSAC Presidency at the time.[83] The task of the liaison officer was then to keep national parliaments abreast of the progress towards a yellow card and to encourage other potentially interested parliaments to adopt a reasoned opinion.[84] They succeeded in mobilising the Swedish Riksdagen and the French Senate who then both became very active too.[85] Finally, the Dutch Tweede Kamer changed its mind and decided to adopt a reasoned opinion on the very last day, in part because they knew that the threshold for a yellow card had almost been reached.[86] Both in Portugal and in Belgium the staff at home and their liaison officers in Brussels were seen as playing a key role in mobilising their MPs.[87]

(iv) European Public Prosecutor's Office Regulation

In the case of the second yellow card on the proposal regarding a European Public Prosecutor's Office (EPPO), the Dutch Tweede Kamer was very active. They too used their liaison officer to inform the other parliaments that this was a Dutch priority and to proactively ask what other parliaments were planning to do.[88] As in the case of the first yellow card, there was a 'bandwagon effect', with other parliaments joining in gradually. Even Denmark—which has an opt-out in Justice and Home Affairs—considered adopting a reasoned opinion out of solidarity, but decided in the end that it could not legitimately adopt a subsidiarity complaint on an issue that would not affect it.[89]

[81] Parliamentary Liaison Officer in Brussels, 13/10/2011, n 14 above; Högenauer and Neuhold, 'National Parliaments after Lisbon: Administrations on the Rise', n 1 above at 347.

[82] Interview with a Danish EU advisor, 15/04/2014; Interview with a Dutch committee clerk, 18/04/2014; Interview with a Dutch committee clerk, 18/04/2014; Parliamentary Liaison Officer, 31/05/2012, n 12 above.

[83] cf M Buskjær Christensen, 'Is the Danish model of parliamentary scrutiny still best practice?' in C Heffler, C Neuhold, O Rozenberg and J Smith (eds), *The Palgrave Handbook of National Parliaments and the European Union* (Basingstoke, Palgrave Macmillan, 2015).

[84] Interview with a Dutch EU advisor, 16/04/2014; Interview with a Belgian committee clerk, 23/04/2014.

[85] Parliamentary Liaison Officer, 31/05/2012, n 12 above.

[86] Dutch committee clerk, 18/04/2014, n 80 above.

[87] Parliamentary Liaison Officer, 31/05/2012, n 12 above.

[88] Dutch committee clerk, 18/04/2014, n 80 above.

[89] Danish EU advisor, 15/04/2014, n 80 above.

In spite of the success NPs achieved in the Monti II and EPPO Regulations, there are also critical voices. One permanent representative expressed the view that parliaments were often no longer able to adopt a reasoned opinion within the EWS deadline, if they really only started their work once they had heard about the proposal from liaison officers.[90] Yet, the last-minute reasoned opinions from the Dutch and Belgian parliaments show that it is possible to react if parliaments are determined to do so. Since the eight-week deadline of the Early Warning System is relatively short, national parliaments are most effective if they have already earmarked a proposal as potentially problematic before it has been officially published.

(v) European Parliament's Administration in the Early Warning System

The role of the EP administration in the EWS is to translate and disseminate reasoned opinions. Whether a yellow card is reached or not, the EP, like other EU institutions, is obliged to take into account the opinions of national parliaments.[91] For this reason the Directorate for Relations with National Parliaments reviews all the documents that reach the EP within the EWS eight-week deadline. The main responsibility of the Directorate is to make reasoned opinions and contributions accessible to MEPs.[92] After it reviews the documents, the Directorate sends them to concerned committees and to the Legal Affairs Committee, which is responsible for the issue of subsidiarity and verifies whether a document is in fact a reasoned opinion and not a contribution.[93] All the reasoned opinions are then translated into the official languages of the EU (except for Maltese and Gaelic).[94] The committee secretariat, which is responsible for the legislative dossier of given reasoned opinions, informs the committee Chair and Rapporteur, who then schedule a debate. In addition to committees, the Conference of Committee Chairs (ie, the EP body bringing together the chairs of all the EP committees) is systematically informed on the state of play on reasoned opinions, which the Directorate for Relations with National Parliaments prepares monthly. Thus, the EP administrators play a role of information. The extent to which MEPs take into account reasoned opinions when writing reports and tabling amendments does, ultimately, depend on their political will.

IV. CONCLUSION

This chapter has reviewed administrative interparliamentary cooperation in terms of actors and activities. Our analysis has shown that the administration of interparliamentary relations is in the hands of the European Parliament, the Parliamentary Troika and the Presidency Parliament. Both national parliaments and the EP have invested resources to develop their administrative network since the 1990s. The EP has set up a Directorate, which provides assistance to MEPs, but takes up also the general role of contact facilitator between

90 Parliamentary Liaison Officer, 12/01/2012, n 12 above.
91 Art 7, Protocol No 2 to the Treaty of Lisbon.
92 EP Official, 26/01/2012, n 29 above.
93 ibid.
94 This is not the case for contributions, which are translated only at the request of committees. All the translations of the reasoned opinions are available in the EP's Public Register of Documents.

the EP and NPs. While the Directorate for Relations with National Parliaments provides successful tools for the coordination between the EP and individual NPs (eg, Directory of Corresponding Committees, database of reasoned opinions, etc), it is mainly the role of the COSAC Secretariat and the respective liaison officers of parliaments in Brussels to guarantee mutual coordination between NPs. This is a difficult, but important task, since under the EWS national parliaments have the power to force the European Commission to revise its legislative proposal when a yellow card is reached.

While the EWS has given individual national parliaments the channel to express their views, national parliaments are stronger when they act collectively. Therefore, the administrative capacity for coordination is essential for NPs. This has been shown in the yellow card cases for the Monti II and EPPO Regulations. As the working relations among liaison officers consolidate, we would expect NPs to increasingly use their prerogatives in the area of EU legislation. Nevertheless, human resources for relations with the EP are not the only problem of national parliaments in the scrutiny of EU legislation. The eight-week deadline prescribed in Protocols No 1 and 2 to the Treaty of Lisbon tests the capacity of NPs to scrutinise EU legislation. In order to effectively use their rights under the Lisbon Treaty, national parliaments might have to invest more resources in a proactive scrutiny of the European Commission legislative agenda. Thus, NPs might consider investing time and resources at a much earlier stage of the EU legislative cycle than presently.

While there is little doubt that administrative resources play an important role in the scrutiny of EU legislation, less firm conclusions can be drawn on the value of administrative contacts per se. These occur on a technical, but also on a policy substantive level. The core of administrative contacts consists of the exchange of best practices on technical matters, such as the scrutiny of legislation, communication with citizens, management of research, etc. The meetings of Secretary-Generals of EU Parliaments are the most prominent example of administrative interparliamentary relations on a policy substantive level, where Secretary-Generals discuss and coordinate the agenda of the EU Speakers' Conference. Albeit with smaller margins of manoeuver, policy discussions occur also in meetings between low-level officials. Every interparliamentary encounter (political or administrative) can thus represent an opportunity for communication on policy-relevant issues. The value of such communication does not only depend on the hierarchy level, but also on the administrative culture within each Member State of the EU.

Given the dynamic nature of EU politics, it is difficult to predict how the role of parliamentary administrations in interparliamentary cooperation will develop in the future. Thus far, European integration has fostered this type of relations. Examples outside the scrutiny of EU legislation, such as the OECD Network of Parliament Budget Officials, show that there is a scope for administrative contacts on policy issues. This has not yet occurred for the scrutiny of EU legislation, where the network of liaison officers is formally in charge only for maintaining relations with the EP.

Part IV

Euro-national Parliamentary Procedures

9

The Instrumental Value of Horizontal Parliamentary Cooperation: Subsidiarity Review and the Political Dialogue

MARCO GOLDONI

I. THE EMERGENCE OF INTERPARLIAMENTARY COOPERATION

INTERPARLIAMENTARY COOPERATION IS a challenging topic for political scientists and constitutional lawyers because it sits in a grey area. Its nature—whether it is a form of political dialogue, of political action or 'just' parliamentary diplomacy—is still open to contestation and far from being a settled question. Cooperation among parliaments might have a diplomatic dimension or a substantially political core built on dialogue, but its dynamics have not captured the imagination of lawyers as much as the dialogue among courts. As a consequence, the relevance of cooperation for European integration and law-making is still both underrated and undertheorised.[1] Moreover, it does not help that academics, practitioners and politicians themselves have different opinions on this issue, ranging from quite an optimistic outlook to sheer indifference to the value of cooperation. Yet, in the current predicament of the EU one cannot imagine national parliaments staying relevant without resorting to certain forms of cooperation. It is difficult to imagine national parliaments to be effective, also in their national functions, in an EU with 28 Member States without resorting to formal and informal cooperation. How one or more parliaments are acting (or not) in the European context might have an effect on other parliaments and of course on European institutions. This circumstance constitutes an incentive to participate into forms of cooperation. The proliferation of forums of cooperation

[1] There are many reasons behind this underestimation. Among these reasons, it is worth noting the neglect of parliamentary politics and law by public lawyers attached to the idea that constitutional law takes place mostly in the realm of constitutional or supreme courts.

confirms the willingness to find space for parliamentary interaction. Last but not least, given how the practice of cooperation is evolving, in particular after the inception of the Euro crisis, one might see in some of its instantiations a potential erosion of the principle of loyal and sincere cooperation. As will be made clear below, channels of cooperation might be manipulated in order to pursue aims of sheer national interest. It is therefore unavoidable to try to make sense of this practice and its boundaries.

A caveat has to be introduced at this stage: the scope of the inquiry of this chapter is limited to a special kind of cooperation among national parliaments, despite the fact that cooperation takes place through many networks which are growing together with the Europeanisation of parliaments.[2] The scope of this chapter is limited to horizontal forms of cooperation[3] and its focus is on subsidiarity review and the so-called political dialogue.[4] Both practices are supposed to achieve two outcomes: infusing some form of democratic legitimacy into EU law-making and at the same time protecting some of the parliaments' competences by raising concerns to the European Commission.

After having reconstructed the point of interparliamentary cooperation in its horizontal dimension, an argument in favour of the exceptionalism of cooperation in the context of subsidiarity review will be made. This entails that some principles of interparliamentary cooperation might not apply with the same degree of intensity in the case of subsidiarity. For the political dialogue, in particular if understood as a channel for asserting national parliaments' political will in the EU law-making process (possibly through a 'green card'), a more demanding conception of cooperation ought to be adopted. In that section, the focus will be on the recent proposals of a 'green card', as they seem to entail a stronger form of cooperation in order to be realised.

II. THE CONTEXT AND FUNCTION OF HORIZONTAL INTERPARLIAMENTARY COOPERATION

Before plunging into the analysis of how interparliamentary cooperation unfolds in the contexts of the Early Warning System (EWS) and the Political Dialogue, it is necessary to evaluate the point of this practice. When addressed from this perspective, questions around an institutional practice tend to revolve around its context, functions and purpose.[5] As mentioned above, the context of the practice is rather clear: national parliaments are operating in a politically and constitutionally complex environment which, unsurprisingly, is often described as a stratified reality: a 'multilevel parliamentary field', 'a composite

[2] See, for a recent assessment, D Fromage, 'A mapping of recent trends in interparliamentary cooperation within the EU' in C Fasone, D Fromage and Z Lefkofridi (eds), *Parliaments, public opinion and parliamentary elections in Europe*, (2015) EUI Max Weber Working Paper Series.

[3] This form of cooperation is grounded on Art 12 TEU, letter F and on arts 9 and 10 of Protocol No 1 of the Lisbon Treaty. Before the Lisbon Treaty, interparliamentary cooperation was not recognised by EU primary law. It is also important to remind that according to letter F of article 12 TEU, national parliaments do exercise their European functions in complete autonomy from their national governments. As it will be reminded below, this is one of the main points of interparliamentary cooperation.

[4] D Jančić, 'The Barroso Initiative: Window Dressing or Democracy Boost?' (2012) 78 *Utrecht Law Review*.

[5] For an analysis of public law of this kind see M Loughlin, *Foundations of Public Law* (Oxford, Oxford University Press, 2010) 164.

constitution', a 'two-level game' or a 'Euro-national parliamentary system'.[6] Because of the limited availability of time and resources, a single national parliament cannot cope with such a highly complex institutional environment. In an environment saturated by many kinds of pressure, parliaments are exposed to the double risks of irrelevance and transfiguration into something different from a parliamentary institution. Indeed, not all parliamentary functions can easily be translated into interparliamentary cooperation. This is why the nature of cooperation among parliaments—ie, whether it is a political dialogue or a form of diplomacy—is still discussed.[7]

This situation has pushed parliaments, in order to stay relevant, outside the comfort zone of their domestic jurisdictions to reach out to other parliamentary and European institutions. In such a context, the interaction among parliaments has generated multiple functions of interparliamentary cooperation.[8] In the context of horizontal cooperation, a first important function is to raise the awareness of the European role played by national parliaments' decisions. Certain forums of cooperation like COSAC and the conferences of specialised parliamentary committees have strengthened parliaments' awareness of the European relevance of their politics. At the same time, national parliaments have become more aware of the impact of European integration on their domestic role and begun to understand that only by engaging with other parliamentary institutions through processes of learning, exchange and sharing they can actually protect or shape their institutional position in their jurisdiction.

It is not surprising that, as stated by the guidelines on interparliamentary cooperation, an important function is related to the exchange of information and so-called best practices. Interaction among parliaments has made visible the availability of different models of scrutiny and accountability and the different institutional setting undergirding them. Again, this form of interaction pushes parliaments to question their own approach to EU affairs and their relation to national governments.[9] Intriguingly, parliaments through cooperation would also discharge one of the functions attributed to them by Bagehot; more specifically, the expressive and learning function.[10]

Related to this function of interparliamentary cooperation is the partial recognition of COSAC as one of the main forums for exchange of information. Protocol no 1 of the Lisbon Treaty amends the provisions on COSAC and attributes to it the official function of exchanging information and good practices between parliaments, and extends that role to

[6] See, respectively, J Fossum and B Crum, 'Multi-level Parliamentary Field: A Framework for Theorizing Representative Democracy in the EU' (2009) 11 *European Political Science Review* 452; I Pernice, 'Multilevel Constitutionalism in the European Union' (2002) 27 *European Law Review* 511; R Bellamy and A Weale, 'Political Legitimacy and European Monetary Union: Contract, Constitutionalism and the Normative Logic of Two-Level Games' (2015) 22 *Journal of European Public Policies* 257; A Manzella and N Lupo (eds), *Il sistema parlamentare Euro-nazionale* (Torino, Giappichelli, 2014).

[7] See, for example, C Decaro and N Lupo (eds), *Il dialogo fra parlamenti* (Roma, LUISS University Press, 2009).

[8] Most of the following account is based on practices of cooperation after the Lisbon Treaty. For an analysis of interparliamentary cooperation until 2007 see C Bengtson, 'Interparliamentary Cooperation within Europe' in J O'Brennan and T Raunio (eds), *National Parliaments within the Enlarged European Union* (London, Routledge, 2007) 46–65.

[9] This seems to be the case of the (back then) new Member States, whose observation of the practices of Scandinavian countries seems to have deeply influenced their national arrangements for the scrutiny of national executives: see A Buzogány, 'Learning from the Best? Interparliamentary networks and the parliamentary scrutiny of EU decision-making' in B Crum and J Fossum (eds), *Practices of Interparliamentary Coordination in International Politics* (Colchester, ECPR, 2013) 17.

[10] W Bagehot [1867], *The English Constitution* (Cambridge, Cambridge University Press, 2011) 95.

specialised committees. The Protocol also provides for COSAC to 'organise interparliamentary conferences on specific topics' (Article 10, Protocol no 1).[11] These potential improvements remain often frustrated, as it is for the latter case (ie the organisation of conferences among specialised committees), and they are not revolutionary changes, but they are quite significant for tracing the development of interparliamentary cooperation. On the one hand, the exchange of information at the level of specialised committees favours addressing the lack of expertise, which represents one of the hurdles in interparliamentary cooperation. On the other hand, the possibility of making direct contributions to the European institutions is also a significant improvement because, in this way, discussions that would take place in COSAC can assume a much more concrete form, like, for example, the case of an opinion sent to the Commission or the Council.

A second important function is the coordination of administrative practices in order to maintain a constant flux of information and contacts. This function is unjustly underrated, possibly because national parliaments are not regarded by doctrine as comprising different political and administrative layers, but just as a sum of parliamentarians or, at best, political groups or parties. In fact, the interaction among administrative units of parliaments is often essential for the preparation of interparliamentary meetings.[12] Plenty of contacts take place behind the scenes, usually aside the COSAC meetings or other types of parliamentary conferences. The setting-up of IPEX under the impulse of the EU Speakers' Conference[13] and the meetings among permanent representatives of national parliaments in Brussels have become permanent features of the current system of cooperation. At this stage of European integration there is a constant interaction among the administrative apparatuses of national parliaments and it is not an overstatement to note that this aspect plays a crucial role in the success of parliamentary cooperation. Besides consolidating the links among parliamentary offices, the interaction among parliamentary staff favours the circulation of best practices and procedures.[14]

[11] Article 10 Protocol no 1 states that 'A conference of Parliamentary Committees for Union Affairs may submit any contribution it deems appropriate for the attention of the European Parliament, the Council and the Commission. That conference shall in addition promote the exchange of information and best practice between national Parliaments and the European Parliament, including their special committees. It may also organise interparliamentary conferences on specific topics, in particular to debate matters of common foreign and security policy, including common security and defence policy. Contributions from the conference shall not bind national Parliaments and shall not prejudge their positions'.

[12] This point is rightly highlighted by A Esposito, 'La cooperazione interparlamentare: principi, strumenti e prospettive' in Manzella and Lupo (eds), *Il sistema parlamentare Euro-nazionale* (n 6 above) at 181. He explains that the underestimation by the doctrine might be due to the impossibility of measuring this practice.

[13] National parliaments have created various functions and forums to support the functioning of IPEX: the IPEX steering group, the IPEX board and the IPEX correspondents. The first website was created in 2004, fully launched in 2006 and substantially revised in 2011. The Guidelines for Interparliamentary Cooperation in the European Union set up by the Conference of the Speakers in July 2004 states the role of IPEX: 'The Objective of IPEX (Interparliamentary EU Information exchange) is to support interparliamentary cooperation in the European Union by providing a platform for the electronic exchange of EU-related information between parliaments in the Union including a calendar of meetings and forums for exchange of views on subsidiarity control. Each parliament/chamber has an IPEX correspondent to represent the parliament'. For the use of IPEX in subsidiarity review see V Knutelská, 'Cooperation among National Parliaments: An Effective Contribution to EU Legitimation?' in Crum and Fossum (n 9 above) at 41–45.

[14] For an overall assessment of the role of administrative bureaucracies in interparliamentary cooperation see N Lupo, 'Il ruolo delle burocrazie parlamentari alla luce dei mutamenti dell'assetto istituzionale, nazionale e sopranazionale' (2012) 54 *Rassegna parlamentare* 51, 88. For an evaluation of the rise of administrators in European parliamentary politics see AL Högenauer and C Neuhold, 'National Parliaments after Lisbon: Administrations on the Rise?' (2013) 20 *Journal of European Public Policy* 335. See, also, A Pegan and AL Högenauer, 'The Role of Parliamentary Administrations in Interparliamentary Cooperation', Ch 8 in this volume.

A third function of parliamentary cooperation can be seen at the level of the relationship of parliaments with their national governments. Interaction with other parliaments—both formally and informally—provides information without having to resort to the government's expertise and in this way stimulates parliaments' independence and autonomy in European affairs. This seems to be in line with what is prescribed by Protocol no 1 of the Lisbon Treaty, which establishes a right of national parliaments to get information without the help of the national government.[15] Access to information concerning the position adopted by other institutions on European affairs gives parliaments more leverage in the relations with their governments. Overall, interparliamentary cooperation opens up a space of relatively autonomous action in the realm of European politics. Obviously, autonomy here does not mean separation: parliaments are embedded in their national political systems and it is natural that their members will interact with other people. But at this level, interparliamentary cooperation can truly make a difference and secure an autonomous political space for national parliaments.

III. THE AIM OF HORIZONTAL INTERPARLIAMENTARY COOPERATION

What is then the purpose of interparliamentary cooperation in light of the previous considerations? Basically, scholars and practitioners understand it according to two broad ideal types: either interparliamentary cooperation is seen as a contribution to the 'good functioning of the EU' (ex article 12 TEU)[16] or as a way to protect the autonomy and the jurisdiction of national parliaments against the centripetal force exercised by European institutions.

In the former case, it is mostly thought to be functional to the promotion of the national channel of parliamentary representation into EU law-making. It is, in other words, an interaction among parliamentary actors with deliberative properties. From this perspective, what makes cooperation valuable is its deliberative input into representative politics. Yet, this perspective seems to be too optimistic because it overlooks the idea that deliberative politics is conceived as a dialogue among actors with a view to reaching a common rational consensus based on the best argument. Deliberative politics is supposed to be guided by communicative and not instrumental rationality.[17] The intuition behind this conception is based on the absence of concrete decision-making power of national parliaments in EU law-making. This lack of power would open up a space free from instrumental considerations which might prove adequate for increasing the creation of a transnational public sphere:

> democratic legitimacy at the EU level is dependent on arenas where it is possible to talk relatively unrestrained by strategic considerations pertaining to national or party interests, interests which may be activated as soon as a concrete decision has to be taken.[18]

[15] For a commentary of this Protocol (whose scope encompasses, interestingly enough, information and cooperation) see: PG Casalena, C Fasone and N Lupo, 'Commentary on the Protocol no. 1' in HJ Blanke, S Mangiameli (eds), *Treaty on the European Union. A Commentary* (Heidelberg/New York, Springer, 2013).

[16] S Roland, 'Quand le performatif tient lieu d'argumentatif: la contribution des Parlements nationaux au bon funcionnement de l'Union' (2012) 556 *Revue du marché commun et de l'Union Européenne* 178.

[17] An important introduction to the topic is represented by J Bohman and W Rehg (eds), *Deliberative Democracy* (Boston MA, MIT Press, 1997).

[18] L Blichner, 'The Anonymous hand of public reason: Interparliamentary discourse and the quest for legitimacy' in E Eriksen and J Fossum (eds), *Democracy in the European Union: Integration through deliberation* (London, Routledge, 2000).

To remedy the absence of power, parliaments would be pushed to deliberate around the best argument on a European issue. Only in this way they would be capable of drawing the attention of European institutions. However, both from a practical and from a normative perspective, this conception is rather weak. Parliaments resort to cooperation not to come up with a compelling argument to be communicated either to the Commission or their national government: to the contrary, national parliaments think it necessary to resort to cooperation because, on the one hand, they often perceive their informational asymmetric disadvantage toward governments and, on the other hand, they are increasingly aware that, at least in certain cases, only a strengthened form of parliamentary discourse might have an impact on European institutions. From a normative perspective, it is not evident how interparliamentary cooperation would in itself enrich parliamentary representation at the European level. While it is obvious that cooperation is politically more salient than diplomacy, there is no structured forum where parliaments, or some of their representatives, can articulate a form of representative politics.

The second ideal type reduces interparliamentary cooperation to a form of sheer networking among parliamentarians.[19] While this is the case in some instances, this conception is not accurate and does not take into account the stratified and multi-layered structure of agents involved in formal and informal cooperation. It also portrays cooperation or interparliamentary discourse as basically a kind of lobbying or bargaining activity among parliamentarians. The official recognition of interparliamentary cooperation in the Treaties seems to suggest that the European legislator itself does not consider cooperation as merely an exercise in lobbying. Yet, parliaments (and the agents involved in parliamentary activities) are increasingly conscious of the intricacies of their relations with other parliaments and, therefore, of the formal and material constrains introduced by the interparliamentary discourse. A network-based explanation of cooperation is also oblivious to the phenomenon of bureaucratic exchange and interaction across the EU. For institutional reasons linked to their position, the actions of administrative officials can be motivated by different reasons from those of professional politicians. While the idea of networking is compatible with the autonomy of national parliaments—which would be motivated by their own entrenched institutional preference[20]—it does not offer an accurate account of the functions and purposes of cooperation.

So, while the two ideal types of interparliamentary cooperation are useful for mapping the current practices, the question about which one is more accurate cannot be answered in any definitive way because both the practice and the text of the Treaties leave open enough leeway to support different interpretations.[21] EU primary law states that interparliamentary

[19] See, for a classic reference, A-M Slaughter, *A New World Order* (Princeton NJ, Princeton University Press, 2004).

[20] Yet, there is a limit also in the available options for institutional preference. This is, again, a limit introduced by the context and the point of the practice. For example, the definition of what counts as a national parliament cannot be entirely left to the discretion of the Member State. It would stand against the point of the involvement of national parliaments and in plain contrast to the common constitutional traditions: N Lupo, 'National Parliaments in the European Integration Process: Re-aligning Politics and Policies' in M Cartabia, N Lupo and A Simoncini (eds), *Democracy and Subsidiarity in the EU. National Parliaments, regions and civil society in the decision-making process* (Bologna, Il Mulino, 2013) 113.

[21] Antonio Esposito (n 12 above) has rightly noted that the norms on interparliamentary cooperation are included in the Treaties and therefore they have to be interpreted in a coherent way against the background of primary EU law.

cooperation has to be employed in a complementary way to the forms of European law-making. In other words, the contribution of national parliaments has to favour and not hamper European politics. In terms of practice, by examining cooperation in the EWS and in the political dialogue it will be possible to outline how diversified is their conception by national parliaments. At this point, one should note that talking of national parliaments is rather abstract and somehow vague. Who are the real actors of cooperation? As previously mentioned, they are mostly politicians and the administrative staff of parliament. It is therefore possible to postulate that even within the same national parliament one might register a variety of understandings of cooperation.

The two ideal types previously sketched rather represent the two poles of a wide spectrum of a large number of different conceptions of cooperation. In between these two polarities, other proposals have been put forward as an attempt to cope with the complex nature of interparliamentary relations. The idea of a 'multilevel parliamentary field' seems to be the most successful and it certainly captures some of the dynamics of cooperation. It is a sociological perspective based on Bourdieu's idea of the field and it aims to explain vertical and horizontal parliamentary relations. As such, the relative force of the actors involved in the interaction constitutes the primary factor in shaping the field. Counter-intuitively, the perspective of the field suggests that

> interparliamentary relations serve as 'a weapon of the weak'. This is an obvious field effect and relates to the general notion that while strong, established actors can get by with the resources they command, weak actors benefit disproportionately from regulated interaction.[22]

The field itself, however, does not contain precise parameters for evaluating strong and weak parliaments. It is not clear, within the field, whether strength is measured vis-à-vis a parliament's own government, or against the background of the strength of the Member State they represent, or in the comparison to other national parliaments. Yet, this might represent a strength of the field concept because of its elasticity. What is more troubling is the admission by the authors that, ultimately, 'the added value of many interparliamentary relations hinges on the involvement of some strong parliaments; if they are just an exclusive gathering of weak parliaments no one is likely to benefit much in the overall scheme of things'.[23] There seems to be a potential contradiction between the recognition that interparliamentary relations are the weapon of the weak and that it is essential to have strong parliaments involved because this latter condition gives to those parliaments an ample margin of manoeuvre.[24]

A second aspect where the multilevel parliamentary field does not seem entirely convincing concerns its emphasis on deliberative qualities. Fossum and Crum argue that 'the aspect on which the multilevel parliamentary field appears most evolved is *deliberation*'.[25] Upon a closer look, the emphasis on deliberation is misplaced if one takes deliberation

[22] J Fossum and B Crum, 'Toward a Democratic Multilevel Parliamentary Field?' in Crum and Fossum (n 9 above) at 260.

[23] ibid.

[24] Fossum and Crum recognise that the advantages for weak parliaments are less clear when it comes to political parties: 'we find that big and well-established parties and party groups are particularly well-positioned to reap the benefits from interparliamentary cooperation because they control prominent positions at the different levels and have the facilities to maximise the connections between them': ibid at 261.

[25] ibid at 264.

seriously. Research shows that there is mutual observation and links established around important political points, but this is far from ensuring that the field is productive of a deliberative interaction.[26] Given that the field is still held together by the political will of the parliaments, an invitation to promote interparliamentary cooperation from this perspective sounds rather vague. In fact, Jürgen Neyer has noted that the multilevel parliamentary field cannot prescribe how parliaments ought to cooperate at any level.[27] The idea recently advanced of a Euro-national parliamentary system is more promising because it can account for the role and the functions of cooperation at the European and the national level.[28] It is also more attentive to the state-related dimension of European integration and of the attachment of national parliaments to the executives of their Member States.[29]

Where do these considerations lead to? It is proposed here that, in light of the previous considerations, interparliamentary cooperation at the horizontal level has an instrumental and not intrinsic value.[30] Its purpose, then, it is not to enhance the democratic legitimacy of EU law-making processes or to support the European politics of national executives by enhancing political accountability. Note that from a descriptive point of view, this conception of interparliamentary cooperation can account for national parliaments' different views on the point of cooperation. Some consequences stem directly from this assumption, at least as far as concerns the EWS and the political dialogue. The most relevant thing is that the only way to anchor to an objective standard the point of interparliamentary cooperation is to derive it from the function that it is supposed to serve. This entails that interparliamentary relations concerning, say, the Common Foreign and Security Policy (a case of both vertical and horizontal cooperation) might take place according to a different logic than interaction relative to the political dialogue. This is not enough to ensure that parliamentary relations will be conducted by parliaments according to the same understanding, but it gives to the observer an objective perspective.

Establishing the instrumental value of interparliamentary cooperation is also essential to assessing the values of transparency and accountability in relation to different forms of cooperation. In fact, while transparency and accountability are important goods in the process of EU law-making (and in the EU these are scarce goods), they are not intrinsically valuable when they are associated with parliamentary cooperation. The different standard of assessment is determined by the fact that parliaments are not supposed to operate as if they were an assembly or a third chamber of the EU. Their cooperative meetings do not strictly work according to the principles of parliamentary representation. Again, according to the circumstances, respective parliamentary positions on a European topic have to be made visible to the public at the national level, but how a single parliamentary chamber or committee extracts information or builds alliances with other parliaments is not always

[26] B Crum and E Miklin, 'Interparliamentary Coordination in Single Market Policy-Making: The EU Services Directive' in Crum and Fossum (n 9 above) at 71.

[27] J Neyer, 'Justified Multilevel Parliamentarism' (2014) 21 *Journal of Legislative Studies* 125.

[28] Lupo and Manzella, *Il sistema parlamentare Euro-Nazionale*, n 6 above.

[29] cf A Manzella, 'Lo Stato Comunitario' (2003) *Quaderni costituzionali* 273; C Bickerton, *European Integration* (Oxford, Oxford University Press, 2012).

[30] A practice instantiates an intrinsic value when its properties are good in themselves and internal to the practice, while it instantiates an instrumental value when its properties serve for the realisation of goods which are external to the practice. For a distinction see, for example, J Raz, *Engaging Reason* (Oxford, Oxford University Press, 1999).

subject to the same level of scrutiny as other more politically salient practices. Furthermore, it would not make sense to demand the same kind of transparency and accountability to the parliamentary bureaucracies involved in cooperation. Sometimes, a request for transparency might pose an unnecessary burden upon these actors and hamper the development of interaction. Hence, the legitimacy of the practice is not harmed even when parliamentary cooperation, as it happens sometimes, is instantiated in informal settings.

IV. INTERPARLIAMENTARY COOPERATION IN THE EARLY WARNING SYSTEM

Despite its mixed outcome, subsidiarity review has attracted a lot of attention from practitioners and scholars. The empowerment, so to say, of national parliaments in checking the application of the principle of subsidiarity by the Commission has opened up a space for national parliaments to act at a European level and to protect their own competences.[31] The perception of the importance of this new instrument was unevenly spread across legislatures. But some of the most active legislatures had both advocated and supported the EWS. Hence, the potential value of cooperation in order to make the mechanism work was soon recognised. Before the entry into force of the Lisbon Treaty, COSAC lent itself as the forum for eight tests of subsidiarity review on important legislative drafts.[32] On these occasions, the COSAC general meetings were used to perform a quasi-collective scrutiny of the Commission's proposals. It must be immediately added that, after the end of the experimental period, COSAC decided to stop these trials because for many parliaments this was not its mandate and it also was difficult to coordinate the issuing of reasoned opinions when they were often left to the competence of different sectoral committees according to each Member State.

The importance of cooperation in the framework of the subsidiarity review is further highlighted by the guidelines for interparliamentary cooperation as adopted by the EU Speakers' Conference, gathering together the Speakers of the European and the national parliaments, at the Lisbon meeting in 2008. In the objectives, it is first stated that interparliamentary cooperation is organised in order 'a) To promote the exchange of information and best practices between the national parliaments and the European Parliament with a view to reinforcing parliamentary control, influence and scrutiny at all levels', and after that, it is made clear that the second objective is 'b) To ensure effective exercise of parliamentary competences in EU matters in particular in the area of monitoring the principles of subsidiarity and proportionality'.[33] More generally, since the Convention for the Constitutional Treaty, it has been clear that subsidiarity review was one of the main interests for national parliaments. As a matter of fact, given the procedure for triggering a yellow or an orange card, that is, the threshold of necessary votes, the limited resources and the time at their disposal (eight weeks), some form of cooperation among parliaments is unavoidable.

Even a cursory look at the way the most successful initiatives in the field of subsidiarity review have been conducted shows that cooperation was critical for its accomplishment.

[31] For a general introduction to the EWS see P Kiiver, *The Early Warning System for the Principle of Subsidiarity* (London, Routledge, 2012).

[32] For an analysis of these tests, see ibid, chapter 4.

[33] Guidelines for Interparliamentary Cooperation in the European Union, Lisbon, June 2008, p 3.

The two yellow cards triggered until now (Monti II and the European Public Prosecutor's Office, EPPO) are the most evident proof of the importance of cooperation in the context of subsidiarity review.[34] An analysis of the Monti II proposal 'can reveal the extent of interparliamentary coordination'.[35] In this case, cooperation and interaction took place in different places and times. The threshold was reached only thanks to a number of factors: the activism of certain parliaments (in particular the Danish Folketing); a timely COSAC meeting; and the interaction occurring among the permanent representatives in Brussels. The first lesson to be drawn from this first yellow card is that cooperation *matters*. And its relevance extends beyond the exchange or networking of parliamentarians. Insightfully, Ian Cooper has noted that

> the National Parliament Representatives in Brussels played an indispensable role by sharing with one another real-time information about the state of play regarding the scrutiny of Monti II in their respective parliaments. Only with this network of representatives in place was it possible to compile an accurate and up-to-date picture of the likelihood of a reasoned opinion from each chamber, and thus a rough 'vote count' as the process unfolded and thus the knowledge that a yellow card was within reach. The representatives shared this information with their home parliaments.[36]

Given that some parliaments had not heard or noticed the Monti II proposal, interparliamentary cooperation in formal and informal settings (from COSAC to information exchange on IPEX) was instrumental to the mobilisation of some legislatures. The leading legislatures were able to convince other parliaments of the potential impact of the Monti II proposal upon their constituencies, overcoming in this way the issue of lack of incentive.[37]

In the case of EPPO, the context was rather different because, in light of the topic (already 'announced' in the Lisbon Treaty) and the coincidence of the summer break (which does not count for the EWS), parliaments were already aware of the importance of the proposal before the beginning of the eight-week period. A pattern of instrumental cooperation can be detected also in this case. The leading parliamentary chamber was the UK House of Commons, followed by the two Dutch chambers. Very early in the process of review, concerns about the proposal were raised in the Monday morning meetings of the permanent representatives in Brussels and through this channel it became public that some legislatures had already chosen to issue a reasoned opinion. An intensive interaction among permanent representatives and use of the IPEX platform[38] took place, leading to the reaching of the necessary threshold.[39] In this case, the COSAC general meeting did not take place during

[34] For a recent reconstruction of these two cases see A Pintz, 'National Parliaments Overcoming Collective Action Problems Inherent in the Early Warning System: The Cases of Monti II and EPPO' (2014) *LUISS School of Government working papers* 22/2014.

[35] I Cooper, 'A Yellow Card for the Striker' (2015) 22 *Journal of European Public Policy* 1406.

[36] I Cooper, Oral Evidence to the UK Parliament: available at: www.publications.parliament.uk/pa/ld201314/ldselect/ldeucom/151/15108.htm#n112: last visit: 20 April 2015).

[37] This does not mean that often parliamentarians do not have incentives to participate in subsidiarity review, but it shows that if left to exceptional and rare occasions, MPs can be mobilised. In the case of Monti II, it is not surprising that the Nordic parliaments were easily co-opted because convinced that their peculiar model of industrial relations was at stake.

[38] OJ Gstrein and D Harvey, Written Evidence, in House of Lords/European Select Committee, *The Role of National Parliaments in the European Union*, 9th Report of Session 2013–14, §§ 53–59.

[39] Note that in the process some parliamentary chambers changed their opinion on the EPPO or contradicted the position of their governments.

the eight-week period and could not be used as a forum for information exchange and agenda-setting.

From these two cases of a yellow card it is fair to infer that interaction and coordination among parliaments was a necessary precondition in order to trigger the yellow card. Note that in the absence of parliamentary leadership, many parliaments would not have realised the strategic importance of these proposals and certainly no yellow card would have been triggered. This is an important aspect to be taken into account when evaluating the relation between cooperation and subsidiarity review. It takes the leadership of some of the most active parliaments to mobilise the sufficient amount of effort for the prospect of triggering a yellow card. This leaves the EWS open to the agenda-setting powers of some of the most active national parliaments. The latter might want to use the yellow card for reasons entirely related to their own domestic political dynamics. In other words, at play in the EWS is a mix of collective and individual activity. The collective dimension, however, is functional to the individual motivation. Subsidiarity is supposed to protect the autonomy of parliaments' jurisdiction, but parliaments themselves can raise a subsidiarity issue only as long as they coordinate with a significant number of other legislatures.[40]

As reminded above, a proper understanding of parliamentary cooperation requires an explanatory framework which makes possible to assess the qualities of different institutional practices (ie, subsidiarity review, political dialogue, economic governance) according to the function they are supposed to instantiate. As far as concerns subsidiarity review, there seems to be two possible ways of understanding parliaments' participation in the EWS. Either the instrument empowers parliaments as a collective group or individually, a question which is strictly connected to the nature of subsidiarity review (whether it is only a collective good, or also an individual one).

Obviously, the standard for cooperation varies according to the conception of subsidiarity review. Notoriously, Ian Cooper advocates the idea that when they act in the subsidiarity review mode, national parliaments are actually forming a virtual third chamber.[41] This means that they are acting with the awareness of being a collective agent and not just an aggregation of individual parliaments. Given that the yellow and the orange card do not amount to a formal veto power, Cooper argues that if parliaments want to be effective they have to produce solid arguments through a genuinely deliberative process. Deliberation works here in two directions: horizontally, as a form of argumentation among the national parliaments and, vertically, as the elaboration of a common position on subsidiarity to be submitted to the Commission with the sheer 'force of the argument'. This necessity would then augment parliaments' consciousness of their collective status as actors in the European Union. In brief, the EWS would provide a deliberative platform for 'Europeanising' national parliaments and make them the bearers of a third channel of political representation beyond those provided by the Council and the European Parliament. It goes without saying that, from this point of view, interparliamentary cooperation in subsidiarity review ought to be conducted as an exercise in deliberation. Cooper's proposal is intriguing but unconvincing

[40] This is a consequence, among many things, of the fact that national parliaments differ profoundly across the EU. Their institutional configuration and political culture, for example, are strictly related to the constitutional identity of their Member State.

[41] I Cooper, 'A "Virtual Third Chamber" for the European Union? National Parliaments after the Treaty of Lisbon' (2012) 35 *West European Politics* 441.

if put against the background of the current practice and, broadly, the point of subsidiarity review.

While it is true that some parliaments have tried to impose an interpretation of the EWS as a collective device (in particular the Dutch parliament and the French Senate), the majority have adopted an individual stance.[42] Some factors point to this conclusion. First of all, the principle of subsidiarity is understood in different ways by national parliaments and it is scrutinised according to different procedures. Secondly, sometimes subsidiarity review is conducted not by the EAC but by another specialised committee. Finally, COSAC has not been able to represent a constant point of reference for the practice of subsidiarity review, both because members of EACs see in this institution different purposes and because its general meetings take place only twice per year (which makes it difficult to become the point of reference for coordinating an effort for triggering a yellow card). As it has been summed up, 'to date, the early warning system has, above all, been used mainly as an *individual* instrument at the disposal of each national parliament, and not as a *collective* instrument at the disposal of the "front" of the national parliaments'.[43] In conclusion, interparliamentary coordination—understood as the sum of interaction at different levels of the parliamentary structure (ie, political and administrative), information exchange and agenda-setting—is essential for the well-functioning of the EWS. However, this does not entail a duty upon national parliaments to cooperate. As explained in the previous sections, cooperation is instrumental to the functional aspect of an institutional practice. Subsidiarity review has a negative function in EU law-making: it tries to pre-empt European legislation which might encroach upon essential tenets of the national compact.[44] In that respect, subsidiarity review is not aimed at injecting democratic legitimacy into EU law-making, but is a tool for empowering those institutions more affected by a spillage of power toward the EU. Being an activity concerning the individual parliament, subsidiarity review invites a strategic form of parliamentary cooperation.

V. THE POLITICAL DIALOGUE: COOPERATION AND THE GREEN CARD

Rather interestingly, the need for strengthening cooperation is by now strongly advocated by some national parliaments for the so-called political dialogue. This procedure allows national parliaments to interact with the Commission without the same time-constraints imposed upon the EWS. Parliaments have an opportunity to take a position or to simply comment on all draft legislative acts and also non-legislative acts, of the European Union. They are free to comment on several aspects of the proposal: the legislative form chosen by the Commission (regulation or directive), its content and its merit, and the principle of proportionality. Initiated as an informal procedure by the Barroso Commission in 2006, the political dialogue was aimed at establishing a cooperative environment between the Commission and national parliaments. The Commission promised to take into account all remarks sent by national legislatures. As an instrument, the political dialogue partially

42 Not to mention that even an active parliament as the Finnish Eduskunta is usually dismissive of the relevance of the EWS. See the written evidence submitted to the House of Lords enquiry: §§ 43–48.

43 Lupo et al (n 20 above) at 124–25.

44 B Guastaferro, 'Reframing subsidiarity inquiry from an 'EU value-added' to an 'EU non-encroachment' test?' in Lupo et al (n 20 above) at 133.

overlaps with the EWS but its philosophy is different because it is not the negative logic of obstruction but the logic of positive contribution to EU law.

The political dialogue has produced mixed results, but it would be unfair to dismiss the whole procedure as a mere cosmetic operation. In practice, the political dialogue has strengthened parliaments' awareness of their potential role and in some instances has actually produced a real impact on the legislative draft.[45] Coordination in the political dialogue is not a necessary feature because the interaction is supposed to take place between the European Commission and the individual national parliaments. But it is quite telling that COSAC embraced fully this new channel of communication, highlighting that 'the opportunity (under the political dialogue) for national parliaments to feed views into the pre-legislative phase of the EU proposals is particularly important'.[46]

It is indeed in the context of the political dialogue that an attempt to overcome some of the alleged limits of the EWS has been formulated. The idea is to use the political dialogue as an informal influencing channel of communication with the Commission with the aim of achieving an active parliamentary participation in the EU law-making process. The most recent development in this field concerns the possible introduction of the green card. Interestingly, the idea of a green card, advocated by some parliaments, has received attention in interparliamentary forums in the first place and it is going to be properly discussed during the next COSAC meeting in Riga at the end of May 2015. In this case, cooperation is going to be instrumental also for the formulation of a coherent and shared understanding of what the green card ought to be.

While the trajectory of the proposal is clear and points toward a more active role for the national parliaments in the EU, there are different available ways of conceiving the green card. This is due, partly, to the causes behind the request for a green card. Fasone's and Fromage's explanation for the causes behind a request for a green card is the most plausible. They list, as important factors,

> the disappointment expressed by most national parliaments about the replies provided by the Commission to their opinions, the perception of scarce impact on the content of EU legislation, and the understanding of their role as mere negative-veto player in the EU.[47]

The 'Dutch approach' entails the creation of 'a group of parliaments that is gathered around a theme (cluster of interest) [and that] could propose ideas for new European policies to the European Commission, or could propose the amending or revoking of existing legislation'.[48] The 'Danish approach' suggests that the green card ought to operate in way similar to the EWS and, in contrast to the Dutch proposal, it would intervene only once a legislative proposal has already been made by the EU Commission. A third approach is represented by the House of Lords' take on the green card as giving the opportunity to make proposals to change already proposed legislation. It also suggests that 'there should be a way for a group of like-minded national parliaments to make constructive suggestions for EU policy

[45] A classic case is represented by the regulation on the European Citizens' Initiative. For a reconstruction, see C Fasone, 'Competing Conceptions of Subsidiarity in the Early Warning System', in Cartabia et al (n 20 above) at 189–91. Other cases are mentioned in the House of Lords, Report on the role of national parliaments (n 38 above) § 45.

[46] COSAC, Contributions and Conclusions to the XLVII meeting, Copenhagen, April 2012.

[47] C Fasone and D Fromage, 'National parliaments and the EU Commission's agenda: limits and recent developments of a difficult partnership' in C Fasone, D Fromage and Z Lefkofridi, n 2 above.

[48] Dutch *Tweede Kamer*, 'Ahead in Europe. On the Role of the Dutch House of Representatives and national parliaments in the European Union' *Final Report on Democratic Legitimacy*, 9 May 2014, p 14.

initiatives, which may include reviewing existing legislation'.[49] A discussion paper has been prepared by Lord Boswell for an interparliamentary meeting in January 2015, on the basis that 'the green card procedure could build on the existing political dialogue'.[50]

While there seems to be a majoritarian consensus on the green card by national parliaments, it has still to be seen which version will prevail in the end. The questionnaire submitted to national parliaments in preparation for the COSAC plenary meeting in Riga, May 2015, lists four possible tasks for the green card: 'suggestions for new legislation, suggestions to amend existing legislation, suggestions to repeal existing legislation and suggestions to amend or repeal delegated or implementing acts'. In order to frame how cooperation will have to take place it is necessary to understand the function of the green card, and much depends on its aim. Whether national parliaments ought to act more as a 'virtual third chamber' or, again, just as individual national parliaments trying to find alliances with a view to triggering a green card is relative to the objective of the green card. If the green card is thought to inject democratic legitimacy into the process of EU law-making[51] then one might expect interactions more attentive 1) to the European dimension of the proposal and 2) more prone to favour a deliberative attitude over a national-interest-based approach. If the green card were used to infuse EU law with the impetus coming from national parliaments, then cooperation ought to be less instrumental in promoting the national interests or preferences of a single chamber or group of chambers. If, on the other hand, a 'reactive' conception of the green card were to prevail (and this would happen if the green card were to be limited to the repeal of a piece of EU legislation) then it would be possible to envisage a more individualistic approach toward the necessary cooperation. In the latter case, horizontal interparliamentary cooperation could still be made operative according to an instrumental logic and it would function as a precious tool for reaching the threshold required to repeal a specific piece of European legislation.

VI. CONCLUSION: THE RISE OF ASYMMETRIC COOPERATION

One of the side effects of the Euro crisis is the incipient distrust toward the legitimacy of European institutions, which reflects scepticism on the legitimacy credentials of EU law-making. Together with the innovations introduced by the Lisbon Treaty, the Euro crisis has brought about an acceleration in the proliferation of forms of parliamentary cooperation as one of the responses to this distrust. Plenty of bilateral and multilateral meetings (formal and informal) among parliaments are taking place with an accelerated speed. As the House of Lords noted in its report on the role of national parliaments in the EU, 'as national parliaments increasingly engage with key EU policies, it is likely that there will be informal conferences to discuss major policy issues'.[52] In this context, the Danish parliament has suggested that it is time to move toward meetings based on 'clusters of interest' with a view to pressure the EU Commission. To these meetings are usually invited members

[49] UK House of Lords European Union Committee, 'The Role of National Parliaments in the European Union' (n 38 above) §§ 55–59.

[50] Lord Boswell, *The Green Card discussion paper*, 1.

[51] D Chalmers, *Democratic Self-Government in Europe* (London, Policy Network, 2013).

[52] House of Lords (n 38 above) § 132.

of the EACs and sometimes of other sectoral committees. In certain cases, representatives from the European Parliament have also been invited. The organising parliament (the leading one) makes sure to submit a discussion paper before the meeting and to coordinate the discussion which might end up with a common declaration or the adoption of a common position to be communicated to the European Commission.[53]

How to assess then the proposal of clusters of interest made, among others, by the Danish Folketing and the British House of Lords? Antonio Esposito, while praising the first meetings around clusters of interest for their political vibrancy, has made a powerful argument against the 'trade unionisation' of groups of national parliaments because this might hamper EU law-making as a whole.[54] Other issues might affect meetings based on clusters of interest. Given their changing composition, these meetings might not form a coherent pattern. It could be the case, for example, that MPs have subscribed to two contradictory declarations.[55]

This asymmetrical form of cooperation might become extremely circumstantial and encourage a patchy approach to EU law-making. In light of previous considerations, while presenting a real risk, the value of these forms of asymmetric cooperation should be at least tested on a long-term perspective. Their emergence is related to processes of differentiation in European integration and parallel phenomenon of the increased weakness of certain parliaments in affecting or controlling EU legislation in its pre-legislative or law-making phases.[56] In fact, given the asymmetrical development of European integration, it is going to be extremely difficult to pre-empt asymmetric forms of cooperation as a kind of reaction.[57] A parliament of a Member State which is in the position of being a debtor or it is outside the Eurozone, might not have much interest in participating in formal and informal meetings with parliaments whose Member States have a different status in the dynamics of the economic governance.

It is urgent to impose some principles upon these forms of cooperation as a way to limit their disruptive and potentially manipulative setting: first, it should be made mandatory to invite always all national parliaments (or in cases of asymmetric cooperation, at least those involved) to these meetings. Given the political nature of these meetings, participation should remain on a voluntary basis. But every parliamentary chamber should have the right to articulate its position. Secondly, in light of the duty of sincere and loyal cooperation, conclusions and proposals should always show that there is an attempt at bringing together both the European and the Member States respective common goods. The latter requirement would not rule out the possibility of using 'clusters of interest' meetings to contrast EU initiatives but at least introduce a procedural aspect for pushing parliaments to make an effort to bring together national and European interests.

[53] In the first of these meetings, organised by the Danish parliament on 21 October in Copenhagen on the freedom of movement of persons, 14 parliamentary chambers were present. The French National Assembly hosted an interparliamentary meeting on the EPPO and on personal data protection in September 2014 in the framework of a Franco-German initiative.

[54] Esposito (n 6 above) at 177.

[55] D Fromage, 'A mapping of recent trends in interparliamentary cooperation within the EU', n 2 above.

[56] Fromage notes that those parliaments using a mandate-based system of accountability have partially lost control over the EU law-making process with the increase of trialogues.

[57] For recent analyses of differentiated integration: J Fossum, 'Democracy and Differentiation' (2015) 22 *Journal of European Public Policy* 799; B Leruth, 'Operationalising National Preferences on Europe and Differentiated Integration' (2015) 22 *Journal of European Public Policy* 816.

10

Parliamentary Involvement in the Economic and Monetary Union after the Euro Crisis

DAVOR JANČIĆ*

I. INTRODUCTION

AS ONE OF the most arresting events in the EU since the establishment of the common currency, the sovereign debt crisis has had an incisive impact on both the Union and its Member States. When the former European Council President, Herman van Rompuy, declared in his 2012 speech at the Humboldt University in Berlin that national parliaments (NPs) retain their budgetary sovereignty 'as long as national policies do not threaten the financial stability of the euro itself',[1] what he was describing is precisely the EU principle of sincere cooperation, which epitomises deep interdependence between the Union's component political communities.[2] This principle requires the EU and the Member States to act in a politico-legal symbiosis and with full mutual respect while assisting each other in performing the tasks flowing from the founding treaties. It also obliges the Member States to take adequate measures to fulfil the agreed objectives of European integration and enjoins them from taking those that frustrate their attainment.[3] It is submitted here that these duties of loyalty in the relations between the EU and the Member States also refer to NPs as prime carriers of the popular will. When Mr Van Rompuy further stated that

* Research for this chapter was conducted while I was British Academy Newton Fellow at the Law Department of the London School of Economics and Political Science (LSE), UK, and was funded by the British Academy through its postdoctoral Newton International Fellowship scheme. The author wishes to thank Prof Damian Chalmers, Dr Floris de Witte, Dr Michael Wilkinson, and LSE students for invaluable comments and discussions, not least during my guest lecture on this topic as part of the 'Philosophy of EU Law' course at the LSE.

1 Speech no EUCO 21/12, Walter Hallstein Institute for European Constitutional Law.

2 Art 4(3) TEU.

3 See further M Klamert, *The Principle of Loyalty in EU Law* (Oxford, Oxford University Press, 2014); E Neframi, 'Le Principe de Coopération Loyale comme Fondement Identitaire de l'Union Européenne' (2012) 556 *Revue du Marché Commun et de l'Union européenne* 197–203.

domestic legislatures ought to and do indeed keep a close watch over each other's budgetary laws and that they have now become European institutions,[4] he invoked the necessity of NPs appropriating the process of what, for want of a more suitable label, can be viewed as a piecemeal process of fiscal federalisation in the EU,[5] whereby certain rules on the use of public moneys are no longer decided exclusively by the Member States but with the input of EU institutions.[6]

The Union's intervention in domestic budgetary procedures, the rise of the executive branches of government, and the consequent upsetting of the constitutional balance in the EU are well acknowledged in scholarly milieus.[7] The former European Commission President, José Manuel Barroso, is thus right that 'tighter economic governance needs tighter democratic control'.[8] For these reasons, calls abound for a more thorough involvement of NPs in EU affairs both in terms of domestic scrutiny and in terms of EU-level cooperation.[9] The UK Prime Minister David Cameron has been particularly vocal in this regard, arguing that NPs are 'the true source of real democratic legitimacy and accountability in the EU' and that they 'instil proper respect—even fear—into national leaders'.[10]

One of the key democratic implications of these developments is how NPs have responded to these challenges, what vehicles of influence they retain, and what new individual and collective channels of democratic intervention they have created. As Curtin rightly notes, the 'networked role' of parliaments in Europe, whereby they combine efforts at both levels to incentivise public debate, might alleviate the executive dominance accentuated by the debt crisis.[11] This chapter carries out a legal analysis thereof: (a) by delving into the repercussions for NPs of the post-euro crisis reform of the Economic and Monetary Union (EMU), which was implemented by means of changes to the Stability and Growth Pact (SGP) through the adoption of the Six Pack, Fiscal Compact and the Two Pack; and (b) by examining the domestic and EU parliamentary channels of participation in the

[4] Speech during the Interparliamentary Meeting on the European Semester for Economic Policy Coordination, doc no EUCO 31/12, Brussels, 27 February 2012.

[5] A Hinarejos, 'Fiscal Federalism in the European Union: Evolution and Future Choices for the EMU' (2013) 50 *Common Market Law Review* 1621–42.

[6] K Armstrong, 'The New Governance of EU Fiscal Discipline' (2013) 38 *European Law Review* 616.

[7] See in this regard: K Tuori and K Tuori, *The Eurozone Crisis: A Constitutional Analysis* (Cambridge, Cambridge University Press, 2014); P Craig, 'Economic Governance and the Euro Crisis: Constitutional Architecture and Constitutional Implications' in M Adams et al (eds), *The Constitutionalization of European Budgetary Constraints* (Oxford, Hart Publishing, 2014); U Puetter, 'Europe's Deliberative Intergovernmentalism: The Role of the Council and European Council in EU Economic Governance' (2012) 19 *Journal of European Public Policy* 161–78; MW Bauer and S Becker, 'The Unexpected Winner of the Crisis: The European Commission's Strengthened Role in Economic Governance' (2014) 36 *Journal of European Integration* 213–29; M Dawson and F de Witte, 'Constitutional Balance in the EU after the Euro Crisis' (2013) 76 *Modern Law Review* 817–44; D Schwarzer, 'The Euro Area Crises, Shifting Power Relations and Institutional Change in the European Union' (2012) 3 (Issue Supp, s 1) *Global Policy* 28–41; M Dobbels, 'The Implications of the New Economic Governance for Democracy in the EU' (2014) 10 *Journal of Contemporary European Research* 203–20; N Scicluna, 'EU Constitutionalism in Flux: Is the Eurozone Crisis Precipitating Centralisation or Diffusion?' (2012) 18 *European Law Journal* 489–503; G Majone, 'From Regulatory State to a Democratic Default' (2014) 52 *Journal of Common Market Studies* 1216–23.

[8] Speech to the EP, 'Report on the European Semester for Economic Policy Coordination: Annual Growth Survey 2014', Strasbourg, Plenary session of 25 February 2014.

[9] See also chapter by Ian Cooper, 'The Interparliamentary Conference on Stability, Economic Coordination and Governance in the European Union (The "Article 13 Conference")', Chapter 13 in this volume.

[10] D Cameron PM, Bloomberg Speech of 23 January 2013, www.gov.uk/government/speeches/eu-speech-at-bloomberg.

[11] D Curtin, 'Challenging Executive Dominance in European Democracy' (2014) 77 *Modern Law Review* 31.

EMU and budgetary affairs. The objective of the chapter is to evaluate the composite EU fiscal law-making process and argue that, despite the restriction of their autonomy, NPs have countered the euro crisis using various constitutional avenues including interparliamentary cooperation.[12]

II. THE ROLE OF NATIONAL PARLIAMENTS IN EU ECONOMIC AND FINANCIAL GOVERNANCE

A. The Six Pack's Encroachment on Domestic Budgetary Sovereignty

One of the Six Pack regulations establishes a new form of economic policy coordination called the European Semester.[13] The European Semester lasts from January to June each year and operationalises the adoption and implementation of broad economic policy guidelines.[14] The European Council defines economic priorities and gives Member States general policy orientations based on the Commission's Annual Growth Survey. Taking these into account, Member States submit to the Commission their stability programmes (for euro area Member States) or convergence programmes (for non-euro area Member States). Stability and convergence programmes outline the Member States' fiscal plans, while national reform programmes expound their plans for structural reforms with a view to boosting growth and jobs. The Commission then drafts country-specific recommendations, which are endorsed by the European Council and adopted by the Council. The second half of the year is called the National Semester and it culminates with the NPs' adoption of annual budgets on the basis of country-specific recommendations. Both Semesters operate according to a common EU budgetary timeline, which leaves NPs a very short period of time in which to react and adjust their budgetary plans. This hamstrings their fiscal prerogatives insofar as NPs are forced to rearrange their decision-making procedures and schedules in order to meet the 'Semestral' deadlines.[15] The European Parliament (EP) is virtually sidestepped too,[16] which is why it is essential to bolster the NPs' involvement in the European Semester.

NPs are only marginally mentioned in the Six Pack. All five regulations underline in their recitals the necessity of a closer and more timely involvement of the EP and NPs to increase the transparency of and accountability for the decisions taken.[17] The Regulation amending the preventive component of the SGP demands that each stability or convergence

[12] D Jančić, 'Countering the Debt Crisis: National Parliaments and EU Economic Governance' (2014) 1 *LSE Law Policy Briefing Paper*.

[13] Article 1(3) Regulation (EU) No 1175/2011 of the European Parliament and of the Council of 16 November 2011 amending Council Regulation (EC) No 1466/97 on the strengthening of the surveillance of budgetary positions and the surveillance and coordination of economic policies [2011] OJ L306/12 (inserting Section 1-A).

[14] See further on the EU and national phases of the European Semester process in: EP Study 'An Assessment of the European Semester' (Mark Hallerberg et al), September 2012.

[15] C Hefftler and W Wessels, 'The Democratic Legitimacy of the EU's Economic Governance and National Parliaments' (2013) 13 *IAI Working Paper* 10.

[16] C Fasone, 'European Economic Governance and Parliamentary Representation. What Place for the European Parliament?' (2014) 20 *European Law Journal* 164–85; D Hodson, *Governing the Euro Area in Good Times and Bad* (Oxford, Oxford University Press, 2011) 4.

[17] Recital 16 Regulation 1175/2011.

programme and national reform programme include information: (a) on its status in the context of national procedures and particularly whether the programme has been presented to parliament; (b) whether parliament has had a chance to discuss EU recommendations; and (c) whether parliament has approved the programme.[18] Yet the Regulation does not stipulate an obligation for NPs to be involved in formulating these programmes. As Chalmers rightly argues, this is a lost opportunity, because NPs may de facto be brought to a fait accompli.[19] Yet it remains contentious whether the EU is entitled to impose such an obligation in the first place, given that any regulation of legislative-executive relations falls within the ambit of domestic constitutional law and national sovereignty. The duty for the Union to respect the national identity of the Member States provides a safeguard against any such encroachment.[20] As demonstrated in Section III of this chapter, domestic law has provided a remedy for this in several Member States.

B. The Fiscal Compact's Attempted Constitutional Onslaught

In order to further remedy the fiscal fallacies befalling the Eurozone, all EU Member States—except the United Kingdom (UK) and the Czech Republic—signed on 2 March 2012 and outside the EU framework the Treaty on Stability, Coordination and Governance in the Economic and Monetary Union (TSCG or Fiscal Compact).[21] This Treaty mandates the implementation of the balanced budget rule, requiring the structural deficit not to exceed 0.5 per cent of GDP or 1 per cent of GDP where the public debt is significantly below 60 per cent of GDP.[22] This is to be performed by enacting binding and permanent domestic provisions, preferably of a constitutional nature, or by otherwise guaranteeing full adherence to these rules throughout the national budgetary process.[23] In case of significant deviation from these targets, an automatically triggered correction mechanism shall be put in place at the national level and 'shall fully respect the prerogatives of NPs'.[24]

However, it has been argued that the Fiscal Compact marks the end of the Westphalian paradigm because it 'strikes at the heart of the institutions of parliamentary democracy by dislocating as a matter of constitutional principle the budgetary autonomy of the Member States'.[25] Still, this did not happen because the provision requiring the constitutionalisation

[18] Arts 3(4) and 7(4) Regulation 1175/2011.

[19] D Chalmers, 'The European Redistributive State and a European Law of Struggle' (2012) 18 *European Law Journal* 686–87.

[20] See further in: LFM Besselink, 'National and Constitutional Identity before and after Lisbon' (2010) 6 *Utrecht Law Review* 36–49; E Cloots, *National Identity in EU Law* (Oxford, Oxford University Press, 2015).

[21] P Craig, 'The Stability, Coordination and Governance Treaty: Principle, Politics and Pragmatism' (2012) 37 *European Law Review* 231–48; S Peers, 'Stability Treaty: Permanent Austerity or Gesture Politics?' (2012) 8 *European Constitutional Law Review* 404–41.

[22] Art 3(1)(a) and (b) TSCG. See: F Fabbrini, 'The Fiscal Compact, the "Golden Rule", and the Paradox of European Federalism' (2013) 36 *Boston College International and Comparative Law Review* 19.

[23] Art 3(2) TSCG. See more in M Adams et al (eds), *The Constitutionalization of European Budgetary Constraints* (Oxford, Hart Publishing, 2014).

[24] Arts 3(1)(e) and 3(2) TSCG.

[25] Editorial, 'The Fiscal Compact and the European Constitutions' (2012) 8 *European Constitutional Law Review* 5–6. See more: A Hinarejos, 'The Euro Area Crisis and Constitutional Limits to Fiscal Integration' (2012) 14 *Cambridge Yearbook of European Legal Studies* 243–68.

of the balanced budget rule was watered down several times during negotiations.[26] Constitutional form is now thus merely a preferred manner of internalising the balanced budget rule, but no longer a mandatory one. Yet a requirement for the Member States to constitutionalise this rule could have widened the democratic deficit of EU economic governance.[27] This requirement would also likely have been at variance with Article 4(2) TEU, which enshrines respect for the national identity and constitutional structure of the Member States.[28] Emphatically, national identity encompasses 'parliamentary identity',[29] because an essential part of the domestic constitutional structure pertains to the prerogatives of parliament. If the manner in which a Member State regulates its structural deficit is put on a constitutional footing, this significantly reduces parliaments' autonomy because changing the constitution requires a higher majority in parliament, or potentially, popular approval in a referendum. Furthermore, in Member States such as the UK and the Netherlands, parliament enjoys legislative supremacy that is incompatible with this requirement.[30] Legal tension arises here regardless, however, because fiscal prerogatives of parliaments are encroached upon externally, allowing exogenous influence on an inherently endogenous process. The Fiscal Compact hence represents an attempted, but failed, constitutional attack on the NPs' fiscal competence, because implementation of the balanced budget rule may be performed through sub-constitutional legal instruments. Nonetheless, budgetary limitations remain a consequence of the Fiscal Compact.

C. The Two Pack's Hidden Messages on Domestic Politics

In a move to hone EU economic governance, the EP and the Council adopted the Two Pack regulations. Though these legal acts establish a further layer of supranational supervision over domestic budgeting, they also foresee modest avenues for NPs' liaison with EU institutions.

The Regulation on the fiscal surveillance of Member States with serious difficulties with financial stability envisages several rights for NPs. When the Commission decides to subject a Member State to enhanced surveillance, the latter shall adopt appropriate measures and the Commission shall, where relevant and in accordance with national practice, inform the NP of these measures.[31] On the one hand, this provision reveals an important shortcoming of the EU economic coordination process in general, since it implies that the national government might not inform parliament of these measures. It is indeed possible for these

[26] Craig, n 21 above, at 237.

[27] R Baratta, 'Legal Issues of the "Fiscal Compact". Searching for a Mature Democratic Governance of the Euro' in B de Witte et al (eds), *The Euro Crisis and the State of European Democracy* (Florence, EUI, 2013) 58.

[28] CM Cantore and G Martinico, 'Asymmetry or Disintegration? A Few Considerations on the New "Treaty on Stability, Coordination and Governance in the Economic and Monetary Union"' (2013) 19 *European Public Law* 465.

[29] A von Bogdandy and S Schill, 'Overcoming Absolute Primacy: Respect for National Identity under the Lisbon Treaty' (2011) 48 *Common Market Law Review* 1426.

[30] M Gordon, 'The United Kingdom and the Fiscal Compact: Past and Future' (2014) 10 *European Constitutional Law Review* 35.

[31] Art 3(1)(2) Regulation (EU) No 472/2013 of the European Parliament and of the Council of 21 May 2013 on the strengthening of economic and budgetary surveillance of Member States in the euro area experiencing or threatened with serious difficulties with respect to their financial stability [2013] OJ L140/1.

measures to be agreed between the Commission and the government without much prior parliamentary participation. Moreover, informing the NP is a matter of discretion for the Commission, which may well decide not to provide information. The alienation of NPs is therefore tangible. On a more positive note, the provision guarantees parliamentarians' access to information. This may enable them to prevent the government from playing the blame game by accusing Brussels of imposing these measures.[32] This direct communication between the Commission and NPs is harmonious with Protocols No 1 and 2 appended to the Lisbon Treaty.

The second Regulation calls for a 'commensurate involvement of the EP and NPs as appropriate'[33] and entitles NPs to request from the Commission its opinion on draft budgetary plans and its recommendations on the correction of the excessive deficit, but only once these documents have been made public and submitted to the executive branches.[34] These are unfortunate prescriptions for two reasons. First, while the Commission's opinions and recommendations are presented to the Eurogroup and the governments automatically, NPs must place a specific request to gain access to these documents. If such a request is not made, the manner in which EU requirements concerning the domestic budget are fulfilled may be thrashed out between the Commission and the government in isolation from the NP, which is de facto sidelined. Secondly, there is no political added value in sending to parliaments information that has been made public anyway, because this does not increase their capacity for timely reaction.

The following headings analyse the arrangements at the national and EU levels that are aimed at improving NPs' oversight over EMU decision-making. This is imperative given that no less than 20 domestic parliamentary chambers have introduced new procedures in relation to the European Semester.[35]

III. NATIONAL-LEVEL REACTIONS TO EMU REFORMS

At the national level, changes in view of the European Semester and other EMU reforms are rather diverse. They are inspected below on the basis of examples drawn from the French, British, German and Portuguese (F, UK, DE, PT) legal systems with occasional references to other systems where relevant. These Member States have been selected because they exemplify different legislative, political and judicial channels for internalising and taking ownership of the EU economic governance. Furthermore, they provide insights from the perspectives of both euro area (F, DE, PT) and non-euro area Member States (UK), as well as of both parliamentary (UK, DE) and semi-presidential systems of government (F, PT).

[32] A Benz, 'Accountable Multilevel Governance by the Open Method of Coordination?' (2007) 13 *European Law Journal* 517.

[33] Recital 6 Regulation (EU) No 473/2013 of the European Parliament and of the Council of 21 May 2013 on common provisions for monitoring and assessing draft budgetary plans and ensuring the correction of excessive deficit of the Member States in the euro area [2013] OJ L140/11.

[34] Arts 7(3) and 11(2) Regulation 473/2013.

[35] COSAC, *21st Bi-Annual Report* (June 2014) 39.

A. Legislative Enhancement of the Budgetary Prerogatives of Parliaments

(i) Greater Approval Rights

As the most powerful asset in the hands of parliamentarians, the right of approval during the course of the budgetary procedure has been upheld or fortified in a number of Member States in response to the euro crisis.

In France, EU constraints on fiscal policy-making have been counterbalanced by enacting two rights of approval in budgetary process.[36] One was adopted in 2010 and entitles Parliament, thus both the Assemblée nationale and the Sénat, to receive a draft stability programme from the government at least two weeks before it is transmitted to the Commission, then to debate it in the plenary, and to vote on it.[37] A constitutional amendment on the balancing of public finances was adopted by both Houses of Parliament on 13 July 2011,[38] but was not definitively approved because a 3/5 majority in the Congrès could not be secured.[39] Had it become law, these rights would have become a constitutional obligation and thus more difficult to repeal. The right to vote on draft stability programmes does not apply to national reform programmes and they are scrutinised by the relevant finance committee in the form of information reports. In early 2014, however, the Assemblée nationale requested for NPs to partake in the preparation of national reform programmes as well as to be given the right formally to approve them.[40] The other approval right stems from the implementation of the Fiscal Compact in 2012 by an organic law. It enables both chambers of Parliament to approve the government's detailed report on revenues and spending. This report must address France's position with regard to both general EU strategic objectives and the concrete Six Pack requirements, and it must justify any differences between the government's and the Commission's estimates of the GDP and conjunctural fluctuations.[41]

In a non-euro area Member State, such as the UK, where EU economic rules apply with the exception of the Two Pack and of the Six Pack provisions on sanctions,[42] Parliament's right to approve the government's assessment of the medium-term economic and budgetary position in relation to public investment expenditure, which was enacted in the wake of the Maastricht Treaty,[43] extends to Britain's European Semester obligation to submit convergence programmes to the Commission. However, while convergence programmes

[36] See the prior situation in: E Grossman and N Sauger, 'Political Institutions under Stress? Assessing the Impact of European Integration on French Political Institutions' (2007) 14 *Journal of European Public Policy* 1117–34.

[37] Art 14 *Loi no 2010-1645 du 28 décembre 2010 de programmation des finances publiques pour les années 2011 à 2014.*

[38] *Projet de loi constitutionnelle relatif à l'équilibre des finances publiques*, www.assemblee-nationale.fr/13/dossiers/equilibre_finances_publiques.asp.

[39] M Saoudi, 'La Régulation Européenne des Finances Publiques Nationales' (2013) 567 *Revue du Marché Commun et de l'Union Européenne* 210.

[40] Assemblée nationale, *Résolution européenne no 284 sur les progrès de l'union bancaire et de l'intégration économique au sein de l'Union économique et monétaire* of 30 January 2014, point 13.

[41] Art 5 *Loi organique 2012-1403 relative à la programmation et à la gouvernance des finances publiques* of 17 December 2012.

[42] The UK has negotiated an EMU derogation, which is expounded in Protocol no 15 annexed to the founding treaties. See more: A Dashwood, 'The United Kingdom in a Re-Formed European Union' (2013) 38 *European Law Review* 737–56.

[43] Section 5 European Communities (Amendment) Act of 1993.

need parliamentary approval, national reform programmes do not. The House of Lords specifically rejected the need for national reform programmes to be approved, because they do not introduce new policy but merely restate the policies already pursued in the government's Comprehensive Spending Review and Pre-Budget Report, which are subject to the usual budgetary procedure.[44] The House of Commons' Treasury Committee scrutinises the Pre-Budget Report and produces a report thereon on the basis of oral and written evidence from Her Majesty's Treasury and external stakeholders.[45] While there is no systematic mechanism for ex ante parliamentary scrutiny of the Comprehensive Spending Review, which is principally a process whereby the Treasury negotiates expenditures with other government departments, the Commons select committees can be involved in the consultations on the spending review and seek relevant information from the government.[46] Furthermore, as of 2011 Her Majesty's Treasury has been obliged to set out its fiscal policy in a Charter for Budget Responsibility and lay it before Parliament. This Charter cannot enter into force unless it is approved by a resolution of the House of Commons and this gives an opportunity to Parliament to exert upstream influence over the formulation of budgetary parameters.[47]

Similar rights of approval in the course of the European Semester have been established in Latvia[48] and Spain.[49] In Italy, although there is no formal right of approval a comprehensive process of prior parliamentary consultation has been put in place,[50] and both chambers can adopt resolutions on stability programmes and national reform programmes.[51] In yet other Member States where no approval right in the European Semester exists whatsoever, Parliament has proven capable of exerting significant pressure on the government through non-EU-related instruments of accountability, such as the vote of no confidence.[52] For instance, in the cases of Sweden and Portugal,[53] government was toppled because Parliament's budgetary preferences were ignored. In the latter case, the fall of the Socrates Government in 2011 was directly rooted in the Assembly's rejection of the fourth Portuguese stability programme and the austerity measures contained therein.[54] As a consequence, the stability programme had to be revised. The political process can thus mitigate the deficiencies of the legislative frameworks for parliamentary scrutiny of EU economic coordination processes.

[44] HL 81 'The EU Strategy for Economic Growth and the UK National Reform Programme', *5th Report 2010–2011*, paras 8–9 and 30.

[45] HC, Committee Office Scrutiny Unit, 'Financial Scrutiny Uncovered: How the Government Manages Its Finances and How Parliament Scrutinises Them' (March 2007) 14.

[46] ibid, 12.

[47] Section 1(7) Budget Responsibility and National Audit Act of 2011.

[48] COSAC, *21st Bi-Annual Report* (June 2014) 41. See also: Rule 185(3) Rules of Procedure of the Latvian Saeima.

[49] Art 15(7) *Ley Organica 2/2012 de Estabilidad Presupuestaria y Sostenibilidad Financiera.*

[50] Art 2 *Legge no 39/2011* amending *Legge no 196/2009 di contabilità e finanza pubblica.*

[51] COSAC, *21st Bi-Annual Report* (June 2014) 43.

[52] Editorial, 'The European Council and the National Executives: Segmentation, Consolidation and Legitimation' (2012) 8 *European Constitutional Law Review* 165.

[53] The Swedish Prime Minister Stefan Löfven was defeated in December 2014 and the Portuguese Prime Minister José Socrates in March 2011.

[54] *Reunião plenária* of 23 March 2011, DAR-I/67, 77–79. See more in: PC Magalhães, 'After the Bailout: Responsibility, Policy, and Valence in the Portuguese Legislative Election of June 2011' (2012) 17 *South European Society and Politics* 309–27.

(ii) Intensified Public Debate, Strengthened Scrutiny, and Streamlined Information Access

Due to the high salience of economic and fiscal policy, steps have been taken in a number of Member States to ensure greater parliamentary debate and sharper scrutiny of the EU economic governance. However, without possessing adequate information and without receiving it in good time, parliaments cannot have much clout. Information is the key munition a parliament needs in order to set in motion instruments of policy-making influence, and the euro crisis has led to an improved parliamentary access to it.

To facilitate the fulfillment of the requirements of the European Semester process, in France debates can be organised in both the Assemblée nationale and the Sénat to provide them with 'the best information' in a timely manner.[55] Both chambers may also debate all Council decisions related to France's excessive deficit. Additionally, they may at any time increase their information base by organising hearings with the members of the fiscal council established under the name of High Council of Public Finances.[56] The latest Act on the Programming of Public Finances for 2014–19 further ameliorates Parliament's scrutiny and information rights by obliging the government to send both chambers its reviews and evaluations of fiscal expenditure as well as its public debt estimations in relation to the EU excessive deficit procedure.[57]

Furthermore, both chambers of the French Parliament underwent significant developments in scrutinising EU economic governance either informally or by passing European resolutions. In the Assemblée nationale, since 2010 the adoption of a resolution on the Commission's observations on the stability programme and national reform programme has been customary practice.[58] This was coupled in 2012 with a more general request for the government to consult Parliament at all key stages of the European Semester.[59] In 2013, MPs on several occasions provided constructive input on the economic policy preferences of the government, the European Council and the Commission in the context of the European Semester and discussed the democratic legitimacy of this process.[60] For their part, the Sénat passed a reasoned opinion on the draft Two Pack Regulation on the monitoring of budgetary plans. The senators deplored the Commission's failure to explain subsidiarity compliance, raised proportionality concerns, and approved the proposal only under the condition that key legal standards be interpreted widely.[61] They further invited the Commission to involve them in the economic dialogue and called upon the government

[55] Art 10 *Loi organique 2012-1403.*

[56] Art 20 *Loi organique 2012-1403.*

[57] Arts 22–23 and 32 *Loi no 2014-1653 du 29 décembre 2014 de programmation des finances publiques pour les années 2014 à 2019.*

[58] See: COSAC, *15th Bi-Annual Report–Annex* (May 2011) 50.

[59] Assemblée nationale, *Résolution européenne no 48 sur l'ancrage démocratique du gouvernement économique européen* of 27 November 2012, point 5.

[60] Assemblée nationale, *Résolution européenne no 95 sur les orientations européennes de politique économique* of 15 March 2013, point 5; *Résolution européenne no. 204 sur l'approfondissement de l'Union économique et monétaire* of 11 August 2013, points 7 and 14; *Résolution européenne no 205 sur l'avis de la Commission européenne sur les programmes de stabilité et de réforme de la France* of 11 August 2013, points 5, 6 and 10.

[61] Sénat, *Résolution européenne no 53 portant avis motivé sur la conformité au principe de subsidiarité de la proposition de réglement établissant des dispositions communes pour le suivi et l'évaluation des projets de plans budgétaires et pour la correction des déficits excessifs dans les Etats membres de la zone euro* of 24 January 2012.

to permit enhanced parliamentary control of Eurozone affairs.[62] In 2014, the Sénat made substantive recommendations on how to deepen and democratise the EMU and called for 'regular contradictory debates' with the Commission and the establishment of specialised bodies of euro area parliamentarians at the EU level.[63] In this regard, both chambers avidly supported the interparliamentary conference on economic and financial governance.

In the UK, convergence programmes are debated and adopted in plenary debates. The House of Lords has seen another related informal development. Sparked by discussions between the EU Committee and the government, the latter agreed to include national reform programmes in plenary debates on the convergence programmes.[64] When it comes to parliamentary scrutiny of the EU economic governance reform, the Six Pack was scrutinised by Westminster in its entirety. The House of Commons analysed this legislative package in the European Scrutiny Committee and in the plenary.[65] During the latter session, MPs noted with approval the government's commitment to present budgetary and fiscal information to Parliament before these are sent to EU institutions.

In the House of Lords, the Six Pack was examined in detail by the EU Sub-Committee on Economic and Financial Affairs, which resulted in an in-depth report and an exchange of letters with the Financial Secretary to the Treasury.[66] This report is a clear endorsement of the EU economic governance reform, which was welcomed as a step in the right direction that promotes 'national ownership of EU rules'.[67] Their Lordships also commented on matters that do not apply to Britain, expressing 'strong reservations' about the imposition of sanctions within the excessive imbalance procedure.[68] This is a sign of their proactive approach to EU scrutiny, which is aimed at informing the wider debate and not only at appraising UK policy. Yet as they maintained, Britain is indeed directly affected because the debt crisis puts pressure on British banks.[69] Most importantly, their Lordships were very positive about the European Semester, holding that the Member States will 'benefit greatly' from what they saw merely as 'advice' from the Commission.[70] They concluded that, rather than downgrading the role of NPs, the European Semester could strengthen parliamentary scrutiny of the executive by yielding more information.[71] However, the Lords EU Committee also warned that it is crucial to ensure democratic legitimacy of the European Semester because an integrated economic policy could take electoral power away from the citizens and prevent them from deciding at the ballot box how taxes are raised and how public money is spent.[72]

[62] Sénat, *Résolution européenne no 106 pour un renforcement du contrôle démocratique de la gouvernance économique et budgétaire de l'Union européenne* of 6 March 2012.

[63] Sénat, *Résolution européenne no 73 sur l'approfondissement de l'Union économique et monétaire* of 4 February 2014.

[64] COSAC, *15th Bi-Annual Report–Annex* (May 2011) 156.

[65] HC 428-v, *5th Report 2010–11*, chapters 1 and 2; HC Deb of 10 November 2010, vol 518, cols 359–388.

[66] Ministerial correspondence for 1 December 2010–31 May 2011: www.parliament.uk/documents/lords-committees/eu-sub-com-a/CWM/CwMSubADec10-May11.pdf, pp 40–44.

[67] HL 124-I 'The Future of Economic Governance in the EU–Volume I', *12th Report 2010–11*, paras 245 and 265.

[68] HL 124-I, para 273.

[69] HL 124-I, paras 247–248.

[70] HL 124-I, para 169.

[71] HL 124-I, para 170.

[72] HL 134 '"Genuine Economic and Monetary Union" and the Implications for the UK', *8th Report 2013–14*, paras 195 and 222.

They advocated a reinforcement of NPs in overseeing Eurozone developments.[73] The euro crisis has furthermore attracted an ongoing parliamentary attention, especially in the Lords, who continue to put pressure on the government to release details of European Council negotiations.[74] Finally, both chambers scrutinise the European Semester using regular instruments, such as reports, scrutiny reserves, ministerial correspondence, and plenary and committee debates.[75]

As a Member State that has undergone a bailout programme, Portugal has promptly revised parliamentary scrutiny of EU economic governance.[76] In May 2012 the European Scrutiny Act was amended to introduce plenary debates with the government on various instruments of EU economic governance,[77] including the European Semester and the stability programme, which was initially called the Stability and Growth Programme (*Programa de Estabilidade e Crescimento*) and later the Fiscal Strategy Document (*Documento de Estrategia Orçamental*).[78] Since 2004 the Assembly has had the right to receive from the government the final version of the stability programme before it is sent to EU institutions. In addition, a plenary debate in the presence of the Prime Minister is henceforth held *before* each European Council meeting to enable prior parliamentary discussion inter alia of Eurozone matters.[79]

Moreover, the 2001 Budgetary Framework Act (*Lei de Enquadramento Orçamental*) enacted the right of MPs to receive from the government in a timely fashion all information needed for the scrutiny of the execution of the budget, including the financial flows between Portugal and the EU.[80] This Act also provides for a plenary debate on the government's spending policy and stability programme revisions, allowing questions from parliamentary groups.[81] In the debt crisis period, this Act underwent a four-fold amendment, of which three merit special attention.[82] The fifth amendment (May 2011) clarified that the budgetary process now begins with an annual revision of the government's stability programme, which must be 'duly justified'.[83] The seventh amendment of this Act (June 2013) transposed the Six Pack Directive on the requirements for budgetary

[73] HL 151 'The Role of National Parliaments in the European Union', *9th Report 2013–14*, para 167.

[74] HL 260 'The Euro Area Crisis', *25th Report 2010–2012*, para 150. See also HL 163 'Euro Area Crisis: An Update', *11th Report 2013–2014*.

[75] COSAC, *15th Bi-Annual Report–Annex* (May 2011) 154 and 157.

[76] *Lei 21/2012* amending *Lei 43/2006 Acompanhamento, apreciação e pronúncia pela Assembleia da República no âmbito do processo de construção da União Europeia* (European Scrutiny Act). See more in: D Jančić, 'The Portuguese Parliament: Blazing the Trail to the European Scrutiny Trophy?' (2011) 1 *Interdisciplinary Political Studies* 93–108; D Jančić, 'The European Union in the Portuguese Assembly: Scrutinising Primary and Secondary EU Decision Making' in A Cunha et al (eds), *Portugal e as Organizações Internacionais: Comportamentos, Mensagens e Impactos* (Lisbon, Observatório Político, 2014); D Jančić, 'The Portuguese Parliament and EU Affairs: From Inert to Agile Democratic Control' in C Hefftler et al (eds), *The Palgrave Handbook on National Parliaments and the European Union* (Basingstoke, Palgrave Macmillan, 2015).

[77] Art 4(1)(d) European Scrutiny Act.

[78] Conselho das Finanças Públicas, *Relatório 3/2013*, May 2013, 2; *Resolução 79/2012*, DAR-I/111, 2945.

[79] Art 4(1)(a) European Scrutiny Act.

[80] Art 56 thereof (later renumbered Art 59). This parliamentary right was further affirmed in Art 86 thereof (later renumbered Art 89), which was introduced by the first amendment of this Act, carried out by *Lei 2/2002*.

[81] This debate was given a European tone by the third amendment of this Act (August 2004) by obliging the government to submit to the Assembly a report outlining general economic policy orientations and budgetary consolidation specifically in the context of the EU.

[82] *Lei 91/2001*, DAR-I/192, 5352, 20 August 2001.

[83] Art 12-B as amended by *Lei 22/2011*.

frameworks and implemented the Fiscal Compact. It established the government's duty to present to the Assembly a comparison between the macroeconomic and budgetary forecasts laid down in its draft budget and those made by European Commission and obliged it to 'explain in a reasoned manner' any significant differences between them.[84] In case of deviations from the balanced budget rule, the government must submit to the Assembly a plan of measures to rectify them.[85] The determination of the existence of exceptional circumstances that justify significant deviation from this rule must also be sent to MPs for consideration.[86] Since the eighth amendment (July 2014) the measures aimed at correcting such deviations must be inserted into the stability programme, whereby they become subject to additional scrutiny and debate.[87] An empirical study unveils that the increase in the number of plenary debates held from 2009–11 was partly due to debates on the stability programme.[88] Besides, the European Semester has indeed been the MPs' top scrutiny priority.[89]

The information flow and debate between governments and parliaments have thus been streamlined. Innovative solutions for scrutinising EU economic governance have been devised in yet other Member States. For example, in December 2013 the Croatian Parliament established a Special Fiscal Policy Committee, which is in charge inter alia of the European Semester process.[90]

B. Political Practice and the Scrutiny of the European Semester

To depict the actual NPs' involvement in EU economic affairs following the debt crisis, I have carried out a qualitative empirical analysis into the scrutiny by all five parliamentary chambers in Portugal, France and Britain of the annual growth surveys, stability or convergence programmes, national reform programmes and country-specific recommendations drafted in 2011—the first year of operation of the European Semester. To this are added two strategic documents on ways to reform the EMU: the 2012 Commission Communication entitled 'Blueprint for a Deep and Genuine Economic and Monetary Union—Launching a European Debate' (Blueprint)[91] and the 2012 Report by the former European Council President, Herman van Rompuy, entitled 'Towards a Genuine Economic and Monetary Union' (Van Rompuy Report).[92] The empirical data, summarised in Table 1, exhibit the marked intensity and frequency of government–parliament interactions as well as keen parliamentary interest in the future of the EMU architecture.

[84] Art 36 as amended by *Lei 37/2013*.

[85] Art 72-C as amended by *Lei 37/2013*.

[86] Art 72-D as amended by *Lei 37/2013*.

[87] Art 72-D(3) as amended by *Lei 41/2014*.

[88] MT Paulo and A Cunha, 'A Europa no Discurso Parlamentar Português: Os Debates Plenários entre 1985 e 2011' (2013) 40 *Relações Internacionais* 191.

[89] *Resolução 73/2011*, DAR-I/66, 1980. See also: www.en.parlamento.pt/EuropeanAffairs/EuropInitiativesPriorities.html.

[90] Rule 45 Rules of Procedure of the Croatian Sabor.

[91] COM(2012) 777.

[92] See: www.consilium.europa.eu/uedocs/cms_Data/docs/pressdata/en/ec/134069.pdf.

Table 1: Parliamentary scrutiny of the 2011 European Semester and the strategic EMU documents

	AGS	SCP	NRP	CSR	Blueprint	VRR
PT Assembly	EAC SC	Plenary SC	EAC SC	–	EAC SC	Plenary EAC
FR Assemblée nationale	EACs jointly with MEPs	Plenary EAC SC	Plenary EAC SC	Plenary* SC	Plenary EAC	Plenary EAC
FR Sénat		Plenary SC	–	Plenary* SC	–	Plenary EAC
UK House of Commons	EAC	Plenary	EAC	EAC	Plenary EAC	Plenary EAC
UK House of Lords	EAC	Plenary	Plenary EAC	EAC	Plenary EAC	Plenary EAC

Source: Own research based on surveys, parliamentary documents, COSAC data and the 2012 EP study on the European Semester.

Legend: EAC–European Affairs Committee; SC–sectoral committee; AGS–annual growth surveys; SCP–stability or convergence programmes; NRP–national reform programmes; CSR–country-specific recommendations; VRR–Van Rompuy report.

* The resolutions were adopted by the relevant sectoral committees and, pursuant to the respective Rules of Procedure of the two Houses, considered adopted by the plenary after 15 days if the applicable conditions have been met.

With the exception of country-specific recommendations, there is a discernible tendency towards European Semester documents being effectively scrutinised by all parliamentary chambers under inspection. While the annual growth surveys saw a dominant engagement of sectoral committees, the plenary prevailed with regard to stability or convergence programmes. An interesting finding concerns country-specific recommendations, which were not scrutinised in Portugal but were scrutinised in Britain, where the Commons examined not only draft country-specific recommendations for the UK but also for all other Member States.[93] This shows that Eurozone membership is not correlative with the scrutiny of the European Semester. Thanks to their strategic importance, the Blueprint and the Van Rompuy Report have triggered a massive response in all chambers, which examined them on a variety of occasions, concluding that these documents poorly addressed the democratic legitimacy and accountability in the EMU. The British House of Commons in particular expressed great concern about the presumption of the EP's precedence in democratising the EMU,[94] underlining that the 'constitutional primacy' of the UK Parliament must be respected.[95]

The foregoing analysis shows that, irrespective of the constitutional differences, a number of Member States have successfully internalised the European Semester, whether through enactments or practical adjustments. It also reveals that NPs by no means refrain from utilising their rights and that the crisis has ignited rather than suppressed their scrutiny.

[93] HC 428-xxx, *34th Report 2010–12*, pp 20–34; HC 428-xxxii, *36th Report 2010–12*, pp 9–14.

[94] HC 86-xiv 'Banking Union and Economic and Monetary Union', *14th Report 2012–13*, para 2.11.

[95] HC 86-xxviii 'Economic and Monetary Union', *28th Report 2012–13*, paras 1.22 and 1.24. See above text accompanying n 30 above.

C. Judicial Protection of the Budgetary Prerogatives of Parliaments

The budgetary competence of NPs in the context of the euro crisis is also protected by courts. The most notable example hereof is Germany, where the Federal Constitutional Court, the Bundesverfassungsgericht (BVerfG), has continued its traditional role of the 'guardian of Parliament'. In a series of crisis-related judgments,[96] the Bundestag's place in the budgetary process has been safeguarded and EU fiscal integration vindicated as long as the principle of democracy is respected.[97] This was made most apparent in its *Greek Aid and European Financial Stability Facility* case from September 2011,[98] where the BVerfG ruled that the Bundestag must retain not only the right to approve every large-scale financial rescue measure of the Federal Government that impacts on its budgetary autonomy but that it must also be able to exercise 'sufficient parliamentary influence' in the management of any such financial undertaking.[99] A prior consent of the Bundestag's Budget Committee must be obtained before Germany may engage in both international and EU mechanisms that impinge on Parliament's fiscal prerogatives.[100]

In February 2012, another BVerfG judgment ruled against allowing a down-sized composition of the Bundestag's Budget Committee to decide on budgetary matters in cases of urgency and confidentiality.[101] Similarly, on the occasion of the ratification of the Fiscal Compact and the European Stability Mechanism (ESM) Treaty, the BVerfG ruled in September 2012 that Germany's financial liability beyond the agreed share in the ESM (€190 billion) cannot be assumed without the approval of the Bundestag.[102] The latter's overall budgetary responsibility was also flagged as a matter of concern in the BVerfG's preliminary ruling reference in the case related to the European Central Bank's (ECB) unlimited bond-buying programme, dubbed Outright Monetary Transactions (OMT).[103]

In Germany, the euro crisis has also helped reaffirm that Parliament's constitutional right to be comprehensively informed on EU matters at the earliest possible time is not a dead letter.[104] Quite to the contrary, it is justiciable and inviolable. In relation to the intergovernmental negotiations on the ESM and the Euro Plus Pact, the BVerfG ruled in June 2012 that the Federal Government had infringed this right by failing to provide Parliament with

[96] PM Huber, 'The Rescue of the Euro and Its Constitutionality' in W-G Ringe and PM Huber (eds), *Legal Challenges in the Global Financial Crisis: Bailouts, the Euro and Regulation* (Oxford, Hart Publishing, 2014) 18; G Beck, 'The Court of Justice, the Bundesverfassungsgericht and Legal Reasoning during the Euro Crisis: The Rule of Law as a Fair-Weather Phenomenon' (2014) 20 *European Public Law* 553.

[97] I Pernice, 'Domestic Courts, Constitutional Constraints and European Democracy' in M Adams et al (eds), *The Constitutionalization of European Budgetary Constraints* (Oxford, Hart Publishing, 2014) 305. See the 'democracy Solange' argument in: D Jančić, 'Caveats from Karlsruhe and Berlin: Whither Democracy after Lisbon?' (2010) 16 *Columbia Journal of European Law* 355.

[98] C Calliess, 'The Future of the Eurozone and the Role of the German Federal Constitutional Court' (2012) 31 *Yearbook of European Law* 407.

[99] BVerfG, 2 BvR 987/10, 1485/10 and 1099/10, judgment of 7 September 2011, 128.

[100] ibid, 141.

[101] BVerfG, 2 BvE 8/11, judgment of 28 February 2012, 100.

[102] BVerfG, 2 BvR 1390/12, 1421/12, 1438/12, 1439/12, 1440/12, and 2 BvE 6/12, judgment of 12 September 2012, 171.

[103] BVerfG, 2 BvR 2728/13, 2729/13, 2730/13, 2731/13, 2 BvE 13/13, judgment of of 14 January 2014, 43, 102–3. See also: M Wilkinson, 'Economic Messianism and Constitutional Power in a 'German Europe': All Courts are Equal, but Some Courts are More Equal than Others' (2014) 26 *LSE Law, Society and Economy Working Paper*.

[104] Art 23(2) *Grundgesetz*.

European Commission documents and information on the relevant European Council meetings.[105] A few months later, in the aforesaid judgment of September 2012, the BVerfG reiterated that the ESM Treaty provisions on the confidentiality of documents and professional secrecy must not preclude Parliament's right to information.[106]

D. Assessment of the Post-Crisis Domestic Legal Changes

While the crisis-propelled legal evolution in the position of NPs represents a small step in countervailing EU intervention in domestic fiscal policy, it does carry a broader constitutional importance.

For France, the significance lies in the fact that ever since the birth of the Fifth Republic, Parliament has been 'rationalised' to enable governmental stability and this has been the key structural hindrance to parliamentary empowerment in EU affairs.[107] Namely, despite the July 2008 constitutional strengthening of Parliament, the latter enjoys few budgetary powers. Beyond voting on the budget (*loi de finance*),[108] Parliament may neither increase expenditures nor lower revenues.[109] In contrast, the Government drafts the budget and may propose amendments thereto throughout the budgetary year (*loi de finance rectificative*). Further, the government may enact the budget in the form of an ordinance if Parliament does not act within 70 days.[110] One of the most idiosyncratic instruments of governmental dominance is the Prime Minister's right to make the adoption of the budget a matter of parliamentary confidence, in which case the budget is considered adopted unless a motion of censure is tabled within 24 hours and duly passed.[111] This is embedded within a more general trend,[112] set out in 2001,[113] towards enhancing Parliament's budgetary control,[114] which a former Chairman of the Sénat's Finance Committee and the current Chairman of the EP's Budget Committee describes as 'efficient and listened to' thanks to its access to quality information and the agility of committees.[115]

In the UK, any increase in parliamentary involvement in the budgetary sphere is noteworthy because, due to the political polarisation and tight party discipline, Westminster is traditionally one of the world's weakest parliaments when it comes to budgetary autonomy. The German and Portuguese Parliaments have also received significant legal and political

[105] BVerfG, 2 BvE 4/11, judgment of 19 June 2012, 133.

[106] BVerfG, 2 BvR 1390/12, 1421/12, 1438/12, 1439/12, 1440/12, and 2 BvE 6/12, judgment of 12 September 2012, 256.

[107] A Dyevre, 'The French Parliament and European Integration' (2012) 18 *European Public Law* 530. See more generally: P Avril et al, *Droit Parlementaire* (Paris, LGDJ, 2014).

[108] Arts 34(4) and 47(1) French Constitution.

[109] Art 40 French Constitution.

[110] Art 47(3) French Constitution.

[111] Art 49(3) French Constitution.

[112] C Le Bris, 'Le Droit de Regard du Parlement Français sur la Norme Supranationale en Formation' (2012) 128 *Revue du Droit Public* 950.

[113] A Lambert, 'Vers un Modèle Français de Contrôle Budgétaire' (2010) 134 *Pouvoirs* 47.

[114] J-F Amédro, 'L'Évaluation des Politiques Publiques: Structure et Portée Constitutionnelle d'une Nouvelle Fonction Parlementaire' (2013) 129 *Revue du Droit Public* 1138 and 1142.

[115] J Arthuis, 'La Dégradation des Finances Publiques: La Loi en Échec, le Contrôle et l'Évaluation en Recours' (2010) 134 *Pouvoirs* 88.

recognition of their budgetary prerogatives. The euro crisis has therefore triggered a defensive mechanism in a good number of Member States against encroachments on the power to collect public revenue.

IV. EU-LEVEL REACTIONS TO EMU REFORMS

Whereas the juridico-political response at the national level has been as varied as there are Member States, the EU level response is characterised by three chief institutional arrangements for interparliamentary cooperation in the European Semester process. They include the so-called economic dialogue, the Interparliamentary Conference on Economic and Financial Governance (ICEFG), and the European Parliamentary Week (EPW).

A. Economic Dialogue

The economic dialogue is the principal formal mechanism for enhancing the transparency and accountability of EU economic governance. It allows for interinstitutional discussions between the EP on the one hand, and the Commission, the Council, the European Council, and the Eurogroup, on the other. Its aim is to spark public debate on the spillover effects of national decisions and enable peer pressure to be put on relevant actors.[116] The economic dialogue is envisaged by both the Six Pack and the Two Pack.

The Six Pack outlines that, within the European Semester, the dialogue focuses on the evaluations, conclusions and reports concerning multilateral surveillance conducted by EU institutions. The dialogue also foresees the involvement of relevant stakeholders on main policy issues in accordance with EU law and domestic legal and political arrangements,[117] but falls short of mentioning NPs. The economic dialogue further extends to the imposition of sanctions, including deposits and fines, both within the framework of the SGP and within that for the correction of excessive macroeconomic imbalances. Since these discussions have a direct bearing on domestic fiscal and economic policy, in all of the above situations the competent EP committee may invite the Member State concerned, typically the minister in charge of the economy or finance, to participate in an exchange of views.[118] By March 2015, there were some 14 economic dialogues or exchanges of views with different Member States.[119] It is lamentable that NPs are not directly involved,[120] although they may organise ex ante and ex post hearings with the competent minister and seek information on the discussions held at the EU level.

[116] Recital 12 Regulation 1173/2011.

[117] Art 2-a(4) Regulation 1466/97 as amended by Regulation 1175/2011.

[118] Art 3 Regulation 1173/2011; Art 6 Regulation 1174/2011; Art 2-ab(3) Regulation 1466/97 as amended by Regulation 1175/2011; Art 14(2) Regulation 1167/2011; Art 2a(1)(3) Regulation 1467/97 as amended by Regulation 1177/2011.

[119] EP Briefing Note: 'Economic Dialogues and Exchanges of Views with the Member States under the European Semester Cycles' (Kajus Hagelstam), 25 March 2015.

[120] MP Maduro et al, 'The Euro Crisis and the Democratic Governance of the Euro: Legal and Political Issues of a Fiscal Crisis' in *The Democratic Governance of the Euro, RSCAS Policy Papers no 2012/08*, 9; Fasone (n 16 above) at 177.

The Two Pack lays down a reverse procedure too, whereby the NP of the Member State concerned may, during the course of the enhanced surveillance process, invite representatives of the Commission, the ECB and the International Monetary Fund for an economic dialogue.[121] Specifically, it is foreseen that the NP concerned may invite the Commission for an exchange of views after the latter has made public its recommendation on the precautionary corrective measures or a macroeconomic adjustment programme.[122] Such an exchange of views is also possible in order to discuss progress in implementing the adjustment programme.[123] If a Member State is subjected to post-programme surveillance the Commission is obliged every six months to communicate to the parliament of that Member State its assessment of the latter's economic and fiscal situation. The parliament concerned may also invite the Commission for an exchange of views at any time of the post-programme surveillance.[124] Finally, once the Commission publishes its opinion on the draft budgetary plans of a given Member State, it is obliged to present it to the NP concerned if the latter makes such a request.[125] These linkages between NPs and the Commission represent a new channel of 'communication and moral suasion' between them.[126] However, a greater emphasis on ex ante consultations would have been more advantageous to NPs. These possibilities may nonetheless upgrade their information access and contribute to bringing EU goals into harmony with the domestic fiscal exigencies and socio-economic policies.

Yet while the economic dialogue might foster better overall oversight of EU institutions, it is insufficient to guarantee full democratic legitimacy because parliamentarians at both levels continue to have no power of decision.[127] The economic dialogue complements the ongoing trend of greater participation of finance and budgetary committees of NPs in the European Semester, whereby some of them—like those in France, Portugal and the UK—frequently organise hearings with EU officials, typically Commissioners and MEPs.[128] In this regard, the economic dialogue may help to put fiscal policy deliberations on a more permanent footing and narrow the communication gap between the two levels of governance.

B. Interparliamentary Conference on Economic and Financial Governance

To facilitate the collective discussion of budgetary policies, the Fiscal Compact called for the organisation of a conference of competent committee representatives.[129] This materialised

[121] Art 3(9) Regulation 472/2013.

[122] Art 3(8)(b) Regulation 472/2013.

[123] Art 7(11) Regulation 472/2013.

[124] Art 14(5) Regulation 472/2013.

[125] Art 7(3) Regulation 473/2013.

[126] EP Study: 'An Assessment of the European Semester' (Mark Hallerberg et al), September 2012, 19.

[127] Chalmers (n 19 above) at 691; M Ruffert, 'The European Debt Crisis and European Union Law' (2011) 48 *Common Market Law Review* 1801.

[128] C Krolik, 'Le Renouveau des Commissions Parlementaires Permanentes?' (2014) 98 *Revue Française de Droit Constitutionnel* 357; COSAC, *19th Bi-Annual Report–Annex* (May 2013) 145; *Comissão de Orçamento, Finanças e Administração Pública, Relatório de Atividades* of 18 July 2012, 3, 9 and 11–12. See also the six-monthly evidence sessions that the House of Lords EU Sub-Committee on Economic and Financial Affairs organises in the context of the euro crisis with the Financial Secretary to the Treasury, external experts, and members of EU institutions: www.parliament.uk/business/committees/committees-a-z/lords-select/eu-economic-and-financial-affairs-and-international-trade-sub-committee-a/inquiries/parliament-2010/update-on-the-euro-area-crisis.

[129] Art 13 TSCG.

during the EU Speakers' Conference in Nicosia on 23 April 2013, when the Interparliamentary Conference on Economic and Financial Governance (ICEFG) was set up.[130] The conference convenes twice a year and is coordinated with the European Semester cycle.[131] It may adopt non-binding conclusions, which are sent to EU institutions.[132]

The first ICEFG meeting (Vilnius, 16–17 October 2013) proclaimed that its goals are to spark debate and exchange information and best practice in the fiscal area. This meeting also espoused the principle of right balance between the EP and NPs, whereby each of them should scrutinise decisions made at their level. The added value of ICEFG, however, is notably to avoid having 28 unconnected, parochial parliamentary debates that would disregard the perspectives of other Member States.[133] Cooperation and a stable alliance between the European and national parliaments have indeed been widely regarded as an essential tool for legitimising EMU decision-making,[134] not least by nurturing a dialogue on key normative issues of EU integration.[135] Yet while MEPs, the Commission and the European Council strongly support the EP's primacy in democratising EMU governance, most NPs are against it.[136] ICEFG is hence a compromise solution that reconciles the EP's and NPs' endeavours to preserve their autonomous sphere of influence in the budgetary field.

Certainly, networking between national and European parliamentarians is a welcome development if they are to 'mirror and keep pace with their networking national and European executives, who have long ago jumped the fence of national constitutional systems'.[137] Given the spillover effect of national budgetary processes and the high level of economic interlacement in the EU, there is significant added value in having parliamentarians liaise and debate the EU-wide implications of their fiscal legislation.[138] This contributes to a 'common discursive field of representative democracy in a multilevel setting'[139] and could mitigate the negative repercussions of isolated budgetary engineering. Indeed, while parliamentarians may have relatively few incentives for multilevel interparliamentary dialogue,[140] the lack thereof could speed up the drifting apart of national economic policies,

[130] V Kreilinger, 'The New Interparliamentary Conference for Economic and Financial Governance' (2013) 100 *Notre Europe Policy Paper*; R Fox, 'Europe, Democracy and the Economic Crisis: Is it Time to Reconstitute the "Assises"?' (2012) 65 *Parliamentary Affairs* 468.

[131] Art 3.1 TSCG.

[132] Art 7.1, 7.3 TSCG.

[133] Hefftler and Wessels (n 15 above) at 13.

[134] A Maurer, 'From EMU to DEMU: The Democratic Legitimacy of the EU and the European Parliament' (2013) 11 *IAI Working Paper* 4; T Kunstein and W Wessels, 'The New Governance of the Economic and Monetary Union: Adapted Institutions and Innovative Instruments' (2013) 3 *IAI Working Paper* 8; DM Viola, 'Interparliamentary Cooperation in the European Union: Towards Multilevel Governance' in GPE Walzenbach (ed), *European Governance: Policy Making Between Politicisation and Control* (Farnham, Ashgate, 2006) 177.

[135] R Bellamy and D Castiglione, 'Legitimising the Euro-"Polity" and Its "Regime": The Normative Turn in EU Studies' (2003) 2 *European Journal of Political Theory* 8.

[136] EP Study (Hallerberg) (n 14 above) at 10 and 77.

[137] M Bovens et al, 'The Real World of EU Accountability: Comparisons and Conclusions' in M Bovens et al (eds), *The Real World of EU Accountability: What Deficit?* (Oxford, Oxford University Press, 2010) 195.

[138] I Pernice, 'How Can the Process of European Unification Be Organised Democratically on a Medium and Long-Term Basis?' (2012) 3 *WHI Paper* 6–7.

[139] A Buzogány, 'Learning from the Best? Interparliamentary Networks and the Parliamentary Scrutiny of EU Decision Making' in B Crum and JE Fossum (eds), *Practices of Inter-Parliamentary Coordination in International Politics: The European Union and Beyond* (Colchester, ECPR Press, 2013) 20.

[140] See the limits of interparliamentary cooperation in O Costa and M Latek, 'Paradoxes et Limites de la Coopération Interparlementaire dans l'Union Européenne' (2001) 23 *Journal of European Integration* 139–64.

which Member States ought to adopt with a view to achieving common EU objectives.[141] Conversely, tighter ties between parliaments could lead to shared role perceptions about the economic backbone of the common currency.[142] Namely, although most contacts between MEPs and MPs occur through political parties rather than through interparliamentary bodies,[143] the latter could facilitate the opening up of these channels of communication. In the eyes of a German MP, ICEFG could prompt parliamentarians to articulate common standpoints, policy alternatives and red lines to EU institutions.[144] In effect, however, ICEFG merely complements domestic practices, because, as the Finnish Parliament rightly submits, 'no conference can replace the work done in parliaments'.[145]

Nevertheless, it could be argued that interparliamentary cooperation has gained momentum in the past several years. The increase in the frequency and forms of interparliamentary cooperation is the consequence of the growing understanding that an exchange of policy-relevant ideas is a necessary ingredient of effective scrutiny.[146] It is in this sense that, following in the footsteps of COSAC and the Interparliamentary Conference for CFSP and CSDP established in 2012,[147] ICEFG adds a valuable new layer to EU parliamentarism. However, the euro crisis also reveals the difficulties in organising interparliamentary cooperation due to the vastly different interests of NPs in the fiscal field.[148]

C. European Parliamentary Week

The EPW originates in a 2011 EP initiative to bolster interparliamentary cooperation on the implementation of the European Semester by determining the priorities for each cycle of economic coordination on the basis of the Commission's Annual Growth Survey.[149] Beginning in 2013, the EPW has taken place every year in January on the premises of the EP in Brussels. As of 2014, ICEFG was held under the EPW aegis.[150] While the former focuses on structural deficit reduction and the maintenance of a balanced budgetary policy, the

[141] See also: W Wessels, 'National Parliaments and the EP in Multi-Tier Governance: In Search for an Optimal Multi-Level Parliamentary Architecture' in *Compendium of Notes 'Challenges of Multi-Tier Governance in the European Union: Effectiveness, Efficiency and Legitimacy'* (Brussels, European Parliament, 2013) 108.

[142] V Knutelská, 'Cooperation among National Parliaments: An Effective Contribution to EU Legitimation' in Crum and Fossum (n 139 above) 46.

[143] E Miklin and B Crum, 'Interparliamentary Contacts of Members of the European Parliament: Report of a Survey' (2011) 8 *RECON Online Working Paper* 12.

[144] A Schäfer and F Schulz, 'A Conference of Parliaments for Europe: New Ways of Interparliamentary Cooperation' (2013) *FES International Policy Analysis* 2.

[145] Eduskunta, Grand Committee, 'Banking Union and the Future of EMU', Statement no 4/2012 of 13 December 2012, p 9.

[146] M Larhant, 'La Coopération Interparlementaire dans l'UE: l'Heure d'un Nouveau Départ?' (2005) 16 *Notre Europe-Jacques Delors Institute Policy Paper* 29.

[147] See: J Wouters and K Raube, 'Seeking CSDP Accountability through Interparliamentary Scrutiny' (2012) 47 *The International Spectator* 155.

[148] A Benz, 'An Asymmetric Two-Level Game: Parliaments in the Euro Crisis' in Crum and Fossum (n 139 above) 140.

[149] EP Resolution of 1 December 2011 on the European Semester for Economic Policy Coordination, points 46 and 47.

[150] See: www.europarl.europa.eu/webnp/cms/pid/1975;jsessionid=500EB9255EF1DF79BDE2E17473AE377B.

latter provides for discussions not only on budgetary matters, but also on broader themes such as the social dimension of the EMU, employment policies and the overall EU economic agenda.

The EPW discussions are organised in plenary sessions and in the form of interparliamentary committee meetings under the helm of the competent EP committees. The EPW is also an occasion for gatherings of EP political groups with their party colleagues from NPs. All of this facilitates the exchange of best practices among parliamentarians in charge of implementing the European Semester. It also serves to acquaint NPs with the policies of EU institutions, which are represented at the EPW by their presidents.

The primary goal of the EPW is for the EP and NPs to formulate an informed but separate response to EU economic plans for the attention of the Spring European Council meeting. A secondary goal is to spur political togetherness in the EU 'in a spirit of constructive partnership'[151] between parliaments at the EU and national levels and raise their awareness of the impact that domestic fiscal policies have on other Member States in an economically highly interdependent Union. This may be a far cry from reality, however. The EPW bears little resemblance to a genuine parliamentary debate and instead comprises a collection of unrelated statements.[152] This initiative is arguably yet another in the line of the EP's forums for cross-level interparliamentary cooperation that has had mixed results and minor impact.[153]

Yet this 'soft', discourse-oriented model of interparliamentary cooperation in fiscal matters is unsurprising if one recalls the EP's warnings that 'a new joint parliamentary body … would be both ineffective and illegitimate from a democratic and constitutional point of view' and that 'there is no substitute for a formal strengthening of the full legitimacy of the European Parliament'.[154] This kind of approach, coupled with the EP's strong protagonism and leadership in organising the EPW and ICEFG, might provoke a sense among NPs that the EP seeks to control the agenda and this could harm the benefits that the EPW and ICEFG could produce.

V. CONCLUSION

The euro crisis has shaken the EU from economic complacency, challenged fiscal decentralisation, and, once again, brought the question of the quality of the underlying democratic fundament of European political integration back to the fore.[155] The national-level responses to the crisis have resulted in significant recalibrations of the way budgets are

151 EP Resolution of 11 March 2015 on the European Semester for Economic Policy Coordination: Annual Growth Survey 2015, point 39.

152 EUobserver, 'National MPs Show Varied Interest in EU Parliament Event', 2 February 2015: euobserver.com/institutional/127467.

153 C Fasone, 'Interparliamentary Cooperation and Democratic Representation in the European Union' in S Kröger and D Friedrich (eds), *The Challenge of Democratic Representation in the European Union* (Basingstoke, Palgrave Macmillan, 2012) 42; B Crum, 'Saving the Euro at the Cost of Democracy?' (2013) 51 *Journal of Common Market Studies* 627.

154 EP Resolution of 12 December 2013 on Constitutional Problems of a Multitier Governance in the European Union, point 32.

155 See essays in: B de Witte et al (eds), *The Euro Crisis and the State of European Democracy* (Florence, EUI, 2013).

made in favour of NPs. These relate to greater approval rights in the course of the budgetary procedure, improved scrutiny, intensified plenary and committee debates on EU economic coordination, and better access to information on fiscal policy-making. The responses at the EU level were more modest and remain limited to discursive and deliberative efforts organised in interparliamentary forums that cannot exert decisive influence over EU economic decisions. This asymmetric outcome stems from the difference in the gravity of constitutional power in the budgetary field. It continues to reside at the national level and this is why domestic legal and political changes have been more pronounced. Yet even at the national level, there is a colourful variety in the manner in which NPs have tackled the crisis.[156]

A marked facet of the post-crisis EMU reform is the fundamental uncertainty as to the nature of the political beast that is being shaped by the initiatives of EU institutions and the Member States. At the heart of this uncertainty is the tension between the EU trying to shield itself against perceptions that the Union is invading domestic fiscal authority and the Member States scrambling to protect their budgetary autonomy and thereby their national sovereignty.

On the one hand, the Commission asserts that NPs 'retain their full rights in the national budgetary processes. The Commission does not have a veto, does not have the right to change the draft national budgets'.[157] It merely gives 'independent policy advice … to facilitate the assessment of the draft budgets' compliance with EU fiscal rules'.[158] On the other hand, some scholars see the Commission's expanded competence as pre-empting domestic parliamentary democracy.[159] The concern is a valid and strong one. Yet as this chapter shows, NPs have not given in despite the constraints placed on the exercise of their fiscal prerogatives. Nevertheless, one of the most constant characteristics of European integration is its spillover capacity. This means that measures taken to stem the crisis are not likely to stop at that, as shown by the creation of the Banking Union.[160] There also are other tendencies, such as the mounting euro-sceptic rhetoric in the UK, Greece's continuing economic predicament, and the decreasing support for enlargement, which point in the opposite direction. We find ourselves at a critical juncture in the EU's maturation process. Is the Union headed towards greater integration, a period of impasse and status quo, or perhaps even disintegration?

If unaddressed, the uncertainty provoked by this monumental question can grow into fear, resentment and rejection of the EU project and this is precisely where NPs find their greatest utility. It is squarely their calling to nurture the environment in which the direction of the Union will be debated, scrutinised and analysed for its politico-legal benefits. If a portion of the decision-making authority has been transferred to the EU, this does not mean that parliaments no longer bear responsibility for European unity. On the contrary,

[156] K Auel and O Höing, 'National Parliaments and the Eurozone Crisis: Taking Ownership in Difficult Times?' (2015) 38 *West European Politics* 390.

[157] JM Barroso, Speech to the 2nd EPW, p 5. See: www.europarl.europa.eu/webnp/webdav/site/myjahiasite/shared/EPW%202014/President%20Barroso.pdf.

[158] European Commission, '2015 Draft Budgetary Plans: Overall Assessment', COM(2014) 907, p 5.

[159] F Scharpf, 'Monetary Union, Fiscal Crisis and the Pre-Emption of Democracy' (2011) 9 *Zeitschrift für Staats- und Europawissenschaften* 163–98.

[160] N Moloney, 'European Banking Union: Assessing Its Risks and Resilience' (2014) 51 *Common Market Law Review* 1609–70.

it is their task to ensure that European integration proceeds in keeping with the preferences and political sentiments of the electorate. It is the NPs' sacred competence for this process to unfold in an informed manner and the euro crisis has aided the realisation of this objective.

This is where transnational interparliamentary cooperation—embodied by the economic dialogue, ICEFG and the EPW—can be usefully employed. In fact, we are witnessing the emergence of an ever greater number of interparliamentary networks in the EU. Their mushrooming is exemplary of the heightened pace of the disaggregation of state sovereignty at the hands of European integration.[161] The incremental process of deepening the poly-centricity of the Union is an enormous challenge, because it can become both a constructive as well as a destructive force. Europe's crisis is not only one of economic downturn and fiscal irresponsibility but also that of miscommunication and disconnect between policy-makers and policy addressees. The role of NPs in overcoming these problems, which carry truly palpable consequences for the European citizen, is and will remain paramount.

[161] A-M Slaughter, 'Disaggregated Sovereignty: Towards the Public Accountability of Global Government Networks' (2004) 39 *Government and Opposition* 161.

Part V

Old and New Interparliamentary Conferences

11

COSAC: Birth, Evolution, Failures and Perspectives

ADAM CYGAN

I. INTRODUCTION

IN JANUARY 1989, Mr Laurent Fabius, the then Speaker of the French Assemblée nationale, proposed establishing an interparliamentary body composed of members of national parliaments specialised in European affairs.[1] The primary reason behind this initiative was the feeling in many national parliaments that they were losing contact with Community policies following the introduction of direct elections to the European Parliament in 1979. This reason of disconnection between the citizens and the EU integration project has not subsided and if anything has become more acute in the intervening period.

At the meeting of the Presidents of the Parliaments of the Member States of the European Community in Madrid in May 1989, agreement was reached to reinforce the role of national parliaments in the Community process of decision-making. The agreement—which established what has become known as COSAC[2]—has, since the beginning, served the primary objective of bringing together the various committees in the national parliaments specialising in European affairs. However, COSAC cannot be said to have bridged the gap between the citizens and the EU and has remained a forum for interparliamentary cooperation primarily with regard to technical parliamentary matters.

[1] See the report from Mr Laurent Fabius: 'Les Parlements Européens dans la perspective de l'Europe de 1993. Le traitement des affairs communautaires et la collaboration entre les chambres', presented at the meeting of the Speakers' Conference, gathering together the Speakers of the Parliaments of the EC-12 in Madrid on 20 May 1989.

[2] Usually known by COSAC, the French acronym for: *Conférence des organes spécialisés dans les affaires communautaires.*

During the French Presidency in the second half of 1989 these committees met with representatives of the European Parliament and agreed:

— to intensify the exchange of information; and
— to meet twice a year in the country holding the presidency of the Council to discuss issues of common concern.[3]

As can be seen, these objectives are forged in terms of parliamentary procedure and do not address the constitutional status of national parliaments within the EU, nor do they enhance the relationship between parliaments and the citizens.

The first COSAC formally met in Paris on 16–17 November 1989. Since this first meeting COSAC has developed its modus operandi to reflect the developments that have taken place with each Treaty revision. The current COSAC rules of procedure,[4] setting out the mission statement of the forum, state clearly that the aim is not to create a supra-national procedure for the scrutiny of legislative proposals or policy documents. COSAC should not therefore be viewed as a 'third chamber' after the Council and European Parliament, nor is its purpose to harmonise parliamentary procedures. On the contrary, COSAC accepts the diversity of individual scrutiny arrangements within each national parliament and that these reflect political and constitutional priorities[5] within Member States. Soon after its inception, the Select Committee on European Legislation in the United Kingdom described the role of COSAC in the following manner:[6]

> COSAC was conceived as consultative in nature, and has remained so; delegations do not have a mandate from their Chambers. In our view, the Conference has been most successful when it has considered the technique and practice of parliamentary control and scrutiny rather than engaging in inconclusive political debate.

The House of Commons identified that COSAC has a role to foster and promote scrutiny including best practice and not to undertake a formal scrutiny function itself. This continues to be the case and since the Treaty of Lisbon came into force, one objective of COSAC has been to devise an effective procedural mechanism, the purpose of which is to maximise interparliamentary cooperation under Protocol no 2. In addition, under Article 1.2 of COSAC's Rules of Procedure it may be suggested that COSAC has moved forward since the Select Committee on European Legislation made its assessment in 1994.[7]

Article 1.3 of the Rules of Procedure incorporates the provisions of Protocol no 1 on the Role of National Parliaments and envisages a more proactive political function for COSAC. While this seeks to integrate parliaments within the EU polity through, inter alia, directly representing political opinions within the policy-making process, this does not sufficiently address the core problem of de-parliamentarisation that remains an enduring consequence of integration. Article 1.3 does not offer new prerogatives for COSAC nor does it constitute

[3] Fabius (n 1 above) at 3.

[4] Rules of Procedure of Conference of Parliamentary Committees for Union Affairs of Parliaments of the European Union, (2011/C 229/1), 4.8.2011.

[5] Article 1.3 COSAC Rules of Procedure.

[6] HC 239-I (Session 1994–95), paragraph 116.

[7] M Knudsen and Y Carl, 'COSAC—its Role to Date and its Potential in the Future' in G Barrett (ed), *National Parliaments and the European Union: The Constitutional Challenge for the Oireachtas and Other Member State Legislatures* (Dublin, Clarus Press in association with the Institute of European Affairs, 2007) 455.

COSAC as a third chamber which speaks with a uniform single voice for all national parliaments. The right 'to submit any contribution it deems appropriate for the attention of the European Parliament, Council and Commission' is a rudimentary acknowledgment that EU decision-making needs to have an anchorage in national parliaments. Moreover, this may be considered as part of the wider objective of reconnecting with the citizen that was first identified in 1989.

After the Treaty of Lisbon, it is the provisions of Article 12 TEU and the prerogatives within Protocols no 1 and 2 which are central to the activities of national parliaments, and which necessitate the application of significant time and resources within the overall scrutiny activities. Thus, interparliamentary cooperation through COSAC is an important ingredient within the process of subsidiarity monitoring, especially as subsidiarity monitoring remains sporadic and lacks coordination. Yet COSAC is not the only mechanism through which national parliaments may secure influence and as such COSAC should not be considered as a comprehensive mechanism or panacea through which national parliaments may influence EU governance. For example, since 2006, the Barroso Initiative for Political Dialogue with National Parliaments has arguably offered more effective and direct input for national parliaments to engage in a dialogue with the Commission. The Barroso Initiative differs from the cooperation through COSAC as it is vertical cooperation between each national parliament and the Commission, and to this extent reinforces the individual or monist function of national parliaments in EU affairs by which ministerial accountability remains the priority.

Post Lisbon, COSAC has responded to the prerogatives within Article 12 TEU and Protocols no 1 and 2 through seeking to foster a more coherent response to subsidiarity monitoring and interparliamentary cooperation more generally. However, this chapter argues that this cooperation falls far short of securing the necessary coordinated institutional framework that is required in order for subsidiarity monitoring to be synchronised to an extent which ensures that national parliaments will secure the agreement necessary to regularly meet the thresholds within Protocol no 2. Moreover, extra-Treaty opportunities for national parliaments to improve their activities, for example through the Barroso Initiative, further challenge the proposition that synchronised horizontal collective interparliamentary coordination is the most effective form of interaction in EU affairs for national parliaments.

II. FROM PARIS TO LISBON: THE DEVELOPMENT OF COSAC

The benefits of interparliamentary cooperation have been identified for many years, but identification of the successes remains more elusive. Since the early 1990s academic literature has consistently identified considerable value in interparliamentary cooperation.[8] The primary justification for extending interparliamentary cooperation and making it more formal is that through the creation of such networks the ensuing dialogue will deliver practical added value to the work of national legislatures.[9] Meetings of national parliamentarians would facilitate the sharing of best practices and the identification of mutual problems,

[8] Knudsen and Carl (n 7 above) at 470.

[9] T Raunio, 'National Parliaments and European Integration: What we Know and Agenda for Future Research' (2009) 15 *Journal of Legislative Studies* 317–34.

through regular dialogue with the European Parliament, national MPs would receive information that contributes to effective government scrutiny.

The period of integration which has been categorised by the definition of 'Eurosclerosis' represented a point within EU cooperation where Treaty reform was difficult to agree upon. National interests and the future role of the veto remained contentious issues for all Member States and a concern that the loss of further legislative competence could undermine the ability of Member States to control economic and social development. In order to counteract this view, and as part of the move to closer integration, there was a recognition of the need to involve national parliaments in the integration dialogue more directly in European affairs. By the end of the 1980s, concerns had already been expressed about the existence of a possible democratic deficit within EU integration and that there was a disconnect between EU Institutions and EU citizens. In particular, the involvement of national executives at EU level was reducing the scope of national parliamentary power.[10]

It was against this justification—that interparliamentary cooperation will enrich domestic scrutiny—that the proposal for the creation of COSAC was put forward. Though COSAC was originally conceived as an initiative of national parliamentarians, its subsequent development and contribution since that first meeting in Paris in November 1989 should be evaluated within the overall context of EU Treaty reform. COSAC exists, at least in part, as a response to the criticism of 'de-parliamentarisation' that has accompanied EU integration. Thus, one measure of COSAC's achievements should be the success with which it has responded to the significant transfer of competences that have accompanied all new Treaties since the Treaty of Maastricht 1993. In particular, do national parliaments retain sufficient control over ministers and their actions within the Council and can they exercise effective sanctions against ministers who fail to represent the wishes of the national parliament? This task is made especially difficult by the absence of a harmonised procedure in the operation of scrutiny systems across national parliaments and the extent to which EU affairs are considered a priority amongst national parliamentarians.[11] However, COSAC has sought to fill this vacuum.

At the first meeting of this interparliamentary conference, convened by the French National Assembly in November 1989, parliamentarians from 10 of the 12 Member States participated, even though at that time not all national parliaments had specialised European Affairs Committees. The meeting was co-chaired by the Chairmen of the European delegations of the French National Assembly and Senate, Mr Charles Josselin and Mr Jacques Genton. The European Parliament was absent from this first meeting, signalling an issue that has continued to concern COSAC to this day; namely how should it interact with the European Parliament and to what extent does cooperation with the European Parliament offer opportunities to create effective parliamentary mechanisms to control the decision-making process.

Since 1989, the COSAC agenda has focused on a fundamental issue which is still valid today: how to increase parliamentary control of EU affairs within a decision-making process which is both remote and does not correspond to a traditional parliamentary method of decision-making. To that extent, the first COSAC identified the concern articulated by many academic commentators and parliamentarians, which is that one

[10] Knudsen and Carl (n 7 above) at 471.

[11] Resolution recognising the diversity of national parliaments was adopted by the 26th COSAC meeting in Madrid on 12–14 May 2002.

consequence of EU integration and the decision-making process is that these have led to a de-parliamentarisation within the EU.[12]

In 1989, the main focus was on how to reinforce the involvement of national parliaments in EU affairs arising in large part as a consequence of the de-parliamentarisation which, at that point of EU integration, arose from the completion of the Internal Market Programme and the demise of the veto. The parliaments discussed different options, for example, strengthening parliamentary control at the national level, enhancing interparliamentary cooperation between parliaments, or strengthening the role of the European Parliament. Indeed one proposal from the Speaker of the French Senate was to create a 'European Senate' composed of representatives of national parliaments. However, in the conclusions from this first conference, the parliaments limited themselves to considering ways in which they could improve their 'reciprocal information through systematic exchange of texts concerning European affairs adopted by the Parliaments'.[13] Moreover, the establishment of an EU institution which represents national parliaments and engages in scrutiny and review of the decision-making process is not on COSAC's agenda, and the commitment to enhancing the position of national parliaments in EU affairs remains central to its mission statement.

The first COSAC therefore identified the fundamental question of the timely and substantive provision of information to national parliaments and the need for this information to be made available simultaneously to all national parliaments.[14] The timely provision of documents is central to effective scrutiny, be it ministerial or subsidiarity monitoring, and it may be judged a success of COSAC that it has forced this agenda on to the Treaty negotiators who have responded. Clearer deadlines for the provision of documentation in the Protocol on National Parliaments were included within the Treaty of Amsterdam and this has been taken further in Protocol no 1 of the Treaty of Lisbon 2009 by requiring direct transmission to national parliaments without the need for intermediate involvement of national executives.[15] Under Article 2, national parliaments now receive all draft legislative acts sent to the European Parliament and Council. This is hugely beneficial in order to meet the tight deadlines for scrutiny contained within Article 4 of Protocol no 1 and provides a degree of certainty to the scrutiny process. When taken together with the continuing recognition of scrutiny reserves within Protocol no 1 it may be argued that, at least from a procedural perspective, COSAC has made a difference to the exercise of the procedural prerogatives which national parliaments enjoy.

III. COSAC AND SUBSIDIARITY MONITORING

For national parliaments, the key question post Lisbon is whether, and if so to what extent, does COSAC improve the operation of Protocol no 2. Formally, COSAC has no role within

[12] A Cygan, 'The Parliamentarisation of EU Decision-Making? The Impact of the Treaty of Lisbon on National Parliaments' (2011) 36 *European Law Review* 478.

[13] Conclusions of the Interparliamentary Conference of European Affairs Committees, Paris, 16–17 November 1989, paragraph 1.

[14] Resolution of the 1st COSAC meeting, 20 May 1989.

[15] C Fasone and N Lupo, 'Comment on Protocol No. 1, on the role of national parliaments in the European Union annexed to the Treaty of Lisbon' in Blanke and Mangiameli (eds), *The Treaty on European Union (TEU)—A Commentary* (Vienna/New York, Springer, 2013) 1529–40.

the operation of Protocol no 2; however, given its coordinating role, it is not uncontroversial that COSAC would wish to place itself within the framework of subsidiarity monitoring.[16] One question that has been discussed within this context is whether interparliamentary cooperation between national parliaments within Protocol no 2 raises possibilities that this may constitute the beginnings of a new 'EU organ' representing national parliaments.[17] Cooper considers that the Early Warning Mechanism and improved interparliamentary cooperation which develops from the existing COSAC structures could evolve into a 'virtual third chamber'.[18] This sits alongside Kiiver's proposal that improved interparliamentary cooperation could morph in to national parliaments constituting an advisory Conseil d'Etat.[19] New designations which indicate engaged and proactive national parliaments working collectively can be readily attached, but, within the existing Treaty framework, parliamentary priorities and overall parliamentary workloads, any enlarged function is most appropriately viewed as aspirational.

Neither the Treaty, nor, for that matter the Barroso Initiative, refers to institutional representation for national parliaments whether through COSAC or some other forum. Furthermore, proposals for a second EU parliamentary chamber comprising representatives from national parliaments were rejected within the Constitutional Convention as inconsistent with institutional balance.[20] With the exception of IPEX and COSAC as forums to exchange information—and both pre-Lisbon developments—the Early Warning Mechanism is not bound to result in a significant increase of interparliamentary cooperation.

Under the Council's Rules of Procedure, the Committee of the Permanent Representatives of each Member State (COREPER) ensures that the subsidiarity and proportionality principles are respected. In the European Parliament compliance is verified by the committees in charge of specific legislative dossiers, together with the Committee on Legal Affairs. The Council and the European Parliament each have their own procedures for implementing the subsidiarity control mechanism. The European Parliament's Rules of Procedure ensure that the reasoned opinions of national parliaments are taken into consideration within parliamentary discussions. The Council's Rules also stipulate that national parliaments are consulted on legislative initiatives originating from a group of Member States. These procedural obligations offer national parliaments several opportunities for interventions but do not presuppose collective action by national parliaments. Moreover, the evidence to date suggests that COSAC has not galvanised parliaments into a methodology which systematically delivers coordinated responses.

In 2005, COSAC organised a Subsidiarity Monitoring Pilot Project on the 3rd Railway Package[21] to test the subsidiarity early warning mechanism that was proposed by the Constitutional Treaty. The COSAC Secretariat received reports on the pilot project from 31 of

[16] HL 151 *The Role of National Parliament in the European Union* (2013–14) at paragraph 24.

[17] D Jančić, 'A New Organ of the European Union: "National Parliaments Jointly"' (February 2008) *Federal Trust Policy Commentary*. Available at: www.fedtrust.co.uk/uploads/Parliaments_Jointly.pdf.

[18] I Cooper, 'The Watchdogs of Subsidiarity: National parliaments and the Logic of Arguing in the European Union' (2006) 44 *Journal of Common Market Studies* 281–83.

[19] P Kiiver, 'The Early Warning System for the Principle of Subsidiarity—The National Parliament as a Conseil d'etat for Europe' (2011) 36 *European Law Review* 98.

[20] See CONV 353/02 at paragraph 33.

[21] COM(2004) 104 final, 3.3.2004. Communication from the Commission, 'Further Integration in the European Rail System: Third Railway package'. See also P Kiiver, *The Early Warning System for the Principle of Subsidiarity: Constitutional Theory and Empirical Reality* (London, Routledge, 2012) 77–79.

the 37 national parliamentary chambers that participated in the test. In total 14 parliamentary chambers indicated that they found that one or more of the legislative proposals in the 3rd Railway Package breached the principle of subsidiarity and 11 of these chambers adopted a reasoned opinion. In addition, a further three national parliaments expressed doubts as to whether one or more of the four proposals conformed to the principle of subsidiarity. The national parliaments did not, however, identify problems with the same legislative proposals, indicating a wide variation of the definition and application of subsidiarity and reinforcing the point that the absence of a normative definition of subsidiarity hinders the operation of the early warning mechanism.

Subsequent projects carried out in 2009, including a proposal for a Directive on Standards of Quality and Safety of Human Organs Intended for Transplantation[22] and a proposal for a Council Framework Decision on the Right to Interpretation and Translation in Criminal Proceedings[23] both highlight that the lack of consensus on both the definition and application of subsidiarity remained an obstacle to improved subsidiarity monitoring. In the case of the latter inquiry the objections raised by several national parliaments, including the Maltese and Irish parliaments, that the proposal went too far suggest an evaluation by these parliaments with the principle of proportionality rather than confining their inquiry to determining subsidiarity compliance, and illustrate a common mistake made by national parliaments.

In its 18th Report on Better Lawmaking the Commission noted[24] that, since 2006, it had, within the framework of the political dialogue of the Barroso Initiative,[25] transmitted all new proposals to national parliaments, and replied to their opinions.[26] As from 1 December 2009, this framework of the Barroso Initiative and the improved transmission of a greater variety of documents direct to national parliaments have been used in parallel to the subsidiarity control mechanism. By the end of 2010, the Commission had sent out in that year 82 draft legislative proposals falling within the scope of Protocol no 2 and received 211 opinions. While most of the opinions concentrated on the content of the proposal, a total of 34 opinions did raise specific subsidiarity concerns. In 2010, the Commission received, in the case of five legislative proposals, more than one reasoned opinion,[27] but in all of these cases the threshold for a 'yellow card' was far from being reached.

In 2011, the Commission received 64 reasoned opinions from national parliaments, an increase of almost 75 per cent by comparison with the 2010 statistics, the first year of functioning of the subsidiarity control mechanism following the conclusion of the ratification process for the Treaty of Lisbon. Despite this increase, these 64 reasoned opinions still represent slightly less than 10 per cent of the total number of 622 opinions received by the Commission in 2011 as part of its broader political dialogue with national parliaments.[28] This

[22] Directive 2010/5/ EU of the European Parliament and Council of 7 July 2010.

[23] COM(2009) 338 final.

[24] COM(2011) 344 final *Report from the Commission on Subsidiarity and Proportionality* (18th Report on Better Lawmaking Covering the year 2010) at pp 6–10.

[25] ibid. See also fn 16 of COM(2006) 211 *Communication from the Commission to the European Council—A Citizens' Agenda—Delivering Results for Europe.*

[26] ibid.

[27] Directive 2010/5/ EU and further details are available on the IPEX website.

[28] COM(2012) 373 final, Report from the Commission on Subsidiarity and Proportionality (19th Report on Better Law-Making covering the year 2011).

can be in large part put down to the fact that the focus of national parliaments' reasoned opinions remains quite disparate. Of the 64 reasoned opinions received in 2011, 28 related to different Commission proposals. Moreover, most of the reasoned opinions focused on legislative proposals in the fields of taxation, agriculture, internal market and justice. The proposals which elicited the highest number of reasoned opinions concerned the Common Consolidated Corporate Tax Base (nine opinions), the temporary reintroduction of border controls at internal borders in exceptional circumstances (six), the Common European Sales Law (five) and the Single CMO Regulation (five). The national parliaments most active in issuing reasoned opinions were the Swedish Riksdag, the Luxembourg Chambre des Députés and the Polish Sejm and Senat (lower and upper chambers).[29]

For none of the 2011 legislative proposals were the thresholds for triggering the yellow or orange cards met, thereby questioning both the extent and effect of coordination by COSAC. In the case of the proposed Directive for a European Sales Law[30] the overriding subsidiarity concerns of the United Kingdom Parliament that the measure failed to meet the necessity and value added tests required for EU legislation, were not shared by many other parliaments with only five reasoned opinions in total. Apart from the above mentioned legislative proposals the vast majority of the 28 legislative proposals on which national parliaments issued a reasoned opinion in 2011 elicited at most three reasoned opinions. This evidence points to the existence of a weak horizontal dialogue and no consensus on how to apply the principle of subsidiarity, leading to criticisms that political dialogue constitutes no more than a talking shop.[31]

Until the end of 2011, the success of the Early Warning System to secure coordinated agreement on the application of the subsidiarity principle can be described, at best, as largely ineffective. COSAC cannot share sole responsibility for this and it may be concluded that achieving this level of coordination on a consistent basis was unreasonable from the outset. There is no doubt that different political priorities, heterogeneous constitutional arrangements and the absence of a single definition of subsidiarity that is accepted by Member States continues to hamper the Early Warning System and COSAC should not be considered as being able to bridge this.

While it may be the case that indeed none of the legislative measures reviewed have raised any *real* subsidiarity questions, it cannot be ignored that even when national parliaments did raise an objection, this was often for different reasons by comparison to other parliaments and which usually related to political priorities within the Member State. However, on one occasion in 2012 the political consensus was reached with respect to the proposal for a Draft Regulation concerning the posting of workers and the right to take collective action (the so-called *Monti II* Regulation).[32] On this occasion, national parliaments reached the threshold to show a yellow card, but what made this legislative proposal stand out from

[29] ibid at 4.

[30] COM(2011) 635 final *Proposal for a Regulation of the European Parliament and of the Council on a Common European Sales Law.*

[31] C Bengston, 'Interparliamentary Cooperation in Europe' in J O'Brennan and T Raunio (eds), *National Parliaments within the Enlarged European Union: From 'Victims' of Integration to Competitive Actors* (New York, Routledge, 2007) 46–61.

[32] COM(2012) 130 Draft Regulation on the exercise of the right to take collective action within the context of the freedom of establishment and the freedom to provide services.

previous ones where only a few subsidiarity objections were raised and which did not result in a yellow card? Can this yellow card merely be dismissed as being only coincidental[33] it being inevitable that there will always be a few instances where the subsidiarity interests of national parliaments are more broadly aligned? In the case of the *Monti II* proposal this yellow card may be explained, in large part, by the politically and constitutionally controversial nature of the proposal. However, does this yellow card indicate that collective action between national parliaments *may* function and that COSAC has fostered a change in the approach within national parliaments—who, after early hesitation with political dialogue, are beginning to work more closely together—and which may have helped to determine a clearer understanding of the application of subsidiarity principle?

This chapter questions the efficacy of the yellow card and COSACs role in delivering it primarily because Protocol no 2 fails to systematically bring together national parliaments to directly deliberate on a legislative proposal and on whether it conforms to the principle of subsidiarity. To this extent COSAC can be said to have not achieved one of its objectives of promoting horizontal parliamentary coordination within Protocol no 2. Parliaments continue to be primarily individual actors in EU affairs and use their own diverse procedures to determine if the principle of subsidiarity has been breached. To this extent, the use of the yellow card can at best be described as sporadic and overwhelmingly the requisite thresholds are not attained.

To date there have been two instances of a yellow card being raised. The first, mentioned above, related to the proposed Regulation on the exercise of the right to take collective action within the context of the freedom of establishment and the freedom to provide services—the so-called *Monti II* Regulation—which was eventually withdrawn. This proposal, being made under the ordinary legislative procedure, required a threshold of 18 reasoned opinions from 54 chambers. The second occurrence concerned a proposal for the establishment of a European Public Prosecutor's Office (EPPO)[34] designed to combat fraud and waste in the EU as provided for under Article 86 TFEU. As this was a legislative proposal submitted on the basis of Article 76 TFEU, the special legislative procedure was used. By contrast to the *Monti II* proposal the legislative procedure of Article 76 TFEU requires only 14 chambers to deliver reasoned opinions for a yellow card to be raised, which together represent one quarter of the votes allocated to national parliaments.

With regard to the proposal for the EPPO, the circumstances surrounding this yellow card largely confirm both the procedural flaws of COSAC—through which the process of subsidiarity review fails to consistently generate a coherent and uniform response from a significant number of national parliaments—as well as the substantive weakness of the yellow card to stop the legislative process. Within the deadline laid down in Article 6 of Protocol no 2, 14 chambers from the national parliaments raised a reasoned opinion on the EPPO proposal, which accounts for exactly one quarter of the allocated votes. As with *Monti II* the EPPO proposal barely reaches the requisite threshold, notwithstanding that a lower number of reasoned opinions are required, thereby further reinforcing the observation that

[33] P Kiiver, *The National Parliaments in the European Union: A Critical View on EU Constitution Building* (The Hague, Kluwer Law International, 2006) 162–64, who described any such consensus on the application of a yellow card as amounting to no more than a 'phantom collective' which would be achieved by coincidence rather than by design.

[34] COM(2013) 534 Council Regulation on the Establishment of the European Public Prosecutor's Office.

the yellow card procedure suffers from an absence of uniformity and agreement among national parliaments on the substantive question of when a measure breaches the principle of subsidiarity.

Despite the yellow card, and unlike with the *Monti II* proposal, the Commission elected to proceed despite the yellow card. The primary justification for this given by the Commission in its response was that the drafters of the Treaty have expressly provided for the possibility of establishing the EPPO in Article 86 TFEU. This included among its powers and responsibilities the ability to investigate and prosecute crimes affecting the EU's financial interests in the courts of the Member States. As far as the Commission viewed this, the existence of a specific Treaty base gives a strong indication that the establishment of the EPPO cannot be considered either per se or in the abstract to be in breach of the principle of subsidiarity. COSACs ineffectiveness is underscored because it was constitutionally powerless to challenge the Commission's decision.

The Commission's decision to press on with the EPPO proposal, notwithstanding the yellow card, is not an altogether surprising one and indicates that the Commission perhaps has only limited regard for the constitutional status of COSAC. In particular, as the Commission points out on several occasions, only 14 chambers submitted a reasoned opinion and this fails to constitute an overwhelmingly negative response to the EPPO proposal. This point is undoubtedly correct and the numbers speak for themselves. To this extent it is necessary for COSAC to consider whether and how it can improve parliamentary coordination; yet what should be of some concern to national parliaments is that the Commission would, in the light of its response to the EPPO yellow card, appear to view Protocol no 2 as a procedural inconvenience to endure rather than a mechanism which seeks to inject greater legitimacy into the legislative process.

The tone of the Commission's response to the yellow card is dismissive and pays only lip service to genuine concerns relating to the operation of the EPPO in Member States. The evidence is still thin, and with only two yellow cards definitive conclusions are premature, but judging by the Commission's dismissal of subsidiarity as a relevant consideration in the context of both the *Monti II* and the EPPO proposals this raises future concerns about the operation of Protocol no 2, and COSAC. This is especially so as both instances appear to indicate that there is some distance between how national parliaments and the Commission interpret and apply the principle of subsidiarity. Moreover, the procedure within COSAC has not been able to bridge this gap. If this trend continues to develop then Protocol no 2 runs the risk of being nothing more than an empty vessel and this will have the effect of undermining both the credibility and relevance of COSAC.

In these circumstances, what can COSAC do? To help make the early warning mechanism as effective as possible a coordinating role by COSAC is central and this is recognised by Article 10 of Protocol no 1. That said, interparliamentary cooperation is not a new development introduced by the Treaty of Lisbon and sharing information amongst national parliaments as part of the scrutiny process has been in existence since COSAC was first established in 1989. However, parliamentary coordination has not been a priority for individual parliaments and Protocol no 1 has not altered this position. Post Lisbon the need for horizontal coordination to secure the necessary consensus has become more pressing in order to for Protocol no 2 to function because this can be considered as a pre-requisite of the early warning mechanism and is strongly implied by the overall aims of Protocol no 2. It is, however, questionable whether national parliaments will be able, with sufficient regularity, to coordinate any more effectively than they already have achieved pre-Lisbon or in the examples of *Monti II* and the EPPO proposals.

The Treaty of Amsterdam Protocol on national parliaments formally recognised COSAC and its role in improving parliamentary scrutiny by enabling it to inter alia 'address to the EU Institutions any contribution it deems appropriate on the legislative activities of the Union'. Article 10 Protocol no 1 of the Treaty of Lisbon goes further with COSAC identified as a forum to debate policy and an information exchange[35] which suggests that the respective activities are more than complimentary. Through cooperation 'in accordance with the Protocol on the Role of National Parliaments',[36] this will inevitably require some consensus between the European Parliament and national parliaments on the application of the subsidiarity principle, but as already discussed in this chapter, such coordination is not a given and largely presupposes that national parliaments broadly share the same subsidiarity concerns, but the evidence to date indicates that this will not necessarily be the case.[37]

Despite the limitations of parliamentary coordination and document repositories such as IPEX,[38] the principle of national parliaments seeking to act with greater unity should not be dismissed. Improved interparliamentary communication and coordination in the context of subsidiarity monitoring with COSAC at the centre will only be for the benefit of improving subsidiarity monitoring. So far, COSAC has led a shadowy existence despite its good intentions and efforts and needs to reposition itself and play a more direct leadership role within the early warning mechanism. However, the overriding question remains whether national parliaments view COSAC as integral to their scrutiny work and that it may bring a substantive value added contribution to subsidiarity monitoring under Protocol no 2. On the evidence thus far, such an assertion remains, at the very least, questionable.

IV. INTEGRATING NATIONAL PARLIAMENTS INTO EU AFFAIRS

Despite the shortcomings with COSAC within the operation of Protocol no 2, it would be wrong to conclude that COSAC has not made a positive contribution to raising the profile of the scrutiny work of national parliaments across the EU. For example, interparliamentary networking in COSAC and other forums has facilitated the sharing of 'best practices', with the individual parliaments assessing the strengths and weaknesses of the scrutiny arrangements in the other legislatures.[39] This peer learning of best practices is particularly applicable to those countries that have joined the EU since 2004 and offers a mechanism through

[35] The conference may communicate with the European Parliament; the Council and the Commission may not bind national parliaments or 'prejudge their positions'; 'shall' promote exchange of information and best practice; may organise interparliamentary conferences.

[36] Article 12 (f) TEU.

[37] See for example the outcome of the Subsidiarity Monitoring Pilot Project on the 3rd Railway Package to test the early warning mechanism that was proposed by the Constitutional Treat. In the course of this pilot project several subsidiarity objections were raised by a number of national parliaments, but these were on different provisions within the legislative proposals and suggested the absence of a single definition of subsidiarity and how it was to be applied. See further Kiiver (n 19 above) at 77–78.

[38] IPEX is the Interparliamentary EU Information Exchange and contains parliamentary documents and information from national parliaments concerning the EU. It also includes all Commission documents since 2006 and a parliamentary calendar. All information is available on-line at: www.ipex.eu.

[39] K Auel and A Benz, 'The Europeanisation of Parliamentary Democracy' (2005) 11 *Journal of Legislative Studies* (Special Issue) 3–4.

which to provide shared solutions to common problems. Indeed, the evidence from these newer Member States indicates that their parliaments have on average implemented more comprehensive scrutiny mechanisms than the legislatures of the older EU countries.[40] But, despite the general trend towards tighter scrutiny, there remain, as noted above, significant national differences with respect to both how powerful national parliaments and their EU affairs committees are, and the extent to which the regular standing committees become involved in EU affairs.

It may be accurate to suggest that national parliamentary scrutiny of EU affairs is heterogeneous, at least with respect to the question of the constitutional objectives of scrutiny—procedural cooperation, for example—through an exchange of ideas among the parliaments, has developed. Raunio has suggested that there has been a gradual institutional convergence in relation to procedural matters among the parliamentary EU scrutiny systems,[41] which may be attributed to a combination of factors including the role of COSAC. First, COSAC has provided a forum for communication and this dialogue has prompted exchange visits between parliamentarians who have integrated useful procedural devices in to the modus operandi of their scrutiny committee.[42] Secondly, notwithstanding the problems with securing the thresholds, subsidiarity monitoring has created a single function for all parliaments to engage in, and through COSAC, as well as through bilateral parliamentary contacts, parliaments have sought to maximise the prerogatives that subsidiarity monitoring affords them and to coordinate responses in order that the Protocol no 2 thresholds can be met. Finally, and perhaps most importantly, recognition of scrutiny reserves by Protocol no 1, of the kind that exist in the United Kingdom Parliament and which are extremely effective to mitigate against unaccountable ministerial conduct, have been adopted by most parliaments. This development may be seen as recognition by national parliaments that control of *their* minister in Council remains the primary objective of parliamentary scrutiny and that procedural coordination of this activity is important.

The pursuit of interparliamentary cooperation since the late 1980s has reflected the normative paradigm of parliamentary governance that exists within all Member States. While Member States (to greater or lesser degrees) are accepting of EU integration, they simultaneously recognise that national parliaments remain the primary representative institutions for citizens and it is this requirement of effective representation for citizens within the decision-making process that, at least in part, led to the formation of COSAC. It also is indicative of the argument that the European Parliament does not sufficiently provide this representation, primarily because it lacks the parliamentary traditions that exist within domestic legislatures as well as failing to find direct relevance in the lives of EU citizens.[43]

COSAC remains the primary forum for interparliamentary cooperation, but it has not been alone in offering opportunities for national parliaments to participate at the EU level and it would not be inaccurate to suggest that COSAC has felt politically threatened through other forms of interparliamentary cooperation. One such example were the Assises, which were held in 1990, and brought together delegations from national legislatures and the

[40] Kiiver (n 33 above) at 46.

[41] Raunio (n 9 above).

[42] See HL Report 2014.

[43] K Auel, 'Democratic Accountability and National Parliaments: Redefining the Impact of Parliamentary Scrutiny in EU Affairs' (2007) 13 *European Law Journal* 487 at 491.

European Parliament in the run up to the Maastricht IGC on 27–30 November 1990. The Assises comprised 173 members of national parliaments and 85 Members of the European Parliament. The idea of organising the Assises had been proposed by the French President, Mr François Mitterrand, in a speech on 25 October 1989 before the European Parliament and was later supported by two resolutions of the European Parliament, who saw this as an opportunity to gain support for its proposals in the Spinelli Report,[44] providing a blueprint for a Treaty Establishing a European Union.

With the benefit of hindsight it may be suggested that the establishment of the Assises was a first formal attempt to address the issue of the future representation of citizens within the integration process by seeking to directly involve parliamentarians within the IGC process. The issue of citizen disconnection and the democratic deficit arsing from the EU's institutional architecture spurred on the debate for improved parliamentary representation in EU affairs amid concerns that the integration process had to be relevant to EU citizens and that it should be rooted in democratic values.

COSAC welcomed the principle of organising the Assises to discuss possible Treaty changes at its meeting in Cork in May 1990,[45] but wanted to influence its organisation. Hence delegations considered it necessary that a restricted meeting of the Chairmen of the European Affairs Committees and the European Parliament be held with a view to preparing the Assises. A number of organisational issues were addressed at that meeting, which took place in the Belgian Parliament on 26 June 1990. However, the formal decision to convene the Assises and settle the organisation of the event was taken by the Speakers' Conference at a meeting on 20 September 1990. Apart from settling issues such as the composition, working method and presidency of the Assises, they also ensured a link to COSAC by establishing a drafting committee composed of the Chairmen of the European Affairs Committees plus five MEPs charged with the task of drafting the final declaration of the Assises.

At its Conference on 1 and 2 October in Rome (just eight weeks before the Assises) COSAC attempted to influence the agenda of the Assises by recommending that the debate be divided into four general topics: 1) the new goals of the Community; 2) strengthening democratic legitimacy; 3) allocation of competences; and 4) relations with other countries and institutions of Europe. Coincidentally, these were also priorities for COSAC. It was agreed that the Chairmen of the European Affairs Committees plus five MEPs (identical with the 'drafting committee' established by the Speakers' Conference) should finalise preparations for the Assises. However, at a meeting on 12 November the 'triple presidency' of the Assises (the two Italian Chambers and the European Parliament) refused to accept the proposal by COSAC for the agenda, which they found would effectively alter the decision reached by the Presidency of the Assises. At the end of the Assises, a final declaration was adopted that endorsed a number of proposals for treaty reform. This declaration, though symbolic, in an aspirational sense, could not be said to empower national parliaments or advance their agenda, and the experiment of the Assises has not been repeated prior to subsequent IGCs.

[44] Alterio Spinelli, 'Report on the Future of Europe' (1973).

[45] Knudsen and Carl (n 7 above) at 461.

Recognition that COSAC has a role to play in EU affairs is not disputed; the outstanding and as yet unresolved question is precisely what this role should be. COSAC does not exist as an EU Institution which represents national parliaments in EU decision-making, nor should it be viewed as the forum through which the objectives of Protocol no 2 should be achieved. Similarly, COSAC has a different modus operandi from the Assises and indeed the Convention method adopted in 2004. In Working Group IV of the Convention on the Future of Europe the discussions confirmed that the overwhelming majority of national politicians were essentially in favour of maintaining the status quo and not introducing a secondary forum for parliamentary coordination, nor did they consider the need to transform COSAC into some type of EU Senate. Constitutionally, this is understandable; national parliaments are anchored within Member States where they pursue democratic accountability of the executive. On this basis, the objective of COSAC should be to materially improve the capacity of national parliaments to fulfil this function. In particular, the primary focus needs to be to improve national scrutiny of governments in EU affairs through, inter alia, better access to information and a willingness for national parliaments to use more effectively the prerogatives within Protocol no 2.

The final conclusions of Working Group IV[46] did not indicate any enthusiasm for the establishment of a new collective body which should represent national MPs or for changing the functions of COSAC. More generally, the Conclusions of Working Group IV confirmed the ambivalence within national parliaments with respect to the question of collective representation within the EU. Working Group IV concluded that

> the mandate of COSAC should be clarified to strengthen its role as an interparliamentary mechanism. It could usefully act as a platform for a regular exchange of information and best practices, not only between European Affairs Committees, but also between specialised committees. It should become a stronger network for exchange between parliaments.[47]

In the Treaty of Lisbon, this vague and unambitious statement manifests itself as Protocol no 1, on the Role of National Parliaments in the European Union. The Protocol merely confirms the status quo, explicitly stating that 'contributions from the conference shall not bind national parliaments and shall not prejudge their positions'.

Protocol no 1 therefore appears to confirm that national parliaments have determined that COSAC should fulfil a consultative and advisory function. However, this decision should not determine that, by undertaking this role, COSAC is wholly devoid of influence. For example, COSAC continues to provide an effective forum for the exchange of best scrutiny practices and sharing of policy expertise and has undoubtedly assisted new Member States in establishing effective European Affairs Committees within their parliaments. However, it is difficult to see how COSAC may move beyond this role.

V. INTERPARLIAMENTARY COOPERATION: A POLITICAL FICTION?

Interparliamentary cooperation, despite its recognition within the Treaty, remains a peripheral issue. Relationships between national parliaments tend to be informal and sporadic

[46] CONV 353/02 Working Group IV The Role of National Parliaments, Final Report of Working Group IV on the Role of National Parliaments.

[47] ibid at p 5.

and there is only limited interest in this form of interparliamentary cooperation or in EU affairs more generally.[48] Kiiver, amongst others, suggested[49] that such interparliamentary networks and relationships are destined to remain of limited importance. Moreover, with the obligation within Protocol no 1 for the Commission to transmit documents directly to national parliaments, interparliamentary cooperation, as a means to secure information sources, is probably less significant. This development may have the unintended consequence that, with easier access to information, national parliaments see less need for interparliamentary cooperation and revert to executing what remains their primary objective, namely securing effective accountability of the executive in EU affairs.

Protocols no 1 and 2 represent a modest re-alignment from the 'monist' position of national parliaments. The main effect has been to alter the focus of national parliaments away from *only* pursuing ministerial accountability to recognising that securing a single 'centralised' opinion representing the collective views of parliaments on the question of subsidiarity compliance is a valuable and achievable objective. This more 'polycentric' form of methodology has been considered a shift towards a single EU scrutiny paradigm through which parliaments cease to function as isolated individual actors and evolve into a proactive horizontal bloc.[50] Ostensibly this may be viewed as national parliaments re-centred, but the early evidence indicates that, notwithstanding Protocols no 1 and 2, systematic subsidiarity monitoring which is underpinned through collective action is yet to be achieved.[51]

Under Article 12(f) TEU national parliaments and the European Parliament participate in 'inter parliamentary cooperation in accordance with Protocol no 1. This Protocol expands the concept of the 'collective' and implies that subsidiarity monitoring should not be an exclusively horizontal task. Article 9 of Protocol no 1 requires the European Parliament and national parliaments to determine together 'the organisation and promotion of regular interparliamentary cooperation within the Union'. When considered alongside the requirements of Protocol no 2, this vertical cooperation must include consensus on the application of subsidiarity.

Interparliamentary political cooperation is not a new idea. COSAC has promoted information and best practice exchange between national parliaments and with the European Parliament since 1989. The Amsterdam Protocol formally recognised COSAC, enabling it to, inter alia, 'address to the EU Institutions any contribution it deems appropriate on the legislative activities of the Union'. Article 9 of Protocol no 1 goes further and COSAC is identified as a forum to debate policy and exchange information.[52] Horizontal and vertical collaboration between these actors is important but establishing a framework for dialogue is not the challenge. For example, cooperation within COSAC originated *without* the need for Treaty amendment and has been supplemented by other informal initiatives such as the IPEX database.

The *real* test of this relationship arises within the ordinary legislative procedure. Significant scope for disagreement exists because the input legitimacy provided by the European

48 M Larhant, 'La cooperation interparlementaire dans l'UE' (2005) 16 *Notre Europe Policy Paper*.

49 Kiiver (n 33 above) and Cygan (n 12 above).

50 Kiiver (n 33 above) at 122.

51 Cygan (n 12 above) at 491.

52 The conference may communicate with the European Parliament; the Council and the Commission may not bind national parliaments or 'prejudge their positions'; 'shall' promote exchange of information and best practice; may organise interparliamentary conferences.

Parliament may not necessarily correspond to the acceptable limits of output legitimacy defined by national parliaments through subsidiarity monitoring. Put bluntly, it is questionable that the European Parliament will share an expansive interpretation of subsidiarity with national parliaments, for example, making the European Parliament an unreliable partner in circumstances of an orange card be shown. Moreover, as already suggested and the evidence demonstrates, national parliaments remain divided on a definition of subsidiarity. The problem is further compounded because the Court of Justice remains unwilling to provide an interpretation of subsidiarity that is inconsistent with Europeanisation.[53]

Some academic commentators[54] and parliamentarians[55] have argued that the creation of a coherent 'collective' of national parliaments is an unlikely and even undesirable goal, which cannot be achieved through a Treaty or through the activities of COSAC. Notwithstanding this, the Preamble to Protocol no 1 includes the statement of 'desiring to encourage greater involvement of national parliaments in the activities on the Union'. This complements the objective in Article 12 TEU that 'national parliaments contribute actively to the good functioning of the Union'.

The original English language draft of Article 12 TEU included a statement that 'national parliaments *shall* contribute actively to …', suggesting a positive requirement to participate in subsidiarity monitoring and by implication within COSAC. The final English language version omits any mention of 'shall', but this omission does not necessarily suggest the absence of a mandatory connotation to the provision.[56] The United Kingdom Government disagreed with a purposive interpretation of Article 12 TEU and responded that the provision was purely declaratory indicating that parliamentary coordination and COSAC created no explicit prerogatives or obligations. Notwithstanding this assertion, it may be argued that Article 12 TEU does create a prescriptive function for parliaments which requires them to, inter alia, pursue subsidiarity monitoring.[57] If this is the case, then COSAC, as a forum which brings together national parliaments, could be considered as a normative part of the decision-making process.

Article 12 TEU, if read together with the Protocol no 1 'desire to encourage participation' creates an expectation, if not an explicit requirement on the part of national parliaments. The Treaty of Lisbon identifies subsidiarity monitoring as the key task for them; they are the ones losing power to the institutions of the Union and are best placed to make the

[53] See Case C-49/01 *R v Secretary of State for Health ex parte British American Tobacco and Imperial Tobacco* [2002] ECR I-11453 in particular paragraphs 177 and 185. The Court held that once it was considered necessary to adopt common rules to regulate the Internal Market this could only be achieved through EU action and must inevitably comply with subsidiarity.

[54] See, for example, A Maurer, 'National Parliaments in the Architecture of Europe after the Constitutional Treaty' in G Barrett (ed), *National Parliaments and the European Union: The Constitutional Challenge for the Oireachtas and Other Member State Legislatures* (Dublin, Clarus Press in association with the Institute of European Affairs, 2007) 60–61.

[55] See House of Commons European Scrutiny Committee 35th Report HL 104 (2006–07) *European Union Intergovernmental Conference* and House of Lords EU Committee 35th Report HL 180 (2006–07) *The EU Reform Treaty: Work in Progress.*

[56] The original language French version reads '*Les parlements nationaux contribuent…*' which can be translated literally as 'national parliaments contribute…'.

[57] National parliaments are not just limited to subsidiarity monitoring and will also be involved in reviewing activities under Eurojust as well as other EU policies, but the extent of this activity this will depend upon resources within the Parliament. National parliaments are also involved in Treaty revision, though this is far less common by comparison to subsidiarity monitoring.

political judgement of how to apply this principle. The concern within several parliaments, for example the Danish Folketing, was that a synchronised opinion on subsidiarity could be obtained at the expense of ministerial accountability. Such an individual approach to parliamentary scrutiny does not sit comfortably with the objectives of COSAC or indeed Article 12 TEU. The parliamentary EU Committee of the Folketing is an influential strong Committee which mandates the minister to vote in advance of the Council meeting.[58] It is not prepared to sacrifice this tradition of executive accountability to pursue political dialogue, whether through COSAC or otherwise, with parliaments who have historically been considered as 'weak' actors.[59] This brings into sharp focus the distinction between the individual and collective functions of national parliaments which Protocols no 1 and 2 were intended to address. Because, even post Lisbon, differentiated levels of participation in EU affairs remain, national parliaments can only continue to effectively and systematically fulfil the individual function and not the collective obligations within Protocol no 2, thereby further questioning the efficacy of COSAC.[60]

Ministerial accountability and subsidiarity monitoring are not mutually exclusive tasks, and coordination through COSAC may help to facilitate either. The exercise of inquiry and review of draft legislation will generally inform both activities. Yet these remain detailed and onerous tasks for parliaments to complete within an eight-week period and parliaments considered 'weak' are unlikely to engage. By contrast, strong parliaments will remain primarily focused on securing accountability of the minister. More generally, the problems of time and resources may lead parliamentarians to conclude that, politically, there is little to be gained from subsidiarity monitoring and to this extent Article 12 TEU and COSAC will not radically change their priorities.[61]

VI. CONCLUDING REMARKS

The new powers which have been conferred by the Treaty of Lisbon upon national parliaments have led to some national parliaments amending their rules of procedure to adapt to the requirements of subsidiarity monitoring.[62] From research conducted by COSAC[63] it is evident that there is no normative or single model by which national parliaments have implemented the requirement of Article 12 TEU and Protocols no 1 and 2. Notwithstanding the internal parliamentary reforms to procedure and practice post Lisbon, significant disparity continues to exist between the internal modus operandi of national parliaments which enables the criticism to continue that national parliaments are classified as either

[58] See D Arter, 'The Folketing and Denmark's "European Policy": The Case of an Authorising Assembly' (1990) 13 *Western European Politics* (*Special Issue*, '*Parliaments in Western Europe*') 110.

[59] See P Riis, 'National Parliamentary Control of EU Decision-making in Denmark' in O Tans, C Zoethout and J Peters (eds), *National Parliaments and European Democracy: A Bottom-UP Approach to European Constitutionalism* (Groningen, Europa Law Publishing, 2007) 185 at 199.

[60] See also Kiiver (n 33 above) at 163 commenting on the Constitutional Treaty arrangements.

[61] See Tans, Zoethout and Peters (n 59 above) at 229.

[62] Parliamentary procedures were amended in the Belgian Chambre des Députés, the Czech Poslanecka, the Finnish Eduskunta, the French Assemblée nationale, the Dutch Ereste Kamer and Tweede Kamer, the Swedish Riksdag and the House of Lords.

[63] See COSAC Secretariat, *Thirteenth Bi-annual Report: Developments in European Union. Procedures and Practices Relevant to Parliamentary Scrutiny*, Madrid (2010).

'strong' or 'weak' actors in respect of their EU oversight activities. Moreover, improved parliamentary coordination through COSAC will not materially alter this. Indeed, it may be argued that it will only be those parliaments which are considered as strong parliaments that will amend their internal procedures in an attempt to ensure that their scrutiny activities remain relevant and perhaps view COSAC as a valuable forum. COSAC may help to share this best practice amongst parliaments, but peer learning is a slow process and does not guarantee results.

The Treaty of Lisbon sought to address the criticism of strong and weak actors through assigning to national parliaments the task of subsidiarity monitoring[64] and introduces a harmonised minimum standard for their EU scrutiny activities. This presumes that effective subsidiarity monitoring necessitates a political dialogue within an organised horizontal collective of parliaments. Moreover, subsidiarity monitoring undertaken by a 'collective' bloc of national parliaments implies that citizens are more likely to accept legislation if their national parliaments have uniformly confirmed its compliance with the exercise of EU competences. To secure this level of consent Protocol no 2 includes a process of political dialogue which has been singled out as an opportunity through which national parliaments may be reposition themselves within the EU polity. For example, Passos has argued that national parliaments have become a 'new actor in the European Union legislative process to be added to the existing European Parliament—Council—Commission triangle'.[65] However, whether national parliaments are elevated to an institutional or even quasi-institutional status through COSAC can be challenged on several grounds, not least because simply by executing the task of subsidiarity monitoring, which the evidence post Lisbon indicates is itself sporadic, COSAC does not collectively institutionalise national parliaments within the EU polity. COSAC and other interparliamentary conferences may offer representation for national parliaments in the EU, but it does not constitutionalise their status.

There is a broad consensus about the impact of European integration on national parliaments and any recognition of them as a collective entity misinterprets or exaggerates the prerogative offered to national parliaments under the Treaty. In the context of the negative effects of EU integration, most of the literature on the role of national parliaments in the EU polity has considered them as victims of European integration.[66] Constitutionally, this is probably correct and relatively straightforward to explain. Powers which previously were under the jurisdiction of national legislatures have been shifted upwards to the European level. In the Council of Ministers the increased use of Qualified Majority Voting has made it increasingly difficult for national parliaments to force governments to make ex ante commitments before taking decisions at the European level, thereby impeding parliamentary scrutiny. Moreover, the extensive involvement of national ministers and civil servants in drafting and implementing EU legislation insulates or marginalises national parliaments, regardless of the Council's decision. The resulting information deficit has reduced the ability

[64] For a comprehensive comparison of the provisions in the Constitutional Treaty and Treaty of Lisbon see G Barrett, '"The King is Dead, Long Live the King": The Recasting by the Treaty of Lisbon of the Provisions of the Constitutional Treaty Concerning National Parliaments' (2008) 33 *European Law Review* 66.

[65] See further R Passos, 'Recent Developments Concerning the Role of National Parliaments in the European Union' (2008) 9 *ERA Forum* 25 at 35.

[66] Maurer (n 54 above).

of MPs to control their governments in European matters and COSAC has not mitigated against this.[67] Nor can it be suggested that COSAC has significantly alleviated the assertion that national parliaments are somehow losers in the integration process. In fact, through the centrality of technical expertise in the EU policy process, the true winners of European integration have arguably been bureaucrats and organised private interests at all levels of government and not directly-elected representatives who are considered as the traditional holders of legitimacy in European systems of parliamentary government.[68] If this analysis is correct and parliamentarians really are the 'losers' within the integration process it is hard to see how COSAC can materially alter this position in the future.

Going forward COSAC continues to be faced with many challenges, not least within the EU's response to the Financial Crisis and economic governance.[69] The EU's strategy for addressing the challenges which arise from the Financial Crisis may be criticised for marginalising national parliaments, which in turn leaves only limited opportunities for COSAC to make material input. A common problem is identified with respect to reviewing economic governance, namely the time available for national parliaments to review proposals.[70] In a questionnaire issued by COSAC to national parliaments which sought responses on best practice employed in the field of economic governance, all parliaments indicated that even the eight-week time frame applied within Protocol no 2 will not usually be considered as sufficient to examine a Commission proposal.[71] The consensus was that the politically sensitive and technical nature of the proposals would necessitate more detailed review which cannot be completed within eight weeks. Though the Report indicates[72] that legislatures are gradually becoming more involved in reviewing economic governance, the conclusion must be that domestic parliamentary scrutiny of European economic governance is far from optimal and COSAC does not have the constitutional standing to change this.

It is essential that the opportunities for debate and discussion about major matters of economic and financial policy between parliamentarians of all Member States are increased. A 'variable geometry' of interparliamentary cooperation on the consequences of the Financial Crisis is undesirable and would inhibit valuable debate.[73] Thus COSAC should seek to develop effective mechanisms through which it may coordinate interparliamentary

[67] *COSAC Twentieth Bi-annual Report: Developments in European Union Procedures and Practices Relevant to Parliamentary Scrutiny* (COSAC, 2013) 26.

[68] See T Bergman and E Damgaard (eds), *Delegation and Accountability in European Integration: The Nordic Parliamentary Democracies and the European Union* (London, Frank Cass, 2000); H Kassim, G Peters and V Wright (eds), *The National Coordination of EU Policy: The Domestic Level* (Oxford, Oxford University Press, 2000); and W Wessels, A Maurer and J Mittag (eds), *Fifteen into one? The European Union and its Member States* (Manchester, Manchester University Press, 2003).

[69] HL 151 *The Role of National Parliament in the European Union* (2013–14) at paragraph 125.

[70] K Auel and O Hönig, 'Scrutiny in Challenging Times—National Parliaments in the Eurozone Crisis' (2014) 1 *European Policy Analysis* 1.

[71] *COSAC Nineteenth Bi-annual Report: Developments in European Union Procedures and Practices Relevant to Parliamentary Scrutiny* (COSAC, 2013).

[72] ibid. There is a clear belief expressed in the Report among those parliaments which responded that the key documents of the Six-Pack and Two-Pack do not adequately consider the issues of democratic legitimacy and accountability and, in particular, the role of the national parliaments and the European Parliament. Fifteen out of 21 (71.4%) of those who responded believe this to be the case with the Van Rompuy Report and the European Council conclusions of December 2012. The Commission Blueprint for implementing the Six-Pack and Two-Pack, at 13 out of 19 (68.4%), fared only marginally better.

[73] Auel and Hönig (n 70 above).

cooperation on economic and financial matters which involves all 28 Member States. This, however, will be a significant challenge in the light of the diverse economic conditions that exist within the EU.

It would be incorrect to view COSAC as being an irrelevant mechanism through which to secure improved parliamentary accountability. COSAC has demonstrated that it can be a positive forum though which to improve democracy because it allows national parliaments to have a structured dialogue on EU affairs which transcends national capitals. However, it remains open to question to what extent this may be expanded in order to enable COSAC to substantively address the challenges of improving accountability and democracy within the EU. Perhaps after 25 years of activity and the limited Treaty recognition that it enjoys, COSAC has reached the limit of its influence.

12

The Interparliamentary Conference on Common Foreign and Security Policy: A Quest for Democratic Accountability in EU Security Governance

JAN WOUTERS AND KOLJA RAUBE

I. INTRODUCTION

THIS CHAPTER DEALS with interparliamentary cooperation in the recently established Interparliamentary Conference for the Common Foreign and Security Policy and the Common Security and Defence Policy ('Conference'). In other words, we focus on the cooperation between national parliaments and the European Parliament in the context of EU external action, and, more specifically, the Common Foreign and Security Policy ('CFSP') and the Common Security and Defence Policy ('CSDP') of the European Union ('EU' or 'Union').[1] In light of its peculiar status as a parliamentary conference in a decidedly intergovernmental domain such as CFSP and CSDP,[2] the Conference has been seen as a test case for further interparliamentary settings in EU governance.

[1] The Conference has been established by the decisions of the EU Speakers' Conference at its meetings in Brussels, 4–5 April 2011 and in Warsaw, 20–21 April 2012. At its first meeting in Paphos, Cyprus on 9–10 September 2012, the Conference adopted its Rules of Procedure. See for more background Doc 53, 2442/001 (Senate), 5-1806/1 (Chamber), Report on the Paphos meeting by D Van der Maelen and K Vanlouwe, 11 October 2012.

[2] JC Piris, *The Lisbon Treaty—A legal and political analysis* (Cambridge, Cambridge University Press, 2010) 132–33.

Following security governance[3] and democratic accountability approaches,[4] we aim to identify the *drivers* of interparliamentary cooperation in the areas of CFSP and CSDP and point to those factors which concretely *shape* such cooperation. Focusing on both approaches, rather than on just one of them, allows us not only to explain why parliamentary networks (and their relationships) are becoming more intertwined between the national and the European level in EU foreign, security and defence policy—ie, for reasons relating to information exchanges and parliamentary contributions to foreign policy and security output—but also why such enforced relationships matter in view of democratic representation and accountability.[5] Overall, the assessment of the Conference will not only shed light on the potential challenges, but also the achievements of this novel entity in view of its contribution to (a) parliamentary networks in security governance and (b) democratic accountability in European security cooperation.

Against the background of our analysis, four factors are identified that concretely *shape* parliamentary cooperation and accountability in security governance: (i) a (lack of) solid Treaty foundation on the basis of which parliamentary cooperation can blossom; (ii) status questions concerning the parliamentary cooperation framework, in addition to status and membership questions concerning the parliaments involved; (iii) a (lack of) common understanding among parliaments regarding what parliamentary cooperation should achieve; and (iv) financial constraints.

Based on desk research and expert interviews, we advance the thesis that the work of the Conference, in its first years of existence, has mainly focused on mutual information exchange and network building. Its contribution to democratic accountability remains rather low. Cooperation in respect of the latter is undermined by unresolved status questions and the lack of a common understanding regarding what exactly such accountability entails. Nevertheless, information exchanges with senior executives in an interparliamentary context, for example with the High Representative of the European Union for Foreign Affairs and Security Policy, are seen as added value to the parliamentary dimension of the EU's foreign and security policy.

II. WHAT DRIVES AND SHAPES INTERPARLIAMENTARY COOPERATION IN EUROPEAN SECURITY GOVERNANCE?

The European Parliament has gained considerable powers under the Lisbon Treaty, including EU external action. Whereas its powers have been formalised with regards to trade and other international agreements, it has also become more assertive in the field of EU foreign

[3] HG Ehrhart, H Hegemann and M Kahl, 'Putting security governance to the test: conceptual, empirical, and normative challenges' (2014) 23 *European Security* 119; E Krahmann, 'Conceptualizing Security Governance' (2003) 38 *Cooperation and Conflict: Journal of the Nordic International Studies Association* 5; M Webber, S Croft, J Howorth, T Terriff and E Krahmann, 'The governance of European security' (2004) 30 *Review of International Studies* 3.

[4] B Crum and JE Fossum, 'The Multilevel Parliamentary Field: a framework for theorizing representative democracy in the EU' (2009) 1 *European Political Science Review* 249.

[5] ibid.

and security policies.[6] At the same time, with the Lisbon Treaty, interparliamentary cooperation has become an essential cornerstone of EU policy-making.[7]

The subsidiarity principle and the application of the Early Warning System[8] led to increasing interactions between the European Parliament and national parliaments. Some scholars have interpreted the implementation of interparliamentary powers in the multi-level polity of the EU as the emergence of a 'third legislative chamber' (after the Council and the EP).[9] Furthermore, authors have highlighted Article 9 of Protocol No 1 to the Treaty on European Union ('TEU'):

> The European Parliament and national Parliaments shall together determine the organisation and promotion of effective and regular inter-parliamentary cooperation within the Union.[10]

In view of Article 9, the European Parliament and national parliaments are currently undertaking a large range of formalised and informal meetings in various formats. More specifically and with a particular view to Article 10 of Protocol No 1, which refers to the establishment of 'interparliamentary conferences on specific topics, in particular to debate matters of common foreign and security policy, including common security and defence policy', academics have pointed out that both provisions of Article 9 and Article 10 of the Lisbon Treaty provide entry points for the cooperation of national parliaments and the European Parliament in the otherwise intergovernmental CFSP/CSDP.[11] We will discuss Articles 9 and 10 of Protocol No 1 and the creation of the Interparliamentary conference on CFSP/CSDP in in greater detail below (see Section IV.A).

Studies have described and analysed the role of national parliaments in EU politics, as well as the relationship between Members of the European Parliament and national parliamentarians, in order to conceptualise the role of inter-parliamentary cooperation in the EU, and to measure Europeanisation effects on national parliaments.[12] However, despite

[6] M Furness, 'Who controls the European External Action Service? Agent autonomy in EU external policy' (2013) 18 *European Foreign Affairs Review* 103; K Raube, 'The European External Action Service and the European Parliament' (2012) 7 *The Hague Journal of Diplomacy* 65; K Raube, 'Parliamentarisation Approach: Parliamentary Control in EU Foreign Policy' in M Wilga and P Karolewski (eds), *New Approaches to EU Foreign Policy* (Abingdon, Routledge, 2014) 125–41; E Wisniewski, 'The Influence of the European Parliament on the European External Action Service' (2014) 18 *European Foreign Affairs Review* 81.

[7] By EU policy-making, we understand initiatives, legislative procedures and policy-implementation in the multi-level governance of the EU.

[8] Protocol No 2 to the Treaty on European Union.

[9] I Cooper, 'A "Virtual Third Chamber" for the European Union? National Parliaments after the Treaty of Lisbon' (2012) 35 *West European Politics* 441.

[10] R Corbett, 'Evolving Roles of European Parliament and national Parliaments' in A Biondi et al (eds), *EU Law after Lisbon* (Oxford, Oxford University Press, 2012) 260.

[11] C Caballero-Bourdot, 'Interparliamentary Scrutiny of the CFSP: Avenues for the Future', *Occasional Paper no 94* (Paris, EU Institute for Security Studies, October 2011); European Parliament, 'Report on 'Interparliamentary Cooperation between the European Parliament and national Parliaments under the Treaty of Lisbon' (Brussels, 2012) 4–5; European Parliament, '*2011 Yearbook National Parliaments and the European Parliament*' (Directorate General for relations with national Parliaments, Brussels, 2011) 10–11; A Herranz-Surrallés, 'The EU's Multilevel Parliamentary (Battle)Field: Inter-parliamentary Cooperation and Conflict in Foreign and Security Policy' (2014) 37 *West European Politics* 957; J Wouters and K Raube, 'Seeking CSDP accountability through interparliamentary scrutiny' (2012) 47 *International Spectator* 149.

[12] T Raunio, 'National Parliaments and European Integration: What We Know and Agenda for Future Research' (2009) 15 *Journal of Legislative Studies* 317; E Miklin, 'Inter-Parliamentary Cooperation in EU Affairs and the Austrian Parliament: Empowering the Opposition? (2013) 19 *Journal of Legislative Studies* 22; E Miklin and B Crum, *Inter-parliamentary contact of Members of the European Parliament—Report of a Survey* (RECON Report 2011/8).

various attempts to describe the new developments in terms of EU law and integration, the advent and conduct of interparliamentary cooperation in European security governance, including in the largely intergovernmental field of CFSP/CSDP, is yet to be explained. To cure this shortcoming in the literature, we focus on two approaches, which have tried to explain institutional cooperation from two different perspectives. These are (i) a security governance approach and (ii) an approach concentrating on democratic accountability and representation.

Following European (and global governance) approaches, transnational and transgovernmental relations are seen as key to understanding global and EU-wide policy-making by means of 'governance'.[13] As the Commission on Global Governance wrote in 1995, 'governance can be seen as the sum of the many ways individuals and institutions, public and private, manage their common affairs'. Accordingly, authors have pointed out that security governance, understood as the management of common affairs in the field of security, allows us to conceptualise cooperation on security issues beyond governmental affairs.[14] Hence, it has been argued that, in security governance, a plentitude of actors form networks in order to shape security outcomes, and that executive actors are but one element next to non-governmental actors.[15] Moreover, in light of the move from 'government' to 'governance', security governance is seen as being not so much about hierarchical decision-making but rather about 'the fragmentation of political authority among a diversity of public and private actors across levels of analysis'.[16] In this view, the advent of parliamentary actors, national parliaments and the European Parliament, as part of European security governance, with decision-making powers being vested both on the national and EU level, is hardly surprising.

Transnational cooperation across levels and actors is seen as a channel to coordinate action in multi-level governance frameworks.[17] In such governance arrangements, supranational and national actors enter networking arrangements and create relationships with other actors. Depending on the policy domain, they can collectively impact upon the policy itself.[18] Respective approaches are concerned with the establishment of such relationships under the umbrella of multi-level governance. However, as has been pointed out elsewhere,[19] governance approaches focus mainly on the operation and interactions of network arrangements and lack the concern generally shared by approaches focusing on democratic accountability. This is especially clear in light of the current conceptualisation of European security governance, which in its institutional dimension focuses mainly on the interrelationship between executive Member State actors (governments), executive non-state actors (European Commission, European External Action Service), and non-governmental actors.[20] While it has been pointed out, especially in the field of internal

[13] A-M Slaughter, *A New World Order* (Princeton NJ, Princeton University Press, 2004) 61 ff.

[14] M Webber, S Croft, J Howorth and E Krahmann, 'The governance of European security' (2004) 30 *Review of International Studies* 3; E Krahmann, 'Conceptualizing Security Governance' (2003) 38 *Cooperation and Conflict: Journal of the Nordic International Studies Association* 5.

[15] ibid, 5–6.

[16] ibid, 6.

[17] Slaughter, *New World Order* (n 13 above) 23 ff.

[18] ibid.

[19] Crum and Fossum, 'Multilevel Parliamentary Field' (n 4 above) 257–59.

[20] P Norheim-Martinsen, 'Beyond Intergovernmentalism: European Security and Defence Policy and the Governance Approach' (2009) 48 *Journal for Common Market Studies* 1351.

security governance, eg counterterrorism policies, that the European Parliament has gained considerable powers and adds a parliamentary dimension to the institutional level of security governance,[21] the role of parliaments in the external domain of security governance has received less attention.

Complementing the security governance literature, accountability approaches have focused on the question of whether parliamentary and interparliamentary arrangements beyond the nation state in supranational and international organisations can make up for the lack of executive control at the national and European level.[22] In this context, parliamentary involvement in EU security governance can contribute to the control and scrutiny of institutional actors by means of parliamentary mechanisms, eg parliamentary vetoes, reports, hearings, etc.[23] Several studies have pointed to the role of national parliaments in exercising war powers, including their agreement with troop mobilisation in the context of international missions,[24] the European Parliament's competences in the non-military budget of the CFSP/CSDP, and its access to security information.[25] These studies pay critical attention to democratic accountability and the question whether interparliamentary cooperation is able to fill the democratic accountability gap in EU foreign and security policy. According to existing literature, multi-level governance poses a key problem for parliaments: it hollows out legislative control functions of governments who willingly transfer decision-making powers to European or global levels of governance, which are beyond parliaments' reaches.

Control of governments is linked to parliamentary instruments by which executives can be sanctioned for their actions in foreign policy: for example, by the use of parliamentary prerogatives and related legislative veto options. *Scrutiny*, on the other hand, is less advanced, as here parliaments can request information on governmental external action but without the opportunity to sanction. Still, scrutiny can have effects on governmental action, as in principle it can generate public debates and awareness on otherwise non-transparent executive behaviour.[26] In multi-level governance, security cooperation often shows a double democratic deficit in the form of a lack of democratic accountability at both the national and the European level.[27] In this context it needs to be analysed whether and to what extent interparliamentary cooperation can be of an added value.

[21] J Monar, 'EU internal security governance: the case of counter-terrorism' (2014) 23 *European Security* 195.

[22] C Lord, 'The Political Theory and Practice of Parliamentary Participation in the Common Security and Defence Policy' (2011) 18 *Journal of European Public Policy* 1133–50; D Peters, W Wagner and N Deitelhoff, 'Parliaments and European Security Policy: Mapping the Parliamentary Field' in S Vanhoonacker, H Dijkstra and H Maurer (eds), *Understanding the Role of Bureaucracy in the European Security and Defence Policy* (2010) *European Integration Online Papers* (Special Issue 1) vol 14; G Rosen, 'EU Confidential: The European Parliament's Involvement in EU Security and Defence Policy' (2015) 53 *Journal of Common Market Studies* 383; Wouters and Raube, 'Seeking CSDP accountability' (n 11 above) 153–55.

[23] Wouters and Raube, 'Seeking CSDP accountability' (n 11 above) 151–53.

[24] D Peters and W Wagner, 'Between Military Efficiency and Democratic Legitimacy: Mapping Parliamentary War Powers in Contemporary Democracies, 1989–2004' (2011) 64 *Parliamentary Affairs* 165.

[25] Raube, 'The European External Action Service and the European Parliament' (n 6 above) 69; Rosen, 'EU Confidential' (n 22 above), 384–85, 388 ff.

[26] Wouters and Raube, 'Seeking CSDP accountability' (n 11 above) 150.

[27] W Wagner, 'The Democratic Control of Military Power in Europe' (2006) 13 *Journal of European Public Policy* 200, 203 ff.

Building on security governance and accountability approaches that have focused on interparliamentary relations, three *driving factors* for interparliamentary cooperation in security governance are advanced.

1) First, following governance approaches, parliamentary cooperation is seen as a response to the need of members of parliaments to exchange information and to arrive at a mutual understanding in particular domains (here: security governance).
2) Secondly, and related to the first factor, parliamentary cooperation constitutes a way of fostering parliamentary networks that help to enhance multi-lateral security frameworks such as the EU. Here, following governance approaches, relations between parliaments are seen as a function of the security governance system which produces an overall policy output.
3) Thirdly, following accountability approaches, interparliamentary cooperation is seen as being driven by the need to enhance the accountability vis-à-vis parliaments of otherwise uncontrolled security policies.

As regards the *shape* of interparliamentary cooperation, one can expect different outcomes of inter-parliamentary cooperation and accountability in security policies, depending on whether one looks at it from an intergovernmental or supranational perspective. From an intergovernmental perspective one would assume that cooperation of parliaments needs to be restricted to information exchanges and mutual understandings, while scrutinising governments remains, if at all, reserved to the national parliamentary setting. From a supranational angle, the role of interparliamentary cooperation should not interfere with supranational prerogatives. However, interparliamentary cooperation could be a complementary alternative in such domains, for example where a supranational parliament like the European Parliament has not (yet) successfully gained powers, such as in the field of CFSP/CSDP. Essentially, these understandings will have an impact on the nature and organisational dimension of parliamentary cooperation (eg, a formal decision-taking assembly or an informal conference), questions of membership (eg, equal distribution of members or unequal size of delegations) and working arrangements (eg, institutionalised fact-finding reports or loose exchanges of views). In essence, the diversity of understandings will impact upon the organisation and could constrain its shape and working methods.

III. WHY INTERPARLIAMENTARY COOPERATION IN CFSP/CSDP?

A. Exchanging Information Among Parliaments

In the context of EU foreign policy and security governance arrangements, in which governments increasingly take decisions at the European level, interparliamentary cooperation is first of all based on the need of parliamentarians to exchange information and—if possible—to arrive at a mutual understanding. In other words, parliaments create a network of relations in order to attract information about governance decisions which they would not be able to obtain nationally. In general, while information is accessible easily in today's world, it remains difficult for parliaments to access information on security-related issues, especially when it is seen as confidential information. Moreover, parliaments lack the resources to process information about all 28 Member States. Under such circumstances, exchanges of information and mutual understandings are most easily accomplished if parliamentarians meet, interact or listen to others' interactions in interparliamentary settings.[28] The substance of the communication will depend upon the structure of the setting. The more informal and closed the settings, the more information will flow. By way of contrast, in formal, transparent and publically accessible meetings, participating parliament members may choose not to communicate sensitive information.[29]

However, a systematic information exchange on European foreign and security policy—including decision-making processes in Brussels and policy implementation by EU and national actors—needs to take account of the various policy instruments at EU level and the capacities, needs and limitations of the EU and its Member States. In a Union with almost 30 Member States it is important to obtain a comparative overview of capacities, limits and opportunities in foreign and security policy. The former Western European Union (WEU) Assembly, comprising parliamentarians of all Member States of the WEU, offered a good example of how methods could be developed to reach a comparative overview encompassing all Member States. To this end, it gathered information on EU crisis management from Member States, which it digested and presented in a comparative manner in WEU Assembly reports. Moreover, in an interparliamentary context, the European Parliament, which oversees the budget of nearly all aspects of EU external policies, is in a unique position to identify interdependent links between security and other areas of EU policy-making. This means that, alongside comparative perspectives across Member States, information can be exchanged between parliaments at different levels. Bringing these two perspectives together potentially provides added value, contributes to mutual understanding and generates a trans-parliamentary sphere in which genuine European security cooperation can be embedded.[30]

B. Fostering Parliamentary Networks to Enhance Multi-lateral Security Governance

Parliamentary cooperation can also be seen as a way to foster parliamentary networks that help to enhance multi-lateral security frameworks, such as the EU. According to this governance perspective, mutual exchanges between parliaments not only lead to an enhanced understanding of the EU's foreign and security policy, but also to an informed position whereby parliaments actively take part in EU foreign policy. Parliaments can add to the making of security cooperation and generate overall policy outputs. For example, it has been demonstrated that national parliaments are able to influence national defence spending and—to varying degrees—national interventions abroad.[31] Moreover, parliamentary diplomacy adds to the toolkit of European foreign and security policy by actively seeking contacts with parliamentarians and civil society in third countries.[32]

[28] Interview, European Parliament, February 2013.

[29] ibid; in such a case, corridor talks and exchanges during the coffee breaks might be more enlightening than plenary sessions.

[30] Wouters and Raube, 'Seeking CSDP accountability' (n 11 above) 160–62.

[31] Wagner, 'The Democratic Control of Military Power in Europe' (n 27 above) 204–6.

[32] Raube, 'Parliamentary Control in EU Foreign Policy' (n 6 above) 135; D Jančić, 'World Diplomacy of the European Parliament and Democratic Legitimacy' (2016) 11 *Hague Journal of Diplomacy*, forthcoming.

Incentives to cooperate can be an outcome of exchange of information and mutual understanding between national parliaments and the European Parliament.[33] Such a 'support culture' can manifest itself in reports and resolutions on specific policy issues in security. In this perspective, there are two ways in which information exchanges can support multi-lateral cooperation. First, in interparliamentary settings, parliament members exchange views and try to persuade each other that security cooperation matters and that, subsequently, steps have to be taken in the direction of collective action and closer cooperation. Secondly, parliament members are informed about the necessity for collective security action by high-level executive staff from the EU and Member States, such as the High Representative or senior staff of the EEAS, or, conversely, parliament members inform such high-level staff about their views on collective action.

In order for these mechanisms to support security cooperation, parliamentarians need to be persuaded not only that multi-lateral European security cooperation is to be supported, but also that they need to bring home these beliefs and persuade fellow domestic parliamentarians.

C. Enhancing Democratic Accountability

Interparliamentary cooperation can also be driven by the need to enhance democratic accountability of otherwise uncontrolled executive-driven security frameworks.[34] This must be seen in light of the challenges that a multi-layered and multi-level policy like CSDP poses to democratic accountability. In the EU, CSDP decisions are no longer taken in a 'security world' only, but increasingly function as 'nexus decisions'. In view of what is called the 'comprehensive approach' to EU foreign policy,[35] policies on the ground are increasingly about bringing various policy tools together from various dimensions of security, trade, development and human rights. As such, the nexus between security and other policies is ever closer and arguably needs to be reflected in the way how parliaments scrutinise and control the field.

CSDP decisions are planned, made and implemented across various policy-making levels. Intergovernmental and trans-governmental settings involve sensitive information and policy planning. Security trans-governmental networks interact, consult and shape decisions in intergovernmental settings. For example, in the case of CFSP/CSDP it has been pointed out that national executives can try to circumvent domestic controls and increase their autonomy by establishing foreign and security decision-making at the EU level.[36] For parliaments, this poses problems. Often, parliaments are said to have insufficient access to the information in trans-governmental networks. Hence, parliaments increasingly find

[33] Interview, European Parliament, February 2013.

[34] Peters, Deitelhoff and Wagner, 'Parliaments and European Security Policy' (n 22 above) p 15.

[35] J Wouters, G De Baere, B Van Vooren, K Raube, J Odermatt, T Ramopoulos, T Van der Sanden and Y Tanghe, *The Organisation and Functioning of the European External Action Service: Achievements, Challenges and Opportunities* (Brussels, European Parliament, 2013) 28–29.

[36] M Koenig-Archibugi, 'The democratic deficit of EU foreign and security policy' (2002) 37 *The International Spectator* 61, 67.

themselves in situations in which they do not receive crucial information on policy preparation, decisions and implementation, or they receive such information too late.[37]

As regards the multi-layered and multi-level nature of security policy, Bieber has argued that, in a situation in which the EU increasingly has to take complex foreign policy decisions, all policy perspectives, including those of parliaments, need to be taken into account.[38] Security actors are only able to find democratically legitimised answers to global policy problems if the perspective of parliaments—which represent citizens, not states—is also heard by executive decision-makers. This argument is applicable to CSDP, but also to other intergovernmental organisations like NATO.

Security and defence decisions need to take into account as many concerns as possible (input legitimacy)[39] in order to arrive at acceptable effective and coherent policy solutions (output legitimacy).[40] What is more, given the multi-faceted and multi-layered nature of EU external action—of which CSDP is only one part—and given that the dividing lines between 'the external' and 'the internal' are becoming more and more blurred, the complexity of security and defence decisions must be checked against the interests and needs of those who are actually affected by such a policy. This also implies that CSDP as an area of intergovernmental policy-making is inseparable from other, more supranational, policy fields. It follows that an interparliamentary setting can be a unique forum for considering the overall complexity of CSDP. Pooling information from various decision-making levels in an interparliamentary forum and making comprehensive trans-parliamentary suggestions (embracing the concerns of national parliaments and the EP) could help to determine which CSDP policies should be adopted.

IV. THE INTERPARLIAMENTARY CONFERENCE ON CFSP/CSDP

A. Treaty Legal Basis

Article 9 of Protocol No 1 stipulates:

> The European Parliament and national parliaments shall together determine the organisation and promotion of effective and regular inter-parliamentary cooperation within the Union.

This provision arguably underlines in general the objective of cooperation between the European Parliament and national parliaments. It can potentially serve as an entry point for inter-parliamentary cooperation even outside well-established fora (such as COSAC).[41] In this case, the European Parliament and national parliaments shall 'together determine' the ways of interparliamentary cooperation.

[37] This is a more general problem which applies to many areas of so-called 'informal international law-making': see J Pauwelyn, RA Wessel and J Wouters (eds), *Informal International Lawmaking* (Oxford, Oxford University Press, 2012), in particular 16 and 332–33.

[38] R Bieber, 'Democratic Control of European Foreign Policy' (1990) 1 *European Journal of International Law* 152–53.

[39] FJ Scharpf, *Regieren in Europa—Effektiv und demokratisch?* (Frankfurt, Campus, 1999) 20 ff.

[40] M Zürn, 'Global Governance and legitimacy problems' in D Held and M Koenig-Archibugi (eds), *Global Governance and public accountability* (Malden/Oxford, Blackwell, 2005) 162.

[41] Herranz-Surrallés, 'The EU's Multilevel Parliamentary (Battle) Field' (n 11 above) 968.

Article 10 of Protocol No 1 introduces interparliamentary cooperation in the field of CSDP with regard to COSAC. It stipulates that a

> conference of Parliamentary Committees for Union Affairs ... shall promote the exchange of information and best practice between national parliaments and the European Parliament, including their special committees.

Article 10 adds that this conference

> may also organise interparliamentary conferences on particular topics, in particular to debate matters of common foreign and security policy, including common security and defence policy.

Finally, Article 10 underlines that '*[c]ontributions from the conference shall not bind national parliaments and shall not prejudge their positions*'. In other words, it foresees that COSAC could not only foster interparliamentary exchanges between parliaments in the EU, but also that it can organise specialised conferences on CFSP/CSDP matters.

Well into the first decade of the twenty-first century, the (former) WEU Assembly fostered the cooperation of parliaments in the intergovernmental area of security and defence.[42] However, the Modified Brussels Treaty ended on 30 June 2011, and with it the work of the WEU and the WEU Assembly. Since this date, there has been no form of formalised interparliamentary cooperation in place within the CSDP framework. However, the statement of the Member States terminating the WEU reads:

> The Assembly of WEU has contributed substantially to the development of a European culture on security and defence. In accordance with the specific nature of CSDP, we encourage as appropriate the enhancement of interparliamentary dialogue in this field including with candidates for EU accession and other interested states. Protocol 1 on the role of national parliaments in the European Union, annexed to the Lisbon Treaty, may provide a basis for it.[43]

Despite the emphasis of parliamentary cooperation in both the Lisbon Treaty and the statement of WEU Member States, these texts leave open and, in fact, unclear how the interparliamentary cooperation should be established, what a potential future conference should look like and how it should function. Also unclear is whether this future conference is meant to make any contribution to democratic accountability in CFSP/CSDP. In this sense, the Treaty leaves decision-makers with an incomplete scenario.

At the same time, the explicit mentioning of a conference in the field of foreign policy, security and defence in the Treaty (Article 10 of Protocol No 1) may imply a foreseen formalisation of interparliamentary meetings in security and that the conference could serve as a template for interparliamentary conferences in other policy domains.[44] In other words, the demise of the informal and in-camera meetings of Chairmen of Foreign Affairs Committees (COFACC) seems to have been anticipated.[45] Still, the Rules of Procedures of the eventual established Conference only make a reference to Protocol No 1 in general, but not explicitly to Article 10.[46] In fact, the establishment of the Conference and the prominent

[42] 'Statement of the Presidency of the Permanent Council of the WEU on behalf of the High Contracting Parties to the Modified Brussels Treaty—Belgium, France, Germany, Greece, Italy, Luxembourg, The Netherlands, Portugal, Spain and the United Kingdom', Brussels, 31 March 2010: www.weu.int/Declaration_E.pdf.

[43] ibid.

[44] Interview, European Parliament, 2013.

[45] ibid. Conference of Foreign Affairs Committee Chairpersons (COFACC).

[46] Preamble, Rules of Procedure.

role of the EU Speakers' Conference suggest that Article 9 (see below) rather than Article 10 (COSAC) served as the real Treaty basis of the Conference.

From an institutional point of view, the presence or lack of a solid Treaty legal basis has a strong impact on interparliamentary cooperation and democratic accountability. This is especially true in an intergovernmental policy, such as CFSP/CSDP. In order to carry sufficient weight in terms of cooperation and accountability, it seems essential that parliamentary interaction would be given a strong Treaty basis. The WEU, established by the Modified Brussels Treaty of 1954, was a case in point of an intergovernmental security and defence organisation which explicitly provided for the establishment of a parliamentary assembly, the WEU Assembly.[47] In case of a weak, or even non-existent, formal Treaty legal basis, alternative informal arrangements need to be found among the relevant parliaments and vis-à-vis executive actors. Such arrangements face the problem of watered-down objectives and working methods because of the variety of interests of the actors involved, including competing parliamentary interests.

B. Establishing the Interparliamentary Conference

After initial deliberations between the Belgian Presidency, the European Parliament and national parliaments in 2010, the EU Speakers' Conference on 4–5 April 2011 ended with no common consensus.[48] Parliamentarians from several national parliaments and the European Parliament could reach no final consensus as to what their 'conference' should look like. Special attention was given to numbers of members from individual parliaments (especially the question of how large the European Parliament's delegation could be) and the location and work of the secretariat (especially the question of whether it was supposed to be embedded in the European Parliament or not). The Presidency concluded by saying that 'given the diverging views, the Speakers did not reach an agreement on all aspects of the establishment of an inter-parliamentary Conference'.[49]

Despite the failure to achieve an overall agreement, the Presidency Conclusions of the EU Speakers' Conference announced, among other things, a consensus on the following courses of action: to call for a CFSP/CSDP conference, composed of 'delegations of the national parliaments of the EU Member States and the European Parliament'; to replace the Conference of Foreign Affairs Committee Chairpersons (COFACC) and the Conference of Defence Affairs Committee Chairpersons (CODACC) to open up for observers, coming from national parliaments of EU Candidate States and European Members of NATO; to determine that the Conference takes place two times per year, either being hosted by the EU Council Presidency or the European Parliament; to agree that the rotating presidency shall chair the meetings 'in close cooperation' with the European Parliament; to foresee that

[47] Article IX Modified Brussels Treaty of 23 October 1954, 19 *UNTS* 51, 211 *UNTS* 342: 'The Council of Western European Union shall make an annual report on its activities and in particular concerning the control of armaments to an Assembly composed of representatives of the Brussels Treaty Powers to the Consultative Assembly of the Council of Europe'.

[48] Wouters and Raube, 'Seeking CSDP accountability' (n 11 above) 156.

[49] 'Presidency Conclusions, 'Conference of the Speakers of the Parliaments of the EU', Brussels, 4–5 April 2011, www.ipex.eu/IPEXL-WEB/euspeakers/getspeakers.do?id=082dbcc530b1bef60130b64f909f0023.

the High Representative is present at the meetings to 'set out the outlines and strategies' of CFSP/CSDP; and, finally, to decide that 'non-binding conclusions by consensus' can be issued during the conferences.[50]

After these preliminary conclusions, a formal compromise was found at the next Speakers' Conference on 20–21 April 2012 in Warsaw after several exchanges of letters between the Polish Presidency of the Speakers' Conference, the European Parliament and all other national parliaments in November 2011.[51]

The statement of the general secretaries of parliaments in February 2012 mentioned that, given the 'importance' of setting up an interparliamentary conference,[52] a consensus should be communicated even if some Member States' parliaments still disagreed with the overall formula. The final compromise, reached on 20 April 2012, provided that 16 members of the European Parliament would be able to participate in the conference, whereas only six parliamentarians would be sent by each national parliament. How the delegations are composed is to be determined by individual parliaments.[53] Moreover, another question was 'solved' by introducing a secretariat that would be provided by the hosting country 'in close cooperation' with the European Parliament. Currently, the Conference has set up a review mechanism which looks into adaptations of the present Rules of Procedure. To this end, a special seminar, which convened in Athens in February 2014, and an ad hoc Review Committee, which convened during the conference in Athens in April 2014, have come up with further suggestions of how to change the rules of procedure, including the identification of best practices.[54]

C. Composition and Participation: Lack of Interest?

The composition of the Conference is organised along the lines of the originally foreseen compromise. 16 members of the European Parliament and six members of each national parliament can be represented. Parliaments from candidate countries and from 'European Member Countries of NATO' can be represented by four observers each.[55]

Prior to the consensus on the size of delegations, the European Parliament and a number of national parliaments, including Belgium and Italy, proposed that the European Parliament should be represented by 54 delegates. This proposal provided that Member State parliaments would each be represented by four members.[56] A later Belgian compromise foresaw that the European Parliament should be represented by 27 MEPs, while four members per national parliament were to be represented.[57] In a Resolution of 7 July 2011, the

[50] Wouters and Raube, 'Seeking CSDP accountability' (n 11 above) 156.

[51] ibid, 159.

[52] 'Meeting of the Secretaries-General of EU Parliaments', Warsaw, 5–6 February 2012.

[53] 'Presidency Conclusions', Warsaw, 20 April 2012, www.ipex.eu/IPEXL-WEB/euspeakers/getspeakers.do?id=082dbcc530b1bef60130b6491e6c001d.

[54] See also Synopsis of the Proceedings of the Interparliamentary Conference in Athens, 3–4 April 2014 at: www.ipex.eu/IPEXL-WEB/euspeakers/getspeakers.do?type=082dbcc5420d8f48014247cca6f04248.

[55] Art 2.1 and 2.2 Rules of procedure.

[56] EU Speakers' Conference, Topic: Parliamentary Scrutiny of the Common Foreign and Security and Defence Policy (CSDP)—Overview of the Responses of the Belgian Presidency Proposal', Brussels, 4–5 April 2011, www.ipex.eu/IPEXL-WEB/euspeakers/getspeakers.do?id=082dbcc530b1bef60130b64f909f0023.

[57] ibid.

European Parliament stressed that, in a conference of interparliamentary cooperation, it would opt for a size of representation that reflected its role in holding CFSP/CSDP accountable, recognised the European nature of such policies and satisfied the need to reflect its internal political diversity.[58] Moreover, it argued that its delegation had to be larger than individual parliament delegations because it needed experts from all sorts of committees working on issues related to CSDP beyond those in the Security and Defence (SEDE) Committee to scrutinise CSDP.

Conversely, several national parliaments argued that CFSP/CSDP constitutes an intergovernmental field and that, accordingly, the European Parliament could not be represented by larger numbers than individual parliaments.[59] If national parliaments were supposed to be represented by six parliamentarians, then the European Parliament should also send six MEPs. This system would have resembled the COSAC formula (27+1), which gives equal size of delegations to the 'old' 27 Member States and the European Parliament. A British proposal suggested that out of the six members of the European Parliament three could have come from the Foreign Affairs Committee (AFET) and three from the Security and Defence Committee (SEDE).

One of the outcomes in the review process was that the Rules of Procedure concerning the participation of the European Parliament and national parliaments were to be positively reviewed.[60] At the same time, the 'light' construction of the Conference does obviously lead to questions why the mandates have problematised at all. Do formally 'fixed' delegation seats make a difference in a conference which is based on consensus and non-majority voting? Moreover, the findings of the conference are supposed to be non-binding; hence, the outcome of the conference does not impede future actions of its members.

However, the debate centered not only on the overall size of delegations but also on the question of which issues the Conference was supposed to tackle. For example, would the Conference engage in discussions on CFSP/CSDP *only*, or would the Conference consider CFSP/CSDP as interlinked with other policy fields and instruments, like development cooperation, humanitarian aid, the Instrument for Stability, the African Peace Facility, etc?

Looking at the Conference in Cyprus in Autumn 2012, it becomes evident that most of the delegations participated with fewer than six delegates.[61] This has become a trend in the other conferences as well, but with a considerable amount of variation between delegations. Interestingly, this fact stands in clear contrast to the original struggle among parliaments to find a compromise on how many delegates would have to be represented. The absence of parliamentarians can be explained by increasing financial constraints on national parliaments, especially if interparliamentary conferences take place in relatively distant places.[62] Overall, financial constraints and the limited number of participating members point once again to the informal character of the Conference. What is more, Member State parliaments and the European Parliament can change the participating member lists from one Conference meeting to another. The European Parliament, for example, makes its choices

[58] Caballero-Bourdot, 'Interparliamentary Scrutiny of the CFSP' (n 11 above) 45.

[59] Wouters and Raube, 'Seeking CSDP accountability' (n 11 above) 157.

[60] See also Synopsis of the Proceedings of the Interparliamentary Conference in Athens, 3–4 April 2014 at www.ipex.eu/IPEXL-WEB/euspeakers/getspeakers.do?type=082dbcc5420d8f48014247cca6f04248.

[61] Participants list, Interparliamentary Conference, 9–10 September 2012.

[62] Interviews, February 2013.

primarily on the basis of the subjects discussed at the Conference. By this, parliamentary participation is not consistently linked to specific members and/or committees; rather, an in-built flexibility means parliamentarians can decide, from one Conference to the next, whether they are interested in participating or not.

D. Secretariat and Organisational Structure: Lack of Funding?

Prior to the above mentioned consensus, the role and location of the secretariat remained a contentious issue. The European Parliament supported the idea of having the Conference secretariat in its premises. It also suggested that its premises could be used for the conference meetings. By making these suggestions, it underlined its ambition to impact upon the agendas of the Conference. At the same time, Member States wanted to hold on to their influence on agendas of the Conference through a secretariat that was closer to their own concerns. Overall, the suitability of a secretariat with a wide range of functions and a large number of staff members was doubted.

Finally, however, parliamentarians agreed on what appeared to be the bottom line, not only regarding the Conference in general, but also regarding the secretariat: 'We wanted something light and flexible'.[63] While the Conference takes place two times a year (each rotating presidency hosts one conference), it is organised by the host parliament 'in close cooperation' with the European Parliament. In practice, the Presidency parliament, in close cooperation with the European Parliament and with the preceding and following Presidencies, works to prepare the Conference and, when necessary, to coordinate positions on current or urgent matters linked to the Conference.[64] In the case of the Cyprus Conference 2012, coordination between the host and the European Parliament was said to be smooth. Also, in the case of the Irish Conference 2013, the coordination was said to be good.[65] Hence, the conference is not run by a centralised secretariat. Rather, the hosting parliament coordinates with the European Parliament the agenda of each Conference. The review process concluded: 'for the sake of efficiency and in order to guarantee cost effectiveness and the involvement of all delegations to the Inter-Parliamentary Conference, the establishment of a permanent secretariat as well as any other form of institutionalization is considered inappropriate'.[66]

When analysing the precise content and scope of the issues addressed, delineated by previously agreed agendas, it becomes clear that Conference Presidencies have a tendency to address particular external action challenges in view of their own interests. Both the Cypriot (September 2012) and Lithuanian Presidency (September 2013) addressed the Arab Spring, the Southern Neighbourhood and the Eastern Neighbourhood, while the Irish Presidency (March 2013) focused on the 'comprehensive approach to instability in Africa—the experience of the Horn of Africa', the human rights situation in Russia, and the broader EU objectives concerning the 'Middle Eastern Peace Process'.[67] The Greek Conference in April 2014

[63] Interviews, February 2013.

[64] See also Synopsis of the Proceedings of the Interparliamentary Conference in Athens, 3–4 April 2014 at: www.ipex.eu/IPEXL-WEB/euspeakers/getspeakers.do?type=082dbcc5420d8f48014247cca6f04248.

[65] Interviews, February 2013.

[66] ibid.

[67] Conclusions of the Inter-Parliamentary Conference for the Common Foreign and Security Policy and the Common Security and Defence Policy, Dublin, 24–25 March 2013, para 7.

focused on 'security challenges in Southern and Eastern Europe' and 'current priorities for the CFSP and CSDP, including the situation in Ukraine'.[68] The latest Conferences in Rome and Riga, in Autumn 2014 and Spring 2015 respectively, paid particular attention to 'the Mediterranean and the crises at the borders', the 'Libya crisis', 'state of play of the European Neighborhood Policy' and 'European Common Security and Defence Policy and NATO—better cooperation in view of the new security challenges'.[69]

Obviously, the Conference runs the risk of becoming incoherent and addressing various issues linked to special concerns of the Presidencies. At the same time, in discussing Conference agendas with national parliaments beforehand, the role of the European Parliament can be seen as a corrective one here (see below, Section IV.E).

Interparliamentary cooperation and accountability are affected by shortened public budgets: organisations cut spending which, in turn, impacts upon the employment of staff and maintenance of resources. The closure of the WEU and the interparliamentary WEU Assembly cannot be understood solely as a functional 'friendly takeover' by the EU in the field of security and defence: it was also a means to cut expenses. Taking this into account, international organisations have to justify their existence in terms of their functional and substantial added value. More concretely, they have to justify their costs in view of their overall organisational policy output. Hence, interparliamentary cooperation and accountability will be dependent, in part, upon how much stakeholders are willing to invest in interparliamentary endeavours. If stakeholders are not willing to invest financially, this can have an impact on the organisation and working methods of interparliamentary cooperation.

E. Institutional Arrangements and Interparliamentary Action: Parliamentary Interactions, But Lack of Accountability?

The first 'Interparliamentary Conference for the Common Foreign and Security Policy and the Common Security and Defence Policy' decided upon the Rules of Procedure. The Rules of Procedure underline the aims of the Conference:

> 1.1 The Inter-Parliamentary Conference shall provide a framework for the exchange of information and best practices in the area of CFSP and CSDP, to enable national Parliaments and the European Parliament to be fully informed when carrying out their respective roles in this policy area.
>
> 1.2 The Inter-Parliamentary Conference shall debate matters of Common Foreign and Security Policy, including Common Security and Defence Policy.
>
> 1.3 The Inter-Parliamentary Conference shall replace the Conference of Foreign Affairs Committee Chairpersons (COFACC) and the Conference of Defence Affairs Committee Chairpersons (CODACC). Taking into account these matters dealt with by the Conference, Parliaments shall freely and autonomously decide on the composition of their delegations.

[68] See also Synopsis of the Proceedings of the Interparliamentary Conference in Athens, 3–4 April 2014 at: www.ipex.eu/IPEXL-WEB/euspeakers/getspeakers.do?type=082dbcc5420d8f48014247cca6f04248.

[69] See Programme of the Inter-Parliamentary Conference for the Common Foreign and Security Policy and the Common Security and Defence Policy, Rome, 5–7 November 2014, at: www.ipex.eu/IPEXL-WEB/euspeakers/getspeakers.do?id=082dbcc5465372690146f166b8b1146e, and Programme of the Inter-Parliamentary Conference for the Common Foreign and Security Policy and the Common Security and Defence Policy, Riga, 4–6 March 2015, at: www.ipex.eu/IPEXL-WEB/euspeakers/getspeakers.do?type=082dbcc5420d8f48014247cca6f04248.

1.4 The Inter-Parliamentary Conference may in accordance with the procedures laid down in article 7 adopt conclusions on matters related to the CFSP and CSDP of the EU. The conclusions do not bind national Parliaments or the European Parliament or prejudge their positions.[70]

These stated aims point to the Conference's ambition to move towards an 'exchange of information' within parliamentary cooperation. Parliamentarians are to debate and to take non-binding decisions. Moreover, the Conference foresees that 'best practices' shall be identified. Interestingly, these aims seem to be in line with the comparative approach taken by the WEU Assembly, identified above. Ideally, through the work of the Conference, parliaments are to 'be enabled' and 'to be fully informed when carrying out their respective roles'.[71]

Overall, the Rules of Procedure indicate an exchange of information rather than an active networking aiming to convince and build support for multi-lateral security policies. However, using the Conference to network and build support for multi-lateral security policies cannot be ruled out. Talking to European Parliament officials, it becomes evident that the European Parliament does not see its role in the Conference only as one of advocating European cooperation through information sharing.[72] Rather, it wants to contribute to a 'culture on security' which, according to European Parliament officials, is currently absent in the EU.[73] From this point of view, a collection of foreign and security policy tools need to be assessed, and 'win-win-situations' to be identified.[74] In that respect, the European Parliament and national parliaments who generally support a common European approach towards security imitate efforts of like-minded governments on the executive level. Furthermore, whereas views from within national parliaments are relatively sceptical about gains for accountability via the Conference,[75] the European Parliament does see an added value for such accountability.[76] In view of its expected gains for 'policy support' and 'democratic accountability', it has to face different attitudes on the side of national parliaments. The compromise of the Rules of Procedure and its focus on 'exchange of information' also needs to be seen in this light.

From the second Conference onwards, a small number of so-called 'workshops' have been held in addition to the plenary meetings. This implies that alongside the plenary meeting, members of the Conference can exchange their views on more specialised issues in smaller settings. Discussions in the workshops are, however, not prepared through special rapporteurs or input by the secretariat. Rather, parliamentarians decide on the spot which workshop they want to attend.[77] Overall, workshop conclusions are non-binding without any accompanying reports or recommendations. In one workshop in Dublin 2013, the parliamentarians discussed 'the Middle East peace process' and upon the request of the European Parliament another workshop dealt with the 'comprehensive approach to instability in Africa—the experience of the Horn of Africa' (see above).[78] The latter topic

[70] Article 1.1, 1.2, 1.3, Rules of Procedure.
[71] Article 1.1. Rules of Procedure.
[72] Interviews, February 2013.
[73] ibid.
[74] ibid.
[75] ibid.
[76] ibid.
[77] Interviews, February 2013.
[78] Interviews, February 2013.

mirrors the European Parliament's current concern regarding the comprehensiveness of the EU's external action and the question of how the many instruments of the EU, including military and civilian crisis management and other external relations instruments, can be most effectively used in cases like the Horn of Africa or the Sahel region. It also indicates the Parliament's intention to link CFSP/CSDP with other policy fields and instruments, beyond a purely intergovernmental understanding of CFSP/CSDP.

Interactions in the field of human rights provide another example of active exchanges. The Conference has dealt with human rights on a number of occasions and has thus proven to be an arena where human rights policy is dealt with in the context of foreign and security policy. The first dialogue between the European Parliament, national parliaments, and High Representative Catherine Ashton about the effective implementation of the Strategic Framework on Human Rights was held at the Cyprus Conference 2012.[79] The High Representative and parliaments agreed to talk about human rights issues in the subsequent Conferences in Dublin and Vilnius in 2013.[80] For example, at the Vilnius IPC in September 2013, the High Representative addressed the question of human rights in the Eastern Partnership. In the run up to the Vilnius Eastern Partnership Summit in late 2013, the High Representative underlined the importance of the implementation of human rights in the Eastern Partnership, with a particular view on Ukraine.[81] In the end, the Vilnius Conference conclusions underlined the role of human rights, not only in the Eastern Partnership but also in the 'comprehensive approach of the EU.[82] Moreover, the document stressed that EU 'strategic partnerships must be based upon a common vision, not least a commitment to democracy and human rights, and should be reviewed regularly including through parliamentary cooperation'.[83]

Alongside exchanges with national parliaments, the European Parliament is interested in interparliamentary scrutiny in CSDP matters. In this domain, its role remains relatively limited. In this respect, it is worth mentioning that the High Representative can be invited 'to the meetings of the Inter-Parliamentary Conference to set out the priorities and strategies of the EU in the area of CFSP and CSDP'.[84] At the same time that the High Representative's relationship with the European Parliament has been tightened in Brussels, her presence may rather have added value for national parliaments, who hardly have the opportunity to get in contact with the High Representative in national capitals. After the first appearance and participation of the High Representative at the inaugural Conference in Cyprus, it was believed that her presence would become a given during future Conferences.[85] The fact that

[79] First Meeting of the Interparliamentary Conference on Common Foreign Policy and Security Policy and on Common Security and Defence Policy. Second Part: Current developments in the area of CFSP and CSDP—Military and non-military operations of the EU, Exchange of opinions with the High Representative for CFSP issues, Baroness Catherine Ashton, Paphos, 9–10.9.2012.

[80] Conclusions of the Interparliamentary Conference for the Common Foreign and Security Policy and the Common Security and Defence Policy, 4–6.9.2013, Vilnius.

[81] European Union, Remarks by EU High Representative Catherine Ashton to the Interparliamentary Conference (IPC), Vilnius, 5.9.2013 (A 443/13) 6.9.2013, p 5.

[82] Conclusions of the Interparliamentary Conference for the Common Foreign and Security Policy and the Common Security and Defence Policy, 4–6.9.2013, Vilnius, para 9.

[83] Conclusions of the Interparliamentary Conference for the Common Foreign and Security Policy and the Common Security and Defence Policy, para 10.

[84] Art 2.3 Rules of Procedure.

[85] Interviews February 2013.

the High Representative attends the Gymnich Meetings of the EU Foreign Affairs ministers, which are planned by the rotating Presidency before and/or after the IPC, helps to facilitate her presence. In Dublin at the Conference of 24–25 March 2013, the High Representative spoke once again about priorities in CFSP/CSDP and about exchanging views with participating members.[86] During the Conference in Athens on the 3–4 April 2014, the High Representative informed the parliamentarians about latest developments, including those in Ukraine.[87] In Rome and Riga, in Autumn 2014 and Spring 2015 respectively, the new High Representative, Federica Mogherini, made her first appearances in the Conference, addressing priorities, strategies and tasks of CFSP/CSDP.[88]

Overall, however, the Conference is yet to develop a profile for how it can actually contribute to democratic accountability in CFSP and CSDP. The identification of best practices in the current review process positively highlighted 'the consistent participation of the High Representative in the Inter-Parliamentary Conference [as] both fruitful as well as useful to the debate on the priorities and strategies of the EU in the area of CFSP-CSDP'.[89] In general, the best practices also highlight that there should be a 'balance from lengthy plenary presentations by the speakers to more time for questions and answers, in particular between delegates … to ensure that each Parliament/Chamber present is able to contribute during each debate'.[90]

On a first look, the informal setting of the Conference, while perhaps benefiting debate and exchange mechanisms, seems to undermine efforts of proper parliamentary control and scrutiny. At the same time, and related to the fact that the Conference will be organised in the country of the rotating Presidency, there will be exchanges not only with the High Representative, but also with national executives. This is a theme that was already developed at the first Conference in Cyprus and appeared in the preliminary schedule of the Conference in Dublin in May 2013. In the future, Ministers of Foreign Affairs and Defence will be invited to inform national and European parliamentarians about their views on general and more specific themes of European foreign and security policy.[91] As such, hosting parliaments will have an interest to offer exchanges with their domestic ministers.[92] In the long term, this could imply that parliamentarians are able to gain a comparative view on national executives' perceptions on EU foreign and security policy. However, given the limited tools of the Conference in terms of scrutinising measures, the first impacts of parliamentary-executive exchanges might be on exchanges of views and supporting the ongoing quest for a security culture within the EU.

[86] See also the Dublin conference programme at: www.parleu2013.ie/meetings/interparliamentary-conference-on-common-foreign-and-security-policy-cfsp-and-common-defence-and-security-policy-cdsp/.

[87] See also Synopsis of the Proceedings of the Interparliamentary Conference in Athens, 3–4 April 2014 at www.ipex.eu/IPEXL-WEB/euspeakers/getspeakers.do?type=082dbcc5420d8f48014247cca6f04248.

[88] See Programme of the Interparliamentary Conference for the Common Foreign and Security Policy and the Common Security and Defence Policy, Rome, 5–7 November 2014, at: www.ipex.eu/IPEXL-WEB/euspeakers/getspeakers.do?id=082dbcc5465372690146f166b8b1146e, and Programme of the Interparliamentary Conference for the Common Foreign and Security Policy and the Common Security and Defence Policy, Riga, 4–6 March 2015, at: www.ipex.eu/IPEXL-WEB/euspeakers/getspeakers.do?type=082dbcc5420d8f48014247cca6f04248.

[89] ibid.

[90] ibid.

[91] Interview, February 2013.

[92] ibid.

V. CONCLUDING REMARKS

This chapter started with the assumption that three different *driving factors* can explain inter-parliamentary cooperation in European security governance, with a special focus on CFSP/CSDP. In the first place, parliamentary cooperation could be seen as a response to the need of members of parliaments to exchange information and to arrive at a mutual understanding in EU security governance. Secondly, parliamentary cooperation could be seen as a way of fostering parliamentary networks that help to enhance the EU security frameworks. Thirdly, interparliamentary cooperation in EU security governance could be seen as being driven by the need to enhance the democratic accountability of otherwise uncontrolled security policies. While the first two driving factors proved to correspond to realities, the third one appears to be a much less influential driving force for interparliamentary cooperation. However, it may be observed that the European Parliament seems to interpret the Conference as a setting in which a security culture—and even greater democratic accountability—can be fostered amongst parliaments.

Against this background we also identified four factors that concretely *shape* parliamentary cooperation and accountability in European security governance: (i) a (lack of) solid Treaty legal foundation on the basis of which parliamentary cooperation can blossom; (ii) status questions concerning the parliamentary cooperation framework, in addition to status and membership questions concerning the parliaments involved; (iii) a (lack of) common understanding among parliaments regarding what parliamentary cooperation should achieve; and (iv) financial constraints.

The lack of a solid Treaty legal basis not only invites parliaments to argue about the actual purpose of the Conference, but it also means that, after all, the Conference will be interpreted merely as an informal (non-binding) arrangement (in line with Protocol No 1 to the Lisbon Treaty). Status questions have also impacted upon the final arrangements. The hard-fought compromise between the European Parliament and national parliaments regarding a formal formula for the size of delegations has been somewhat undermined by the parliaments' practice of sending parliamentarians very flexibly. Indeed, most delegations sent by parliaments have been incomplete, being composed of fewer than six participants. Again, this situation is linked to the informal 'light' construction of the Conference: why would one need to have formal 'delegations' and 'seats' in the Conference in the first place, if the conclusions are consensual and non-binding? Moreover, status questions have impacted upon the question of where the secretariat should be located and where Conferences should be held. Finally, it has become evident that different understandings of the purpose of the Conference as well as financial constraints have impacted upon its final shape. On the one hand, from the beginning, financial constraints ruled out the option of a 'real' secretariat of the Conference. Further, the working mechanisms of the Conference point to a very 'light' structure, without the possibility of preparatory work or reports which would help to shape discussions. On the other hand, different understandings matter when it comes to the organisation of the Conferences themselves. In light of the current evidence, the European Parliament is likely to propose one workshop topic to the hosting Presidency, while the national parliaments will also introduce topics close to their own interests. The same holds true for the exchange of views with the High Representative and national executives.

13

The Interparliamentary Conference on Stability, Economic Coordination and Governance in the European Union (the 'Article 13 Conference')

IAN COOPER

I. INTRODUCTION: A WORK IN PROGRESS

THIS CHAPTER TELLS of the genesis and early history of the EU's newest Interparliamentary Conference (IPC), created in 2013 to discuss and oversee the new regime of economic governance that has arisen in the wake of the financial crisis. It is commonly called the 'Article 13 Conference' because the impetus for its creation was Article 13 of the Treaty on Stability, Coordination and Governance in the EMU (the 'TSCG', also known as the 'Fiscal Compact'), which foresaw that the representatives of the relevant committees of the European Parliament (EP) and national parliaments (NPs) would come together in a conference 'to discuss budgetary policies and other issues covered by this Treaty'. In fact, there was considerable debate over what the conference should be called, and its first four meetings took place under four different names.[1] While the choice of name may seem a trivial matter, it has a bearing on which substantive issues should be discussed at the conference. Should the conference focus narrowly on the budgetary rules arising

[1] These were the 'Interparliamentary Conference on Economic and Financial Governance of the European Union' (October 2013, Vilnius), the 'Interparliamentary Conference on Economic Governance of the European Union' (January 2014, Brussels), the 'Interparliamentary Conference Under Article 13 of the Fiscal Compact' (September 2014, Rome), and the 'Conference under Article 13 of the Treaty on Stability, Coordination and Governance in the Economic and Monetary Union' (February 2015, Brussels). When this chapter had already been finalised, this Interparliamentary Conference eventually adopted its rules of procedure in November 2015.

from the Fiscal Compact, or should it also tackle broader financial issues? A narrow remit is implied by the title employed in Rome ('Interparliamentary Conference Under Article 13 of the Fiscal Compact') whereas the Vilnius title ('Interparliamentary Conference on Economic and Financial Governance') implies a broader sphere of concern. This issue was tentatively resolved by the EU Speakers' Conference which, at its meeting in Rome in April 2015, decided that the new conference should be called, 'Interparliamentary Conference on Stability, Economic Coordination and Governance in the European Union'.[2] Despite this resolution, the controversy over the conference's name is emblematic of deeper disagreements over its nature and purpose, which have yet to be resolved.

Surprisingly, the principal controversy that dogged the early days of the Article 13 Conference was not an ideological debate about EU economic policy—ie, right vs left, pro- vs anti-austerity, ordo-liberalism vs Keynesianism—but rather an institutional debate about how the structure and functioning of the new conference should be organised. Around the time of the creation of the conference, it was possible to summarise this controversy as a dispute between two positions: on one side was the EP and a small number of NPs (including Germany's) favouring a weak conference with a narrow scope; and on the other side was a larger group of NPs (including those of Lithuania and France) favouring a strong conference with a broad scope.[3] Nearly two years later, this debate was still unresolved, but a more nuanced picture could be discerned from a closer examination of NPs' evolving views regarding the conference. The differing preferences of the various parliaments regarding the institutional structure and functioning of the conference could be found in abundant detail in their positions regarding the conference's Rules of Procedure.[4] These reveal that

[2] For the sake of brevity, however, it will be referred to as the 'Article 13 Conference' throughout this chapter.

[3] See I Cooper, 'Parliamentary oversight of the EU after the crisis: on the creation of the "Article 13" interparliamentary conference' (2014) 21 SOG Working Papers, available at: sog.luiss.it/sites/sog.luiss.it/files/SOG%20Working%20Papers%20WP21-2014%20Cooper.pdf.

[4] Most, but not all, of the relevant documents are publicly accessible, either on national parliaments' websites or on the IPEX website, which serves as an online archive of documentary materials pertaining to the EU Speakers' Conference, the CFSP-CSDP Conference, and the Article 13 Conference (ie, all the major EU IPCs except for COSAC). They form five groups of documents, ordered chronologically. First (early 2013), most parliamentary opinions on the Article 13 Conference that were voiced prior to its establishment may be accessed from the webpage dedicated to the EU Speakers Conference in Nicosia: www.ipex.eu/IPEXL-WEB/conference/getconference.do?id=082dbcc53782a3ff0137bbfaafe71dbb. This includes the Presidency Conclusions of the EU Speakers' Conference (held in Nicosia) that set the general parameters for the conference. Secondly (late 2013), documents relating to the first meeting in Vilnius in October 2013 are available on the website of the Lithuanian parliament: www.lrs.lt/intl/presidency.show?theme=284&lang=2&p_eventguid=0f6147e3-6125-40b9-93d8-edc7c31e085f. This includes, most importantly, a document prepared by the *Seimas* of the draft Rules of Procedure incorporating the amendments proposed by other parliaments prior to the meeting ('Draft RoP with Amendments 2013'). Thirdly (early 2014), further amendments submitted to the Greek parliament are compiled on the IPEX webpage dedicated to the Article 13 Conference: www.ipex.eu/IPEXL-WEB/conference/getconference.do?id=082dbcc5428b1a43014298b2999d0f06. Fourthly (late 2014), the Italian parliament prepared a new text of the Rules of Procedure, including different options for controversial passages, to facilitate the debate that took place at the Rome meeting of the Article 13 Conference. A number of proposed amendments from various parliaments were gathered together in a single document ('RoP Amendments File 2014'). These documents were circulated at the Rome meeting but not uploaded to the website, and so are not readily available to the public (but were obtained by this author). Fifthly (early 2015), various parliaments proposed further amendments to a compromise draft produced by the Italian parliament in December 2014, which were brought together in a single document ('RoP Amendments File 2015'). The EU Speakers' Conference, meeting in Rome in April 2015, agreed a set of principles regarding the Rules of Procedure of the Article 13 Conference in its Presidency Conclusions ('EU Speakers' Conference Rome Conclusions'). These documents are available at: www.ipex.eu/IPEXL-WEB/conference/getconference.do?id=082dbcc54a393144014a4d75e8690dec.

there were not just two positions but several; moreover, while the principal line of conflict was still over institutional questions, it was cross-cut by an undercurrent of ideological conflict over EU economic policy. In practical terms, these differences amount to a debate over whether the Article 13 Conference should be merely a discussion forum in which parliamentarians converse about the economic policies of the EU, or an oversight body that exercises a kind of joint scrutiny over the new regime of EU economic governance.

While it is useful to study the whole range of opinions among the various EU parliaments, the views of three parliaments in particular—the EP, the German parliament, and the French parliament—will receive close attention here because they embodied strongly held, contrasting views concerning the future of the Article 13 Conference. The preferences of the EP and the German parliament generally coincided, in that both preferred the conference to be a discussion forum. But their ultimate concerns were different. The EP's principal concern was institutional: it wished to avoid the creation of any new assembly that could threaten its position as the preeminent parliamentary body at EU-level. Therefore the EP's preferences for the Article 13 Conference were to deny it any independent decision-making authority or appearance of democratic legitimacy, while at the same time ensuring that the conference recognised the EP's special status among EU parliaments. But the EP was less concerned about ideology: while it sometimes proposed substantive moderation in the economic policies of the EU,[5] it was much more engaged in insisting that such policies should be brought within the realm of oversight of the EP. In the same vein, the EP wanted to limit the substantive focus of the Article 13 Conference so it would not encroach on the field of EU economic policies already subject to the EP's own oversight. The German parliament's ultimate concern, by contrast, was ideological: it aimed for the adoption across the EU of economic policies premised on fiscal discipline and structural reform—policies exemplified by the TSCG—and saw the Article 13 Conference as a vehicle for the promotion of that policy. Thus the EP and the German parliament both believed that the conference should be merely a discussion forum rather than a decision-making body, but for different reasons: the EP wanted to avoid the creation of an institutional rival, and the German parliament wanted a policy discussion on its approved ideological terms.

The French parliament's view was opposed to the other two, principally on institutional grounds but also to some extent on ideological grounds. It thought that the Article 13 Conference should be able to take political decisions, at least in the form of the adoption of non-binding conclusions, and that it should have a semblance of democratic legitimacy. Moreover, the French parliament proposed that the Article 13 Conference should exercise an oversight function with respect to EU economic policy: the meetings should be timed to coincide with key dates in the European Semester,[6] and the top officials responsible for EU economic policy should be invited to speak and take questions from the assembled parliamentarians. This was very different from the German view, which saw the conference more as an opportunity for NPs to scrutinise one another's economic and budget plans, rather than to oversee the top EU officials. Ideologically, the French parliament did not by any means advocate a radical policy shift, but only suggested that the prevailing fiscal orthodoxy should be relaxed, for example by taking the 'social dimension' into account.

[5] See C Fasone, 'European Economic Governance and Parliamentary Representation. What Place for the European Parliament?' (2014) 20 *European Law Journal* 164.

[6] See also D Jančić, Parliamentary Involvement in the Economic and Monetary Union after the Euro Crisis, Ch 10 in this volume.

The remainder of this chapter is organised as follows. In order to contextualise the Article 13 Conference within this volume, Section II explains how it relates to the other major interparliamentary conferences (IPCs) within the EU. Section III revisits the document that provided the foundation for the Article 13 Conference, the TSCG, in order to assess its suitability as a platform for an interparliamentary debate on EU economic policy. Next (Section IV) there is a short history of the Article 13 Conference in operation, with a brief summary of its first four meetings, which took place between October 2013 and February 2015. After that (Section V) there is a closer examination of various parliaments' opinions regarding the Rules of Procedure of the conference, with a particular focus on the EP, the French parliament and the German parliament. Finally (Section VI), the chapter concludes by bringing the story up to date, explaining the outcome of the discussion of the Rules of Procedure that took place at the EU Speakers' Conference in Rome in April 2015. This resolved some outstanding issues regarding the Article 13 Conference, but it did not resolve the basic question of whether it ought to be a discussion forum or an oversight body.

II. RELATIONS WITH THE OTHER INTERPARLIAMENTARY CONFERENCES

This volume allows us to put the Article 13 Conference into the context of interparliamentary cooperation in the EU generally, and it illuminates in particular its relationship with the other three major IPCs—COSAC, the Conference on the Common Foreign and Security Policy and the Common Security and Defence Policy (the CFSP-CSDP Conference), and the EU Speakers' Conference.[7] Much of the controversy about the institutional design of the Article 13 Conference may be seen as a debate on whether it should be modelled more closely on COSAC or on the CFSP-CSDP Conference: while many NPs (such as the Lithuanian Seimas) preferred the model of COSAC, which enjoys greater institutional permanence and autonomy, the EP preferred the model of the CFSP-CSDP Conference, which is subject to greater influence by the EP.

To the casual observer, COSAC and the CFSP-CSDP Conference may seem broadly alike in that they are both large meetings of representatives of all the EU parliaments that take place twice a year in the Member State holding the Council presidency; yet there are significant institutional differences. COSAC, which has been around much longer (since 1989), enjoys greater institutional permanence and autonomy, in particular with regard to five attributes: it actually has *four* meetings each year, with two during each six-month presidency (there is not only a plenary meeting but also a preparatory chairs' meeting); its functioning is aided by a well-established presidency *troika* of previous, current and upcoming Presidency parliaments (which is actually a *quartet*, as it also includes the EP); it has a staff secretariat which, among other things, helps to arrange meetings and produces

[7] See the respective chapters in this volume. In addition, on COSAC, see M Knudsen and Y Carl, 'COSAC—Its Role to Date and its Potential in the Future' in G Barrett (ed), *National Parliaments and the European Union: The Constitutional Challenge for the Oireachtas and Other Member State Legislatures* (Dublin, Clarus Press, 2008) 455–83. On the CFSP-CSDP Conference, see A Herranz-Surrallés, 'The EU's Multilevel Parliamentary (Battle) Field: Inter-parliamentary Cooperation and Conflict in Foreign and Security Policy' (2014) 37 *West European Politics* 957–75; A Huff, 'Executive Privilege Reaffirmed? Parliamentary Scrutiny of the CFSP and CSDP' (2015) 38 *West European Politics* 396–415; J Wouters and K Raube, 'Seeking CSDP Accountability Through Interparliamentary Scrutiny' (2012) 47 *The International Spectator: Italian Journal of International Affairs* 149–63.

a bi-annual report; it can adopt some decisions by qualified majority vote (QMV); and it is not institutionally dependent on the EU Speakers' Conference. By contrast, the CFSP-CSDP conference meets just twice a year, its *troika* does not meet regularly (just two of the first six conferences included a *troika* meeting), it has no permanent secretariat, it adopts conclusions only by consensus, and its ongoing operations are subject to review by the Speakers' Conference.[8]

In addition, the EP enjoys a less privileged position within COSAC than within the CFSP-CSDP conference. While the EP has permanent representation in COSAC's *troika* and secretariat, it otherwise has a status equal to each of the 28 NPs. By contrast, the Rules of Procedure of the CFSP-CSDP conference state that the EP can send a much larger delegation—16 MEPs, as opposed to six members from each NP (Article 2.1). It specifies that the conference may take place not only in the country of the Presidency parliament but also 'at the European Parliament in Brussels' (Article 3.1)—although up to now this has never happened. Furthermore, it stipulates that the conference 'shall be presided over by the Presidency Parliament, in close cooperation with the European Parliament' (Article 3.2). Even though it is the Presidency parliament that hosts and chairs the meeting, the EP assumes a role much like a 'quasi-co-host' of the meeting.[9] For example, at the start of each conference there is a place on the programme for opening words of welcome from the chair of the EP's Foreign Affairs Committee.[10] In similar ways, the EP's preferences for the Article 13 Conference (discussed in Section V below) reflect the fact that the CFSP-CSDP Conference is its preferred model.

Another point of comparison between the Article 13 Conference and other IPCs concerns its subject-matter. In addition to the two long-standing IPCs that deal with issues of European scrutiny and cooperation generally, COSAC and the EU Speakers' Conference, the Article 13 Conference is—along with the CFSP-CSDP Conference—one of two new IPCs that have a functionally-specific policy focus. Yet the subject-matter of the Article 13 Conference is quite ill-defined in comparison to that of the CFSP-CSDP Conference: the function of the latter is to enable the discussion and oversight of an established set of EU policies that are well-defined in the Treaty of Lisbon, and are in large part executed by a particular EU agency, the European External Action Service. The Article 13 Conference, by contrast, finds its impetus in the TSCG, a non-EU treaty that does not define the whole field of EU economic policy but merely sets out a specific set of policy measures within that field—measures which are not necessarily conducive to meaningful parliamentary oversight (see Section III, below).

Finally, a further aspect of the relations between the IPCs is illustrated by the early history of the Article 13 Conference: it demonstrates the growing importance of the EU Speakers' Conference as the IPC that establishes and supervises the development of new forms of interparliamentary cooperation. The Speakers' Conference established the basic parameters for the Article 13 Conference at its Nicosia conference in 2013, much as it had done for the CFSP-CSDP Conference at its Warsaw meeting in 2012. Furthermore, after the Article 13

[8] Documents relating to the CFSP-CSDP Conference, including its Rules of Procedure and the Programmes of the meetings, can be found on the IPEX website: www.ipex.eu/IPEXL-WEB/conference/getconference.do?type=082dbcc5420d8f48014247cca6f04248.

[9] I am grateful to an anonymous national parliament official for pointing this out to me.

[10] At all six conferences that have taken place thus far (between late 2012 and early 2015) this has been the MEP Elmar Brok.

Conference failed to agree upon its own Rules of Procedure at its first four meetings, the Speakers' Conference revisited the Article 13 Conference at its 2015 meeting in Rome, and provided further guidelines as to its structure and functioning (see Section VI, below).

III. THE TREATY ON STABILITY, COORDINATION AND GOVERNANCE AS A PLATFORM FOR INTERPARLIAMENTARY DEBATE

The Article 13 Conference is an outgrowth of the TSCG, which was negotiated between November 2011 and February 2012 and signed in March 2012 by 25 EU Member States, and which entered into force in January 2013. The original intention had been to adopt a treaty that would simply amend the existing EU treaties, but this was not possible as a unanimous agreement could not be reached; a new stand-alone treaty was adopted under international law instead.[11] The purpose of the TSCG, which was promoted in particular by the German government, was to strengthen the Stability and Growth Pact by requiring Eurozone Member States to entrench stringent fiscal rules into national law, preferably in national constitutions. It should be emphasised that, despite its name, the 'Fiscal Compact', as it is sometimes called, did not in any way strengthen the fiscal capacity of the EU itself; it only strengthened the power of the EU to enforce a set of fiscal rules that apply to the Member States.

The TSCG was signed at the height of the sovereign debt crisis in the EU, when the idea had firmly taken hold that its root cause was fiscal profligacy, and that therefore the correct policy response was greater fiscal discipline. This was, it should be said, a dubious diagnosis of the problem: with the exception of Greece, in Member States worst hit by the crisis, high public deficits were the consequence, not the cause, of the financial crisis.[12] Earlier in the crisis, there was a period of about 12 months—from mid-2009 to mid-2010—when EU policy in this area had actually moved in a Keynesian direction, towards an economic policy of fiscal stimulus. But by the time the TSCG was signed, EU policy was once again focused squarely on fiscal consolidation, with the reigning idea that this would restore 'confidence' and, ultimately, growth. The new EU regime of enforced fiscal orthodoxy included not only the TSCG, an international treaty, but also two packages of ordinary EU-level legislation from this period, the 'Six-Pack' and the 'Two-Pack', which were intended to achieve the same ends by establishing systems of fiscal and macroeconomic surveillance and budgetary coordination.

It should be noted that the specific substantive measures contained in Titles III, IV, and V of the TSCG (concerned with stability, coordination and governance, respectively) do not provide much material for wide-ranging policy debate at an interparliamentary conference. Title III ('Fiscal Compact') was the heart of the treaty, requiring each Contracting Party whose currency is the euro to incorporate a 'balanced budget' rule and a self-correcting mechanism into national law, subject to review by the European Court of Justice. This one-time legal reform, which was completed within a year of the TSCG's entry into force, would

[11] The UK and the Czech Republic have never signed the TSCG. Neither has Croatia, which acceded to the EU in July 2013, after the TSCG entered into force.

[12] For an extended critique of EU policy during this period, see ch 3 of M Blyth, *Austerity: The History of a Dangerous Idea* (Oxford, Oxford University Press, 2013).

seem to provide little basis for discussions over the ensuing years within a permanent interparliamentary conference. Title IV ('Economic Policy Coordination and Convergence') did not actually create any new mechanisms of economic policy coordination which could in turn be discussed and overseen by an interparliamentary conference; rather, it merely affirmed the Contracting Parties' commitment to coordinate their economic policies, and to make use of existing mechanisms such as Eurozone-specific measures (under Article 136 TFEU) or enhanced cooperation. By contrast, Title V ('Governance of the Euro Area') did create a new mechanism for the governance of the single currency, in that it institutionalised the regular 'Euro Summit' of Heads of State and Government of Eurozone Member States. But Title V, unlike Titles III and IV, specified that the EP would have at least a minimal role of parliamentary involvement in this area: the President of the EP 'may be invited to be heard' at the Euro Summit, and the President of the Euro Summit must present a report to the EP after each meeting. By contrast, the treaty did not specify any role for an interparliamentary conference to oversee the Euro Summit.

Indeed, despite the fact that the Article 13 Conference has its origins in the TSCG, the specific substantive measures contained in the treaty have rarely, if ever, been discussed at the conference. For example, in all of the debates that took place during the first four meetings of the Article 13 Conference, there was never—not once—a discussion either about (1) how states are incorporating the balanced budget rule into national law, or (2) how the Euro Summit is functioning. Yet these are arguably the only two concrete institutional changes actually mandated by the TSCG, apart from the creation of the Article 13 Conference itself.

It is important to point this out because one of the ongoing disputes about the Article 13 Conference concerns its scope—specifically, whether it should be narrowly focused on the terms of the TSCG/Fiscal Compact, or whether it should also address broader economic and financial issues. Those favouring the former approach, including the German Bundestag, sometimes imply that the conference is legally or constitutionally bound to adhere to a narrow scope because it must be confined to matters covered by the TSCG. As Norbert Lammert, Speaker of the Bundestag, wrote in March 2014,

> Finally, with regard to the subjects to be dealt with by the Conference, I wish to reiterate that it was decided by consensus in Vilnius that the meetings should deal with economic and financial policy coordination, as envisaged by the Fiscal Compact.[13]

This is a common view, but the actual text of the TSCG provides little support for it. The term 'Fiscal Compact' is often used not specifically to refer to the TSCG in whole or in part, but as shorthand for the whole regime of economic governance put in place to respond to the crisis; Mr Lammert seems to be using it in this way. While the TSCG is part of this regime, it is of far less practical importance than the Six-Pack and the Two-Pack, measures passed through the normal EU legislative process.[14] These provisions set out the specific measures of budgetary surveillance and coordination with which the Member States must comply, within an annual policy cycle—the European Semester. In reality, it is these legislative measures, which are not part of the TSCG per se, that set the terms of the 'economic

[13] Letter from the President of the German Bundestag to the President of the Hellenic Parliament, 21/03/2014.

[14] For an argument along these lines, see D Gros and C Alcidi, 'The case of the disappearing Fiscal Compact' (2014) CEPS Commentary. Available at: www.ceps.eu/system/files/Fiscal%20Compact.pdf.

and financial policy coordination' to which Mr Lammert refers. Therefore, those who advocate an Article 13 Conference solely focused on budgetary discipline and structural reform need to be reminded that to narrow the focus in this way is not a legal or constitutional obligation but a political choice.

If the scope of the Article 13 Conference were expanded beyond the terms of the TSCG to include the whole new post-crisis economic regime for the EU, this would raise a broader problem with respect to the ideological range of potential policy options that may be discussed there. Certainly, it is logical to involve NPs in the discussion and oversight of the new budgetary rules, including the Six-Pack and the Two-Pack, as these measures have their most immediate impact on NPs themselves, the institutions that must enact national budgets. It is these legislative instruments, rather than the TSCG, that contain the measures of stability, coordination and governance that most affect national parliaments: 'stability' through the strengthened Stability and Growth Pact, 'coordination' through the European Semester, and 'governance' in the form of the Commission's increased powers of budgetary surveillance. Yet these measures are quite prescriptive, in that they dictate a set of fiscal and economic rules that are largely determinative of policy outcomes, and therefore tend to prevent a wide-ranging discussion of economic policy choices. They seem to preclude, for example, a Keynesian analysis of the sources of the EU's economic crisis, or a set of policy prescriptions premised on fiscal stimulus rather than budget-balancing.[15] In this light, what, exactly, are the gathered parliamentarians supposed to discuss? To put it another way, meaningful political deliberation among parliamentarians is about both *ends* and *means*: what policy outcome do we seek, and what course of action should we take to achieve it? Yet the rules of the EU economic regime are so heavily prescriptive that they seem largely to determine not only the policy ends sought, but even the means required to achieve them.

This broader problem is illuminated if we compare the Article 13 Conference to the other two major IPCs, COSAC and the CFSP-CSDP Conference. There is an argument to be had about whether these IPCs themselves have an oversight function vis-à-vis EU institutions or, on the other hand, they merely enable the sharing of best practices and information which enables individual parliaments to better exercise oversight either of their own governments' conduct of EU affairs (in the case of NPs) or of the EU institutions (in the case of the EP): in practice, each IPC involves a combination of the two. But it is relatively clear in both cases what the object of their oversight is. COSAC excels as a forum in which members of the European Affairs Committees from the various NPs can share information and best practices in monitoring the continuous stream of EU legislation, helping them to oversee, and perhaps control, their respective governments' position regarding particular legislative measures. In a like manner, the CFSP-CSDP Conference enables members of the foreign and defence committees of NPs to exchange information and best practices as regards their oversight of their respective governments' involvement in EU foreign and defence matters. But the conference itself also to some extent directly oversees these EU policies, which largely involve executive (non-legislative) action as performed by a particular EU agency, the European External Action Service, and its head, the High Representative, who always attends the CFSP-CSDP Conference in person to make a statement and answer questions from the assembled parliamentarians.

[15] See Cooper (n 3 above), 16–18.

By contrast, the object of the Article 13 Conference's oversight is genuinely uncertain, and this is the case whether such oversight is understood as exercised by the conference as a whole or by individual parliaments. This is because the EU policy in question, the post-crisis regime of economic governance, is not easily identifiable either as a continuous stream of EU legislation or as the executive actions of an EU agency. Rather, this new economic regime is a set of rules imposed on Member States (by their own consent) placing strictures on their fiscal and economic policies; while these rules were originally passed by EU legislation, they are enforced on an ongoing basis by EU institutions, in particular the Commission, mainly using 'soft' legal instruments such as recommendations, although in the background there lies the threat of very costly sanctions that could be applied by the Council against a persistent rule-breaker. So what should the members of the budget and economics committees of the NPs and the EP focus their attention on when they gather for the Article 13 Conference? Should they be sharing information and best practices as to how best to obey the rules and/or to scrutinise their own governments to ensure they are obeying the rules? By the same logic, should they engage in a kind of 'peer review' of *one another's* economic and fiscal plans to ensure that everyone is obeying the rules? Or, on the other hand, should they *question* the rules? By extension, should they be 'watching the watchers', overseeing the actions of the EU institutions in the course of implementing and enforcing this new economic regime? These are the questions that arise in defining whether the conference is primarily a discussion forum or an oversight body.

IV. THE ARTICLE 13 CONFERENCE: A BRIEF HISTORY

When it was signed in early 2012, the TSCG anticipated the creation of an interparliamentary forum of some kind, but it was initially unclear what form it should take or even how it was to be created. The outcome of these questions was influenced by the successful creation of the CFSP-CSDP Conference, the basic parameters of which were established by the EU Speakers' Conference in Warsaw in April 2012, and which met for the first time in Cyprus in September 2012. Following this precedent, the Speakers' Conference set the parameters for the new Article 13 Conference at its next meeting, in Nicosia in April 2013. In late 2012 and early 2013, various suggestions as to how the conference should be organised were put forward by the EP and by NPs, both individually and in groups; these were sent to the Speaker of the Cypriot Parliament, who would host the meeting. Particularly influential was a 'working paper' of the speakers of the parliaments of the six founding EU Member States and the President of the EP,[16] suggesting that the conference meet twice per year, with at least one meeting held in Brussels and co-hosted and co-chaired by the EP and the

[16] 'Working paper of the meeting of the Speakers of Parliament of the Founding Member States of the European Union and the European Parliament in Luxembourg', 11 January 2013. This working paper also proposed that one conference meeting should take place 'notably before the European Council in June, before or after the adoption of the relevant documents—namely the recommendations on the stability and reform programmes, the orientation of economic policies, the Growth Survey and the Alert Mechanism Report'. This proposed timing was in line with the French parliament's idea of the Article 13 Conference as an oversight body with respect to EU institutions. However, despite the fact that both the EP and the German parliament endorsed the idea of a June conference in this working paper, only the French parliament continued to support the idea later (see Section V, below).

parliament of the Member State holding the Council presidency (the 'Presidency parliament'). This general formula was adopted by the EU Speakers' Conference in Nicosia.

This Conference managed to resolve, at least temporarily, a number of potentially controversial questions regarding the organisation of the conference. It decided, for example, that the parliaments of all EU Member States should attend the conference, even if they have not signed the TSCG and/or they are outside the Eurozone.[17] Furthermore, the Speakers' Conference decided, 'the composition and size of each delegation rests upon each Parliament'. This avoided specifying exactly which parliamentary committees should be represented at the conference (eg budget, finance, social affairs, and/or European affairs), and it also defused a possible argument over whether the EP delegation should be larger than national delegations (as at the CFSP-CSDP conference) or the same size (as at COSAC meetings). Thus, many of the practical questions regarding how the conference should be established and organised were resolved, at least temporarily, in Nicosia; this paved the way for the first Article 13 Conference to take place just a few months later in Vilnius, within the framework of the 'parliamentary dimension' of the Lithuanian presidency of the Council.

A. Vilnius, October 2013

Despite the short notice, the Lithuanian parliament, the Seimas, prepared an ambitious agenda for the Vilnius meeting in October 2013. In addition to wide-ranging discussions of substantive issues, the Seimas proposed that the conference should debate and adopt two documents—the 'Rules of Procedure' setting out its internal operating rules, and a set of 'Conclusions' describing the substantive issues discussed there. This was hardly a radical proposal, considering that just the previous year the first meeting of the CFSP-CSDP conference had adopted 'Rules of Procedure' and 'Conclusions' by consensus. More provocative was the provision in the Seimas's draft Rules of Procedure that the conference may, like COSAC, adopt Conclusions by a three-quarters qualified majority if consensus were unobtainable; this aggravated the EP, which prefers a rule of strict consensus within IPCs, as this affords it a veto over major decisions.

After the Seimas circulated its draft Rules of Procedure, a number of other parliaments suggested amendments on the assumption that the document would be debated and adopted in Vilnius. Yet it elicited a furious response from the EP, in the form of a letter from President Martin Schulz, who objected not only to the inclusion of qualified majority voting but to the very idea of the Article 13 Conference adopting Rules of Procedure and Conclusions at all. This position was supported by the German Bundestag: Norbert Barthle, head of the German delegation to the conference and Spokesperson of the CDU/CSU Parliamentary Group on budget policy, sent a letter stating that it would be 'premature' to adopt Rules of Procedure in Vilnius. Moreover the President of the Bundestag, Norbert Lammert, sent a letter stating that 'the speakers in Nicosia had agreed that the conference should be a … purely advisory body which serves solely as a forum for an inter-parliamentary exchange of views, experience and intent in the field of economic and financial policy', implying that the conference should not adopt Conclusions at all, and certainly

[17] Critically, on this decision, see N Lupo, 'La Conferenza interparlamentare sulla governance economica e finanziaria: la deludente attuazione dell'art. 13 del Fiscal Compact' (2014) 1 *Quaderni costituzionali* 113–15.

not by qualified majority.[18] In the face of these objections, the Seimas removed the debate and adoption of the Rules of Procedure from the agenda—it was replaced with a more general discussion of the 'purpose and vision' of the conference—but left in place the debate and adoption of Conclusions.

In the event, these procedural questions provoked the most discussion in Vilnius, in addition to a substantive agenda that included discussion of post-crisis economic governance, banking union, and budgetary consolidation and structural reform. The Seimas had sought in particular the participation of Olli Rehn, then the Commissioner for Economic and Monetary Affairs and the Euro, as he was the EU official most closely associated with and responsible for the EU policy in this field. Rehn did participate, though not in person but by video-conference, a format which prevented a lively exchange with the assembled parliamentarians. At the beginning of the conference there was a contentious *in camera* meeting of the presidency *troika* (the Irish, Lithuanian, and Greek parliaments) and the EP; the EP and the Seimas clashed over, among other things, the inclusion on the conference agenda of the debate and adoption of Conclusions, with the Irish delegation supporting the Lithuanian position, and the Greek parliament lending tacit support to the EP position (there was no *troika* meeting at the next three Article 13 Conferences.) During the debate over the 'purpose and vision' of the conference, a number of parliamentarians expressed annoyance that the debate on the Rules of Procedure had been removed from the agenda at the behest of the EP. In the meantime, a compromise approach was developing, in which a working group would be given the task of studying the Rules of Procedure and reporting back to a future meeting of the Article 13 Conference. The postponement of debate on the Rules of Procedure was supported by the EP as expressed, for example, in an intervention by Swedish MEP Göran Färm:

> If we shall be able to take our cooperation a step further, and actually develop a joint strategy for a more democratic economic policy in Europe, we have to tread carefully, and find a real consensus approach based on unanimity. It's more important to get it right than to get it quickly … So let's create a good working party to prepare Rules of Procedure to be adopted in January, as a basis for the future effective cooperation between the European Parliament and the national parliaments.[19]

This approach was received sceptically by many national parliamentarians. One Dutch MP, Anne-Wil Lucas, responded that she found it absurd that instead of debating the Rules of Procedure, as originally planned, the conference was having a procedural debate over whether to debate the Rules of Procedure. She effectively accused the EP of obstructing the proceedings.

> We can agree with the Rules of Procedure in their current form, and for us an extra draft from a report is not necessary. And actually I believe for about 28 of the 29 delegations this would be the same. We have indeed an elephant in the room … But that elephant is not the Rules of Procedure; that elephant is the role of the European Parliament in this conference. I believe we have created a Kafkaesque reality where one parliament solely dodges a lengthy procedural discussion on the Rules of Procedure by invoking an even lengthier discussion on the desirability of that discussion. And honestly, I cannot explain that to my citizens. We would like to leave the discussion on procedures behind us so we can actually exchange views on substantial issues.

[18] This correspondence may be found on the website of the Seimas, available at: www.lrs.lt/intl/presidency.show?theme=284&lang=2&p_eventguid=0f6147e3-6125-40b9-93d8-edc7c31e085f.

[19] Video of this exchange may be found on the website of the Seimas, available at: www.lrs.lt/intl/presidency.show?theme=284&lang=2&p_eventguid=0f6147e3-6125-40b9-93d8-edc7c31e085f.

These remarks were greeted with applause from many other national parliamentarians.

In the end, the Rules of Procedure were not adopted in Vilnius. Even so, an agreement was made in principle to begin a 'Vilnius Process' wherein a working group would aim to agree upon Rules of Procedure in 2014, using the Seimas's draft as a basis. Moreover, in the face of opposition from the EP and some others, the conference as a whole did not adopt 'Conclusions'. After a search for a new label, the conference adopted, by consensus, a 'Contribution'—the term normally used to denote the concluding political document adopted by COSAC—to which was eventually annexed a summary of the proceedings of the conference. In addition, the Seimas, acting on its own authority—after a short debate, but without a vote—adopted 'Presidency Conclusions', which is the form of concluding document adopted at the EU Speakers' Conference.[20]

B. Brussels, January 2014

The second Article 13 Conference took place in the EP premises in Brussels, co-chaired by the EP and the Greek parliament. This meeting differed from the one in Vilnius in a number of ways. The Article 13 Conference was held in Brussels in the context of the European Parliamentary Week, a series of interparliamentary meetings that had been held for the first time the previous year, in January 2013. Some national parliaments were dismayed by the organisation of the conference, as they had thought that the Article 13 Conference would either replace the European Parliamentary Week or be entirely separate from it. Instead, the Article 13 Conference had appeared to be subsumed within the European Parliamentary Week, merely one of many interparliamentary meetings hosted by the EP.[21] Another difference from the Vilnius conference is that there was no discussion of the Rules of Procedure, and no Conclusions were adopted: these were left off the agenda entirely. During the opening session, a parliamentarian from the Lithuanian delegation decried the absence of these items from the conference agenda. In response to the Lithuanian complaints, the co-chairs from the Greek parliament and the EP assured them that the Greek parliament would continue the Vilnius Process by making consultations with other national parliaments, with a view to finalising Rules of Procedure under the Italian Presidency in the latter half of 2014.[22] Another difference from Vilnius was that many more top EU officials spoke at the conference: the opening session was addressed by the presidents of the EP, the Council and the Commission. In addition, Olli Rehn, the Economics Commissioner, attended the meeting in person rather than by video-conference, which made for a more lively exchange with the assembled parliamentarians. One national MP whose tough, strident questions were out of place in the otherwise placid atmosphere was Dimitrios Papadimoulis, the sole representative from the Greek Syriza party in attendance at the conference.

[20] See Cooper (n 3 above) 22–23.

[21] See ibid, 14–15.

[22] In February 2014, the chairs of the committees on European and Economic Affairs of the Greek parliament sent a letter to the other parliaments soliciting their suggestions for amendments to the Rules of Procedure, to which numerous parliaments responded. This correspondence may be found on the IPEX website: www.ipex.eu/IPEXL-WEB/conference/getconference.do?id=082dbcc5428b1a43014298b2999d0f06 (accessed 15 June 2015). There was a brief, inconclusive discussion of the Article 13 Conference at the EU Speakers' Conference in Vilnius in April 2014.

C. Rome, September 2014

The third meeting took place in Rome in September 2014. It differed from the previous two in that no Commissioner attended to answer questions about EU policy, because the new Commission had not yet taken office after the EP elections which had taken place in May 2014. As it happens, Olli Rehn did attend the meeting, but by then he had resigned as Commissioner to take up his position as a newly elected MEP, and Vice-President of the EP. The Italian parliament decided to organise the conference sessions much like a series of academic seminars, rather than political exchanges between legislative and executive branches of government.

A debate over the Rules of Procedure was on the agenda of the Rome conference, and the Italian parliament had produced a new draft as a basis for discussion. However, at the outset of the conference the Speaker of the Italian Camera dei Deputati, Laura Boldrini, announced that the Rules of Procedure would not be adopted there, but would instead be approved by the next EU Speakers' Conference, in Rome in the spring of 2015. In pronouncing this, she was putting herself in a position in which she would likely wield considerable influence over the outcome, because she personally would co-preside over that Conference in Rome, along with the speaker of the Italian Senate. This pronouncement meant that the debate on the Rules of Procedure, when it occurred, was robbed of its significance, because no decision was to be taken. During the debate a number of national MPs—including representatives from the French, German, Lithuanian and Polish parliaments—criticised this move, and argued that consensus on the Rules of Procedure was within reach and that the conference could and should adopt its own Rules of Procedure there and then, rather than leave the matter to the Speakers' Conference. The Italians chairing the meeting stuck to their position, however, and received vocal support from two senior MEPs, Olli Rehn (Vice-President of the EP) and Roberto Gualtieri (chair of the ECON committee), who agreed that the decision should be left to the EU Speakers' Conference, which is where matters stood when the meeting came to a close. The Italian parliament promised to consult further and to produce a compromise draft of the Rules of Procedure. A final draft was produced in December 2014, and national parliaments were given until late February 2015 to propose amendments to the new draft. The Rules of Procedure were not discussed at the fourth Article 13 Conference—a request by the Polish parliament to debate them there was rebuffed—as the consultation period was still ongoing and the discussion and possible adoption of the Rules of Procedure was on the agenda of the EU Speakers' Conference in Rome in April 2015 (see Section VI, below).

D. Brussels, February 2015

The fourth meeting took place in Brussels in February 2015, again within the framework of the European Parliamentary Week. Initially, the Latvian parliament, the Saeima, sought to make the Article 13 Conference an entirely separate event from the European Parliamentary Week, and looked for a date in April, close to the time in when Member States must present their National Reform Programmes and their Stability or Convergence Programmes detailing their plans for economic and budgetary policies. This could not be arranged. However, in the event, in contrast to the 2014 European Parliamentary Week, a clearer distinction was made between the Article 13 Conference, which took place on February 4 and was chaired by the Saeima and the EP together, and an event on the previous day, the 'Interparliamentary meeting on the European Semester Cycles 2014 and 2015', hosted and chaired by the EP alone.[23] In organising the two meetings, the EP and the Saeima coordinated to avoid them overlapping thematically, but they also tussled over which top EU officials would attend which meeting, as this could indicate which meeting was more important. The new Commission President, Jean-Claude Juncker, attended the EP meeting, to speak about his investment plan. Having the conference in Brussels turned out to be no guarantee against no-shows: Donald Tusk, European Council President, was supposed to attend the EP meeting but cancelled; and Eurogroup President Jeroen Dijsselbloem was scheduled to attend the Article 13 Conference but cancelled at the last minute. The story of one invited speaker reveals an interesting difference in approach between the EP and the Saeima. Jyrki Katainen, Commission Vice President in Jobs, Growth, Investment and Competitiveness, could attend one of the meetings to give a speech but would not commit to staying for the full two-hour session for the 'exchange of views' after the speeches; the Saeima did not want him to address the Article 13 Conference under those circumstances, and so he attended the EP event instead. Evidently, the Saeima attached greater importance than the EP to having the Commissioner stay to answer questions from the assembled parliamentarians.

The fourth Article 13 Conference took place just days after the Greek elections that brought the left-wing Syriza party to power on a platform that rejected the terms of Greece's bailout which had imposed harsh austerity on the country. By extension, the election result was a challenge to the entire EU economic governance regime, and it raised anew fears that Greece could be forced out of the Eurozone, which would permanently damage the common currency. Unfortunately, no Greek MPs attended the Article 13 Conference on this occasion, because the new parliament had not yet had a chance to elect a speaker or form new parliamentary committees.[24] Thus while Greece was frequently spoken of during the meeting—with comments along the lines of, 'We respect the democratic decision of the Greek people, but Greece must keep its commitments'—there were no political representatives present to defend the Greek position. In this way, an opportunity was lost to have a wide-ranging debate about the justice and the efficacy of the EU's economic regime. In general the tone of the debate at the conference reflected the fact that the orthodoxy of fiscal discipline had relaxed slightly under the new Commission. Juncker's new investment programme represented a small fiscal stimulus, and there was slightly more emphasis on the possibility of 'flexibility' in the application of the rules of the Stability and Growth Pact. The basic policy, however, remained unaltered.

[23] Another difference concerned the attendance of candidate countries. While they had been invited to the Vilnius and Rome conferences, they were not invited to the 2014 Brussels conference. For the 2015 Brussels conference, the EP was disinclined to invite them, but they were invited at the insistence of the Saeima. Among candidate countries, only representatives from the parliament of Montenegro attended; the parliaments of two non-candidate countries, Norway and Switzerland, also sent representatives.

[24] 'National MPs show varied interest in EU parliament event', *EuObserver.com*, 2 February 2015, available at: euobserver.com/institutional/127467.

V. THE PARLIAMENTS' VIEWS ON THE FUTURE OF THE ARTICLE 13 CONFERENCE

The preferences of NPs are not as easily discerned as those of the EP, because there is great variation not only in the views among NPs but also in the extent to which they have been articulated, if at all. The relevant paper trail for examining NPs' views is their correspondence: for the period prior to the Speakers' Conference in Nicosia, this includes the various letters sent by NPs, individually and in groups, concerning the major organisational questions, most of which were addressed to the Speaker of the Cypriot parliament; after Nicosia, as the 'Vilnius process' progressed, there were proposed amendments to different versions of the draft Rules of Procedure submitted by various national parliaments to the Lithuanian, Greek, and Italian parliaments. Each of the Presidency parliaments had an opportunity in turn to shape the Rules of Procedure, but not all of them took advantage of it. The Seimas took up the task with alacrity and, despite limited time and resources, produced the draft Rules of Procedure that provided the basis for all future debate. This draft envisioned a relatively strong and independent conference, modelled on COSAC, that was strongly supported by the French delegation. The Greek parliament, by contrast, showed little interest in debating the Rules of Procedure or producing its own text; rather, it continued the 'Vilnius process' by collecting the opinions of other parliaments regarding the Seimas's draft and passing them along to the Italian parliament. In its turn, the Italian parliament took a very active role, producing its own draft to provide a basis for discussion at the Rome meeting in September 2014, and then a further compromise draft in December 2014; these texts brought the Rules of Procedure much closer to the position of the EP. The aim was to produce a final agreement the following April when the Italian parliament chaired the EU Speakers' Conference in Rome (see Section VI, below). The next Presidency Parliament, the Latvian Saeima, acquiesced in this move, even though it left them with little or no role in shaping the Rules of Procedure.

As for other NPs, their involvement varied. The parliaments of six Member States—Austria, Bulgaria, Croatia, Malta, Portugal, and Spain—seem to have expressed no discernable opinion on the Article 13 Conference apart from endorsing the Nicosia conclusions of the Speakers' Conference and the 'Contribution' adopted in Vilnius. Many other parliaments were only concerned with specific or minor issues. Prior to Nicosia, a number of parliaments expressed concern that they might be excluded from the conference if their Member State was not a signatory to the TSCG or in the Eurozone, before the Nicosia Conclusions clarified that the parliaments of all EU Member States could participate.[25] After Nicosia, many NPs weighed in with more specific opinions on unresolved questions such as the conference name, the numbers of participants, the relation of the first-semester conference to the European Parliamentary Week, etc. However, the remainder of this section is devoted to a detailed study of the positions of just three parliaments—the EP, the French parliament, and the German parliament. These three are chosen not because of their inherent importance, but because, of all the parliaments involved (with the possible exception of the Lithuanian and Italian parliaments), these three have articulated their positions most extensively, and as a result they provide the best contrast between visions of the Article 13 Conference as a discussion forum (the EP and the German parliament) or as an oversight body (French parliament).

[25] See Cooper (n 3 above) 9–11.

A. The European Parliament

As discussed above (in Section II), the EP preferred that the Article 13 Conference conform to the model of the CFSP-CSDP Conference in having a weak institutional structure within which the EP enjoys a privileged position. In fact, the EP has advocated an even weaker institutional structure than that of the CFSP-CSDP Conference: after all, the CFSP-CSDP Conference adopted Rules of Procedure and Conclusions (by consensus) at its very first meeting, but the EP strongly objected when the Seimas proposed that the Article 13 Conference should do the same at its first meeting in Vilnius. Later, in its suggested amendments to the Italian draft, the EP proposed that the Rules of Procedure should not be adopted by the conference itself but by the EU Speakers' Conference: the EP proposed a textual change (in the Preamble) to state that the latter Conference did not just 'deliberate on' the document, as in the Italian draft, but positively 'adopted' it.[26] To diminish its importance, the EP also suggested that the document should not be called the 'Rules of Procedure' at all, but merely the 'Practical Arrangements' for the conference.[27] Furthermore, the EP preferred that the Article 13 Conference not adopt any Conclusions, and to that end proposed that the entire Section 6, devoted to 'Conclusions', be stricken from the text.[28] Moreover, if no Conclusions were to be adopted, then there would be no need for the conference to vote on decisions of any kind, even on a consensus basis; therefore, the EP proposed that the reference to 'Voting' (Article 2.6) be changed to 'Modus Operandi', with text reading as follows: 'Throughout its workings the Conference shall operate on the basis of the principle of consensus'.[29]

Despite its attempts to make the Article 13 Conference a body of marginal importance with no independent decision-making authority, the EP also strove to increase its own influence within it. Most notably, it sought to establish the system whereby the EP is the host and the co-chair of the first-semester meeting of the Article 13 Conference. Moreover, it also proposed new language, stating that the second-semester conference should be presided over by the Presidency parliament 'in close cooperation with the European Parliament'[30] (Article 2.1); just as was the case with the CFSP-CSDP Conference, the EP was trying to position itself as 'quasi-co-host' of the second-semester Article 13 Conference. Similarly, the EP proposed adding language to state that the agenda for the second-semester conference would be drawn up by the presiding Parliament 'in close cooperation with the European Parliament'[31] (Article 4.1). This would replace the original text stating that, 'The draft agenda shall be drawn up by the presiding Parliament(s) in close cooperation with the Presidential Troika', which would have involved two additional NPs—those immediately preceding and following as Presidency Parliament—in drafting the agenda for a given meeting of the conference. Indeed, the EP wanted to eliminate the Presidential *troika* from the Article 13 Conference altogether, and proposed cutting the relevant provision (Article 2.2), as well as all other references to the *troika*, from the Rules of Procedure.[32] The EP would

[26] RoP Amendments File 2015, 2.
[27] RoP Amendments File 2015, 1.
[28] RoP Amendments File 2015, 9.
[29] RoP Amendments File 2015, 6.
[30] RoP Amendments File 2015, 4.
[31] RoP Amendments File 2015, 8.
[32] RoP Amendments File 2015, 4–5.

evidently have preferred to maximise its influence over the conference by dealing with the Presidency Parliament on a one-to-one basis, with a minimum of involvement from other NPs.

B. The French Parliament

The position of the French parliament (with the two chambers generally in agreement) provided the strongest contrast to the view of the EP. The French position was that the IPC itself—not just the individual parliaments—should have a collective role in ensuring the democratic legitimacy of EU economic governance. The Seimas's original draft Rules of Procedure merely said that the conference provides 'a framework for debate and exchange of information and best practices on matters of economic and financial governance of the EU'. The French delegation in Vilnius proposed amending the text to read that the conference, 'contributes to ensuring democratic accountability and legitimacy of the decisions taken in the area of economic and financial governance in the EU'.[33] The French idea was that the conference should directly exercise an oversight function with respect to EU economic governance. In keeping with this, the French supported the Lithuanian idea that the Article 13 Conference should be able to adopt Conclusions—in effect, to make a common political statement addressed to the EU institutions; moreover, to avoid such Conclusions being watered down, they should be adopted by qualified majority vote if consensus were unobtainable.[34] The French parliament also proposed that the conference should take account of the 'social dimension',[35] which would temper somewhat the single-minded focus on fiscal discipline. These changes were incorporated into the compromise text drafted by the Italian parliament.

The French approach was evident in two further proposed amendments. Whereas the Lithuanian draft had proposed only that the conference should invite 'Member(s) of the Commission responsible for economic and monetary affairs', the French proposed that the presidents of the Eurogroup and the European Council should also be invited to address the conference and answer questions from the assembled parliamentarians.[36] Moreover, the French suggested audaciously, that the timing of the Article 13 Conference meetings should be completely changed. They proposed that the first-semester meeting should take place 'after the presentation by the Commission of its Country-Specific Recommendations' (ie in June) and that the second-semester meeting take place after the Commission's Annual Growth Survey (ie, in December).[37] If this proposal were carried through, both meetings would be tied in with the events of the European Semester, one coming at the beginning

[33] Draft RoP with Amendments 2013, 1–2.

[34] The French Sénat supported the proposal of the Seimas that side events may be organised within the conference. The French Sénat proposed that there should be a sub-committee of the Conference devoted to the democratic oversight of banking supervision. It also suggested a meeting solely of Eurozone parliaments, which could be organised by a parliament other than the Presidency parliament, if the latter is not from a Eurozone Member State. (French Sénat letter of 27/3/2014.) For fear of being excluded from such side events, the UK delegation proposed the following amendment to the Seimas draft: 'Any delegate to the conference may attend and participate in such side events'. (Draft RoP with Amendments 2013, p 3.)

[35] Proposed Amendments of French Assemblée Nationale (1/4/2014).

[36] Proposed Amendments of French Assemblée Nationale (1/4/2014).

[37] RoP Amendments File 2014, 2–3.

(December) and the other close to the end (June), and each one timed to respond to a Commission initiative. It would effectively eliminate the second-semester meeting as it has taken place up to now—in the autumn, outside of the European Semester calendar. The combined effect of the French proposals would be that the top EU officials responsible for the EU's economic policies would be summoned to answer questions from national parliamentarians, much the same way as, in domestic politics, a minister will come before a parliamentary committee to answer questions on government policy. However, this proposed change in timing ran into two problems, one practical and one political. The practical problem was that in many parliaments December is a busy month in the committees whose members would attend the Article 13 Conference, as they are preparing the budget for the coming year. The political problem was that while the French proposal was intended to make the responsible EU officials the target of the conference's oversight, some parliaments were concerned that their own economic and budget plans might become the target: they worried that an Article 13 Conference taking place at that time could become a kind of 'peer review' process with national parliaments examining one another's budgets.[38] Indeed, while the latter was not the French intention, it seems to be not far off from what the Germans had in mind.

C. The German Parliament

The German parliament (the Bundestag, with the full support of the Bundesrat) suggested more amendments to the draft Rules of Procedure than any other national parliament. Concerning the conference's scope, the German parliament wanted to reject the French amendment to Article 1.1 stating that the conference 'contributes to ensuring democratic accountability and legitimacy', and to retain only the text referring to it as a 'framework for debate and exchange of information and best practices', with the following rationale: 'The delegation from the German Bundestag feels that an interparliamentary conference does not itself convey democratic legitimation; only the national parliaments and the European Parliament can decide at their respective levels'.[39]

Furthermore, the Bundestag wanted to add text narrowing the conference's scope to the terms of the treaty, stating that it 'shall maintain a special focus on the budgetary issues and procedures covered by the TSCG'; moreover, it would also remove the reference to the 'social dimension', as it 'risks losing the general theme of the conference'.[40]

Furthermore, like the EP, the Bundestag did not think that the Article 13 Conference should collectively adopt Conclusions:

> The German delegation regards the Conference as a forum for parliaments to share views and experience. The German delegation is therefore opposed to Conclusions which could be viewed as a political statement. However, the presiding Parliament could, on its own responsibility, summarise the outcome of the meeting and publish this summary.[41]

Concerning the above points, the German position was close to that of the EP and in opposition to the French. However, unlike the EP, the Bundestag wanted there to be a clear

[38] I am grateful to the anonymous national parliament official who shared this insight with me.
[39] Amendments of the German Delegation (9/3/2015), 3.
[40] Amendments of the German Delegation (9/3/2015), 3.
[41] Amendments of the German Delegation (9/3/2015), 8.

separation between the events of the European Parliamentary Week and the Article 13 Conference. The German parliament proposed text stating that the Article 13 Conference 'shall be clearly distinguishable from other parallel events', and also advocated changing the date of the first-semester meeting, not to June (as proposed by the French) but rather to April:

> The German delegation advocates that the Article 13 Conference be held in April … after the relevant Council has discussed the policy guidelines of the European Semester at its Spring meeting and before the Member States present their National Action Plans to the European Commission by the end of April.[42]

An April meeting would occur right in the middle of the European Semester, around the time when each Member State must submit two reports to the Commission, a National Reform Programme outlining their detailed plans for structural reform, and a Stability or Convergence Programme detailing their long-term fiscal plans. This timing would have made it more likely that the Member States' reports themselves, rather than the Commission's subsequent Country-Specific Recommendations, would be the topic of discussion at the Conference. This proposed timing accorded with Germany's preference that the Article 13 Conference be a 'forum for parliaments to share views and experience' but not one to make a 'political statement'. It is difficult to escape the conclusion that the German parliament would like the conference to be one where parliaments engage in a form of 'peer review' of one another's fiscal and structural reform plans.

Another of Germany's demands was for a new language regime wherein German would be made a working language of the conference in addition to English and French, which are the customary working languages of interparliamentary meetings. In explanation, the Bundestag defended this proposal not only on practical grounds, but also because it would give some recognition of Germany's role in managing the crisis:

> German is the mother tongue of nearly 20 per cent of EU citizens and thus the language with the most native speakers in the EU. At the same time, Germany is playing a key role is managing the economic and financial crisis. The German delegation thus requests that the debates and meeting documents are also made directly available in German.[43]

Whereas the TSCG has sometimes been described, in figurative terms, as an instance of 'Europe Speaking German', this proposal would make that prospect literally true of the IPC that arose from the treaty.[44]

VI. CONCLUSION: THE EU SPEAKERS' CONFERENCE IN ROME

In early 2015, the Article 13 Conference still had no Rules of Procedure. The Italian parliament proposed that the Rome meeting of the EU Speakers' Conference should adopt the Rules of Procedure in its stead, which would have in effect pre-empted the Article 13 Conference's adoption of them on its own authority. This proposal received the support of the representatives of the EP, the French and German parliaments, and a number of others.

[42] Amendments of the German Delegation (9/3/2015), 5.

[43] Amendments of the German Delegation (9/3/2015), 7.

[44] See L Besselink and JM Reestman, 'The Fiscal Compact and the European constitutions: "Europe speaking German"' (2012) 8 *European Constitutional Law Review* 1–7.

However, at the Rome meeting the representatives from a number of parliaments (those of the Netherlands, the UK, Ireland, Sweden, and the Polish Sejm) objected, questioning whether it was the proper role of the EU Speakers' Conference to adopt Rules of Procedure for another IPC. As a compromise, the Rome Speaker's Conference 'discussed and agreed principles regarding the Rules of Procedure of the Conference', which 'shall be transposed in detailed Rules of procedure' by the next Article 13 Conference, which would meet in Luxembourg in November 2015. While some of these 'principles' reiterated the Nicosia conclusions—for example, that 'the composition and size of delegations shall be determined by each Parliament'—others effectively established new rules for the conference. In this way, the EU Speakers' Conference made a number of decisions regarding the structure and functioning of the Article 13 Conference—including the name, the 'Interparliamentary Conference on Stability, Economic Coordination and Governance in the European Union'.

The Speakers' Conference made decisions regarding the scope, timing, invited speakers, *troika*, conclusions, and language regime of the conference. The set of principles adopted by the Speakers was in many ways a compromise between the positions of the EP, the French and the German parliaments set out above—although the opinions of other parliaments no doubt influenced the outcome as well. Concerning the scope of the conference, the Speakers' Conference adopted language that reflected the concerns of both sides, stating not only that it 'should provide a framework for debate and exchange of information and best practices', the German parliament's preferred text, but also that it should 'contribute to ensuring democratic accountability in the area of economic governance and budgetary policy in the EU … taking into account the social dimension',[45] as proposed by the French parliament. As for timing, the Speakers' Conference specified: 'In order to enhance the parliamentary role, the Conferences should be convened before the presentation of the Annual Growth Survey and the adoption of the National Reform Programmes'.

While this wording was somewhat ambiguous (how long before is 'before'?), it was broadly in keeping with the Bundestag's proposal that the first-semester conference be held in April (around the time of the National Reform Programmes) and the current practice of holding the second-semester conference in the autumn. It was a clear rejection of the French proposal, which would have probably entailed meeting in June and December. On the other hand, the EU Speakers' Conference adopted the French proposal to invite the top EU officials to speak to the conference:

> The President of the European Council, the President of the Eurogroup and the relevant members of the European Commission and other EU Institutions should be invited to the Interparliamentary Conference to set out the priorities and strategies of the EU in the areas being discussed by the Conference.

Against the wishes of the EP, the EU Speakers' Conference also institutionalised the role of the presidential *troika* (consisting of the 'delegations of the current, preceding and following Presidency Parliaments and of the European Parliament') in drafting the conference agenda. On Conclusions, it stated, 'The Presidency Parliament may present non-binding conclusions on the outcome of the meeting'. This was closely aligned with

[45] However, whereas the Italian compromise text referred to 'ensuring democratic accountability *and legitimacy*' (emphasis added), the last two words were removed—an amendment proposed by the EP. The EP had also proposed changing the word 'ensuring' to 'enhancing'—implying that the conference is helpful but not essential for democratic accountability—but this change was not adopted. (RoP Amendments File 2015, 2).

the position of the German parliament, which was a middle way between that of the EP (which wanted no conclusions at all) and that of the French parliament (which wanted the conference to adopt conclusions as a body, by QMV if necessary). Instead the 'Presidency parliament' may adopt 'non-binding' conclusions on its own behalf, in a form more akin to a summary of the proceedings than to a collective political statement. Finally, the German parliament did not get its way on the language regime, as the Speakers' Conference confirmed that, 'The working languages of the Interparliamentary Conference should be English and French'.

While the Rome Conclusions settled many issues related to the Article 13 Conference, there were still a number of questions yet to be resolved. For example, whereas the EU Speakers' Conference confirmed that the first-semester conference would take place in Brussels and be co-hosted and co-presided over by the Presidency parliament and the EP, it did not clarify whether it would be combined with the European Parliamentary Week (even if it were moved to a later date, eg April) and, if so, whether it would be parallel to or absorbed within it. Other practical, unresolved questions were whether non-EU parliaments, from candidate countries or other affiliated countries (eg Norway, Switzerland) should be invited to attend, or whether the conference should include side events.

The ultimate still-unresolved question is: what is the nature and purpose of the Article 13 Conference? Is it fundamentally a discussion forum or an oversight body? As noted in the introduction, the EP and the German parliament both prefer to see it as a discussion forum, but for different reasons: the EP wishes to avoid the creation of an institutional rival, whereas the German parliament wants to promote the policies of the TSCG, to which it is ideologically committed. The French parliament, by contrast, would prefer it to become an oversight body, with at least an element of independent democratic legitimacy and a minimal ability to take collective decisions. This dispute is mainly institutional, concerning the structure and functioning of the conference. But there is also an ideological element to the institutional debate, in that the choice of institutions influences the breadth and depth of discussion that they foster. If the Article 13 Conference is conceived solely as a discussion forum institutionally tied to the TSCG, then it will foster a discussion of how best to implement the terms of the TSCG rather than a broader debate about the wisdom of the policy dictates that spring from that treaty. Alternatively, if the conference is conceived as a political body whose function is to oversee the EU's economic and financial governance regime, then this arguably leads it to a more critical stance, tending towards a questioning of the prevailing policies in this field. Some elements of the EU Speakers' Conference Rome Conclusions implied a strong conference with a broader remit: the references to 'democratic accountability' and the 'social dimension' in the conference's scope; the listing of top EU officials as invited speakers; and the institutionalisation of the *troika*. On the other hand, some elements implied a weak conference with a narrow field of concern: the conference name, which closely mirrors the title of the TSCG; the timing of the meetings, which are oriented more towards parliaments exercising a 'peer review' of one another's economic policies rather than questioning EU policy; and the weakness of the conclusions, which are specifically 'non-binding' and issued by the Presidency parliament, rather than the conference as a whole. However, it should be emphasised that Rules of Procedure shape, but do not determine, the nature and purpose of an IPC of this kind. Ultimately, it is the task of the parliaments themselves, through their choice of a conference agenda and their participation in it, to define its political importance into the future.

14

Ruling the (Dis-)Order of Interparliamentary Cooperation? The EU Speakers' Conference

CRISTINA FASONE

I. INTRODUCTION

THE EU SPEAKERS' Conference is the oldest interparliamentary conference in the European Union, after the European Parliamentary Assembly,[1] its inaugural meeting dating back to 1963.[2]

Its role and prestige have grown with the development of interparliamentary cooperation in Europe and largely derive from its composition. Indeed, the highest authorities in each national parliament or chamber thereof, the Speakers, sit in this conference; an element that, as will be pointed out (III), represents at the same time a strength and a weakness of such a forum.

Because of the role gradually achieved by the European Parliament and national parliaments in the EU,[3] the EU Speakers' Conference has undertaken a gradual process of

[1] In 1962 the European Parliamentary Assembly unilaterally changed its name to the 'European Parliament', but was officially recognised as the 'European Parliament' only by the Single European Act of 1986, ie, seven years after its first direct elections. cf European Parliament, 'The European Parliament: Historical Background' (2015) *Factsheet on the European Union*, available at: www.europarl.europa.eu/ftu/pdf/en/FTU_1.3.1.pdf.

[2] O Costa and M Latek, 'Paradoxes and limits of interparliamentary cooperation in the European Union' (2007) 23 *Journal of European Integration* 139, 142.

[3] See A Buzogány, 'Learning from the Best? Interparliamentary Networks and the Parliamentary Scrutiny of EU Decision-Making' in B Crum and JE Fossum (eds), *Practices of interparliamentary coordination in international politics the European Union and beyond* (Colchester, ECPR Press, 2013) 17.

adaptation, which is still ongoing. As soon as interparliamentary cooperation 'exploded' as a new constitutional phenomenon and the Treaty of Lisbon entered into force on 1 December 2009, expectations have risen about the leading role the EU Speakers' Conference would have played in the Euro-national parliamentary system, where an EU fragmented executive, composed of national and European executives, and multiple parliamentary forums must coexist.[4] However – it is argued in this chapter – despite the adoption of guidelines and rules by the Conference, these aspirations have not been fulfilled effectively in practice both because of the constraints inherent in its composition and the lack of actual legal authority to push its new rule-making role further, which might not even be desirable. Precisely for these reasons, today the EU Speakers' Conference has an ambiguous placement in interparliamentary cooperation, as it cannot be considered either as just one among the many interparliamentary forums, like the sectoral conferences on CFSP/CDSP and on Stability, Economic Coordination and Governance, or the leading interparliamentary site in the EU, in contrast with its aspirations.

This chapter sets out to respond to the following research question: Has the EU Speakers' Conference been able to rule the (dis-) order of interparliamentary cooperation we have been witnessing in the EU? The chapter proceeds as follows. It first offers an account of the origins of the Conference, when and how it was established and took on the shape it has today (Section II). Secondly, it looks into the composition of the Conference, also explaining why it is difficult to reconcile its (supposedly) leading role with the constitutional status of its member Speakers (Section III). Thirdly, the chapter examines the way the conference functions, its organisation, procedures and decision-making rules (Section IV) as well as its *finalités* (Section V). Fourthly, it sheds light on the role the conference has acquired in the aftermath of the entry into force of the Lisbon Treaty and in the setting up of new forums of interparliamentary cooperation (Section VI). Finally, it presents some closing remarks and highlights potential avenues for developing the EU Speakers' Conference in the future (Section VII).

II. THE ORIGINS

The first meeting of the EU Speakers' Conference was organised in 1963 in Rome upon the initiative of the then President of the European Parliamentary Assembly, Gaetano Martino, aiming to gather together the parliaments of Europe at apical level. More than 10 years elapsed before the following meetings were summoned in Strasbourg and Rome in 1975,[5] when, in a few years, the European Parliament (still called Parliamentary Assembly at that time) was to become a directly elected Parliament.

[4] The idea of a Euro-national parliamentary system has been first outlined in A Manzella and N Lupo (eds), *Il sistema parlamentare euro-nazionale. Lezioni* (Torino, Giappichelli, 2014) and is further developed here, in the Introduction and the Conclusions to this volume.

[5] On the gradual engagement of national parliamentary assemblies with European affairs through the Speakers' Conference, see the keynote speech given by L Elia, 'Relazione di sintesi sul tema: contributo delle assemblee parlamentari nazionali alla presa di coscienza europea ed alla costruzione comunitaria', on the occasion of the Conference of the Speakers of the European Parliamentary Assemblies held in Rome, Palazzo Montecitorio on 26–27 September 1975, and now published in (2009) 3 *Il diritto dell'Unione europea* 465, next to the editorial note by E Cannizzaro, 'Il ruolo dei Parlamenti nazionali nel processo di integrazione europea: in margine ad uno scritto inedito di Leopoldo Elia' (2009) 3 *Il diritto dell'Unione europea* 457.

In its first period (1975–79) the Conference met on a regular basis every year, but besides the President of the European Parliament, it involved the Speakers of the Parliaments from all Member States of the Council of Europe, also including the President of the Parliamentary Assembly of this international organisation. Subsequently, from 1980 to 1998, this enlarged format of the Conference, also named 'Big Conference', alternated every two years with the 'Small Conference', which comprised only the President of the European Parliament and the Speakers of the national parliaments within the European Community. Hence every year either the 'Small' or the 'Big' Conference was convened. This peculiar arrangement made the Conference a sort of unique *trade d'union* at parliamentary level between the two main international-supranational organisations established in the post-World War II Europe.

As, after the Treaty of Maastricht of 1991 and, even more so after the Treaty of Amsterdam of 1997, the European Parliament and national parliaments were acknowledged a much more prominent constitutional role than in the past, the 'Small Conference' was transformed into an autonomous interparliamentary forum regularly summoned at least on a yearly basis. Furthermore, informal and extraordinary meetings have been organised, in particular on the occasion of celebrations, like the fortieth anniversary since the entry into force of the Treaty of Rome, or in the aftermath of Treaty revisions, so as to agree on a common position among the parliaments while intergovernmental conferences were taking place.[6]

Although the Speakers' Conference was initially seen merely as a forum for discussion on topics such as parliaments and globalisation and the role of parliaments in the EU and in the scrutiny of their executives, the reforms of European Treaties, especially starting from the (failed) Constitutional Treaty of 2004, have triggered the construction of a new 'institutional' role for the EU Speakers' Conference, oriented to pose the basis for a coherent and coordinated development of interparliamentary cooperation in the EU under this Conference's supervision. Yet, the EU Speakers' Conference has never been explicitly recognised by the EU Treaties, unlike COSAC, which possibly places the Speakers' Conference in between institutionalisation and informal governance.[7]

III. THE COMPOSITION OF THE CONFERENCE AND THE DIFFERENT ROLES OF THE SPEAKERS

Since it became an autonomous forum of cooperation in 1999, the EU Speakers' Conference has been made up of the Speakers of national parliaments and the President of the European Parliament, who participate on an equal basis. If needed, they can be represented

[6] See, for example, Conférence informelle des Présidents des Parlements des États Membres et du Parlement Européenne, *La situation actuelle de l'Union européenne et les tâches des Parlements nationaux qui en découlent concernant la democratization et les reformes institutionelles. Rapport de L Lagendries*, 1 December 1998, 11. For an overview of the history of the EU Speakers' Conference and its meetings, see EU Speakers' Conference, *The History of the EU Speakers' Conference* 2013, available at: www.ipex.eu.

[7] COSAC is the acronym, from French, for Conference of parliamentary bodies dealing with European Affairs. See, for instance, A Cygan, 'COSAC: Birth, Evolution, Failures and Perspectives' (Chapter 11) and A Esposito, 'The Role of COSAC in EU Interparliamentary Cooperation: An (Endless) Quest for an Identity' (Chapter 19), in this volume.

by the Deputy Speaker or the Vice-President of their chamber. No hierarchies are admitted between national legislatures or between them and the European Parliament.[8]

Compared to many other interparliamentary conferences, like COSAC or the newly established CFSP-CDSP Conference, the EU Speakers' Conference is a small forum, with only 29 members (28 from the Member States plus the European Parliament). Its size has allowed the conference to work with a good degree of effectiveness as far as regards the role it has played in the last few years.

Nevertheless, there are constitutional constraints that limit what the Speakers and the European Parliament's President can actually do. Those limitations are fixed at domestic level for them and in principle cannot be overcome when they act in the Conference at supranational level. In other words the way these Speakers can perform their tasks in the EU is inevitably shaped by the institutional standing and powers enjoyed in their respective constitutional systems.[9] Indeed, this principle is expressly acknowledged by the Conference's Guidelines, in Article 1(2): 'The activities of the Conference respect the autonomy and the constitutional position of each participating Speaker'. This provision is further emphasised in Article 2, where the objectives of the Conference are listed and it is specified that their fulfillment cannot violate the different powers vested in its members.

When looking at the constitutional status of the Speakers and the President, in fact, a great variety of situations can be found. In the two Houses of the French parliament, for example, the Speakers are prominent politicians who are certainly asked to apply the rules of procedure and standing orders impartially, but they undoubtedly pursue the interest of the majority and are allowed to vote without special restrictions.[10] By contrast in the UK House of Commons, the Speaker is deemed to be an impartial arbiter of parliamentary proceedings, s/he cannot vote or take a stance in parliamentary and political debates in general—although sometimes the practice departs from this constitutional convention—and when running for the next Parliament the election of the Speaker is uncontested (with no other candidates) in her/his constituency.[11] In the Nordic countries the style of the parliamentary Speakership resembles the UK model much more than the French case.[12] The case of the Italian Speakers is somewhat halfway between the French and the UK examples in that the Speakers do not usually vote in parliament but they have a great political (constitutional) influence and they are not expected to be *super partes*.[13] A constitutional convention has been gradually established providing for the Speakers of either Houses, most likely of the Chamber of Deputies, to be elected among MPs from the opposition (1976–92) and, more recently (1994–2013), among the MPs elected within the second ranking party of the winning majority coalition, while the President of the Senate comes from the main ruling

[8] Art 1 of the Guidelines for the EU Speaker's Conference, last revised in Stockholm in 2010. The Speakers of the Parliaments of the candidate countries for accession to the EU take part in the conference's meetings as observers.

[9] cf F Longo, 'I Presidenti di Assemblea e la politica estera: fra rappresentanza istituzionale e attivismo internazionale' in E Gianfrancesco, N Lupo and G Rivosecchi (eds) *I presidenti di assemblea parlamentare: riflessioni su un ruolo in trasformazione* (Bologna, Il Mulino, 2014) 367–74.

[10] A Martin, *Les Présidents des Assemblées parlementaires sous la V Republique* (Paris, LGDJ, 1996) and P Avril and J Gicquel, *Droit parlementaire*, 4th edn (Paris, Montchrestien, 2011) 70 ff.

[11] A Torre, *Il magistrato di assemblea* (Torino, Giappichelli, 2000)

[12] M Iacometti, *I Presidenti di assemblea parlamentare* (Milano, Giuffrè, 2001).

[13] See among others, A Manzella, 'Il parlamento' in G Amato and A Barbera (eds), *Manuale di diritto pubblico*, II (Bologna, Il Mulino, 1997) 110.

party of the governmental coalition. In other words, the Italian Speakers' political role has definitely increased.[14]

Moreover, the President of the European Parliament, whose mandate usually lasts only half of the parliamentary term—hence two and a half years—is usually elected based on a political compromise between the two major European political groups, the socialists (S&D) and those of the people's party (PPE), depending on the case, with or without the support of the liberals (ALDE). While the President enjoys great visibility outside the European Parliament in the relationship with the other European institutions and the media, inside the Parliament his role is rather weak and is overlooked by the decisions of political groups and the Conference of Groups' Chairpersons.[15]

Furthermore, it cannot be denied that in bicameral legislatures, which are 13 out of 28 national parliaments, a further diversification may occur at national level between the two Houses,[16] where, in the light of their composition and powers, the two Speakers enjoy a different constitutional standing and autonomy.

The ability of parliamentary delegations to bind their own parliaments through the position they take within interparliamentary conferences is always problematic, according to whether a prior mandate has been voted by the parliament to direct the delegation (which happens in few cases) or not. Even more challenging, from a constitutional point of view, is the case of the Speakers within the EU Speakers' Conference. Not only do many of them have an autonomy within their parliament that does not allow other MPs to tell the Speaker what to do, but besides this, where a Speaker is considered as a *super partes* arbiter under constitutional law, s/he could not take a political stance abroad, ie voting within the EU Speakers' Conference, that would result in a binding determination at national level. This is why the conclusions, prepared by the Presidency of the Conference following the meeting just to disclose the content of the debates—ie, by the Speaker of the parliament holding the rotating Presidency of the EU in the second half of a calendar year—are by no means binding on individual parliaments (Article 5 of the Guidelines).[17] Moreover, taking into account the fact that many Speakers do not vote in their own parliament, any decision in the Conference (for example, declarations) is adopted by consensus (Article 1(4) of the Guidelines).[18]

[14] See E Gianfrancesco, N Lupo and G Rivosecchi (eds), *I Presidenti di Assemblea parlamentare. Un ruolo in trasformazione* (n 9 above).

[15] See O Costa, 'The President of the European Parliament', in V Lippolis and N Lupo (eds), *Le trasformazioni del ruolo dei Presidenti delle Camere* (Napoli, Jovene, 2013) 143 and L Gianniti and N Lupo, 'The Role of the European Parliament President in Parliamentary Diplomacy' (2016) 10 *The Hague Journal of Diplomacy*, forthcoming.

[16] On this point and, in particular, in relation to the EU, see A Baraggia, 'Bicameralism and Interparliamentary Cooperation' (Chapter 5), in this volume.

[17] The conclusions are drafted in such a way as to ascribe them to the Speakers rather than to the Conference as a whole.

[18] The only exception is represented by the decision to convene an extraordinary meeting of the Conference, to be proposed by one of the Speakers and to be seconded by two-thirds majority of the members (Art 3(6) of the Guidelines). Under Art 5(2) of the Guidelines, any member of the Conference is entitled to disclose her/his disagreement with the position endorsed by the majority of the Conference and should state clearly that that opinion has not been confirmed by the Conference as a whole. An interesting case of 'dissenting opinion' has emerged in the aftermath of the EU Speakers' Conference held in Rome on 20–21 April 2015. The Speaker of the Hungarian National Assembly sent a letter to the Speakers of the Italian Chamber of Deputies and Senate contesting the fact that the conclusions of the Conference had been adopted by consensus, according to the Conference's Guidelines. In particular this Speaker objected to the allegation contained in the conclusions addressed against Hungary for the violation of fundamental rights.

Interestingly and consistently with the *sui generis* status of the Speakers and the European Parliament's President compared to ordinary MPs and MEPs, the EU Speakers' Conference is devoid of 'standing orders' or 'rules of procedure'. It is rather based on very generic 'Guidelines', equally passed and amended by consensus, that just provide guidance for the Conference organisation and procedure so as not to legally constrain their members.[19]

The remarkable differences existing between the Speakers and the President participating in the EU Speakers' Conference, in terms of functions and autonomy in their own domestic sphere, amount to a limitation on the Conference's leading role in interparliamentary cooperation in the EU. Although the Conference would be the perfect candidate to undertake this role, being composed of the highest authority in each parliament of the EU, the constitutional variation between the Speakers' institutional positions and the lack of decision-making powers outside their parliament constitute a brake on the Conference's proper performance of this task. It cannot be neglected to mention, however, that if, on the one hand, the domestic rules on the speakership condition the functioning of the Conference; on the other hand, this Conference, with its debates and documents (conclusions and declarations) adopted, affects the status a Speaker is accorded in her/his jurisdiction by making her/him inevitably less *super partes* and more political, even in the case of the Speaker of the UK House Commons. So that a sort of two-way influence, between the style of speakership and activities of the EU Speakers' Conference, can start to be detected.

IV. THE FUNCTIONING

A second feature of the EU Speakers' Conference that undermines its potential leadership in interparliamentary cooperation is the – too low – yearly frequency of its meetings. How could a Conference that strives for the coordination of the whole interparliamentary activities be able to reach this objective if it meets on a regular basis only once a year? The Conference is devoid of permanent bodies, capable of ensuring continuity to its functions if one excludes the steady support of parliamentary administrations and their continuous exchange of information. Nevertheless, it is the political and crucial dimension of the Conference, the one involving the Speakers, that lacks continuity. To be more precise the Speakers of the European and national parliaments take part in a variety of meetings within the EU, many of them informal and with the participation of only few parliaments – often those of the EU founding Member States[20] – and at the global level, within the Interparliamentary Union and the parliamentary dimension of the G7. These 'side' meetings, which certainly help in creating an informal network of relationships among Speakers, nevertheless are not placed in the framework of the EU Speakers' Conference – although they might become instrumental to fulfilling its tasks and to putting forwards new initiatives – nor are they able to gather together the Speakers of all 28 national parliaments plus the President of the European Parliament.

[19] See A Esposito, 'La cooperazione interparlamentare: principi, strumenti e prospettive' in A Manzella and N Lupo (eds), *Il sistema parlamentare euro-nazionale. Lezioni* (n 4 above) 157–59.

[20] In this regard, in terms of organisation of informal meetings, the most active Speakers are those of the French, the German and the Italian Parliament. See, for instance, the Conference organised in Rome, at the Italian Chamber of Deputies, on 'Greater European Integration: The Only Way Forward', on 14 September 2015.

There is a rotating Presidency. Until 2010, the Conference was summoned upon the initiative of any Speaker of a participating parliament who wished to host the next meeting, regardless of the system of rotating Presidency in the EU. In order to schedule the activities at least one year in advance, the only condition posed by the Guidelines at the time was to define the hosting parliaments for the two next meetings at the end of the annual meeting. As a consequence, problems of coordination between the programme of the EU Presidency and the priorities of the Conference's annual Presidency arose. The reform of the Guidelines has tried to link the two Presidencies, but the system has remained schizophrenic and inefficient in that, while the EU Presidency changes every six months, the Conference's Presidency, although inspired by the former, changes on a yearly basis and is anchored to the Member State holding the Presidency in the second half of the year, as noted above. Moreover, the Speakers remain free to disregard this guideline and this is why, like in the past, at the end of each meeting the Conference confirms the next two Presidencies. A practice has been developed, however, aiming to avoid the fragmentation of the Conference's work by Presidency: a Presidency trio has informally been set up by putting together the former, the ongoing and the next Presidencies in an effort to coordinate their activities like other interparliamentary forums, eg, the Troika role within COSAC.

The Presidency starts at the end of the previous meeting (Article 3(5) of the Guidelines) and is able to direct the work of the Conference, to provide it with its inputs, to prepare the final draft agenda taking into account the suggestions from other Speakers and parliamentary officials and to write down the conclusions, based on the debate taking place during the annual meeting, organised in the first half of the year. When writing the conclusions, the Presidency enjoys a remarkable degree of discretion and, rather than being a formal and bureaucratic document, sometimes these conclusions have in fact been highly significant political acts, able to shape the contours of interparliamentary cooperation in the EU in the years to come. Depending on the style of the Presidency and the constitutional constraints posed on the Speaker(s) at domestic level, the Presidency can draft the conclusions in a way that lets the member Speakers in the Conference take a stance on the issues at stake, in spite of the general prohibition of any binding effects. The same holds true for the political pressure the Presidency can exert on the adoption of the declarations in the Conference.[21] Usually parliaments like those of Belgium, France, Italy and Luxembourg have favoured an expansion of the role of the EU Speakers' Conference, whereas parliaments that acknowledge a more limited political discretion to their Speakers, like in the UK and Nordic countries, tend to promote the Conference's self-restraint, despite the new trend towards policitisation of the speakership all over Europe, highlighted above.[22]

Temporary bodies set up from time to time by the Conference and reporting to it are working groups 'aimed at addressing matters concerning the role of parliaments and the organisation of interparliamentary cooperation and parliamentary functions' (Article 6(1) of the Guidelines). Examples of working groups were those on the quality of legislation in

[21] See, for example, the number of background notes, documents (including draft rules of procedures of other interparliamentary conferences and their amendments) and declarations discussed on the occasion of the EU Speakers' Conference of 20–21 April 2015 as well as the political tone of the Presidency conclusions published later on: see www.ipex.eu/IPEXL-WEB/euspeakers/getspeakers.do?id=082dbcc54a393144014a4d75e8690dec. Declarations are typically adopted on topical issues when the Conference is organised, eg Treaty revisions, economic governance, migrant crisis.

[22] See section III of this chapter.

the EU, set up in 1999 at the Conference held in Lisbon, and the working group on assistance to parliaments of new and emerging democracies that presented its conclusions at the Conference of Copenhagen in 2006. The Conference defines the modus operandi of a working group, its coordinator and when the group is expected to deliver its conclusions. Once the mission of a working group is accomplished, the body is dissolved.

By contrast it is the administrative side of the Conference that, as said above, ensures a fair degree of stability to its activities, while the political dimension of the cooperation alone appears currently looser and this might become problematic from the point of view of democratic responsiveness and accountability.[23] A crucial role in this regard is thus played by the Secretaries General of the member parliaments, to whom the Conference's Guidelines in fact devote an ad hoc article (Article 8).[24] The Secretaries General assist the Speakers during the annual Conference and meet to consult on the draft agenda of the Conference and on any other issue that might arise for which consultation is needed. Perhaps the EU Speakers' Conference is the only forum of interparliamentary cooperation in the EU that envisages a regular meeting of parliamentary administrations at the top level two to three months before the (political) Conference takes place while being devoid of a permanent secretariat on the COSAC model.[25] Although, as is widely acknowledged, the role of parliamentary administrations in interparliamentary cooperation has become a key feature of this constitutional phenomenon, also giving rise to criticism of its bureaucratisation and low democratic credentials,[26] a specific position for parliamentary officials is formally recognised only within the EU Speakers' Conference as a condition for the fulfillment of the Conference's mandate. As Secretaries General are the counterparts of the Speakers at administrative level, their decisions within the Conference are able to set the general directions of cooperation in the EU between parliamentary administrations.

V. THE AIMS

The EU Speakers' Conference pursues three main objectives, although only two of them have accompanied the Conference's mandate from the start. The first aim is to promote and safeguard the role of parliaments in the EU and to work in support of interparliamentary activities (Article 2(1) of the Guidelines). Under this objective, the Conference and its member Speakers are supposed to be promoters of interparliamentary cooperation in the EU. It is not by chance that basically all the permanent forums of interparliamentary cooperation in the EU have been subsequently established upon the actual initiative of member

[23] A-L Högenauer and T Christiansen, 'Parliamentary Administrations in the Scrutiny of EU Decision-Making' in C Hefftler et al (eds), *The Palgrave Handbook of National Parliaments and the European Union* (Basingstoke, Palgrave Macmillan, 2015) 116.

[24] Moreover, also the Guidelines for interparliamentary cooperation in the EU refer to the role of coordination of interparliamentary administrative cooperation of the Secretaries General, mirroring the coordinating task of the EU Speakers' Conference at political level.

[25] Unlike COSAC, which foresees at least six meetings per year under different formats (plenary meetings, meetings of the Chairpersons, meetings of the Presidential Troika), the EU Speakers' Conference, as highlighted, only meets once a year. Hence, the need for a permanent secretariat can hardly be justified.

[26] See A-L Högenauer and C Neuhold, 'National Parliaments after Lisbon: Administrations on the Rise?' (2015) 38 *West European Politics* 335; A Pegan and A-L Högenauer, 'The role of parliamentary administrations in interparliamentary cooperation', (Chapter 8) in this volume.

Speakers – eg Laurent Fabius, Speaker of the French National Assembly, for COSAC in 1989 – or of the Conference itself – eg the Interparliamentary Conferences on CFSP/CDSP, in 2012, and on Stability, Economic Coordination and Governance in the EU, in 2013.[27]

A second aim of the Conference is to be a forum of exchange of opinions, information, and experiences among the Speakers on the role of parliaments and the organisation of parliamentary functions (Article 2(2) of the Guidelines).[28] Unlike the sectoral conferences set up in 2012 and 2013 the EU Speakers' Conference does not have a precise policy focus. Nor does it have a clear organisational commitment, unlike COSAC, which in principle is tasked with the organisation of interparliamentary conferences, in particular in the field of CFSP. According to the Guidelines of the Conference (Article 5(3)), in order to give visibility to the results of its debates that are usually not held in public and are rarely televised,[29] the Presidency is asked to send the conclusions to the President of the European Commission, the President of the European Council, the President-in-office of the General Affairs Council and to the COSAC Troika (the latter in an attempt to coordinate the work of the two conferences). Furthermore these conclusions are published also in the EU Speakers' Conference section within the EU Interparliamentary Exchange Online Platform (IPEX).

Perhaps the most important success achieved by the EU Speakers' Conference when looking at the issue of exchange of information, promotion of research activities and common action among parliaments is the launch of the IPEX in 2006.[30] The initiative, which derived from a recommendation adopted by the EU Speakers' Conference in 2000, has involved a considerable amount of work on the part of parliamentary administrations and in particular the Secretaries General.[31] It has resulted in the most widely used – by politicians, parliamentary administrations and academics – platform of interparliamentary cooperation, providing for a calendar of all interparliamentary activities and a comprehensive database of all EU draft legislative acts and documents subject to the Early Warning System (EWS) and the political dialogue, and inclusive of the opinions of national parliaments and the replies by the European Commission. Put under the political supervision of the EU Speakers' Conference, the IPEX has been able to increase the level of cooperation among parliaments, in particular national legislatures, on EU decision-making and, besides COSAC, has given a major input to the interparliamentary coordinated scrutiny of EU legislative proposals.

Aiming to strengthen the parliamentary influence on EU decision-making through the Conference's debates, during the 1998 informal Conference, the Speaker of the Belgian Chamber of Representatives, Raymond A Langendries, had proposed linking the meeting of this interparliamentary forum with those of the European Council, which then was not yet acknowledged as a EU institution. Mr Langendries' idea to convene the Conference prior to any European Council meeting would have definitely enhanced the political appeal

[27] These dates correspond to the year of their first meeting.

[28] See M Dicosola, 'I Presidenti di Assemblea nella cooperazione interparlamentare in Europa' in E Gianfrancesco, N Lupo and G Rivosecchi (eds) *I presidenti di assemblea parlamentare* (n 9 above) 359.

[29] One of the few exceptions has been the last EU Speakers' Conference organised under the Italian Presidency in Rome, on 20–21 April 2015, whose videos are available at: ue2014.parlamento.it/34?appuntamento=36#video_0.

[30] cf Esposito (n 19 above) 151–53.

[31] At present each parliament (or chamber thereof) sends its IPEX national correspondent to the annual meeting to define and debate the technical aspects of the platform, whereas the Secretaries General retain a supervisory role and address the financial issues, in particular the system of co-financing.

of the exchange of views taking place within the Conference and would have forced it to be summoned more often. However, the proposal was never put into practice and has partially lost its potential since the Treaty of Lisbon, as the President of the European Parliament is usually invited to speak and be heard before the European Council at the beginning of its meetings (Article 235(2) TFEU).[32] This circumstance highlights the different standing of the President of the European Parliament vis-à-vis the national Speakers when it comes to the relationship with the European institutions and the individual role the European Parliament prefers to play, as it is also fostered by the Treaties, rather than investing in the collective dimension of interparliamentary cooperation on an equal footing with national parliaments.

Finally, the third and nowadays most contested objective of the EU Speakers' Conference has been taken up at a later stage, when the rate of interparliamentary activity in the EU had at least doubled, that is while the saga of the Constitutional Treaty, which strengthened the role of the European Parliament and the national parliaments in the EU, was taking place. Facing a conundrum of permanent and mostly temporary interparliamentary forums, the Conference aims to 'oversee the coordination of interparliamentary EU activities' (Article 2(3) of the Guidelines). Indeed, it was precisely at the meeting in The Hague in 2004 when the EU Speakers' Conference adopted the first version of the Guidelines for interparliamentary cooperation in the European Union, which were then substantially revised in June 2008, when the Treaty of Lisbon had already been signed.[33] Since then the coordinating function of the Conference has become a major task, although not easy to perform because, on the one hand, the number of interparliamentary meetings in the EU has further increased, most often in an informal way; whilst on the other hand, it potentially clashes with the role of coordinators that COSAC, first, and, now, the European Parliament alone tend to play.[34]

VI. THE CONFERENCE IN THE POST-LISBON ERA

Taking advantage of its long 'cursus honorum' and composition, the EU Speakers' Conference has certainly grown in prestige and authority in the Post-Lisbon era. Yet it has not gained any official recognition in the Treaties compared to COSAC (Article 10, Protocol no 1 annexed to the Treaty of Lisbon) or the Interparliamentary Conference on Stability, Economic Coordination and Governance in the European Union (Article 13 of the Fiscal Compact).[35] In spite of the role the EU Speakers' Conference has tried – and sometimes successfully managed – to play as the centre of coordination of interparliamentary forums and activities, it has not even been mentioned by the revised Treaties.

Its (weak) legal basis can be found in Article 9 of Protocol no 1, since this Conference is supposed to be the main 'device' through which 'The European Parliament and national Parliaments shall together determine the organisation and promotion of effective and

[32] See Costa (n 15 above); Gianniti and Lupo (n 15 above).

[33] The Treaty of Lisbon was signed by the contracting parties on 13 December 2007.

[34] See Esposito (n 19 above) 155–57.

[35] The recognition of COSAC in the EU Treaties dates back to 1997 and the first version of Protocol no 1 on the role of national parliaments in the EU.

regular interparliamentary cooperation within the Union', without further specifications on the substantive goals the cooperation must achieve. This does not help in dealing with problems of inconsistencies and overlapping functions, in particular with COSAC, the European Parliament and the new—post-Lisbon—interparliamentary conferences.

Besides the limitations of the EU Speakers' Conference already outlined with regard to its peculiar composition, in the following it is argued that the three roles this Conference seeks to undertake—as a representative body, as a locus of coordination and as a rule-making authority—are potentially impaired by the lack of reform of its rules of functioning which have not been updated, taking into consideration the transformations that have meanwhile been achieved in the EU constitutional system.

A. A Representative Body

The Speakers of national parliaments and the President of the European Parliament, gathered together in the EU Speakers' Conference, have tried to validate their role of representatives of their own legislatures and, indirectly, of the European citizens, at an apical level. Indeed, as clarified, there is no authority in a parliament placed above the Speaker or the President. Hence, as the Speakers are the main 'ambassadors' of their parliaments, with all the limits set out in terms of autonomy and bindingness, in an ideal hierarchy of the forums and activities of interparliamentary cooperation, the EU Speakers' Conference could be located at the top, by mirroring the Speakers' institutional position at domestic level.

However, the variety of powers and status of the Speakers in the EU has grown further as a consequence of the EU's eastward enlargement, and the size of the Conference, although remaining relatively small compared to other forums, has been almost doubled since 2004. The Guidelines of the Conference have not been reformed so as to adapt to such a structural change, for instance by setting up governing bodies that can ensure the coordination between each of the 29 member parliaments and the Conference during the whole year and to set up sectoral committees in the areas that are of major concern for interparliamentary cooperation, such as CFSP and economic governance, in order to look closely at the activities of the two new conferences established in those fields. In other words the enlarged size of the Conference, while representing a challenge, could have allowed it to improve its organisational arrangements and the continuity of the business, now dependent upon the initiative of the Presidency alone or the Presidency Trio.

A second feature of the post-Lisbon EU constitutional system that the Speakers' Conference has failed to accommodate is the powers of the European Parliament and its President. The European Parliament has not just been promoted by the Treaty of Lisbon as ordinary co-legislator next to the Council. It has also been granted scrutiny and oversight powers over the European Commission, the European Council and now, to some extent, also the European Central Bank (ECB) that this legislature had never enjoyed before.[36]

While the European Parliament's empowerment and the entitlement of its President to be heard before the European Council and the Euro Summit and to be involved in

[36] See the Interinstitutional Agreement between the European Parliament and the European Central Bank on the practical modalities of the exercise of democratic accountability and oversight with regard to the exercise of the tasks conferred on the ECB within the framework of the Single Supervisory Mechanism, OJ L 320, 30.11.2013, 1.

the strategic process of construction of the Eurozone sharpen the asymmetric—much stronger—position of this President compared to the Speakers of national parliaments, the Conference could have used these constitutional developments to strengthen its standing as a representative arena. The information collected by the President of the European Parliament thanks to its new powers could have been discussed and shared among parliaments within the Conference. By the same token, if summoned with greater frequency, the EU Speakers' Conference could have influenced the position of the European Parliament's President in the fulfillment of its post-Lisbon tasks with the other European institutions and bodies aiming to take into account the stance of parliamentary institutions in the EU, including national parliaments.

Considering its role of representative body, the transparency and visibility of the Conference's activities could also have been enhanced, starting from amending the Guidelines that do not pay any attention to the link between the Conference and the public (media, electoral constituencies, citizens). Information and Communication technologies have undergone a revolution since the setting up of the Conference in the 1970s. Perhaps the Conference's meetings could be televised and made available online in addition to the publication of the Presidency conclusions, declarations, and the background notes on the IPEX website.

B. A Locus for Coordination

Since 2004 the EU Speakers' Conference has presented itself as the main locus for coordination of the interparliamentary activities in the EU.[37] In 2008 the Conference adopted new Guidelines for interparliamentary cooperation while the ratification of the Treaty of Lisbon was still pending. That means that the substantive novelties put forward by the Treaties and protocols concerning the European and national parliaments in the EU could have oriented the revision of the Guidelines. Indeed, in the 'Preamble' to the Guidelines it is acknowledged that national parliaments contribute actively to the good functioning of the EU (Article 12 TEU) and that their role is complementary to that of the European Parliament (Article 10 TEU).

However, despite the constitutional significance assigned by the Treaty of Lisbon to interparliamentary cooperation,[38] according to the 2008 Guidelines adopted by the EU Speakers' Conference, this cooperation should focus primarily on the effective exercise of parliamentary competences in EU matters, in particular on monitoring compliance with the principles of subsidiarity and proportionality, in the promotion of relationships with parliaments of third countries (Article I.(b) and I.(c)), and in the exchange of information and best practices on the procedures for parliamentary scrutiny (Article III.(a)): the picture provided by these Guidelines appears to describe an arrangement that dates back to the Treaty of Amsterdam, ie, more than 10 years before.

[37] See Dicosola (n 28 above) 359.

[38] R Corbett, 'The Evolving Roles of the European Parliament and of National Parliaments' in A Biondi, P Eeckhout, and S Ripley (eds) *EU After Lisbon* (Oxford, Oxford University Press, 2012) 248; PG Casalena, C Fasone and N Lupo, 'Comment on Protocol no. 1, on the role of national parliaments in the European Union annexed to the Treaty of Lisbon' in H-J Blanke and S Mangiameli (eds), *The Treaty on European Union (TEU) A Commentary* (Vienna/New York, Springer, 2013) 1529–1634.

Although the Early Warning System has been described as one of the most important post-Lisbon procedures for national parliaments, the control of compliance with the principle of subsidiarity in a different form had already been established under the Treaty of Amsterdam and its Protocol no 2.[39] Furthermore, the Guidelines disregard many other areas that the Lisbon Treaty has disclosed to the cooperation between national parliaments and the European Parliament: treaty revisions (Article 48 TEU), accession to the EU (Article 49 TEU), use of implied powers (Article 352 TFEU), early transmission of EU legislative proposals and documents (Article 12(a) TEU), scrutiny of specific policy areas, like the area of freedom, security and justice, especially Europol and Eurojust (Article 12(c) TEU), and CFSP (Article 10, Protocol no 1).

The Guidelines have not been amended since 2008, whereas the constitutional practice has pushed interparliamentary cooperation in a direction that perhaps was not even foreseen at the time of the entry into force of the Treaty of Lisbon. The 2008 Guidelines consider the framework of interparliamentary cooperation as being characterised by the following actors: the Conference itself; COSAC; the joint meetings on topics of common interest organised by the European Parliament and the parliament of the Member State holding the EU Presidency; the meetings of sectoral committees of national legislatures and the European Parliament; the Secretaries General, the representatives of national parliaments to the EU, ie parliamentary officials.[40]

The overview provided on the main players of interparliamentary cooperation in the EU is outdated as there have been the following developments in the meantime.

(i) The cooperation has become more and more policy-oriented, and occasional joint meetings on topics of common interest have been gradually replaced by permanent interparliamentary conferences – two already established and a third, on the scrutiny of Europol and the evaluation of Eurojust, is underway – on areas subject to eminently intergovernmental decision-making. Likewise in other policy domains the meetings of the same sectoral parliamentary committees take place several times a year, although an ad hoc conference has not been set up on the relevant subject-matter.

(ii) The increase in the number of the EU Member States and, hence, of the member parliaments has led to significant asymmetries in interparliamentary cooperation, whereby a variable geometry of interparliamentary activities can be detected, according to cluster of interests, geographical areas and economic performance.[41] This trend is coupled by the rise in the number of such meetings and their level of informality, so that this phenomenon of interparliamentary cooperation 'à la carte' can hardly be controlled, even by the EU Speakers' Conference based on its current arrangements.

(iii) COSAC, once the most important political avenue for interparliamentary cooperation, has undergone a deep identity crisis for multiple reasons. Other interparliamentary forums have been established limiting the COSAC's ability to engage in discussions on policies as this would entail a duplication of their activities. The coordination on the

[39] See M Goldoni, 'The Instrumental Value of Horizontal Parliamentary Cooperation: Subsidiarity Review and the Political Dialogue' (Chapter 9), in this volume.

[40] See Esposito (n 19 above) 145–48.

[41] See D Fromage, 'A mapping of recent trends in interparliamentary cooperation within the EU' in C Fasone, D Fromage and Z Lefkofridi (eds), *Parliaments, public opinion and parliamentary elections in Europe* (2015) 18 EUI Max Weber Working Paper and M Goldoni (n 39 above).

control of compliance with the principle of subsidiarity by national parliaments has been taken away from COSAC by the Treaty of Lisbon. Since the COSAC's mandate has been reshaped, potential overlappings may arise with the EU Speakers' Conference as the locus of coordination of interparliamentary activities. Both Conferences are not deemed to cover a specific policy field, can promote exchange of information and best practices between national legislatures and the European Parliament, and can address contributions to the European institutions. Moreover, just like the Speakers' Conference, COSAC is enabled to shape the organisation of interparliamentary activities by summoning interparliamentary conferences. Indeed, an actual overlapping has occurred in the field of CFSP, where COSAC can organise conferences, according to Article 10, Protocol no 1, but in the end the Speakers' Conference has succeeded in setting the rules of a new interparliamentary body by departing from the COSAC model.

(iv) Finally, the European Parliament and its President, also thanks to the remarkable endowment of powers determined by the Treaty of Lisbon, act as 'shadow-coordinator' of interparliamentary cooperation. Except for the activities involving only some national parliaments, always on a voluntary basis, there is virtually no interparliamentary meeting of which the European Parliament is not a co-organiser or an organiser.

It follows that the Guidelines for interparliamentary cooperation design a coordinating role for the EU Speakers' Conference that is not updated to the EU changing constitutional landscape, after the Treaty of Lisbon. A suitable locus of coordination for interparliamentary cooperation today would require combining policy specialisation with flexibility and differentiation among parliaments – between the European Parliament and national legislatures, but also among national parliaments. At the same time, it should give directions for defining a new role for COSAC that could be complementary with the sectoral conferences and the EU Speakers' Conference at the same time. Therefore it is clear that, without reforms, an effective coordination of interparliamentary activities can by no means be provided by a body like the EU Speakers' Conference that meets only once a year, although being significantly supported by the Secretaries General. Yet, performing such a coordinating role would definitely be needed at present, in a Euro-national parliamentary system where the competing claims in terms of authority and powers of many different interparliamentary forums confront, systematically, but in a disorderly way – as if there were no structured system of relationships – the rising EU intergovernmentalism on some policies and, by contrast to the parliaments, the effective coordination among national and EU executives.

C. A Rule-Making Authority

Rather than revising the Guidelines for interparliamentary cooperation and its own Guidelines in an attempt to restore its (intended) coordinating role and to rule the (dis-)order reigning in the field of interparliamentary activities, the EU Speakers' Conference has preferred to shape the setting up of two new interparliamentary conferences, in one case, the conference dealing with CFSP-CDSP,[42] substantially defining the content of the rules of

[42] A Herranz Surráles, 'The EU's Multilevel Parliamentary (Battle) Field: Inter-parliamentary Cooperation and Conflict in Foreign and Security Policy' (2014) 37 *West European Politics* 957 and J Wouters and K Raube, 'The Interparliamentary Conference on Common Foreign and Security Policy: A Quest for Democratic Accountability in EU Security Governance' (Chapter 12), in this volume.

procedure in their original version. The Speakers' Conference has done so even though it possibly lacked a clear rule-making power in this respect.

Indeed, the legal basis for the adoption of other conferences' rules is vague and is identified in Article 9 of Protocol no 1, annexed to the Treaty of Lisbon, only through a creative interpretation of the provisions assigning to the European Parliament and the national parliaments together (hence within the Speakers' Conference) the determination of effective and regular interparliamentary cooperation in the Union. This way the EU Speakers' Conference has 'stolen' from COSAC the possibility to set up, based on the model provided by Article 10, Protocol no 1, the Interparliamentary Conference for the CFSP-CDSP.[43]

The fact that this legal basis is somewhat questionable is shown by the circumstance that, while the Conference could exercise this rule-making power for the first time on the occasion of the setting up of a new interparliamentary body, it is very unlikely that it could modify the rules of procedure of already established interparliamentary conferences, like COSAC, or adopt a revised version of the rules of the Interparliamentary Conference for the CFSP-CDSP.

The approval of the rules of procedure or just 'binding' principles for the subsequent adoption of rules of procedure was then justified by the inertia in the creation of interparliamentary conferences that, nonetheless, were felt desirable by national parliaments and which the European Parliament greatly needed, but on whose format they did not manage to agree. Given the authority of its members and the role of coordinator of interparliamentary cooperation in the EU, the Conference of the Speakers was the only viable solution to overcome the impasse. Therefore the rule-making authority of the EU Speakers' Conference can be seen as causally linked to the setting up of the conferences and temporally limited to the initial stage of operation of the new body.

In the case of the Interparliamentary Conference on CFSP-CDSP, the new interparliamentary body was set up upon decisions of the EU Speakers' Conference taken at the meetings in Brussels, 4–5 April 2011, and in Warsaw, on 20–21 April 2012. In the meeting of 2011 the Speakers had diverging views on some aspects of the new conference, like the size of the delegations, but fixed principles regarding, for example, the frequency of the conference's meeting, its decision-making rule, the Presidency, the role of the High Representative for Foreign Affairs and Security Policy. Those principles were defined in the conclusions of the EU Speakers' Conference's Presidency as rules by which the new Interparliamentary Conference had to abide in adopting the rules of procedure and working methods. One year later and as the Interparliamentary Conference for CFSP-CDSP had not yet held its first meeting (which took place in Nicosia in September 2012), the EU Speakers' Conference convened in Warsaw and supplemented those principles, by eventually defining the composition of the delegations and the arrangements for the secretariat. Furthermore, the Speakers' Conference recommended the future CFSP-CDSP Conference to carry out a review of those principles and rules subsequently adopted after two years and to submit the results of such review (again) to the Speakers. The first meeting of the new interparliamentary conference, held a few months later, strictly followed the principles set out by the Speakers' Conference and entrenched two provisions in the rules of procedure that enhanced the

[43] It has to be highlighted that in the Preamble of the Rules of Procedure of the Interparliamentary Conference for CFSP-CDSP the legal basis for its setting up is identified in general terms as Protocol no 1 to the Treaty of Lisbon, without further specification.

rule-making authority of the Speakers. Article 8(2) affirmed that any amendment to those rules 'must be in accordance with the framework set out by the Conference of Speakers of the EU Parliaments' and Article 9 assigned to the EU Speakers' Conference the final say over the recommendations adopted within 18 months by the ad hoc review committee on the rules of procedure.

When the review took place, however, the final decision on updating and amending the rules of procedure was taken by the Interparliamentary Conference on CFSP-CDSP itself at its meeting in Rome on 6–7 November 2014; a decision that was later on endorsed also by the EU Speakers' Conference in Rome, on 20–21 April 2015.

The fact that the new interparliamentary conference regained jurisdiction on its own rules – it is argued here – has to be seen as a positive development, whereby the body demonstrates that it enjoys autonomy and is able to make the choices that are more consistent with the features of the peculiar field in which it is called upon to operate. The EU Speakers' Conference can help to coordinate the activity of the Interparliamentary Conference on CFSP-CDSP with the remaining interparliamentary activities of the Union,[44] but, from a normative point of view, it would certainly not be desirable for the Speakers rather than the members of the sectoral conference to rule on its organisation and functioning years after its initial establishment.

Even more controversial has been the setting up of the Interparliamentary Conference on Stability, Economic Coordination and Governance in the EU, for reasons linked to the contingency of the financial crisis and lack of democratic accountability of the Euro-crisis decision-making, to the disputable legal basis, provided in part by an international agreement outside the EU Treaty framework, and to the divide between Eurozone and non-Eurozone member parliaments as well as the position of the European Parliament.[45]

The first meeting of the Interparliamentary Conference on Stability, Economic Coordination and Governance in the EU took place in Vilnius in October 2013 and since then the Conference has not been able to adopt its rules of procedure, causing a series of spillover effects on the performance of this body, lacking any basic standards for its operation. Because of the gridlock, the EU Speakers' Conference has stepped in to try to address the problem of the postponement in the adoption of the rules of procedure.[46] The Italian Parliament, holding the Presidency in the second half of 2014, proposed its own draft rules at the Interparliamentary Conference on Stability, Economic Coordination and Governance

[44] An actual problem of coordination lies in the fact that while the Presidency of the EU Speakers' Conference is assigned to the parliament of the Member State holding the EU Presidency in the second half of the calendar year, the organisation of the new interparliamentary conference, every six months, mirrors the rotating Presidency of the EU.

[45] See, at length, V Kreilinger, 'Inter-Parliamentary Cooperation and its Challenges: The Case of Economic and Financial Governance' in F Fabbrini, E Hirsch Ballin and H Somsen (eds), *What Form of Government for the European Union and the Eurozone?* (Oxford, Hart Publishing, 2015) 271 and I Cooper, 'The Interparliamentary Conference on Stability, Economic Coordination and Governance in the European Union (the 'Article 13 Conference')' (Chapter 13), in this volume, who provided a first appraisal in Cooper, 'Parliamentary oversight of the EU after the crisis: on the creation of the "Article 13" interparliamentary conference', 2014 *LUISS School of Government Working Paper Series* 21.

[46] After the first meeting, three more meetings of the Interparliamentary Conference on Stability, Economic Coordination and Governance in the EU were organised under the Greek and Italian Presidencies in 2014 and the Latvian Presidency in 2015 without the rules of procedure being adopted.

in the EU of October 2014, and, following the amendments submitted by other legislatures, prepared a compromise text in December 2014. At the EU Speakers' Conference of April 2015 the revised draft rules were expected to be finally adopted, since they could count on the support of the European Parliament, the French and the German Parliaments, among others. However, other parliaments – for instance, the UK, the Polish and the Dutch Parliaments – stood against the approval of the new conference's rules of procedure by the EU Speakers' Conference, which would have requested the consensus of all the Speakers. They objected that the Speakers' Conference would have acted beyond its mandate, if it had adopted the rules of another conference on its own. The debate on whether to defer the decision to the next Interparliamentary Conference on Stability, Economic Coordination and Governance in the EU entailed a reflection on the right balance to strike between the rule-making power of the Speakers' Conference and the sectoral interparliamentary conferences' autonomy, which in the end prevailed. In line with the conclusions of the Speakers reached in 2011 and 2012 on the Interparliamentary Conference for CFSP and CDSP, the Speakers' Conference in Rome only agreed on a set of principles to 'be transposed in detailed Rules of procedure by the next Interparliamentary Conference on Stability, Economic Coordination and Governance in the EU', as in fact happened in Luxembourg on 9–10 November 2015.[47] The Speakers addressed issues such as the participating parliaments (from all the Member States and not just the contracting parties of the Fiscal Compact), the focus of the Conference, the timing and the linguistic regimes, but they did not touch upon the most debated questions of the size of the delegations and the relationship between the European Parliament and the national parliaments in the new forum.

All in all, however, the rule-making authority of the EU Speakers' Conference has to be reappraised compared to the initial expectation it created in 2011–14, that the Speakers would have shaped interparliamentary cooperation in the EU through their rules. One can even wonder how a Conference that is devoid of the power to provide itself with binding rules of procedure could – indeed, it bases its activity on Guidelines, according to the special status of the Speakers – adopt those rules for other interparliamentary bodies. Even if this argument is disregarded, the institutional practice confirms that the EU Speakers' Conference's rule-making authority is limited to a very initial stage of operation of other conferences and it rather serves the purpose of promoting interparliamentary cooperation. In other words, in the two cases of the Interparliamentary Conferences for CFSP-CDSP and for Stability, Coordination and Governance in the EU, by ruling on the organisation and procedures of those bodies – in particular, their founding principles – the Speakers had just found a way to fulfill their supervisory role of coordination of interparliamentary cooperation, when this cooperation got stuck because of the disagreements among national parliaments and between these legislatures and the European Parliament. As a matter of

[47] See EU Speakers' Conference, 'Conclusions of the Presidency', Rome, 20–21 April 2015, 5, available at: www.ipex.eu/IPEXL-WEB/euspeakers/getspeakers.do?id=082dbcc54a393144014a4d75e8690dec. See also the Rules of Procedure of the Interparliamentary Conference on Stability, Economic Coordination and Governance in the European Union available at: http://www.ipex.eu/IPEXL-WEB/conference/getconference.do?type=082dbcc5420d8f480142510d09574e02. Interestingly Art.7(2) of the Rules of procedure of this Conference mirrors Art.8(2) of the Interparliamentary Conference for CFSP and CDSP's Rules of Procedure, since, as clearly requested by the European Parliament at the meeting in Luxembourg in November 2015, it provides that any amendments to these new Rules 'must be in accordance with the framework set by' the EU Speakers' Conference.

fact, the discipline of the two interparliamentary conferences has been set down only in part by the EU Speakers' Conference. By contrast, it is up to those conferences to adopt the detailed rules of functioning and, eventually, to amend them in compliance with the guiding principles of the EU Speakers' Conference, which by no means can be seen as having a force comparable to the 'eternity clauses' of some national Constitutions.

Moreover, the initial rule-making authority of the Speakers' Conference cannot be generalised for all new interparliamentary sectoral conferences and is accomplished on a case-by-case basis. For example it does not appear that the Speakers' Conference will have a say – in terms of setting down the rules of procedure – on the much discussed interparliamentary forum aiming to promote a joint scrutiny of Europol and a joint evaluation of Eurojust between the European and national parliaments (Article 12 TEU). The EU Speakers' Conference has debated the topic on several occasions, but never as if it would take the lead in the setting up of a new sectoral conference.[48] This is not just because the European Parliament was in principle against the establishment of a new interparliamentary conference;[49] rather, the legal arrangements of interparliamentary cooperation in this sector, according to the European Commission, are to be provided directly by EU law, in particular an EU regulation.

Concerning Europol, in 2010 the European Commission presented a Communication on the procedures for the scrutiny of Europol's activities by the European Parliament, together with national parliaments, in preparation for a subsequent EU legislative act.[50] Indeed, the new legal basis for Europol, Article 88 TFEU, stipulates that Europol must be governed by regulation(s) adopted under the ordinary legislative procedure. Hence the rule-making of the EU Speakers' Conference could only be marginal, if not absent.

In the 2010 Commission Communication the idea of setting up a permanent joint—between the European Parliament and national legislatures—interparliamentary forum was outlined. It would have been composed of representatives of the parliamentary committees responsible for police matters and could have invited the Director of Europol and the competent Commissioner to be heard. Furthermore 'a formal mechanism would be established for information exchange and coordination between national parliaments and the European Parliament with a view to unifying parliamentary control at European Union level (without prejudice to national parliamentary procedures)'.[51] The European Parliament's legislative resolution on the subsequent EU draft Regulation proposed by the European Commission – at early second reading negotiations in November 2015 – put forward the idea of setting up a Joint Parliamentary Scrutiny Group on Europol that could liaise directly with this agency.[52] The format would depart from that of the new interparliamentary conferences as, rather than establishing new bodies of a considerable size, the

[48] See, for instance, EU Speakers' Conference, 'Overview of the presentations and debates of the Conference of Speakers of the European Union Parliaments', Vilnius, 6–8 April 2014, 7.

[49] ibid, 8.

[50] See European Commission, Communication from the Commission to the European Parliament and the Council *on the procedures for the scrutiny of Europol's activities by the European Parliament, together with national Parliaments*, COM(2010) 776 final, Brussels, 17 December 2010.

[51] ibid, 15.

[52] See the amendments passed by the European Parliament in the legislative resolution of 25 February 2014 on the proposal for a regulation of the European Parliament and of the Council on the European Union Agency for Law Enforcement Cooperation and Training (Europol) and repealing Decisions 2009/371/JHA and 2005/681/JHA (COM(2013) 0173), at first reading (P7_TA(2014)0121).

Joint Parliamentary Scrutiny Group would associate national legislatures and the European Parliament in the procedures to control Europol and to hold its governing bodies (as well as the European Commission) accountable.

Although the reception of the European Parliament's amendments in the final text of the regulation is uncertain, it is clear that the design of these new procedures of inter-parliamentary scrutiny could never have been advanced by the EU Speakers' Conference, whose rule-making powers, de iure and de facto, are marginal and subject to the constraints already pointed out.

VII. CONCLUSIONS. THE AMBIGUOUS PLACEMENT OF THE CONFERENCE IN EU INTERPARLIAMENTARY COOPERATION

The transformation of the role(s) of the EU Speakers' Conference has by and large reflected the developments that have taken place in a Euro-national parliamentary system 'in the making' and its growing complexity as well as the rise of interparliamentary cooperation as an ordinary activity for the European and national parliaments, on a daily basis.[53]

Established originally in 1963 as the 'Small Conference', the EU Speakers' Conference first became a permanent forum of interparliamentary cooperation in 1999, after the Treaty of Amsterdam, and then tried to validate itself as the main locus of coordination for inter-parliamentary activities. Indeed, in 2004, in the aftermath of the signature of the Constitutional Treaty, which would have greatly enhanced the role of the European Parliament and national legislatures in the EU, the EU Speaker's Conference adopted the first version of the Guidelines for interparliamentary cooperation. These Guidelines were subsequently revised in 2008 while the process of ratification of the Treaty of Lisbon was still ongoing. However, on the one hand, the new version failed to take into account the many novelties introduced by this Treaty on parliaments in Europe; while on the other hand, it was not able to fully grasp the evolving practice of interparliamentary cooperation, the crisis of COSAC and the setting up of new interparliamentary conferences, especially when confronted with a well-structured system of intergovernmental relationships.[54] In fact, the Guidelines were never amended afterwards.

The circumstance of being composed of the Speakers of national parliaments and the President of the European Parliament has represented for the Speakers' Conference a reason for prestige and authoritativeness in the reign of interparliamentary cooperation. By the same token, however, that feature has prevented this Conference until recently from giving clear political directions to the EU interparliamentary activities and from fully exercising rule-making powers towards the other sites and avenues of cooperation between national legislatures and the European Parliament.

The Treaty basis of the EU Speakers' Conference is rather weak – Article 9, Protocol no 1 annexed to the Treaty of Lisbon – and has not supported this body in defining clear boundaries between its mandate and goals and those of other interparliamentary conferences,

[53] C Hefftler and K Gattermann, 'Interparliamentary Cooperation in the European Union: Patterns, Problems and Potential' in C Hefftler et al (eds), *Palgrave Handbook of National parliaments and the European Union* (n 23 above) 95.

[54] See S Fabbrini, *Which European Union?: Europe After the Euro Crisis* (Cambridge, Cambridge University Press, 2015) 124–52.

such as COSAC, or the growing role of the European Parliament in interparliamentary activities. The internal and volatile cleavages arising within the EU Speakers' Conference, also dependent on the variety of domestic constitutional status of its member Speakers and further fostered by the eastward enlargement of the Union, have certainly not helped. By the same token, the new powers acquired by the President of the European Parliament to participate—although with a *sui generis* role—in the meetings of EU intergovernmental institutions and bodies and to co-define with other European institutions the long-term strategy for the EU integration process, have not been properly exploited by the EU Speaker's Conference either to control ex post the intergovernmental decision-making more closely or to try to provide ex ante inputs.

From this viewpoint and with all the constraints deriving from its composition, if the EU Speakers' Conference wants to present itself as a democratic representative and the main locus of coordination for interparliamentary activities, it should probably undertake a reform of its rules of functioning, starting from the Guidelines for its organisation and procedures of 2010 and ending up with an update of the 2008 Guidelines for interparliamentary cooperation according to the current shape of the EU constitutional system. Indeed, it is not feasible for a body committed to a leading role, like the Speakers' Conference, to meet just once a year with no continuity that might ensure the fulfillment of its tasks during the whole year, with the exception of the activity of the Secretaries General and the growing role of parliamentary administrations or informal 'side' meetings of some EU Speakers in other forums.

Rather the Speakers' Conference could meet at least twice a year, once per semester, in plenary and as many times at the level of the Presidency Troika. Sectoral committees within the Speakers' Conference could be created to supervise the activities of the new bodies and formats of interparliamentary cooperation (economic governance, CFSP, the cooperation in criminal matters, for example) and to address possible inconsistencies and lack of coordination among the sites of interparliamentary cooperation in those fields. As it is relatively small in size, compared to other interparliamentary conferences, the Speakers' Conference and its internal bodies could potentially be much more effective. With such changes also the problem of the disconnected Presidency of the Conference—currently rotating once a year in spring, after the plenary meeting—vis-à-vis the EU six-month Presidency would be dealt with. The Presidency of the EU Speakers' Conference would follow the Presidency of the Union by alternating every semester and being in charge of the organisation of one of the two plenary meetings. At the same time, the role of the Presidency Troika, gathering together the current, the past and the next presidencies of the Conference, should be acknowledged by the Conference Guidelines and strengthened in terms of agenda-setting.

Finally the setting up of the Interparliamentary Conferences for CFSP-CDSP in 2012 and on Stability, Economic Coordination and Governance in the EU in 2013 has been a test bench for the Speakers' Conference and has triggered the exercise of a sort of rule-making authority by the Speakers collectively. Facing an impasse in the establishment of these new conferences—all parliaments advocated for them but they fundamentally disagreed on the mandate, composition and organisation—the EU Speakers' Conference has helped to overcome this stalemate by defining compromise principles among the many parliamentary positions confronting one another and to set a framework for the adoption of the conferences' rules of procedure. This does not imply, however, that the EU Speakers' Conference has suddenly become entitled to rule on other interparliamentary conferences and enjoy generic rule-making powers. By contrast, the founding principles that the Speakers' Conference has adopted for these sectoral interparliamentary conferences are limited to the initial stage of their setting up and are justified by the gridlock which all the parliaments contributed to create as well as the uncertainties concerning the legal basis. Therefore, because of its members, the highest authority in interparliamentary cooperation found itself legitimised to intervene. However, it cannot be said that the Speakers' Conference rule-making authority extends also to the ordinary life of the new interparliamentary conferences or to the amendments of those rules. The Speakers' Conference lacks a legal basis to undertake this task, nor would its fulfillment be desirable as it would interfere with the autonomy of another interparliamentary body with a specific policy-oriented mandate, that goes beyond the Speakers' Conference remit. Nor is this Conference mandated to intervene in the establishment of any new interparliamentary body, as the case of the joint parliamentary scrutiny on Europol quite clearly shows.

Part VI

Debating the Role of COSAC

15

The Role of COSAC in the Europeanisation of National Parliaments and in the Evolution of Interparliamentary Cooperation

DAVIDE A CAPUANO*

I. INTRODUCTION

THE ROLE OF COSAC in the Europeanisation of national Parliaments and in the evolution of the interparliamentary cooperation has been pivotal, representing an example of a body in which topics of European interest are discussed and sometimes voted on by parliamentarians of both the European Parliament and national Parliaments, gathered together.

The first meeting of COSAC dates back to 1989; so, it has to be considered as a well consolidated and—after its inclusion in the Treaty of Amsterdam and in the Treaty of Lisbon[1]—a well institutionalised body.[2]

* The opinions of the author are personal.

[1] Art 10 of Protocol no 1 annexed to the Treaties states that 'A conference of Parliamentary Committees for Union Affairs may submit any contribution it deems appropriate for the attention of the European Parliament, the Council and the Commission. That conference shall in addition promote the exchange of information and best practice between national Parliaments and the European Parliament, including their special committees. It may also organise interparliamentary conferences on specific topics, in particular to debate matters of common foreign and security policy, including common security and defence policy. Contributions from the conference shall not bind national Parliaments and shall not prejudge their positions'.

[2] For the history of COSAC, see the paper 'COSAC: historical development'(2015), available at: www.cosac.eu/documents; see, also, Chapter 11 in this volume, A Cygan, 'COSAC: Birth, Evolution, Failures and Perspectives'; for a view from the Italian perspective, see DA Capuano and C Fasone, *La Conferenza degli Organi specializzati negli affari europei (COSAC). Evoluzioni e prospettive* (Roma, Senato della Repubblica, 2010).

The current practice of COSAC meetings varies according to the different approaches of the single Chambers of the Member State holding the rotating Presidency of the Council, given the great flexibility offered by the Rules of Procedure. Some Chambers prefer more general and political issues, while some others prefer more procedural arguments.

The aim of this contribution is to address a series of issues, also taking into account the results of the LII Meeting of COSAC, held in Rome at the Plenary Hall of the Italian Senate, on 1–2 December 2014, and prepared by the Conference of Chairpersons, held in Rome in the same premises on 18 July 2014.

These issues represent the most advanced positions in the attempt to involve national Parliaments more directly in real European debates. All the powers granted to national parliaments by the Treaty of Lisbon, directly linked with the good functioning of the European Union (Article 12 TEU), need in fact a framework of fruitful cooperation not only between national Parliaments themselves,[3] but also in the necessary connection with the European Parliament, declined in terms of effective and regular interparliamentary cooperation, within the Union, by Article 9 of Protocol no 1.

In this perspective, the role of COSAC, since its establishment in 1989, has been constantly proactive in promoting—directly or indirectly—the contribution of national parliaments to the good functioning of the European Union, mainly through the questions related to subsidiarity (later on codified in Article 12 of TEU) and the enhancement of political dialogue with the EU Institutions.[4] The COSAC-coordinated subsidiarity checks, conducted in the last part of the 2000 decade, have been in fact a successful exercise in helping national Parliaments to directly involve themselves in the scrutiny of the draft EU legislation, even well before the entry into force of the Treaty of Lisbon.[5]

Obviously, due to its peculiar composition, COSAC strengthened most clearly the role of the European Affairs Committees in their respective national Parliaments, permitting them to have a special say in European matters, autonomously from the position of the other sectoral Committees and of the Plenary Assemblies. This role is now codified in specific national constitutional provisions for some Chambers,[6] while the role of COSAC is also codified in some national Parliaments'/Chambers' Rules of Procedure, as it is, for example, the case of the Italian Senate.[7]

It is important to underline that, each European Affairs Committee being part of a single national Chamber, their strengthened role is reflected in their respective Chamber, the latter benefiting from the Europeanisation of the former.

[3] According to Article 12, letter f), TEU, the contribution of national Parliaments to the good functioning of the Union is assured also 'by taking part in the inter-parliamentary cooperation between national Parliaments and with the European Parliament, in accordance with the Protocol on the role of national Parliaments in the European Union'. For this approach, see DA Capuano, 'The role of national parliaments in the legislative process of the EU. A view from the Italian Parliament', in M Cartabia, N Lupo and A Simoncini (eds), *Democracy and Subsidiarity in the EU* (Bologna, Il Mulino, 2013), 252 ff.

[4] On the political dialogue, see DA Capuano, 'The role of national parliaments' (n 3 above), 233 ff.

[5] See DA Capuano and C Fasone, '*La Conferenza degli Organi specializzati negli affari europei (COSAC)*', n 2 above.

[6] As it is for Art 88(4) of the French Constitution or Art 45 of the German Constitution.

[7] Art 23 of the Rules of Procedure states that the Committee on European Union Policies shall also be responsible for relations with the Conference of European Affairs Committees of Parliaments of the European Union.

II. THE COORDINATING ROLE OF COSAC IN THE EARLY WARNING SYSTEM (IN DECLINE)

A first theme that is worth considering further in taking stock of the evolution of COSAC meetings is its role in the Early Warning System. After the role played during the exercises of the subsidiarity checks, with the Treaty of Lisbon COSAC ceased to play a promotional activity with reference to this task, mainly due to the negative position taken by some Parliaments/Chambers.[8] This fact ultimately led to the decision of the XLIII COSAC of Madrid,[9] stating that 'the coordinated subsidiarity checks should no longer be a priority for the Conference, although these checks may be conducted on an ad hoc basis on the proposal of each Presidency'.

In this perspective, the driving role of COSAC in transmitting European inputs to national Parliaments, via their respective European Affairs Committees, has rapidly declined; the presence of a permanent Secretariat of COSAC—due to its narrow mandate, limited to assisting the Parliament of the Member State holding the rotating Presidency of the Council—has not had any effect in this regard.

As a direct effect of this minor involvement of COSAC, national Parliaments lost their collector of inputs as regards the scrutiny of EU proposals. By consequence, in the absence of a collective body able to organise and coordinate the collective scrutiny of draft legislative proposals—and with the time-limit of eight weeks fixed by Protocol no 2—the reaching of the thresholds foreseen by the Treaty of Lisbon for raising a 'yellow card' has been accomplished only twice.[10]

Therefore, after having verified the inefficiency of the subsidiarity checks, as envisaged by the Treaties with all their technicalities (but without a political 'body', able to organise them), there was a general request for a more efficient and more streamlined use of the Early Warning System, the main input coming from the EU Speakers' Conference of 2014 in Vilnius, which asked COSAC to explore some practical solutions.[11]

COSAC replied shortly to this engagement and the Conclusions of the LII Meeting of Rome, taking into account the replies to the 22nd Bi-annual Report, suggested that a more efficient use of subsidiarity checks may be achieved, among others, by: (a) prioritising proposals selected from the Commission's Annual Work Programme before 31 January; (b) giving out early information on the findings of other Parliaments/Chambers, especially through IPEX and the network of national parliaments' representatives in Brussels.

This may not constitute a real change, but it is certainly a better focusing of the instruments already at its disposal; and it is in no way comparable to the leading role of COSAC in the pre-Lisbon phase.

[8] See A Esposito, 'La cooperazione interparlamentare: principi, strumenti e prospettive', in A Manzella and N Lupo (eds), *Il sistema parlamentare euro-nazionale* (Torino, Giappichelli, 2014), 140 ff and A Cygan, 'COSAC: Birth, Evolution, Failures and Perspectives', Chapter 11 in this volume.

[9] Held on 30 May–1 June 2010.

[10] See A Pintz, 'National Parliaments overcoming collective action problems inherent in the early warning mechanism: the cases of Monti II and EPPO' (2014), *LUISS Guido Carli School of Government Working Papers* 2014/22, available at: sog.luiss.it/sites/sog.luiss.it/files/SOG%20Working%20Papers%20WP22-2014%20Pintz.pdf.

[11] Point no 22 of the EU Speakers' Conference Conclusion of Vilnius (6–8 April 2014) proposed to COSAC the exploration of the possibilities for more efficient use of subsidiarity checks, and that the next Conference of Speakers could consider any such work undertaken by COSAC.

Another effect of the minor involvement of COSAC was that the political pressure for its active role in giving guidance to the collective exercise of the early warning system rapidly moved towards new alternative forms. Some Chambers tried to find an autonomous way to seek practical solutions to their need for a collective role of national Parliaments in scrutinising EU proposals. As an example, they succeeded in organising meetings related to specific topics, in addition to COSAC meetings or to meetings falling within the general interparliamentary cooperation with the European Parliament, but with the participation of only a limited number of Parliaments/Chambers (the so-called clusters of interests, like the meeting held in 2013 in Copenhagen to discuss the 'free movement of workers and National Welfare Systems').

In this sense, the cooperative and inclusive format of COSAC meetings—with the participation of all EU Chambers and the European Parliament—has not been considered as essential.

III. THE COORDINATING ROLE OF COSAC IN THE CONSIDERATION OF THE COMMISSION'S ANNUAL WORK PROGRAMME (IN DEVELOPMENT)

We could therefore assume that the role of COSAC in promoting the cooperation amongst national Parliaments on the subsidiarity checks—and, via that tool, in promoting the Europeanisation of the national Parliaments—was a positive one, especially before the entry into force of the Treaty of Lisbon.

However, after this period, its role in promoting the formation of a collective position of national Parliaments was strongly opposed by some Parliaments/Chambers, also because of the wording of Article 10 of Protocol no 2. This circumstance led to a lack of political influence of COSAC on the 'European' national agendas of the European Affairs Committees, and consequently on the European agendas of their respective Parliaments.

In this context, the absence of an institutionalised body for determining a collective position weakened the use of the procedure of the subsidiarity check, making it scarcely significant. The national Parliaments' representatives in Brussels could not remedy this deficiency due to the absence of a coordinating body, and given their merely administrative functions.

So, the main political instrument for enhancing the process of acting together in the scrutiny of EU draft legislative acts—Europeanising the agendas—and the sharing of information about the proposals under consideration in the single Chambers had to be found in a different, more flexible and generally accepted, tool, coherent with the provisions of the Treaties, as Commissioner Timmermans clearly affirmed in his intervention at the LII COSAC of December 2014.

That is why the Conclusions of LII COSAC of Rome stressed the importance of the consideration of the Commission's Annual Work Programme. The Final Report of the Friends of Presidency Group, submitted to the General Affairs Council of 16 December 2014, also admitted that the discussions on the Commission's Annual Work Programme were important in order to devote particular attention to the respect of the subsidiarity and proportionality principles, in connection with the fact that 'subsidiarity is not about "less Europe", but rather about "better" Europe'. In this framework, as the Report states, the 'necessary tools and legal instruments to verify the respect of these principles are already in place'.

And, it is possible to add, these tools and legal instruments—which are in force to make a better Europe—involve primarily the national Parliaments, according to the procedure laid out in Protocol no 2 annexed to the Treaties.

Therefore, the consideration of the Commission's Annual Work Programme becomes crucial. By examining the Programme at the beginning of the year and prioritising, within the time limit of 31 January of each year, the proposals to be considered, national Parliaments could reciprocally signal their main political issues. In this perspective, they could facilitate not only the formation of coalitions of national Parliaments that could more easily pool together in order to reach the thresholds fixed by the Treaties—as a certain view of the procedure may suggest—but also a decisive input for a timely and coherent consideration of the proposals by all national Parliaments/Chambers involved.

If this approach succeeds, the pivotal role of COSAC, through the support for the consideration of the Commission's Programme, would be recognised again—after the shady period following the XLIII COSAC of Madrid—as the engine of the enhancement of national Parliaments' capacity to Europeanise themselves by a more structured and significant scrutiny of draft legislative proposals (or other documents falling into the more general political dialogue) and by a more effective interparliamentary cooperation.

If this approach does not succeed, the model of clusters of national Parliaments acting together in the early warning system outside a European legal framework such as COSAC, would rapidly increase and stabilise, with the risk that legitimacy is given to the wish of some national Parliaments to scrutinise draft legislative acts in order to reach the thresholds envisaged by the Treaties for blocking EU legislation.

However, this last solution does not seem to fit with what the EU requires and with the necessary involvement of national Chambers in the integration process. That is why COSAC must be provided with all necessary tools and political support in promoting the coordination of the early warning system and of the political dialogue with the European Commission and with the European Parliament.

Following this approach, the organisation of side events during the plenary sessions of COSAC seems a good practice. The recent Presidencies have always hosted such events providing a room for the meetings and all other facilities, save for translation services, the latter not envisaged as necessary in these cases by COSAC's Rules of Procedure.

The confirmation of this practice and its extension to the organisation of side events also during the Chairpersons' meetings would increase the level of the debates, also contributing to the transformation of the COSAC into a real political Assembly, and would channel the political pressure of the clusters of interests into a more institutionalised framework.

IV. COSAC MOVING TOWARDS A MORE POLITICAL STANDING

A second issue that is worth mentioning is the enhanced political dimension of COSAC and the political influence that its model exerted on the other forums of the interparliamentary cooperation.

The debates of COSAC are not limited only to procedural matters that concern, for example, the sharing of information and best practices amongst European Parliaments, but have been more and more connected with real political 'European' issues, as it became evident in the last four meetings of COSAC,[12] where the themes linked to the economic crisis of the Eurozone and questions connected with the tensions in the Mediterranean and in the East of Europe were widely and passionately discussed.

The relevance of the political issues in the recent COSAC meetings is appreciable because nearly all the sessions have been prepared on real, actual, European topics and taking into account requests coming from a significant number of national Parliaments/Chambers, having their representatives as keynote speakers on the points on the agenda. In this perspective, the political level of the debates of COSAC was particularly evident, contributing to the awareness of all the participants of the importance of discussing together European issues, with specific points to be consequently incorporated in the final documents of the meetings.

This aspect may imply a possible overlapping with the debates of other interparliamentary forums or even of the European Parliament, but it is a problem that must be solved within the Parliament organising the parliamentary dimension of the bi-annual rotating Presidency of the Council in connection with the European Parliament. However, the organisation of interparliamentary cooperation should take into account the willingness of national Parliaments/Chambers to discuss real European issues, and not limit them to only procedural or institutional ones.

The increasingly political attitude of COSAC meetings has also been certified with the update of the document on practices regarding voting on Contributions.[13] This document, drafted by the permanent member of the COSAC Secretariat in 2012, was updated by the Italian Presidency, after an analysis conducted with the assistance of the Secretariat and previous consultation of the Troika.

The necessity to update arose because, on the occasion of the Chairpersons' Meeting held in Rome on 18 July 2014, 14 Parliaments/Chambers circulated a draft letter, then submitted a few weeks later, asking for the clarification of some concepts as regards the voting of COSAC's Contribution.

In this sense, taking into account an unclear practice followed during previous COSAC meetings on the role of the Troika of COSAC,[14] this letter recommended that all amendments tabled by delegations on the final Contribution of COSAC should be discussed and voted on, without a power of the Troika to adopt some of them without discussion. Consequently, all amendments tabled should be given equal weight and treatment. Another question was related to the specification that the amendments were examined in the order in which they appeared in the text, not in the order of submission.

The document, updated by the Italian Presidency before the meeting held in Rome, on 1–2 December 2014, took a positive position on the issues underlined in the letter and, more concretely, the procedure followed for the adoption of the Contribution paid regard to this new clearer procedure.

During the Chairpersons' meeting, in fact, several votes took place, with the Presidency often using Rule 7.5 of the COSAC Rules of Procedure. According to this Rule, COSAC

[12] XLIX Meeting of Dublin (first semester of 2013), L Meeting of Vilnius (second semester of 2013), LI Meeting of Athens (first semester of 2014) and LII Meeting of Rome (second semester of 2014).

[13] According to COSAC's Rules of Procedure, 'COSAC may address contributions for the attention of the European Parliament, the Council and the Commission pursuant to the Protocol on the Role of National Parliaments in the European Union to the Treaty of Lisbon' (rule 7.1).

[14] According to COSAC's Rules of Procedure, the Troika is composed of the delegations of the national Parliaments of the Presidency, the preceding Presidency, the following Presidency and the European Parliament.

generally seeks to adopt the Contribution by consensus; however, if this is not possible, the Contribution should be adopted by qualified majority of three quarters of the votes cast, representing at the same time at least half of all votes. Each of the 29 parliamentary delegations has two votes (Rule 7.6).

According to the document, although the Rules of Procedure of COSAC do not stipulate a voting procedure at this stage in the Chairpersons' meeting, in cases where no consensus can be reached, the Presidency has the discretion to put any amendments or parts of the draft text to a vote using the guidance of Rule 7.5, which provides the basis for voting in COSAC. Consequently, in the Chairpersons' meeting, the Presidency used the document on the voting procedure widely, often calling for a vote and using a special table to verify if an amendment has to be considered adopted, even by considering the number of votes constituting a blocking minority.[15]

Then, the texts of the Contribution and Conclusions of LII COSAC, prepared and amended with this procedure by the Chairpersons, were adopted in the final session of 2 December 2014.

The long debates and the general attitude of the delegations showed clearly the political level of the LII COSAC, which benefited in terms of efficiency from the adoption of the document on voting on the Contribution. The wide use of that document pressed the delegations of EU Affairs Committees of national Parliaments and of the European Parliament to engage constructively to find compromise solutions on real European issues such as the role of the EU in the Mediterranean and in Eastern Europe or, if necessary, to vote, collectively, as if it was a real political assembly, as with the topic of the mid-term review of Europe 2020 Strategy.[16]

In this perspective, the Europeanisation was particularly self-evident and the role of the COSAC deliberations in the debate at the European level cannot be underestimated, also given that, after adoption, the Contributions are published in the *Official Journal of the European Union* (Rule 7.7).

Therefore, the voice of national Parliaments in Europe—via the COSAC channel—can find a stronger audience if the deliberations are taken with a real discussion amongst the participants on real European issues. And, obviously, the importance of these deliberations, and their aim to influence the EU institutions, is directly linked with the involvement also of the delegation of the European Parliament, as an active member of the Troika and a co-legislator of the European Union.

V. COSAC AS THE POLITICAL LABORATORY OF THE EUROPEANISATION OF NATIONAL PARLIAMENTS

Trying to fix some points of reference, it must be underlined that the need for efficiency in the interparliamentary cooperation, and in the COSAC meetings, is strictly related to the

[15] The document contained also a table useful to quickly calculate the votes needed to gain the qualified majority depending on the number of votes cast. The table contained also the number of votes necessary to form a blocking minority.

[16] In particular, point 1.6 of the Contribution has been voted on with the new procedure. According to this point, COSAC called for public expenditure related to the implementation of programmes co-financed by European and Investment Funds to be completely excluded by the definition of Stability and Growth structural deficit.

adoption by those meetings of some sort of political conclusions, to be drafted in a document and circulated afterwards amongst the institutions and other interested bodies.

Interparliamentary cooperation is in fact connected to the terms of regularity and effectiveness by Article 9 of Protocol no 1 annexed to the Treaty of Lisbon. This concept of effectiveness is similar to a sort of political influence that can be exerted through these meetings. But to make it effective, a document must be adopted and circulated.

These are the reasons for the attention given to the document on the voting of the Contribution at the LII COSAC. Only the political relevance of the issues discussed and the positions taken by national Parliaments may justify the strong pressure put on the Italian Presidency to change the rules of voting. The results have been quite satisfactory, indeed.

Another relevant point concerns the role of COSAC in dealing with real European issues and real pieces of legislation. The rising pressure put by the clusters of national Parliaments/Chambers, gathered together to discuss draft legislative acts and trying to adopt common positions in order to influence the reaching of the thresholds foreseen in Protocol no 2, needs some serious reflection.

These clusters of interests are a positive tool to support further engagement of national Parliaments/Chambers in an Europeanisation process, in the sense that they oblige the participant Chambers to discuss real European pieces of legislation. So, a positive effect cannot be denied.

Conversely, these meetings have the not minor problem that not all the national Parliaments/Chambers participate actively, for several reasons (eg, time constraints, agenda-setting). That is why it seems politically significant to convene those clusters meetings when there is already a European meeting in place, in order to offer to all Chambers the possibility to participate.

An even better solution would be the strategic use of the COSAC itself. If the clusters meetings have only a function of orientating the decisions that Parliaments/Chambers would take autonomously, the same function could be accomplished, in a more structured way, by the COSAC meetings. This, with the positive effect that it would be a 'European' function, given the peculiar structure of COSAC, composed by all the EU Affairs Committees of the Member States and by a delegation of the European Parliament, as both strategic parts of the European interparliamentary cooperation.

In this regard, the influence that the COSAC model has had on the composition of other stable interparliamentary forums cannot be denied, such as the CFSP-CSDP Conference and the Article 13 Conference, both composed, as they are, of members of national Parliaments and European Parliament and both aiming to discuss themes drawing on political conclusions.[17]

The strong emphasis put by the Lisbon Treaty on the interparliamentary cooperation between national Parliaments and with the European Parliament testifies to the importance of their connective role that could enormously increase the effectiveness of their activities and of their deliberations.

[17] See J Wouters and K Raube, 'The Interparliamentary Conference on Common Foreign and Security Policy: A Quest for Democratic Accountability in EU Security Governance' (Chapter 12), and I Cooper, 'The Interparliamentary Conference on Stability, Economic Coordination and Governance in the European Union (the "Article 13 Conference")' (Chapter 13), both in this volume.

In this framework, the role of COSAC resembles that of a political laboratory. The LII COSAC of Rome paved the way for 'new style' COSAC meetings, in which the roles of national Parliaments are more interconnected—also through the fundamental presence of the European Parliament—with real European dossiers and real European decisions.

The Europeanisation of national Parliaments, in other words, must be associated with a political engine that operates autonomously in a European body, as does the COSAC, but which has its connection in each Chamber of the EU, through their specialised Committees on European Affairs.

16

The Role of COSAC in the Changing Environment of National Parliaments in the EU: An Identity Crisis?

BRUNO A DIAS PINHEIRO*

I. INTRODUCTION

THIS CONTRIBUTION IS a critical review of COSAC from the standpoint of a practitioner and a direct observer of these phenomena for some years. In fact, the author has been attending COSAC meetings from November 2006 up until now, first based in a national capital as a Clerk to the European Affairs Committee of the Portuguese Assembleia da República, then from within COSAC as a member of the Presidential troika of the COSAC Secretariat (2007–08) and finally from Brussels as the Permanent Representative of the Portuguese Parliament to the European Institutions (2010–14).

In terms of methodology the first remark to be made is: the following evaluation, critical review and identification of challenges have been developed from the views of someone who has simultaneously being working *for* and *at* COSAC, but who has also developed an academic perspective of this scientific area, namely through research[1] on the subject of the Representatives of national Parliaments in Brussels and in collaboration with different Universities (eg, LUISS and Uppsala) or think-tanks (eg, the European Academy of Law).

Thus, the approach followed is mostly empirical and heuristic, which is a standard technique based on professional experience to promote and develop a more in-depth knowledge of a scientific area, oriented towards problem-solving and the identification of new

* The views expressed here are strictly personal and do not bind or reflect in any way the political and institutional position of the Portuguese Assembleia da República.

[1] BA Dias Pinheiro, *The Treaty of Lisbon and the adaptation of national Parliaments to the challenges of European integration: the case of the permanent representatives of national Parliaments to the EU institutions*, (2012) ISCSP, Lisbon, abstract available at: www.repository.utl.pt/bitstream/10400.5/5124/1/ABSTRACT%20Bruno%20Dias%20Pinheiro%5b1%5d.pdf.

patterns of behaviour of the institutional actors which operate in this environment, ie, national Parliaments.

Finally, and as far as the structure of this contribution is concerned, it starts with a critical evaluation of the proceedings of COSAC so far, its results and achievements, and it casts some light onto the challenges this interparliamentary conference is currently facing. The last section of this contribution is dedicated to an exercise in forward-thinking, namely questioning whether COSAC is facing an identity crisis and discussing the possible ways to overcome any such crisis.

II. CRITICAL REVIEW: AN EVALUATION

There is a current trend to evaluate COSAC in a negative way, ie, to look at the Conference only regarding the difficulties it now faces in affirming its role. This, in my view, is a common mistake which neglects its history and its importance for the role of national Parliaments themselves since COSAC was established in 1989. This trend is sometimes unconsciously present and can be illustrated by the introductory remarks enshrined in Chapter 1—'Future of COSAC' of the 21st Bi-annual report,[2] that 'whilst interparliamentary cooperation has been blossoming in importance and a number of significant fora have been created in recent years, it can be argued that COSAC has not evolved significantly'. Even though the chapter itself goes in a different, and more positive, direction about COSAC, there is a certain mindset to refer to it only considering its recent past and overlooking its 25 years history.

From the author's perspective, COSAC should be considered as one of the most important pillars of interparliamentary cooperation and of the development of the role of national Parliaments in the EU. It is worth reading the historical overview of COSAC prepared by its Secretariat in January 2014[3] to realise that, since its origins in 1989, COSAC has been, for many years, the only forum where parliamentarians from all Member States, the EP and candidate countries could meet to discuss and exchange views and best practice on the most relevant issues of European integration.

In this historical overview, references can be found, for instance, to the Assises, held in Rome in November 1990, on the eve of the Maastricht Intergovernmental Conference (IGC), and to a debate held at the COSAC meeting in Lisbon in 1992, proposing the convening of an IGC on budgetary control of Community finances. On some occasions, one could easily argue that COSAC was even ahead of its time. At its eighth meeting, for example, it is stated that COSAC 'focused on economic growth, competiveness and employment. The situation in Eastern and Central Europe … was also debated'.

More recently, and in the framework of the so-called constitutional process which began with the Convention on the Future of Europe, and finally ended with the entry into force of the Treaty of Lisbon, COSAC played a decisive role. In fact, COSAC followed the proceedings of the Convention both closely and actively, because many national parliamentarians participating in COSAC were at the same time also representatives of their Parliaments in the Convention, which created a certain synergy between the two processes.

[2] Presented at the COSAC in Athens in June 2014, available at: www.cosac.eu/documents/bi-annual-reports-of-cosac/e2-21st%20Bi-annual%20Report.pdf.

[3] Available at: www.cosac.eu/documents/History%20of%20COSAC%20SEPTEMBER%202014%20EN.pdf.

One of the most important achievements of COSAC in recent years was the initiative of coordinating joint subsidiarity and proportionality checks in relation to specific Commission proposals, which began in 2006 and lasted until the Treaty of Lisbon entered into force.[4] This initiative was considered to be very useful for a majority of national Parliaments, because it helped them organise internally, streamline scrutiny procedures and learn from the examples of other national Parliaments to overcome difficulties such as complying with the six- or eight-week period to issue a reasoned opinion.

At this point, a preliminary evaluation about COSAC indicates that it has succeeded in fulfilling its mission of 'promoting the exchange of information and best practice between national Parliaments and the EP' stated in its Rules of Procedure (Article 1.2) in several different domains. Together with the valuable *acquis* gathered in the bi-annual reports, COSAC has enabled Parliaments to enter into and maintain a level of exchange and cooperation amongst themselves that would not exist otherwise. Moreover, its importance is confirmed by that fact that it is the only interparliamentary conference recognised by the EU Treaties.

But at same time, when evaluating what COSAC is, and what it can and cannot do, one must always bear in mind that, as MacCártaigh notes, 'national parliaments are not a homogenous group, and do not act collectively to influence the EU system of governance' adding that 'it is for individual member states to explore how best they see their representative assembly and executive dealing with the challenges of EU governance'.[5] Therefore, different Parliaments expect different things from their participation in COSAC: some see the Conference playing a more active role, while others give it a lesser and more restrictive responsibility. From an empirical point view, it would be enough to attend a COSAC plenary meeting and to observe how difficult and controversial it always is to get 41 parliamentary chambers and the European Parliament to agree on the Contribution to be adopted by the Conference.

Notwithstanding, and as Chapter 1 of the 21st Bi-annual report clearly states,[6] there are several past and current successes of COSAC that are highlighted by a vast majority of Chambers and Parliaments, namely the networking between Members of Parliament, and the exchange of best practice amongst Parliaments.

Based upon on the experience as an observer of the evolution of COSAC and the impact and influence it has had on the advancement of the work of national Parliaments in EU affairs, it seems evident that COSAC has fostered a learning process among Parliaments throughout the years. It has provided them with comparative information and practice on how to tackle the challenges of EU integration (eg, subsidiarity checks) and has been especially helpful in strengthening their capacities to deal with the prerogatives enshrined in the Treaty of Lisbon. Therefore, one can conclude that COSAC has helped to Europeanise national Parliaments, influencing their procedures and institutional behaviours towards EU affairs. It has also assisted them in streamlining their approaches to the difficulties they have been facing in adapting to the changing environment of EU multi-level governance.

[4] For more information, cf the 6th bi-annual report at: www.cosac.eu/documents/bi-annual-reports-of-cosac/a8-sixthREPORT.pdf.

[5] M MacCárthaigh, 'Conceptualising the role of national parliaments in the EU system of governance' (2005) *Geary Institute Discussion Paper Series*, No 9.

[6] Presented at the COSAC in Athens in June 2014, available at: www.cosac.eu/documents/bi-annual-reports-of-cosac/e2-21st%20Bi-annual%20Report.pdf.

On the other hand, and without detriment to the role played by the EU Speakers' Conference, COSAC has been the main forum ensuring institutional continuity and memory, coherence and stability in interparliamentary cooperation. To this effect, the set up and development of the COSAC Secretariat (the only permanent secretariat of interparliamentary cooperation) has been an outstanding landmark. It is the unique feature of COSAC and one of its most important working tools, and is of benefit to all national Parliaments and the EP.

III. COSAC: CURRENT CHALLENGES AND SHORTCOMINGS

It has been alluded to earlier that 'interparliamentary cooperation has been blossoming in importance and a number of significant fora have been created in recent years'.[7] Indeed, and as paradoxical as this might sound, this development presents COSAC with unprecedented challenges, both external and internal.

First, other than the EU Speakers' Conference, COSAC had been, until very recently, the only established and structured forum of regular meetings between parliamentarians dealing with EU affairs in which the EP participated. This meant that the scope of the topics COSAC could cover was quite broad, because there was no other meeting point for Members to network and exchange best practice.

Gradually, this scenario evolved: a) within the framework of the rotating EU Council Presidency, a so-called parliamentary dimension of the Presidency was developed, comprising a set of meetings of the Chairpersons of the different sectoral Committees of all national Parliaments, besides COSAC; b) the EP has widened its interaction with national Parliaments, namely through Joint Parliamentary Meetings, Joint Committee Meetings, and meetings of corresponding committees on specific topics; c) after the entry into force of the Treaty of Lisbon and of the intergovernmental Treaty on Stability, Coordination and Governance (TSCG) in the Economic and Monetary Union (Fiscal Compact), two interparliamentary conferences were established, the Conference on CFSP/CSDP and the Conference foreseen in Article 13 of the TSCG, on economic and financial governance.

This trend illustrates a shift in the ownership of EU issues within national Parliaments from the sphere of the EU Affairs Committees alone, which are no longer the sole driving force within national Parliaments in this domain, towards the remit of sectoral Committees, which are increasingly more involved in the monitoring of EU policies.[8]

Although COSAC is composed only of Members of the EU Affairs Committees of national Parliaments, it somehow lost the prerogative of being the unique forum available to debate any EU-related issue. In fact, the establishment of the Interparliamentary Conference on CFSP and CSDP, of the Interparliamentary Conference foreseen by Article 13 of the Fiscal Compact and the likely establishment of a Joint Parliamentary Scrutiny Group in the framework of the EUROPOL regulation,[9] have consolidated a trend towards

[7] 21st COSAC bi-annual report.

[8] On the involvement of committees in interparliamentary cooperation, please see the contribution from D Fromage, 'Standing committees in interparliamentary cooperation in the post-Lisbon era: towards the end of the European Affairs Committees' predominance?', Ch 6 in this volume.

[9] COM/2013/173: Proposal for a Regulation of the European Parliament and of the Council on the European Union Agency for Law Enforcement Cooperation and Training (Europol) and repealing Decisions 2009/371/JHA and 2005/681/JHA.

the empowerment of other Committees in the scrutiny of sectoral EU affairs and to the development of a multi-polarised system of interparliamentary cooperation, where the EU Affairs Committees are no longer the sole engine of reflection, but merely one of its components.

In parallel, and to somehow legitimise and oversee this trend and this multi-polarisation, the EU Speakers' Conference has taken responsibility for the leadership and steering role in interparliamentary cooperation after the entry into force of the Treaty of Lisbon, promoting debates on current and future developments, and adopting the necessary decisions to foster and strengthen that cooperation.[10]

This has led to an external pressure on COSAC. In fact, despite its decisive contribution to the development of tools of parliamentary scrutiny through the process of mutual learning it fostered for years and which are now of benefit to other parliamentary committees, COSAC itself is now faced with a certain ambiguity regarding its role and scope as a consequence of the empowerment of other fora.

Adding to this exogenous pressure, COSAC faces some internal dilemmas related to its own functioning, which were profusely highlighted in the replies to the 21st COSAC bi-annual report. These may be outlined as follows; first, many Parliaments and Chambers thereof (15 out of the 29 responding) state that the quality of the debates has been the least successful aspect of the COSAC meetings. This reflects a certain dilemma that COSAC faces: is it more important to have high-level speakers (Prime-Minister, Minister of Foreign Affairs, Commissioners) who deliver a long speech on the priorities of an EU Council Presidency (or a certain policy field) not necessarily linked with the main concerns of Parliaments, or to structure COSAC meetings around topics that promote an actual exchange of views and best practice amongst parliamentarians? This is an issue that COSAC, namely the forthcoming Presidencies, will have to deal with. In fact, delegations often criticise the very little time available for debate (often restricted to one minute per member) and the lengthy presentations given by some of the speakers, which are then not followed up with questions or which do not have any concrete impact on the work of COSAC.

Secondly, COSAC is currently structured around two main events: a meeting of the Chairpersons, which is of a 'preparatory nature' and to 'be held prior to each plenary meeting', and which is attended by the Chairmen of all EU Affairs Committees and the relevant member of the EP; and the COSAC Plenary meeting itself. However, there is room for substantial improvement in the links and interdependence between the two. In fact, if the agendas of the Presidencies for the past six or eight years are analysed, it is possible to conclude that the only contact point between the Meetings of the Chairpersons and the COSAC Plenary meetings is the approval of the agenda and of the outline of the bi-annual report. Indeed, the COSAC Chairpersons' meeting is often viewed as a 'mini-COSAC Plenary', with an agenda of its own, that is then not followed up throughout the semester leading to the actual Plenary meeting. It is argued here that COSAC, as a Conference for exchange of best practice and information, would benefit from a certain degree of streamlining and coordination between these two meetings.

Thirdly, and also a clear example of the two issues mentioned above, more importance should be given to the bi-annual report that each Presidency presents, outlined at

[10] More information on the EU Speakers' Conference available at: www.ipex.eu/IPEXL-WEB/euspeakers/getspeakers.do.

the Chairpersons' meeting and then endorsed at the COSAC Plenary meeting. Despite the intense amount of work invested by all delegations and by the COSAC Secretariat in the preparation and drafting of each bi-annual report, a very low degree of attention is dedicated to it, especially at the Plenary meeting, where it is often treated like a procedural item, instead of one COSAC's most substantial outputs.

Fourthly, regarding the Contribution adopted by each COSAC Plenary meeting and addressed to the EU institutions, it is the most politically visible output produced by COSAC at present. Therefore, it is often also the most controversial part of every Plenary meeting. In this process the Presidency puts forward a draft with its proposals, aiming at an adoption by consensus. At the same time a significant number of delegations may be quite active in trying to leave their own influence on the final document and it can even be the case that issues set out in the Contribution may not have actually been addressed at the debates. It is my view that this type of controversy is provoked by differing views across delegations on what purposes COSAC should serve: exchange of best practice and information? Taking political stances on issues of common interest? Steering the development of interparliamentary cooperation? Therefore, delegations tend to see the Contribution according to the perspective they have on the role of COSAC itself, which often leads to long, declarative, and less targeted Contributions.

It should however be noted that the political effectiveness of these Contributions was clearly demonstrated in the framework of the two 'yellow cards' on subsidiarity issued so far (Monti II and EPPO):[11] by calling upon the European Commission to respond directly to the concerns raised by national Parliaments in both cases, COSAC used the Contribution to put political pressure on the Commission to react, which it eventually did. Therefore, the Contribution, if used in a targeted and results-oriented way, can be a valuable asset at the disposal of COSAC.

The final remark in this section addresses the interaction between COSAC and other fora of interparliamentary cooperation. Notwithstanding the fact that the establishment of other interparliamentary conferences (CFSP/CSDP, Article 13) is a recent trend, COSAC should give particular attention to this development and, put special emphasis on setting up channels of communication with these fora. This would serve, not only to promote synergies, exchange of information and avoid unnecessary duplications, but also to affirm its role within this new constellation of interparliamentary cooperation, or 'Euro-national parliamentary system'. The same applies, with acute relevance, to the dialogue and contact with the EU Speakers' Conference, given the coordination and steering role the latter plays in this context.

IV. THE FUTURE OF COSAC: SOME PROPOSALS

From all the challenges and shortcomings outlined in the previous section, it is legitimate to conclude that the purpose, scope, organisation and role of COSAC are currently under question, and possibly heading for some sort of identity crisis—i) is it a political body, aiming at steering and coordinating the role of national Parliaments in the EU, as the only

[11] COM/2013/534, Proposal for a Council Regulation on the establishment of a European Public Prosecutor's Office.

interparliamentary conference foreseen in the Treaty? Or is it, instead, a forum for the mere exchange of information and best practice? ii) Where should COSAC be placed within the constellation of interparliamentary conferences—is it a *primus inter pares* Conference or, nowadays, just one among many? iii) Which issues can/should COSAC cover—any salient EU issue it deems appropriate? Or should it avoid addressing issues now under the remit of other interparliamentary Conferences? iv) Which relationship and communication channels should COSAC establish with these fora?

Finding answers to these questions is of the utmost importance for COSAC, and in particular to respond to the above-mentioned 'blossoming' of other interparliamentary fora and to avoid any stagnation that might lead to it becoming irrelevant. Therefore, this contribution aims at putting forward some concrete proposals for further reflection on the strengthening of COSAC, its proceedings and output.

With regard to the organisation of the meetings, its structure and the correlation between the meeting of the Chairpersons of COSAC and the Plenary meeting, the following proposals could be considered.

First, the choice of topics to be discussed in each meeting should focus on the issues that bring direct added value to the scrutiny work that national Parliaments perform: specific legislative proposals, exchange of best practice on the scrutiny of the activity of national Governments, debates on how to strengthen democratic legitimacy and accountability and exchange of views on policy fields that relate directly to the competences of national Parliaments (eg criminal law, banking union, taxation).

Secondly, the debates ought to be structured to promote the development of a parliamentary perspective around the topics chosen, ie, for each panel and issue to be discussed, parliamentarians should always be included as key-note speakers, alongside Commissioners and members of Government.

Moreover, the Presidency should try, as much as possible, to steer the debates towards this parliamentary perspective, in a way which enriches the scrutiny of the same policy fields or specific proposals being done in the capitals. For the same reason, the Contribution to be adopted should mirror the debates and exchanges that actually took place during the meeting, seeking to influence and obtain a reply from the European institutions to the issues and concerns raised by Parliaments therein.

In addition to that, the correlation between the Chairpersons meeting and the Plenary could be strengthened. In the first semester, one suggestion would be to use the two meetings to promote a sustained monitoring of the European semester, since in any event the Chairpersons meeting usually takes place in January, after the publishing of the Annual Growth Survey and on the eve of the Interparliamentary Conference on Article 13, and that the COSAC Plenary usually occurs in May, around the time the European Commission publishes its Country-Specific Recommendations.

With regard to the bi-annual report, it is considered that it should be mainstreamed in the COSAC agenda, ensuring a greater linkage between the content of the report and the debates scheduled for the Plenary debates.

Concerning the relationship of COSAC with the new interparliamentary conferences and with the EU Speakers' Conference, a good practice that has been implemented in the past is worth signalling: on some occasions, the Presidency of the EU Speakers Conference was invited to deliver a short briefing at the COSAC Plenary, highlighting and giving notice of its main decisions and achievements. This approach should be generalised as a standing invitation between the various Conferences (namely COSAC, CFSP/CSDP and Article 13) to host a representative from each other in order to give a briefing on the latest developments and achievements within their remits. This would facilitate dialogue, create synergies, and avoid duplications, besides functioning as a confidence building measure between the different players. At the national level, it might also be valuable to help the EU Affairs Committees balance their relationship with the other Committees.

On the other hand, in relation to the more effective role to be played by COSAC in the new *Euro-parliamentary system*, some suggestions can also be formulated. COSAC has been very effective in promoting the exchange of best practice and information on parliamentary scrutiny procedures in the preparation for the entry into force of the Treaty of Lisbon. Currently, and especially after the two 'yellow cards' reached under Protocol no 2, COSAC should promote a more in-depth analysis in the aftermath of this development. In fact, particular attention should be devoted to the follow-up carried out by Parliaments not only regarding the proposals that met the threshold foreseen by Protocol no 2 (eg EPPO), but also those which, despite falling short of the required votes, raised a significant number of opinions from Parliaments (eg, seasonal workers,[12] Schengen,[13] tobacco directive).[14]

This exchange of information should address not only the dialogue with the European institutions, but mostly with the Commission, but also the interaction at the national level with the Governments, which might be useful to share among Parliaments. From this perspective, and regarding scrutiny as a dynamic process that encompasses several dimensions beyond the eight-week period dedicated to subsidiarity, there are evident gains to be had for COSAC if it could establish itself as the promoter of a learning process amongst Parliaments in the context of what some scholars label as the 'multi-level parliamentary field'.[15]

On a concluding note it has to be highlighted that COSAC indeed looks very different from the Conference established in 1989: despite the influential and decisive role it has played since then in promoting the role of national Parliaments in the EU, it now faces the unprecedented challenges that are outlined in this contribution. Overcoming these challenges requires boldness and creativity from COSAC to reinvent itself, affirming its new position in the interparliamentary design by doing what it does best: anticipating the needs of national Parliaments (eg, gathering information on parliamentary practice), raising awareness of issues of common concern (eg, democratic accountability and legitimacy), and being politically assertive in those fields where Parliaments wish to show their strength (eg the follow-up to the yellow cards). Finally, COSAC should strive to establish a relationship of complementarity, instead of rivalry or competition, with other interparliamentary fora.

It should be noted, however, that COSAC is what national Parliaments make of it. Therefore, this contribution ends by quoting a realistic assumption by Philipp Kiiver: 'national Parliaments have the potential to change things. It is up to them whether they do so'.[16]

[12] COM/2010/379.

[13] COM/2011/560.

[14] COM/2012/788.

[15] B Crum and JE Fossum, 'The Multilevel Parliamentary Field: a framework for theorizing representative democracy in the EU' (2009) 1 *European Political Science Review* 249.

[16] P Kiiver, *The National Parliaments in the European Union: A Critical View on EU Constitution-Building* (The Hague, Kluwer Law International, 2006).

17

The Role of the COSAC Secretariat within the Evolving Landscape of Interparliamentary Cooperation: Challenges for the Future

CHRISTIANA FRYDA

I. INTRODUCTION

COSAC (*Conférence des organes spécialisés dans les affaires communautaires*) was established in 1989 and has been evolving ever since.[1] Initially recognised in the Treaty of Amsterdam, it is now a formally recognised forum of interparliamentary cooperation enshrined in Article 10 of the Protocol No 1 annexed to the Treaty of Lisbon, on the role of national Parliaments in the EU:

> A conference of Parliamentary Committees for Union Affairs may submit any contribution it deems appropriate for the attention of the European Parliament, the Council and the Commission. That conference shall in addition promote the exchange of information and best practice between national Parliaments and the European Parliament, including their special committees. It may also organise interparliamentary conferences on specific topics, in particular to debate matters of common foreign and security policy, including common security and defence policy. Contributions from the conference shall not bind national Parliaments and shall not prejudge their positions.

In exploring the role of COSAC in the evolving landscape of interparliamentary cooperation, a discussion on the role of the COSAC Secretariat assisting the Presidency Parliament

[1] For a detailed account of the historical development of COSAC, see M Knudsen and Y Carl, 'COSAC—Its Role to Date and its Potential in the Future' in G Barrett (ed), *National Parliaments and the European Union—The Constitutional Challenge for the Oireachtas and Other Member State Legislatures* (Dublin, Clarus Press, 2008) and the 'History of COSAC' on the COSAC website: www.cosac.eu/documents/.

in its tasks is essential. Thus, this contribution focuses on this very specific aspect of COSAC and aims at summarising the ideas submitted by Parliaments on the role of the Secretariat and presented in the 21st Bi-annual Report of COSAC of June 2014 under the Hellenic Presidency[2] (section III) and raising certain points as food for thought for further discussion and reflection (section IV), while briefly presenting, at the beginning, the history of the establishment of the COSAC Secretariat and its status today (section II).

II. A BRIEF PRESENTATION OF THE HISTORY OF THE COSAC SECRETARIAT AND ITS STATUS TODAY

The establishment of a secretariat was a sensitive issue. The decision to form a secretariat was taken in Rome in 2003 after an agreement on a set of guidelines for the establishment of a permanent secretariat in the XXIX COSAC in Athens, under the Hellenic Presidency, in 2003. COSAC agreed the formula for establishing a secretariat to facilitate its work; to this end, it endorsed a set of guidelines proposing a secretariat comprising one Permanent Member and four members seconded from the three national Parliaments of the Presidential Troika (the former, the current and the future Presidency Parliaments) and the European Parliament. It was designed to improve the way that meetings were prepared, to facilitate exchange of information between participating Parliaments, and to present a report every six months on 'developments in EU procedures and practices relevant to parliamentary scrutiny'.[3]

The Secretariat assumed its tasks in 2004 and, according to Rule 9 of the Rules of Procedure of COSAC, it is composed of officials from the Parliaments of the Presidential Troika, appointed for a non-renewable period of 18 months, and a Permanent Member, an official of a national Parliament, for two years with the possibility of one renewal. It is located in the European Parliament in Brussels; the post of its Permanent Member and its technical needs are co-financed by Parliaments.[4] At the XXXVII COSAC in Berlin in 2007, a political consensus[5] was reached on a Presidency draft for the inclusion of a COSAC Secretariat and its Permanent Member in the COSAC Rules of Procedure.

According to Rule 9.4 of the Rules of Procedure, which provides a general description of the Secretariat's role, the Secretariat shall assist the Presidency Parliament in all its tasks; its members shall perform their duties under the political responsibility of the COSAC Presidency and the Presidential Troika or according to the decisions taken by COSAC meetings. Its Permanent Member shall coordinate the activities of the COSAC Secretariat under the direction of the Presidency Parliament.

[2] See full report on the COSAC website: www.cosac.eu/documents/bi-annual-reports-of-cosac/.

[3] H Haenel and H De Croo, 'Evolution of COSAC over the last 20 years', COSAC website: www.cosac.eu/spain2010/ordinary-meeting-of-the-xliii-cosac-30-may-1-june-2010/.

[4] See report of the working group following the link below (n 5 below).

[5] The establishment in September 2006 of a working group dealing with the co-financing of the Permanent Member of the COSAC Secretariat preceded the agreement. In its report, the dissenting views of the Italian Camera dei Deputati and Senato della Repubblica are documented. 'Only the Italian and the Hungarian delegation argued against the co-financing mechanism as they consider a mere rotating system of secretariat members more suitable than having a permanent member': Minutes of the XXXVI COSAC, Helsinki, 2006. See relevant documents on the COSAC website: www.cosac.eu/finland-2006/ordinary-meeting-of-the-xxxvi-cosac-19-21-november-2006/.

In practice, in general terms, on the basis of Rules 8 and 9, the Secretariat, under the coordination of the Permanent Member, assists the Presidency in the preparation and circulation of the documents relating to the meetings organised, drafts the minutes of the meetings, drafts the Bi-annual Report of COSAC, drafts background documents that may be deemed useful in preparation of the meetings and updates the COSAC website. Additionally, in this context, the Secretariat, and particularly its Permanent Member working closely with the Presidency, may advise the Presidency on any potential issue arising in relation to the organisation of the COSAC meetings.

III. THE IDEAS SUBMITTED BY PARLIAMENTS ON THE ROLE AND FUNCTIONING OF THE COSAC SECRETARIAT IN THE CONTEXT OF THE 'FUTURE OF COSAC'[6]

Following discussions and reforms of COSAC in recent years and building upon the 13th and the 14th Bi-annual Reports of COSAC under the Spanish and Belgian Presidencies of May and October 2010 respectively, the 21st Bi-annual Report of June 2014 under the Hellenic Presidency,[7] identifying a significant lack of evolution, explores the 'Future of COSAC'. In this context, Chapter 1 presents Parliaments' views on the effectiveness of COSAC as a forum of interparliamentary dialogue and exchange of information and best practice, and collects their opinions on how COSAC should adapt to the evolving landscape of interparliamentary cooperation.

In the questionnaire for the Report, Parliaments were asked, among other things, '*whether the role and functioning of the COSAC Secretariat should be improved or reformed within the evolving landscape of interparliamentary cooperation*'. Twenty-two out of 37 responding Parliaments/Chambers replied negatively.

Six of those which responded positively and which commented on the issue (French Sénat, Luxembourg Chambre des Députés, Irish Houses of the Oireachtas, UK House of Commons, Italian Senato della Repubblica and Danish Folketing), proposed an expanded role for the COSAC Secretariat in supporting other interparliamentary meetings, such as:

— the Inter-Parliamentary Conference for the Common Foreign and Security Policy (CFSP) and the Common Security and Defence Policy (CSDP) (French Sénat, Luxembourg Chambre des Députés, Irish Houses of the Oireachtas, UK House of Commons, Danish Folketing);
— the Interparliamentary Conference based on Article 13 of the Treaty on Stability, Coordination and Governance in the Economic and Monetary Union (French Sénat, Luxembourg Chambre des Députés, Irish Houses of the Oireachtas, Danish Folketing);
— the future mixed parliamentary committee in the area of EUROPOL and the evaluation of EUROJUST (French Sénat);
— the EU Speakers' Conference (Luxembourg Chambre des Députés);
— all interparliamentary meetings organised in national Parliaments and the European Parliament (Italian Senato della Repubblica).

[6] This section is based on Chapters 1 and 2 of the 21st Bi-annual Report of COSAC.
[7] See full report on the COSAC website: www.cosac.eu/documents/bi-annual-reports-of-cosac/.

The Luxembourg Chambre des Députés referred to 'a certain experience of the Secretariat in the field of interparliamentary cooperation' supporting that it 'could offer its competences to the benefit of the respective Presidencies, being reinforced, where appropriate, with a second or third or fourth permanent member for co-financing amongst Parliaments'. The UK House of Commons referred to an expanded role for cost and efficiency reasons.

Certain Chambers referred to a role in relation to a 'yellow card' issued according to the provisions of Protocol No 2 annexed to the Treaty of Lisbon on the application of the principles of subsidiarity and proportionality:

- the COSAC Secretariat should give priority to the improvement of a structural coalition-formation in the context of the 'yellow card' procedure by facilitating discussion on the Commission Work Programme, exchange of priorities amongst the members of COSAC and identification of potential coalitions on specific topics (Dutch Tweede Kamer);
- more online tools could be used, such as a Facebook web page or email lists (Dutch Tweede Kamer);
- there may be a role for the COSAC Secretariat to more actively facilitate interparliamentary activities between COSAC meetings, both at official and political level, for example on occasions when a 'yellow card' is reached (UK House of Commons).

The UK House of Lords saw a role if simultaneous workshops, topic debates or working groups were organised and identified a need for a potential increase of the resources available to COSAC and its Secretariat should COSAC modify its working practices to include the above or ad hoc working groups of members preparing discussion papers. The same Chamber added that, subject to guidelines set down by COSAC, there could be a role for the COSAC Secretariat in providing logistical or other support and advice in order to facilitate ad hoc 'cluster' meetings of parliamentarians, given the increasing frequency of these.[8]

Others proposed a reinforced role within the existing framework and arrangements:

- a role in relation to the content (ie, preparation of notes for reflection) rather than a purely formal role (Belgian Chambre des représentants);
- the COSAC Secretariat may work to further encourage and trigger cooperation and awareness, ie, by maintaining a database of requests/questionnaires on parliamentary procedures, accessible through the COSAC webpage (Greek Vouli ton Ellinon);
- the COSAC Secretariat could, under the political responsibility of the COSAC Presidency and the Presidential Troika, play a greater role in distributing/circulating the COSAC Bi-annual Report and in preparing information notes (European Parliament's Committee on Constitutional Affairs).

The Latvian Saeima identified a potential role in exploring ways to improve the functioning of COSAC; the COSAC Secretariat could, in cooperation with the Presidency, contribute by exploring ways to improve the functioning of COSAC, to strengthen its role and increase the role of national Parliaments in the legislative process of the EU.

[8] Such meetings have been proposed by the European Affairs Committee of the Danish Folketing in a paper titled 'Twenty-three recommendations—to strengthen the role of national parliaments in a changing European governance'. According to proposal 14, '[m]embers of national parliaments could benefit from meeting with European colleagues in small informal sessions organised along shared interests'.

The Dutch Tweede Kamer noted that the Secretariat should implement its duties within the existing financial arrangements.

The Italian Camera dei Deputati expressed the view there was no need to change the role, the composition and the functioning of the COSAC Secretariat; it should continue to concentrate on the preparation of Bi-annual Reports and to assist the Presidency Secretariat in all its tasks.

Chapter 2 of the 21st Bi-annual Report collects Parliaments' views on whether, in the context of recent developments, there is a need to update the Guidelines for interparliamentary cooperation in the European Union (Lisbon guidelines)[9] and, among others, on how COSAC may provide a useful input to future EU Speakers' Conferences. The guidelines in question were adopted by this Conference at its meeting in Lisbon, 20–21 June 2008, before the entry into force of the Treaty of Lisbon. They refer to three main objectives of interparliamentary cooperation in the EU, namely the promotion of the exchange of information and best practices between national Parliaments and the European Parliament with a view to reinforcing parliamentary control, influence and scrutiny at all levels; ensuring effective exercise of parliamentary competences in EU matters, in particular in the area of monitoring the principles of subsidiarity and proportionality; and the promotion of cooperation with Parliaments from third countries.[10]

The majority of Parliaments/Chambers (21 out of 35) responded that the guidelines in question should be updated, several of which mentioned that an update should reflect new recent interparliamentary fora. Furthermore, in the related questionnaire, Parliaments were asked whether COSAC could provide some useful input to future EU Speakers' Conferences in relation to a possible reflection on the Lisbon guidelines for interparliamentary cooperation of June 2008. Twenty-eight out of 35 responding Parliaments/Chambers gave a positive reply.

The most favoured means (21 replies) for such potential input was the submission of a working document based on the replies to the COSAC questionnaire on the guidelines in preparation of the EU Speakers' Conference. Fourteen Parliaments/Chambers supported submitting the 21st Bi-annual Report to the Speakers' Conference. Considering the replies received, it is argued that a potential role for the Secretariat could be explored in such a context.

A concrete proposal was submitted by the Greek Vouli ton Ellinon; the latter expressed the view that, in preparation of the EU Speakers' Conference, the COSAC Secretariat could produce a more elaborate working paper based on the replies to the COSAC questionnaire on the guidelines in question.

IV. CHALLENGES AND FURTHER REFLECTION ON THE FUTURE ROLE OF THE COSAC SECRETARIAT IN AN EVOLVING INTERPARLIAMENTARY LANDSCAPE

The COSAC Secretariat and the creation of the post of its Permanent Member have gone a long way in contributing to the continuity and institutional memory of COSAC's activities. Parliaments' mostly negative reply to the question whether its role should be improved or

[9] See the document available at: www.europarl.europa.eu/webnp/webdav/site/myjahiasite/shared/About%20us/Guidelines/Guidelines%20Interparl%20Cooperation_Lisbon%2008.pdf.

[10] Para I.

reformed may be interpreted as confirming this statement. However, should the evolving landscape of interparliamentary cooperation require reconsideration of the Secretariat's role, it is argued that certain issues should be addressed. These should inform any further reflection that might be undertaken in the future.

In the light of the above, the challenges that would need to be addressed as regards the role of the COSAC Secretariat could be seen as relating to four basic themes in the context of which certain questions are inevitably raised: first, the role of the COSAC Secretariat and its Permanent Member as envisaged in the Rules of Procedure of COSAC; secondly, COSAC's relationship with new interparliamentary fora; thirdly, the political discussion on COSAC's role and raison d'être; and fourthly, the implementation of proposals should an improvement or a reform be deemed necessary in the future.

First, focusing on the primary source of the Secretariat's and the Permanent Member's tasks, ie the relevant provisions of the Rules of Procedure of COSAC, in section II it was noted that these are described in a general way. The question is raised as to whether a revision is needed and whether these tasks should be more concretely defined to reflect any possible reform. However, is the general character of the wording in COSAC's Rules of Procedure in relation to the tasks of the Secretariat a weakness or strength? How much regulation and/or flexibility are needed for the Secretariat, especially its Permanent Member, to successfully fulfil its role? What is more, to what extent, in the context of the existing institutional framework, can the abovementioned functions fundamentally be revised? How easy would the adoption of a revision proposal be considering the requirement in Rule 11 of the Rules of Procedure for unanimity among the delegations present at the meeting?

Secondly, how does COSAC constructively coexist with other existing interparliamentary meetings, such as the Inter-Parliamentary Conference for the Common Foreign and Security Policy (CFSP) and the Common Security and Defence Policy (CSDP) and the Interparliamentary Conference based on Article 13 of the Treaty on Stability, Coordination and Governance in the Economic and Monetary Union? In this context, should the Lisbon guidelines for interparliamentary cooperation be updated to reflect these?[11] Moreover, how do other different, smaller, formal and informal meetings of members of Parliaments potentially submitting contributions to COSAC fit in with the overall discourse on the future of COSAC?[12]

Thirdly, it is argued that COSAC has provided some rationalisation of interparliamentary cooperation and has enabled national Parliaments to contribute actively to the good functioning of the Union (Article 12 of TEU).[13] How far are we in the exploration of the raison d'être and functioning of COSAC as a political forum? Article 10 of Protocol no 1 annexed to the Treaty of Lisbon provides for exchange of information and best practice between national Parliaments and the European Parliament extending this function to special committees. It also offers the possibility for COSAC to organise conferences on specific topics.

In addition, the establishment of new interparliamentary fora, as well as potential initiatives regarding the right of national Parliaments to issue a 'yellow card'[14] and even a

[11] See views on these meetings in Part 2.2 of Chapter 2 of the 21st Bi-annual Report of COSAC under the heading 'Lisbon guidelines for interparliamentary cooperation'.

[12] See views on these meetings in Part 1.3 of Chapter 1 of the 21st Bi-annual Report of COSAC under the heading 'Formal and informal meetings of members of Parliaments/Chambers'.

[13] Haenel and De Croo, 'Evolution of COSAC over the last 20 years' (n 3 above).

[14] See Protocol no 2 annexed to the Treaty of Lisbon.

proposed 'green card'[15] in the context of political dialogue with the EU institutions, allowing national Parliaments to make suggestions regarding policy or legislative proposals to the European Commission without amending the Treaties may trigger a reflection on the future of COSAC as a political forum of interparliamentary cooperation and exchange of best practice.

In the light of the above, is COSAC going through an identity crisis in today's evolving landscape? Do delegations/politicians of both national Parliaments and the European Parliament agree on the role and potential of COSAC and its Secretariat? Can we identify some common ground in this regard? To what extent should a discussion on a possible reform of the Secretariat's role reflect the discussion on the future of COSAC?

Finally, the practical implementation of proposals, should an improvement or a reform be deemed necessary in the future, is inextricably linked to the discussion above. If COSAC, as an interparliamentary forum of exchange of information and best practice between national Parliaments and the European Parliament functioning since 1989, after 25 years of activities, is indeed in an identity crisis, how do we transform this crisis into a constructive, and not a destructive, discussion? How do we implement practical proposals, which would reflect common ground at a political level? Amidst differing views regarding the role of COSAC and its Secretariat, how do we reform considering also the question of human resources, if deemed necessary, while maintaining neutrality and/or balance in the Secretariat's work and the work of its Permanent Member assisting the Presidency Parliament and facilitating the functioning of COSAC?

V. CONCLUSION

This contribution has cast light on the views expressed by Parliaments in the 21st Bi-annual Report of COSAC on the need to explore further the potential of the role of the COSAC Secretariat; amidst differing positions, it is argued that such a discussion should necessarily reflect the wider discussion on the future of COSAC as a political forum of interparliamentary cooperation and exchange of best practices. Practical proposals in this regard should aim at a constructive approach and reflect common ground at a political level. The 21st Bi-annual Report is indicative of the degree of variation in the views of Parliaments in this regard. In the context of a potential quest for a revision of the Secretariat's role, taking into consideration a dynamically changing political landscape in the area of interparliamentary cooperation in relation both to the Treaty of Lisbon and to the political dialogue between national Parliaments and the EU institutions, especially the European Commission, certain vital questions and challenges for the future should be addressed.

[15] See proposal no 2 in the document of the European Affairs Committee of the Danish Folketing, in n 8 above, and a discussion paper circulated by the UK House of Lords, 28 January 2015.

The topic of the 'green card' procedure is discussed in the 23rd Bi-annual Report of COSAC published under the Latvian Presidency in May 2015. According to para 2.13 of the Contribution of the LIII COSAC adopted in Riga, a working group of COSAC on strengthening the political dialogue by introducing a 'green card' and improving the reasoned opinion procedure ('yellow card') was established under the Luxembourg Presidency, which met on 30 October 2015. See related documents on the COSAC website: www.cosac.eu/54-luxembourg-2015/cosac-working-group-30-october-2015/.

18

Interparliamentary Cooperation in the Context of COSAC: A View from the European Parliament

FRANCISCO GÓMEZ MARTOS*

I. INTRODUCTION

THE PRESENT CONTRIBUTION offers a view on interparliamentary cooperation from inside the European Parliament and thus it adopts a specular standpoint, compared to the other contributions of this Part that are based on the positions of different national parliaments.

The analysis carried out focuses on two main dimensions. The first aims to reconstruct the contribution of the European Parliament to directly reinforcing interparliamentary cooperation during the last 25 years, in particular through COSAC membership, and indirectly to the 'Europeanisation' of national parliaments. The second dimension of analysis aims to present the philosophy of the European Parliament towards the evolving role of COSAC.

No one can doubt that the European Parliament has always endeavoured to strengthen the democratically elected representation within the EU. The European Parliament did not want to have the monopoly of democratic projects, but instead spread its value by associating the NPs as closely as possible in the institutional structure, which is built from the

* The views expressed by the author are personal and do not necessarily reflect the official position of the European Parliament.

bottom-up approach instead of the top-down. The EP does not see itself as the exclusive representative of the citizens and guarantor of democracy, and the role of NPs is therefore deemed very important.

As a recent report of the European Parliament on the relations with national parliaments points out, the EU operates on the basis of a representative democracy and a two-fold democratic legitimacy: stemming from the European Parliament, directly elected by the citizens, and the Member States as represented in the Council by their governments, which are accountable to their national parliaments and citizens.[1]

II. SIGNS OF A COOPERATIVE ATTITUDE OF THE EUROPEAN PARLIAMENT TOWARDS NATIONAL PARLIAMENTS UNDER THE PRE-LISBON REGIME

Following Declaration no 13 of the Maastricht Treaty, on the role of national parliaments in the European Union, the European Parliament has been hosting national representatives from the national parliaments' administrations at its premises since the very beginning and has promoted interparliamentary contacts and sectoral meetings. Indeed, according to this Declaration, 'it is important for contacts between national parliaments and the European Parliament to be stepped up, in particular through the granting of appropriate reciprocal facilities and regular meetings between the members of Parliament interested in the same issues'.

Later, the Convention method, with the experience of the Conventions on the Charter of fundamental rights and on the future of Europe, has given strength to democratically elected representatives from national parliaments and the European Parliament and has allowed them to work together, achieving impressive results as reflected eventually in the Charter itself and in the Lisbon Treaty.[2] This treaty is a breakthrough in European democracy and a common success of national parliaments and the European Parliament. As a result of the dramatic increase of the quantity and the quality of interparliamentary cooperation, the Convention method was finally entrenched in the Treaties (article 48 TEU) as part of the ordinary revision procedure.

Furthermore, since the launch of the Interparliamentary EU Information Exchange (IPEX) in 2006, the European Parliament has been more than supportive in terms of financial and human resources provided in order to ensure the smooth functioning of this electronic platform, which has proved to be very useful to exchange information among parliaments in the European Union.

III. SIGNS OF 'RIVALRY' BETWEEN NATIONAL PARLIAMENTS AND THE EUROPEAN PARLIAMENT

Nevertheless, relations between the European Parliament and national parliaments have never been free of a certain rivalry and on some occasions overshadowed by some ambiguity.

[1] European Parliament, Committee on Constitutional Affairs, 'Report on relations between the European Parliament and national parliaments', Rapporteur Mr Carlo Casini, A7-0255/2014, 27 March 2014. See also art 10 TEU.

[2] On the role of parliaments in the Conventions, see C Pinelli, 'The Convention method', Ch 3 in this volume.

A clear proof of this tension can be seen regarding the structure and the functioning of COSAC.

First of all, since the very beginning, in 1989, the European Parliament has never been satisfied with the institutional model of COSAC, as the European Parliament's delegation was assimilated to each individual national parliament, regardless of the complexity of the European institution in ideological, national and geographical terms. It is worth remembering that six members of the European Parliament's delegation are asked to represent the views of more than 200 national political parties in 28 Member States. Needless to say, it is not easy to guarantee full representation of the European Parliament in its delegation to COSAC in order to reflect European political pluralism.

In this respect, the shortcomings deriving from the composition of COSAC parallel, to some extent, the mistrust of some national parliaments towards the so-called 'Assises', held in Rome in 1990. The two forums of interparliamentary cooperation, COSAC and 'Assises', show precisely the same though the opposite problems, in terms of lack of representation, respectively for the European Parliament and national parliaments. The 'Assises' brought together 173 national parliamentarians and 85 MEPs, with a clear over-representation of the European Parliament. For this reason the idea of convening a Conference of Parliaments, as proposed in Declaration 14 of the Maastricht Treaty, did not materialise. By contrast, COSAC has remained in place still today, despite the disproportionality between the number of seats available for MEPs and for members of national parliaments.

Secondly, the European Parliament has always been opposed to the idea, strongly supported by the French Parliament, of converting COSAC into a third chamber within the European institutional architecture, next to the Council and the European Parliament. The report presented in 2002 by the then President of the European Parliament's Committee on Constitutional Affairs (AFCO)—who later on became President of the Italian Republic—Giorgio Napolitano, was very clear in rejecting such an institutional development.[3]

Thirdly, the European Parliament considered that the monitoring of the respect of the subsidiarity principle should be ensured by each national parliament individually. Therefore, COSAC should not be entitled to have a collective and coordinating role in the monitoring of this essential principle, and the Lisbon Treaty is very clear in this respect. No reference is made to subsidiarity in article 10 of Protocol no 1 and the only role of COSAC is to promote the exchange of information in this context. Furthermore, articles 6 and 7 of Protocol no 2 annexed to the Treaty of Lisbon establish the individual nature of the early warning system.

IV. THE CHANGING LANDSCAPE OF INTERPARLIAMENTARY COOPERATION AFTER THE TREATY OF LISBON

During the last five years a great deal of change in interparliamentary cooperation has been experienced. Since the entry into force of the Lisbon Treaty, this cooperation has become increasingly intense in particular as regards to sectoral committees, while COSAC seems

[3] European Parliament, Committee on Constitutional Affairs, 'Report on relations between the European Parliament and the national parliaments in European integration', Rapporteur Mr Giorgio Napolitano, A5-0023/2002, 23 January 2002.

to lag behind. It appears evident that in the last few years an important shift of paradigm in the cooperation between national parliaments and the European Parliament has taken place.

Before the Lisbon Treaty, cooperation was mainly focused on institutional and constitutional issues and was concentrated on the role and activities of the AFCO Committee, in the European Parliament, and on the European Affairs Committees, in national parliaments. COSAC has therefore played an important role. However, as a result of the entry into force of the Lisbon Treaty, the scope of interparliamentary cooperation has significantly widened: the subsidiarity check needs to involve expert parliamentarians on the case, in specialised and sectoral committees as well. As a matter of fact, interparliamentary cooperation is moving from the exchange of information between institutional experts to political dialogue among specialists.

To meet this need, new formats of cooperation are being developed which are more adapted to 'specialist to specialist' interparliamentary dialogue. This has been reflected in recent years in a record number of interparliamentary committee meetings organised on the premises of the European Parliament or by the Parliament of the Member State holding the rotating Presidency of the Union dealing with dossiers at an early legislative phase. These dossiers are mainly linked to the adoption of the multiannual financial framework and of major reforms of EU policies, such as regional policy, agriculture, fisheries and other sectorial themes.[4]

A shift can be detected from smaller meetings, dealing with broad political questions but with a limited direct impact on the ongoing parliamentary activity, towards more specialised meetings on specific policies or pieces of draft legislation. In the near future, this tendency could include new 'made-to measure' meeting formulas, technically supported by the use of video-conferencing.[5]

V. IS THERE ROOM FOR COSAC'S PARTICIPATION IN THIS NEW MODEL OF INTERPARLIAMENTARY COOPERATION?

Which role could COSAC play in this new shifting scenario? In the last two years, two other new Interparliamentary Conferences have been established besides COSAC, giving rise to the prospect of a greater degree of parliamentary scrutiny in the area of CFSP-CSDP, following the dissolution of the WEU Parliamentary Assembly, and on economic governance, according to Article 13 of the Treaty on Stability, Coordination and Governance.

In this new context, COSAC is experiencing some difficult challenges, as the COSAC model for interparliamentary cooperation was not considered suitable for this 'second generation' of interparliamentary forums. Nevertheless, it remains to be seen whether these

[4] European Parliament, DG Presidency, Directorate for relations with national parliaments, Report on 'Interparliamentary relations between the European Parliament and national Parliaments under the Treaty of Lisbon 2009–2014, Annual Report 2013/2014', in particular chapter 7 on Trends in interparliamentary relations 2009–2014, pp 17–21.

[5] This trend was explicitly encouraged by the EP in its resolution of 7 May 2009 (Brok report) and developed by the Steering Group on relations with national Parliaments (Report on 'Interparliamentary relations between the European Parliament and national Parliaments under the Treaty of Lisbon, 2010–2011').

Interparliamentary Conferences can constitute a competitive and more effective model for more democratic accountability and parliamentary scrutiny of EU policies.

Likewise the relationship with the EU Speakers' Conference can represent a challenge for COSAC. In the last two years, the Speakers' Conference has risen in importance due to the role attributed to interparliamentary cooperation by article 9 of the Protocol no 1 on the role of national parliaments, and has led the way in shaping the future of interparliamentary relations. The EU Speakers' Conference has achieved agreements on setting up two new formats for interparliamentary scrutiny, on CFSP/CSDP and on economic governance, as a counterbalance to the trend of intergovernmental decision-making among Member States within the European Council and Ecofin. It appears that the Speakers' Conference rather than COSAC is exercising a coordinating and supervisory, if not rule-making, authority in shaping interparliamentary cooperation in the EU.[6] In the new shifting scenario of interparliamentary cooperation, COSAC is coping with further challenges that are only partly caused by the (problematic) composition.

Indeed, a dichotomy can be detected between COSAC's 'generalist' Members from EU Affairs Committees and more expert 'specialist' Members of sectoral committees who participate in other and more numerous interparliamentary forums.[7] The stability of COSAC's membership over time also derives from its highly institutionalised character and its strict rules of procedures, unless members of committees on EU affairs form part at the same time of sectoral committees.

A second weakness of COSAC lies in the fact that, instead of providing enough space for interparliamentary dialogue, debates and interaction between EU parliamentarians, which is COSAC's statutory purpose, it has become more a forum for national and European executives to pass down their views to parliamentarians. Currently, Prime Ministers, ministers, members of the European Commission and other representatives from the executive branches account for almost two-thirds of Speakers at COSAC's meetings. On the other hand, parliamentarians introducing the debate account for 16 per cent of keynote speakers and are therefore the exception.

Even if 'vertical' dialogue with national and European representatives from the executive branch is always very welcome,[8] some COSAC innovations are needed to create intense 'horizontal' interparliamentary dialogue. In this respect, it can be noted that the Irish and Lithuanian Presidency Parliaments made interesting attempts to innovate and refresh the format of COSAC meetings by, inter alia, introducing panel discussions, providing a forum to young citizens representing minority groups and scheduling informal sessions on parliamentary practices in selective EU scrutiny experiences and on the role of national parliaments in scrutinising EU decision-making.

[6] See C Fasone, 'Ruling the (Dis-)order of Interparliamentary Cooperation? The EU Speakers' Conference', Ch 14 in this volume, who highlights the many problems arising from the exercise of this rule-making function by the EU Speakers' Conference.

[7] See D Fromage, 'Standing committees in interparliamentary cooperation in the post-Lisbon era: towards the end of the European Affairs Committees' predominance?', Ch 6 in this volume, arguing that the creation of new interparliamentary and more specialised forums has not yet led to a marginalisation of the European affairs committees in the national parliaments.

[8] See the findings of the COSAC 21st Bi-Annual Report, Developments in European Union Procedures and Practices Relevant to Parliamentary Scrutiny, 19 June 2014, p 11.

A second direction of transformation of COSAC could be that of its politicisation. Indeed COSAC's plenary meetings are traditionally preceded by meetings of the main political groups at European level, which are either presided or co-presided over by the Co-chairs of the European Parliament's delegations.[9] The recent adoption of the Regulation on funding of the European Political Parties and Foundations constitutes an important step in the creation of a genuine European political space.[10] In this context, COSAC, by formalising more articulated and substantial debates within political families, could certainly play a leading role.

VI. CONCLUSION

In the past COSAC has played a key role in the configuration of interparliamentary cooperation, by making it more efficient and innovative compared to the framework pre-1989. For instance, COSAC actively promoted the idea of minimum time limits for consideration of EU legislative documents by national parliaments, on the occasion of the COSAC meeting in Dublin in October 1996. COSAC has also supported making fuller use of the electronic transmission of Commission and other EU documents to national parliaments and the need for an informal involvement of NPs at an early stage of legislative planning.

Nevertheless, since the very beginning, COSAC has faced a paradox. On the one hand, this is the unique instrument for interparliamentary cooperation recognised by the Treaties since 1997. On the other hand, its scope and its limited mandate are not clearly defined, which results in a series of consequences.

First, COSAC is constantly looking for its institutional identity. It does not have the necessary capacity at its disposal to adapt to current changes and therefore lacks flexibility.

Secondly, without having either clear and ambitious objectives or a clear mandate, its place in the institutional design of the EU can hardly be defined.

Given these limitations, it is difficult to determine what the real added value of this organ is, beyond the promotion of information and best practices among parliaments. The lack of institutional definition creates a sort of overlapping and competitive situation which adversely affects COSAC in comparison to other more concrete and new models of informal meeting (like interparliamentary committee meetings and joint parliamentary meetings) and a new generation of interparliamentary conferences in the framework of CFSP/CSDP and economic governance. COSAC has indeed a potential to be exploited but that is quite difficult to use, since the scope, mandate and the rules of procedure which govern its functioning cannot be easily modified.

Finally, COSAC has to find its place in the new scene of interparliamentary cooperation by demonstrating its added value, its efficiency and attractiveness. The institutional sky is full of stars: the question is which one will light the best way forward.

[9] See N Brack and T Deruelle, 'Towards a more politicised interparliamentary cooperation? The European Parliament's political groups and the European Parliamentary week', Ch 7 in this volume.

[10] Regulation (EC) No 2004/2003 of the European Parliament and of the Council of 4 November 2003 on the regulations governing political parties at European level and the rules regarding their funding, as it has been subsequently modified in [2007] OJ, L343/5, 27 December 2007.

19

The Role of COSAC in EU Interparliamentary Cooperation: An (Endless) Quest for an Identity

ANTONIO ESPOSITO

I. COSAC AND THE ANTINOMIES OF INTERPARLIAMENTARY COOPERATION

SINCE ITS ESTABLISHMENT in 1989, COSAC (Conference of the Parliamentary Committees for Union Affairs of Parliaments of the EU) has been engaged in an endless quest for an identity within the EU constitutional framework.

While (and because) it is the only form of interparliamentary cooperation explicitly referred to in the Protocols annexed to the Treaties, COSAC has been the main battleground—in the institutional debate as well as in the literature[1]—for conflicting positions about the role of the National Parliaments (NPs) in the EU and their relations with the European Parliament (EP).

As a consequence, the role of the Conference has been underestimated or, more often, overestimated, by neglecting or misconceiving the relevant legal framework.[2] COSAC has

[1] See A Cygan, 'COSAC: Birth, Evolution, Failures and Perspectives', Chapter 11 in this volume, and the authors cited by him.

[2] The legal framework of interparliamentary cooperation results from the combination of different sources, which can be ordered in five hierarchical levels:

a) Treaties on the European Union (TEU) and on the functioning of the EU (TFEU), annexed Protocols on the role of national parliaments (Protocol no 1) and on the application of the principles of subsidiarity and proportionality (Protocol no 2). In particular, Art 12(f) TEU and Title II (Interparliamentary cooperation, including Articles 9 and 10) of Protocol no 1 are the specific legal basis of cooperation. Such provisions do not provide just a symbolic recognition of the cooperation but have a normative content resulting from a systematic interpretation along with other provisions of the Treaties (in particular, Art 10.2 TEU) and with the general principles of the EU legal system;
b) Guidelines on interparliamentary cooperation, adopted by the EU Speakers' Conference in 2004 and revised in 2008, which can be considered as a direct implementation of the function of 'organisation and promotion of effective and regular cooperation' set out in Article 9 of Protocol no 1. They are therefore at a higher hierarchical level than the rules of procedure of each conference;
c) General principles of cooperation, well established in the practice and recalled in the Guidelines;

been over time thought of as an EU Institution[3] or consultative and overseeing body[4] as a coordinator of the cooperation among NPs,[5] as the core of a second (third) EU Chamber,[6] as a mere forum for the exchange of information and views.[7]

The actual role of COSAC results from a fragile compromise among contrasting views that can be traced back to five antinomies.

The first concerns the position of COSAC in the framework of EU interparliamentary cooperation and notably its relationship with the EU Speakers' Conference. Such antinomy has focused—after the Lisbon Treaty entered into force—on the interpretation of Articles 9 and 10 of Protocol no 1.

Under Article 9 the EP and NPs 'shall together determine the organisation and promotion of effective and regular interparliamentary cooperation within the Union'. Such provision does not establish a specific model of cooperation but leaves a wide discretion to the parliaments themselves, provided that the EP and NPs decide 'together' the framework of the cooperation. Article 10 is the legal basis of COSAC and entrusts it with three tasks:

— Submitting any contribution it deems appropriate for the attention of the EP, the Council and the Commission. The contributions do not bind NPs and do not prejudge their positions;
— Promoting the exchange of information and best practices between NPs and the EP (including their special committees). This task (which was not mentioned in the Protocol annexed to the Treaty of Amsterdam previously in force) is, significantly, the only one expressly conferred upon COSAC by the Guidelines on interparliamentary cooperation (Section II.b));
— Organising 'interparliamentary conferences on specific topics, in particular to debate matters of common foreign and security policy, including common security and defence policy'. The scope of this task—which was in part mentioned in the Protocol on the role of NPs annexed to the Treaty of Amsterdam—has raised a highly controversial debate over the interpretation of Articles 9 and 10.

According to one interpretation, advanced by NPs which aim at strengthening the role COSAC and at reducing the influence of the EP on interparliamentary cooperation, Article 10, as a *lex specialis* in relation to Article 9, would enable COSAC to establish new conferences between specialised committees of EU parliaments.[8] To this end, COSAC could

d) Decisions of the EU Speakers' Conference on the organisation of specific conferences, forums or tools of cooperation (such as IPEX);
e) Rules of procedure of each conference (EU Speakers' Conference, COSAC, Conference on CFSP/CFDP).

[3] See R Hrbek, 'The Role of National Parliaments in the EU' in H Blanke and S Mangiameli (eds), *The European Union after Lisbon* (Heidelberg, Springer, 2012) 137.

[4] See M Olivetti, 'Parlamenti nazionali nell' Unione europea' in *Digesto discipline pubblicistiche. Aggiornamento V* (Torino, Utet, 2012) 485, 567.

[5] See especially M Houser, 'La COSAC, une instance européenne à la croisée des chemins' (2005) 2 *Revue du Droit de l'Union Européenne* 357.

[6] See J Neyer, 'Justified Multi-level Parliamentarism: Situating National Parliaments in the European Polity' (2014) 20 *Journal of Legislative Studies* 135.

[7] See JV Louis, 'National Parliaments and the Principle of Subsidiarity—Legal Options and Practical Limits' in I Pernice and E Tanchev (eds), *Ceci n'est pas une Constitution—Constitutionalisation without Constitution?* (Baden-Baden, Nomos Verlag, 2009) 144.

[8] See especially the position of the EACs of 16 NP/Chambers (Czech, Danish, Irish, Hungarian, Lithuanian, Estonian, Luxembourg, Latvian, Slovenian, Slovak, Finnish and Swedish parliaments as well as the House of Lords,

vote, as provided in its Rules of procedure, by a majority of three-quarters even against the position of the EP (which has two votes, within COSAC, as does each national parliament). As a result, COSAC would mostly ensure the organisation of 'regular' cooperation, while the EU Speakers' Conference could only set out general principles of cooperation.

An opposite interpretation, supported by other NPs[9] and the EP, sees in Article 9 the exclusive legal basis to organise interparliamentary cooperation even by establishing new conferences. In particular, this provision would give a legal ground to the competence of coordinating the interparliamentary cooperation conferred on the EU Speakers' Conference well before the Lisbon Treaty entered into force.[10] As it always decides by consensus, the latter Conference ensures that EP and NPs decide 'together'. In addition, the Speakers, despite the different role they play in their respective assemblies, are in the best position to establish the general rules applicable to conferences or meetings involving various parliamentary bodies. Conversely, COSAC, while including only representatives of the EU Affairs Committees (EAC), would not be entitled as such to take any decision on the establishment or organisation of other conferences, forums or tools for cooperation among sectoral committees or other parliamentary body.

According to this interpretation, Article 10 as well as any other Treaty provision envisaging, directly or indirectly, the establishment of forms of interparliamentary cooperation[11] should be applied in compliance with the principles established by EU Speakers' Conference. COSAC could convene only ad hoc (rather than permanent) conferences on specific topics.

The latter interpretation is more consistent with the wording of Protocol no 1 (Article 9 refers specifically to the promotion of an 'effective and regular' cooperation', while Article 10 enables COSAC to organise conferences 'on specific topics') and with the general principles of the EU constitutional system. If COSAC were responsible for organising the cooperation between sectoral committees, this would determine a serious breach of the principle of institutional autonomy stated in Article 4.2. TEU and recalled in the first paragraph of the preamble of Protocol no 1. Indeed the EAC would be conferred a competence of coordination of the cooperation among the sectoral committees of NPs despite the different powers they have in their respective parliamentary systems.

It is therefore not surprising that the second proposed interpretation of Articles 9 and 10 of Protocol no 1 has prevailed over the first. The EU Speakers' Conference decided on the establishment and the organisation of the Conference for the CFSP/CSDP and of the Conference under Article 13 of TSCG despite the EACs of some parliaments having asked COSAC to proceed for this purpose.[12]

Belgian and Romanian Senates) who sent a letter to the EU Speakers' Conference in March 2013, proposing to hold the Conference under Art. 13 of the TSCG in the margins of the COSAC-meetings. The letter is published on the website of the Conference's meeting in Nicosia in April 2013 (www.ipex.eu/IPEXL-WEB/euspeakers/getspeakers.do).

[9] Especially the Italian Parliament.

[10] On the role of the EU Speakers' Conference see C Fasone, 'Ruling the (dis-)order of interparliamentary cooperation? The EU Speakers' Conference', Ch 14 in this volume.

[11] See Art 13 of the Treaty on Stability, Coordination and Governance in the Economic and Monetary Union ('TSCG') and Arts 70, 85 and 88 TFEU.

[12] See n 8 above. On the establishment of the Conference on CFSP/CSDP and of the Conference under Art 13 TSCG see, respectively, J Wouters and K Raube, 'The Interparliamentary Conference on Common Foreign and Security Policy: A Quest for Democratic Accountability in EU Security Governance' (Ch 12), and I Cooper,

A second antinomy concerns the object and scope of COSAC. According to Article 5.2 of the COSAC Rules of procedure, 'the principal business on every draft agenda shall be derived from the role of COSAC as a body for exchanging information and best practices between parliaments of the EU, in particular on the practical aspects of parliamentary scrutiny'. Invoking this Article, some NPs propose that COSAC, in order to make its meetings more effective, should focus on the role of parliaments at EU level, including their relations with the EU Institutions, as well as on important horizontal dossiers and on relevant aspects of EU decision-making.

Instead most NPs claim that the Conference is competent to discuss any EU-related issue, including specific legislative proposals or pre-legislative documents. As this position tends to prevail, the agenda of COSAC meetings usually includes various items, even concerning EU sectoral policies falling within the scope and the objects of other interparliamentary conferences or meetings. This causes a duplication of interparliamentary debates on the same issue and a tendency of COSAC meetings to have an overfull and unfocused agenda, which affects the quality of the plenary debates and of the final contributions.

A third antinomy concerns the role of COSAC in relation to the Early Warning System (EWS) introduced by the Lisbon Treaty. Some NPs argue, more or less explicitly, that COSAC should facilitate the triggering of the thresholds of the yellow or orange card. To this end it should identify, even before their formal presentation (notably scrutinising the Annual Working Programme of the Commission), legislative proposals that raise subsidiarity concerns; once submitted, such proposals could be discussed during the ordinary (or ad hoc) Chairpersons' (see next section) and/or plenary meetings or even by working groups. The COSAC Secretariat could support this exercise.

Other NPs and the EP counter that in this way COSAC would end up exercising collectively the EWS, against the wording and the principles of the Treaties. Indeed Article 10 of Protocol no 1, unlike the Protocol on the role of NPs annexed to the Amsterdam Treaty, does not make any reference, among the COSAC tasks, to subsidiarity and the examination of specific legislative proposals. This significant innovation—surprisingly neglected by several NPs and scholars[13]—seems aimed at preventing COSAC from interfering in the conduct of the subsidiarity checks by individual NPs. According to Article 6 of Protocol no 2 each national parliament or chamber can, following its procedures and practices, issue a reasoned opinion and decide if and how to share information and its subsidiarity assessment with the others.[14] COSAC would therefore be entitled to promote the exchange of information and best practices on how NPs carry out the EWS. Conversely, it should not stimulate or coordinate the conduct of the subsidiarity check on specific legislative proposals.

This second position has prevailed as the XLIII COSAC (Madrid, 30 May–1 June 2010) decided that the coordinated subsidiarity check—conducted from 2005 to 2009—'should no longer be a priority for the Conference'. This decision was taken not so much to maintain

'The Interparliamentary Conference on Stability, Economic Coordination and Governance in the European Union (the "Article 13 Conference")' (Ch 13), both in this volume.

[13] See especially P Kiiver, *The Early Warning System for the Principle of Subsidiarity. Constitutional theory and empirical reality* (Abingdon, Routledge, 2012) 132; A Cygan, 'COSAC: Birth, Evolution, Failures and Perspectives', Ch 11 in this volume.

[14] On the individual or collective use of the EWS see M Goldoni, 'Interparliamentary cooperation in the EWM and in the "political dialogue"', Ch 9 in this volume.

consistency with the Treaties, but because of the sheer practical difficulty of coordinating the action of NPs in the EWS, due to three factors:

a) In several parliaments the sectoral committees and/or the plenary have a primary competence to issue a reasoned opinion. Therefore the coordination of COSAC, which includes only the EACs, would be inappropriate or ineffective;
b) NPs carry out the subsidiarity check following heterogeneous criteria, methods and objectives.[15] A few parliaments assess only the compliance of draft legislative acts with subsidiarity; most of them scrutinise also the legal basis and some appraise the proportionality compliance. The proposal to adopt guidelines clarifying the scope of the subsidiarity check—advanced by some NPs—has been considered within COSAC but has not been agreed;
c) After five years of application of the EWS, it is clear that each parliament uses it to assert its respective national interests. Reasoned opinions are issued on the basis of political rather than of legal appraisal, as evidenced by the fact that they concern a very broad variety of legislative proposals.

A fourth antinomy concerns the relationship between NPs and the EP within COSAC. Some NPs consider the EP as a competitor or even an antagonist (in particular in relation to the EWS) and often take positions that underline this potential conflict. Others support instead the complementarity of the roles of the EP and of NPs. These approaches often face each other in the debates on the contributions and in the conclusions of COSAC.

A fifth antinomy regards the scope of the relations between COSAC and the EU Institutions. In some NPs' view COSAC should promote a 'collective' political dialogue with the Commission, with the aim of enhancing the direct influence of NPs on EU policy-making or even of making the Commission de facto accountable to them. Other NPs instead argue that COSAC, in compliance with the institutional balance established in the Treaties, could just allow and promote an exchange of views with the Commissioners (and representatives of other EU Institutions).

The latter position is prevailing: COSAC does not (and should not) play any advisory, policy-setting or overseeing function in the EU Institutions. It has no specific role in the EU decision-making or policy-framing process. Its contributions, while addressed to the EU Institutions, contain general statements on various aspects of Union activity. The Commission's replies, symmetrically to the contributions, are quite generic and often recall measures or positions already taken by the Commission itself.

II. COMPROMISE AND AMBIGUITY IN THE COSAC RULES OF PROCEDURE

The compromise among the contrasting views on the role of COSAC is reflected in its Rules of procedure (RoP), which provide unique organisational arrangements compared to those of other EU interparliamentary conferences:

a) The equal size of the delegations of EP and each NP (six members) while in the Conference on CFSP/CSDP the EP has 16 representatives and the NPs six. In the

[15] See N Lupo, 'National parliaments in the European integration process: re-aligning politics and policies' in M Cartabia, N Lupo and A Simoncini (eds), *Democracy and Subsidiarity in the EU* (Bologna, Il Mulino, 2013) 107.

Conference under Article 13 of Fiscal Compact each parliament decides the size of its delegation;

b) The regular meetings of the Chairpersons (not provided for in any other Conference), which were established with an amendment to the RoP in 2003 proposed by some NPs. The ultimate objective was to strengthen the role of COSAC by creating a body more agile and informal than the plenary, so as to take a position more rapidly and frequently on specific issues or draft legislation. This strategy has not been successful, due to the opposition of other NPs and of the EP; the bi-annual meeting of the Chairpersons—apart from the (formal) adoption of the draft agenda of the plenary—just debates generic or specific policy issues without providing any added value to the activities of COSAC. More significant is the meeting of the Chairpersons which adopts the final draft contribution and conclusions to be submitted to the plenary meeting;

c) The Presidential Troika (formally not provided for in any other Conference), which has to be consulted by the Presidency Parliament on the agenda of the plenary and on all matters relating to the functioning of COSAC;

d) The voting procedures for its deliberations, including the possibility of qualified majority voting. Unlike the EU Speakers' Conference and the other interparliamentary conferences, where consensus is the rule, COSAC's contributions and conclusions may be adopted, if a broad consensus cannot be achieved, with a majority of at least three-quarters of the votes cast, representing at least half of all votes;

e) The COSAC Secretariat composed of officials from parliaments of the Troika and a Permanent Member (an official of a NP appointed by the COSAC Chairpersons for two years). The decision to create the Secretariat was taken on a transitional basis in 2003 after long and contentious negotiations, and codified in the RoP in 2007. NPs wishing to strengthen the role of COSAC (even in view of a coordination of the positions of NPs vis à vis the EU institutions) had proposed to entrust the Secretariat with broad powers and to give the Permanent Member a prominent role (a sort of Secretary general of the Conference); conversely, other NPs and the EP opposed the creation of the Secretariat and the appointment of a Permanent Member; in their view the Presidency Secretariat could fulfil effectively all the tasks required for the functioning of COSAC. The compromise codified in Articles 8.7 and 9 RoP confers upon COSAC secretariat mere tasks of support to the Presidency Secretariat, under the political responsibility of the Presidency and the Troika. The Permanent Member in turn coordinates, just for the organisational aspects, the activities of the Secretariat.

Despite the efforts put in place by some NPs, since its establishment the COSAC Secretariat has not performed any task of coordination or promotion of the EWS or of other NPs' activities. Its most significant and valuable contribution to COSAC is the drafting of the Bi-annual Report on the developments in procedures and practices in the EU that are relevant to parliamentary scrutiny.

III. CONCLUSION: ACHIEVEMENTS AND POTENTIAL OF COSAC

The oscillation of COSAC between strongly different aspirations evinces a contest among (at least) three contrasting views about the role of NPs at EU level and the scope and object of interparliamentary cooperation.

Those who would entrust COSAC (or other conferences) with oversight powers over EU Institutions, and/or with functions of coordination for the purpose of the EWS and/or of the political dialogue, express a dissatisfaction with the current role of NPs and with the state of cooperation among them and the EP. In their view, the ultimate objective of interparliamentary cooperation should be the creation of a more effective democratic counterweight to the EU Institutions, in addition to the scrutiny by each NP of its own government. Most supporters of this view see collective or coordinated action by the NPs as a way to influence EU policy-making more effectively and even to require (a sort of) accountability of the Commission to the NPs themselves. Others make the case for joint scrutiny involving the EP and national parliaments together, especially in areas where EU decision-making is largely intergovernmental, such as foreign and security policy and economic governance.

Those who want COSAC to remain a forum for the exchange of information, views and best practices adhere to a strict interpretation of the legal framework of interparliamentary cooperation.

Crucial in this context is Article 10.2 TEU which, recognising the complementarity between direct and indirect representation for the democratic legitimacy of the EU, states that the primary role of NPs in the EU composite constitutional system is to ensure the accountability of their respective governments. The powers of direct intervention of the NPs in EU decision-making introduced by the Treaty of Lisbon as well as the political dialogue are therefore an additional and ancillary channel to ensure the democratic legitimacy of the EU.

It follows that the primary object of interparliamentary cooperation should be to contribute to the best performance of the functions of the EP and NPs, according to the logic of complementarity and not of competition among them.

Some NPs and most scholars[16] counter that interparliamentary cooperation, if resulting only in the exchange of information and views, would give little contribution to enhancing the position of NPs in the EU. COSAC (and the other conferences) should instead enable the national parliaments to reach a critical mass around common positions to be taken into account effectively by the EU Institutions. Taking note of the opposition of EP and other NPs to such approach, several NPs are engaging in forms of enhanced cooperation (clusters of interests) among themselves with the aim of coordinating their positions on specific topics or draft legislation for the purposes of the political dialogue or the EWS.

Such an approach seems to be based on an underestimation of the achievements of COSAC (and, more in general, of the current framework of cooperation).

A first achievement consists in the enrichment of the information base for policy-making and decision-making both in the EP and in NPs. COSAC meetings (including the informal contacts among MPs) and bi-annual reports prepared by the Secretariat provide a valuable survey of the positions as well as of the procedures and methodologies of other parliaments (and sometimes of the EU Institutions).

A second achievement is the increasing awareness in the NPs of the European dimension of national policies. COSAC (and other interparliamentary fora) have contributed to an unprecedented shift in the political culture in the NPs by overcoming purely national visions and the short-termism that pervades decision-making in most Member States.

[16] See A Cygan, 'COSAC: Birth, Evolution, Failures and Perspectives', Ch 11 in this volume.

A third achievement is the hybridisation and cross-fertilisation of the procedures and practices for the EU scrutiny in the NPs which have been significantly stimulated by the exchange of information and best practices within COSAC (and other interparliamentary forums). Amendments to constitutions, legislation or rules of procedure adopted by most Member States, especially after the entry into force of the Treaty of Lisbon, evince an emulation of the best practices of other Member States.

A fourth achievement is the consolidation of multilateral and bilateral relations between NPs and the European Commission, both at a political and at an administrative level. Together with the EU Speakers' Conference, COSAC has contributed to improving the political dialogue and the other channels of direct interaction among the NPs and the Commission.

A fifth achievement consists in the enhancement of administrative cooperation among NPs that ensures a constant contact among the assemblies, managing important information flows and facilitating cooperation at the political level. In addition to IPEX and to the network of representatives of NPs in Brussels, the contacts among officials attending COSAC meetings (and other standing conferences) promote a convergence of working methods and best practices that complete the process of cross-fertilisation mentioned above.

Through such achievements COSAC has contributed to two important developments of the EU constitutional system:

— the Europeanisation of NPs, made evident by the cross-fertilisation of the procedures and practices related to the EU scrutiny and by the increasing focus on the EU dimension in national policy-making;[17]
— the consolidation of a European parliamentary system consisting of a network of interparliamentary meetings, conferences and tools for administrative cooperation. Such a system, overseen by the EU Speakers' Conference, allows de facto a mutual influence of each parliament on the others in framing EU policies as well as in national decision-making.

The potential of COSAC and of the overall euro-national parliamentary system,[18] despite the results mentioned above, has not been fully exploited. The debates during COSAC meetings are often uninteresting due to various factors: too many items on the agenda of the meetings; limited speaking times for the delegates who often read pre-prepared speeches; keynote speakers from NPs as well as from EU Institutions who do not provide great added value. COSAC contributions and conclusions, while debated at length, end up containing vague and heterogeneous statements. Too much time and too many resources are wasted before and during the meetings in sterile claims for new powers to be vested in NPs. Few EAC report back to their parliaments on the outcomes of COSAC meetings.

[17] See DA Capuano, 'The Role of COSAC in the Europeanisation of National Parliaments and in the Evolution of the Interparliamentary Cooperation', Ch 15 in this volume.

[18] On the concept of the euro-national parliamentary system see N Lupo, 'Parlamento europeo e Parlamenti nazionali nella Costituzione "composita" dell'UE: le diverse letture possibili' in A Ciancio (ed), *Nuove strategie per lo sviluppo democratico e l'integrazione politica in Europa* (Roma, Aracne, 2014) 365–96 and A Manzella, 'Parlamento europeo e parlamenti nazionali come sistema' in *Rivista AIC*, 1/2015, available at: www.rivistaaic.it/parlamento-europeo-e-parlamenti-nazionali-come-sistema.html.

Such shortcomings do not stem from structural weakness of COSAC (and of the existing framework of interparliamentary cooperation) but from organisational failures and deficiencies in the political and administrative culture of individual parliaments.

COSAC can therefore find an identity by improving its organisation with a view to a more focused and in-depth exchange of information and views instead of re-proposing at every meeting debates on its future and indulging in the rhetoric of the democratic deficit of the EU.

The insistence of some NPs within COSAC on calling for new tools to interact collectively with the European Commission (such as the 'green card' allowing groups of NPs to propose to the Commission new legislative action, or the review, amendment of repeal of existing legislation) seems more a sign of weakness than a way to enhance parliamentary democracy in Europe. On the one hand, such an approach seems to reaffirm a competitive relationship between the EP and NPs that could affect the overall functioning of the euro-national parliamentary system; on the other hand, it evinces distrust in the effectiveness of the scrutiny by each NP of its own government.

20

Reshaping COSAC as a Dynamic Venue for Interparliamentary Exchange

MENDELTJE VAN KEULEN

I. INTRODUCTION

'MAY YOU LIVE in interesting times!', as the Chinese proverb allegedly goes. This certainly goes for one particular pillar in the EU's already rather intricate institutional architecture: national parliaments (NPs). In the past decade, the number of parliamentary practices and subsequent academic followers of these developments have blossomed. Increased parliamentary activity and awareness of European Union policy-making has put the spotlight upon one particular corner of European cooperation: that of COSAC, a venue which has been in operation for 25 years and has thereby witnessed the most lively period of the European integration process.

Other contributions in this volume have fleshed out the legal foundations and historical development of COSAC, a key venue for horizontal cooperation between national parliamentarians and their staff and representatives of the EU institutions (Commission and European Parliament (EP)). The acronym is generally used for their quarterly meeting in the respective capitals of the rotating Presidency. There is a distinction between the chairpersons'-COSAC, gathering together committee chairs of parliamentary European Affairs Committees at the beginning of each Presidency and the plenary meeting (with larger delegations) at the end. During each meeting, current EU policies and parliamentary affairs are discussed.

Few EU scholars have discussed the potential role of COSAC in interparliamentary cooperation, and even fewer academics have actually visited its meetings—which makes most analyses of its functioning and potential improvement somewhat hypothetical. And the focus on the alleged lack of concrete results of interparliamentary contacts (for example the rarity of yellow cards) has made the informal governance system, which has effectively been established amongst parliaments of EU Member States, less appreciated.[1]

This contribution aims to bridge the gap between academics and practitioners. Observations and suggestions stem from my own personal experience of subsequent COSAC meetings as secretary to the Dutch Tweede Kamer delegation in the past few years, following a decade of European academic study.

In a short presentation of common complaints and suggestions for improvement, it is argued that COSAC has not yet risen to its potential to become a true market place for the exchange of recent developments, positions and best practices in the parliamentary scrutiny of EU affairs.

II. WHAT MAKES COSAC UNIQUE?

The caveats are well known: there is a lot that COSAC is *not*. It is not an EU institution; it is not an agency; it is not a formal decision-maker for parliaments (this is the legal domain of the annual EU Speakers' Conference), and it is a particularly heterogeneous club. At the biannual full meetings, prepared by a meeting of EU Affairs Committee chair meetings, six Members represent each parliament. In addition, the NPs of the candidate countries are invited to participate with three observers each. These MPs, called together by their President (chair of the European Affairs Committee of the rotating Presidency), represent many different cultural backgrounds, legal cultures and constitutional mandates. The plenary summer meeting of COSAC constitutes one of the lesser-known, but larger meetings during the biannual rotating national Presidency in the EU capitals. As a COSAC conference of more than 300 attendees can be larger in size and duration than certain informal Council meetings, it is often, but mistakenly, undervalued during national Presidency preparations.

Apart from its overwhelming internal diversity, there are a number of other features that make COSAC rather peculiar in the EU's institutional architecture. For a long time, it was the only interparliamentary venue with a legal basis: namely article 9 of the Protocol on the role of National Parliaments in the European Union, annexed to the Treaty of Lisbon. Over the years, more specialised conferences have been given legal status, including the biannual economic and financial interparliamentary conference established with the Treaty on Stability, Coordination and Growth ('the article 13 conference'). And indeed, upon its founding as early as 1989, COSAC was meant to form a new room in the EU institutional building, as is argued elsewhere in this volume.[2] The conference was formally recognised in a Protocol on the Role of National Parliaments in the European Union to the Treaty of Amsterdam that was concluded by the Heads of State or Government in June 1997, and which entered into force on 1 May 1999.[3] From the first meeting onwards, the participants agreed that the main aim was a systematic exchange on the state of play in European affairs within the NPs and in the EU context. Later in this contribution, I will come back on the issue of to what extent this ambition has succeeded.

[1] See for a critical appraisal K Sohn and S Czuratis, *Reviving the principle of subsidiarity* (Freiburg, Centrum fur Europaische Politik, 2015). On informal governance, see T Christiansen and C Neuhold (eds), *Informal Governance in the European Union* (Cheltenham, Edward Elgar, 2012).

[2] A Cygan, 'COSAC: birth, evolution, failures and perspectives', Ch 11 in this volume.

[3] See COSAC Secretariat, *History of COSAC*, September 2014, available at: www.cosac.eu.

The second characteristic is that COSAC since 2004 has worked with a Permanent Secretariat, comprising one permanent member and four members seconded from the three NPs on the Presidential Troika (the former, the current and the future Presidencies) and the EP. The Secretariat's composition was a compromise between an OECD-like permanent Secretary General, and rotating administrative support provided by the parliament of the national Presidency. COSAC Secretariat's office is located at the EP's office, in the same building as the National Parliamentary Representatives. The Secretariat forms the administrative backbone of each conference and prepares the biannual reports.[4] Compared to the Secretariats of the NATO and BENELUX Parliamentary Assemblies (respectively 35 and 60 permanent staff), the four-person COSAC Secretariat obviously draws on limited capacity. Although there have been regular calls to upgrade its administrative support, until now the majority of its Member State parliaments have not been willing to add to its capacity in times of increasing Euroscepticism.

Thirdly, COSAC is the only EU interparliamentary conference with a strong history of producing substantial products on a regular basis: the Biannual Reports. These reports, addressing the state of play on a particular EU policy topic as reported by NPs, are increasingly used by practitioners and scholars in their search for parliamentary practices. As substantial output, they may be compared to the products delivered to the assembly by the NATO Secretariat. However, their reports in the field of international defence co-operation are drafted in smaller groups of committee officials and parliamentarians, whereas the biannual reports are essentially derived from the replies to questionnaires drafted by its member parliaments and edited by the Secretariat—one of its main functions during the period from conference to conference.

Finally, there is one feature of COSAC which is not at all unique, but rather common to all EU institutions. This concerns the fact that it is an institution in flux, which has evolved over the past 25 years of its existence and witnesses a dynamic period of change once again. This contribution assesses the developments at COSAC in the past few years and suggests practices for improvement of its workings in order to match the evolving role of NPs after the 2009 Lisbon Treaty.

III. COMPLAINTS ON COSAC

From the 21th Biannual Report of June 2014, a volume biannually compiled by the Secretariat on the basis of parliamentary responses, emerges a clear picture of the perception of pros and cons of COSAC co-operation as seen by its members.[5]

Most parliaments (27 out of the 31 parliamentary Chambers which responded to the question) consider *networking* as the most successful aspect of COSAC meetings. This networking function became particularly visible when the first yellow card (Monti II) was issued, as has been vividly described by one of few recent academic reporters live from COSAC.[6] Several parliaments mention that the timing of the COSAC meeting and

[4] C Fryda, 'The role of the COSAC secretariat within the evolving landscape of interparliamentary cooperation: challenges for the future', Ch 17 in this volume.

[5] COSAC, *21st Bi-annual Report on EU Practices and Procedures* (Brussels 2014), available at: www.cosac.eu.

[6] I Cooper, 'A Yellow Card for the Striker: How National Parliaments Defeated EU Strikes Regulation' (2015) 22 *Journal of European Public Policy* 1406 (published online on 1 April 2015).

networking during the conference was highly effective, as proponents of a yellow card used the conference actively to amass support amongst fellow MPs.[7]

Notwithstanding the stalled experiments with centrally administered common subsidiarity checks through COSAC, in recent years COSAC has become an important forum for coordinating the submission of reasoned opinions as part of the early warning system (EWS).

A second reason for praise for COSAC by its member parliaments is its being a venue for the regular exchange of best practices between parliaments. There are at least three topics for interaction between and during conferences. First, it is clear that all member parliaments face the same challenge of scrutinising their governments actively in EU negotiations. Secondly, since the Lisbon treaty, all parliaments also have the competence in the so-called EWS, the requirements of which (for example the numerical threshold and strict eight-week deadline put similar demands on parliamentary administrative and political capacity). Thirdly, in responding to the EU negotiating process, most parliaments discuss substantial EU dossiers at the same time, for example such packages as the European Semester, the EU common neighbourhood policy or migration challenges. This gives opportunity for exchange of opinions and experiences.

Whereas, on paper, COSAC may prove its worth as a relevant forum for interparliamentary exchange, there is critique on its current format and functioning. Many NPs, as interviewed in the report, consider the quality of debate during COSAC meetings as the least successful aspect of this type of interparliamentary cooperation. One problem is that practical issues often preclude actual attendance at the meeting by MPs, as participation or votes during domestic political debates are often prioritised by national fractions in parliaments above their members being away on working visits abroad. As the COSAC plenary session convenes on week days, for certain parliaments, such as the Dutch Tweede Kamer, there is often also a formal requirement to be present at recurrent—and sometimes unexpected—voting sessions in the plenary.

A second problem is that there is wide variation in the process of how the COSAC 'mandate' for the delegation is drawn up. In some parliaments, there is no previous discussion to set the mandate for Members visiting COSAC, so that each MP speaks on his or her own behalf. In other Chambers, written contributions are coordinated beforehand with the relevant standing committees to ensure that the delegation expresses a majority view. As a result, at COSAC meetings, certain participants can hardly make any new statements to developing discussions, nor improvise, whereas other delegations lack the power to bind their own assembly or to make commitments on its behalf.

Also, the outcome of deliberations is vague. Conclusions on amendments are generally decided on by consensus, although there can be voting by a qualified majority, as was the case with the paragraphs on migration after lengthy discussions in the November 2015 COSAC meeting in Luxembourg. However, according to article 10 of Protocol no 1, the conclusions and contributions are not binding upon NPs, in contrast to the annual EU Speakers' Conference. After a particularly difficult final session in Athens in June 2013, there have been calls to clarify the procedure of getting to conclusions, which according to

[7] On the yellow card and horizontal interparliamentary cooperation, see M Goldoni, 'The Instrumental Value of Horizontal Parliamentary Cooperation: Subsidiarity Review and the Political Dialogue', Ch 9 in this volume.

some should be more concise and focus on concrete and current issues.[8] But although the COSAC conclusions have no binding value, over the years, they have expressed in depth views both on current policy developments as well as procedural matters relevant for all delegations.

A related observation is the recurrent criticism of the large degree of formalism during COSAC conferences. Delegations often change composition, for example after national elections, with the effect that interpersonal contacts are difficult to sustain. Also, the conference programme as drawn up by the presiding parliament generally does not purposefully facilitate informal contacts between delegation members or staff. For example, there are generally no pre-determined seating plans during lunch or dinners, so that the networking aspect is rather random. The list of participants distributed by the Secretariat shortly before meetings does not include political affiliation or contact details. There is no practice of staff meetings foreseen before or during the political meetings, where particular aspects of the programme could be discussed. Therefore, a perceived weakness of COSAC is that its success is very much dependent on accidental personal contacts, which makes continuity a problem. It is partly due to this that horizontal contacts between MPs beyond COSAC meetings remain rare. There is no coordinated contact list of European Affairs Committee chairs, which hampers the occurrence of political coalition making at the moment when this is necessary, for example when an eight-week subsidiarity deadline is coming up.

IV. WHAT MAY BE IMPROVED?

A. The Content: More Focus on Substance …

In the aforementioned 21st biannual report, a majority of respondents suggested that COSAC meetings should focus more on substantive issues, allowing for dialogue and exchange of views—amongst NPs and with the EP. Here appears an important cleavage. On the one hand, there are parliaments which do actively value COSAC as a venue for discussing policy issues, such as regional issues (EU Mediterranean; EU Eastern Partnership). On the other side, there are those preferring a more procedural role for the conference, suggesting that COSAC focuses more on institutional issues, such as the role of NPs in EU decision-making or the functioning of the political dialogue.

The first position continues a tradition started with the very first COSAC meetings, which became at the time a debating venue for proposals for a Political Union and an Economic and Monetary Union, and prepared for the then-imminent Intergovernmental Conference in 1991. In some cases, discussing concrete policy domains indeed heats up the debate, as Member State parliaments tend to differ strongly regarding, for instance, the future of the EU's common agricultural policy, the quality of EU development aid or Turkish accession to the EU. In other cases, the quality of guest speakers, the static format of most contributions, as well as the large number of interruptions make for long sessions on rather specialised topics, such as 'improving economic governance'. This points

[8] See for example the letter by the European Affairs Committee Chairman of the German Bundestag, Gunther Krichbaum, on the occasion of the LII COSAC, Rome, 30 November–2 December 2014, available at: www.cosac.eu.

towards a more principled objection against a too substantial role of COSAC, which after all unites European Affairs spokespersons, instead of thematic parliamentary MP's. There is the potential risk of duplication with the proliferation of thematic conferences, organised by the presiding parliament and the EP, which focus on concrete policy domains such as CFSP/CDSP, economic and financial governance or ad hoc conferences on, for example, migration or gender rights.

A concrete proposal in order to facilitate a debate on content and to give more focus on the substance could be for the European Commission to be invited to COSAC meetings to present the ins and outs of recently published initiatives for new EU legislation or policy. The focus of the Commissioners' presentation could then be on the perceived impact of new EU proposals, based on the assessment of congruence with existing national and European law and the subsidiarity principle. For parliaments, this has the advantage of becoming quickly familiarised with a current topic. For the Commission, the COSAC forms a relevant format for discussion on topics to be negotiated between the Member States, in which the parliamentary waters can be tested concerning, for example, a new (Multi-)Annual Work Programme or new consultation documents, including Green or White papers or proposals for directives or regulations.

B. … Or on Process?

I argue in this contribution that the added value of COSAC for its participants could improve with the discussion of recent legislative and policy initiatives for the sake of upcoming national scrutiny. Another potential for improvement lies in organising discussions on those topics, which are core to the position and functioning of the participating parliaments.

The most obvious topic for interparliamentary exchange is the functioning in practice of the subsidiarity checks. It is well known that the current system of early warning in case of alleged breaches of the subsidiarity principle is a source of many complaints. During the November 2013 COSAC meeting in Rome, a group of interested parliaments led by the Danish Folketing, the House of Lords and the Dutch Tweede Kamer took the initiative to put forward different ways to improve the procedure. For some changes to take effect, parliaments are dependent on other parties, for example the flexibility by the European Commission to consider substantial contributions after the legal (eight-week) deadline and the quality and timing of its responses to reasoned opinions. But the main improvement to the Early Warning System to which national parliaments themselves have the key, is better co-ordination before, during and after the eight-week procedure to draft and send reasoned opinions to the Commission.

There are two concrete examples to be elaborated of regular interparliamentary contacts which may improve the quality and effectiveness of their interaction. First, if parliaments would care for a timely exchange of their individual political priorities on the basis of the (Multi-)Annual Legislative programme of the European Commission, they may find each other easier to deal with when those priorities are translated into concrete proposals eligible for a subsidiarity check. At the moment, this idea is elaborated upon the initiative of the Dutch Tweede Kamer. After an informal meeting of NPs' representatives in Brussels in January 2015, a request in the network of parliamentary representatives resulted in an overview of the priorities of 20 chambers, which was sent, on behalf of the participants, to the coordinating Commissioner Timmermans in May 2015.[9] In developing this procedure into standard practice, lies a potential role for the COSAC Secretariat.

A second suggestion is to have subsidiarity complaints more visible with the introduction of a fixed opening sentence of a reasoned opinion. That way it is immediately clear to the European Commission if it concerns a reasoned opinion and it will not be possible anymore for the Commission to decide itself on the status of an opinion. This initiative has been followed up in Spring 2015, by the installation of an ad hoc working group under the chairmanship of the Polish Sejm.

Much inspiration can be found in the biannual reports which function as an open source on interparliamentary practices. Searchable online at www.cosac.eu, everyone can take as they please procedures or smart ideas from the report that are appropriate for the processes and culture in their own parliament. During each plenary meeting, the new report is presented by the Secretariat. This presentation could easily be turned into an interactive discussion, by projecting the results in the form of statistics or statements and inviting participants to respond, or, alternatively, by giving room to certain participants to explain their best practices as mentioned in their responses. In this part of the conference programme, academic experts could be invited to contribute to the discussion on parliamentary scrutiny and co-operation within and between parliaments—a topic which enjoys more and more academic attention in the European Studies domain.[10] The biannual report has effectively had this effect, as was demonstrated by the successful attempt of the Dutch parliament to gain access to an internet database, containing all relevant Council agendas and legislative documents (Extranet), by using the information from other parliaments' experiences as described in the 15th biannual report published during the Polish Presidency in 2011. Confronted with the results of this report, attached to a letter of the European Affairs Committee explaining how the Dutch Tweede Kamer risked becoming a latecomer in access to this EU document database, in 2012, then-Foreign Minister Timmermans granted both Chambers access to the document database.

As mentioned in the above, most NPs are often concerned with the same topics at the same time. Exchanges on these matters and how parliaments deal with them could inspire and give way to new working methods, in particular if items addressed are given follow up by the Presidency in the next half year. During the chairpersons' COSAC Meeting in Rome in 2014, on the eve of the EP's elections, there was a call to invite other parliaments to propose national MEPs to question the candidate-Commissioners on their commitment to national parliamentary involvement. Although there seemed to be a positive reaction by those present at the conference, the follow up of this initiative by parliaments—and the effective response by national MEPs as well as individual Commissioners during the hearing—have remained unclear, through lack of any evaluation at a subsequent meeting.

[9] Letter of the European Affairs Committee Chairman, Dutch Tweede Kamer, Malik Azmani, to the Vice-President of the European Commission, Frans Timmermans, on the overview of national Parliaments' priorities selected from the European Commission Work Programme 2015, on the occasion of the LIII COSAC, Riga, 31 May–2 June 2015.

[10] See, for example, E Mastenbroek et al, *Engaging with Europe. Evaluating National Parliamentary Control of EU Decision-making After the Lisbon Treaty* (Nijmegen, Radboud University, 2014).

C. On the Conference Format

(i) Side Meetings

When asked about the potential for the venue, most respondents to the biannual reports support the suggestion to allow for more informal interaction at COSAC, such as ad hoc meetings or side meetings, given the absence of national mandates and the fact that it is not a decision-making body. For a number of years, there has been scant experience of meetings outside the plenary room. For example, during the 49th COSAC in June 2012 in Dublin, the Dutch Tweede Kamer initiated an informal lunch-time debate on parliamentary practices in selective EU scrutiny. The pilot session highlighted the annual exercise of extracting political priorities from the Commission Work Programme. In a smaller room with a Powerpoint introduction and walking microphone, some 60 MPs of different NPs attended the meeting and commented on the opportunities for priorities selection. The working language was English, as it was in Vilnius in October 2013 during an informal lunch-time session at the 50th COSAC, initiated by the House of Lords of the United Kingdom, on the role of NPs in shaping and scrutinising EU decision-making. It was highly appreciated by the participants as a rare opportunity to be engaged in a spontaneous, dynamic and open exchange of views, inter alia, with the European Commissioner responsible for inter-institutional relations.

During the 51th COSAC in Athens in June 2014, the Dutch Tweede Kamer hosted a side meeting focusing on experiences and potential best practices for the accountability of EU funds, and at the subsequent plenary in Rome, in December 2014, the practices of EU policy-making of health and safety at work were discussed. Although these meetings attracted considerable attention, responsiveness depends much on the commitment of the presiding parliaments, for example by listing the side session in the formal programme or providing sufficient time for discussion. Until now, the practice of regularly proposing side events, although actively initiated by the Dutch Tweede Kamer and the House of Lords, has depended on the degree to which they are actively taken up by successive Presidencies or other parliaments.

In contrast to other parliamentary assemblies, such as NATO and OSCE Parliamentary Assemblies, COSAC does not have the practice of preparatory meetings of delegation officials.[11] In an attempt for change, during a pilot session in Copenhagen in April 2012, delegation clerks and EU advisors gathered informally for a reception in the margins of the formal meeting. A second more substantial 'secretaries of delegation' meeting was organised in the margins of the 49 COSAC in Dublin, in Spring 2013. The topic was the quality and timeliness of information on EU scrutiny delivered by national governments, and introductions were held by the clerks of the Bundestag, Tweede Kamer and Italian Senate delegations. Notwithstanding positive evaluation by most participants, the meeting format was not repeated by subsequent Presidencies. In contrast to the aforementioned assemblies, which actively use social media such as email or Facebook in order to prepare assembly meetings logistically, COSAC also lacks a virtual meeting place of delegation officials.

[11] A Pegan and A-L Högenauer, 'The role of parliamentary administrations in interparliamentary cooperation', Ch 8 in this volume.

(ii) Real Interparliamentary Debates

The agenda of COSAC is drawn up by the Presidential Troika; composed of the current, former and future Presidencies, together with a representative of the EP. During the 5th COSAC meeting, in November 1991 in The Hague, where the rules of procedure were set, the practice of involving the full group of committee chairs in setting the agenda was dropped. However, apart from the issue of who determines the final agenda, there could be more activism by parliaments suggesting agenda items to be explored, in order to increase mutual commitment. The agenda of COSAC, primarily a meeting place of NPs, is influenced by the EP, as part of the Troika preparing the meetings. During the meetings, the EP gladly delivers speeches and at every conference, a number of European Commissioners fly in to address national parliamentarians. This gives the chance to debate policy fields with EU insiders. The key to improvement lies in the format; as the speech is often rather static and the opportunity for questions and answers not very structured. It has been suggested that the impact of these contributions could be easily improved by using modern technological facilities, such as telescreens projecting statements for discussion. Videoconferencing is a cost-effective option but for obvious reasons does not stimulate face-to-face exchange or networking opportunities.

V. CONCLUSION: ASSESSING COSAC

This contribution has focused on potential improvements to COSAC, a venue with a large potential. In general, the conference is highly valued as a place for networking and information exchange. Rather paradoxically, the current format of the conference suffers from too much formality, at times when there could be more interaction (for example in the presentation of the results from the biannual report). At the same time, its workings are too informal, where a little bit of structure could improve its effectiveness (for example in providing for contact details of the participants). As COSAC is considered by many as static, over-long and ready for improvement, its format may only change through concrete initiatives. Nevertheless, a focus on COSAC should not underestimate ongoing parliamentary practices. After all, only COSAC convenes four times per year. Increasingly, there is more regular exchange through the other venues; those of the Brussels' network of parliamentary representatives; the digital venue IPEX and other interparliamentary conferences such as the biannual meetings on CFSP/CSDP and economic and financial governance ('article 13').

Another potentially enriching practice outside but related to COSAC is that parliaments are working more and more together in so called 'clusters of interest'.[12] Within those meetings, which could take the form of informal conferences, parliaments could discuss recent initiatives and proposals to adapt, improve or withdraw EU legislation or scrutinise best practices. The Danish Parliament took the lead to initiate one such meeting in 2013, and it has been followed up by the Dutch Tweede Kamer in a meeting between almost 20 Chambers in January 2015 at the venue of the Netherlands Permanent Representation to the EU.

[12] A Esposito, 'The role of COSAC in the EU interparliamentary cooperation: an (endless) quest for an identity', Ch 19 in this volume.

As COSAC gains more academic attention, more questions for exploration remain. One is to what extent COSAC, as the first formal EU interparliamentary conference, can prove itself a model for interparliamentary cooperation. Article 9 of the Treaty Protocol no 1 annexed to Treaty of Lisbon determines a competing model as the EP and NPs may design alternative forms of cooperation.

Another issue to explore in depth is the relation between COSAC and the EU Speakers' Conference: to what extent is the role of COSAC weakened, and the role of the latter strengthened because of the new interparliamentary meetings conferences of article 13 of the Treaty on Stability, Coordination and Governance and on CFSP-CSDP? Should COSAC develop into a forum for primarily sharing best practices, relevant substantial discussions could increasingly be dealt with in thematic venues, such as the aforementioned conferences or on a more ad hoc basis in 'clusters of interest'.

A second avenue to explore is to stretch thinking out of the boundaries of the existing, rather closed-door format of interparliamentary cooperation.

In 1992, the COSAC held in London rejected a proposal to open up deliberations for the press. However, recent venues have been live-streamed and press communiqués tend to be drawn up after the meeting. The lack of transparency involves not only COSAC: most interparliamentary fora and conferences lack transparency and thus there is not enough awareness among governments, let alone media or the general public, as well as among scholars, that every week bilateral or multilateral meetings among parliaments take place in the EU, both at national and at European level.

This contribution has assessed some novel ways for formatting COSAC, the prime venue for those within and around national parliaments and the EP interested in the current state of European parliamentary affairs. Ultimately, the proof of the pudding in this particular case is, first and foremost, in the eating. Obviously, the gradual reshaping of COSAC into a dynamic market place for the exchange of relevant EU information between parliaments, relies upon the discretion of subsequent national presidencies and the EP, which each have their say in designing the format, style and focus of respective conferences. However, given the broad interest demonstrated by many recent Presidencies to push for innovation, the issue has been announced to be at centre stage during the Presidency of the Netherlands (first half of 2016).

Conclusion

Interparliamentary Cooperation in the Framework of a Euro-national Parliamentary System

CRISTINA FASONE AND NICOLA LUPO

I. DISAGREEMENT ON INTERPARLIAMENTARY COOPERATION IN THE EU

MANY DISAGREEMENTS SEEM to have accompanied the evolution of interparliamentary cooperation in the EU. As shown in the previous chapters, every form of interparliamentary cooperation has experienced and is still experiencing profound disaccord and ambiguities regarding its structure, powers and procedures. This applies equally to the old interparliamentary conferences, like the EU Speakers' Conference and COSAC, whose role has tended to be redefined and questioned also in recent years;[1] as well to the newest one, like the two Conferences on CFSP-CSDP and on Stability, Economic Coordination and Governance in the European Union, whose setting-up, in the last five years, has been all but smooth.[2]

Also the other forms of involvement of national parliaments in EU affairs conceived in more recent years, since the Treaty of Lisbon, do not appear to be the result of a clear mindset or design regarding the role and aims of interparliamentary cooperation. Although national parliaments are often considered as a unitary block of institutions for explanatory purposes, in fact they do not enjoy the same powers in EU affairs under the national Constitutions, nor do they agree on how interparliamentary cooperation should look: a matter

[1] See the chapters by C Fasone, 'Ruling the (dis-)order of interparliamentary cooperation? The EU Speakers Conference' (Ch 14) and A Cygan, 'COSAC: Birth, Evolution, Failures and Perspectives' (Ch 11), as well as all the contributions in the sixth part of the volume.

[2] See, respectively, the chapters by J Wouters and K Raube, 'The Interparliamentary Conference on Common Foreign and Security Policy: A Quest for Democratic Accountability in EU Security Governance' (Ch 12), and I Cooper, 'The Interparliamentary Conference on Stability, Economic Coordination and Governance in the European Union (the "Article 13 Conference")' (Ch 13), in this volume.

that often triggers the creation of unstable alliances of parliaments, either in a 'coalition' with the European Parliament or not, depending on the subject-matter.

In some cases, like the early warning system (EWS), it is even debated whether and to what extent we could talk of an instrument of interparliamentary cooperation, as, according to some interpretations, the EWS would be better conceived as an essential individual procedure, to be exercised first of all by a single national parliament or a chamber thereof. Interparliamentary cooperation is however necessary in case the objective is to reach the threshold for the 'yellow card' or the 'orange card', but not for issuing a reasoned opinion or just sending a contribution in the framework of the political dialogue (although, again, it might become necessary for proposing an initiative according to the 'green card' experimental procedure, where thresholds have not been clearly fixed yet).[3] Interparliamentary cooperation then appears just instrumental to fully exploit a procedure and to increase its legitimation, given the number of national parliaments raising subsidiarity concerns.

In other cases, like the Economic and Monetary Union (EMU) and the European Semester, the space for interparliamentary cooperation has seemed rather limited so far. Indeed, budgetary and financial policies are defined by each national government, and then by each national parliament, through programmes and legislation that have to comply with the guidelines and the recommendations decided by the EU institutions, although now following the same common annual timeline. In this case, interparliamentary cooperation is called upon to play a complementary role: either in the sense of helping the European Parliament to get a more complete picture of the different national financial policies; or else, reciprocally, to allow national parliaments to better understand the strategy of EU institutions, to compare their situation to those of Member States which are in similar conditions, or, based on the system of peer review, to use other countries as a benchmark. With this regard, the cooperation between the European Parliament and national parliaments can show great potential in the setting up and implementation of the Banking Union and can be further developed in the framework of the European Semester, as argued in the five Presidents' Report.[4]

It is also thanks to these disagreements that an apparent odd phenomenon took place. At least in some phases, and also very recently, the case for an involvement of the national parliaments and later on for an increase of their role has been advanced both by supporters of further and deeper European integration, in order to have it more democratically legitimised, and by Eurosceptics, willing to multiply (national) brakes and veto powers in the EU decision-making process.[5]

[3] D Jančić 'The Game of Cards: National Parliaments in the EU and the Future of the Early Warning Mechanism and the Political Dialogue' (2015) 52(4) *Common Market Law Review* 939.

[4] *Completing Europe's Economic and Monetary Union*, Report by J-C Juncker, in close cooperation with D Tusk, J Dijsselbloem, M Draghi and M Schulz (Brussels, 2015), 17. See also R Ibrido, 'The Banking Union and the "Euro-national parliamentary system". Constitutional implications', paper presented at the 2nd Annual Conference of the Erasmus Academic Network on Parliamentary Democracy in Europe—PADEMIA, Brussels, 2–3 July 2015.

[5] A Groen and T Christiansen, 'National Parliaments in the European Union: Conceptual Choices in the European Union's Constitutional Debate' in C Hefftler et al (eds), *The Palgrave Handbook of National Parliaments and the European Union* (Basingstoke, Palgrave MacMillan, 2015) 43, 57. See also R Bin and P Caretti and G Pitruzzella, *Profili costituzionali dell'Unione europea* (Bologna, Il mulino, 2015), 151–60 (underlying the uncertainty and ambiguity of the increased role of national parliaments).

II. ALTERNATIVE VISIONS ON PARLIAMENTS IN THE EU

These disagreements can be explained rightly by the fact that there is not a clear vision on what the role of parliaments in the EU is. As anticipated in the Introduction, at least four different models could be envisaged, each one with its own normative implications for parliaments in the EU: 1) a rigid separation between the European Parliament and national parliaments; 2) national parliaments as a (virtual) 'Third Chamber' of the European Union; 3) the 'multilevel parliamentary (battle)field'; 4) the 'euro-national parliamentary system'.

1) The first model, embraced by the supporters of the 'federalist' approach, depicts parliamentary democracy in the EU as based on a sharp separation of functions and competences between the European Parliament and national parliaments. According to this model, the former scrutinises the EU executive (identified with the European Commission), while the latter oversee their respective governments' decisions in EU affairs, as any other policy, in their national capitals.[6] This model has characterised the European integration process for a long time, inspiring both the institutional behaviour of national parliaments and the response of the European Parliament to the democratic legitimacy challenges of the EU. In both cases, however, the results achieved have proved unable to cope with the atypical nature of the European supranational decision-making.

This failure explains why article 12 TEU and Protocols No 1 and 2 annexed to the Treaty of Lisbon, creating stable links between each national parliament and the EU institutions, actually seem to have overcome this model, which is therefore to be considered outdated, at least in its original and quite rigid version. However, this model still resurfaces in those who argue in favour of a further strengthening of the European Parliament as the only way to solve the democratic problems of the EU and also, although less clearly, in the scholarship that tends to diminish the significance of the EWS or to qualify it as a mere legal instrument.

2) According to the second model, essentially based on Protocol No 2, and specifically founded on the provisions and the practice of the EWS, the cooperation among parliaments, and especially among national parliaments, would give origin to a sort of a (virtual) 'Third Chamber' in the EU next to the European Parliament and the Council, seen as the EU 'Second Chamber'.[7] In fact, although never meeting in the same place, members of national parliaments of the EU lead to a unique deliberative process, that can trigger remarkable effects in the EU decision-making, in case of the raising of a 'yellow card' or an 'orange card'.[8] Such model tends to emphasise the 'collective' dimension of national parliaments, underestimating the individualistic and often contrasting approaches and behaviour that usually drive such assemblies in their relationship with EU affairs.

[6] T Raunio, 'Holding Governments Accountable in European Affairs, Explaining Cross-National Variation' (2005) 11 *Journal of Legislative Studies* 319; P Caretti, 'Il ruolo dei Parlamenti nazionali prima e dopo il trattato di Lisbona' in *Studi in onore di Franco Modugno* (Napoli, Editoriale scientifica, 2011) 535; RD Kelemen, 'Towards a New Constitutional Architecture in the EU?' in F Fabbrini, EH Ballin and H Somsen (eds), *What Form of Government for the EU and the Eurozone?* (Oxford, Hart Publishing, 2015) 208.

[7] The interpretation of the Council as the EU second Chamber is, especially after the Treaty of Lisbon, absolutely dominant: see, among many, S Hix and B Høyland, *The political system of the European Union*, 3rd edn (Basingstoke, Palgrave Macmillan, 2011) 68 ff and R Schütze, *European Union Law* (Cambridge, Cambridge University Press, 2015) 173 ff. Nevertheless, it does not seem fully convincing, especially when assessing the Council from a structural, instead of functional, viewpoint.

[8] See I Cooper, 'A "virtual third chamber" for the European Union? National parliaments after the Treaty of Lisbon' (2012) 35 *West European Politics* 441 and I Cooper, 'Bicameral or tricameral? National parliaments and representative democracy in the European Union' (2013) 35 *Journal of European Integration* 531.

This model evokes, at least from its denomination, an old proposal, frequently put forward especially by the French Parliament, aimed at setting up another parliamentary assembly in the EU, composed of representatives of national parliaments of all the EU Member States. This proposal—obviously strongly rejected by the European Parliament alongside several national legislatures—has more recently been refreshed and re-submitted, arguing that, for what concerns the Economic and Monetary Union, this 'Third Chamber' should be composed of national parliamentarians of the Eurozone countries only.[9] In other words, the increasing variable geometry of the EU, matched with the inability of the European Parliament to properly represent these asymmetries, has led some to suggest again the establishment of a new collective and permanent interparliamentary body, but where only the parliaments of the participating countries would be represented.

3) A third model assumes the existence of a 'multilevel parliamentary field', as a space for close interaction between parliaments at different levels (European, national, subnational), without fixed hierarchies and with overlapping constituencies.[10] This model seems rather consistent with the most recent developments of interparliamentary cooperation, which have seen a multiplication of interparliamentary forums without a clear structure or a coordinated design. As these developments have sometimes shown strong contrasts between the European Parliament and national parliaments, on the one hand, and between national legislatures themselves, on the other, they have also somehow supported the idea of a sort of multilevel parliamentary 'battle-field'.[11] An image, of course, particularly suitable to describe the struggle that preceded the setting up of the Interparliamentary Conference on CFSP-CSDP.

The advantage of this model—on which many scholars agree[12]—is to show that it requires all parliaments in the EU, including regional parliaments with legislative powers, involved in the early warning system by article 6 of Protocol No 2, to acknowledge that their respective representative and oversight functions are no longer exclusive, but rather and necessarily overlapping and that each parliament 'is becoming an intrinsic part of the others' operating environment'.[13] The shortcomings of this model are however, on the one side, that it does not trace the existent structured interparliamentary relationships convincingly enough and, on the other side, that its adoption could lead each parliament to act autonomously on the 'field', irrespective of their Executive (and, in the 13 bicameral systems of the EU, even of the other Chamber).

[9] R Dehousse, 'Inter-institutional balance in the EU: is the community method still relevant?', *Challenges of Multi-tier Governance in the EU*, Workshop held at the European Parliament, Brussels, 4 October 2012, available at: www.europarl.europa.eu/document/activities/cont/201210/20121003ATT52863/20121003ATT52863EN.pdf, p 23; T Piketty, 'Il faut donner un parlement à l'euro', interviewed by C Gatinois and A Salles, *Le Monde*, 20 May 2014.

[10] B Crum and JE Fossum, 'The Multilevel Parliamentary Field: a framework for theorizing representative democracy in the EU' (2009) 1 *European Political Science Review* 249.

[11] See A Herranz Surálles, 'The EU's Multilevel Parliamentary (Battle)Field: Explaining Inter-parliamentary Cooperation and Conflict in the Area of Foreign and Security Policy' (2014) 37 *West European Politics* 957.

[12] See, among others, C Lord, 'The European Union: Parliamentary Wasteland or Parliamentary Field?' in B Crum and JE Fossum (eds), *Practices of Inter-parliamentary Coordination in International Politics: The European Union and Beyond* (Colchester, ECPR Press, 2013) 235; E Eriksen, *The Normativity of the European Union* (London, Palgrave MacMillan, 2014) 98 ff. Others authors speak of a 'multilevel parliamentary system': B Rittberger and T Winzen, 'The EU's multilevel parliamentary system' in J Richardson and S Mazey (eds), *European Union. Power and policy-making* (Abingdon, Routledge, 2015) 107–33.

[13] B Crum and JE Fossum, 'Conclusion: towards a *democratic* multilevel parliamentary field?' in B Crum and JE Fossum (eds), *Practices of Inter-parliamentary Coordination in International Politics: The European Union and Beyond* (Colchester, ECPR Press, 2013) 251–68, at 252.

4) Finally, the fourth model, envisaging a 'Euro-national parliamentary system',[14] assumes that the EU democracy is founded and characterised by the confidence relationship that links each national government to its parliament (as already seen, with the only exception of Cyprus) and asks for the coordination of four different types of relationships shaping the system: first, the relationship between the European Parliament and the other EU institutions; secondly, the relationship between the European Parliament and national parliaments; thirdly, the relationship between national parliaments and EU institutions; fourthly, the relationship between each national parliament and its respective government, whose relevance for the EU democracy is acknowledged by article 10 TEU. Indeed interparliamentary cooperation can be used by each parliament to strengthen its ability to set the political directions for the executives of the EU and to control their actual respect more effectively.

The 'system' of relationships just detected is constituted by procedures, ruled by a composite parliamentary law, made up of EU as well as national provisions, and based on the idea that the functions of representation, political direction and oversight are now necessarily shared between parliaments of different levels of government.[15]

The fulfilment of this model calls for the further diffusion and strengthening of parliamentary and interinstitutional procedures, both bilateral and multilateral, able to structure a real and effective 'system': among parliaments, but also, and especially, between each parliament and its own Executive, conceived as a part of the fragmented EU Executive, or with other bodies which are components of the same Executive (the European Council, the Council, the Commission, and even, to some extent, the European Central Bank).

Based on the contributions of the different authors and on the ways the research questions identified in the Introduction have been addressed, the preference for the fourth vision appears confirmed. It is true that all the four models still seem to coexist in some regards. However, the fourth model is better suited to explain most of the current trends in interparliamentary cooperation, is more consistent with the logic of a composite European Constitution, and at the same time is more capable to reconcile the national and European dimensions of parliamentary democracy, and to address the need to counterbalance the EU 'fragmented' Executive. Finally, it looks better suited than the other models to reduce the level of conflicts between the European Parliament and national parliaments.

III. EUROPEAN PARLIAMENT AND NATIONAL PARLIAMENTS: AN UNAVOIDABLE COMPETITION?

From the analyses conducted in this volume, it is quite clear that the stabilisation of the instruments of interparliamentary cooperation is not eased by the fact that the European Parliament and national parliaments are naturally competing for the same good: that is, the

[14] A Manzella and N Lupo (eds), *Il sistema parlamentare euro-nazionale. Lezioni* (Torino, Giappichelli, 2014); N Lupo, 'Parlamento europeo e Parlamenti nazionali nella Costituzione "composita" dell'UE: le diverse letture possibili' in A Ciancio (ed), *Nuove strategie per lo sviluppo democratico e l'integrazione politica in Europa* (Roma, Aracne, 2014) 365–96; A Manzella, 'Parlamento europeo e parlamenti nazionali come sistema' in *Rivista AIC*, 1/2015, available at: www.rivistaaic.it/parlamento-europeo-e-parlamenti-nazionali-come-sistema.html.

[15] A Manzella, 'Verso un governo parlamentare euro-nazionale?' in A Manzella and N Lupo (eds), n 14 above. See also, although talking of a multilevel parliamentary field, T Winzen, C Roederer-Rynning and F Schimmelfennig, 'Parliamentary Co-Evolution: National Parliamentary Reactions to the Empowerment of the European Parliament' (2015) 22 *Journal of European Public Policy* 75.

political representation of the interests of EU citizens. This means that, notwithstanding some frequent and vague appeals to an 'alliance among parliaments', the European Parliament inevitably tends to reserve for itself the role of promoter and coordinator of any form of interparliamentary cooperation. At best, in some cases it can agree to co-promote and co-chair a meeting, together with the parliament of the Member State holding the Council presidency (and the Troika, composed also of the former and the next presidency of the EU), but it does not accept being left out of the control panel and leaving it only to representatives of national parliaments. To some extent the leadership of the European Parliament has also good reasons, starting from its past experience of being a permanent interparliamentary institution until 1979, of being originally multilingual and provided with financial resources and administrative support that by no means are comparable to those of most national parliaments, especially in a time of crisis.

This notwithstanding, some important steps forward have certainly been accomplished in recent years. It is no longer the time for the European Parliament to oppose almost any attempt of cooperation among national parliaments, as happened in the aftermath of the 1979 elections, when the European Parliament needed to acquire its own role and legitimation, without the concurrence of powerful national legislatures (and their members).

Now the European Parliament expressly promotes interparliamentary cooperation together with national parliaments, also according to article 9 of Protocol No 1 to the Treaty of Lisbon, and even favours the presence of permanent representatives of national legislatures in Brussels (obviously, also in an attempt to monitor and coordinate their activity).[16] However, the European Parliament acts this way on the condition of being able to control, direct and coordinate these forms of interparliamentary cooperation. At the same time, it is still opposing any new form of cooperation among national parliaments which excludes it or which in any case tends, consistently with the COSAC model, to put the European Parliament on the same level as any national parliament.

By the same token and because of the strengthened position in the EU deriving from the Treaty of Lisbon,[17] national parliaments have also become more sensitive and reactive to what the European Parliament proposes in matters of interparliamentary cooperation and more and more able to pursue autonomous strategies, as the rise of horizontal but at the same time of asymmetric forums of cooperation between national legislatures, often based on 'clusters of interests', demonstrates.[18] The 'green card' initiative and the very difficult setting up of the new interparliamentary conferences, from those on the CFSP-CDSP and on Stability, Economic Coordination and Governance in the European Union, not to mention the not yet defined interparliamentary cooperation in the field of Europol and Eurojust (article 12, letter C TEU), prove that the position of the European

[16] A Pegan and A-L Högenauer, 'The Role of Parliamentary Administrations in Interparliamentary Cooperation' (Ch 8) and F Gómez Martos, 'Interparliamentary Cooperation in the Context of COSAC: A View from the European Parliament', Ch 18 in this volume.

[17] R Corbett, 'The Evolving Roles of the European Parliament and the National Parliaments' in A Biondi, P Eeckhout and S Ripley (eds), *EU After Lisbon* (Oxford, Oxford University Press, 2012) 248.

[18] See M Goldoni, 'The Instrumental Value of Horizontal Parliamentary Cooperation: Subsidiarity Review and the Political Dialogue', Ch 9 in this volume; D Fromage, 'A mapping of recent trends in interparliamentary cooperation within the EU' in C Fasone, D Fromage and Z Lefkofridi (eds), *Parliaments, public opinion and parliamentary elections in Europe* (2015) 18 EUI Max Weber Working Paper Series.

Parliament has been at least partially challenged by its national counterparts (which, as said above, nevertheless often disagree among themselves). A great deal of time has passed since the experience of the 'exclusively European Parliament-dominated' Assises in Rome in 1990. As has been recently argued, the developments and outcomes of the relationships between the European and national parliaments are necessarily based on a history of 'co-evolution' between those institutions.[19]

This competition between the European Parliament and national parliaments was not formally contemplated in the first 'federal' model, as their respective representative areas were not overlapping, at least in theory. The convergence or rather the divergence of viewpoints is also influenced by the European Parliament's institutional position. Indeed, it appears that the tension may increase when the European Parliament only enjoys weak powers in the EU decision-making, such as in the Economic and Monetary Union and the CFSP-CDSP, as any further enhancement in the position of national parliaments in the EU can threaten the European Parliament's authority. By contrast, in the fields where the European Parliament has the status of co-legislator, its powers can hardly be challenged by national parliaments through the procedures provided for under the Treaty of Lisbon.

The competition is also likely to be encouraged every time national parliaments tend to act as a 'virtual third chamber', thus finding a collective position which is naturally seen as somewhat alternative to that expressed by the European Parliament. Also the model of 'multilevel parliamentary field' normally eases the development of this kind of institutional/representative competition: in an open field, characterised by loose and non-structured relationships, every parliament, as already remarked, is quite free to act as it wishes and to gain the political space it obtains thanks to its concrete activity and representative capacity, on a case by case basis. In both models, a sort of confrontation and balancing of different positions, expressed by the European Parliament as well as by national parliaments—individually and collectively—has to be concretely provided, depending on the case at stake and the specific procedure.

On the contrary, the coming onto the scene of the executives and the formation and recognition of more formalised procedures, like those required by the Euro-national parliamentary system, is probably better able to limit the areas of conflict and competition between the European Parliament and national parliaments or to frame them in such a way that in the end they can contribute to the good functioning of the European democracy.

IV. OVERCOMING THE EU 'POLITICAL DEFICIT'?

Besides parliaments and executives, there are nevertheless other prominent institutional players in the EU that cannot be disregarded.[20] It is well known that traditionally the construction of the EU constitutional order has been mainly, if not exclusively, a matter of courts. In particular, a prominent role in designing the essential feature of the composite

[19] See T Winzen, C Roederer-Rynning and F Schimmelfennig, 'Parliamentary co-evolution: national parliamentary reactions to the empowerment of the European Parliament' (2015) 22 *Journal of European Public Policy* 75.

[20] See G Martinico, 'Inter-judicial Dialogue and Interparliamentary Dialogue in the Constitution of the Union', Ch 2 in this volume.

EU constitution has been played by the Court of Justice of the EU and some national courts entitled to carry out constitutional review.

Needless to say that the prominent role of these courts in shaping EU constitutionalism has contributed to the marginalisation of national parliaments. Not only has the principle of primacy of EU law weakened their legislative powers and prompted a passive attitude among some of them towards the process of European integration,[21] but also their 'constitutional' function has been significantly weakened by the activity of judges, European and national, easily able to talk and understand each other, since the first decades of the European integration process.[22] In other words, in the construction of the major elements of the composite EU Constitution the main cornerstones have been shaped by judges and only later on have they partially been codified by the Treaties. This process has then been followed by the explicit acknowledgment either by the European Treaties or by case law of the main typical instruments of this Constitution: ie, common constitutional traditions, national constitutional identity and 'counter-limits'.[23]

This prominent role played by courts is perfectly consistent with the elitist nature of the first stages of the European integration process.[24] In fact, courts, and especially European and national constitutional courts, are naturally composed of members of the dominant elites.[25] In the first decades of the European Communities, these members, who generally had strong memories of the Second World War, were keen to contribute to the European construction, taking advantage of the 'permissive consensus' that, in many national public opinions, supported the progress of the European integration process.[26] Of course, this construction could also benefit from other elites that, in the EU institutions as well as in some national governments, shared the same fundamental aims and thus contributed to progressively building up the *acquis communautaire*.

[21] P Craig and G de Búrca, *EU Law: Texts, Cases, and Materials*, 5th edn (Oxford, Oxford University Press, 2011) 256–96; D Chalmers, G Davies and G Monti, *European Union Law*, 3rd edn (Cambridge, Cambridge University Press, 2014) 235–42; R Schütze, *European Union Law* (Cambridge, Cambridge University Press, 2015) 127–44.

[22] JHH Weiler, 'The Transformation of Europe' (1991) 8 *Yale Law Journal* 2403–83 and, more specifically on the German and Italian cases, B Davies, *Resisting the European Court of Justice. West Germany's Confrontation with European Law, 1949–1979* (New York, Cambridge University Press, 2009) and M Cartabia, 'The Italian Constitutional Court and the Relationship Between the Italian legal system and the European Union' in A-M Slaughter, A Stone Sweet and JHH Weiler (eds), *The European Court and National Courts. Doctrine and Jurisprudence* (Oxford, Hart Publishing, 1998) 133–46.

[23] See, inter alia, A-M Slaughter, A Stone Sweet and JHH Weiler (eds), n 22 above, M Claes et al (eds), *Constitutional Conversations in Europe. Actors, Topics and Procedures* (Cambridge, Intersentia, 2012) and G Martinico, *The Tangled Complexity of the EU Constitutional Process. The frustrating knot of Europe* (Abingdon, Routledge, 2014).

[24] On the elitist character of the European integration process see, for all, L Hooghe and G Marks, 'A postfunctionalist theory of European integration: from permissive consensus to constraining dissensus' (2008) 39 *British Journal of Political Science* 1, and JHH Weiler, '60 Years since the First European Community: Reflections on Political Messianism' (2011) 22 *European Journal of International Law* 303.

[25] See generally R Hirschl, *Towards Juristocracy. The Origins and Consequences of the New Constitutionalism* (Cambridge MA, Harvard University Press, 2007) and, more specifically, on European judges and the community of lawyers, A Vauchez and B De Witte (eds) *Lawyering Europe. European Law as a Transnational Social Field* (Oxford, Hart Publishing, 2013).

[26] Among many, see A Hurrelmann, 'European Democracy, the "Permissive Consensus" and the Collapse of the EU Constitution' (2007) 13 *European Law Journal* 343, and S Kröger and R Bellamy, 'Beyond a Constraining Dissensus: The Role of National Parliaments in Domesticating and Normalising the Politicization of European Integration' (2016) 14 *Comparative European Politics*, early view, 1–23.

The enlargement of the EU, as a consequence of the end of the Cold war, and the new objectives pursued by European policies, also in reply to the financial crisis, changed the picture rather dramatically. European policies are no longer classifiable as exclusively regulatory for the purpose of enhancing competition and the four freedoms in the internal market, but clearly involve also redistributive elements,[27] which cannot be decided without letting national parliaments, and hence the public opinions they represent, participate.

As has been correctly underlined,[28] any attempt to rebalance the features of EU constitutionalism should therefore go in the direction of increasing its 'political' elements, to counterbalance the traditional dominance of its 'legal' elements. This imbalance was clearly detected more than 20 years ago, when talking about the 'political deficit' in the EU,[29] and has now become even more urgent to address, after the economic crisis.[30]

At the same time, the intergovernmental approach adopted since the Treaty of Maastricht for some important European policies has shown that the cure for this 'political deficit' of the EU cannot consist only in a further strengthening of the European Parliament nor in a 'parliamentarisation' of the EU form of government, with a politicisation of the European Commission.[31] Neither could it be solved by the mere presidentialisation of the EU form of government, with the direct election of the President of the European Council.[32] All these transformations could be deemed important, but in any case not sufficient to adequately address the problem at stake as they only involve the European level of government.[33]

Public opinions are still mainly nation-based, and they feel themselves represented better in their national parliaments than in the European Parliament.[34] At the same time, decisions taken by intergovernmental bodies need to be accountable before some parliaments,

[27] See G Majone, *Rethinking the Union of Europe Post-Crisis. Has Integration Gone Too Far?* (Cambridge, Cambridge University Press, 2014) 196 ff.

[28] J Habermas, 'The Crisis of the European Union in the Light of a Constitutionalization of International Law' (2012) 23 *The European Journal of International Law* 335–48; K Nïcolaidis, 'European Democracy and Its Crisis' (2013) 51 *Journal of Common Market Studies* 351–69; R Bellamy, '"An Ever Closer Union Among the Peoples of Europe": Republican Intergovernmentalism and Demoicratic Representation within the EU' (2013) 35 *Journal of European Integration* 499–516, J Habermas, 'Democracy, Solidarity And the European Crisis' and K Nicolaïdis, 'Pragmatism, Idealism and European Demoicracy' in A-M Grozelier (ed), *Roadmap to a Social Europe* (Social Europe Report, 2014) respectively, 4–13 and 19–24; R Bellamy and A Weale, 'Political legitimacy and European monetary union: contracts, constitutionalism and the normative logic of two-level games' (2015) 22 *Journal of European Public Policy* 257–74; J Neyer, 'Empowering the Sovereign. National Parliaments in European Union Monetary and Financial Policy' in S Piattoni (ed), *The European Union. Democratic Principles and Institutional Architectures in Times of Crisis* (Oxford, Oxford University Press, 2015) 219–35.

[29] R Dehousse, 'Constitutional Reform in the European Community. Are there Alternatives to the Majority Avenue?' in J Hayward (ed), *The Crisis of Representation in Europe* (London, Frank Cass, 1995) 118, 124.

[30] See, recently, Kaarlo Tuori and Klaus Tuori, *The Eurozone Crisis. A Constitutional Analysis* (Cambridge, Cambridge University Press, 2014), N Scicluna, *European Union Constitutionalism in Crisis* (Abingdon, Routledge, 2015) and A Hinarejos, *The Euro Area Crisis in Constitutional Perspective* (Oxford, Oxford University Press, 2015).

[31] C Antpöhler, 'The Proposal to Politicise the Election of the European Commission's President—Enhancing European Democracy in Times of Crises?' in F Fabbrini, EH Ballin and H Somsen (eds) (n 6 above) at 217 ff.

[32] See S Fabbrini and S Micossi, Una proposta istituzionale per l'Europa: legittimazione ed efficienza (2013), available at: www.aspeninstitute.it/aspenia-online/article/una-proposta-istituzionale-l%E2%80%99europa-legittimazione-ed-efficienza, and S Fabbrini, *Which European Union? Europe After the Euro Crisis* (Cambridge, Cambridge University Press, 2015) 275 ff.

[33] LFM Besselink, 'The Place of National Parliaments within the European Constitutional Order', Ch 1 in this volume, who suggests for the EU not to take into consideration only the most traditional institutional form of parliamentary accountability established in the framework of nation states.

[34] PL Lindseth, *Power and Legitimacy. Reconciling Europe and the Nation-State* (Oxford, Oxford University Press, 2010).

according to the 'European model' of parliamentary form of government.[35] Even a direct election of the President of the European Council cannot substitute the oversight and scrutiny that need to be exercised by one or more parliaments.

Without interparliamentary cooperation it is clear that the parliaments of Europe will not be able to play any crucial role in European constitutionalism. Their ability to effectively intervene in the EU dynamics presupposes, in fact, some knowledge about the behaviour of the other actors involved and also about the margins of manoeuvre at their disposals. These are all elements that can potentially be acquired thanks to an increased interparliamentary cooperation.

It is probably not by chance that the first use of the Convention method was conceived in order to codify a Charter of fundamental rights in the EU. That is, the first attempt by the political bodies to take upon themselves one of the main tasks of constitutionalism, the protection of fundamental rights, until then entirely left to the courts.[36] Although a Convention has not been summoned since 2003, when the Convention on the future of Europe ended its mandate, the Convention method has been entrenched in the European Treaties as part of the ordinary revision procedure (article 48 TEU), with the assurance that a parliamentary component made up of MEPs and MPs is represented. Therefore, for future decisions triggering further constitutional advancements in the EU integration process some form of parliamentary participation should be guaranteed, unless national governments decide to bypass the Convention method and resort to a purely intergovernmental dynamic.

Courts and legal constitutionalism have nonetheless played a very significant role not only in shaping the European integration process itself, but also in protecting parliamentary democracy in Europe. For example, the Court of Justice of the European Union has decisively supported the struggle of the European Parliament for its empowerment, in particular for what concerns its legislative powers.[37] By the same token, some national Constitutional Courts, and first of all the German Bundesverfassungsgericht, have been the first guarantors of national parliamentary prerogatives 'against' the European Union in the name of democratic principles and citizens' rights,[38] even when national parliaments had deliberately decided to give up their powers. Indeed, parliaments need the protection of the Courts. Otherwise, if they are left alone, even if in the presence of constitutional and treaty provisions that formally guarantee parliamentary powers, parliaments—as the history of the authoritarian regimes in Europe during the first part of the twentieth century has dramatically shown—tend to passively renounce those prerogatives or not fully exercise them.

[35] See W Wessels and O Rozenberg (eds), *Democratic Control in the Member States of the European Council and the Euro zone summits* (Brussels, European Parliament, January 2013), available at: www.europarl.europa.eu/committees/en/studiesdownload.html?languageDocument=EN&file=90910.

[36] See C Pinelli, *Il momento della scrittura. Contributo al dibattito sulla Costituzione europea* (Bologna, Il Mulino, 2002) 211 ff.

[37] See, for instance, the well-known *Isoglucose case*: Case 179/80, *SA Roquette Frères v Council of the European Communities*, 19 October 1982, [1982] ECR 3623.

[38] The German Constitutional Court has developed its reasoning on the protection of national parliamentary powers since the *Maastricht-Urteil* of 12 October 1993 (BVerfGE 89, 155); a case law that has been confirmed and further strengthened in the judgments on the Treaty of Lisbon and later on of the Euro-crisis measures. See, for example (2009) 10 *German Law Journal*, Special Issue on 'The Federal Constitutional Court's Lisbon Case'.

Because the national parliaments' role in the EU is ultimately influenced by the judicial protection provided by Constitutional and Supreme Courts, the citizens' rights to participate in EU affairs through national parliaments, although deemed a core element of EU democratic legitimation and additional to the right to be represented in the European Parliament (article 10 TEU), are enforced in an asymmetric way. Their enforcement, in fact, depends not only on the form of government of each Member State, but also on the extent to which each system of constitutional review protects and guarantees its own national parliament's prerogatives.[39] This trend is even more evident in the aftermath of the Eurozone crisis and can only be countered by an expansion of politics. That is, by the ability of national parliaments to retrieve an autonomous and independent space of action that allows them to scrutinise and give political directions to the executive. A development which has already occurred in some Member States, either by means of constitutional amendments, like in Austria, or by the fulfillment of a sort of 'political' constitutional review by the parliament, like in Finland.[40]

V. INTERPARLIAMENTARISM BY COMMITTEE

In conclusion, based on the contributions proposed in this Volume, two trends can be detected in interparliamentary cooperation in the EU. The first is the increasing need for specialisation by policy and subject-matters of the many interparliamentary forums blossoming in Europe,[41] regardless of whether they enjoy some degree of formalisation and stability—like the new interparliamentary conferences—or whether they are summoned ad hoc and more and more often with the participation of just few parliaments. This also explains the identity crisis experienced by COSAC as a 'generalist body' as long as it does not convert itself in the interparliamentary forum where the constitutional fundamental choices surrounding the EU are tackled.

[39] C Closa, 'National Higher Courts and the Ratification of EU Treaties' (2013) 36 *West European Politics* 97; O Höing, 'Differentiation of parliamentary powers. The German Constitutional Court and the German Bundestag within the financial crisis' in M Cartabia, N Lupo and A Simoncini (eds), *Democracy and Subsidiarity in the EU* (Bologna, Il Mulino, 2013) 259–83; C Pinelli, 'La giurisprudenza costituzionale tedesca e le nuove asimmetrie fra i poteri dei parlamenti nazionali dell'eurozona' (2014) *Costitutionalismo.it*: www.costituzionalismo.it/articoli/470/, 25 March 2014, and S Theil, 'What Red Lines, If Any, Do the Lisbon Judgments of European Constitutional Courts Draw for Future EU Integration?' (2014) 15 *German Law Journal* 601.

[40] On this point, see C Fasone, 'Eurozone, non-Eurozone and "troubled asymmetries" among national parliaments in the EU. Why and to what extent this is of concern' in R Castaldi and G Martinico (eds), Special Issue on 'The Never-Ending Reform of the EU: Another Chain in the Semi Permanent Treaty Revision Process?' (2014) 6 *Perspectives on Federalism* E1–41. More specifically, on Austria see S Puntscher Riekmann and D Wydra, 'Representation in the European State of Emergency: Parliaments against Governments?' (2013) 35 *Journal of European Integration* 565–82. On Finland, P Leino-Sandberg and J Salminen, 'The Euro Crisis and Its Constitutional Consequences for Finland: Is There Room for National Politics in EU Decision-Making?' (2013) 9 *European Constitutional Law Review* 451–79.

[41] On this point, identifying a 'new trend for specialization in interparliamentary cooperation', see C Hefftler and K Gattermann, 'Interparliamentary Cooperation in the European Union: Patterns, Problems and Potential' in C Hefftler et al (eds), above n 5, 94–115, 98 ff, and, although wishing for a revamping of EU affairs committees' role, D Fromage, 'Standing committees in interparliamentary cooperation in the post-Lisbon era: towards the end of the European Affairs Committees' predominance?', Ch 6 in this volume.

After more than five years since the entry into force of the Treaty of Lisbon, almost all national parliaments have overcome the stage of the mere Europeanisation of their activities and organisation, and also thanks to the early warning system and the political dialogue, they are ready to engage in the EU, in coordination with the other legislatures, in more in-depth and comprehensive examination and debate on policy proposals and ongoing European developments. Furthermore, this is confirmed by the fact that while the national parliaments' European Affairs Committees and the European Parliament's Committee on Constitutional Affairs have for a long time been primary actors in the cooperation with other parliaments, today sectoral committees are taking the lead.

A second trend in interparliamentary cooperation concerns the increase of contacts between parliaments, sometimes all together, some others with asymmetric and selected participation, either by geographic area in the EU (Nordic, Southern and Eastern countries; or founding Member States, or Benelux) or by issue of concern (immigration, Eurozone, criminal cooperation). This trend seems linked to the former in that it triggers a more flexible organisation of interparliamentary cooperation, moving away from heavy structured interparliamentary sessions, with lengthy debates sometimes even on non-clearly identified issues (the future of Europe, the protection of fundamental rights in the EU, sustainable development) and arranged just once or twice a year.

As highlighted in most contributions this format is not effective. Here it is argued that the lack of effectiveness of interparliamentary cooperation does not derive—or, at least, not directly—from the absence of binding decisions on the executives and the other EU institutions taken as a result of interparliamentary meetings or coordination, like in the subsidiarity scrutiny where the last word lies nevertheless with the European Commission in the event of a 'yellow card' (and potentially with the European Parliament or the Council on the 'orange card'). Rather, one of the original sins in the format of the interparliamentary conferences is that they resemble those of plenary sessions in Parliament, with hundreds of MPs and MEPs. With the 'little' difference that the *finalité* of those conferences, according to their rules (if adopted), is to exchange views and debate or to adopt contributions and conclusions, and hence the final vote does not assume the same value as when a law or a resolution is passed. Speaking time for MPs and MEPs is very limited and the debates are often constrained by the need to listen to interesting but out-of-context keynote speeches by external speakers, not only members of the EU fragmented executives, but also experts on the subject-matter. Furthermore, these conferences, with the exception of COSAC, are summoned only twice a year—just once in the case of the EU Speakers' Conference—without any permanent arrangement or coordination in between those sessions. By contrast, these conferences are sometimes used by MPs for purposes other than those 'institutionally' provided, like the informal coordination on EU legislative proposals, pending the deadline for the EWS. Although these non-public side meetings can lead to building up regular contacts between MPs and MEPs, in particular committee chairmen, and hence can also have positive implications, they are not just the signal of a 'malaise' regarding the current functioning of interparliamentary conferences (which sometimes do not constitute the primary reason for a parliamentary delegation to travel to Brussels or to another European capital). They also prove that parliaments are likely to use interparliamentary cooperation more intensively when they perceive themselves unable to shape the government's action and wherever a lack of influence of their own executive in particular in the intergovernmental venues of the Council and European Council is observed. The rise of informal and side (interparliamentary) meetings on ongoing EU decision-making procedures and legislative packages testifies the dissatisfaction of parliaments with the information gained from their executives and with the achievements of their own governments in the EU context.[42]

Moreover, the 'plenary-like' format of the interparliamentary conferences is not fully coherent with the features of the Euro-national parliamentary system, where the parliaments of the EU are placed. Every parliamentary system needs many specialised representative bodies, with continuity of relationships and some common expertise to share without necessarily this leading to a process of institutionalisation, in contrast with the idea that the setting up of a 'Third Chamber' appears to embrace. Hence interparliamentary meetings, in presence or by using the Internet, should become more frequent, but smaller in size and with a more clearly policy-oriented 'order of business'. Information technologies nowadays also make it possible to dramatically reduce the costs of the missions and meetings, which sometimes could be arranged via the web. Existing online platforms, such as IPEX, could be further developed for this purpose so as to encourage more frequent contacts not just on the part of parliamentary officials but also politicians.

The higher frequency of meetings should also allow a slightly higher turnover in the participation,[43] assuring an increased involvement of the opposition groups. These groups should be equally given the opportunity to be involved in interparliamentary cooperation in the EU and to benefit from the socialisation and the mutual learning process it fosters. The added value of parliaments, compared to governments, in the EU is rightly endowed by the participation of opposition parties in the decision-making process, which otherwise could be blamed of being in the hands only of the executives and their majority parties.[44] In this way, interparliamentary cooperation could play an integration function with regard to anti-EU and populist parties, to have their voices heard by the EU executives at an early stage and to offer some opportunities for them to contribute to the agenda setting and to the actual drafting of EU legislation.[45]

A larger involvement of opposition groups in the interparliamentary cooperation on economic and fiscal policies could actually soften one of the problems affecting some national democracies, especially when dealing with the adoption and implementation of austerity measures. In fact, this involvement could somewhat counter the pressure coming from the EU and from other member states to form wide coalition governments called

[42] For an attempt to classify national parliaments according to their positions towards interparliamentary cooperation see V Kreilinger, *Inter-parliamentarry Cooperation and its Challenges: The Case for Economic and Financial Governance* in F Fabbrini, EH Ballin and H Somsen (eds) (n 6 above) 280 ff.

[43] See, consistently, the proposals put forward by DA Capuano, 'The Role of Cosac in the Europeanisation of National Parliaments and in the Evolution of the Interparliamentary Cooperation' (Ch 15); BA Dias Pinheiro, 'The Role of COSAC in the Changing Environment of National Parliaments in the EU: An Identity Crisis?' (Ch 16), A Esposito, 'The Role of COSAC in EU Interparliamentary Cooperation: An (Endless) Quest for an Identity' (Ch 19), and M Van Keulen, 'Reshaping COSAC as a Dynamic Venue For Interparliamentary Exchange' (Ch 20), in this volume.

[44] On the possible role exercised by 'Euro-national austerity coalitions' and the problematic lack of responsible parliamentary oppositions see C Fasone, 'Taking budgetary powers away from national parliaments? On parliamentary prerogatives in the Eurozone crisis' (2015), EUI LAW Working paper no 37, available at: hdl.handle.net/1814/36658.

[45] Under this viewpoint, a proposal recently advanced by S Kröger and R Bellamy (n 26 above) seems extremely interesting, as it aims at allowing also national parliamentary minorities to activate a parliamentary legislative initiative. Although a unique threshold at 1/3 of each national parliament may be a bit too rigid, depending on the feature of each national form of government and electoral system, the proposal seems to move along in the right direction.

to adopt structural reforms.[46] The active participation of the main opposition groups in interparliamentary forums, where they can interact with European Commissioners and Council's members, and the opportunity for these groups to express their positions also in a European arena could diminish, of course up to a certain extent, the temptation to take irresponsible and populist positions afterwards. For instance, once an opposition group has publicly supported, in an interparliamentary forum, the policy objectives of its own national government it becomes slightly more difficult to reverse its position in the national debate in the event, after the next elections, it gets the majority to rule a country. At the same time, formal debates and informal contacts between the leaders of national opposition groups and the members of the European 'fragmented' Executive that take place during interparliamentary meetings could help legitimising each other's respective role at national and European level. Furthermore, this can even reduce the risk, for the European Commission and the European Council, to have the policy objectives negotiated and agreed with a previous government overturned or disregarded following a change of the ruling majority (former opposition) in a member state.

These proposals would entail the establishment of a new format of interparliamentary cooperation, not only specialised in subject-matter, but fully 'committee-based'. Therefore, the EU experience of interparliamentary cooperation would become closer to 'parliamentarism by committee',[47] shifting away from the plethoric 'conference-based' interparliamentarism, shaped according to international assemblies, in which parliamentarians try to play a diplomatic role, far away from their actual domestic powers and the free mandate they enjoy.

In order to complete this transformation it would be necessary for the European political parties to play a greater role in the EU decision-making as well as in the European public opinion. Of course, this step looks rather distant from where we are now and here we can only make some recommendations for the future and add new items for a research agenda on interparliamentary cooperation. What can be done, for the moment, is to give more external relevance, in all the formats of interparliamentary cooperation, to the membership of a certain political group. For instance, wherever possible, MPs and MEPs should sit by political family rather than by nationality, and political groups should be provided with time to meet and coordinate before and after interparliamentary conferences are summoned. The rigid format of national delegations, obliged to speak only with one voice, clearly does not fit the needs of the current intense and lively (inter)parliamentary dynamics in the EU.

The history of parliamentarism itself suggests that such a perspective should be seconded. After all, especially in Europe, the twentieth century has witnessed the reorganisation of

[46] On the pressure of EU institutions and other Member States in favour of wide coalition governments, which accompanies the interest of majority parties to include the main oppositions in bearing the burden of austerity measures (thus opening political space for populist movements), see, for some hints, P Mair, *Bini Smaghi vs. the parties: representative government and institutional constraints*, EUI Working paper, 2011 (available at: hdl.handle.net/1814/16354) 13 ff, P Craig, 'Economic Governance and the Euro Crisis: Constitutional Architecture and Constitutional Implications' in M Adams and F Fabbrini and P Larouche (eds), *The Constitutionalization of European Budgetary Constraints* (Oxford, Hart Publishing, 2014) 39 ff, and N Lupo, 'I "governi tecnici". Gli esecutivi Ciampi, Dini e Monti nel difficile equilibrio tra tenica e politica' (2015) 57 *Rassegna parlamentare* 57–120.

[47] For this expression see A Manzella, 'Is the EP legitimate as a parliamentary body in EU multi-tier governance?', European Parliament, Directorate-General for Internal Policies, *Challenges of multi-tier governance in the EU*, Workshop, 4 October 2012, at 37.

parliaments through committee systems, in which all the parliamentary groups could be proportionally represented. In fact parliamentary committees are the only bodies with a specific competence by subject-matter that allow a rational and specialised division of the parliamentary work, they decisively lead parliamentary procedures and, eventually, the decisions of the plenary and, most of all, committees ensure a continuous and incisive oversight of the Executive.[48] The same development—it is proposed here—should be followed at the level of interparliamentary cooperation, for example by increasing the participation of MPs in the meetings of the standing committees of the European Parliament and, at the same time, the involvement of MEPs in national committee meetings.[49] As said above, in order to contain the costs, the increased number of interparliamentary meetings can be ensured by exploiting virtual Internet platforms and video-conferences much more than has been done so far.

'Interparliamentarism by committee' would by no means entail the setting up of a 'Third Chamber' in the EU, composed of several committees. Rather this concept supports the intensification of contacts between MPs and MEPs by policy or subject-matter, with an attendance of nearly half of the current members of interparliamentary conferences. This can be achieved, especially in bicameral parliaments, by a more accurate balance in the participation of the two chambers that do not necessarily need to be represented on an equal footing (it would depend on the subject-matter at stake in the light of the constitutional features of each bicameral system). A size limit of the delegations should be set, for instance by allowing a maximum of four members per parliament with opposition groups represented, although balancing the principle of representation with that of proportionality. Furthermore, in the areas currently subject to EU differentiated integration, only national parliaments from the countries involved should be allowed to participate. MPs and MEPs are to be appointed according to the membership of the relevant parliamentary committees at national and European level and with a higher turnover compared to their current practice, in the light of the increased number of meetings. Each interparliamentary committee should meet in presence at least four times per year with two meetings co-organised by the European Parliament and one by each parliament holding the rotating presidency of the EU. The Troika, composed of the committee chairmen of the three parliaments involved in the organisation of the meetings, should meet virtually or in person at least twice a semester and should promptly inform the other parliaments. In consultation with the Troika, any parliament however remains able to take the initiative to organise a meeting on a specific subject-matter relevant for the committees' competence under the condition that either it will support the whole cost of the meeting or it will summon it through online platforms and video conferences. It is likely however that some committees, namely those covering the fields subject to the intergovernmental method (CFSP), the open method of coordination (social policies) and those that have been more recently placed under the Community

[48] C Fasone, *Sistemi di commissioni parlamentari e forme di governo* (Padova, Cedam, 2012) chs 5 and 6. W Wilson [1885], *Congressional Government. A study in American politics* (New Brunswick NJ, Transaction Press, 2009) 110 and M Debré, 'Trois caractéristiques du système parlementaire français' (1955) 5 *Revue française de science politique* 21, despite referring to different forms of government, highlight the strong influence standing committees have on the Executive, sometimes acting as veto players.

[49] For some experiences see C Hefftler and K Gattermann (n 41 above, at 102) and N Brack and T Deruelle, 'Towards a More Politicised Interparliamentary Cooperation? The EP's Political Groups and the European Parliamentary Week', Ch 7 in this volume.

method (criminal matters), will meet more often than others, because in those areas the integration is weaker and requires a more frequent exchange among parliaments. The meetings should be televised and a transcript of each meeting should be published online, on the website of each committee.

The idea of 'interparliamentary cooperation by committee' also nicely adapts to another inherent feature of the Euro-national parliamentary system: the need for the many parliaments of Europe to scrutinise the fragmented executive in the EU. The participation of Commissioners, members of the Council and the European Council has not so far been systematic in the interparliamentary conferences. However, when it has been foreseen, like in the latest Interparliamentary Conferences on CFSP-CSDP, the quality of the debate and the scrutiny on the executives, in particular on the High Representative for foreign affairs and security policy, has been enhanced to a great extent.

The participation of the European Commission, also through Director Generals, should be turned into a permanent feature of the new format of interparliamentary cooperation, likewise during national standing committee meetings a representative of the executive is always asked to attend and to reply to questions if so requested. Indeed, rather than from renown keynote speakers and besides their mutual exchange of views, parliaments participating in interparliamentary meetings could obtain first-hand information directly from the EU executives, even having them attending the same meeting together and comparing their own respective responsibilities. All this would enormously strengthen the effectiveness of the scrutiny at domestic level. As the appearance of the Greek Prime Minister Tsipras before the European Parliament's plenary on 8 July 2015 on the request for a third bailout package shows, the same importance should also be given to the supply of information from national governments to the European Parliament, which in this way can better scrutinise the activity of the EU intergovernmental institutions.

In the end, it is the very formula used in article 9 Protocol No 1 to the Treaty of Lisbon, in contrast with that of article 10, that triggers an adaptation of the current formats on interparliamentary cooperation when it asks the European Parliament and the national parliaments to determine together and promote 'an *effective* and *regular* interparliamentary cooperation in the Union' [emphasis added]. The format of interparliamentarism by committee described can accommodate this need for effectiveness and regularity and can then be applied also to new venues of cooperation to be established, for instance those dealing with the scrutiny of Europol and the evaluation of Eurojust under article 12 TEU.[50] In fact, the opportunity to go beyond article 10 and the COSAC model, as it stands, is also demonstrated by the current institutional practice as they have not been applied for the setting up of the two new interparliamentary conferences on CFSP-CDSP and on economic governance and, yet, the shape chosen for those conferences has not proved to be really instrumental to the parliaments' active contribution to the good functioning of the EU (article 12 TEU).

[50] Indeed, the features of the interparliamentarism by committee, regarding the policy-oriented focus, the continuity of the scrutiny, the small size and the flexible organisation of the cooperation, appear to be endorsed by the proposed Joint Parliamentary Scrutiny Group on Europol, according to the amendments passed by the European Parliament in the legislative resolution of 25 February 2014 on the proposal for a regulation of the European Parliament and of the Council on the European Union Agency for Law Enforcement Cooperation and Training (Europol) and repealing Decisions 2009/371/JHA and 2005/681/JHA (COM(2013) 0173), at first reading (P7_TA(2014)0121).

Index

www.ingramcontent.com/pod-product-compliance
Lightning Source LLC
LaVergne TN
LVHW080016210926
848481LV00011B/3035
9781509924424